A History
of Ancient Israel
and Judah

Also published by The Westminster Press

By John H. Hayes

Introduction to the Bible

Edited by John H. Hayes and J. Maxwell Miller

Israelite and Judaean History (The Old Testament Library)

A History
of Ancient Israel
and Judah

J. Maxwell Miller
and John H. Hayes

The Westminster Press
Philadelphia

Grateful acknowledgment is made to the following
for the use of copyrighted material:

The British Museum, for selections from *Chronicles of Chaldean Kings (626–556 B.C.) in the British Museum* by D. J. Wiseman.
British School of Archaeology in Iraq, for extracts from *Iraq* 16, 17, 18, and 35. Quoted by permission.
Harvard University Press, William Heinemann, and The Loeb Classical Library for lines from the works of Josephus, Eusebius, and Dio Cassius. Reprinted by permission.
National Council of the Churches of Christ in the U.S.A., for verses from the Revised Standard Version of the Bible copyrighted 1946, 1952, © 1971, 1973 by the Division of Christian Education of the National Council of the Churches of Christ in the U.S.A.
The Oriental Institute of the University of Chicago, for passages from *Ancient Records of Assyria and Babylonia,* vols. I and II, by Daniel David Luckenbill, © 1926, 1927 The University of Chicago Press. Reproduced by permission.
Princeton University Press, for excerpts from *Ancient Near Eastern Texts: Relating to the Old Testament,* 3rd ed. with Supplement, ed. by James B. Pritchard. Copyright © 1969 by Princeton University Press. Reprinted by permission.
Society of Biblical Literature, for excerpts from *Handbook of Ancient Hebrew Letters: A Study Edition* by D. Pardee. Reprinted by permission.

First edition

Published by The Westminster Press®
Philadelphia, Pennsylvania

PRINTED IN THE UNITED STATES OF AMERICA

9 8 7 6 5 4 3 2 1

Library of Congress Cataloging in Publication Data

Miller, James Maxwell, 1937–
    A history of ancient Israel and Judah.

    Bibliography: p.
    Includes indexes.
    1. Jews—History—To 70 A.D. 2. Bible. O.T.—History
of Biblical events. I. Hayes, John Haralson, 1934–
II. Title.
DS117.H36 1986   933   85-11468
ISBN 0-664-21262-X

Contents

List of Charts, Illustrations, Maps, and Texts

Texts

Preface

Any attempt to write a history of ancient Israel and Judah must depend primarily on the biblical record and necessarily presupposes a moderate position between two extremes. On the one hand, there are those who, usually on theological grounds, insist that the biblical record itself already provides a completely accurate and adequate account of biblical times. On the other hand, there are those who, viewing the Bible fundamentally as a collection of folk legends, miracle stories, theological treatises, and the like, deny that it has much valid historical information to offer. We expect this volume to receive negative responses from both directions—from those who regard our treatment as overly skeptical of the biblical story, and from those who regard it as overly gullible.

One thing is certain: writing a history of biblical times, or a history of any period, is not a simple matter of collecting "facts" and arranging them in chronological order. It entails the highly subjective task of analyzing and interpreting sources—different kinds of sources, which rarely provide in any straightforward manner exactly the kinds of information the historian seeks. Thus we have devoted considerable space to describing the sources relevant to the various periods of Israelite and Judean history and explaining how we have used each of them. The bibliographies for each chapter at the end of the book include items from essentially three categories: (1) publications pertaining to the primary sources utilized in the chapter; (2) technical studies upon which our treatment is dependent to some degree; and (3) selected publications by other scholars who have taken approaches that differ from ours. Readers who desire fuller documentation are directed to our earlier edited volume, *Israelite and Judaean History* (1977). This collection, containing contributions of fourteen different authors, reviews the various scholarly debates over the past century pertaining to biblical history and seeks to summarize the present status of research. In effect, therefore, it serves as a prolegomenon for the present volume.

Two matters of terminology may require some advance explanation. The biblical books of Genesis through II Kings (excluding the book of Ruth) provide an essentially continuous narrative with coverage from creation to the Babylonian exile. This Genesis-II Kings narrative will be the primary source of information in chapters 2–11 of the present volume. We are well aware of the various theories pertaining to the composition of Genesis-II Kings and corresponding terminology such as "Pentateuch," "Hexateuch," "Tetrateuch," and "Deuteronomistic History." Here, however, taking into account that some readers will not be familiar with the various theories, we refer to this sequence of books simply as "the Genesis-II Kings account." The other matter of terminology is our tendency to refer to "Israelite and Judean" history rather than to "Israelite" history. Again, we are aware that the name "Israel" often has a broadly inclusive connotation in the Bible and that certain biblical passages specifically identify Judah as a subunit of Israel. For reasons that will be explained in chapter 3, however, we are convinced that Israel and Judah were regarded as essentially separate entities during Old Testament times, and our terminology is an attempt to respect this fact.

The two of us share a common approach to Israelite and Judean history, as is illustrated by the fact that we collaborated on the earlier volume and now on this one. Yet our views are not identical. Moreover, simply as a matter of practicality, it was necessary for us to divide our labors on both projects. Thus, while there was constant interchange between the two of us during every stage of the writing of chapters 1–9 of the present volume, with Hayes making valuable contributions, these chapters are essentially the work of Miller, and he takes full responsibility for their contents. The reverse is true for chapters 10–12. Miller was involved especially at the research stage of these chapters, but Hayes determined the direction they would take and is responsible for their contents. Chapters 13–14 are entirely the work of Hayes.

The original manuscript extended through the Bar Kochba revolt. It was decided, however, in view of its length, to conclude the volume with the Persian period. Eventually we hope to offer a second volume which will focus on the Jewish and early Christian communities during Classical Times.

Biblical quotations are from the RSV, except where we have provided our own translations as explained in context. We wish to offer special thanks to Lelia Rotch and Dorcas Ford-Doward for typing the manuscript, to Lori Ann Adelmann for assistance in preparing the maps, to Frank Gorman, Paul Hooker, and other graduate students of Emory University for various services and suggestions, and to Professors Peter Ackroyd and John Gammie, who read and commented on earlier drafts of several of the chapters.

Finally, we express our gratitude to those persons and institutions who provided the photographs which illustrate this volume. A special mention is due in this regard to materials supplied to us from the *Bible Lands Exhibit.* This exhibit is one of several teaching packages of posters, transparencies, maps, and satellite imagery now available from Pictorial Archive, The Old School, P.O. Box 19823, Jerusalem. Teachers of biblical history are recommended to apply to Pictorial Archive for additional information.

July, 1985   J. M. M.
                                                                     J. H. H.

Abbreviations

ABC *Assyrian and Babylonian Chronicles,* by A. K. Grayson. Locust Valley, N.Y.: J. J. Augustin, 1975

ABR *Australian Biblical Review*

AEL *Ancient Egyptian Literature: A Book of Readings,* by M. Lichtheim. 3 vols. Berkeley and London: University of California Press, 1973–1980

AfO *Archiv für Orientforschung*

AGS *Assyrische Gebete an den Sonnengott für Staat und königliches Haus aus der Zeit Asarhaddons und Asurbanipals,* by J. A. Knudtzon. Leipzig: Eduard Pfeffer, 1893

AJBA *Australian Journal of Biblical Archaeology*

ANET *Ancient Near Eastern Texts Relating to the Old Testament,* ed. J. B. Pritchard. 3d ed. Princeton: Princeton University Press, 1969

AnSt *Anatolian Studies*

Ant *Jewish Antiquities,* by Josephus

AOAT *Alter Orient und Altes Testament*

AP *Aramaic Papyri of the Fifth Century* B.C., by A. E. Cowley. Oxford: Clarendon Press, 1923

ARAB *Ancient Records of Assyria and Babylonia,* by D. D. Luckenbill. 2 vols. Chicago: University of Chicago Press, 1926–1927

ARE *Ancient Records of Egypt,* by J. H. Breasted. 5 vols. Chicago: University of Chicago Press, 1905–1907

ARI *Assyrian Royal Inscriptions,* by A. K. Grayson. 2 vols. Wiesbaden: Otto Harrassowitz, 1972–1976

ASTI *Annual of the Swedish Theological Institute in Jerusalem*

AUSS *Andrews University Seminary Studies*

BA *Biblical Archaeologist*

BAR *Biblical Archaeology Reader*

BASOR *Bulletin of the American Schools of Oriental Research*

BETL *Bibliotheca Ephemeridum Theologicarum Lovaniensium*

Bib *Biblica*

BJRL   *Bulletin of the John Rylands Library*
BR   *Biblical Research*
BTB   *Biblical Theology Bulletin*
CBQ   *Catholic Biblical Quarterly*
CCK   *Chronicles of Chaldean Kings (626–556 B.C.) in the British Museum,* by
        D. J. Wiseman. London: British Museum, 1961
CDP   *Catalogue of the Demotic Papyri in the John Rylands Library,* ed. F. L.
        Griffith. 3 vols. Manchester: University Press, 1909
CTM   *Concordia Theological Monthly*
EI   *Eretz—Israel*
GS   *Gesammelte Studien*
HAHL   *Handbook of Ancient Hebrew Letters: A Study Edition,* by D. Pardee. Chico,
        Calif.: Scholars Press, 1982
HUCA   *Hebrew Union College Annual*
IAKA   *Die Inschriften Asarhaddons Königs von Assyrien,* by R. Borger. Graz:
        Archiv für Orientforschung, 1956
IASHP   *Israel Academy of Sciences and Humanities*
IEJ   *Israel Exploration Journal*
Int   *Interpretation*
Iraq   London: British School of Archaeology in Iraq
JAAR   *Journal of the American Academy of Religion*
JANES   *Journal of the Ancient Near Eastern Society of Columbia University*
JAOS   *Journal of the American Oriental Society*
JARCE   *Journal of the American Research Center in Egypt*
JBL   *Journal of Biblical Literature*
JCS   *Journal of Cuneiform Studies*
JNES   *Journal of Near Eastern Studies*
JNSL   *Journal of Northwest Semitic Languages*
JSOT   *Journal for the Study of the Old Testament*
JSS   *Journal of Semitic Studies*
JTS   *Journal of Theological Studies*
KS   *Kleine Schriften*
OP   *Old Persian: Grammar, Texts, Lexicon,* by R. G. Kent. New Haven:
        American Oriental Society, 1950
Or   *Orientalia*
OTS   *Oudtestamentische Studiën*
PEQ   *Palestine Exploration Quarterly*
RB   *Revue Biblique*
SAK   *Studien zur altägyptische Kultur*
SVT   Supplement to *Vetus Testamentum*
TA   *Tel Aviv*
ThLZ   *Theologische Literaturzeitung*
TNAS   *Two Neo-Assyrian Stelae from Iran,* by L. D. Levine. Toronto: Royal
        Ontario Museum, 1972
VT   *Vetus Testamentum*

War   *The Jewish War*, by Josephus
ZAW   *Zeitschrift für die Alttestamentliche Wissenschaft*
ZDMG *Zeitschrift der Deutschen Morgenländischen Gesellschaft*
ZDPV   *Zeitschrift des Deutschen Palästina-Vereins*

CHAPTER 1

The Setting

The immediate setting of the history of ancient Israel and Judah was ancient Palestine, between approximately the twelfth and fourth centuries B.C.E. Yet this history, as the history of any people, must be understood in its broader geographical and chronological context. Actually Palestine represents only a tiny portion of Middle Eastern territory, and the period of ancient Israelite and Judean history only a small segment of the long sweep of Middle Eastern history.

The Chronological Context

Middle Eastern history is not very well known to most Westerners and is in fact rather difficult to follow for several reasons. This history spans an enormous length of time. Geographical terms and place-names change in kaleidoscopic fashion. Peoples and rulers with strange-sounding names surface, survive for a time, and then melt back into the landscape. In order for one to gain an overview, and thus understand ancient Israelite and Judean history in proper chronological context, it is useful to divide the Middle Eastern past into four major phases. (For a more detailed chronological outline of Middle Eastern history from earliest times to the present, see Chart I.)

Prehistoric Times. There are no written records prior to about 3200 B.C.E., but archaeological findings indicate human occupation in the Middle East extending back hundreds of thousands of years. The long period of time prior to written records is often designated "prehistoric" and subdivided into four main "ages": Paleolithic, Mesolithic, Neolithic, and Chalcolithic.

Ancient Times. Covering approximately three thousand years, this first "historical" phase began late in the fourth millennium B.C.E. with the appearance of urban centers and the earliest written records. It is subdivided into the Bronze Age and the Iron Age and came to an end during the fourth century B.C.E.

CHART I. Chronological Outline of Middle Eastern History*

Prehistoric Times   From the earliest evidences of human occupation to the first
appearance of cities. No written records are available.

Paleolithic Period   before ca. 14,000 B.C.E.

Mesolithic Period   14,000 to 8000 B.C.E.

Neolithic Period   8000 to 4000 B.C.E.

Chalcolithic Period   4000 to 3200 B.C.E.

Ancient Times   From the emerging urban centers of the Nile and Euphrates rivers
come our earliest written records. This was the era of the ancient
empires of Egypt, Mesopotamia, and Anatolia. The kingdoms of
Israel and Judah belong to the Iron Age.

Early Bronze Age   3200 to 2000 B.C.E.
                     EB I 3200–3000
                     EB II 3000–2800
                     EB III 2800–2400
                     EB IV (earlier MB I) 2400–2000

Middle Bronze Age   2000 to 1550 B.C.E.
                     MB I (earlier MB IIA) 2000–1800
                     MB II (earlier MB IIB) 1800–1650
                     MB III (earlier MB IIC) 1650–1550

Late Bronze Age   1550 to 1200 B.C.E.
                     LB I 1550–1400
                     LB II 1400–1200

Iron Age   1200 to 332 B.C.E.
                     Iron I 1200–900
                     Iron II 900–600
                     Persian Period 600–332

Classical Times   For approximately a millennium, beginning with Alexander's
conquests, the Middle East was dominated by Greek- and
Latin-speaking peoples.

Hellenistic Period   332 to 63 B.C.E.

Roman Period   63 B.C.E. to 324 C.E.

Byzantine Period   324 C.E. to 640 C.E.

Islamic-Medieval Times   Palestine and much of the Middle East had fallen into Arab
hands by 640 C.E. Since that time, Islam and the Arabic
language have been dominant cultural features of the region.

Early Islamic Period 640 to 1099
      Umayyad Caliphate 661–750
      Abbasid Caliphate 750–969
      Fatimid Caliphate 969–1171

Crusader Period   1099 to 1260

Mamluk Period   1260 to 1517

Ottoman Period   1517 to 1918

Modern Times World War I and the fall of the Ottoman Empire set the stage for the current scene of Middle Eastern politics. Key features have been the establishment of the State of Israel and the emergence of national Arab states.

---

*The dates provided here must be regarded as very approximate, especially for the periods prior to Classical Times. Where more precise dates are provided, for Classical Times and later, they apply primarily to Palestine.

Classical Times. Following Alexander the Great's conquests in the fourth century B.C.E., a Macedonian version of Greek culture and politics began to pervade the Middle East. For roughly the next thousand years (subdivided by historians and archaeologists into the Hellenistic, Roman, and Byzantine periods), the Mediterranean region was a basin of common culture and the Middle East was dominated by Greek- and Latin-speaking peoples.

Islamic-Medieval and Modern Times. With the rise of Islam in the early seventh century C.E., the Middle East fell under Arab rule and the domination of Arab culture. It still is predominantly an Arab realm in spite of various invasions by Turks, Crusaders, and Mongols as well as the emergence of the modern State of Israel.

The Israelites and Judeans as "Late-Comers"

Roughly two thousand years of recorded history and impressive cultural achievements preceded the beginnings of Israelite and Judean history. This earlier span of time witnessed major literary, technological, and scientific developments, particularly in Mesopotamia and Egypt. Known written materials from these civilizations include business documents, royal inscriptions, biographical and autobiographical narratives, epic poems, correspondence, love songs, wisdom collections, theological and mythological treatises, hymns and prayers, and even recipes, both pharmaceutical and culinary. Technological and scientific achievements can be seen not only in the development of fortified cities, monumental and domestic architecture, tools, weapons, household utensils, and jewelry but also in the development of mathematics and astrology. While most of our knowledge of these pre-Iron Age developments comes from Egypt, Mesopotamia, and Syria (particularly Ebla and Ugarit), artifactual remains

unearthed at ancient sites in Palestine—such as Megiddo, Gezer, and Hazor—
illustrate that in Palestine also the Israelites and the Judeans were heirs to a long
and sophisticated civilization.

Their Origins in the Late Bronze–Early Iron Age

During the Late Bronze Age (about 1550–1200 B.C.E.), Egypt was the dominant empire in the Middle East, with its control and influence extending deep
into Asiatic territory. Palestine in particular, the homeland of Israel and Judah,
was essentially Egyptian territory. Egypt's primary competitor was the Hittite
empire centered in Anatolia. These two empires fought to a draw in the second
quarter of the thirteenth century and then established amicable relations (see
ANET 199–203). As the century drew to a close, however, both empires
virtually collapsed. This latter turn of events may have been brought about in
large part by major population movements that are known to have been occurring about that time. Indo-European movements from the northwest, of which
the "Sea Peoples" were a part, disrupted normal life from Greece to the Nile
Delta. There may have been similar disruptive migrations from the southeast
as well—Semitic tribal groups from the steppes and fringes of the Arabian
Desert.

The origins and early history of Israel and Judah have as their immediate
backdrop these turbulent times at the end of the Bronze Age and the beginning
of the Iron Age. A new political configuration began to emerge in Syria-
Palestine during the Iron Age which favored local particularities—tribal politics, small national states, and petty kingdoms. The kingdoms of Israel and Judah
were among the small Early Iron Age states that resulted.

The Impact of Alexander's Conquest

Alexander's conquest in the fourth century B.C.E. marked a significant turning
point in Middle Eastern affairs—the end of Ancient Times and the beginning
of Classical Times, according to the chronological divisions indicated above—
and had particular implications for the remnants of Israel and Judah. Preclassical
Israelite and Judean history can be understood as unfolding primarily in the
context of the Fertile Crescent. After Alexander, it unfolds primarily within the
context of the Mediterranean World. The transition involved a wrenching
culture shock.

The invading Macedonians brought with them an impressive cultural heritage
which differed radically from that of the east. Even later in the Hellenistic
period, when closer contacts with other civilizations had modified their sense
of elitism, the Greeks still felt themselves greatly superior to the barbarians—
non-Greek-speaking peoples. And the Greeks had good reason for regarding
as unrivaled their highly self-conscious culture. It treasured the freedom of man,
the values of education, realism in art, the worth of dialogue, discussion, and
independence of thought, not to mention its superiority in battlefield tactics and
military organization. Yet Judaism too, even in the fourth century, was highly

self-conscious. Clash ("thy sons, O Zion, against thy sons, O Greece"; Zech. 9:13) and synthesis ("there was such an extreme of Hellenization and increase in the adoption of foreign ways"; II Macc. 4:13) between the two cultures were inevitable.

Place-Names and the Succession of Dominating Cultures

The interchange and succession of dominating cultures throughout the long sweep of Middle Eastern history are reflected in the geographical terminology and place-names of Palestine. That is, any particular city or locale typically will have been known by different names in the past, corresponding to the different historical periods.

The most ancient geographical terms and place-names naturally are Semitic, since the basic population stock of the Middle East, excluding Egypt, spoke Semitic languages. "Semitic," a term borrowed from the name of one of Noah's sons (Shem), refers to a group of related languages (a language family), which includes Hebrew, Aramaic, Akkadian, Arabic, and others. During Classical Times many of these older Semitic names apparently remained in use among the indigenous Palestinian population but tended to be replaced or modified by the new upper and official class which spoke Greek and Latin. Still later, with the Arab expansion, many of the old preclassical Semitic names came back into official use, although usually with different pronunciation and spelling. And of course new Arabic names were coined as well, especially for places whose old names had been forgotten and for new settlements. Finally, with the establishment of modern Israel, there has been a move within Israeli territory to revert to biblical names and to Hebraize Arabic ones.

In short, place-names in the Middle East in general and in Palestine in particular reflect the complexities of Middle Eastern history and can be understood much better when it is realized that name changes have tended to occur in accordance with the last three of the four major chronological phases outlined above. Chart II illustrates the sort of changes that have occurred. It will be our

CHART II. Ancient Names–Modern Names

Ancient Name	Classical Name	Arabic	Modern Hebrew
Jerusalem	Aelia Capitolina	el-Quds	Jerusalem
Beth-shean	Scythopolis	Beisan	Beth Shean
Shechem	Neapolis	Nablus	
Rabbath-ammon	Philadelphia	Amman	
Acco	Ptolemais	Akka	Acco
Samaria	Sebastos	Sebastiyeh	

practice in this volume to use the ancient and classical forms of place-names, depending on the context.

The Geographical Context

Center stage for the history of ancient Israel and Judah was a small area of mountainous terrain, the central Palestinian hill country, lying between the coastal plain and the great depression of the Jordan Valley. In modern times we have come to think of all of Palestine as the "Holy Land." And it is true that certain biblical texts claimed the whole of the land and even beyond for the Israelite tribes. The fact is, however, that ancient Palestine was shared by a diversity of people not limited to the Israelites and Judeans, and that only during certain periods of strength were the Israelite and Judean kings able to exercise authority beyond the limits of the central hill country. While the central hill country was the immediate geographical context, however, Israelite and Judean history must be understood also in relation to four broader and overlapping geographical contexts: the Fertile Crescent with Egypt, the Mediterranean World, the Eastern Mediterranean Seaboard, and of course Palestine as a whole.

The Fertile Crescent with Egypt

The early history of Israel and Judah unfolds in the broader context of the so-called Fertile Crescent and adjacent regions, particularly Egypt. The name "Fertile Crescent," of modern coinage, refers to the region considered to be the cradle of earliest Asiatic civilization. Specifically, it denotes the crescent-shaped band of cultivable land that begins near the head of the Persian Gulf, where the Tigris and Euphrates rivers empty their waters. From there the crescent extends toward the northwest, following the plains and valleys of these two rivers and their tributaries to the borders of the Anatolian plateau. The band bends then to the southwest, to include the Eastern Mediterranean Seaboard, and ends finally in the wastelands of Sinai (see Map 1). The Fertile Crescent, as the name implies, stands out from its surroundings which, except for Egypt, are less inviting or even hostile to human settlement. To the north and northwest, the crescent is limited by a series of mountain ranges. The Mediterranean Sea on the west completes, with these mountains, the borders of the convex edge of the crescent. The concave edge is limited by the northern and western reaches of the Sinai, Syrian, and Arabian deserts, which are lands only seasonally usable and which were, until the widespread use of the camel, a nearly impassable barrier to travel.

Fed by spring rains, the Tigris and Euphrates rivers are subject to periodic violent flooding, threatening life and harvest. Their windswept river plain (or "Mesopotamia," which means "between the rivers" in Greek) is fertile, however, and through the use of irrigation canals was already highly productive in Ancient Times. Ancient Mesopotamian affairs tended to be dominated by two rival city-states, both of which emerged as empires during the late Iron Age:

Assyria in the north (Upper Mesopotamia) and Babylonia in the south (Lower Mesopotamia). The Assyrian empire flourished first, during the eighth and seventh centuries B.C.E., and eventually incorporated the whole of the Fertile Crescent and Egypt as well. The collapse of the Assyrian empire was followed by a period of Babylonian imperialism during the sixth century, after which Persia emerged as the dominating power of the whole Middle East for approximately the next two centuries. Indeed, the Indo-European Persians, whose center of power was located in the Iranian plateau east of the Fertile Crescent, produced the most expansive empire up to its day. This Persian empire extended eastward to the Indus Valley, northwest to the Greek city-states of Asia Minor (threatening even the mainland of Greece itself), and southwest as far as the Sudan and North Africa.

Southwest of the Eastern Mediterranean Seaboard, which we will consider more closely below, was Egypt. Although actually a part of Africa and separated from the Fertile Crescent by the Sinai Desert, Egypt might be considered as an extension of the Fertile Crescent because of its proximity and the equally important role it played in ancient history. Herodotus, the sixth-century B.C.E. Greek historian, described Egypt as "the gift of the Nile" (*Histories* II.5), which was a very perceptive observation. The land drew its sustenance from the river

View of Amman. Seen from the hill on which ancient Rabbath-ammon, chief city of the Ammonites, was situated. Memory of the Ammonite presence is preserved in the name of the modern city, Amman, which surrounds the ancient site. Central among the buildings of the modern city are the remains of a theater from Roman times, when the city was called Philadelphia (compare Chart II). (*J. M. Miller*)

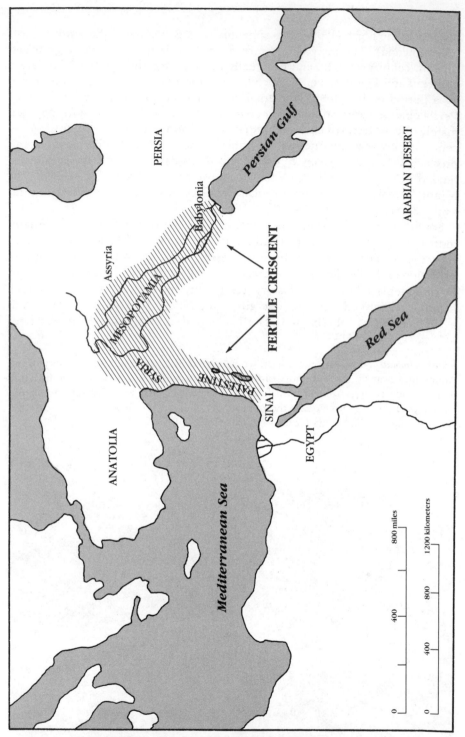

MAP 1. The Fertile Crescent with Egypt

which slithers like a snake through the desert sands, adorning its immediate surroundings with luxuriant growth. The valley of the Nile is bordered to the west by the Libyan wastelands and to the east by an arid plateau which, interrupted by the Red Sea, continues beyond as the Arabian Desert. Fed by equatorial rainfall in the heartlands of Africa, the Nile had an annual rise and fall that was more predictable than that of the Tigris or Euphrates. Its rise always began in July, and by late October all of the agriculturally rich land along the riverbanks was inundated. By January, the river had returned to its banks, leaving behind richly productive silt. The Nile was also more easily navigable than were the Tigris and the Euphrates, so that in addition to feeding Egypt it served as a means of communication and transportation. The heyday of Egypt as an international power had already passed before the emergence of the Israelite and Judean monarchies. As a result of the geographical proximity, however, Egypt was a constant meddler in Syro-Palestinian affairs. And of course there had been a long history of Egyptian control over the area during the Bronze Age—a control that Egypt was never willing to concede even when no longer able to exercise it. Also, under the Ptolemaic rulers following Alexander's conquests, Egypt flourished again for a brief period as a major international power.

As we shall see below, the very location of Palestine and its function as a land bridge between Asia and Africa inevitably involved Israel and Judah in the power struggles between Mesopotamia and Egypt. Moreover, as one would expect, the inhabitants of ancient Palestine shared many cultural characteristics with their neighbors, including the peoples of Mesopotamia and Egypt. In terms of basic cultural patterns—language, literature, mythological and theological perspectives, and the like—there seems to have been a closer kinship with Mesopotamia than with Egypt. The closer geographical proximity of Egypt, on the other hand, meant that Egyptian influence, both political and cultural, was also a fairly constant feature throughout Israelite and Judean history.

The Mediterranean World

While the Fertile Crescent with Egypt is to be understood as the broader geographical context for ancient Israelite and Judean history, the determinative context for Classical Times was the Mediterranean World (see Map 2). Three groups of people—the Phoenicians, the Greeks, and the Romans—figured significantly in the general life of the Mediterranean basin and in the struggle for maritime control. With the Phoenicians and the Greeks, it was a matter of gradual development of commercial and colonizing activity over the years. The conquests of the Macedonian Alexander represented an exception, of course, in the case of the Greeks. The Romans on the other hand, particularly their movement into the eastern Mediterranean, represented overt conquest and domination. The activities and policies of all three powers had impact on the history of Israel and Judah. The Phoenicians, whose main cities were located along the Mediterranean coast from Mt. Carmel northward, dominated the sea

Asiatics in Egypt. "Asiatics" arriving at the royal court, as viewed by the Egyptians. Early Twelfth Dynasty painting from the tomb of Khnum-hotep III at Beni Hasan (near Minya, in Middle Egypt). *(Egypt Exploration Society)*

throughout much of the Early Iron Age and established colonies as far afield as North Africa and Spain. Especially from the tenth century onward, their maritime empire was a source of great wealth, and their colonies were the means of cultural diffusion throughout the Mediterranean World. The two high points of prosperity for Israel and Judah in the tenth and ninth centuries, the reigns of Solomon and Ahab respectively, were to no small extent the consequence of their sharing in the commercial activity and prosperity of the Phoenicians. Some of the Phoenician colonies became major powers themselves. Carthage in North Africa, for example, competed successfully with the Romans for domination of the western Mediterranean during the second century B.C.E. Indeed, the Carthaginians almost succeeded in defeating the Romans in the Punic (Latin for "Phoenician") Wars.

The Greek city-states also colonized widely throughout the Mediterranean, especially along the western and southern shores of Anatolia. After the eighth century, in fact, Assyrian pressure on Phoenicia gave the Greeks an advantage in Mediterranean trade. Still later, as the Persians expanded westward, conquering the Eastern Mediterranean Seaboard and much of southern Anatolia, they clashed with the Greek colonial cities along the Anatolian coastline and eventually invaded the Greek mainland itself. In short, the famous battles of Marathon and Salamis may be seen as part of a larger contest between the Persians and the Greeks for control of the eastern Mediterranean. Moreover, this Greek and Persian maneuvering for power was a crucial element in the background of Jewish history during the fifth and fourth centuries B.C.E. Aspects of the latter, particularly Judean-Persian relations, are best understood in the light of Persia's struggle to retain control of the eastern Mediterranean World. Eventually, with the conquests of Alexander the Great, the Greeks gained superiority and their western culture spread rapidly eastward.

It remained for the Romans, however, who moved into the eastern Mediterranean in the late third and early second centuries B.C.E., following the Punic Wars, to reduce the eastern regions to provinces under the direct control of a

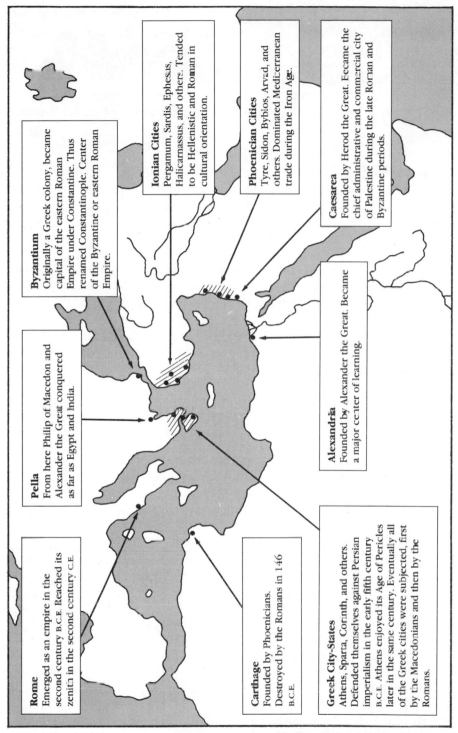

Byzantium
Originally a Greek colony, became capital of the eastern Roman Empire under Constantine. Thus renamed Constantinople. Center of the Byzantine or eastern Roman Empire.

Ionian Cities
Pergamum, Sardis, Ephesus, Halicarnassus, and others. Tended to be Hellenistic and Roman in cultural orientation.

Phoenician Cities
Tyre, Sidon, Byblos, Arvad, and others. Dominated Mediterranean trade during the Iron Age.

Caesarea
Founded by Herod the Great. Became the chief administrative and commercial city of Palestine during the late Roman and Byzantine periods.

Pella
From here Philip of Macedon and Alexander the Great conquered as far as Egypt and India.

Alexandria
Founded by Alexander the Great. Became a major center of learning.

Rome
Emerged as an empire in the second century B.C.E. Reached its zenith in the second century C.E.

Carthage
Founded by Phoenicians. Destroyed by the Romans in 146 B.C.E.

Greek City-States
Athens, Sparta, Corinth, and others. Defended themselves against Persian imperialism in the early fifth century B.C.E. Athens enjoyed its Age of Pericles later in the same century. Eventually all of the Greek cities were subjected, first by the Macedonians and then by the Romans.

MAP 2. The Mediterranean World

western power. By the end of the first century B.C.E., the whole of Anatolia, the Eastern Mediterranean Seaboard, and even Egypt had been incorporated into a gigantic administrative and cultural empire with its center of authority in the city of Rome hundreds of miles away. This situation would continue until the fourth century C.E., when the center of administrative power for the eastern Mediterranean World shifted to Byzantium (itself formally a Greek colony).

The Eastern Mediterranean Seaboard

The Fertile Crescent and the Mediterranean World provided the two larger geographical contexts for the history of Israel and Judah. It is appropriate now to focus more closely on the Eastern Mediterranean Seaboard, the strip of cultivable land extending from Mt. Taurus in the north to the Sinai Desert in the south, sandwiched between the Mediterranean Sea on the west and the Arabian Desert on the east. In short, this is the southwestern horn of the Fertile Crescent, the area where the Fertile Crescent overlaps the Mediterranean World. The seaboard extends about four hundred miles north-south and averages between seventy to one hundred miles east-west (see Map 3).This strip of land between the sea and the desert has served throughout history as a land bridge between Asia and Africa and as a point of maritime contact with Europe. The strip narrows toward the southern end, in the region of Palestine, so that one might think of the land bridge as being shaped like an hourglass, with key routes passing north-south through Palestine and forking off in essentially four directions. The northwestern fork led via the Phoenician ports and Anatolia toward Europe. The northeastern fork led around the desert to Mesopotamia. The southwestern fork led along the Mediterranean coast to Egypt and Africa. The southeastern fork led to the Gulf of Aqabah, itself an arm of the Red Sea, and around the gulf to Arabia.

The topography of this seaboard region is greatly diversified, broken by mountain ranges and valleys. Common to the entire course of the area are four north-south physiographic features. These are most clearly delineated in the north, where they are represented by the Phoenician coast, the Lebanon Mountains, the Bekaa Valley, and the Anti-Lebanon Mountains. At various points this north-south orientation is interrupted by east-west formations which contribute in turn to the variety and brokenness of the terrain. There are no unifying major river valleys comparable to those found in Mesopotamia and Egypt. Agricultural possibilities are reasonably limited and tend toward small-plot farming. The combination of these two physical characteristics predisposed the area to particularistic regionalism. Specifically, the situation favored independent city-states and small localized kingdoms rather than large empires.

The character of the region as lying between continents meant that the population was somewhat heterogeneous and cosmopolitan even in Ancient Times, although the vast majority of the people spoke more or less closely related languages that belong to the "Semitic" family. One would expect this, since the Mediterranean Seaboard is the northwestern part of the Arabian

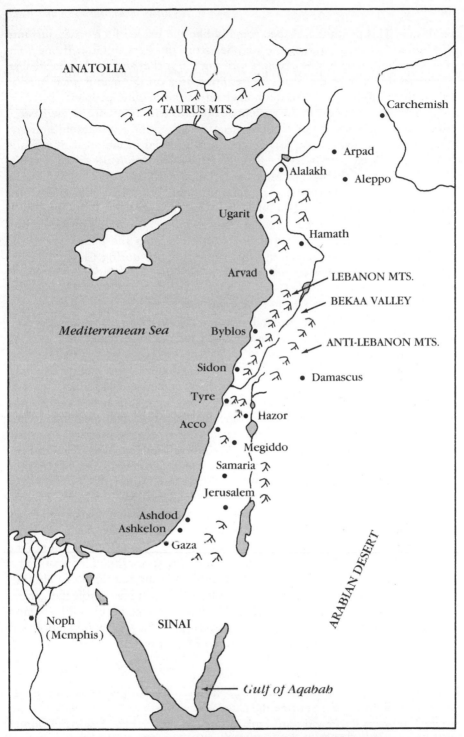

ANATOLIA

TAURUS MTS.

Carchemish

Arpad

Alalakh

Aleppo

Ugarit

Hamath

Arvad

LEBANON MTS.

BEKAA VALLEY

Mediterranean Sea

Byblos

ANTI-LEBANON MTS.

Sidon

Damascus

Tyre

Acco

Hazor

Megiddo

Samaria

ARABIAN DESERT

Jerusalem

Ashdod
Ashkelon

Gaza

Noph
(Mcmphis)

SINAI

Gulf of Aqabah

MAP 3. The Eastern Mediterranean Seaboard

peninsula. This peninsula, shaped roughly like the blade of a hatchet, juts into the Indian Ocean, separating the Red Sea from the Persian Gulf. If one completes the figure, with Mesopotamia forming the socket and the Mediterranean Seaboard the back of the head, the resultant area on the map is what may be called the Semitic Quadrant, the homeland of the Semitic peoples.

Various names appear in the ancient documents with reference to the Eastern Mediterranean Seaboard or subdivisions of it. Often these geographical designations serve as names also for the people who lived in the areas thus designated. The "Arameans" were the people who lived in Aram, for example, while the inhabitants of the land of Moab were known as "Moabites." Sometimes a name was used in different ways in different texts. The name "Canaanite," for example, seems to be used in some texts to refer to the whole indigenous population of Palestine, but in other texts to refer only to one of the various groups that composed this population. Note also that the names we use in English usually derive from terms that came into use during Classical Times. The following are some key names with brief explanations.

Retenu and Hurru. The names "Retenu" and "Hurru" are used in early Egyptian documents for the general seaboard region. Both names had lost their prominence by the time of the Israelite and Judean monarchies.

Amurru (Amorite). The region west of Mesopotamia, including the Mediterranean Seaboard, is referred to in the Mesopotamian (Akkadian) texts as "Amurru" ("the west land"). Variations of this term appear in Egyptian and Hebrew texts also, usually with a somewhat more specific meaning. In the Egyptian texts, for example, the term seems to have referred primarily to a small kingdom in the northern region of the Mediterranean Seaboard (see also Josh. 13:4). The biblical writers often refer to the indigenous population of Palestine as "Amorites," which is the Hebrew equivalent of "Amurru."

Canaan. The name "Canaan" also appears in various ancient texts, from Egypt to Mesopotamia. In the Egyptian texts, Canaan seems to have been used as a designation for Egypt's Asiatic province. In the Bible, Canaan could refer to the whole of Palestine west of Jordan, the ideal inheritance of the Hebrews; but it could also refer to more restricted areas, especially the coastland of Palestine. Correspondingly, the biblical writers occasionally refer to the whole indigenous population of Palestine as "Canaanites" (thus interchangeably with "Amorites"). On other occasions, they seem to distinguish the Canaanites and Amorites from other groups among the occupants of Palestine (compare, for example, Gen. 12:5–6 with Gen. 15:18–21).

Hatti. The Hittites of Anatolia, who spoke an Indo-European language, established a powerful empire during the Late Bronze Age which extended eastward to the Euphrates River and southward into the Mediterranean Seaboard. Important city-states in the northern seaboard region continued to be referred to as

"Hittite cities," moreover, even after the old Hittite empire had ceased to exist (see, for example, I Kings 10:29; II Kings 7:6). In some Mesopotamian texts Hatti is used to refer to the entire seaboard region.

Aram (Syria). The interior of roughly the northern half of the Mediterranean Seaboard is often referred to in the Bible and certain other ancient texts as "Aram." The first indisputable reference to Arameans, the inhabitants of this area, occurs in an inscription of an Assyrian king, Tiglath-pileser I (about 1115–1077 B.C.E.). Carchemish, Hamath, and Damascus were notable Aramean cities. Deuteronomy 26:5 identifies the ancestors of Israel and Judah as Arameans, while other biblical passages describe the wives and concubines of both Isaac and Jacob as Arameans from the region of Haran (see Gen. 24; 29–31). The Greek name "Syria" emerged during Classical Times, apparently derived from "Assyria" and used initially to refer to the Assyrian empire. Later the term was applied to the region west of the Euphrates, then to the whole coastal region, and finally to the interior of roughly the northern half of the coastal zone. In this latter sense, Syria corresponds essentially to Aram; and "Aram" and "Arameans" are normally translated "Syria" and "Syrians" in the Greek and English versions of the Bible.

Phoenicia. The name "Phoenicia," apparently derived from the Greek word *phoinix,* meaning "purple," was applied in Classical Times to the central and northern coastal region of the seaboard. Good ports along this stretch of the coastline, at places such as Tyre, Sidon, and Byblos, allowed the Semitic Phoenicians to develop the extensive maritime and commercial interests throughout the Mediterranean World noted above. The Phoenician cities were somewhat cut off from the Aramean (Syrian) cities of the interior, on the other hand, by the Lebanon Mountains. No doubt this was also one of the factors that encouraged the Phoenicians to turn to the sea.

Arabia. The name "Arabia," apparently deriving from a Semitic word for "nomad," appeared already in Persian texts and came to be used more widely during Classical Times. Specifically, the name referred to the desert regions east and south of the Eastern Mediterranean Seaboard. Some of the inhabitants of Arabia (i.e., "Arabians" or "Arabs") were true nomads, while others followed a more sedentary life-style. The Nabateans were of Arabian origin and deserve special mention in that they became heavily involved in trans-desert commerce and trade. Mentioned first in texts dating soon after Alexander's conquest of the east, they made their capital at Petra and lived astride the important spice and incense trade routes from south Arabia.

Philistia. Along the southern coastal plain of the Eastern Mediterranean Seaboard (roughly south of present-day Tel Aviv) were settled the Philistines. They came to that region as a part of the general "Sea Peoples" migrations at the end of the Bronze Age and inhabited five main cities—Ashdod, Ashkelon, Ekron,

Gath, and Gaza. Although historically the Philistines are to be associated specifically with the coastal plain, during Classical Times the name "Philistia" ("land
of the Philistines") came to be applied more generally to the whole southern
end of the Eastern Mediterranean Seaboard. Syria Palaestina was the name of
the Roman province, for example, which included most of the region that will
be described below as Palestine. In short then, the English term "Palestine"
derives ultimately from "Philistia," "the land of the Philistines."

Being a land bridge between continents, the Eastern Mediterranean Seaboard, or Syria-Palestine as we shall refer to this region, was an active zone of
commerce. Yet while its inhabitants benefited significantly from the commerce,
these benefits came with a heavy price. Syria-Palestine was sucked into virtually
all the major conflicts between the ancient imperial powers. The cost and futility
of military preparedness, the schizophrenia induced by the perpetual need to
choose sides, the agonies of defeat, and the lessons of loss are etched in the
literature of the region, especially in the Hebrew Scriptures. The architectural,
monumental, and inscriptional remains in the region in many instances are not
the work of natives, but reflect the hands and languages of the conquerors—
Hittites, Assyrians, Egyptians, Babylonians, Persians, Greeks, and Romans.

Palestine

A still narrower geographical context for the history of Israel and Judah was
the land of Palestine. This area has reasonably well-defined boundaries—in the
north the foothills of the Lebanon and Anti-Lebanon mountains, in the west the
Mediterranean Sea, in the south the Sinai Desert, and in the east the Arabian
Desert. Lying between 31° and 33° 30′ north latitude and comprising about
9,500 square miles, Palestine is comparable in size to the country of Belgium
or the state of Vermont. Its topography may be divided into four north-south
zones, which are continuations of the four zones delineated above. These are
(1) the coastal plain, continuous with the Phoenician coast; (2) Galilee and the
central hill country, continuous with the Lebanon Mountains; (3) the Jordan
Rift Valley, continuous with the Bekaa Valley; and (4) the Transjordanian
highlands, continuous with the Anti-Lebanon Mountains (see Maps 4 and 5).
The general north-south orientation of the region is interrupted by the Mt.
Carmel range and the Jezreel (or Esdraelon) Valley which parallel each other
in a northwest to southeast direction. The Carmel range is a spur of the central
hill country which juts northwestward into the Mediterranean. Thus it creates
a natural barrier across the coastal plain, forcing traffic along the coastal road
either to detour inward through mountain passes, particularly the one at
Megiddo, or to squeeze through the few hundred feet that separate the precipitous Mt. Carmel promontory from the sea. The Jezreel Valley, which is a
reasonably broad and fertile plain, divides the mountainous backbone of Palestine, separating the Galilean hill country to the north from the central hill
country to the south.

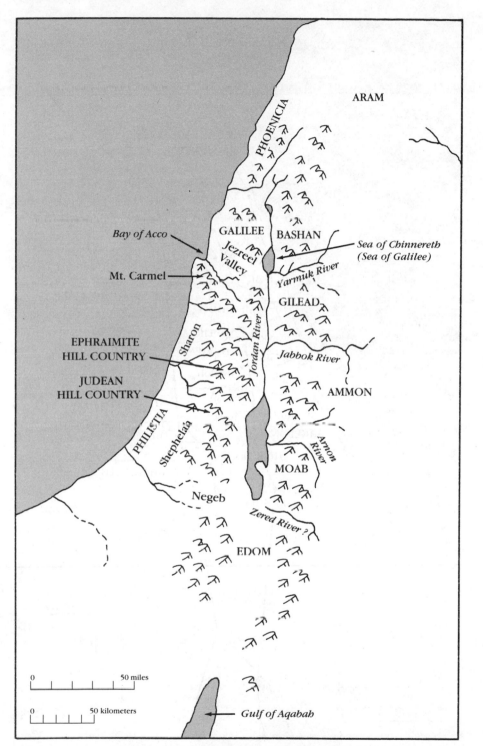

ARAM

PHOENICIA

Bay of Acco

GALILEE   BASHAN

Jezreel
Valley

Mt. Carmel

Sea of Chinnereth
(Sea of Galilee)

Yarmuk River

GILEAD

Sharon

Jordan River

EPHRAIMITE
HILL COUNTRY

Jabbok River

JUDEAN
HILL COUNTRY

AMMON

PHILISTIA

Shephelaa

Arnon
River

MOAB

Negeb

Zered River ?

EDOM

0   50 miles

0   50 kilometers

Gulf of Aqabah

MAP 4. Palestine During Ancient Times

MAP 5. Main Roads and Cities of Ancient Palestine

The Coastal Plain. A characteristic feature of the Palestinian coast is its smooth unaccented line, interrupted only by the Mt. Carmel ridge which juts into the sea and by the Bay of Acco immediately north of Mt. Carmel. The ancient harbor city of Acco was located at the northern end of the bay (in contrast to Haifa, which dominates the bay today from the southern end), and the bay itself represents the northwestern end of the Jezreel Valley. North of the Bay of Acco, the mountains rise almost straight out of the sea. This leaves little true plain, but provided good harbors for the small and fragile ships of Ancient and Classical Times, harbors which the Phoenicians put to good use. South of Carmel the coastline is much smoother, with shallow waters unprotected from the winds—not overly amicable to ancient seafaring. Moreover, much of the southern coast was rendered less accessible by sand dune barriers and low limestone ridges paralleling the shoreline. None of the port cities farther south along the Palestinian coast than Acco—the main ones were Dor, Joppa, Ashkelon, and Gaza—had nearly as good a natural harbor as Acco itself or the other port cities farther to the north. Herod the Great turned the old site of Strato's Tower, just south of Dor, into the successful seaport of Caesarea by constructing an artificial harbor with moles and walls.

The coastal plain is of variable width south of Mt. Carmel, from a few hundred feet at the foot of the mountain to about thirty miles in the vicinity of Gaza. Between Carmel and Joppa, where it was known as Sharon, the plain is fertile but was poorly drained in Ancient Times, thus marshy and forested. From approximately Joppa to Gaza was of course Philistia, the area of the five Philistine cities mentioned above. Here the plain was better suited for agriculture, but there was an increasing degree of aridity toward the south where it eventually merges into the desert.

One of the main international highways through Palestine, "the Way of the Sea" (in Latin called the *via maris*), passed through the coastal plain. Moving up the coast from Egypt, it turned inward at the Carmel ridge and slipped through the Megiddo pass into the Jezreel Valley. At that point it was joined by main roads from the Transjordan and the Aramean cities of Damascus and Hamath, before turning northwestward to follow the Phoenician coast in the direction of Anatolia.

Galilee and the Central Hill Country. The mountainous district between the coastal plain and the Jordan Rift Valley is a range of limestone hills of moderate height and rugged contours, along with their associated features. Essentially two divisions are to be recognized: (1) Galilee, the highlands north of the Jezreel Valley, and (2) the central hill country. The latter may be divided into *(a)* the Ephraimite hill country, also called Samaria, which extends from the Jezreel to approximately Jerusalem; and *(b)* the Judean hill country, from approximately Jerusalem to the Negeb. These are biblical names and are used here rather loosely. "Ephraim," for example, refers to the dominant Israelite tribe that inhabited the mountains north of Jerusalem during Old Testament times. Actually other tribes, particularly Manasseh and Benjamin, also inhabited certain parts of this area. The name "Samaria," on the other hand, derives from the city Samaria, capital from the ninth century on of the northern Israelite kingdom which in turn had as its core this northern part of the central hill country.

Actually two Galilees may be distinguished. Upper, or northern, Galilee is rugged country which reaches an altitude of almost four thousand feet. Lower Galilee's hills are somewhat less rugged and interspersed with fertile valleys. Galilee lay outside the main center of Israelite and Judean territory and at the same time in close proximity to Phoenicia and Syria. Accordingly, the Phoenician and Syrian cities exerted considerable influence on the area.

Josephus, a first-century C.E. historian, reports that there were 204 villages and towns in Galilee in his day (*Life* 245). Elsewhere he writes, with some exaggeration, of this area:

> Although surrounded by such powerful foreign nations, the two Galilees have always resisted any hostile invasion, for the inhabitants are from infancy inured to war, and have at all times been numerous; never did the men lack courage nor the country men. For the land is everywhere so rich in soil and pasturage and produces such variety of trees, that even the most indolent are tempted by these facilities to devote themselves to agriculture. In fact, every inch of the soil has been cultivated by the inhabitants; there is not a parcel of waste land. The towns, too, are thickly distributed, and even the villages, thanks to the fertility of the soil, are all so densely populated that the smallest of them contains above fifteen thousand [!] inhabitants. (*War* III.41–43)

The Jezreel (or Esdraelon) Valley is a broad, flat, and fertile depression which, as indicated above, makes a radical break between Galilee and the central hill country. Throughout history this valley has served as a natural route of overland communication between the Mediterranean and the interior. Add to that the fertility of its soil and it is easy to understand why the Jezreel was the most fought over ground, the natural battlefield, of ancient Palestine. In addition to the port city of Acco, situated, as we have seen, at the northwestern end of the valley, other prominent cities associated with Jezreel were Megiddo, Taanach, and Beth-shean. The name "Jezreel" derives from a small city of that name which was located in the east-central part of the valley and which played an especially prominent role during the period of the Israelite monarchy. Note also that some biblical texts, by referring to the "Plain of Acco" or the "Plain of Megiddo," would seem to reserve the designation "Jezreel Valley" for the more immediate vicinity of the city by that name.

South of the Jezreel Valley, the central mountain range picks up again as the Ephraimite hill country, or Samaria. A key city in this region was Shechem, situated at the pass between the twin peaks of Mt. Ebal (3,083 feet) and Mt. Gerizim (2,889 feet). Generally north of Shechem was the old tribal area of Manasseh, characterized by calcareous hills and valleys of fertile farmland. The valleys lead directly into the heart of the region, thus providing easy accessibility. Three other important cities in this area north of Shechem were Dothan, Tirzah, and Samaria.

Ephraim proper, south of Shechem, is a broad, domed region with heights up to 3,000 feet and more. Jebel Asur, near Bethel, the Baal-hazor of the Bible, reaches 3,332 feet. This was not a region of major cities in Ancient Times, but many of the towns that figure in the biblical narratives were to be found here, including Shiloh, Mizpah, Ramah, Gibeon, and Bethel. In the southern part of Ephraim, in the area occupied by the tribe of Benjamin, two east-west fault lines cut deep into the hill country, thus providing ancient routes into the interior from the coast to the west and the Jordan Valley to the east. Namely, from the west, the Valley of Aijalon (also called "the ascent of Beth-horon") entered the hill country just northwest of Jerusalem. From the east, a double fault line provided two ancient routes from the region of Jericho, one leading to the vicinity of Gibeah and Michmash, the other leading more directly to Jerusalem.

The Judean hill country, from around Jerusalem to the region of Beer-sheba in the Negeb, presents a less fertile, more arid and monotonous countenance than the Ephraimite portion of the central highlands. This is not to say, however, that Judah is barren. In biblical times extensive areas of it were covered by forests. Also then, as well as today, careful husbandry of the somewhat meager resources of soil and moisture produced a relatively successful agricultural economic base for village life. This was particularly true in the better-watered western slopes of the hill country, where, through the utilization of painstakingly constructed terraces, olives, grain, grapes, and other typical Mediterranean products were grown. The chief cities of the Judean highlands were

Jordan River. The Jordan River is shown here near where it leaves the Sea of Galilee. This portion of the river valley is fertile, but as the river flows farther south, it falls lower in altitude and enters less cultivable terrain, eventually emptying into the Dead Sea. (*J. M. Miller*)

Jerusalem and Hebron. Other cities and villages of importance during biblical times were Bethlehem, Tekoa, Beth-zur, and Debir.

Running parallel to the western Judean hill country approximately from Beth-horon to Beer-sheba, and separating the Judean highlands from Philistia proper, lies an area of low foothills known as the Shephelah (meaning "lowland" or "piedmont"). Because of its double importance as Judah's first line of defense and as a fertile, easily farmed strip, the Shephelah was often a source of conflict between the people of Judah and the Philistines.

The eastern edge of the Judean hill country, between the highlands and the Dead Sea Valley, provided a spectacular and even more efficient line of defense. This is the "Wilderness of Judah," a region of arid steppelands, of dizzying naked stone cliffs overlooking the inhospitable waters of the Dead Sea, of caves and hollows where bandits and outcasts have found refuge through the ages, and of dry streambeds down which the waters of occasional heavy rains rush with destructive fury. Some seasonal pasturage of flocks was possible in this wilderness area; otherwise it was essentially uninhabited in Ancient Times.

On the south, the Judean highlands slope quickly to merge into the Negeb (literally, "the dry land"). Specifically, the Negeb begins with the east-west depression of Beer-sheba and ends in the vicinity of Kadesh-barnea, an oasis that marks the southernmost limit of Palestine. Basically the Negeb is a high plateau with very little rainfall—enough to sustain a scrub and grassland vegetation—but with soils which, when irrigated, can produce quite abundantly. In biblical times the Negeb was primarily used by shepherds as pastureland, even though some permanent settlements and military outposts were established in places where natural springs provided a supply of water or military defense was required. In effect, therefore, the Negeb represents an extension of the eastern desert across the southern end of Palestine to the Mediterranean Sea and Sinai.

Although the main international highways through Palestine bypassed the central hill country, a road of some secondary international importance followed approximately the north-south watershed from Shechem via Jerusalem and Bethlehem to Hebron. As indicated above, the main crossroads were provided where valleys cut into the central hill country from the coastal plains to the west and the Jordan Rift Valley to the east—for example, at Shechem, Jerusalem, and Hebron.

The Jordan Rift Valley. The Jordan Rift Valley, with the Jordan River, the Sea of Galilee, and the Dead Sea in its embrace, represents the Palestinian portion of one of the world's most distinctive geological formations. This is the so-called Great Rift, a furrow on the surface of the globe which extends from the Amanus Mountains in Syria to Lake Malaŵi in Africa, forming the Red Sea along the way. It is this deep rift, exacerbating the distinction between the central hill country on the west and the Transjordanian highlands on the east, which gives Palestine its dramatic topographical configurations. The biblical name for the Jordan Rift Valley is Arabah (Ghor in modern Arabic), although some biblical passages seem to use this term specifically for the southernmost end of the valley, south of the Dead Sea.

The sources of the Jordan rise at the foot of Mt. Hermon (itself over 9,000 feet in elevation), in the vicinity of the ancient city of Dan. The river is still above sea level where it parallels Galilee. Here also was located until recently Lake Huleh, a lagoon which was produced by basalt blockage of the river flow and into which several streams drained the marshlands characteristic of the surrounding area in earlier times. On the western bank of the valley along the stretch of the river from Lake Huleh to the Sea of Galilee stood the important city of Hazor. The importance of this city lay in the fact that it was situated at the juncture of the main roads to Hamath and Damascus and at the place where the road to Damascus crossed the Jordan. Below Hazor the river plunges rapidly, so that the Sea of Galilee ten miles farther downstream is almost seven hundred feet below sea level. Bearer of a multiplicity of names (Sea of Chinnereth, Sea of Gennesaret, Sea of Tiberias), the Sea of Galilee is a freshwater lake approximately five miles wide by twelve miles long which supported a fishing industry during Ancient and Classical Times, as it does today.

The main portion of the Jordan Valley lies between the Sea of Galilee and the Dead Sea. Moreover, while the direct distance between the two bodies of water is about sixty-five miles, the meandering course of the river between the two is actually three times that long. Of variable width (averaging about ten miles), this main stretch of the river valley is fertile and cultivable where there are natural springs or where other water is available for small-scale irrigation. This is the case primarily in the north, in the vicinity of the Sea of Galilee. Farther south, as the river approaches the Dead Sea, the valley becomes a virtual wasteland, with the springs at Jericho taking on the character of a desert oasis. Close to the river itself and also becoming more pronounced as it approaches the Dead Sea, the valley drops abruptly, sometimes as much as 150 feet, to form lunar-like eroded gray marly flats of fantastic appearance. These frame the *zor,* the biblical "pride of the Jordan," an impenetrable strip of thorny, tangled growth along the riverbanks, where wild animals, including lions, prowled in biblical times. Its flow through this depressed canyon within the valley rendered the river difficult to cross and relatively useless for any large-scale irrigation purposes. Its rapid flow, on the other hand, and its excessively winding course rendered the Jordan impractical for navigation. In short, the Jordan River was more of a geographical barrier to communication than a link.

Several tributaries join the Jordan in this stretch between the Sea of Galilee and the Dead Sea, the most important of these being the Yarmuk from the east, which drains the area of ancient Bashan and whose waters merge with the Jordan just south of the Sea of Galilee; Wady Far'ah from the west, which provides entrance from the valley to the Ephraimite hill country; and Wady Zerqa from the east, the Jabbok River of biblical traditions, which drains the region of the ancient land of Gilead. Important cities along this stretch of the valley were Beth-shean, at the southeastern end of the Jezreel Valley; Pella, Succoth, and Adam on the east bank; and Jericho with its abundant springs.

The Jordan River ends in the bitter waters of the Dead Sea, the biblical "Sea of the Arabah" or "Salt Sea," also later known as Lake Asphaltitis. This sea is actually a landlocked lake filled with mineral soup (about 25 percent mineral content) produced by evaporation. Throughout antiquity its salt, asphalt, and general features were subjects of fascination and the objects of trade. Josephus gives the following description of the sea.

> Its waters are, as I said, bitter and unproductive, but owing to their buoyancy send up to the surface the very heaviest of objects cast into them, and it is difficult, even of set purpose, to sink to the bottom. Thus, when [the Roman emperor] Vespasian came to explore the lake, he ordered certain persons who were unable to swim to be flung into the deep water with their hands tied behind them; with the result that all rose to the surface and floated, as if impelled upward by a current of air. Another remarkable feature is its change of colour: three times a day it alters its appearance and throws off a different reflection of the solar rays. Again, in many parts it casts up black masses of bitumen, which float on the surface, in their shape and size resembling decapitated bulls. The labourers on the lake row up to these and catching hold of the lumps haul them into their boats; but when they have filled them it is no easy task to detach their cargo, which owing to its tenacious and glutinous character clings to the boat until it is loosened by the monthly secretions of women, to which alone it yields. It is useful not only for caulking ships, but also for the healing of the body, forming an ingredient in many medicines. (*War* IV.476–81)

The Dead Sea is the lowest point on the surface of the earth, with its altitude and the extent of its shoreline varying from time to time, depending on the water level. Typically the water level has been about 1,300 feet below sea level, thus creating a reasonably large lake about 48 miles long, 8 wide, and with a depth of about 1,300 feet in its northern end. The southern end of the sea, below the peculiarly shaped peninsula called the Lisan ("the Tongue") which protrudes from its eastern shore, is very shallow on the other hand, seldom deeper than three or four feet. Several tributaries drain into the Dead Sea from the east, the most important being the Wady Mujib, the River Arnon of the biblical traditions, and the Wady Hesa, possibly the biblical River Zered. Located along the western shores of the Dead Sea were En-gedi, an oasis created by a warm freshwater spring, and Masada, a massive freestanding mountain developed by Herod the Great as a fortified resort and used by the rebels of the First Jewish Revolt as their last refuge. Here also is Qumran, in whose vicinity were discovered the famous Dead Sea Scrolls.

South of the Dead Sea, the Great Rift continues. The land rises rapidly in the direction of the Gulf of Aqabah, reaching its highest point, 650 feet above sea level, some 40 miles north of the gulf. On the gulf itself, actually the eastern arm of the Red Sea, stood Elath, important as a doorway to South Arabia and the East African coast.

The Transjordanian Highlands. Almost in a straight line, running from Mt. Hermon in the north to the shores of the Red Sea in the south, the edge of the

Arabian Plateau rises wall-like alongside the Jordan Valley. North of the Yarmuk River, the plateau is called Bashan, a relatively well watered area with rich soils, famous in biblical times for its fat cattle and fierce bulls. South of the Yarmuk, and roughly paralleling the Ephraimite hill country, lay Gilead, a strip of land from twenty-five to thirty miles in breadth lying along the edge of the plateau and sitting astride the River Jabbok. This is pleasant, bountiful country, with relatively abundant rainfall, which permits the growth of forests and the cultivation of olives and grapes. Gilead being of similar terrain to the central hill country west of the Jordan, it is not surprising that it was inhabited in biblical times by Israelite groups related to those in the Ephraimite area and that Israelite kings attempted to control Gilead. This brought them into confict with the Ammonites and the Moabites, who also made territorial claims in that area.

Rabbath-ammon, the chief city of the Ammonites, was situated at the desert edge on a southeastern branch of the Jabbok. The Moabites, on the other hand, inhabited the rolling plateau east of the Dead Sea. This plateau provides a north-south strip of cultivable land, approximately twenty miles wide, sandwiched between the rugged slopes of the Dead Sea basin and the desert fringe, and bisected by the steep Wady Mujib canyon (the River Arnon). The area is good for grain cultivation and pasturage of goats and sheep. Chief Moabite cities were Heshbon, Medeba, Dibon, and Kir-hareseth.

South of the Wady Hesa (biblical Zered?) was the land of the Edomites, with Bosrah as their chief city. This region becomes increasingly arid as one moves southward; it is similar in this regard to the Negeb and the southern limits of western Palestine. Some biblical texts seem to presuppose that Edom was not limited to the territory east of the Jordan Rift but also extended into the latter region, west of the Arabah. In any case, it is clear that some of the peoples who inhabited the Negeb and southward during Ancient Times were regarded as being of Edomite stock. Later, during the Hellenistic and Roman periods, Nabateans established a commercial empire in the southern Transjordan with its capital at Petra. The Edomites, in the meantime, or Idumeans as they were called during Classical Times, came to be associated with the southern Palestinian region west of the Arabah.

Climate. Palestine has two main seasons: a warm summer that is dry and rainless and a cool winter with rains rolling in from the Mediterranean. Sometime in October the first of the "early rains" moistens the ground enough for plowing and planting. The growing season follows, with most of the necessary moisture coming in the form of sudden downpours rather than the gentler but prolonged periods of precipitation common in more northerly climates. (Jerusalem, for example, gets its twenty or so inches of yearly rainfall, equal to that of London or Paris, in about fifty rainy days, most of them in December, January, and February.) The "late rains" of April and early May are needed to help the crops reach full maturity, and normally they are the last of the rains, although Prov. 26:1 refers to the occasional havoc caused by "rain in harvest" —an anomalous rainfall in early summer. With the onset of spring, vegetation begins to wither and die, especially the winter growth in marginal rainfall areas, and by midsummer drought conditions prevail. The only climatic relief to the summer drought comes in the form of characteristically heavy dews, particularly in the coastal plain and the higher elevations. The hot, dry blast of the sirocco, or khamsin, a southeast wind driving up from the parched desert areas, makes its presence felt from April to early June and from September to November.

Generally speaking, therefore, while some portions of the land receive rain only during the period from December through February, late October through April constitutes the rainy season in Palestine. The "early" and "late" rains mentioned in the Bible are actually the moderate "fall" and "spring" showers which precede and follow the heavy winter storms. The amount of rainfall in any given place in Palestine is controlled by a combination of factors, primarily geographical position and altitude. Namely, the precipitation tends to be heavier toward the north and west and lighter toward the south and east, while at the same time higher elevations tend to get more rain than the lower. As it works out, the central hill country and the Transjordanian highlands usually receive the heaviest rainfall, and within these areas the rainfall tends to be heavier in the north. Thus Upper Galilee averages about 40 inches of rain a year, the Ephraimite hill country (Samaria) around 30, Jerusalem 24, and Hebron 22, while Beer-sheba in the Negeb averages only about 9 inches a year. The coastal plain repeats the pattern, with Acco averaging 26 inches a year and Gaza, in the south, 15, but with the highlands of Carmel receiving as much as 35 inches. In the Jordan Valley, where with the rapid drop in altitude below the Sea of Galilee goes a corresponding increase in aridity, Beth-shean has a mean annual rainfall of 12.5 inches, Jericho 6, and the area around the Dead Sea is true desert, with less than 2 inches of rain a year.

Agrarian-Pastoral Economy. The topography and climate of Palestine predisposed the area to an agrarian-pastoral village economy and life-style. There were no major river valleys comparable to the Tigris-Euphrates or the Nile, and irrigation never played any significant role in Palestinian agriculture. It is "a land of hills and valleys, which drinks water by the rain from heaven" (Deut. 11:11). Accordingly, large cities were the exception rather than the rule. The chief cities in biblical history were small in comparison to their modern or even their ancient Egyptian and Mesopotamian counterparts. Both the Bible and other ancient Middle Eastern literature provide us with descriptions of the crops produced in Palestine: "a land of brooks of water, of fountains and springs, flowing forth in valleys and hills, a land of wheat and barley, of vines and fig trees and pomegranates, a land of olive trees and honey, a land in which you will eat bread without scarcity, in which you will lack nothing" (Deut. 8:7–9). Centuries before the Deuteronomy passage was penned, Sinuhe, an Egyptian traveler, gave the following description of the land:

> It was a good land. . . . Figs were in it, and grapes. It had more wine than water. Plentiful was its honey, abundant its olives. Every kind of fruit was on its trees.

Barley was there, and emmer wheat. There was no limit to any kind of cattle. (*ANET* 19)

Allowing for theological enthusiasm and touristic exaggeration, these two passages provide an accurate glimpse of Palestinian agriculture in biblical times: cereal crops (wheat, barley) which were harvested between April and June, various fruits ripening in the summer months, and grapes and olives gathered in late summer and early fall. From these crops came the basic dietary staples: bread, wine, and oil.

Pastoralism, the raising of sheep and goats, was the second basic element in Palestinian economy—especially in the south and the Tranjordanian highlands. Sheep and goats were well adapted to the Palestinian environment. Both were valued for their secondary products—their wool and hair, and their milk in the case of goats—as well as for the meat they provided. Agrarian and pastoral interests were pursued more in harmony than in competition, although one notices occasional allusions in ancient Middle Eastern literature to differences between the life-styles of the city-village farmer and the life-style of the tent-dwelling shepherd.

Palestine a Land of Contrasts. Perhaps no comparably sized area on the surface of the earth is characterized by such diversity of topographical and climatic features as Palestine. Surely there are not many places other than in ancient Palestine, for example, where one could kill a lion "on a day when snow had fallen" (II Sam. 23:20). As further illustration of the land's topographical and climatic diversity, consider the following hypothetical journey of an ancient traveler from the coastal plain to the eastern desert crossing approximately at Jerusalem. Our hypothetical traveler would have begun the journey, a total distance of less than 80 air miles, by crossing the coastal plain with its tropical climate and growth including palm trees. From there he or she would ascend the rough, low hills of the Shephelah, passing small fields of barley and wheat, vineyards, olive groves, sycamore and other trees, and scrub growth, similar in many respects to the scenery of southern Europe. Climbing then the Judean hills with elevations up to 3,000 feet and above, our traveler would have entered terrain where heavy snowfalls were not unknown and where the land became somewhat more barren, although spotted here and there with growths of forest. After passing Jerusalem and beginning the descent down the eastern slopes of the central hill country, the traveler would have encountered a radically different environment. Namely, the vineyards, olive groves, and cultivated fields would give way to barren ("wilderness") terrain frequented by tent nomads and their flocks of sheep and goats. A few miles farther along, our traveler would have reached the valley of the Jordan, where the summer heat was torrid and the atmosphere heavy. Virtually the whole landscape would have been desolate except for the green oasis of Jericho with its springs and tropical appearance. Within the next twenty miles after passing Jericho, our traveler would descend to the Jordan River approximately at the level of the Dead Sea, itself the lowest spot on the face of the earth, and begin an ascent to the Transjordanian highlands. Rising to an elevation over 3,000 feet, our traveler would have encountered again a landscape of forests and cultivated fields where wheat and barley grew in a plateau setting.

This diversity of east-west topography and climate is matched by a corresponding diversity from north to south. Only 125 miles separate Mt. Hermon with its alpine atmosphere over 9,000 feet above sea level from the Dead Sea with its tropical atmosphere some 1,300 feet below sea level.

Everyday Life in Ancient Palestine

It is difficult for us in modern times to imagine how life was lived and experienced by the inhabitants of Palestine in preindustrial times. Yet we must make an effort to do so, lest we fall into the mentality of medieval artists who depicted biblical characters anachronistically in their own medieval dress and in the physical setting of medieval Europe. Archaeological research is especially useful in this regard. Material remains such as houses, official buildings, tools, weapons, pottery vessels, and coins all contribute to a better understanding of everyday life in Ancient and Classical Times. Moreover, archaeological research is (or can be) more "democratic" than written sources. The latter tend to reflect the life and thought of the wealthy and educated classes. The archaeologist, on the other hand, can excavate in the poorer sections of town as well as in royal palaces and temples.

Perhaps the most important point to be made is that the rhythm and routine of life in preindustrial Palestine was thoroughly immersed in the climatic and agricultural patterns of the land. Fall plowing and sowing, winter pruning, spring harvesting, early summer threshing, and late summer gathering set the dominant agricultural chores. Pastoral pursuits were carried out in the context of this same larger rhythm of life. During the rainy months, when crops were growing, the "wilderness" areas provided pasture; in the summer, the freshly harvested lands could be grazed and the crop residue after threshing used as fodder.

Since there was no means of refrigeration, the diet of fresh food was seasonal. As fruits and vegetables ripened, they were consumed before they spoiled. Some could be cured and preserved in various forms: grapes became raisins and wine, figs were dried, olives were pickled or made into oil, beans and lentils survived dry, and cereal grains needed merely to be preserved from dampness. The diet was essentially vegetarian, with meat consumed only on special occasions.

Living in a marginal rainfall area where cycles of wet and dry years often oscillate, the people were not unfamiliar with famine and hunger. Simply sustaining life required hard and timely labor, and the products of that labor were often unpredictable, being dependent upon uncertain climatic conditions. Even in years of adequate rainfall, locusts and other pests might pose major threats. Thus one can understand why the biblical proverbs warn that people can plan and work but God controls the outcome, and why many of the biblical ideals of life are associated with agricultural and pastoral images of blessedness and plenty.

The routine and the monotony of the agricultural pattern were broken by festival and ceremonial celebrations which were themselves reflective and supportive of the pattern. Based on the two seasons of the year, the religious calendar contained two main periods of worship and festivity (Ex. 23:14–17). Falling near the spring equinox was the festival of Unleavened Bread, celebrating the beginning of the grain harvest. This was followed a few weeks later by the Feast of Harvest, which celebrated the conclusion of the harvest. The main festival of the year, on the other hand, was the Feast of Ingathering, which fell near the autumnal equinox. This fall festival was especially a time of feasting, drinking, and dancing (Judg. 9:27; 21:19–23; I Sam. 1).

The dominant unit of society was the village or town. Farming families lived in small towns or open villages, not in houses on their farming plots. During the harvest seasons, members of the family might stay in the fields in temporary lean-tos. Otherwise they walked to the fields in the early morning and returned in the evening. Inside the walled towns, living quarters were tightly jammed together, with space at a minimum. In such towns of a few hundred, close living quarters allowed and demanded familiarity. This could foster egalitarian and communal concerns but also exacerbate social and economic feelings. The courtyard of the main city gate provided opportunity for gathering and socializing. Here court was held, hawkers sold their wares, speeches were made, the elders philosophized and gossiped, and one could find company and watch the neighbors come and go.

Crafts and special skills tended to be handed down from parents to children. The lack of major technological innovations meant that the skills of one generation rarely differed from those of its predecessor. Even membership in the priesthood tended to be a family and genealogical matter.

Large families were considered a blessing, since they provided labor, social security for a person's future, and continuation of the family name. Because of very primitive medical knowledge, disease was a constant companion. It has been estimated that the infant mortality rate may have been as high as 40 percent and that as many as 30 percent of the women died in childbirth. The elderly and the sick were the responsibility of the family, which was in fact the primary guardian of human status and privilege. To be an orphan or widow without a family was to be in a state of destitution. Although women had few legal rights in the society, they had numerous responsibilities and a multitude of chores. This is apparent from Prov. 31:10–31, for example, which describes the traits of the good wife, obviously in this case from a wealthy family.

Travel and contact with other cultures, at least in pre-Hellenistic times, were rare. Even Solomon with all his power and wealth probably never ventured more than a hundred miles from Jerusalem. Communication was slow, and even the military, the most mobile component of society, traveled primarily on foot. This general lack of outside contacts meant that society tended toward conservatism and was generally suspicious of external influences.

CHAPTER 2

The Question of Origins

The biblical books of Genesis through II Kings, read in sequence, provide a continuous account of Israelite and Judean history from earliest times until the fall of Jerusalem in 586 B.C.E. Genesis through Joshua, the first six of these books, have to do with the origins of the Israelites and how they come to possess the Land of Canaan. The story begins with creation in Genesis and, by the end of the Book of Joshua, has the people at rest in the "land of promise." Since this is the only ancient source that directly addresses the question of Israelite origins, it is appropriate to begin our discussion with a summary of the Genesis-Joshua narrative.

Summary of the Genesis-Joshua Narrative

God created the world in seven days, including all the various land, sea, and celestial formations as well as all vegetation and human life (Gen. 1–2). Adam and Eve, the first human couple, were placed in a garden of paradise. Later, God expelled them from the garden because of their disobedience and initiated a family line which was carried forward by a series of patriarchs. These ancient figures enjoyed unusually long life spans, ranging from Enoch, who lived 365 years, to Methuselah, who lived 969 years. Also, there were giants and "mighty men" in the world in those days, some of these being offspring of the gods (Gen. 2–6). Because of human sin and disobedience, God destroyed all humanity in a universal flood. Only Noah and his immediate family escaped (Gen. 6–9).

The descendants of Noah's three sons (Shem, Ham, and Japheth) began to multiply and migrated to the land of Shinar (Lower Mesopotamia), where they began to construct a great tower with its top to reach the heavens. In order to stop the project, God ordained diversity in human language. No longer able to understand one another, the descendants of Noah's three sons scattered to different parts of the world. Among the distant descendants of Shem, in the ninth generation, was a tent dweller named Abraham. Abraham's father had left

Ur of the Chaldees to migrate to the Land of Canaan but had settled in the vicinity of Haran in Upper Mesopotamia (Gen. 10–11).

After his father's death, Abraham himself migrated from Haran to Canaan. There he lived as a "sojourner" in the land; that is, he maintained his life-style as a tent dweller and resisted integration into the indigenous village-agricultural society of the land. God promised Abraham that someday the whole land would belong to his descendants and that his descendants would be great in number. Eventually Abraham made permanent camp near Hebron and became the father of two sons. The older son, Ishmael, became the father of the desert folk. But the favorite, and the only son of his wife Sarah, was Isaac, born when Abraham was a hundred years old and Sarah was ninety. Meanwhile, Lot, Abraham's nephew, settled in one of the cities of the plain (apparently in the vicinity of the Dead Sea) and barely escaped with his two daughters when God destroyed several cities in that area with fire and brimstone. Lot's wife was turned into a pillar of salt during the escape. His two daughters, in order to continue the family line, seduced their intoxicated father and later gave birth to two sons from these incestuous unions. The two sons became the ancestors of the Ammonites and the Moabites (Gen. 12–22).

After Sarah's death at the age of 127, Abraham remarried and had further offspring by his second wife and by several concubines (Gen. 25:1–11). These became the ancestors of various Arabic tribes. Before his death at the age of 175, he obtained a wife for his son Isaac from their kinsmen living in the city of Nahor near Haran (Gen. 23–24).

Isaac married Rebekah and settled near Beer-sheba. She gave birth to twins: Esau and Jacob. Esau became the ancestor of the Edomites (Gen. 36), and Jacob fathered twelve sons, by his Aramean wives and concubines, who became the ancestors of the twelve tribes (Gen. 25:19–35:29).

One of Jacob's sons, Joseph, was sold as a slave by his brothers and carried into Egypt. In prison, Joseph displayed his ability to interpret dreams. With this power he gained his freedom and eventually became the chief administrative official over all Egypt, second only to the pharaoh. Meanwhile a famine in Palestine forced Jacob and his family to migrate to Egypt in search of food. Joseph arranged for them to settle in a place called Goshen. In Egypt, the families of the twelve brothers multiplied into twelve tribes (Gen. 37–50).

Eventually a pharaoh came to power "who knew not Joseph" and reduced the Hebrews to slavery. God commanded Moses—who, although a Hebrew himself, had grown up in pharaoh's court after being rescued as a babe from the Nile—to lead the people out of Egypt and back to the land he had promised Abraham. The escape from Egypt was surrounded by spectacular miracles, including ten plagues which God sent upon Egypt. After each plague, the pharaoh agreed to allow the Hebrews to leave. Then God "hardened pharaoh's heart" so that he changed his mind, refused to let the Hebrews leave, and thus invited another plague upon his land. When the Hebrews finally did manage to leave, the pharaoh, his heart having been hardened once again, assembled

Dome of the Rock and Haram el-Khalil Mosque. Throughout Palestine are places associated by tradition with the patriarchs and thus regarded as holy spots by Jews, Arabs, and Christians. The Dome of the Rock monument (above) is built over the spot in Jerusalem where, supposedly, Abraham prepared to sacrifice Isaac and Mohammed received his famous vision of Paradise. Solomon's Temple probably stood on or near this spot. The Haram el-Khalil Mosque at Hebron (below) supposedly is built over the cave where the patriarchs and their wives were buried. (Dome of the Rock: *J. M. Miller;* Haram el-Khalil Mosque: *Pictorial Archive*)

his army and chased the people as far as the Red Sea. God parted the waters of the sea, allowing the Hebrews to cross on dry land. When the pharaoh and his army followed, God caused the waters to return and destroy them (Ex. 1–15).

The people made their journey to Canaan in stages. God sent a pillar of cloud by day and a pillar of fire by night to indicate when they should move their camp and where they should pitch their tents. Also he fed them with quail and manna in the wilderness. After three months the people reached a mountain in the wilderness of Sinai. They remained encamped at the foot of the mountain while Moses ascended to the top several times, spoke to God directly, and received from the deity extensive legal and cultic instructions and regulations. These were put into practice with the understanding that they were to be followed by the people from that time on. The people were still encamped at the mountain when they celebrated the first Passover—the anniversary of the escape from Egypt (Ex. 13–Num. 10:10).

On the twentieth day of the second month of the second year the cloud was taken up, signaling that it was time for the people to move on. They set out again and eventually came to a place called Kadesh in the southwestern Negeb. From there they sent twelve spies, one from each tribe, to explore "the promised land." The spies returned with glowing reports about the land's fertility and produce, but they warned that the cities were too strong to be conquered and that the land was inhabited by giants. Caleb, one of the spies, urged the people to attack anyway, with confidence that God would deliver the land as he had promised. The people, however, had lost heart; they began to murmur against Moses and prepared to return to Egypt. Then "the glory of God" appeared at the tent of the meeting and the deity chastised the congregation for their lack of faith, decreeing that the people would wander in the wilderness for forty years—that is, until those who were of age at the time of the incident had been replaced by a new generation. Only Caleb and Joshua (one of the spies who had supported Caleb's urging) were to survive to enter the land. After God's edict, an attempt to enter the land from the south met with defeat (Num. 10:11–14:45).

From Kadesh, Moses sent messengers to the king of Edom, apparently as the forty years drew to an end, and requested permission to pass through Edomite territory as they approached "the promised land" from Transjordan. This permission was denied. They conquered two Amorite kingdoms, however, those ruled by Sihon and Og, thereby gaining possession of the whole of Transjordan exclusive of the Ammonite kingdom on the desert fringe and the Moabite and Edomite territories south of the River Arnon. The newly acquired land was assigned to the tribes of Reuben, Gad, and half the tribe of Manasseh as their possessions (Num. 15–36). While still in Transjordan, Moses gave his farewell address admonishing the people to observe the law after they had entered the land and threatening them with exile from the land if they did not (Deut. 1–34).

After Moses' death in Transjordan, Joshua assumed leadership of the people and began preparations for an invasion of western Palestine. Although some military strategy was involved (for example, sending spies in advance), the crossing of the Jordan and the conquest of Jericho were essentially ritual operations surrounded by miracles. The Jordan River rolled back for the people to cross, as had the Red Sea during their escape from Egypt. When the people marched around the walls of Jericho a specific number of times in a procession led by the priests and the Ark, according to God's instructions, the walls collapsed and the city fell into their hands. With subsequent victories at Ai, Gibeon (where God caused the sun to stand still), Libnah, Lachish, Eglon, Hebron, Debir, and Hazor, virtually the whole land fell into their hands. Joshua then assigned the territory west of the Jordan to the remaining tribes. Only the Levites did not receive a territorial allotment. They, being a priestly tribe, were assigned cities scattered throughout the other tribal territories (Josh. 1–24).

Difficulties with Using the Genesis-Joshua Narrative for Historical Reconstruction

This Genesis-Joshua account of Israel's origins exhibits certain characteristics and makes historical claims that many modern historians, indeed many modern readers in general, find difficult to accept.

Ancient Historical Perspectives

The material in Genesis to Joshua reflects, for example, certain historical perspectives that were popular in ancient times but are no longer in vogue and that raise questions about the material's credibility.

The Concept of a "Golden Age." It was a widespread practice in antiquity to postulate an ideal period in the remote past during which human beings supposedly lived under unique conditions, enjoyed special relationships with the deities, sometimes cohabited with the gods, and lived fantastically long life spans. One sees such a view reflected in the early chapters of Genesis where the earliest ancestors of humanity begin life in a paradise state, are tempted to disobedience by a serpent, intermarry with divine beings, live fantastically long lives, and suffer a universal calamity. Modern understandings of human history informed by geology, archaeology, and paleontology assume a radically different perspective on the origin and early days of human life on earth.

Schematic Chronology. In a manner also typical of historical speculations during ancient times, the Genesis-Joshua narrative sets forth a schematic view of historical chronology. Various manuscript traditions of the Bible—Samaritan, Greek, and Masoretic Hebrew—divide this chronology differently. In the Masoretic or standard Hebrew text, for example, one finds the following schematizations. (1) The unusually long life spans of the earliest ancestors of humanity are understood to have been reduced in four stages. Prior to the Flood, people are said to have lived between 900 and 1,000 years. Mahalalel's 895 years, Enoch's 365 years, and Lamech's 777 years are the exceptions. After the Flood, there is a gradual reduction from Shem's 600 years to Nahor's 148 years. From Abraham to Moses, the typical age limit is between 100 and 200 years. After Moses, the recorded life spans correspond to present-day norms. (2) The exodus from Egypt occurs 2,666 years after creation. This corresponds to the genealogical data which places the exodus during the twenty-seventh generation after creation ($26\frac{2}{3}$ generations with an average of 100 years per generation equals 2,666 years). Moreover, 2,666 is $\frac{2}{3}$ of 4,000 years. By counting forward with the biblical figures and taking into account chronological data that would have been available to later Jews, one arrives at the conclusion that the year 4000 after creation was approximately the date of the rededication of the Temple in 164 B.C.E. following the Maccabean rebellion. (3) Forty and multiples of forty are in evidence throughout Genesis-II Kings. There were forty years of wandering in the wilderness following the exodus, for example. The interval from the exodus to Solomon's building of the Temple is recorded as 480 years (I Kings 6:1). From that point to the return of the exiles from Babylon turns out to be another 480 years. In all of these features, ancient speculative ideas about historical times and chronological periods are in evidence. The modern historian cannot avoid viewing such schematizations with skepticism.

Divine Direction of Human Affairs. Another characteristic of the biblical account of Israel's origins which it shares with ancient literature in general is its emphasis on divine involvement in human affairs. Indeed, in the Genesis-Joshua narrative, divine activity and purpose are considered the primary forces determining the shape and course of the historical process. Yahweh speaks directly with certain selected persons from time to time. His participation in human affairs involved public displays of supernatural power—a great flood removes all of wicked humanity from the earth; the confusion in language scatters humanity abroad; a series of plagues climaxed with the drowning of the pharaoh's army enabled the Hebrews to escape Egypt; miraculously provided manna and quail made it possible for them to subsist in the desert for forty years; abnormal occurrences such as the sudden collapse of Jericho's walls and the sun standing still at Gibeon gave Joshua and his army an edge over the Canaanites; and on and on. While modern historians do not necessarily reject the idea of divine involvement in history, it is a presupposition of modern historiography that the general cause and effect aspects of history are explainable without reference to unique disruptions in natural conditions (such as the waters of the Red Sea rolling back or the sun standing still) or any kind of overt divine involvement in human affairs. In short, modern historians have trouble with miracles.

Lineal Genealogical Descent. A fourth historical perspective which the biblical writers shared with most ancients is the assumption that the origins of the various peoples of the world are to be understood in terms of simple lineal descent from a single ancestor or ancestral line. In such a view, ethnic groups and their relationships are viewed in genealogical categories. Thus the Genesis-

Joshua narrative introduces Israel, Judah, and their neighbors in and around Palestine in terms of extensive family trees. The tribal groups within Israel and Judah are given similar treatment; they are considered to be twelve tribes descended from the twelve sons of Jacob. Modern historians, informed by anthropological studies, recognize that the emergence of population groups normally is a very complex process which cannot be explained or understood in the simplistic categories of lineal genealogical succession.

Common Storytellers' Motifs. Finally, many of the biblical narratives, especially those in Genesis-Joshua, are built on motif patterns that had widespread currency in the ancient world. Consider, for example, the favorite storyteller's motif of "the success of the unpromising" (the Cinderella theme). Stories based on this motif tell how one who seemingly had no chance of success or triumph eventually enjoyed a reversal of fate. Abraham, a man without a country; Joseph, an imprisoned slave in an Egyptian jail; Moses, a babe afloat on the crocodile-infested Nile; the Hebrews, toiling in servitude to a harsh pharaoh— all of these are presented as the unpromising who, with divine help, ultimately succeed and were blessed. The Sodom and Gomorrah story reflects yet another motif pattern known from extrabiblical literature, that of divine beings who visit a city to test the hospitality of its people and eventually destroy the inhospitable city. One can compare in this regard the Greek myth of Baucis and Philemon. The presence of such traditional motifs in the biblical narratives raises the possibility that at least some of these narratives are purely products of the storyteller's art, which of course raises serious questions about their usefulness for historical reconstruction.

General Improbabilities

In addition to the schematic chronology and miraculous events which present the historian with credibility problems of a special sort, there are other aspects that challenge credulity. Some of these relate to chronological matters in addition to the encompassing chronological schema noted above. For example, Jacob presumably would have been at least seventy years old when he went to Mesopotamia to secure himself a wife. He could hardly be accused of acting on romantic impulse in matters matrimonial! Simeon and Levi, sons of Jacob, would have been teenagers when they destroyed the city of Shechem (Gen. 34). Other matters unrelated to chronology raise similar credibility issues. Exodus 12: 37–39 reports that 600,000 Hebrews of fighting age left Egypt. This number plus their wives and children along with the mixed multitude said to accompany them would have totaled some two and a half million. Marching ten abreast, the numbers would have formed a line over 150 miles long and would have required eight or nine days to march by any fixed point. The mere logistics of organizing such a group and sustaining it for forty years of wandering in the wilderness, not to mention the problems two midwives would have had caring for the womenfolk (Ex. 1:15), raise enormous questions for any historian who would seek to use this information. The critical historian must reject some or all of such accounts, qualify them, or develop some nonbiblical scenario large enough to encompass the improbabilities.

Composite and Contradictory Character

As indicated at the beginning of this chapter, Genesis-Joshua is part of a more extensive account, that of Genesis-II Kings, which covers chronologically the time from creation to the exile. Literary analysis reveals that this whole Genesis-II Kings account, from beginning to end, is composite. In other words, many originally independent items (stories, songs, genealogies, collections of laws, and so on), each with its own issues and problems of interpretation as well as historical implications, have been combined to produce the overall account. These various items have been edited, so that the resulting composite account has a degree of unity and coherence. Many ragged edges remain, however, which raise glaring questions for the serious reader and which in some cases present what appear to be blatant contradictions. Some of these questions and apparent contradictions have troubled interpreters since ancient times. Where, for example, did Cain's wife come from (Gen. 4:17)? Do not the genealogies in Gen. 4:17–26 and Genesis 5 present irreconcilable contradictions? Did Abraham present his wife Sarah as his sister on two different occasions (Gen. 12:10–20; 20) and with essentially the same results in both cases, and did Isaac do the same with Rebekah (Gen. 26:1–11)? Or have we here variants of the same event, or merely the literary employment of a common plot motif? Did the Hebrews flee Egypt without the pharaoh's knowledge, in great haste and without preparation (Ex. 12:39; 14:5a)? Or was the departure very deliberate, with the Hebrews organized as an armed military force and only after they had relieved the Egyptians of much of their wealth (Ex. 11:1–2; 12:35–36; 13:18b–19)? What were the laws given to Moses on Mt. Sinai: the Ten Commandments (Ex. 34:28), the Book of the Covenant (Ex. 24:7), or the whole of the Pentateuchal legislation? Was Hebron conquered by Joshua during the initial invasion of western Palestine (Josh. 10:36), or by Caleb (Josh. 15:13–14), or by Judah (Judg. 1:9–10)? If Joshua conquered the whole land of Canaan, destroying its inhabitants (Josh. 10:40–42) and settled the tribes in their allotments (Josh. 13–22), how then can the scene in Judges 1 of Israelites struggling with the Canaanites be explained? Casual readers may not notice such problems in the text or may choose to ignore ragged edges and apparent contradictions of this sort. A historian, however, cannot avoid such problems.

Generally speaking, a historian has essentially two options when the ancient sources present what appears to be contradictory information. One possibility is to challenge the accuracy of some or all of the information provided, choosing one position, source, or passage over against another or discrediting all. The other possibility is to hypothesize a scenario in which the apparent contradiction turns out not to be a real contradiction after all. A historian taking the first option with regard to the conquest of Hebron, for example, might conclude that

Josh. 10:36 is simply mistaken when it attributes the conquest of the city to Joshua, that it probably was the Calebites who conquered Hebron, and that the Calebites have been subsumed under Judah by the editors of Judges 1. A historian taking the second option might hypothesize, on the other hand, that Hebron was conquered more than once. Joshua conquered it; then the indigenous people of the land took it back; then Caleb conquered it; after that it was lost again; then finally the tribe of Judah conquered it. Whereas the first option involves challenging the historical claims of some portions of the text, the second option involves supplementing the text with hypothesized information. Both represent subjective interpretational decisions on the part of the historian.

Folk Traditions and Theological Intentions

In evaluating the Genesis-II Kings account for purposes of historical reconstruction, one must distinguish between the individual compositional units that have been combined to produce this extended account as it stands now and the interests and intentions of the ancient editors who did the compiling. The former may be regarded, for the most part, as "folk traditions."

Most ancient peoples, and modern ones as well, have possessed a repertoire of folk traditions (songs, sayings, stories, and such) which tell how they, their institutions, and customary ways of doing things came into existence and which combine to express their self-understanding as a people. This repertoire, which, taken as a whole, may be regarded as the people's "folk history," tends to be ethnocentric and to focus on certain formative figures and events. Note that the materials in Genesis-Joshua focus on certain key figures each in turn (Abraham, Isaac, Jacob, Joseph, Moses, Joshua) and provide folk explanations for all sorts of things (why snakes have no legs; the reason for so many different and confusing languages among human beings; the origin of the practice of circumcision; how certain holy places in Palestine became holy; the origin of certain unusual personal and geographical names; and so on). A general characteristic of these folk explanations, moreover, is that they project the origins of conditions, practices, and institutions back to early times, the times of the ancestors and heroes of old.

The process by which the Genesis-II Kings account was compiled and edited apparently occurred in several stages and possibly over a long period of time. The final edition seems to be essentially a product of the period of the Babylonian exile or soon thereafter. This is suggested on several grounds, the most obvious being that its coverage of Israelite and Judean history ends rather abruptly with the exile. The characteristic noted above in connection with many of the compositional units of Genesis-Joshua, the tendency to project the origins of contemporary practices and circumstances to the distant past, was characteristic also of the exilic or early postexilic compilers of Genesis-II Kings. They also clearly viewed the time of the patriarchs, Moses, and Joshua as normative for virtually every aspect of later Israelite and Judean history. They would have the reader believe, accordingly, that "Israel" consisted of twelve clearly defined tribes already before the ancestors reached Canaan, each tribe having descended from one of twelve brothers. These early Israelite tribes were presumed to have been monotheistic—worshipers of a single god, except for certain wayward moments, who had revealed himself to the patriarchs and Moses. Standard Israelite life-style would have been governed already in premonarchical times by a code of laws and religious instructions which, in their view, Moses had received at Mt. Sinai. They presumed that Israel was already secure in the Land of Canaan by the end of Joshua's career; that ideal boundaries for eleven of the twelve tribes had been established; and that the twelfth tribe, the Levites, had been installed in key cities throughout the land to serve as priests for all the nation. In short, the exilic or early postexilic compilers of Genesis-II Kings conceived of an ideal Israel which had already emerged, taken its rightful place in Palestine, and settled down to normal life by the time of Joshua's death. Correspondingly, they presented the "pre-Judges" period as normative for later Israelite and Judean history and sought to convey to the exilic/postexilic community that their only hope lay in a return to the ancient socioreligious norms.

Present-day historians recognize that total objectivity is an unattainable goal in historical reconstruction. Unattainable though it may be, however, this is still a practical goal of modern historiography. What is the modern critical historian to do, then, with the folkloric materials in Genesis-Joshua or with the exilic compilers' idealistic views about Israel's origins? Obviously the ancient story-tellers and compilers were not primarily concerned with objective reporting. Moreover, it is not just a matter of deciding what to do with some of the questionable items that the biblical writers did report—folk explanations, incredible historical claims, and the like. Equally problematic is the fact that the ancients, because it was not central to their interests and concerns, often failed to report precisely the sort of information that modern historians consider crucial. Who exactly was the pharaoh "who knew not Joseph," and what was happening on the international political scene at the time of the exodus? What were the sociopolitical circumstances among the Canaanites at the time of Joshua? These sorts of data are basic to the modern historian's interests but were incidental to the theological message that the compilers of Genesis-II Kings wished to convey.

The Search for Contact Points
with Extrabiblical History

The few biblical texts other than Genesis-Joshua that pertain in one way or another to the origins of Israel and Judah provide little or no substantial information, and in some cases even further complicate matters. I Chronicles, for example, offers an alternate reconstruction of Israel's past which reports nothing of the sequence of patriarchs, stay in Egypt, exodus, and conquest. The Genesis-Joshua account itself makes few references to persons or events on the scene of international history; and when these occasional references occur, such as the references to Egyptian pharaohs, usually no names are given. When names are provided, such as the reference to Abimelech king of the Philistines (Gen. 26:1), the persons mentioned are unknown from other sources. The mention of a Philistine king contemporary with Isaac actually raises difficulties, since otherwise we have no knowledge of Philistines in Palestine before about 1200 B.C.E.—that is, much later than the time when Isaac would belong according to the biblical chronology.

With one exception, on the other hand, there is no mention of Israel or the Israelites in extrabiblical sources before the ninth century B.C.E.—that is, until well after the reigns of David and Solomon. The exception is the Merneptah Inscription which, as we shall see below, is of very limited value for dealing with the question of Israel's origins. The biblical Abraham, Isaac, Jacob, Joseph, Moses, and Joshua are not mentioned in any nonbiblical records. Nor is there any reference to an Israelite sojourn in Egypt, the exodus, or the conquest of Palestine in any ancient source contemporary with the time when these events are said to have occurred.

Various attempts have been made, of course, to establish fixed points of contact between the Genesis-Joshua narrative and general Middle Eastern history as known from extrabiblical sources, but none of these proposed contact points bear up under close scrutiny. The following such proposals deserve mention.

Genesis 14 and Mesopotamian History

Attempts have been made to associate the four eastern kings mentioned in Genesis 14 with known rulers of antiquity, an association which it was hoped would provide a general date for Abraham. One such proposal popular during the early decades of the present century was that Amraphel might be identical with the famous Babylonian king, Hammurabi. This was never very convincing, however, because of the philological problems involved in connecting the names Amraphel and Hammurabi. Also there are certain historical difficulties with this proposal. There is no evidence in Mesopotamian records, for example, that Hammurabi ever campaigned in the Palestinian area. In short, about all that can be said of Genesis 14 is that the names seem to have "a ring of authenticity" about them.

The Exodus and Natural Catastrophes

Various hypotheses have been advanced that seek to understand the plagues and other miraculous events associated with the exodus in terms of cosmic and natural catastrophes. It has been argued, for example, that the plagues and the parting of the sea resulted from the close passage of a comet or comets during the Bronze Age. A similar suggestion is that the exodus events were related to Late Bronze Age volcanic activity in the Aegean area, possibly the volcanic eruption that occurred on the Island of Thera about 1450 B.C.E. Supposedly the volcanic ash released in the atmosphere would have produced the phenomena associated with the plagues—darkness, unusual precipitation, and so forth—while the sinking of part of the Island of Thera would have produced massive tidal waves. One of these tidal waves, in turn, would have destroyed the Egyptian forces in its backwash against the southeastern Mediterranean shoreline. Theories of this sort attempt to give naturalistic and scientifically acceptable explanations for the more fantastic and miraculous biblical claims. In our opinion, however, these theories presuppose such hypothetical scenarios, such a catastrophic view of history, and such marvelous correlations of coincidental factors that they create more credibility problems of their own than the ones they are intended to solve.

The Habiru Hypothesis

Texts unearthed in the el-Amarna district of Egypt during the nineteenth century, first through a chance discovery and then through excavation, provide insight into social and political affairs in Palestine during the late fifteenth and early fourteenth centuries B.C.E. These texts, over 350 in number, from the royal Egyptian archives and written in Akkadian on clay tables, are primarily letters addressed to the pharaohs Amenophis III (about 1417–1379 B.C.E.) and

Amarna Letter. One of over three hundred and fifty cuneiform letters discovered in the el-Amarna district of Egypt and dating from the late fifteenth and early fourteenth centuries B.C.E. This particular letter, measuring about 5½ by 3½ inches, was sent to the Egyptian pharaoh by Abdu-Heba, king of Jerusalem (see Text I). *(Staatliche Museen, Berlin)*

Amenophis IV (about 1379–1362 B.C.E.). The latter is better known as a radical reformer under the name Akhenaten. A large portion of these letters were written from Syro-Palestinian rulers subordinate to Egypt or are copies of pharaonic letters to these rulers. In this correspondence, frequent references are made to groups who were causing disruption and turmoil in Palestine by challenging local and Egyptian authority. The name used for one of the groups is Apiru/Abiru, or Hapiru/Habiru, which in turn is strikingly similar to the biblical term *ibri* ("Hebrew"). (See Text I.)

TEXT I. Amarna Letter from Abdu-Heba of Jerusalem

To the king, my lord, say: Thus Abdu-Heba, thy servant. At the two feet of my lord, the king, seven times and seven times I fall. What have I done to the king, my lord? They blame me before the king, my lord, saying: "Abdu-Heba has rebelled against the king, his lord." Behold, as for me, it was not my father and not my mother who set me in this place; the arm of the mighty king brought me into the house of my father! Why should I commit transgression against the king, my lord? As long as the king, my lord, lives, I will say to the commissioner of the king, my lord, "Why do ye favor⸢ the Apiru and oppose the governors?"—And thus I am blamed in the presence of the king, my lord. Because it is said, "Lost are the lands of the king, my lord," thus am I blamed to the king, my lord! But let the king, my lord, know that when the king had established a garrison, Yanhamu took it all away, and . . . the troops of archers(?) . . . the land of Egypt. . . . O king, my lord, there are no garrison troops here! So let the king take care of his land! Let the king take care of his land! The lands of the king have all rebelled; Ilimilku is causing the loss of all the king's land. So let the king take care of his land! I keep saying, "Let me enter into the presence of the king, my lord, and let me see the two eyes of the king, my lord." But the hostility against me is strong, so I cannot enter into the presence of the king, my lord. So may it please the king to send me garrison troops in order that I may enter and see the two eyes of the king, my lord. As truly as the king, my lord, lives, when the commissioners go forth I will say, "Lost are the lands of the king! Do you not hearken unto me? All the governors are lost; the king, my lord, does not have a single governor left!" Let the king turn his attention to the archers, and let the king, my lord, send out troops of archers, for the king has no lands left! The Apiru plunder all the lands of the king. If there are archers here in this year, the lands of the king, my lord, will remain intact; but if there are no archers here the lands of the king, my lord, will be lost!

To the scribe of the king, my lord: Thus Abdu-Heba, thy servant. Present eloquent words to the king, my lord.—All the lands of the king, my lord, are lost! (*ANET* 487–88)

This similarity, plus the fact that a late fifteenth- to early fourteenth-century date for the exodus and conquest would be roughly in keeping with biblical chronology, led many earlier scholars to conclude that the Habiru were none other than the invading Hebrews under Joshua. In other words, the Amarna letters would represent extrabiblical documentary evidence for the Israelite invasion of Palestine while at the same time securing an approximate date of this event.

As more and more ancient documents were discovered by archaeologists, however, it became increasingly apparent that this hypothesis involves an oversimplification of the evidence. Namely, examination of the numerous contexts in which the Habiru are mentioned suggests that Habiru was a rather loose term used for several centuries and over a wide geographical area with reference to various persons and groups on the fringes of society—hired foreign servants and mercenaries, rebels against the government, and the like. In other words, the term apparently was used in widely separated geographical and cultural contexts to refer to an ill-defined social class rather than to a specific ethnic or national group.

A simple equation of the Habiru of the Amarna correspondence with the Hebrews under Joshua seems most unlikely, therefore, and the idea has been abandoned by most biblical historians. Yet there still may be some etymological connection between the terms, and possibly an indirect historical connection as well. Note that the biblical narratives present the Israelite patriarchs as "sojourners" in the lands of Canaan and Egypt. In terms of their social status, therefore, they would have been for all practical purposes Habiru. Assuming that there is an etymological connection between "Habiru" and "Hebrew," therefore, the possible historical connection is that some of the Israelite ancestors may have been Habiru/Hebrews in terms of their political and social standing. This possible connection is of little help, of course, when it comes to dating or confirming the historicity of the biblical account of the conquest.

The Raamesid Period as the Setting of the Exodus

The name Raameses was popular for the Egyptian pharaohs of the Nineteenth and Twentieth Dynasties (about 1320–1085 B.C.E.), and certain of the pharaohs of this period are known to have undertaken major construction projects in the Nile Delta. Thus the period of these two dynasties has been seen as a convincing setting for the notice in Ex. 1:11 which indicates that the Hebrews in Egypt labored on the construction of two store-cities called Pithom and Raameses. Some would argue more specifically that Raameses II (about 1304–1237 B.C.E.) is the most likely candidate for the pharaoh of the exodus, which would allow for the Israelites to reach Palestine in time for their appearance in Merneptah's stela (see next section).

The most obvious problem with this proposed correlation between Egyptian history and the biblical narrative is that it does not square very well with biblical chronology. The Nineteenth and Twentieth Dynasties ruled from the end of the fourteenth century until after the beginning of the eleventh century. Yet biblical chronology seems to place the exodus already in the fifteenth century. And of course there are no references in the Egyptian sources to the Israelite stay in Egypt, their work on the construction projects, or their exodus. Again, as with the mention of the four kings in Genesis 14, one may insist that the notation in Ex. 1:11 has "a ring of authenticity" which could encourage confidence in the historicity of the biblical account. But this falls short of establishing a clearly fixed point between biblical and Egyptian history or, for that matter, even of serving as actual proof of the historicity of the biblical account. One would expect Israelite storytellers to be familiar with and to use authentic Mesopotamian and Egyptian names and customs in their narratives in any case.

Israel in the Merneptah Stela

The only reference to Israel in Middle Eastern sources prior to the ninth century is found in the so-called "Israel Stela" of Pharaoh Merneptah. Inscribed in his fifth year, about 1230 B.C.E., the stela commemorates and extols the pharaoh's victories, some actual, some probably imaginary. Near the end of the final hymnic section, the inscription claims:

> The princes are prostrate, saying, "Mercy!"
>   Not one raises his head among the Nine Bows.
> Desolation is for Tehenu; Hatti is pacified;
>   Plundered is the Canaan with every evil;
> Carried off is Ashkelon; seized upon is Gezer;
>   Yanoam is made as that which does not exist;
> Israel is laid waste, his seed is not;
>   Hurru is become a widow for Egypt!
> All lands together, they are pacified;
>   Everyone who was restless, he has been bound.
>   (*ANET* 378)

Between the references to Canaan and Hurru, which should probably be viewed as essentially synonymous designations in this context, four names appear. Two are names of well-known Palestinian cities—Ashkelon and Gezer. Yanoam may have been a city also. The name Israel, however, is preceded in the inscription by a hieroglyphic sign that normally indicates a people rather than a region or a city. Thus the inscription testifies to the existence of a population group, bearing the name "Israel" and possibly tribal in structure, living in Canaan about 1230 B.C.E. Little more can be concluded from the inscription. The reported encounter between Merneptah and Israel is not mentioned in the Bible. Yet the very fact that this Egyptian inscription reports an Israel as being on the scene in Palestine during the thirteenth century is an important bit of information, and one to which we will return in the next chapter.

The Search for Archaeological Solutions

What of the artifactual evidence recovered by archaeological excavations? Is it possible that this evidence, combined in some fashion with the written materials, might allow us to identify the specific cultural-chronological context or contexts of events recorded in the Genesis-Joshua account? Here again various proposals have been advanced, but none with full success. Basically, four configurations of artifactual evidence have been drawn upon by scholars in their efforts to hypothesize a context against which to understand the biblical account of Israel's origins.

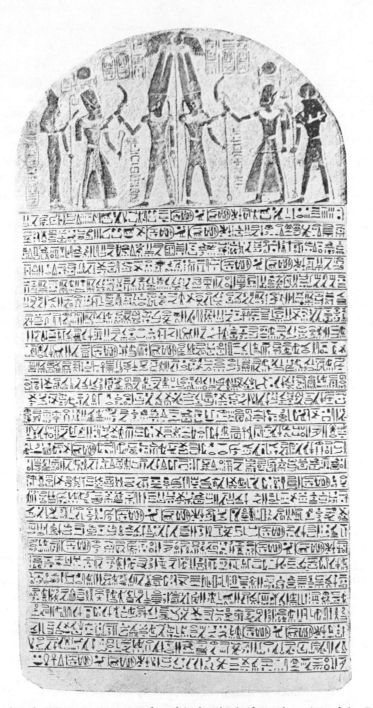

Merneptah Stela. This inscription, 7 feet 6 inches high, from the reign of the Egyptian pharaoh Merneptah (ca. 1230 B.C.E.) contains the earliest reference to Israel in any known nonbiblical document, and the only such reference before the ninth century B.C.E. *(Egyptian Museum, Cairo)*

The Amorite Hypothesis

The beginning of the Middle Bronze Age in Syria-Palestine (early second millennium B.C.E.) was marked by a breakdown of the powerful city-states that had flourished throughout the Early Bronze Age. Parallel disruptions seem to have occurred in Egypt (the First Intermediate Period) and in Mesopotamia (the fall of the so-called Third Dynasty of Ur). This early second millennium disruption of urban life has been attributed to movements of Amorites (Amurru) which begin to be mentioned in the Mesopotamian documents about that time also. Building upon this artifactual and documentary evidence, as well as texts from the later Amorite states of the Middle Bronze Age, scholars formulated during the 1930s what has come to be called "the Amorite hypothesis."

According to the hypothesis, the Hebrew patriarchs entered Palestine as a part of widespread Amorite movements which disrupted the Fertile Crescent during the early second millennium B.C.E. and the patriarchal narratives are to be seen accordingly against the background of early Amorite society. Basically, three arguments were advanced in support of the hypothesis: (1) An early second millennium date for Abraham, Isaac, and Jacob squares essentially with the Genesis-I Kings chronology. Specifically, I Kings 6:1 dates the exodus 480 years prior to the building of Solomon's Temple, while Ex. 12:40 records the Israelite stay in Egypt as having lasted 430 years (however, compare Gen. 15:13; Gal. 3:17). This would mean that Jacob and his sons descended into Egypt approximately during the nineteenth century. Also it would place the Hebrews in Egypt during the so-called Hyksos period (late eighteenth to mid-sixteenth century) when Egypt apparently was ruled by foreigners. (2) The stories of Abraham's migration from Mesopotamia to Canaan and of the later migration of Jacob and his sons into Egypt make sense, it is argued, when viewed against political conditions of the early second millennium. (3) The names of the patriarchs and some of the customs reflected in the patriarchal narratives are similar to those reflected in second-millennium Mesopotamian texts, especially those from Mari (eighteenth century) and Nuzi (fifteenth century).

However, there are some serious problems with this Amorite hypothesis. (1) The idea that the disruption of urban life in Syria-Palestine at the end of the Early Bronze Age and the beginning of Middle Bronze was the result of widespread Amorite movements is itself only a hypothesis which is by no means universally accepted by archaeologists and historians. (2) While the Amorite hypothesis squares fairly well with the schematic chronology of Genesis-II Kings, it creates problems for the associated genealogical data. Genesis 15:16 assumes a four-generation stay in Egypt, for example, and Moses is identified as a fourth-generation descendant of Jacob (Jacob–Levi–Amram–Moses: Gen. 46:8–11; Ex. 6:18–20). These genealogical data can be made to fit the chronological requirements of the Amorite hypothesis, therefore, only if each generation is allowed an average of a hundred years. Note also that the hypothesis places Israel's ancestors on the scene more than six centuries before we hear anything of Israelites in Middle Eastern literature. (3) The parallels between biblical names and customs, on the one hand, and those known from Middle and Late Bronze Mesopotamian texts, on the other, become less impressive when one takes into account that the sorts of names and customs involved were not confined to the second millennium B.C.E. but apparently were characteristic of the first millennium as well. This renders the parallels relatively useless for pinpointing any particular period as "the patriarchal age." (4) Finally, the biblical traditions never associate the patriarchs with the Amorites but rather with the Arameans ("a wandering Aramean was my father," Deut. 26:5) and less directly with other groups (the Moabites, the Edomites, and the Philistines) who cannot in any way be placed in an early second-millennium context.

Transjordanian Occupational Gap

The results of archaeological explorations in southern Transjordan during the 1930s indicated an occupational gap in the territories of ancient Edom and Moab which began about 2000 B.C.E. and ended with a resurgence of village life during the thirteenth century B.C.E. It seemed reasonable, therefore, to associate this thirteenth-century rise of village life with the rise of the kingdoms of Edom and Moab. The biblical account of the Israelite exodus from Egypt and conquest of Canaan reports, on the other hand, that the Israelites had to deal with Edomite and Moabite kings during the last stages of the wilderness wanderings (Num. 20:14–21; 22). An obvious conclusion was that the exodus, the wilderness wanderings, and the conquest must have occurred at least as late as the thirteenth century. If the Hebrews under Moses had passed through the Transjordan at an earlier date, they would not have encountered the kingdoms of Edom and Moab. This line of argumentation was combined with, if not inspired by, the identification of Pharaoh Raameses II as the pharaoh of the exodus (on the basis of Ex. 1:11 and the arguments noted above).

More recent archaeological exploration in southern Transjordan, however, has tended to discredit the idea of a sharp occupational gap prior to the thirteenth century. While there is a noticeable reduction in the amount of surface pottery representing the period in question, especially the Middle Bronze Age, there appears now to have been neither a discrete occupational gap nor a sudden resurgence of settlements that can be dated specifically to the thirteenth century.

Thirteenth-Century Destructions

Archaeological excavations have shown that the end of the Late Bronze Age was a time of widespread city destructions west of the Jordan. Many scholars have been tempted to attribute these city destructions to the invading Hebrews and to see this as confirmation of the historicity of the conquest narratives in the early chapters of Joshua (see Map 6). There are, however, three major problems with this use of the archaeological evidence. (1) It is not clear from the artifactual record that these cities were destroyed simultaneously or as the result of a common enemy. Indeed, it cannot be established archaeologically that they were all destroyed by military action. (2) The sites where artifactual remains indicate city destructions at the end of the Late Bronze Age, with a few exceptions (Lachish, Hazor), are not the ones that the biblical account associates with the conquest under Joshua. (3) The sites that are identified with cities which the biblical account does associate with the conquest, on the other hand, usually have produced little or no archaeological indication of even having been occupied during the Late Bronze Age, much less of having been destroyed at the end of the period. Prominent among the "conquest cities" that fall into this latter category are Arad (present-day Tell Arad), Heshbon (Tell Hisban), Jericho (Tell es-Sultan), Ai (et-Tell), and Gibeon (el-Jib).

The Search for a Distinctively Israelite Material Culture

Claims have been made that certain features of Iron I material culture of western Palestine were specifically "Israelite" in origin. If this is true, if specifically Israelite artifacts can be isolated, this would allow archaeologists, by noting the sites where such artifacts have been found, to trace the course and range of early Israelite settlement in Palestine. The two items that have been given most serious consideration as being distinctively Israelite are the so-called "collared-rim jars" and "four-room houses." Yet there is nothing intrinsically "Israelite" about either of these features, and in fact they show up in the regions of ancient Ammon and Moab as well as in the areas generally associated with Israelite settlement. Clearly these items belonged to a commonly shared culture throughout Iron I Palestine and therefore cannot be used to isolate particular sites, geographical areas, or historical periods as "Israelite."

In summary, while the extrabiblical documents from the ancient Middle East and the artifactual evidence recovered by archaeological excavations in Palestine are very useful for understanding the general background against which Israel and Judah emerged, these have not turned out to be very helpful for tracing the specific origins of Israel and Judah. As for the extrabiblical documents, the tangible evidence reduces for all practical purposes to a single inscription which tells us nothing more than that an entity called "Israel" was on the scene in Palestine near the end of the thirteenth century. Were we dependent on the available artifactual evidence, on the other hand, we would not know even that much. If any specific conclusions are to be reached about the origins and earliest history of Israel and Judah, therefore, these must be based on the biblical materials, primarily the Genesis-Joshua narrative summarized and discussed above.

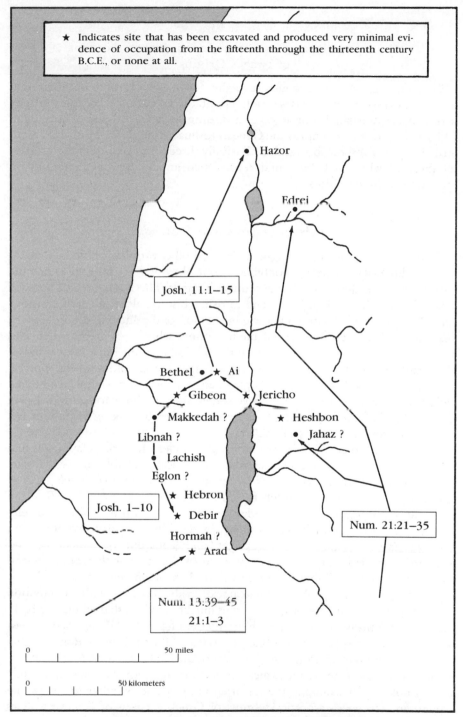

★ Indicates site that has been excavated and produced very minimal evidence of occupation from the fifteenth through the thirteenth century B.C.E., or none at all.

● Hazor

Edrei

Josh. 11:1–15

Bethel ● ★ Ai

★ Gibeon ★ Jericho

● Makkedah ?

Libnah ?

● Lachish

Eglon ?

★ Hebron

Josh. 1–10

★ Debir

Hormah ?

★ Arad

★ Heshbon

● Jahaz ?

Num. 21:21–35

Num. 13:39–45
21:1–3

0   50 miles

0   50 kilometers

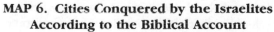

**MAP 6. Cities Conquered by the Israelites
According to the Biblical Account**

Historians' Responses to the Genesis-Joshua Account
of Israel's Origins

Given the fact that we are almost totally dependent on the biblical account
and that this account itself raises serious credibility problems, what approach can
a reasonably cautious historian take in dealing with the origins of Israel and
Judah? Is it possible to employ the Genesis-Joshua materials for historical reconstruction in any responsible fashion? Basically three options present themselves,
all three of which will be found represented among current textbooks on
Israelite and Judean history.

Taking the Account as It Stands

One option, of course, is to ignore the credibility problems noted above, to
disregard the lack of specific nonbiblical control evidence, and to presume the
historicity of the Genesis-Joshua account as it stands. This has been the approach
taken throughout much of Jewish and Christian history, although earlier historians obviously worked without knowledge of most of the ancient Middle Eastern
texts and archaeological data available to modern scholars. If the historian who
follows this option is prepared to take the biblical account fully "as it stands,"
the resulting historical survey will begin with the creation of the world approximately six thousand years ago, presuppose an early period during which human
beings lived enormously long life spans, date the Israelite exodus from Egypt
during the fifteenth century B.C.E., describe the Israelite taking of Canaan as a
miraculous conquest, and so forth.

As might be expected, however, not many modern historians favor this first
option. If the biblical account is regarded as historically reliable and as a satisfactory explanation for the origins of Israel and Judah already as it stands, then
there really is not very much left for a historian to say anyway. In effect, the
historian's task becomes one of finding ways to deal with the miraculous elements and general credibility problems in the biblical story, hypothesizing
scenarios that reconcile the "ragged edges" and "apparent contradictions," and
supporting the resulting "clarified" version of the story with arguments and
illustrations from nonbiblical sources where these seem relevant.

If one does begin to probe the biblical texts in any way even with the intention
of making minor clarifications, it becomes quickly obvious that taking the biblical account entirely as it stands, without discounting or explaining away at least
some of its statements, is impossible. This is true if for no other reason than that
we have no original autograph for any part of the Bible and therefore must rely
on late secondary manuscripts which present variant readings. On such matters
as chronology, for example, the historian must decide whether to follow the
Samaritan Hebrew, Masoretic Hebrew, or Greek versions of Genesis-Joshua,
or some combination of the three. It is not always a question of whether the
biblical account is historically reliable, in other words, but sometimes a question

of which manuscript tradition and which manuscript reading of a particular passage is authentic.

Total Rejection of the Account

The second option, an opposite extreme, is to reject the biblical account as totally useless for purposes of historical reconstruction and to take a thoroughly agnostic position regarding the early history of Israel and Judah. This is a very safe position for one to take, of course, but in our opinion not an entirely satisfactory one either. There is, after all, some positive evidence to be taken into account.

In the first place, it is not a question of whether self-conscious entities known as Israel and Judah appeared on the scene of ancient Palestine and played out their history there, but only a question of when this occurred, under what circumstances, and the details of how their early history unfolded. We have already noted that the Merneptah Stela testifies to the presence of an entity known as Israel in Palestine as early as the last decades of the thirteenth century B.C.E. The narratives in the Book of Judges, which we will examine more closely in the next chapter, seem to presuppose the Early Iron Age in Palestine as their setting.

In the second place, it is not a question of whether the Genesis-Joshua narrative is a valid source of information for the historian's purposes, but rather how it is to be interpreted and what sort of historical information can be derived from it. Potentially, any written document from the past, if it can be understood and interpreted properly, holds valid information for the historian. We must at least hold open the possibility that, in spite of the credibility and interpretational problems which the Genesis-Joshua account presents, many of the old songs, stories, genealogies, and so forth that have been incorporated into this account actually hark back to and may shed some light on, even if only indirectly, the circumstances of earliest Israelite and Judean history. For example, the stories of Jacob's relationship with the Aramean Laban (Gen. 29–31), the listing of Jacob's sons according to whether they were born to his two wives or two concubines (Gen. 29:31–30:24; 35:16–20, 23–26), the attack of Simeon and Levi on the city of Shechem (Gen. 34; 48:22; 49:5–7), the intermarriage of Judah with a Canaanite (Gen. 38), and so on, may reflect intertribal relationships and alignments, and in some cases perhaps actual persons and events, of premonarchical times. The exodus traditions may reflect, regardless of how indirectly or how overlaid with later expansion and exaggerations, an actual memory of slavery in Egypt. Egyptian texts do in fact speak of Syro-Palestinian groups that entered Egypt during time of famine (see *ANET* 259) and of foreigners in Egypt, in some cases Habiru, who worked on pharaonic building projects. One must hasten to say, however, that such texts only allow us to entertain the possibility of some connection between such circumstances in Egypt and the ancestors of Israel and Judah. They do not provide the sort of evidence that can be regarded as historically verifiable.

Searching for a Compromise Position

The third option is to develop an alternate hypothesis for the origins of Israel and Judah which is based to some degree on the biblical material yet which does not follow the biblical account exactly (perhaps not even closely). This is clearly a compromise approach, and obviously not an entirely satisfactory option either, certainly not from a methodological standpoint. Analysis of recent treatments of early Israelite and Judean history reveals that four factors generally contribute to the shaping of such compromise positions.

1. One factor, of course, is the historian's threshold of credibility. It is tempting, for example, to try to follow the general story line of the biblical account, but to begin the story at some point later than creation, to reduce what appear to be unrealistically large numbers, to make selective adjustments in the biblical chronology, and to offer naturalistic explanations for the miracles. Even very biblically conservative historians sometimes avoid the issue of whether the world really was created in just seven days and only six thousand years ago, for example, by beginning their treatment of Israelite history with Abraham (Gen. 12). Other historians are reluctant to draw any historical conclusions for the period prior to Moses (Ex. 1). Still others insist that the first point where there is sufficient and reliable information at hand to begin a treatment of Israelite and Judean history is the time of Joshua and the conquest, or the time of the Judges, or even some later period in the general biblical outline.

2. A second factor is the evidence from ancient nonbiblical documents and archaeology. Note that the various hypotheses reviewed above which sought to correlate the biblical account with the nonbiblical data usually involved a compromise approach. That is, the correlations proposed usually called for some significant adjustments in the biblical account. The patriarchs became Amorites rather than Arameans for the Amorite hypothesis. The date of the exodus was lowered from the fifteenth to the thirteenth century in order to correlate it with the Raamesid period in Egypt and the Transjordanian occupational gap. In order to correlate the Israelite conquest with the Late Bronze Age city destructions in Palestine, it was necessary not only to adjust the biblical chronology and to take liberties with certain items in the biblical account of the conquest but also to interpret somewhat arbitrarily the artifactual evidence from the particular sites involved.

3. A third factor is the results of literary-critical analysis of the biblical materials. Literary critics distinguish, as we have seen above, between the individual compositional units of Genesis-II Kings, on the one hand, and the overall, composite account, on the other. Often the compositional units—the songs, genealogies, stories, and such that have been incorporated into the larger account—appear to be rather old, have a more authentic ring than the compilers' editorial comments, and seem to conflict with the compilers' historical assumptions and claims. This is especially obvious, as we shall see below, in the Book of Judges. As one might expect, therefore, historians who place heavy emphasis on the results of literary criticism tend to place more confidence on the historical

usefulness of the older compositional units and literary strata of Genesis–II Kings than in the final composite and highly editorial story line. There is danger here, of course. The fact that an old narrative can be separated out from later editorial material and sounds authentic does not necessarily mean it is historically reliable. The origin of the narrative still may have been far removed in time from the events that it reports, and naturally any good storyteller would intentionally have given a story "an authentic ring."

4. Finally, historians consciously or unconsciously tend to rely on models. Two such models, one derived from an assumed Middle Eastern cultural pattern and the other from the social sciences, have been widely influential among biblical historians in recent years. The first of these may be referred to as the "nomadic model." Those who utilize this model assume that the Arabian Desert has been, through the ages, a constant source of nomads who infringe from time to time upon the surrounding cultivated areas seeking territory and grazing lands for their flocks. Accordingly, the ancestors of Israel and Judah are believed to have entered Palestine as nomadic groups, gradually settling in unoccupied areas and establishing relationships with the indigenous population. Instead of an initial conquest, therefore, this view postulates a long period of infiltration and settlement during which the newcomers and the settled populations interacted, absorbing and being absorbed. This period of gradual settlement by various and diverse groups would have been followed by a period of consolidation and eventual dominance of the newcomers over the native population. Proponents of this view argue that such a process is reflected in certain of the biblical traditions, especially in the patriarchal narratives of Genesis, the "conquest" traditions of Judges 1, and many of the narratives about the period of the Judges.

The second model seeks to understand the origins of Israel in terms of internal developments within Late Bronze and Early Iron Age Palestine itself. Proponents of this view, while admitting that some of the ancestors may have entered the land from the outside, insist that essentially Israel was the product of a socioeconomic and political upheaval within the Land of Canaan—a revolt of marginal and oppressed elements within the heterogeneous population of the land directed against the economical and political structures of the Canaanite city-states and their monarchical, feudalistic governments. The revolt would have led to a radical retribalization of the population and a restructuring of the socioeconomic orders of society. The outcome, in short, was Israel, a new religiopolitical entity characterized by its covenant allegiance to the god Yahweh and its adherence to a classless and egalitarian social order.

The Approach Taken in the Present Volume

The approach taken in this volume with regard to the question of Israelite and Judean origins can perhaps be described as an extremely cautious and eclectic compromise position, determined to a certain degree by all four of the factors mentioned above, plus a considerable amount of intuitive speculation.

Admittedly, this is not very satisfying from a methodological standpoint. In our opinion, however, this is the best that one can do given the nature of the limited evidence at hand.

1. In the first place, we are cautious about saying anything. The evidence, or lack of evidence, is such that a confident treatment of the origins of Israel and Judah in terms of critical historiography is, in our opinion, simply impossible. This is one of those places where the historian must be willing to concede that anything said is largely guesswork.

2. We are much influenced by the results of literary-critical analysis of the Genesis-II Kings account. The view of Israel's origins advanced by the compilers of this account is idealistic, in our opinion, and in conflict with the historical implications of the older traditions which the compilers incorporated into their account. Specifically, we hold that the main story line of Genesis-Joshua—creation, pre-Flood patriarchs, great Flood, second patriarchal age, entrance into Egypt, twelve tribes descended from twelve brothers, escape from Egypt, complete collections of laws and religious instructions handed down at Mt. Sinai, forty years of wandering in the wilderness, miraculous conquest of Canaan, assignment of tribal territories, establishment of the priestly order and cities of refuge—is an artificial and theologically influenced literary construct. Close examination of certain of the old traditions that have been incorporated into the Genesis-Joshua account, and especially the narratives of the Book of Judges, lead us to doubt that such a politically and religiously unified twelve-tribe Israel existed in premonarchical times.

3. On the contrary, a close literary-critical examination of the Genesis-Joshua materials, particularly the patriarchal narratives in the Book of Judges, strongly suggests, in our opinion, that the various clan and tribal groups that later would compose the kingdoms of Israel and Judah were still, on the eve of the rise of the monarchy under Saul, characterized by ethnic, political, and religious diversity. This corresponds, moreover, to what one might conclude from the ancient nonbiblical documents and archaeological information about the situation in Palestine at the end of the Late Bronze Age and beginning of the Early Iron Age. Palestine at the time was something of a "melting pot," composed of diverse elements living under various "ad hoc" political and religious circumstances. It is our impression, correspondingly, that the early clans and tribes that formed the basis of the later kingdoms of Israel and Judah derived from diverse backgrounds and origins. They too, at least to a certain degree, represented a "melting pot."

Thus an appropriately comprehensive understanding of the origins of Israel and Judah probably would be more complex and variegated than any combination of the hypotheses and models reviewed above. Some of the ancestors may have been part of the old Semitic stock that had occupied Palestine as far back as written records go. Some may have settled the land gradually throughout the Bronze Age, making seasonal use of Palestine's grazing lands. Some may have been counted among the disaffected Habiru known from the Amarna correspondence. Some may have been escaped slaves from Egypt or migrating Arameans who settled in the land. Some may have entered Palestine along with the Sea Peoples, or have been thrust into the hill country as a result of the disturbance and pressure created by the Sea Peoples. Again, there probably is no single explanation to be given for the origins of Israel and Judah; there are many explanations.

4. We decline any attempt to reconstruct the earliest history of the Israelites therefore, and begin our treatment with a description of the circumstances that appear to have existed among the tribes in Palestine on the eve of the establishment of the monarchy. Our primary source of information for this purpose will be the narratives in the Book of Judges.

CHAPTER 3

Before Any King Ruled in Israel

The Merneptah Stela bears witness to the existence of an entity known as Israel on the scene in Palestine during the closing decades of the thirteenth century B.C.E. From Merneptah to the establishment of the monarchy under Saul and David (who must be dated somewhere around 1000 B.C.E.) was approximately two hundred years—the closing years of the Late Bronze Age and the beginning of the Early Iron Age. This would be the so-called "period of the Judges" which the biblical book of Judges describes as a time when "there was no king in Israel [and] every man did what was right in his own eyes" (Judg. 17:6; 21:25). The purpose of this chapter will be to explore the situation among the Israelite tribes during this period—that is, the circumstances out of which the Israelite monarchy emerged. We begin with some observations regarding (1) conditions in Palestine at the close of the Late Bronze Age and the beginning of the Iron Age and (2) the character and historical reliability of the Book of Judges.

Palestine at the Close of the Late Bronze Age
and the Beginning of the Iron Age

Decline of Egyptian Authority

The Late Bronze Age had been the "Empire Period" in Egyptian history. Especially from the reign of Tuthmoses III (about 1504–1450 B.C.E.), Egyptian pharaohs dominated Palestine and even campaigned as far north as the Euphrates River. They administered Palestine through local vassal governors resident in the major cities which were located primarily in the lowlands (the coastal plain and the Jezreel Valley). The population seems to have been rather sparse in the central hill country, and where there were cities of significant size, such as Shechem and Jerusalem, they were farther apart than those in the lowlands. The sparseness of population and the lack of major cities were apparently true of Galilee and southern Transjordan as well. Egypt's hold on Palestine loosened somewhat during the reign of Amenophis IV (= Akhenaten, about 1379–1362 B.C.E.). Later, Horemheb and the early pharaohs of the Nineteenth Dynasty (especially Sethos I, about 1316–1304 B.C.E.; Raameses II, about 1304–1237 B.C.E.; and Merneptah, about 1237–1228 B.C.E.) reasserted Egyptian dominance for a time. Egyptian authority began to fade again after the reign of Merneptah, this time rapidly, and by the reign of Raameses III (about 1206–1175 B.C.E.) of the Twentieth Dynasty, the Egyptians were forced to defend their own homeland against the Sea Peoples (see Text II). Thereafter, Egypt's role in Palestinian affairs was significantly reduced.

A Heterogeneous Population

The population of Palestine in the Late Bronze Age was heterogeneous and became increasingly so near the end of the age as Egyptian hegemony began to loosen and new elements such as the Sea Peoples arrived. This heterogeneous character of the population is evident already in inscriptions of Pharaoh Amenophis II (about 1450–1425 B.C.E.) which report on captives brought back to Egypt from "Retenu":

> (After his first campaign) his majesty reached Memphis, his heart joyful, the Mighty Bull. List of his booty: *maryanu* [apparently a special class of warriors]: 550; their wives: 240; Canaanites: 640; princes' children: 232; princes' children, female: 323; favorites of the princes of every foreign country: 270 women. . . . (After his second campaign) his majesty reached the city of Memphis, his heart appeased over all countries, with all lands beneath his soles. List of the plunder which his majesty carried off: princes of Retenu: 127; brothers of princes: 179; Apiru: 3,600; living Shasu: 15,200; Kharu [settled people?]: 36,300; living Neges [people of northern Syria?]: 15,070; the adherents thereof: 30,652. . . . (*ANET* 245–47)

Other texts provide further glimpses of conditions in the area and illustrate tensions that existed within the heterogeneous population. The Amarna letters, for example, dating from the fourteenth century and written to the Egyptian court from Palestine (see Text I), witness to jealousies, squabbles, political ambitions, and intrigues among the vassal governors. Although answerable to the Egyptian pharaoh, these vassals were not always loyal. It would appear, for example, that some of them cooperated with the local rebels and outlaws occasionally referred to in these letters as Habiru (or Apiru).

A late-thirteenth-century satirical Egyptian letter (Papyrus Anastasi I), in describing the region around Megiddo, spoke of the Shasu nomads who inhabited the area:

> The narrow valley is dangerous with Bedouin, hidden under the bushes. Some of them are of four or five cubits [seven to nine feet] from their noses to the heel, and fierce of face. Their hearts are not mild, and they do not listen to wheedling. (*ANET* 477)

The Assyrian king Tiglath-pileser I (about 1115–1077 B.C.E.) noted in one of his inscriptions that he had crossed the Euphrates River on twenty-eight occasions to fight the Ahlamu and Arameans in Syria (*ANET* 275). Ahlamu, like

TEXT II. Raameses III's War Against the Sea Peoples

Year 8 under the majesty of (Raameses III). . . . The foreign countries made a conspiracy in their islands. All at once the lands were removed and scattered in the fray. No land could stand before their arms, from Hatti, Kode, Carchemish, Arzawa, and Alashiya on, being cut off at one time. A camp was set up in one place in Amor. They desolated its people, and its land was like that which has never come into being. They were coming forward toward Egypt, while the flame was prepared before them. Their confederation was the Philistines, Tjeker, Shekelesh, Denyen, and Weshesh, lands united. They laid their hands upon the lands as far as the circuit of the earth, their hearts confident and trusting: "Our plans will succeed!"

Now the heart of this god, the Lord of the Gods, was prepared and ready to ensnare them like birds. . . . I organized my frontier in Djahi, prepared before them:—princes, commanders of garrisons, and *maryanu*. I have the river-mouths prepared like a strong wall, with warships, galleys and coasters, fully equipped, for they were manned completely from bow to stern with valiant warriors carrying their weapons. The troops consisted of every picked man of Egypt. They were like lions roaring upon the mountain tops. The chariotry consisted of runners, of picked men, of every good and capable chariot-warrior. The horses were quivering in every part of their bodies, prepared to crush the foreign countries under their hoofs. I was the valiant Montu, standing fast at their head, so that they might gaze upon the capturing of my hands. . . .

Those who reached my frontier, their seed is not, their heart and their soul are finished forever and ever. Those who came forward together on the sea, the full flame was in front of them at the river-mouths, while a stockade of lances surrounded them on the shore. They were dragged in, enclosed, and prostrated on the beach, killed, and made into heaps from tail to head. Their ships and their goods were as if fallen into the water.

I have made the lands turn back from even mentioning Egypt; for when they pronounce my name in their land, then they are burned up. Since I sat upon the throne of Har-akhti and the Great-of-Magic was fixed upon my head like Re, I have not let foreign countries behold the frontier of Egypt, to boast thereof to the Nine Bows. I have taken away their land, their frontiers being added to mine. Their princes and their tribespeople are mine with praise, for I am on the ways of the plans of the All-Lord, my august, divine father, the Lord of the Gods. (*ANET* 262–63)

Shasu, seems to have had the connotation of "nomad" or "barbarian," and the inscription suggests disruptive times characterized by migrations of peoples and changing patterns of alliances. Although the Assyrian ruler was describing affairs in Syria, similar conditions probably prevailed in Palestine as well.

New Developments in the Early Iron Age

The standard date given by archaeologists for the end of the Late Bronze Age and the beginning of the Iron Age is 1200 B.C.E. Although no sudden changes in the material culture of Palestine occurred precisely that year, it is appropriate to speak of a new historical and cultural phase as beginning in Palestine at approximately that time. We have noted that some two and a half centuries of Egyptian domination were coming to an end at this turn of the century. Also about the same time, many of the old fortified Bronze Age cities in Palestine met with destruction. Among these cities were Megiddo, Beth-shean, Hazor, Tell Abu Hawam, Aphek, Gezer, Beth-shemesh, Tell Beit Mirsim, and Ashdod. Exact dates and causes are rarely if ever ascertainable, and there is no reason to suppose that the destructions were even related to one another, except insofar as they were part of a general pattern of disturbances throughout Syria-Palestine at the end of the Bronze Age. When new settlements emerged on the sites of these old Bronze Age cities, they were generally much smaller and less impressive than their predecessors. Correspondingly, there occurred a noticeable increase of village settlements in the areas that had been less densely populated during the Late Bronze Age—that is, in the central hill country, Galilee, and southern Transjordan. In short, while Palestine had been dominated during the Late Bronze Age by certain powerful city-states operating under Egyptian supervision and situated primarily in the lowlands, Iron Age Palestine was blanketed with villages in the hill country as well as in the lowlands.

Several factors may have led to the increase of village settlements in the highlands. (1) Population pressure from the influx of new groups in the lowlands—the arrival of Sea Peoples, for example—may have forced people out of these areas and into the highlands where agriculture was possible, even if more difficult and less productive. (2) New peoples, such as the Arameans, may have moved directly into the hill country from outside the region. (3) New technological developments, such as the extensive use of terracing and the increased availability of iron, would have made it easier to clear and farm the forest lands of the hill country and Galilee (see Josh. 17:18). The architectural remains of the Iron Age villages in the hill country are understandably much less impressive than those of the larger cities of the Bronze Age. The same is true of other artifactual remains, such as pottery. On the whole, artifactual remains of the Iron I period represent continuations of the Late Bronze Age traditions, although with a noticeable decline in technique and sophistication.

Thus the close of the Late Bronze Age and the first two centuries of the Iron Age appear to have been turbulent and unsettled times in Palestine. Features of this period—the collapse of Egyptian authority, additional pressures on what was already a heterogeneous population, political disturbances among the old city-states which led to the destruction of many of them, and the surge of village life in areas that previously had been very sparsely occupied—suggest conditions that would have required realignments of sociopolitical structures with a tendency toward smaller units. The old Bronze Age city-states that remained

Raameses III. This statue of Raameses III (1206–1175 B.C.E.) was found standing east of the temple entrance at Karnak. According to his own inscriptions (see Text II), Raameses was successful in checking the advance of the Sea Peoples into Egypt. The presence of these invaders must have been among the factors that brought Egyptian domination in Palestine to an end during the early years of the Twentieth Dynasty. *(University of Chicago)*

A Philistine Warrior. Philistine warriors such as this one, depicted here in Egyptian temple relief at Thebes, would have composed a substantial part of the invading forces of the Sea Peoples. The headdress of this warrior is a stiff encircling crest of either horsehair or feathers; such headgear is characteristic of Egyptian representations of Philistines. *(The British Museum)*

were no longer powerful. Indeed, they probably did well to survive. Conditions gave rise to a new day in which social cohesion would reside primarily in local villages, towns, clans, and tribes. It was in this context that Israel emerged on the scene. Specifically, the Israelite clans and tribes as described in the Book of Judges appear to have been among the Early Iron Age villagers, settled primarily in the central hill country with enclaves in the Transjordan—that is, in precisely those areas which had not been heavily populated during the Late Bronze Age.

Archaeology and the Early Israelite Tribes

While the ancient documents and Palestinian archaeology provide much useful information about general conditions in Syria-Palestine during the Late Bronze Age and the Early Iron Age, one must keep in mind that, with the exception of Merneptah's inscription, these nonbiblical sources shed light only on the general conditions of that time period and provide no specific information about the early Israelite tribes. For example, while archaeologists have excavated several Early Iron Age village sites that are representative no doubt of the sorts of villages inhabited by the early Israelites, it cannot be said for certain that any particular stratum of debris excavated thus far represents specifically an "Israelite" settlement from the "time of the Judges." One or more of the Iron I phases at Beitin (biblical Bethel) are likely candidates. Attempts to equate the Early Iron Age remains at Tell el-Ful with the Gibeah of Judges 19 or those at Izbet Sartah with the Ebenezer of I Sam. 7:12 are tempting, but in our opinion finally unconvincing.

Likewise, as observed in Chapter 2, the claims cannot be sustained that certain ceramic and architectural forms ("collared-rim jars" and "four-room houses") which made their appearance in Palestine at the beginning of the Iron Age were specifically "Israelite" in origin. Such claims are made on the grounds that these forms appear in Palestine at about the same time the Israelites seem to have emerged on the scene there. Yet this is hardly adequate evidence for assigning such items exclusively (or even primarily) to the Israelites. In the first place, the population of Early Iron Age Palestine was heterogeneous. The Israelites did not have even the central hill country to themselves in premonarchical times (see, for example, Judg. 19:10–15). In the second place, there is nothing about the physical character of either of these types that specifically points to the Israelites (as opposed, for example, to the Jebusites, Hivites, Moabites, or others whom the Bible locates in Palestine during the time of the Judges).

The Book of Judges and "the Period of the Judges"

The Book of Judges as a Continuation of the Genesis-Joshua Account

The Genesis-Joshua account, which we explored in the preceding chapter, is, as observed there, part of a more extensive treatment of Israelite and Judean

history which continues through I–II Kings and provides coverage from creation to the Babylonian exile. The entire Genesis-II Kings presentation may be
divided into six parts, corresponding to six discrete historical periods recognized by its compilers.

Genesis 1–11	The beginnings of things (from creation to Abraham)
Genesis 12–50	The Patriarchs (Abraham, Isaac, Jacob, Jacob's sons, the sojourn in Egypt)
Exodus-Deuteronomy	The era of Moses (exodus from Egypt, giving of the law, wilderness wanderings)
Joshua	The conquest of Canaan and the division of the land
Judges	The period of the Judges
I Samuel-II Kings	The rise of the monarchy and the period of the Kings

The Book of Judges therefore represents a continuation of the Genesis-Joshua
account and purports to describe the situation among the Israelite tribes between the era of the conquest and the rise of the monarchy. Specifically, the
Book of Judges consists of a series of stories and brief notes regarding the

Typical Iron-Age Ceramic Styles. Iron II cooking pots excavated at Lahav in the Shephelah.
Every Palestinian household would have possessed such vessels as these during the time
of the Israelite and Judean monarchies. *(Lahav Research Project)*

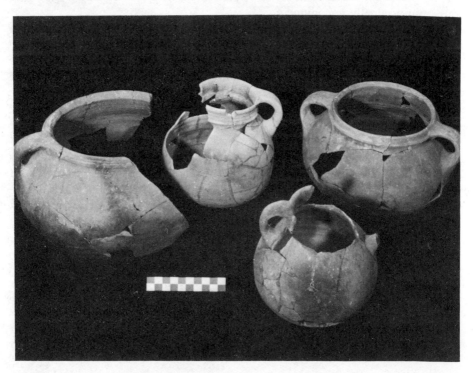

exploits of certain unusual figures who lived in "those days [when] there was no king in Israel [and] every man did what was right in his own eyes" (see Chart III). These figures are identified as deliverers or "judges." The reader is left to suppose that they delivered/judged a unified Israel composed of twelve tribes descended from the twelve sons of Jacob. The chronological data supplied and the present organization of the stories imply further that they were active in chronological sequence.

This Judges account of what is often called "the period of the Judges" presents historians with a situation somewhat comparable to the Genesis-Joshua account of which it is a continuation. It is our only direct source of information for this period of Israelite and Judean history. Yet as it stands, the Book of Judges can hardly be accepted at face value for purposes of historical reconstruction. In addition to matters of detail in the individual stories which strain credulity, the book as a whole reflects a continuation of the Genesis-II Kings editorial scheme which is artificial and unconvincing.

The Book of Judges and Historical Reconstruction

The recurrence of the numbers twenty, forty, and eighty in the chronological data supplied is a warning that we are dealing with a schematic presentation of history rather than with information derived from actual circumstances or preserved records. Compare the following items:

Othniel's deliverance was followed by forty years of peace.

Ehud's deliverance was followed by eighty years of peace.

Jabin oppressed Israel twenty years.

Deborah's deliverance was followed by forty years of peace.

Gideon's deliverance was followed by forty years of peace.

The Philistines oppressed Israel forty years.

Samson judged Israel twenty plus twenty years.

(Judg. 3:11, 30; 4:3; 5:31; 8:28; 13:1; 15:20; 16:31)

Another problem with the chronological data supplied in the Book of Judges is that the total number of years they require for the judges and interim periods, plus forty years for the desert wandering, forty years for Eli's judgeship (1 Sam. 4:18), some years for Samuel and Saul, and still forty years for David's rule, greatly exceeds the 480 years which, according to I Kings 6:1, transpired between the exodus and Solomon's founding of the Temple.

The stories about the deliverers/judges have been arranged and edited by the compilers of Genesis-II Kings in a fashion to demonstrate that conditions in premonarchical times followed, with rhythmic repetitiveness, a cyclic order which proceeded from apostasy to affliction to repentance to rest to apostasy,

CHART III. Outline of the Judges

Othniel
Delivered Israel from the hand of Cushan-rishathaim king of Aram-naharaim (Upper Mesopotamia) and "the land had rest for forty years" (Judg. 3:7–11).

Ehud
Delivered Israel from Moabite oppression and "the land had rest for eighty years" (Judg. 3:12–30).

Shamgar
Killed six hundred Philistines with an oxgoad and also delivered Israel (Judg. 3:31).

Deborah
Urged on Barak, who defeated Jabin king of Canaan. Deborah is described as a prophetess who was "judging Israel at that time," and Jabin is said to have oppressed the people of Israel cruelly for twenty years from his capital at Hazor (Judg. 4–5).

Gideon
Delivered Israel from Midian, who had oppressed the Israelites for seven years (Judg. 6–8). "And the land had rest forty years in the days of Gideon" (Judg. 8:28).

Abimelech
One of Gideon's sons. He killed his seventy brothers, hired a private army with funds contributed by the people of Shechem, was made king by all the citizens of Shechem and Beth-millo, and "ruled over Israel three years" (Judg. 9).

Tola
Judged Israel twenty-three years (Judg. 10:1–2).

Jair
Judged Israel twenty-two years and "had thirty sons who rode on thirty asses; and they had thirty cities" (Judg. 10:3–5).

Jephthah
Commander of a band of "worthless fellows," accepted an invitation to lead Israel in a struggle against Ammonite oppression. It was agreed that he would remain "head and leader" over the people after the Ammonites were defeated. He judged Israel six years (Judg. 10:6–12:7).

Ibzan
Judged Israel seven years and "had thirty sons; and thirty daughters he gave in marriage outside his clan, and thirty daughters he brought in from outside for his sons" (Judg. 12:8–10).

Elon
Judged Israel ten years (Judg. 12:11–12).

Abdon
Judged Israel eight years and "had forty sons and thirty grandsons, who rode on seventy asses" (Judg. 12:13–15).

Samson
A man of amazing strength, made sport of the Philistines and killed many of them at a time when they dominated Israel. Eventually captured and blinded, he killed more than three thousand Philistines at the expense of his own life. He judged Israel in the days of the Philistines "twenty years" (Judg. 13–16).

and so on, again and again. This theological pattern, anticipated in Judg. 2: 11–23 and noticeable with some variations throughout most of Judg. 3:7–17:21, may be outlined as follows:

> Under the leadership of each divinely ordained deliverer or judge the people remained faithful to Yahweh and enjoyed rest in the land.

> With the leader's death, "the people of Israel did what was evil in the sight of Yahweh. . . . They forsook Yahweh, the God of their fathers, who had brought them out of the land of Egypt; they went after other gods, from among the gods of the peoples who were round about them, and bowed down to them."

> "So the anger of Yahweh was kindled against Israel, and he gave them over to plunderers, who plundered them; and he sold them into the power of their enemies round about, so that they could no longer withstand their enemies."

> When the people cried out, "Yahweh was moved to pity by their groanings because of those who afflicted and oppressed them."

> "Yahweh raised up judges, who saved them out of the power of those who plundered them. . . . And he saved them from the hand of their enemies all the days of the judge."

> "But whenever the judge died, they turned back and behaved worse than their fathers."

The basic assumption behind this theological pattern is that fidelity to Yahweh was the determinative factor in the vicissitudes of ancient Israelite history. While such a view possesses theological consistency and homiletical appeal, most historians would have to agree that the dynamics of history are far more complex than this pattern allows. Close scrutiny of the individual narratives that have been utilized to project the theological patterns reveals, moreover, that some of them hardly fit the pattern. One very noticeable conflict between the narratives and the theological pattern they are intended to illustrate is that several of the heroes involved simply do not qualify as divinely ordained deliverers or judges. The Jephthah and Samson narratives are good examples. Shamgar, the son of Anath (a Syro-Palestinian goddess), may even have been a non-Israelite hero (Judg. 3:31).

The implication of the Book of Judges, following as it does upon Genesis-Joshua, is that each successive crisis involved, and that each deliverer/judge exercised leadership over, a politically and religiously unified coalition of twelve tribes, each descended from one of the twelve sons of Jacob. Closer examination reveals, however, that the events narrated in the individual accounts are very localized—usually involving one or two clans or tribes at the most. Moreover, the tribal situation seems to be much more complex than the tribal lists in Genesis-Joshua allow. This is especially obvious from the song of Deborah (Judg. 5), the only place in Judges where as many as ten tribes are mentioned in connection with a single event. The ten tribes mentioned in this list do not correspond entirely to the twelve sons of Jacob. Furthermore, tribal disunity rather than unity is one of the main themes of the song. We will return below to the matter of the tribal situation in early Israel. For the moment, it is sufficient to observe that the concept of judges/deliverers exercising leadership each in turn over a unified twelve-tribe Israel seems to have been superimposed artificially on narratives which originally had to do with localized affairs, usually involving only one or two tribal groups, and which report events that did not necessarily occur in chronological sequence.

The Judges Narratives as Indicative of the General Situation of the Israelite Tribes on the Eve of the Rise of the Monarchy

It is possible, therefore, to make some distinction between the editorial framework of the Book of Judges and the individual narratives that have been incorporated into the book. While the framework gives the impression of an artificial and schematic literary construct, the component narratives often have a more authentic ring. Indeed, the very fact that these individual narratives occasionally depict the deliverers/judges in a fashion that conflicts with the compilers' schematic view of conditions in premonarchical Israel indicates that the narratives were already well established in Israel's folk memory when they were incorporated into the Genesis-II Kings corpus.

To say that the component narratives of the Book of Judges have "a more authentic ring" and that they must have been "well established in Israel's folk memory" is, of course, not necessarily grounds for placing great confidence in their historicity. They are folk legends, not archival material, and studies show that most of them had already undergone changes and reshaping during the process of transmission prior to being included in the Genesis-II Kings account. Actually they are not unlike the patriarchal narratives in Genesis, the similarities becoming all the more apparent when it is recognized that the periodization of the Genesis-II Kings account ("age of the Patriarchs" distinct from "age of the Judges") is itself part of the artificial construct. In other words, the essential difference between some of the patriarchal narratives in Genesis and the deliverer/judge narratives in Judges may not be that they come from a different day and age but that the former focus on tribal and intertribal relationships (expressed in terms of patriarchal figures, family traditions, and genealogies), while the latter focus on individual leaders and events.

Thus, for the same reasons that we declined any attempt to reconstruct "the Patriarchal age" on the basis of the Genesis narratives, or "the age of conquest" on the basis of the material in the Book of Joshua, so also we will not attempt to reconstruct the history of "the period of the Judges" on the basis of the narratives of the Book of Judges. Yet the situation is somewhat different with the Judges narrative in several regards. (1) The contrast between the component narratives and the editorial overlay is much sharper here than in Genesis-Joshua. The individual narratives can be isolated with less difficulty on literary-critical grounds, and the fact that they conflict with the historical perspectives

of the compilers of Genesis-II Kings confirms that they represent earlier traditions. (2) The Judges narratives are not dominated by miraculous events and
extraordinary occurrences as is so much of the material in Genesis-Joshua. (3)
The general sociocultural conditions presupposed by these narratives are in
keeping with what is known about conditions existing in Palestine at the beginning of the Iron Age. (4) The situation reflected in these narratives provides
a believable and understandable background for the rise of the Israelite monarchy as it is depicted in I-II Samuel.

It is our opinion, in short, that the component narratives of the Book of
Judges can serve as a tentative starting point for a treatment of Israelite and
Judean history. While these narratives will not, unfortunately, provide a basis
for reconstructing any kind of detailed historical sequence of people and events,
they probably do offer a reasonably accurate impression of the general sociolog-
ical, political, and religious circumstances that existed among the early Israelite
tribes. It is in this very limited fashion, therefore, that we propose to use them
in the discussion that follows. What can be learned from them about the general
political conditions, social structures, and religious practices among the tribes
on the eve of the establishment of the Israelite monarchy?

Tribal Life and Leadership

Families, Clans, and Tribes

Various texts in the Bible speak of three basic social units in the premonarchical period: the family, the clan, and the tribe (see Josh. 7:16–18; I Sam.
10:20–21). Close examination of the biblical materials, in the light of comparative anthropological research, suggests that the family and the clan tended to
be more basic to the structure of the society than the tribe.

The family, or in Hebrew the *beth ab* ("the house of the father"), was what
today would be called "the extended family." Typically, this would have consisted of several generations (the patriarch, his wife or wives, his married sons
and their wives, their married sons and wives, all unmarried children, grandchildren, and so on) and various related figures (uncles, aunts, cousins) as well as
occasional slaves and strangers. Authority in the family resided with the patriarch. The extended family was probably exogamous, that is, persons generally
married outside the extended family, although marriage to one's maternal first
cousin may have been considered ideal (see Gen. 25:20; 29:9–30). Various
texts even speak of marriage to one's half sister (Gen. 20:8–12; II Sam. 13:
7–14). The extended family generally would have dwelt close together, a
populous specimen perhaps having its own settlement or village. The family was
also the basic unit in the ownership of property, cultivation of land, and care
of pastoral animals.

The clan consisted of several extended families living in nearby areas, inter-
locked by marriage, and employing communal use of land. Since villages and
small towns were characteristic of the areas where we find the Israelite tribes

settled during premonarchical times, there was, no doubt, a high degree of correspondence between villages and clans. In typical cases we may suspect that the families of a village functioned as and conceived of themselves as a clan with a shared past and shared ancestry. The families would have exchanged their daughters in marriage and made common use of surrounding farm and pasture land. Several clans may have been localized in larger towns and their surrounding villages. Government and the administration of justice in the villages/clans were normally in the hands of elders (see Judg. 8:16; Ruth 4:2; I Sam. 11:3), who themselves were the heads of families. Their prominence and position were dependent not upon any elective process but upon social status, wealth, and prestige. Disputes were normally settled and decisions reached in the village gates. The village/clan was also an important unit in cultic and religious life (see I Sam. 20:6, 29).

The tribe would have served as a larger and more strictly endogamous unit than the clan. Also the tribal divisions probably tended to be rather more vague and fluid. Close examination of the biblical materials in the light of comparative anthropological studies reveals (1) that tribal divisions and relationships were far more complex and fluid than a casual reading of the biblical genealogies would suggest and (2) that the tribes tended to be more territorial than genealogical in nature. The biblical genealogies themselves are our best evidence that the twelve-tribe scheme presupposed in the Book of Judges is an oversimplification of historical realities. These genealogies do not agree on the identity of the twelve, much less on the constituency of each tribe. Numerous biblical passages suggest further that the tribal relationships and divisions changed from time to time.

The essentially territorial character of the tribes is suggested, on the other hand, by the fact that several of the tribal names probably originated as territorial designations. Thus the name "Ephraim" probably originated with reference to the people living in the vicinity of Mt. Ephraim. "Gilead" would have been the name applied to people living in the region called Gilead. The same situation was probably the case with "Judah" and Mt. Judah. The name "Benjamin," which means "son of the south," is clearly a geographical name derived from the perspective of Ephraim to the north. References to "the land of Benjamin," "the land of Judah," "the land of Naphtali," and so forth also point to geographical entities.

This is not to claim that the tribe in ancient Israel had nothing to do with kinship relations or that it was purely territorial. The clans constituting a particular tribe no doubt felt a special kinship even if for no other reason than their close proximity and common life-style. Usually they would have shared a similar historical past as well. Thus the constituent clans of a tribe would have tended to think of themselves as having a common ancestry and would have expressed this in their genealogies and marriage patterns.

Against any thought that the biblical tribes may have been purely territorial divisions, it must be remembered that the biblical narratives refer to cities and enclaves of people living within designated tribal territories which for one reason or another were not considered part of the tribe in question. This phenomenon is reflected in the lists of unconquered cities in Judges 1, for example, and in designations such as "the hill country of the Amalekites" (Judg. 12:15), "the territory of the Archites" and "the territory of the Japhletites" (Josh. 16:2–3) for localities within the territory associated with Ephraim and Benjamin. Occasionally clans and even whole tribes may have moved from one territory to another.

Leadership Among the Tribes

As indicated above, political organization in premonarchical times seems to have found its center in the villages/clans rather than in the tribe, and frequent references suggest that the villages/clans were ruled by a body of elders. When the narratives refer to the elders of a region or a tribe, as in Judges 11, these probably were representatives of the villages/clans in a given locale who came together for unified action in the face of a particular situation or need. Several titles are used in the Judges narratives for persons who exercised leadership roles over and above that of elder. Among these titles are "ruler" or "official" (*sar;* Judg. 8:14; 9:30; 10:18), "leader" (*qasin;* Judg. 11:6; see Josh. 10:24, "chiefs"), "head" (*rosh;* Judg. 11:8), and "judge" (*shopet;* Judg. 2:16 and frequently). Note, however, that the title "judge" appears primarily in the editorial passages of the Book of Judges rather than in the component narratives.

We also find a diversity of leadership types reflected in the Judges narratives. Consider the following:

1. Deborah (Judg. 4–5), a prophetess, active in the Ephraimite/Benjaminite region, is said to have sat under a palm where people came to her for judgment (Judg. 4:4–5). This suggests that she was involved in the settlement of disputes and the arbitration of justice. One could compare the statement that Samuel installed his sons, Joel and Abijah, as judges at Beer-sheba, where they took bribes and perverted justice (I Sam. 8:1–3). Deborah is also pictured as rallying Barak and the troops to battle against a Canaanite army.

2. Tola, Jair, Ibzan, Elon, and Abdon were wealthy dignitaries with numerous offspring, which seems to explain their leadership status (Judg. 10:1–5; 12: 8–15).

3. Jephthah (Judg. 11:1–12:7) and Abimelech (Judg. 9) appear to have been semiprofessional paramilitary types with their own private armies (Judg. 9:4; 11:3) which they would have maintained with spoils from raids and "contributions" from those whom they protected. With judicious use of his army, Jephthah was able to achieve official status ("leader," *qasin,* and "head," *rosh*) over the clans of Gilead. Abimelech achieved a similar status over Shechem and the clans in that vicinity—indeed the biblical account indicates that the Shechemites actually proclaimed him "king" (Judg. 9:6). Although it is not stated, Barak may also have already possessed a standing army of some sort when Deborah encouraged him to challenge Sisera (see Judg. 4:6, 10).

4. Ehud (Judg. 3:15–30) and Gideon (Judg. 6—8) seem to have represented another type of leader, daring men who took the initiative to muster voluntary armies from their countrymen and challenge foreign oppression. After the success of his venture, Gideon is said to have been offered the crown and to have accepted some form of permanent leadership (Judg. 8:22–28).

5. Finally, there is Samson (Judg. 13–16), a hero remembered in folk tales for his strength, the trouble he caused the Philistines, and his practical jokes on a heroic scale. Reading the stories about his exploits, one must doubt that he exercised any formal leadership role, even within his own clan.

Tribal Alignments and Territories

As we have seen, the final editors of Genesis-II Kings presupposed a twelve-tribe union during premonarchical times, and Joshua 13–22 states that these twelve tribes held adjoining territorial allotments which, with the exception of certain minor territories that "remained to be conquered," accounted for the entire land of Palestine. Close examination of the materials that compose the books of Joshua and Judges suggests a rather different picture, however, and one that certainly is more accurate.

The Ephraim/Israel Tribes

The first observation to be made is that these materials, especially the narratives in the Book of Judges, tend to focus on the tribe of Ephraim and three neighboring tribal groups—the Benjaminites, the Manassites, and the Gileadites—all three of which appear to have been dominated by or aligned with Ephraim in some fashion. Ephraim proper was that portion of the central hill country between approximately Shechem and Bethel. Joshua himself, although a very hazy and legendary figure, was apparently an Ephraimite. We are told, namely, that he received his inheritance in Ephraim and was buried there (Josh. 19:49–50; 24:29–30).

The Benjaminites ("sons of the south" or "southerners"), associated with Gibeah and surrounding villages, are presumed in some passages to represent an independent tribe but mentioned in others as if they were simply "southern Ephraimites." For example, while Josh. 18:11–20 presumes that the area between Ramah and Bethel belonged to an independent tribe of Benjamin, Judg. 4:5 refers to "the palm of Deborah between Ramah and Bethel in the hill country of Ephraim." The matter of Benjamin's relationship to Ephraim probably was a point of contention at times, as we shall see later. (See Map 7.)

The conquest stories in Joshua 1–9 are primarily local aetiologies pertaining to southern Ephraim/Benjamin. Thus the accounts of the conquest of Jericho (Josh. 6) and Ai (Josh. 7–8) explain the existence of two prominent "tells" in that area (Tell es-Sultan and et-Tell) by attributing their destruction to Joshua. (This does not square with the results of archaeological excavations at the two sites, however, which demonstrate that the ruins actually date primarily from

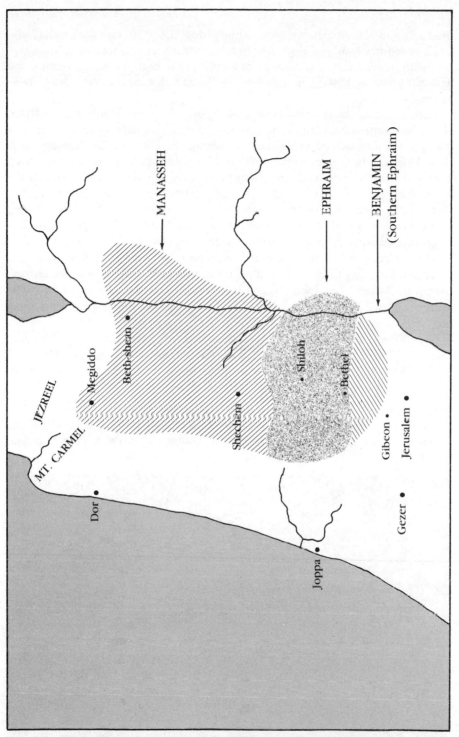

MANASSEH

EPHRAIM

BENJAMIN
(Southern Ephraim)

JEZREEL

MT. CARMEL

Megiddo •

Beth-shean •

Shiloh •

Bethel •

Shechem •

Gibeon •

Jerusalem •

Dor •

Gezer •

Joppa •

MAP 7. Domain of the Ephraim/Israel Tribes

the Early and Middle Bronze ages.) Ehud (Judg. 3:15–30) and Deborah (Judg. 4–5) were from southern Ephraim/Benjamin. Samuel also was an Ephraimite/Benjaminite who served a three-point circuit in the region (Gilgal, Bethel, and Mizpah; I Sam. 7:15–17), and Saul was a Benjaminite who ruled from Gibeah in Benjamin.

Manasseh is associated with the northern part of the central hill country (from about Shechem northward to the Jezreel Valley). Shechem was one of several major cities that existed in this region during the Late Bronze Age and continued into the Iron Age. Apparently the Manassites did not control these cities but lived in surrounding villages. Other major cities in the area not held by the Manassites (according to Judg. 1:27–28) were Beth-shean, Taanach, Dor, Ibleam, and Megiddo. Mention of Beth-shean and Dor (the Dor in the Jezreel Valley) indicates that Manassite clans spilled over into the Jezreel, where they intermingled with the Galilee-Jezreel tribal groups (see Josh. 17:11–13). There may have been some Manassite spillover into the Transjordan as well. For example, the clan of Machir may have been a branch of Manasseh that crossed over into Bashan and Upper Gilead (see Josh. 12:1–6; 13:29–31; 17:1). The same may have been true of Jair and Nobah, although the references to them are obscure (see Num. 32:39–42; Judg. 10:3).

Gideon was a Manassite hero of the Abiezrite clan from the village of Ophrah. We are told that he mustered a volunteer army and expelled Midianite raiders from the Jezreel Valley. In addition to his own tribe, he received support

et-Tell (biblical Ai). Modern et-Tell, the ruins of ancient Ai, is a prominent "tell," in southern Benjamin. Although Joshua 6–8 attributes the destruction of this city to the invading Israelites under Joshua, archaeological excavations reveal that it was in ruins long before the Israelites arrived on the scene. *(J. A. Callaway)*

in this venture from Asher, Zebulun, and Naphtali—that is, from three other tribes settled in the area where the Midianites were raiding (Judg. 6:35; 7:23). Note that the Ephraimites, who were called to arms only after the battle was under way, upbraided Gideon for undertaking the venture without calling them (Judg. 7:24–8:3). Apparently the Ephraimites felt they had some claim on the actions of the Manassites.

A similar situation is reflected in the relationship of Ephraim to Gilead. When the elders of Gilead, led by Jephthah, attacked and defeated the Ammonites, the Ephraimites mustered for war, crossed the Jordan, and threatened to burn the houses of Jephthah's people. They were offended because, specifically, Jephthah and the Gileadites had not summoned them before the battle (Judg. 12:1–6). Here again the Ephraimites seem to have presumed some special claim over the Gileadites. In fact, the Gileadites involved in this episode are described as "fugitives of Ephraim" (Judg. 12:4), which suggests that they may have been Ephraimite settlers in the Transjordan. The presence of Ephraimite settlers in the Transjordan would also explain the mention of "the forest of Ephraim" in II Sam. 18:6. This forest, according to the context of the passage (see II Sam. 18:24–26), must have been in Transjordan roughly opposite Mt. Ephraim.

There seems to have existed in the north-central hill country, therefore, with spillover into the Jezreel Valley and the Transjordanian highlands, a group of loosely associated tribes dominated by Ephraim. Associated with Ephraim in this alliance were Benjamin (sometimes and probably originally considered a part of Ephraim), Gilead (closely associated with Ephraim, probably including Ephraimite clans that had migrated eastward across the Jordan), Manasseh, Machir, Jair, and Nobah (the latter three closely related to Manasseh in the same fashion as Benjamin was related to Ephraim). Probably this loose alliance of tribes was the premonarchical "Israel" to which the Merneptah inscription refers.

The patriarchal narratives would seem to support such a view. Note that the stories about Jacob, also named "Israel" (Gen. 32:27–28; 35:10), have their setting primarily in the territory of these Ephraimite-dominated tribes. Joseph and Benjamin are depicted as favorite sons of Jacob/Israel, with Benjamin as the younger. Manasseh and Ephraim are identified as Joseph's sons, in turn, with Manasseh as the older and Ephraim the one destined to dominate (Gen. 48). The occasional references to "the house of Joseph" in the Book of Joshua clearly pertain to these three related tribes—Ephraim/Benjamin and Manasseh (see Josh. 17:14–18). After the death of Solomon, the territory of these same tribes became the core of the northern kingdom, which in turn is referred to interchangeably as "Ephraim," "Israel," and "Samaria" (after the capital city).

Most of the so-called "minor judges" listed in Judg. 10:1–5; 12:8–15 were from the Ephraim/Israel group. Tola was a man of Issachar but lived and was buried at Shamir in the hill country of Ephraim (Judg. 10:1–2). Jair, like Jephthah, was a Gileadite (Judg. 10:3–5), and Abdon was from "Pirathon in the land of Ephraim, in the hill country of the Amalekites" (Judg. 12:13–15). Only Ibzan and Elon appear to have been from outside the Ephraim/Israel group, but even they may have been associated with the group in one way or another. For example, Elon is said to have been buried at Aijalon in the land of Zebulun (Judg. 12:11–12), but the only Aijalon known in the Bible was in the southwestern Benjaminite area.

While the tribes of the Ephraim/Israel group are to be identified very closely with their respective territories, it cannot be assumed that they represented the total population of these regions. There obviously was some perception of "Israelite" over against "non-Israelite" clans/villages/tribes, as presupposed, for example, in Judg. 19:12. The lines between "Israelite" and "non-Israelite" may have been only vaguely drawn at times, and would have had to do with various ill-defined factors such as ethnic and cultural background, economic arrangements, historical circumstances, cult, and so forth.

These Ephraimite/Israelite tribes command center stage in the biblical traditions pertaining to premonarchical times. Other tribes appear on the periphery of things and usually come into consideration only when their interests overlap those of the Ephraim/Israel group.

The Galilee-Jezreel Tribes

Among the other tribes that figure occasionally in the narratives pertaining to premonarchical times were several located in the Galilee and the Jezreel Valley. Joshua 19:10–39 places the tribes of Asher, Zebulun, Issachar, and Naphtali in the western, southern, and eastern regions of Galilee, respectively, with some spillover into the Jezreel Valley (see Map 8). The tribal sayings in Gen. 49:13 and Deut. 33:18–19 seem to associate Zebulun and Issachar with the sea in some fashion, and the song of Deborah (Judg. 5:17b) does the same for Asher. Perhaps these three were originally coastal clans that had moved into the Galilean mountains, possibly under pressure from (or even including) elements of the Sea Peoples.

These Galilee-Jezreel tribes are described in Judg. 1:30–33 as settled among cities they did not control. The cities that Asher is said not to have taken were primarily Phoenician coastal towns—Acco, Sidon, Ahlab, Achzib, Helbah, Aphek, and Rehob. Nahalol, one of Zebulun's "unconquered cities," was on the River Kishon near modern Haifa. The other, Kitron, has not been located. Naphtali's two unconquered cities, Beth-shemesh and Beth-anath, are also unidentified. Issachar's name, if from *skr,* would mean something like "hired one." This, along with the saying in Gen. 49:14–15, has been taken to suggest that the Issachar clans not only lived among non-Israelites in the fertile Jezreel Valley but also served them as laborers.

The Galilee-Jezreel tribes figure in two of the Judges narratives, both having to do with battles initiated by persons of the Ephraim/Israel group but fought in the Jezreel Valley where the Galilee-Jezreel tribes had interests. (1) Gideon of Ophrah's attack against the Midianite raiders in the Jezreel Valley was supported by Asher, Zebulun, and Naphtali (Judg. 6:35). (2) Deborah of southern Ephraim/Benjamin encouraged Barak from Kadesh in Naphtali to engage

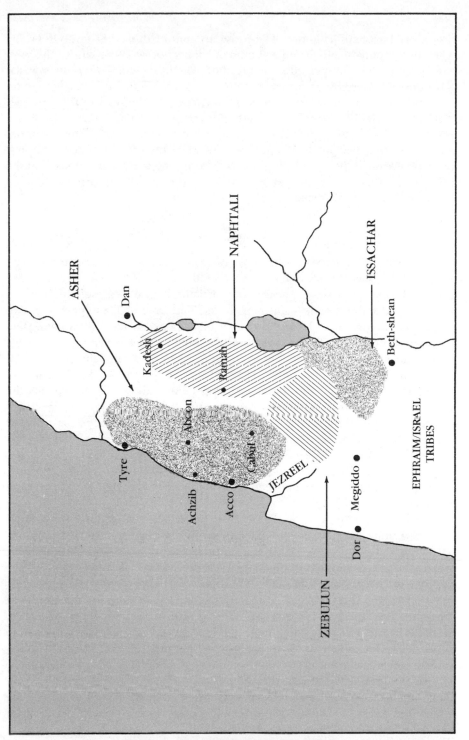

MAP 8. The Galilee-Jezreel Tribes

Sisera of Harosheth-ha-goiim. The prose account of this latter episode (Judg. 4) mentions only Naphtali and Zebulun in connection with the battle, although the fact that Deborah played such a leading role in the affair suggests that the Ephraim/Israel group was involved to some degree. The poetic version (Judg. 5) depicts the Ephraim/Israel group as having taken the lead in the struggle.

Thus the Galilee-Jezreel tribes shared certain common interests with the Ephraim/Israel group which led on occasion to joint endeavors. This commonality came to be expressed genealogically in terms of a common ancestry, perhaps already in premonarchical times. There is no reason to suppose, on the other hand, that the Galilee-Jezreel tribes were bound to the Ephraim/Israel group in any kind of formal tribal league.

Dan, Reuben, and Gad

The territorial domains of the tribes of Dan, Reuben, and Gad are difficult to establish, possibly because elements of these tribes transferred positions during the course of Israel's history or, particularly in the case of Reuben and Gad, ranged far and wide with their flocks. The tribe of Dan appears in two geographical contexts: (1) in the coastal plain between the Ephraimite/Benjaminite section of the hill country and the Mediterranean Sea (see the tribal allotments in Josh. 19, the reference in Judg. 1:34, and the Samson stories in Judg. 13–16) and (2) in the city of Dan (Laish) at the foot of Mt. Hermon in the extreme north of Palestine. The narrative in Judges 17–18 explains the connection of the tribe with the two areas. We are told that the Danites were unable to maintain their position in the coastal region, whereupon a group of them, in search of *Lebensraum,* conquered and inhabited Laish which they renamed Dan. Among the Sea Peoples mentioned in the texts of Raameses III are, in addition to the Philistines, another related group called the Danuna. Possibly there was some connection between these Danuna (or Denyen; see Text II) and the Danites. (See Map 9.)

Danite affairs impinged on those of the Ephraim/Israel group in two ways. (1) The Danite clans, while settled along the Mediterranean Sea, were immediate neighbors of Ephraim/Benjamin. Note, in fact, that according to the tribal distributions presupposed in the Book of Joshua, Dan's allotment would have fallen essentially within Ephraim's allotment. This apparent overlap probably arises from the fact that the boundaries defined in Joshua 16 presuppose a "Greater Ephraim" which extended all the way to the Mediterranean Sea, whereas the Danite section in Josh. 19:40–48 does not. This would explain Judg. 1:29 also, which places Gezer within Ephraim. (2) The Danites, Ephraimites, and Judeans shared a common enemy—the Philistines. Moreover, in the struggles with the Philistines, the Danites would have been the first and most directly affected. By the time Saul appears on the scene, for example, the Philistines had gained superiority over the whole of the southern coastal plain and penetrated into the central hill country. This means that they were in control of all the territory allotted to Dan in Joshua 19.

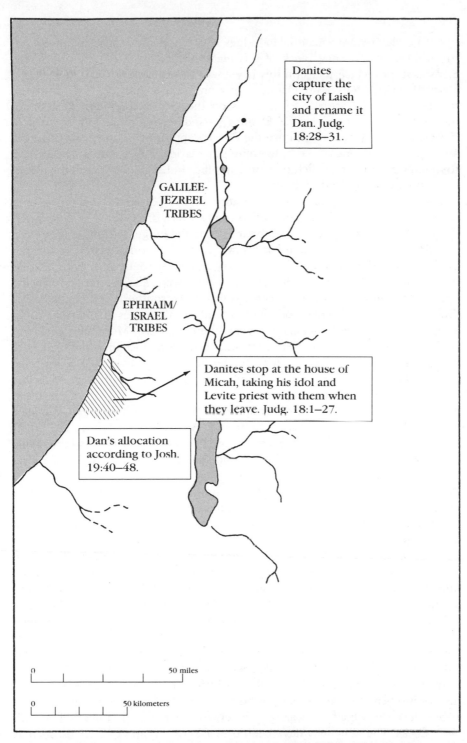

Danites
capture the
city of Laish
and rename it
Dan. Judg.
18:28–31.

GALILEE-
JEZREEL
TRIBES

EPHRAIM/
ISRAEL
TRIBES

Danites stop at the house of
Micah, taking his idol and
Levite priest with them when
they leave. Judg. 18:1–27.

Dan's allocation
according to Josh.
19:40–48.

0   50 miles

0   50 kilometers

MAP 9. The Danite Migration According to Judges 17–18

Most of the narrative material in Judges 13–18 pertains in one way or another to the Danites. The first block of this material (Judg. 13–16) consists of the Samson stories which focus on this legendary strong man of Dan. The second block of material tells of the Danite migration to Laish (Judg. 17–18), although this latter material actually focuses less on the Danite migration than on an incident that happened as the Danites passed through the hill country of Ephraim. Namely, we are told that the Danites appropriated the cultic furniture and a priest from one of the Ephraimite sanctuaries. This priest is said to have founded a priestly line which remained in office in Laish/Dan "until the day of the captivity of the land" (Judg. 18:30).

The tribes of Reuben and Gad figure in the patriarchal narratives and genealogies, with Reuben identified as the firstborn of Jacob (Gen. 29:31–32; 49:3–4). Neither of these tribes is mentioned in the Judges narratives, however, and practically nothing concrete is known about them otherwise. The meager evidence regarding their tribal territory is particularly vague and contradictory. Numbers 32 and Joshua 13 indicate that they were allotted territory in the Transjordanian highlands, from approximately the southern end of the Sea of Galilee to the Arnon River. But while Numbers 32 locates Gad farther south than Reuben, Joshua 13 seems to reverse their positions. Moreover, whatever their relative positions, it is clear from other sources that Reuben and Gad were not alone in this "allotted" territory. Judges 5:17 and 11:1–12:6 place the tribe of Gilead in the area directly east of the Jordan River, for example, while certain prophetical passages seem to presuppose that the entire area east of the Dead Sea (including from the cities of Elealeh and Heshbon southward to the Arnon) was Moabite domain (see Isa. 15; Jer. 48). An inscription left by the ninth-century king Mesha of Moab reaffirms the Moabite claim to this latter area, while at the same time noting the presence there of "men of Gad" (see Text IV). Specifically, the Mesha Inscription associates the Gadites with "the land of Ataroth," which is to be identified in turn with the vicinity of present-day Atarus about eight miles north-northwest of Dhiban.

Finally, certain biblical texts speak of Reubenite and Gadite activity west of the Jordan. Thus Josh. 15:6 (= 18:17) mentions "the stone of Bohan the son of Reuben" near Jericho, while Joshua 22 tells of an ancient tribal conflict which supposedly occurred in the immediate aftermath of Joshua's conquest of Canaan and involved the building of an altar on the west bank of the Jordan by the Reubenites, Gadites, and Manassites. One is tempted to speculate that the actual historical basis of the story, if there is any, was some ancient conflict between the Ephraim/Israel group and the Reubenites (see also Gen. 49:3–4). Perhaps too there was some connection between the "altar" mentioned in this story and "the stone of Bohan the son of Reuben."

In any case, the vague and contradictory information regarding the settlement area of Reuben and Gad probably is best explained by supposing that these two tribes were never confined to a specific territory but ranged rather widely with their flocks. The same may have been true also of certain other tribes, such as the Kenites discussed below. Accordingly, the grazing range of Reuben and

Gad would have partially overlapped territory of the Ephraim/Israel group. There would have been occasional conflicts in the context of symbiotic relations.

Judah and the Southern Tribes

Occupying the southern part of the central hill country and associated areas (the Shephelah, the Negeb, and "the Judean Wilderness"), and separated from Ephraim/Benjamin by an enclave of Hivite and Jebusite villages, were several tribal groups including the Judahites, the Calebites, the Korahites, the Kenizzites, the Jerahmeelites, the Kenites, and the Simeonites. The early history of these southern tribes is very difficult to reconstruct for two reasons. (1) Most of the biblical materials that relate to them presuppose what can be called "Greater Judah," a largely ideal concept which emerged after Judah came to prominence under David and which subsumes the other southern tribes under Judah. (2) The southern tribes do not play a prominent role in the Judges narratives which, as seen above, tend to focus attention on matters pertaining to Ephraim/Israel.

Greater Judah. Judah proper consisted of clans settled in the hill country approximately between Jerusalem and Hebron. However, the twelve-tribe scheme espoused by the compilers of Genesis-II Kings, the supporting genealogies (see also I Chron. 2–5), the tribal allotments in the Book of Joshua, and the brief "conquest reports" in Judg. 1:1–21 all presuppose a "Greater Judah" with ideal boundaries encompassing entire southern Palestine west of the Arabah. Accordingly, all of the various population elements situated within these boundaries, except for the Philistines, Levites, and Simeonites, are treated as belonging to Judah. Even Simeon, while attributed independent status in the twelve-tribe scheme, is subsumed under Judah for all practical purposes in the tribal allotments. Most of the villages assigned to Simeon are also assigned to Judah, and all of them are situated within the boundaries designated for Judah (compare Josh. 15:2–5, 26–32 with Josh. 19:1–9). (See Map 10.)

Two biblical passages require special attention at this point, since both, in their present form and context, pertain to the conquest and settlement of southern Palestine. Namely, Josh. 10:29–42 reports Joshua's capture of several key cities in the hill country and the Shephelah (Libnah, Lachish, Eglon, Hebron, and Debir) and concludes with the sweeping claim that he "defeated them from Kadesh-barnea to Gaza, and all the country of Goshen, as far as Gibeon" (Josh. 10:41). The opening chapter of the Book of Judges, on the other hand, which reports the successes and failures of the various tribes as they attempted to take possession of their respective allotments after Joshua's death, describes Judah as going up first against the Canaanites and taking this same southern territory (Judg. 1:1–21).

These two passages seem to contradict each other on the matter of when and under what circumstances the conquest of southern Palestine occurred. That is, while the former claims an initial conquest of southern Palestine under Joshua,

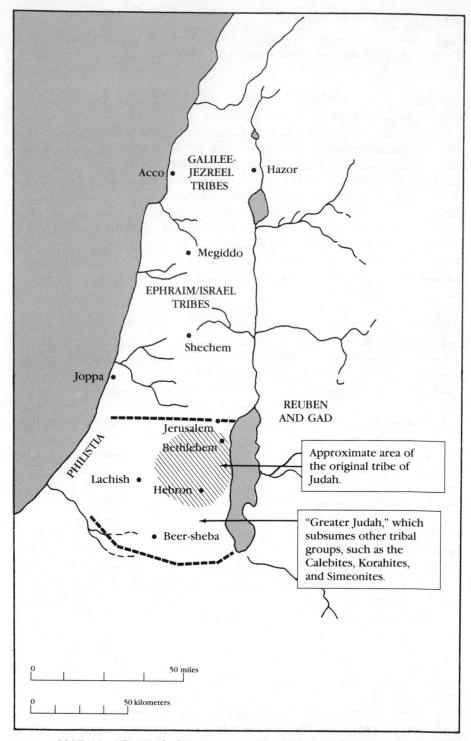

GALILEE-
JEZREEL
TRIBES

Acco •   • Hazor

• Megiddo

EPHRAIM/ISRAEL
TRIBES

• Shechem

Joppa •

REUBEN
AND GAD

PHILISTIA

Jerusalem

Bethlehem •

Lachish •   Approximate area of
            the original tribe of
• Hebron   Judah.

            "Greater Judah," which
• Beer-sheba   subsumes other tribal
            groups, such as the
            Calebites, Korahites,
            and Simeonites.

0   50 miles

0   50 kilometers

MAP 10. The Tribal Territory of Judah and Greater Judah

the latter seems unaware of Joshua's southern campaign and describes independent tribal action on the part of Judah and Simeon. Moreover, the Joshua 10
report of Joshua's southern campaign seems to conflict also with the preceding
story in the Book of Joshua of how the Israelites entered into a nonaggression
pact with the Gibeonites (Josh. 9:3–27). More will be said below about this
problematic campaign report found in Josh. 10:29–42. For the moment it is
sufficient to observe that, while it has the appearance of an authentic report, it
may actually belong in another historical context. Possibly the compilers of
Genesis–II Kings introduced it in its present context in order to "fill out" what
they wished to present as an initial and total conquest of the land under Joshua.

Judges 1:1–21 represents a somewhat similar situation and clearly presupposes the "Greater Judah" concept, although with some lip service given to
Simeon. Upon close examination, these verses turn out to be a motley assortment of individual traditions, most of which appear in variant versions elsewhere. For example, the Adoni-bezek affair reported in vs. 5–7 finds its parallel
in the Adoni-zedek story of Josh. 10:1–5. The Hebron-Debir episode (vs. 10–15;
compare Josh. 15:16–19) is, as we will see below, actually a Calebite/Othnielite
tradition. The reference to Kenite settlement in the Arad region and the explanation of the name of Hormah (vs. 16–17) parallel material found in Num.
14:45 and 21:1–3; and so on. In short, Judg. 1:1–21 is a "contrived" conquest
account in which various traditions pertaining to the actions of different tribal
groups have been combined to suggest a "Greater Judah" conquest of southern
Palestine.

However, there was no such "Greater Judah" conquest. Indeed, while Judah
may have enjoyed some special prominence among the southern Palestinian
tribal groups (as did Ephraim among the north-central tribes), the very idea of
a "Greater Judah" during the premonarchical period is an anachronism.

Judah in the Judges Narratives. As indicated above, Judah and the other southern tribal groups are very much on the periphery in the narratives of the Book
of Judges. Moreover, there is reason to suspect that most of the references to
Judah that do appear in the book were introduced by the compilers of Genesis–II
Kings in a conscious effort to give Judah a more significant role in Israelite affairs
during premonarchical times. Only one of the Judges narratives actually focuses
on a southern hero. Specifically, Judg. 3:7–11 relates how "Othniel the son of
Kenaz, Caleb's younger brother" fought against Cushan-rishathaim king of
Aram-naharaim (Upper Mesopotamia). Several factors suggest that this story is
artificial. (1) The name of the Mesopotamian oppressor, Cushan-rishathaim
("Cushan of Double Evil"), sounds like a scribal caricature. (2) We know from
extrabiblical sources of no time in the Late Bronze Age or Early Iron Age when
Mesopotamian rulers even campaigned in Palestine, much less exercised dominion over that area. (3) The text provides no details about the incident, and does
not even identify the place where the supposed battle occurred. In short, one
has to suspect that this is a fictitious account designed to give Judah ("Greater
Judah") a share of the action in "the period of the Judges."

The mention of Judah in two other passages is suspect on similar grounds. Judges 10:9 states that "the Ammonites crossed the Jordan to fight also against Judah and against Benjamin and against the house of Ephraim; so that Israel was sorely distressed." This statement occurs in a section of the editorial framework of Judges (Judg. 10:6–16) which develops the theological pattern of apostasy-affliction-repentance-restoration. Moreover, the Jephthah story, which this passage introduces, makes it clear that the war with the Ammonites specifically involved Gilead and occurred east of the Jordan. Likewise Judg. 20:18 seems to include Judah unnecessarily in the account of an internal Ephraimite/Israelite conflict.

The two remaining references to Judah in the Book of Judges pertain to Judean clans settled on the western slopes of the hill country close to the Philistines and the Danites. In Judg. 15:9–11 we hear the Judeans complaining to Samson that his harassment of the Philistines was only making things worse. Then, when the Danites made their trek to Laish, they are said to have encamped at "Kiriath-jearim in Judah" (Judg. 18:11). These two passages suggest something of the northern extent or expansion of the Judean settlement in premonarchical days (see also Josh. 15:5–11, where Kiriath-jearim falls within the ideal boundaries of "Greater Judah").

Other Southern Tribal Groups. Associated primarily with the city of Hebron and its agriculturally productive vicinity were the Calebites, as presupposed by Numbers 13–14. This narrative, which reports how Moses sent out an expedition of spies from Kadesh to reconnoiter the Land of Canaan, has been edited also to conform to the schematic views of the editors of Genesis–II Kings. That is, it presupposes that the action involved twelve spies, one from each of the twelve tribes, and that they explored the whole land of Canaan. In its pre-edited version, however, the story probably had to do with a spying expedition specifically directed to Hebron and its vicinity (see Num. 14:22–24), and its main point would have been to confirm the Calebites' right to that area: "My servant Caleb, because he has a different spirit and has followed me fully, I will bring into the land into which he went [that is, Hebron and vicinity], and his descendants shall possess it" (Num. 14:24). This theme reappears in Josh. 14:6–15 and 15:13–19. Note that Judg. 1:10–15, a parallel version of Josh. 15:13–19, has the tribe of Judah—"Greater Judah," that is, which would include the Calebites —taking Hebron.

These last two texts mentioned in connection with the Calebites, Josh. 15: 13–19 and the parallel version in Judg. 1:10–15, describe how Othniel the son of Kenaz the younger brother of Caleb secured the city of Debir south of Hebron. About all that can be deduced from this tale is that Othnielites were settled in the hill country immediately south of Hebron, specifically in the Debir region.

Elements in the biblical genealogies associate the Calebites and Othnielites with the Korahites, Kenizzites, and Jerahmeelites. Thus Num. 32:12 and Josh. 14:6, 14 refer to Caleb as "the son of Jephunneh the Kenizzite," while Judg.

1:13 (see also Judg. 3:9) identifies Othniel as "the son of Kenaz, Caleb's younger brother," and I Chron. 2:42 describes Caleb as the brother of Jerahmeel. Genesis 36:11 and 15–16, on the other hand, present Kenaz and Korah as brothers among the sons of Esau (= Edom), while I Chron. 2:42–43 presents Caleb as the grandfather of Hebron and great-grandfather of Korah. One hardly knows what to do with these passages, and very little is known otherwise about the Korahites, Kenizzites, and Jerahmeelites. All three of these tribal groups appear to have ranged in the foothills of the southern hill country and in the Negeb where they intermingled with and were related to the Edomites. I Samuel 27:10 speaks of "the Negeb of Judah" and "the Negeb of the Jerahmeelites," while I Sam. 30:29 mentions "the cities of the Jerahmeelites." Korah and Kenaz are listed among the descendants of Esau, who in turn is equated with Edom, in Genesis 36.

I Samuel 27:10 speaks also of "the Negeb of the Kenites" and I Sam. 30:29 mentions "the cities of the Kenites" (some Hebrew and Greek manuscripts, however, read Kenizzites instead of Kenites), while Judg. 1:16 identifies the region around Arad as their place of residence. Judges 4:11–22 and 5:24–30, however, place Jael, a tent-dwelling Kenite, as far north as the Jezreel Valley. The father-in-law of Moses, sometimes called Jethro (Ex. 4:18; 18) but at other times Reuel (Ex. 2:18; Num. 10:29) or Hobab (Judg. 4:11), is identified as both a Kenite (Judg. 1:16) and a Midianite (Ex. 3:1). A widely accepted, and probably correct, hypothesis regarding the Kenites is that they (or at least some segment of the tribe) were itinerant metalworkers who enjoyed a special relationship with and protection among the other Palestinian tribal groups (see Gen. 4:1–16, where the characterization of Cain may relate in some fashion to the Kenites).

Religion and Cult

According to the idealistic views of the compilers of Genesis–II Kings, the eleven secular tribes of Israel were led in worship by a twelfth tribe of priests, the Levites. These Levites championed a faith in Yahweh, the national god, which contrasted sharply with the religious beliefs and practices of the indigenous peoples of the Land of Canaan. It was presumed further by these compilers that Shechem and Shiloh served as central cultic shrines for all twelve of the tribes. Joshua is said to have assembled the tribes at Shechem on two occasions and led them in ceremonies pertaining to the Mosaic law and covenant (Josh. 8:30–35; 24). The tent of meeting was brought to rest at Shiloh, according to Josh. 18:1, and Shiloh is presumed to have served as a political center for the tribes thereafter (see, for example, Josh. 21:1–2 and 22:12).

The individual narratives in the Book of Judges, however, as well as certain other biblical and nonbiblical evidence, suggest quite a different situation. Two narratives call for special attention in this regard: the Gideon, Jerubbaal, and Abimelech narrative complex in Judges 6–9 and the story of Micah the Ephraimite in Judges 17–18. Judges 6–9 is a tangle of traditions pertaining to Gideon,

Jerubbaal (equated with Gideon in these narratives), and Abimelech. The scene opens at "the oak at Ophrah," which was owned by Gideon's father, Joash the Abiezrite (Judg. 6:11). The name "Joash" ("Yahweh gives" or "Yahweh has given") presupposes Yahweh worship, and Gideon is said to have encountered an angel of Yahweh (or Yahweh himself, compare Judg. 6:11 with 6:14) at the oak, to whom he offered a sacrifice of meat, bread, and broth. Then, to further commemorate the appearance, Gideon is said to have built an altar to Yahweh and named it "Yahweh is Shalom" (Judg. 6:24). In a second scene (Judg. 6:25–32) Gideon proceeds to pull down an altar of Baal and remove an Asherah (sacred tree? or pole? representing the female deity) also belonging to his father, and to build an altar to Yahweh on top of the "stronghold" (Judg. 6:26). This nocturnally executed destruction of Baal's altar met with opposition from the men of the town, which suggests that it had served as a village shrine (see Judg. 6:24). After defeating the Midianites, Gideon made an ephod (a statue of the deity? some special cultic object?) which he set up in his city, Ophrah.

In the Abimelech episode which follows, we read that seventy pieces of silver were taken from a temple of Baal-berith ("Baal of the Covenant"; Judg. 9:4) in Shechem and given to Abimelech for the hire of a private army. Abimelech was subsequently made king by "the oak of the pillar at Shechem" (Judg. 9:6), no doubt a sacred spot like the oak at Ophrah. Later, when Abimelech attacked Shechem, he approached from the direction of "the Diviners' Oak" (Judg. 9:37). The people of the city fled to "the stronghold of the house of El-berith" ("El of the covenant"; Judg. 9:46).

According to the story of Micah the Ephraimite, Micah took silver consecrated to Yahweh and had it fashioned into a graven/molten image (a statue of Yahweh?). Along with this image, Micah made an ephod and teraphim (statues? vestments? sacred masks?) and placed all three of these items as cultic furniture in what appears to have been essentially a family shrine. Initially he installed one of his sons as priest. Later he replaced the son with a Levite of Bethlehem in Judah. Apparently a Levite priest was regarded as particularly desirable, although it should be noted that "Levite" in this episode does not seem to refer to a genealogical line. This particular Levite is said specifically to have been from the tribe of Judah. Later on in the narrative the Levite is recognized by his voice (Judg. 18:3).

When the Danites passed through Ephraim, they seized the cultic furniture and convinced the Levite to come along with them as their priest, reminding him that it was better to be the priest for a whole tribe than for a single family (Judg. 18:19). The Levite, subsequently installed in the sanctuary at Dan, is identified in Judg. 18:30 as Jonathan the son of Gershom and grandson of Moses; and his priestly line is said to have survived in Dan until the day of the captivity of the land. Micah's image, we are told finally, remained in the Danite shrine "as long as the house of God was at Shiloh" (Judg. 18:31).

Admittedly these two narratives are beset with problems of interpretation. One cannot deny, however, that they reflect a general religious and cultic situation that is quite different from that presupposed by the compilers of

Genesis-II Kings and superimposed by them on the Judges narratives. We would maintain, moreover, that these two narratives present a more accurate picture of the religious and cultic circumstances that pertained among the tribes on the eve of the establishment of the monarchy. Four main generalizations may be made in this regard. (1) Religion and cult among the Israelite clans/villages had much in common with the age-old practices and symbolism of Syria-Palestine. Certainly there was more continuity than contrast. (2) There were numerous shrines, high places, altars, and so forth, scattered among the clans. Some of these sanctuaries were obviously more renowned than others and, correspondingly, would have had a broader constituency. However, the evidence does not suggest a single cultic center even for the Ephraimite/Israelite tribes in premonarchical times. (3) Nor do the narratives suggest that a single priestly tribe had a monopoly on cultic leadership. Indeed, there appears to have been active competition between certain priestly families or guilds. (4) Finally, although Yahwistic religion played a significant role among the people, there appears to have been nothing like a uniform religious faith which demanded the allegiance of all the tribes to the exclusion of other forms of faith and worship.

El, Baal, and Yahweh

Some degree of continuity between the religion and cult of the "Israelite" tribes and that of the general Syro-Palestinian population should be expected, if for no other reason than that the tribes themselves emerged, at least to some extent, from the indigenous population. Also, as even the biblical narratives themselves intimate, many of the shrines that had been active during the Bronze Age continued to be in use among the tribes, in many cases no doubt still with their hereditary priestly families in charge. Several of the patriarchal narratives probably were intended to address this matter. That is, they condone worship at these old Bronze Age shrines by claiming that the Israelite ancestors worshiped at these places long ago and in some instances actually founded the shrines. Thus Abraham is associated with the holy places at Shechem (Gen. 12:6–7), Bethel (12:8), Beer-sheba (21:33), and Mamre near Hebron (13:18); Isaac with Beer-sheba (26:23–25); and Jacob with Shechem (33:18–20) and Bethel (28:10–22).

The Genesis narratives, particularly those which associate the patriarchs with the old Bronze Age sanctuaries, and indeed the name "Israel" itself, imply that Israel's earliest ancestors were primarily worshipers of the deity El (Gen. 16:13; 17:1; 21:33; 31:13; 35:7, 11; 43:14; 48:3). Jacob, for example, is said to have built an altar at Bethel and called it "El-bethel" (Gen. 35:7; see 31:13). Similarly, on property purchased near the city of Shechem, he is said to have erected an altar which he called "El-Elohe-Israel," which would mean "El the God of Israel" (Gen. 33:20). In texts dating from the fourteenth and thirteenth centuries B.C.E. and discovered among the ruins of the ancient city of Ugarit on the Syrian coast, El is the high god, the chief deity in the Syro-Palestinian pantheon. He is presented as the father of years, humankind, and the other gods; and generally depicted as a peace-loving divinity whose will lies behind the operations of the divine and human worlds, although he is at times harassed by the lesser gods and goddesses. In this latter regard, it is interesting to note that the patriarchal worship of El is always placed within a nonmilitary context, unlike the militant Yahwism reflected in the Book of Judges.

The other Syro-Palestinian gods apparently found worshipers among the premonarchical Israelite tribes as well—particularly Baal, known from Ugaritic literature as a dying and rising but virile and active god of vegetation and the seasonal cycle. Often mentioned in connection with Baal altars is the Asherah, probably a symbol of the female consort of Baal. But it was Yahweh, of course, who would emerge as the national god of Israel and Judah, although he probably was never worshiped exclusively by the early Israelites, and certainly not during the early tribal period. Also it must be presumed that Yahweh would have been perceived and worshiped in much the same fashion as the other gods of the Syro-Palestinian pantheon.

Baal. Unearthed in the excavations at Ras Shamra, this stela represents a Canaanite deity, probably to be identified with Baal, the god of storm and rain known throughout the region of Syria-Palestine. Two horns protrude from the front of the headdress, probably imitative of the horns of a bull, an animal often associated with Baal in other representations. He holds in his left hand a lance, the shaft of which is a stylized representation of a tree or lightning bolt. *(The Louvre)*

That Yahwism and Baalism existed alongside each other with essentially the same cultic procedures and paraphernalia is apparent, for example, from the Gideon stories summarized above. Yahweh appears first to Gideon at a sacred oak on the family property. Also Gideon's father's name implies Yahweh worship ("Joash," meaning "Yahweh gives" or "Yahweh has given"). Yet we find that the family had a Baal altar as well and an associated Asherah. It is possible, of course, that the scene in which Gideon destroys the Baal altar and Asherah was introduced by later editors in an attempt to render him a more "orthodox" Yahwist. Even taking into account the possibility of extensive secondary editing of the Gideon stories, one still has the impression that the lines of distinction between Yahwism and Baalism were vague. The Micah story has a graven/molten image—quite possibly an idol of Yahweh himself—in a Yahwistic shrine. A text from the late ninth or eighth century B.C.E. recently discovered at Kuntillet Ajrud in the southern Negeb refers to Yahweh and "his Asherah."

Archaeological evidence indicates an essentially continuous religious and cultic scene throughout Palestine during the Early Iron Age. Nothing has been discovered, in other words, that suggests any notable distinctiveness in temple layout or cultic furniture for the time and territory of the early tribes. Continuity between early Israelite religion and that of the other inhabitants of Syria-Palestine is confirmed further by parallels between the religious and cultic terminology of the biblical materials and the corresponding terminology of extrabiblical documents. Elements of Syro-Palestinian mythology, such as a divine struggle with the cosmic dragon of chaos, also appear here and there in biblical poetry. Occasional biblical passages suggest, in fact, that Yahweh was once viewed as a member of the large pantheon ruled over by El. For example, Deuteronomy speaks of the primordial time

> When the Most High [Elyon] gave to the nations
>   their inheritance,
>   when he separated the sons of men,
> he fixed the bounds of the peoples
>   according to the number of the sons of God.
> For Yahweh's portion is his people,
>   Jacob his allotted heritage.
>
> (Deut. 32:8–9)

The origins of Yahwism are hidden in mystery. Even the final edited form of Genesis-II Kings presents diverse views on the matter. Thus Gen. 4:16, attributed by literary critics to the so-called "Yahwistic" source, traces the worship of Yahweh back to the earliest days of the human race, while other passages trace the revelation and worship of Yahweh back to Moses (Ex. 6:3). Several factors may indicate a southern provenance for early Yahwism. It was in Midian, south of Palestine, according to Exodus 3, that Moses first encountered Yahweh. Moses is said to have married a Midianite wife whose father was, in fact, a priest of Yahweh (Ex. 18). The Midianites seem to have been closely related to the Kenites, who in turn also were associated with southern Palestine and were afforded a special protective status by the Israelites (see, for example, I Sam. 15:6). Israelite poets sang of Jael, a Kenite heroine in Yahweh's wars (Judg. 5:24–30). Finally, it is to be observed that certain poetical texts associate Yahweh in a special way with the south, and speak of Yahweh coming from that area to aid Israel in warfare.

> Yahweh, when thou didst go forth from Seir,
>   when thou didst march from the region of Edom,
> the earth trembled,
>   and the heavens dropped,
>   yea, the clouds dropped water.
> The mountains quaked before Yahweh,
>   yon Sinai before Yahweh, the God of Israel.
>
> (Judg. 5:4–5)

Yahweh came from Sinai,
    and dawned from Seir upon us;
    he shone forth from Mount Paran,
he came from the ten thousands of holy ones,
    with flaming fire at his right hand.

(Deut. 33:2)

Although the location of Mt. Sinai remains uncertain, biblical texts consistently locate the sacred mountain to the south or southeast of Palestine proper.

The spread of Yahwism and its acceptance among the tribal groups were probably gradual phenomena which would have resulted in local forms of Yahwism varying from place to place. Such local varieties are suggested by passages that refer to Yahweh followed by a place-name. Thus I Sam. 1:3 refers to "Yahweh Sebaoth in Shiloh" and II Sam. 15:7 speaks of "Yahweh in Hebron." Depending on a not entirely certain reading, the texts from Kuntillet Ajrud mentioned above may refer to "Yahweh of Samaria" and "Yahweh of Teman." Micah, like perhaps many other prominent heads of extended families, possessed a family shrine dedicated to Yahweh and in which his son served for a time as priest (Judg. 17). The story of Gideon reveals the practice of Yahwism at the clan/village level (Judg. 6:11–32). Tribal Yahwism can be seen in the case of the shrine at Dan and the service of the Levite at the tribal center there (Judg. 18). Trans-tribal Yahwism is probably suggested in the gathering of Naphtali and Zebulun on Mt. Tabor under the direction of the prophetess Deborah.

Perhaps the most noticeable characteristic of Yahweh in Israel's early poetry and narrative literature is his militancy. The so-called "Song of the Sea" in Ex. 15:1–18 and the "Song of Deborah" in Judges 5 are typical in their praise of Yahweh, the divine warrior who could be counted on to intervene on behalf of his followers. At Shiloh he was called "Yahweh Sebaoth," that is, "Yahweh of the armies" (I Sam. 1:3); and the story about David and Goliath has David challenging the giant in the name of "Yahweh Sebaoth, the God of the armies of Israel" (I Sam. 17:45). Most of the Judges narratives point to a strong connection between Yahweh and warfare. Similarly they suggest that it was during military undertakings that the tribes joined together in a common cause which transcended local interest. Thus it may have been primarily in connection with Israel's wars that Yahweh gained status as the national god. During times of peace the tribes will have depended heavily on Baal in his various local forms to ensure fertility. But when they came together to wage war against their common enemies, they would have turned to Yahweh, the divine warrior who could provide victory.

Priestly Lines and Houses

Just as the compilers of Genesis-II Kings tended to subsume numerous and diverse tribal groups under an artificial twelve-tribe scheme, so also they sought to subsume diverse priestly groups under the rubric of the tribe of Levi. The resulting "levitical genealogy" that emerges is shown in Chart IV. That this is an artificial genealogy is indicated both by its internal discrepancies (see the notes to the chart) and the several narratives in the books of Exodus and Numbers that witness to competition and conflict between different priestly lines (Ex. 32; Lev. 10:1–7; Num. 11–12; 16). The Levites themselves probably were a local priestly group from the Judahite city of Bethlehem, David's home, which rose to prominence with the Davidic dynasty. Note that the two Levites who appear in the narratives of Judges 17–21 both had some connection with Bethlehem (17:7–8; 19:1). Also, as we shall see below, David seems to have made extensive use of the Levites in his administration.

The genealogical fragment embedded in Num. 26:58 recognizes five priestly groups, also from the southern hill country, which may or may not have been regarded as Levites during premonarchical times. These are, namely, the Libnites, Hebronites, Mahlites (missing from Greek texts), Mushites (that is, "Mosesites"), and Korahites. The first two of these five correspond to southern towns (Libnah and Hebron). The last two represent priestly lines which appear elsewhere in the biblical traditions. Numbers 16, for example, reports an uprising by the Korahites which supposedly resulted in their annihilation by divine intervention. Yet the Korahites will appear again. In fact, several of the psalms are attributed to them (Ps. 42; 44–49; 84–85; 87–88), and their presence in southern Judah during the late monarchical period is witnessed by an ostracon discovered near the entrance of the Iron Age sanctuary at Arad. The narratives in which Moses functions as a priest or is concerned with priestly matters may reflect, in some indirect fashion, the priestly role of the Mushite (or Moses) line. If so, we may speculate further that the Mushites had connections (as does Moses in the narratives) with the ancient sanctuary at Kadesh(-barnea). Noticeable especially in this regard is Ex. 15:22–26, which assumes that Marah in the vicinity of Kadesh was the place where Moses received the law. Note also that the Levite who figures in the narrative of Judges 17–18 is identified as a direct descendant of Gershom son of Moses and said to have initiated a priestly line which served at Dan "until the day of the captivity of the land" (Judg. 17:7; 18:30).

The Aaronites apparently were another quite separate priestly line in premonarchical times. Moreover, Aaron is presented in a very negative fashion in certain stories which themselves seem to anticipate and serve as polemic against the sanctuary of Jeroboam I at Bethel. Specifically, Exodus 32 depicts Aaron as an apostate priest who builds a golden calf for worship while Moses is away from the camp. The Levites stand over against Aaron in the narrative, siding with Moses and executing vengeance on the people who had participated in the calf worship. Leviticus 10:1–7, on the other hand, relates how Aaron's two sons, Nadab and Abihu, were killed because of improper ritual activities. Note that Jeroboam I, in addition to being accused of introducing golden calves at Bethel and Dan, had two sons who also met untimely deaths. Moreover, their names correspond to the names of Aaron's wayward sons (compare Nadab and Abihu in Lev. 10:1 with Nadab and Abijah in I Kings 14:1–18; 15:25–32). All of this

CHART IV: The Genealogy of the Levites
According to the Compilers of Genesis-II Kings

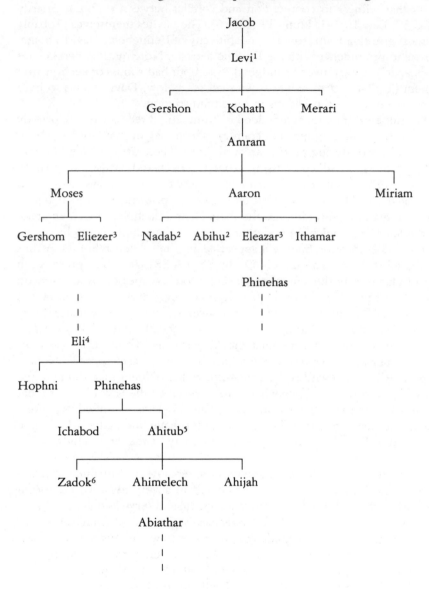

This is a composite genealogy derived from several texts in Genesis-II Kings and must be qualified at several points:

[1] The lineage from Levi through Phinehas is provided in Ex. 6:16–25; 18:3–4; Josh. 21:1; 22:13; 24:33. Miriam is not mentioned in these passages, but is included in this chart on the basis of Ex. 15:20. Note also the genealogical

fragment in Num. 26:58 which recognizes five main Levitical families (the Libnites, the Hebronites, the Mahlites, the Mushites and the Korahites).

[2] It is perhaps not by accident that the first two sons of Aaron (Nadab and Abihu) have names almost identical with those of Jeroboam I (Nadab and Ahijah). Both Aaron and Jeroboam are also associated with apostate worship of golden calves.

[3] Several priestly figures bear variations of the name Eliezar, including Moses' son Eliezer (Ex. 18:4), Aaron's son Eleazar (Ex. 6:23), and Eleazar the son of Abinadab who took charge of the Ark after it had been recovered from the Philistines (I Sam. 7:1). Apparently this was a popular priestly name (see also Ezra 10:18 and I Esdras 9:19). But we must consider also the possibility that an early Eleazar remembered to have been associated with the Ark has been introduced into the Genesis-II Kings account at more than one place.

[4] The priests in charge of the Ark at Shiloh in the books of Joshua and Judges are Eleazar and Phinehas, the son and grandson of Aaron (Josh. 21:1; 22:13; 24:33; Judg. 20:28). As the narration continues in I Samuel we find the Ark still at Shiloh, but in the hands of Eli and his two sons, Phinehas and Hophni. Presumably we are to conclude that Eli was a descendant of Phinehas son of Eleazar son of Aaron. Yet this is never actually stated. Moreover, it must be considered whether Eli is also a variation of the name Eleazar, in spite of the fact that it begins with a different consonant (' ayin rather than ' aleph). In the latter case, we may be dealing with parallel tradition—that is, the Eleazar and Phinehas supposedly associated with the Ark in the days of Moses, Joshua, and the Judges may be none other than Eli and Phinehas of Shiloh whom the compilers of Genesis-II Kings projected back into the earlier period.

[5] The Eli > Phinehas > Ahitub > Ahimelech > Abiathar lineage depicted above is derived from I Sam. 14:3; 22:9; 1 Kings 2:26–27. Yet I Sam. 14:3 which connects Ahitub with the house of Eli appears to have undergone secondary editing. In our opinion, the original text probably read something like "and Ahijah son of Phinehas son of Eli."

[6] II Sam. 8:17 identifies Zadok as the son of Ahitub and thus also a descendant of Eli, assuming of course the Ahitub/Elide connection called into question above. However, this verse is problematic on several grounds: (a) It identifies Ahimelech as the son of Abiathar rather than the other way around (compare I Sam. 22:9). (b) I Chron. 6:1–8 traces Zadok's ancestry back to Aaron by a different line which bypasses the Elides. (c) Other lines of evidence, discussed below, suggest that the Zadokites represented a separate priestly line altogether from either the Levites or the Elides.

---

seems to suggest a connection of some sort between the Aaronites and the Bethel sanctuary. These two narratives which depict Aaron in a negative light contrast with the one in Numbers 17–18, however, which affirms the prominence of Aaron and the Aaronites in Israelite worship. Also, at least one bit of evidence raises the possibility that the Aaronite priests were of southern origin. Specifically, the Aaronite Jehoiada who, according to I Chron. 12:27, was with the Levites who joined David at Hebron may be the same Jehoiada who is identified in II Sam. 23:20 as the father of one of David's officers. This latter Jehoiada, father of Benaiah, was from the southern town of Kabzeel.

Other priestly lines, such as the Elides of Shiloh, the priests of Nob, and the Zadokites, will receive attention in Chapters 4 and 5. As we shall see, the editors of Genesis-II Kings attempted to connect these also with the Levitical line but were not very convincing.

Shechem and Shiloh

The Judges narratives suggest that the typical sanctuary of the Israelite tribes was a local operation serving one or several clans/villages or perhaps one or two tribes at the most. We learn from the Gideon and Micah stories, moreover, how a single family could set up its own shrine, altar, and sanctuary. The Judges narratives do not support, by contrast, the idea that Shechem and Shiloh were key cultic centers for the Israelite tribes during premonarchical times. (See Map 11.)

Shechem. Shechem was one of the ancient Bronze Age cities that continued into the Iron Age, and archaeology has revealed that this city possessed a major temple which apparently remained in use into the Early Iron Age. Also the Abimelech narrative speaks of one or two temples in the city dedicated to Baal/El-berith (Judg. 9). Nearby, but outside the city, was a sacred oak, variously called "the oak of Moreh" and "the Diviners' Oak" (Gen. 12:6; 35:4; Judg. 9:37). This latter sacred spot, along with Mt. Ebal and Mt. Gerizim, may have been the place that the narrator of Genesis 22 had in mind when speaking of the land of Moriah with its mountains (Gen. 22:2; compare Gen. 12:6; Judg. 7:1; but see II Chron. 3:1).

Two passages in Joshua (Josh. 8 and 24) identify Shechem as a place of worship for the tribes, but literary critics have long since recognized that much, if not all, of the material in these passages consists of secondary editorial additions. Actually the Abimelech story seems to treat Shechem as an essentially non-Israelite city. Possibly the editorial stress on Shechem in Joshua 8 and 24 is less reflective of Shechem's actual role among the Israelite tribes during premonarchical times than it is indicative of the importance of the city in the later kingdom of Israel.

Shiloh. The compilers of Genesis–II Kings present Shiloh as the major religious and political center for all the tribes during the post-conquest period (Josh. 18:1; 19:51; 21:1–2; and so forth). If that were the case, however, it is surprising that Shiloh appears in only one of the Judges narratives, Judges 19–21. Even more surprising is the role that Shiloh plays in this particular narrative.

Judges 19–21 describes a conflict between the Benjaminites and the remainder of Israel. At some point during the hostilities, according to the narrative, the other tribes mustered for battle vowed never again to give any of their daughters to Benjaminites in marriage. Once the Benjaminites were defeated, however, they had second thoughts about the matter. Thus the narrative concludes with raids on Jabesh-gilead and Shiloh in order to secure wives for the Benjaminites. Jabesh-gilead was regarded as an appropriate source for wives, since, as it is explained in Judg. 21:12, representatives of this city were not present when the vow was taken. Why Shiloh was considered appropriate is less clear.

> Then the elders of the congregation said, "What shall we do for wives for those who are left, since the women are destroyed out of Benjamin?" And they said, "There must be an inheritance for the survivors of Benjamin, that a tribe be not blotted out from Israel. Yet we cannot give them wives of our daughters." For the people of Israel had sworn, "Cursed be he who gives a wife to Benjamin." So they said, "Behold, there is the yearly feast of Yahweh at Shiloh, which is north of Bethel, on the east of the highway that goes up from Bethel to Shechem, and south

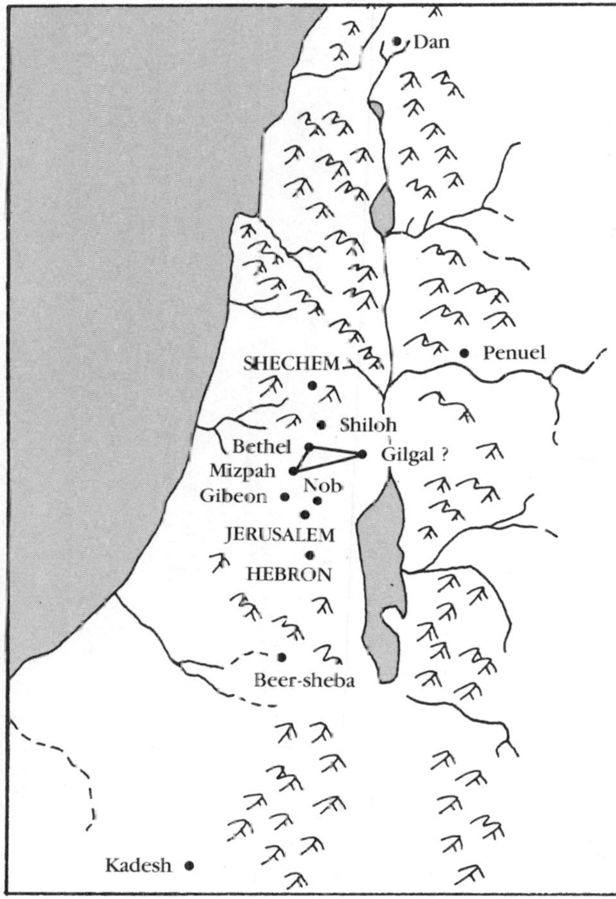

Shechem

Bronze Age city, scene of the assembly that rejected Rehoboam after Solomon's death and thereby established the independent northern kingdom of Israel.

Shiloh

Home of the Elide priests who served before the Ark of Yahweh; declined in importance with the rise of David in Jerusalem.

Nob

Saul massacred the priests of Nob after they aided David. Abiathar, who escaped, served as a chief priest of David's Jerusalem kingdom. Solomon exiled him to Anathoth, near Nob (possibly present-day Mt. Scopus).

Kadesh

Associated with Moses, plays a central role in the exodus story. Possibly the home of the "Mushite" priestly line.

Beer-Sheba

Associated with Isaac. The claim in I Sam. 8:2 that Samuel's two sons judged in Beer-sheba seems doubtful.

Dan

Called Laish until captured by Danites, who established a "Mushite" priestly line. Jeroboam I set up a golden calf at Dan.

Penuel

Associated with Jacob, who is said to have named it after struggling there with an angel; also revived by Jeroboam I.

Bethel, Mizpah, Gilgal

Three hill-country places included in Samuel's priestly circuit. Jeroboam I revived Bethel and placed a golden calf there. The location of Gilgal is uncertain.

Hebron

Ancient Bronze Age city, associated with Abraham and regarded as the burial place of the patriarchs; David ruled from Hebron before conquering Jerusalem.

Gibeon

Sanctuary where Solomon worshiped and Yahweh is said to have promised him great wisdom, possibly the nearby hill, present-day Nebi Samwil.

MAP 11. Important Cultic Centers in the Early Tribal Period

of Lebonah." And they commanded the Benjaminites, saying, "Go and lie in wait in the vineyards, and watch; if the daughters of Shiloh come out to dance in the dances, then come out of the vineyards and seize each man his wife from the daughters of Shiloh, and go to the land of Benjamin. And when their fathers or their brothers come to complain to us, we will say to them, 'Grant them graciously to us; because we did not take for each man of them his wife in battle, neither did you give them to them, else you would now be guilty.' " (Judg. 21:16–22)

The narrative has been edited to bring it into line with the idealistic views of the late compilers of Genesis-II Kings—thus the references to Phinehas' presence with the Ark at Bethel (Judg. 20:27–28), the note about returning to the "camp" at Shiloh after the raid on Jabesh-gilead (Judg. 21:12), and the rather legalistic observation that the Shilonites could not be accused of breaking the vow because their daughters had been taken by force. Scholars have long since suspected that the crux of the conflict was much more limited in scope— possibly a struggle between Benjamin and Ephraim, or between the Ephraimites and the individual town of Gibeah. One gets the impression also that in the pre-edited version of the story Shiloh was regarded as foreign territory. Obviously the note in 21:12 which has the Israelites returning to the camp at Shiloh after the raid at Jabesh-gilead makes no sense in a story which a few verses later will have the "elders of the congregation" explaining to the Benjaminites where Shiloh is located, almost as if they had never heard of the place, and then

Shechem Temple. Remains of a Late Bronze Age temple at Tell Balata (biblical Shechem), which continued in use into the Iron Age. Note the base of a broken pillar in the foreground. The retaining wall surrounding the temple and pillar was built by the excavators for preservation purposes. *(J. M. Miller)*

encouraging the Benjaminites to steal women from there. Moreover, we are still left with the question as to why Shiloh was regarded as an appropriate source for captive women. A very likely explanation, in our opinion, is that the pre-edited version of this story did not presume Shiloh to be an important administrative or cultic center for the Ephraimites/Israelites (or whoever took the vow). Indeed the Shilonites, in spite of the fact that they apparently were worshipers of Yahweh, may have been regarded as foreigners.

Shiloh clearly is later viewed as both Yahwistic and Israelite in the stories about Samuel at Shiloh (I Sam. 1–3), to which we will turn our attention in the next chapter. Yet these stories further complicate matters by indicating that there was a "temple" at Shiloh in addition to a tent of meeting (compare I Sam. 1:7, 24; 2:22; 3:15) and that the temple, housing the Ark (I Sam. 3:3; 4:4), was under the care of the priestly family of Eli.

CHAPTER 4

The Early Israelite Monarchy

In approximately 1000 B.C.E. there emerged an Israelite monarchy under the rule of Saul, a Benjaminite, with its center in the north-central hill country—that is, in the territory of the Ephraimite/Israelite tribes. Our main source of information about this development still is the Genesis-II Kings account, specifically the Book of I Samuel, which concludes with Saul's death. While the end of Saul's reign is not reported until the end of I Samuel, the latter half of the book (from ch. 16 forward) shifts attention to David and prepares the reader for the latter's reign which will be described in II Samuel. We begin, therefore, with a summary of I Samuel 1–15.

Eli, Samuel, and Saul According to I Samuel

Summary of I Samuel 1–15

Samuel, son of an Ephraimite from Ramathaim-zophim (or Ramah?; compare I Sam. 1:1 with 1:19 and 7:17), was dedicated by his parents for service to the temple of Yahweh at Shiloh. The old priest Eli was in charge of the Shiloh temple at the time. Because of the scandalous practices of Eli's two sons, however, Phinehas and Hophni, Yahweh rejected the Elide priestly line in deference to another, not yet identified, priestly line which was to emerge in the future. This divine intention was revealed first to Eli by an anonymous "man of God" and then to the boy Samuel in a dream. As Samuel grew to manhood, Yahweh was with him and he became established as a prophet whose reputation spread throughout the land, from Dan to Beer-sheba (I Sam. 1–3).

In the meantime a battle was fought at Ebenezer between the Israelites and the Philistines. Eli's two sons were killed in the battle; the Philistines were victorious; and the Ark of Yahweh fell into Philistine hands (I Sam. 4). As long as the Philistines held the Ark, however, and in whichever of their cities they placed it, their people were smitten with a plague (apparently tumors of some sort). Finally, under the guidance of their priests and diviners, the Philistines took the Ark with a "guilt offering" of "five golden tumors and five golden mice," one for each of their cities, and placed it on a new cart led by two milch cows and sent them away. The cows pulled the cart to Beth-shemesh, where the Ark came into the custody of Levites, and a monument ("great stone") was erected to commemorate the event. Yet disaster still followed the Ark—Yahweh slew seventy men of Beth-shemesh because they looked into it—so the Ark was transferred from there to Gibeah ("the hill") near Kiriath-jearim, where it was placed in the charge of one Eleazar, whom they consecrated for that purpose (I Sam. 5:1–7:2).

Then Samuel gathered the Israelites at Mizpah and led them in rededication to Yahweh. When the Philistines heard that the Israelites had assembled, they came out for battle, whereupon Yahweh "thundered with a mighty voice that day against the Philistines and threw them into confusion; and they were routed before Israel" (I Sam. 7:10). Samuel erected a monument to the event which he named "Ebenezer," the cities that the Philistines had taken were restored to Israel, and the Philistines no longer threatened Israel as long as Samuel lived.

In the remainder of his life Samuel administered justice to Israel from Ramah, where he built an altar to Yahweh. Also he went on a circuit each year to Bethel, Gilgal, and Mizpah, and judged in these places (I Sam. 7:3–17). When he became old, Samuel installed his two sons as judges over Israel at Beer-sheba. Unfortunately they used the office for personal gain, taking bribes and preventing justice (I Sam. 8:1–3). Eventually the elders of Israel came to Samuel at Ramah and begged him to appoint a king to rule over them. Samuel opposed the idea, but was directed by Yahweh to give them a king anyway, along with a warning of all the evils they could expect from future kings (I Sam. 8:4–9). In the words of Yahweh, Samuel warned them:

> He will take your sons and appoint them to his chariots and to be his horsemen, and to run before his chariots; and he will appoint for himself commanders of thousands and commanders of fifties, and some to plow his ground and to reap his harvest, and to make his implements of war and the equipment of his chariots. He will take your daughters to be perfumers and cooks and bakers. He will take the best of your fields and vineyards and olive orchards and give them to his servants. He will take the tenth of your grain and of your vineyards and give it to his officers and to his servants. He will take your menservants and maidservants, and the best of your cattle [or "young men"] and your asses, and put them to his work. He will take the tenth of your flocks, and you shall be his slaves. (I Sam. 8:11–17)

In spite of this warning, the people insisted on having a king, a desire to which Yahweh again acquiesced and gave his permission (I Sam. 8:19–22).

Saul, the son of a wealthy Benjaminite named Kish, was taller than any of his countrymen and very handsome. On one occasion, while searching for some asses that had strayed, Saul came to a village in the land of Zuph. It so happened that Samuel was conducting sacrifices at the village on that same day—and in fact Yahweh had revealed to Samuel that Saul would be coming and that he should anoint Saul as prince *(nagid)* over Israel. This Samuel did, and sent Saul on his way with certain predictions and instructions: (1) When Saul returned to the land of Benjamin, he was to meet two men who would inform him that the asses had been found. (2) Then Saul was to proceed to the oak of Tabor, where he would meet three men going up to worship God at Bethel. They were to give him two loaves of bread. (3) From there he was to go to Gibeathelohim ("the hill of God") where there was a Philistine garrison (or a Philistine "governor," or some kind of Philistine monument; the precise meaning of *nasib* in I Sam. 10:5 is uncertain) and where Saul would meet a band of prophets coming down from the high place. The prophets would be prophesying to musical instruments, whereupon the spirit of Yahweh would come upon Saul and he would prophesy also. (4) When these three events had transpired as signs that God was with him, Saul was to take some unspecified action: "Do whatever your hand finds to do, for God is with you." (5) Thereafter Saul was to proceed to Gilgal and wait seven days, until Samuel arrived to offer sacrifices (I Sam. 9:1–10:8).

The first three items in Samuel's prediction went as anticipated. Saul arrived at Gibeah ("the hill") and prophesied to the extent that people began to ask, "What has come over the son of Kish? Is Saul also among the prophets?" After prophesying, Saul ascended to the high place ("Gibeah," according to the Greek text). Next we find him in conversation with an uncle (I Sam. 10:9–16).

At this point, Samuel assembled the people again at Mizpah and proceeded to select a king for them by lot. Saul, even though he had hidden himself among the baggage and was not actually present at the time, was selected. When he was found and stood among the people, he was taller than any, from his shoulders upward. All the people shouted, "Long live the king!" Samuel explained the rights and duties of kingship, wrote them in a book, and laid the book up before Yahweh (I Sam. 10:17–25). Saul returned to Gibeah, where he was joined by men of valor (fighting men) and received "gifts" from the people. Not all of the people supported him, however. There were those who expressed lack of confidence in his abilities—"How can this man save us?" they said—and brought him no present (I Sam. 10:26–27).

Soon an occasion arose for Saul to demonstrate his strength. The people of Jabesh in Gilead, their city under siege by the Ammonites, sent messengers to Saul at Gibeah begging for help. Saul called for a general muster of troops, with the warning that he would butcher the cattle of any who failed to respond. Three hundred thousand men of Israel and thirty thousand men of Judah did respond and, under Saul's command, defeated the Ammonites with a great slaughter. The victorious army returned to Gilgal, where they reconfirmed Saul's kingship and offered sacrifices to Yahweh. There were some who urged Saul to take vengeance now on those who had refused to support him initially, but Saul declined to do so (I Sam. 11).

Samuel addressed the people once again, emphasizing the integrity with which he had served as their leader and the folly of their determination to have a king. Yahweh's affirmation of this farewell address was demonstrated by thunder and rain—which frightened the people, because it was the time of the wheat harvest (summer), when rain is unexpected in Palestine (I Sam. 12).

There followed a major battle with the Philistines, touched off when Jonathan or Saul (compare I Sam. 13:3 with 13:4) defeated the Philistine garrison (depending still on the proper translation of *nasib*) at Geba. In response, the Philistines mustered 30,000 chariots, 6,000 horsemen, and innumerable troops at Michmash. Many of the Israelites hid. Those who dared to stand with Saul at Gilgal did so trembling, while he waited seven days for Samuel to come and offer sacrifices. When Samuel did not appear at the appointed time, and fearing that his own warriors would desert if he continued to delay action, Saul offered the sacrifices himself. Samuel arrived then, just as the ceremony was completed, and denounced Saul, proclaiming that Saul's kingdom would not continue.

> You have done foolishly; you have not kept the commandment of Yahweh your God, which he commanded you; for now Yahweh would have established your kingdom over Israel for ever. But now your kingdom shall not continue; Yahweh has sought out a man after his own heart; and Yahweh has appointed him to be prince over his people, because you have not kept what Yahweh commanded you. (I Sam. 13:13–14).

Meanwhile the Philistines had begun to raid in three companies throughout the central hill country and continued doing so until Jonathan conducted a surprise raid on the Philistine garrison *(massab)* at Michmash. The Philistines were routed and the main Israelite army seized the occasion to chase them from the hill country entirely (I Sam. 13:3–14:46). Thereafter Saul was victorious over all of his enemies on every side—including the Moabites, the Ammonites, the Edomites, the Zobahites, and the Amalekites. Also there was more hard fighting against the Philistines throughout Saul's reign (I Sam. 14:47–52).

A battle with the Amalekites occasioned a second angry condemnation of Saul by Samuel. It was on Samuel's command that Saul attacked the Amalekites, and Samuel had specified that everyone and every animal of the Amalekites should be killed: "both man and woman, infant and suckling, ox and sheep, camel and ass" (I Sam. 15:3). Saul did kill all of the people as instructed but spared the Amalekite king, Agag, and some of the best of the animals. Samuel was extremely angry and proclaimed again that Yahweh had withdrawn his blessing from Saul's kingship: "Because you have rejected the word of Yahweh, he has also rejected you from being king" (I Sam. 15:23b).

Yahweh instructed Samuel to go to Bethlehem on the pretense of offering a sacrifice and to anoint for kingship one of the sons of Jesse, a Bethlehemite. David was selected, anointed, "and the Spirit of Yahweh came mightily upon David from that day forward." Simultaneously Yahweh withdrew his Spirit from Saul and sent an evil spirit to torment him. It was decided that a search should be made for someone skillful in playing the lyre in the hope that the music would ease Saul's torment. David was chosen for this purpose and thus was brought to the court to serve as Saul's musician and armor-bearer (I Sam. 16).

From this point on, the I Samuel narrative focuses on David. Occasionally Samuel, Saul, and members of Saul's family enter into the story, but only as secondary characters. Conflict soon developed between Saul and David, we are told, and Samuel among others aided David in his escape from Saul's court (I Sam. 19:18–24). Saul followed close on David's trail while continuing to fight the Philistines (I Sam. 24:1), until finally David himself joined the Philistine camp (I Sam. 27:1–4). According to the narrative as it continues in I Samuel 28–31, David was still associated with the Philistines when Saul met them in his last battle. This battle, which was fought in the vicinity of Mt. Gilboa at the southeastern end of the Jezreel Valley (I Sam. 28:4; 29:1, 11; 31:1), was a disaster for Israel. The Israelites were routed, both Saul and Jonathan were killed, and Saul's kingdom was left in disarray.

General Characteristics of the I Samuel Account

Since the books of I-II Samuel are a continuation of the Genesis-Judges account, it is to be expected that they reflect many of the same literary characteristics that we have recognized in Genesis-Judges. The narrative that they present is composite, for example, consisting of numerous originally independent traditions which have been combined and intertwined to produce the story line as it stands now. Thus, while there is general continuity in this story line, there are also disjunctive elements which cause problems for the historian. For example, whereas Samuel is closely associated with the Elides and plays a central role in the opening chapters of I Samuel, he abruptly drops out of the story between I Sam. 4:1b and 7:2, which describes how the Elides lost possession of the Ark, and then emerges again as the central figure in the next two chapters. The implication of I Sam. 4:1b–7:2 is that the Elides lost possession of the Ark before Saul appeared on the scene, while I Sam. 7:3–14 reports an Israelite defeat of the Philistines under Samuel's leadership with the result that "the Philistines were subdued and did not again enter the territory of Israel" (v. 13a). Only a few chapters later, however, we find the Israelites in desperate battle with the Philistines in the very heart of Israelite territory. Samuel is still on the scene and an Elide priest is there with the Ark as well (I Sam. 13:10; 14:3, 18).

The narration about Saul's search for the asses in I Samuel 9–10 is particularly problematic for literary critics and historians alike in that following 10:5 it presents what amounts to multiple endings: (1) Saul proceeds to Gibeath-elohim, where he prophesies with a band of prophets. Compare the variant version of this tradition in I Sam. 19:18–24 and note that this latter passage locates the incident at Ramah. (2) Saul is instructed to go to Gilgal and wait. Compare I Sam. 13:8–9, where this thread of tradition reemerges. (3) Saul goes to Gibeah, where there was a Philistine garrison (?) and does "what his hand finds to do"—presumably he challenges the Philistines in some fashion (compare I Sam. 13:2–4). (4) Saul returns home (?), where we hear him in conversation with an uncle, and then goes with his family to Mizpah, where he is crowned king.

The various independent traditions that have been combined to produce I-II Samuel are folk legends for the most part. Generally they focus on one or the other of the three outstanding characters of the period: Samuel, Saul, and David. They tend to glorify or condemn the personalities involved, emphasize the dramatic, include novelistic features such as conversations between private individuals, lack any clear chronological framework, and so forth. In some cases we are presented with what appears to be variations of the same folk tradition attached to two different figures. Note, for example, the parallel stories about the righteous priest with two unworthy sons. First it is Eli, then it is Samuel (compare I Sam. 2 and 8). Similarly, there are two stories about a Philistine battle at Ebenezer, one that features Eli and his sons, the other featuring Samuel (compare I Sam. 4 and 7). Less obvious is the confusion in I Samuel 13–14 as to who and what initiated the battle with the Philistines described there. Was it Saul who attacked the Philistine garrison *(nasib)* at Gibeah, or his son Jonathan who attacked the Philistine camp *(massab)* at Michmash across the valley from Gibeah? Apparently two different versions of a daring attack in the vicinity of Gibeah/Michmash survived in the folk memory, and both have been telescoped in I Samuel 13–14. Finally, there is at least one occasion where a tradition that may have pertained originally to Saul has been transferred to Samuel—namely, the story in I Samuel of Samuel's (Saul's ?) birth and dedication at Shiloh. Two things suggest that the story, in an earlier form, may have featured Saul rather than Samuel: (1) The explanation of the child's name in v. 20 corresponds to the name "Saul" rather than "Samuel." (2) Saul is said to have been supported by the Elide priests of Shiloh in his later career (I Sam. 14:3, 18). Samuel, on the other hand, while he is connected with Shiloh in this story and its continuation in I Samuel 2–3, is never associated with Shiloh in other narratives.

Also, as in the case of the materials that compose Genesis-Judges, the old traditions that have been combined and intertwined to produce the story line of I-II Samuel show evidence of having been modified during the process of transmission and then edited still further by the final compilers of the whole Genesis-II Kings presentation. In I-II Samuel, however, these modifications and the editing process took a somewhat different turn. With Genesis-Judges, the inclination was to idealize early Israel and to retroject later circumstances (or ideal circumstances) back into the pre-Judges period. With I-II Samuel the concern is rather to emphasize the legitimacy of the Davidic dynasty (rather than Saul's descendants whom David displaced), the Yahwistic sanction of the Jerusalem cult (over against Shiloh and the Elide priests), and finally, as will become more apparent in II Samuel, to justify Solomon's succession to the throne after David (instead of one of David's older sons). Correspondingly, three tendencies are noticeable in the form of the narratives as we find them now. (1) Saul is played down and presented as an emotionally erratic character rejected by Samuel and Yahweh. (2) David tends to be glorified, presented as Yahweh's man who rarely did any wrong and who repented properly when he did. (3) Samuel plays the role of Yahweh's spokesman, presiding over the demise of the Elide priests at Shiloh and the transfer of God's favor from Saul to David. In order to present him in this role, Samuel has been editorially "written into" several of the stories in which he did not originally appear.

Already we have noted that Samuel may have displaced Saul in the birth story of I Samuel 1 and been connected editorially with Shiloh in the next two chapters. Likewise, as commentators often observe, Samuel seems to have been written into the account of Saul's anointment as *nagid* in I Sam. 9:1–10:16 (originally the story featured an anonymous prophet in "the land of Zuph"), and then introduced secondarily to reconfirm Saul's kingship in I Sam. 11:7, 12–14 and to reject it in I Sam. 13:8–15.

Finally it should be observed that the present arrangement of materials in I-II Samuel is determined to a certain extent by the schematic structure of the Genesis-II Kings presentation. The compilers of this work would have us see Samuel as the last of the great judges, for example, and Samuel's farewell address in I Samuel 12 is intended to conclude the era of the Judges in the same fashion that Moses' farewell address (essentially the book of Deuteronomy) concluded the era of the desert wandering and that Joshua's farewell address (Josh. 23–24) concluded the era of conquest and settlement. I Samuel 13–14 represents Saul's reign, on the other hand, and as such follows the same literary pattern as the presentations of the reigns of the kings which will be treated farther on. Namely, each king's reign will be introduced with a formulaic introduction which presents pertinent chronological data (compare I Sam. 13:1, where the text is corrupt or else the data in the text have been deliberately falsified) and concluded with summary notes about the king's deeds (I Sam. 14:47–52). The point to be made here is that the arrangement of the materials in I-II Samuel is not necessarily an indicator of the historical sequence of events. Thus, for example, Saul's victory over the Ammonites at Jabesh-gilead, which explained how he overcame the early opposition of some of his countrymen, is placed after the account of his election at Mizpah (I Sam. 10:17–24) and before the presentation of his reign proper (I Sam. 13–14), while the account of Saul's victory over the Philistines is placed farther on, in the context of his reign (I Sam. 13:2–14:46). More likely the historical sequence was the other way around. Saul would hardly have been able to muster troops and venture as far as Jabesh-gilead with them if he had not already cleared the Philistines from his own Benjaminite area.

Separating the Traditions in I Samuel

Obviously any attempt to utilize the I Samuel account for purposes of historical investigation must begin with an attempt to disentangle and evaluate the various independent traditions that have been combined to produce the narrative as it stands now. Even this prior step is a speculative task, which means that any resulting "historical" conclusions will be speculative also. We recognize the following main blocks of old traditions underlying the present narrative of I Samuel.

The Samuel-Shiloh Stories (I Sam. 1:1–4:1a). These stories associated the young Samuel with the temple at Shiloh where the old priest Eli and his two sons,

Phinehas and Hophni, were in charge. They are told from an obvious anti-Elide perspective and seek to emphasize that the demise of the Elides was in accordance with Yahweh's will and justified because of the scandalous behavior of Eli's sons. As indicated above, at least the birth story in I Samuel 1 may have pertained originally to Saul rather than to Samuel.

The Ark Narrative (I Sam. 4:1b–7:2 with continuation in II Sam. 6). This narrative explains in rather fanciful fashion how the Ark of Yahweh came to be transferred from the Elide priests of Shiloh into the hands of Levites at Beth-shemesh, from there to Gibeah ("the hill") near Kiriath-jearim, and eventually to Jerusalem. While this narrative must be recognized as independent of the Samuel-Shiloh stories (Samuel is conspicuously absent in the former), it reflects the same overriding theme. Namely, it explains that the demise of the Elides and the transfer of the Ark from their hands to those of the priests in Jerusalem happened in accordance with divine plan. Such a view would have been perpetrated, no doubt, by the Jerusalem priests.

Possibly there is a kernel of historical truth to the Ark Narrative, and certainly the places mentioned were real places (Shiloh, Aphek, Ebenezer, Beth-shemesh, the main Philistine cities, and a prominent "hill" near Kiriath-jearim). However, the story probably strays rather far, chronologically and geographically, from the actual circumstances under which the Ark made its way from Shiloh to Jerusalem. We have already noted that this story conflicts with the account of the Gibeah-Michmash battle in I Sam. 13:2–14:46 which presupposes that the Elides were still in possession of the Ark during Saul's reign. Note also that it has the Israelite and Philistine armies camping at Ebenezer and Aphek respectively prior to the battle in which the Philistines supposedly captured the Ark. It seems more than coincidence that other traditions in I Samuel also remember Ebenezer and Aphek as the scenes of major battles with the Philistines, but place these battles in different contexts. Namely, the Samuel narrative (see below) remembers a major Israelite victory over the Philistines in connection with which Ebenezer received its name (I Sam. 7:3–14), while Saul's last battle with the Philistines, which also turned out to be a disastrous defeat for Israel, began with the Philistines camped at Aphek near Mt. Gilboa (I Sam. 29:1).

The Saul Stories (I Sam. 9:1–10:16; 10:26–11:15; 13:2–14:46). These stories focus on Saul and, in an earlier form, presented both him and his kingdom in an essentially favorable light. The original sequence of these stories was I Sam. 9:1–10:16 . . . 13:2–14:46 . . . 10:26–11:15, thus relating the following sequence of events. The young Saul, in search of his father's asses, encountered an anonymous prophet in the land of Zuph. The prophet anointed him prince *(nagid)*, predicted certain circumstances that would occur as Saul returned home, and instructed him to proceed to Gibeathelohim, where there was a Philistine garrison and where he was to "do whatever your hand finds to do, for God is with you." The story picks up again in I Sam. 13:2–14:46 with the scene at Gibeah, and is somewhat difficult to follow at that point, since it apparently telescopes two versions of a single incident. One of the versions seems to presuppose that Saul attacked the Philistine garrison at Gibeah (see especially I Sam. 13:4), whereupon the Philistines moved a larger military force to Michmash (across the valley from Gibeah) and began to raid the surrounding countryside. The other version credits Jonathan with the raid and has him attacking the Philistine garrison at Michmash. The end result, presumably according to both versions, was that Saul chased the Philstines out of southern Ephraim and established himself with a small army at Gibeah. Thus the story in I Sam. 10:26–11:15 begins with Saul and his soldiers in place at Gibeah and describes how he responded to an urgent call for help from the people of Jabesh in Gilead. Their city was under Ammonite siege at the time and unable to hold out much longer. Saul mustered a large army (in addition to his private soldiers), defeated the Ammonites, and in the wake of the victory was proclaimed (or reaffirmed) king over Israel.

Samuel and the Gilgal episode (I Sam. 10:8; 13:8–15) have been "written into" this narrative complex at some secondary stage of transmission. Also, in the process of compiling the final Genesis-II Kings account, the story in I Sam. 13:2–14:46 has been transposed to its present position (rather than following in sequence after I Sam. 9:1–10:16), introduced with the formulaic introduction to Saul's reign (I Sam. 13:1), and concluded with further notes regarding Saul's deeds in office (I Sam. 14:47–52).

The Samuel Narrative (I Sam. 7:3–8:22; 10:17–25; 12; 15). These passages form a continuous narrative that focuses on Samuel. They present him as the last of the judges, an authentic spokesman for Yahweh who instituted the monarchy in Israel and anointed Israel's first king. Although this Samuel narrative seems to be based on old traditions, these traditions have been largely recast to serve the interests of the late compilers of Genesis-II Kings. As a judge, Samuel is credited with a victory over the Philistines at Ebenezer and discredited by his two sons whom he installed as judges at Beer-sheba. As a king maker, Samuel is depicted first as opposing the institution of a monarchy and warning the people of the many ways in which future kings would take advantage of them. But then, under divine guidance, he is reported to have selected Saul by lot, explained the rights and duties of kingship, and written these in a book to be laid up before Yahweh. Finally, I Samuel 15 has Samuel rejecting Saul and anticipates the shift of divine favor to David.

The Stories About David's Rise to Power (I Sam. 16–II Sam. 5:5). Beginning with the account of Samuel's anointing of David in I Samuel 16 and concluding with the account of David's conquest of Jerusalem in II Samuel 5, one encounters a miscellaneous collection of stories that focus on David. Samuel, Saul, and Saul's descendants are mentioned from time to time when they are relevant to David's career, but otherwise remain very much in the background. Some of these stories seem contradictory and some seem to be duplications, but they all tend to have a common theme—David's rise to power and his rightful claim to the throne. We will explore these stories in more detail in Chapter 5, although it will be necessary to draw on them to a certain extent in this chapter's treatment of Saul's reign and the collapse of his kingdom.

Problem Areas in Historical Reconstruction

If the observations above are even close to the mark, then none of the materials in I Samuel can be taken at face value for purposes of historical reconstruction. We are inclined to suppose that many, perhaps even most, of these stories contain at least a kernel of historical truth. But even that cannot be verified, and, presuming it is the case, there is no way to discern with certainty what is historical kernel and what is legendary elaboration. Unfortunately there are no extrabiblical sources for the period that might serve as outside control. Also, as explained above, while the archaeological record is useful for understanding the general material circumstances of the Early Iron Age, it is not very helpful for clarifying matters of historical detail.

The fact that the compilers of Genesis-II Kings were not so interested in Saul's reign as in David's is an added problem. Actually we are told very little about Saul's kingdom, and much of what we are told is embedded in the stories about David. In short, then, any attempt to explain the historical circumstances of Saul's rise to power and his kingdom must be highly speculative. This is no less true of our attempt below.

Even the matter of establishing an approximate date for Saul is not an easy task. Chronological data provided in I-II Kings and to be discussed below in Chapter 7 would place Solomon's death about 925 B.C.E. (or within a decade of that date). We are told also that Solomon and David reigned forty years each (I Kings 2:11; 11:42). The "forty years" is probably to be regarded as a symbolic or round number in both cases, however, provided by the compilers of Genesis-II Kings in place of more accurate figures which they may not have had available. Allowing a reasonable length of time for the reigns of David and Solomon, Saul's death and the beginning of David's rule would fall not long after 1000 B.C.E. The single verse that provides any chronological information for Saul himself apparently has been corrupted or deliberately distorted during the process of transmission. Literally, I Sam. 13:1 reads: "Saul was a year old when he began to reign; and he reigned two years over Israel." Certainly he was more than a year old by the time he had come to be recognized as king, and one suspects from the deeds credited to him that he ruled longer than two years.

Finally, the materials in I-II Samuel present us with topographical uncertainties which have significant bearing on one's interpretation of the circumstances and the sequence of events described. Particularly problematic is the appellative name "Gibeah" with variant forms "Gibeath," "Geba," and "Gibeon," all of which mean "the hill." This name appears time and again in the early biblical narratives. Clearly more than one place by that name is involved, but it is impossible to say for certain how many different places and which biblical texts refer to which place. As a working hypothesis, we recognize four Gibeahs in the hill country north of Jerusalem. (1) Gibeah of Phinehas (or "Phinehas' hill"), probably somewhere in the immediate vicinity of Shiloh (Josh. 24:33). (2) Gibeah (or "the hill") near Kiriath-jearim where, according to the Ark Narrative, the Ark was temporarily placed in its transition from Shiloh to Jerusalem (I Sam. 7:1–3; II Sam. 6:1–3). (3) Gibeon, the Hivite city with which Saul apparently had unpleasant dealings (II Sam. 21) and where David's troops skirmished with Saul's forces after the latter's death (II Sam. 2:12–17). Later, according to I Kings 3:4–15, Solomon would sacrifice at Gibeon and have his famous dream there. Kiriath-jearim (present-day Deir el-Azar) and Gibeon (el-Jib) were situated on opposite sides of a very prominent height (present-day Nebi Samwil). Possibly this was the common denominator between the two names. Nebi Samwil would have been the Gibeah ("hill") near Kiriath-jearim and Gibeon would have received its name from its proximity to this hill. (4) Gibeah (with the alternate form "Geba," present-day Jeba), sometimes called Gibeah/Geba of Benjamin and sometimes Gibeah/Geba of Saul. This village played a crucial role in the tribal war with Benjamin (Judg. 19–21), Saul's early wars (I Sam. 13:2–14:46), and became Saul's capital (I Sam. 22:6; 23:19; and so on). Gibeathelohim ("the hill of God" in I Sam. 10:5) may have been the same place, or perhaps more specifically the crest of the hill on the side of which Gibeah/Geba was situated. (See Map 12.)

Aphek presents a similar situation. This place-name appears in two different contexts in I Samuel, and in both cases it is the site of the Philistine camp prior to a major battle in which the Israelites were defeated. According to the Ark Narrative, the Philistines camped at Aphek before the battle in connection with which Eli and his sons were killed and the Ark was captured. This context would seem to suggest further that the Aphek involved was somewhere on the frontier between Israelite territory and Philistia. According to I Sam. 29:1, on the other hand, the Philistines camped at Aphek prior to the battle in which Saul and his son Jonathan were killed, and the context places this Aphek somewhere in the vicinity of Mt. Gilboa. One possibility, the one generally assumed, is that these were two different battles involving two different Apheks. As indicated above, however, we are inclined to view the Ark Narrative as a fanciful and biased account (pro-Jerusalem, anti-Elide) which, to the extent that it is based on historical reality, strays rather far from the actual chronology and geography of events. We suspect, namely, that the Ark Narrative is simply misleading in depicting the battle of Aphek in which the Elides lost control of the Ark as some early battle that occurred on the Philistine frontier before Saul's rise to power. More likely it was the same battle of Aphek which occurred in the vicinity of Mt. Gilboa at the end of Saul's reign and in which he and Jonathan were killed. This means that we need search for only one Aphek in connection with the I Samuel narratives, and that this Aphek would have been located somewhere in the vicinity of Mt. Gilboa at the southeastern end of the Jezreel Valley.

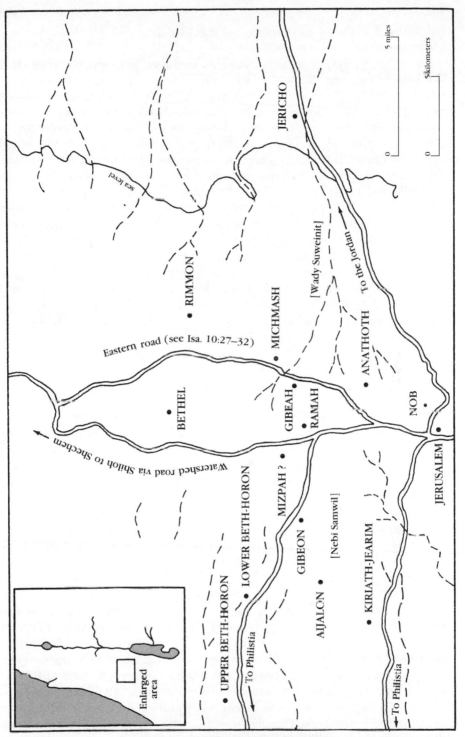

MAP 12. Villages of Benjamin

Shiloh and the Elides

Shiloh clearly played an important role in the early history of Israel, as is indicated by the fact that it appears again and again at crucial points in the biblical materials. The nature of this role is difficult to understand, however, because of what appears to be discontinuity in the Genesis-II Kings account.

According to the Book of Joshua, the people of Israel assembled at Shiloh soon after their entry into the land and from that time forward Shiloh served as the chief political and cultic center for the tribes. The "tent of meeting" was set up at Shiloh and the Ark installed there. Eleazar son of Aaron served as priest until followed in this office by his son Phinehas (Josh. 14:1; 17:4; 19:51; 22:13, 31–32; 24:33). Except for one isolated verse, however, very likely a scribal gloss, one would not get the slightest impression from any of the Judges narratives that Shiloh was, or ever had been, an important political and cultic center for the Israelites. The verse in question, Judg. 21:12, belongs to the story of the tribal war with Benjamin and has the Israelites returning to their camp at Shiloh after a raid on Jabesh-gilead. Yet, as observed in Chapter 3, the overall sense of the narrative about the tribal war seems to require that Shiloh, although Yahwistic, was a non-Israelite cultic center. Thus the Israelites, who had vowed not to give any of their daughters in marriage to the Benjaminites, encouraged the Benjaminites to raid Shiloh for women. The previous raid on Jabesh-gilead for the same purpose is justified in the narrative on the grounds that no one from Jabesh-gilead had been present when the vow was made. But no such explanation is offered in the case of Shiloh. Note also that Shiloh is described in Judg. 21:19 as if the Benjaminites might never have heard of the place.

Whatever interpretation one places on this narrative, it seems out of keeping with the idea that Shiloh served as an important center for the early Israelite tribes. Neither does it prepare us for the opening chapters of I Samuel, where we find Eli and his two sons, Phinehas and Hophni, officiating before the Ark in a temple at Shiloh (I Sam. 1:24; 3:3; note, however, the one reference to "the tent of meeting" in 2:22). These opening chapters of I Samuel anticipate and seek to justify the demise of the Elide priestly line, as we have already noted, and the Ark Narrative goes on to explain how the Ark was captured by the Philistines and found its way eventually to Jerusalem. Nevertheless, the Ark will appear again in the hands of an Elide priest during Saul's reign (I Sam. 14:3, 18).

If one takes a harmonistic approach to these various passages pertaining to Shiloh, the scenario that emerges is somewhat as follows: Shiloh became very early the chief political and cultic center for the Israelite tribes (as reflected in the Book of Joshua); then declined in importance (as seems to be the situation in the Judges narratives); gained prominence again briefly at the time of Eli; and then, with the loss of the Ark, had ceased to function for all practical purposes by the time Saul appeared on the scene. Eli and his son Phinehas would have been direct descendants of Phinehas son of Eleazar son of Aaron. At some point they presumably built a temple alongside the tent of meeting, and somehow one of their descendants contemporary with Saul gained temporary possession of the Ark.

However, we propose an alternate scenario, which admittedly is speculative but which we think takes better into account the surprising attitude toward Shiloh reflected in Judges 19–21, compensates for the strong anti-Elide bias which pervades the opening chapters of I Samuel, and provides an explanation as to why an Elide priest contemporary with Saul would have been in possession of the Ark. Shiloh, in our opinion, was one of the numerous local shrines that dotted the Palestinian hill country during the early tribal period. Its priests, the Elides, were Yahwistic and served before an ark which represented Yahweh's presence. But Shiloh probably was never regarded as a particularly important Israelite cultic center before Saul's day. Indeed it may not even have been regarded as specifically "Israelite." It was when the Elides aligned themselves with Saul and supported him in his early struggles with the Philistines that Shiloh emerged as a sanctuary of national importance. Correspondingly, it was under Saul that the Ark became a national religious symbol for the Israelites.

The disastrous battle near Aphek which left Saul's kingdom in shambles likewise meant the end of Shiloh's brief heyday (although not necessarily the destruction of the village or abandonment of the shrine), the beginning of David's rapid rise to power, and the ascendancy of the Jerusalem cult whose priests eventually would claim authority over all others in Israel and Judah. The Ark was brought to Jerusalem (possibly by an indirect route which may have involved its capture in the battle by the Philistines), where it continued to serve as a national religious symbol. Later, the whole chain of events—the disaster at Aphek, the decline of the Shiloh cult, and the transfer of the Ark to Jerusalem —would be regarded in Jerusalem as the unfolding of Yahweh's will. This is the point of view reflected in the opening chapters of I Samuel, as we have seen, and also in Ps. 78.

> He forsook his dwelling at Shiloh,
>> the tent where he dwelt among men,
> and delivered his power to captivity,
>> his glory to the hand of the foe.
> He gave his people over to the sword,
>> and vented his wrath on his heritage. . . .
> He rejected the tent of Joseph,
>> he did not choose the tribe of Ephraim;
> but he chose the tribe of Judah,
>> Mount Zion, which he loves.
> He built his sanctuary like the high heavens,
>> like the earth, which he has founded for ever.
> He chose David his servant,
>> and took him from the sheepfolds;
> from tending the ewes that had young he brought him
>> to be the shepherd of Jacob his people,
>> of Israel his inheritance.
>
> (Ps. 78:60–62, 67–71)

Jeremiah almost lost his life to an angry Jerusalem mob when he warned that God would reject Jerusalem as he had rejected Shiloh (Jer. 7:12–14; 26:6–9). Still later, the compilers of Genesis-II Kings projected the Ark back into the wilderness period, represented Shiloh as the chief cultic center of their idealized Israel under Joshua, and provided the Elides with a genealogy traced back to Aaron.

The "Historical" Samuel

Samuel is much like Moses and Joshua in that, while the biblical materials assign him a major role at a crucial turning point in Israel's history, he remains a very elusive figure as far as tangible historical information is concerned. Actually three quite different Samuels emerge from the stories about him: there is Samuel the priest-prophet at Shiloh (I Sam. 1:1–4:1a); Samuel the local "seer" from the land of Zuph (I Sam. 9:1–10:16); and Samuel of Ramah, the last of the judges, the king maker and king rejecter (I Sam. 7:3–8:22; 10:17–25; etc.). This threefold picture of Samuel results, in our opinion, from the fact that Samuel has been introduced secondarily into stories and contexts that actually did not involve him originally—particularly the Samuel-Shiloh stories in I Samuel 1–4 and the Saul stories in 9:1–10:16, and so on. Samuel does not appear at all in the Ark Narrative, and rarely appears in the stories about David's rise to power in I Samuel 16 and following. By process of elimination, therefore, the Samuel narrative in I Sam. 7:3–8:22; 10:17–25; 12; 15 is our only hope of catching even a fleeting glimpse of the "historical" Samuel. And this narrative strand, as observed above, while probably based on old traditions, is largely the work of the late compilers of Genesis-II Kings who wished to depict Samuel as the last of the great judges.

Between the lines of their idealized presentation, the Samuel who emerges seems to have been a local cultic leader from Ramah in southern Ephraim/Benjamin who went on a yearly circuit to Bethel, Gilgal, and Mizpah (all three places in close proximity to Ramah). He is described as "judging Israel," which may be the editor's terminology, and reminds one in this regard of Deborah. She likewise is said to have judged Israel "between Ramah and Bethel in the hill country of Ephraim" (see Judg. 4:4–10). The claim that Samuel installed his two sons at Beer-sheba where they took advantage of the office is questionable on at least two grounds. First, the motif of the righteous old priest with two wayward sons is one that we have encountered already in connection with Eli. Second, it seems unlikely that a local Ephraimite priest would have had influence as far south as Beer-sheba, yet this is the sort of thing which the compilers of Genesis-II Kings would have wished to claim for Samuel. Possibly there was another Beer-sheba in the more immediate vicinity of Ramah. But more likely, in our opinion, the whole matter of the two sons judging at Beer-sheba is editorial embellishment of a floating folk motif. We have reservations about the story of the victory over the Philistines at Ebenezer during

Samuel's judgeship on the same grounds. Here again the whole thing sounds like a highly editorialized version of a folk story about how the place called Ebenezer ("the stone of help") got its name.

One motif that persists in the stories about Samuel, however, and cannot be explained away very easily, is that he was involved in some fashion in the official recognition of Saul as king over Israel, but with strong reservations, and then fell into conflict with Saul. This theme of conflict between Samuel and Saul is reflected also in I Samuel 15 (as a secondary addition to the Saul stories) and I Samuel 16 (the first of the stories about David's rise). Presuming that Samuel, in his capacity as religious leader in the Ramah vicinity, did play some ceremonial role in the designation of Saul as king, it is quite understandable that he might have done so under popular pressure rather than in accordance with his own wishes. Saul's new status could only have diminished Samuel's own leadership authority. Nor is there any reason to doubt that what may have been coolness on the part of Samuel toward Saul from the beginning soon developed into open conflict. The explanation given for the break between the two is that Saul failed on two occasions to follow precisely Yahweh's instructions as conveyed by Samuel. Yet one has to suspect that more was involved than matters of ritual detail. Samuel may have recognized that even his status as cultic leader in the Ramah vicinity was being jeopardized by this new king who looked increasingly to the Elide priests of Shiloh for support.

Saul and the Early Israelite Monarchy

The Saul stories read in proper sequence (I Sam. 9:1–10:16 . . . 13:2–14:46 . . . 10:26–11:15) are our primary source of information about Saul's rise to power, and probably bring us nearer to an accurate glimpse of the historical Saul than we have been able to attain for any of the earlier characters of biblical history. This is not to suggest that the Saul stories can be read as historical record. They too represent, at best, a mixture of folk memory and legend. However, at least three observations are to be made in their behalf: (1) In contrast to the Samuel stories, for example, where whatever old traditions are preserved have been thoroughly recast by the late compilers of Genesis-II Kings, the secondary editorial elements in the Saul stories can be separated out with some confidence, as we noted above. (2) When these elements are removed, the material that is left is noticeably free of the anti-Saul and antimonarchical bias which otherwise pervades I Samuel. Indeed, these stories seem to be told from a relatively early "northern" perspective according to which Saul was still remembered as a hero and his kingdom looked upon with favor. (3) The glimpse of Saul that one attains from these stories harmonizes well with the occasional references to him elsewhere in the Samuel materials, particularly in the stories about David's rise during Saul's reign. Specifically, the Saul that emerges from a combination of these sources is depicted in the sections that follow.

Saul's Rise to Power

Saul seems to have been from a prominent and relatively wealthy family (I Sam. 9:1–2) whose ancestral home was the village of Zela in southern Benjaminite territory (II Sam. 21:14; compare Josh. 18:28; Zelza in I Sam. 10:2 may be a variant of the same name). We have noted that the story in I Samuel 1 which describes the unusual circumstances of Samuel's birth originally may have had to do with Saul. If so, it is to be regarded as a "royal legend"—it was not uncommon for kings in ancient times, particularly founders of dynasties, to be credited with unusual births.

Saul came to the fore at a time when the Philistines dominated the central hill country and made a name for himself by attacking a Philistine garrison in the Gibeah-Michmash vicinity (or challenging their authority in some fashion) and then successfully expelling the Philistines from southern Ephraim/Benjamin. The details of this initial victory which launched Saul's career are somewhat confused because of the literary complexity of the narrative in I Sam. 13: 2–14:46. As observed above, this narrative telescopes two versions of the incident, one featuring the young Saul, while the other features the young Jonathan. The result, in any case, was that Saul, having expelled the Philistines from the area, established himself at Gibeah-Michmash with a small standing army. Note that I Sam. 13:2 does not describe the situation at the beginning of the Gibeah-Michmash battle but, in typical biblical narrative style, introduces the account of the battle by summarizing its outcome: "Saul chose three thousand men of Israel; two thousand were with Saul in Michmash and the hill country of Bethel, and a thousand were with Jonathan in Gibeah of Benjamin; the rest of the people he sent home, every man to his tent."

Gibeah and Michmash were situated on opposite sides of a steep valley (present-day Wady es-Suweinit) which cuts into the hill country from the Jordan Valley. Together they were strategically located for dominating southern Ephraim/Benjamin. Michmash, on the northern bank, had access to the territory north of the valley ("the hill country of Bethel"), while Gibeah had corresponding access to the territory southward. (See Map 12.) At the same time, they were in visual communication with each other and together controlled the valley crossing. It is not surprising that the Philistines would have established some sort of outpost in one or both of these villages, or that Saul, having chased the Philistines from the area, would have chosen these twin villages for his own military base.

This is the situation presupposed at the beginning of the Jabesh-gilead affair (I Sam. 10:26–11:15). Saul is residing at Gibeah with a band of soldiers where presumably he and his men have received gifts from the local population who now look to them for protection. Although this is not stated in so many words, it is implied by the reference in I Sam. 10:27 to certain ones who, apparently regarding the Philistine victory as "beginner's luck," doubted Saul's ability to handle a really serious military challenge and thus refused to provide any support: "But some worthless fellows said, 'How can this man save us?' And they despised him, and brought him no present. But he held his peace."

In the meantime the people of Jabesh in Gilead found themselves in a desperate situation. The Ammonites under their king Nahash had laid siege to Jabesh and it was clear that the city would soon fall. When the officials of the city appealed to Nahash for a peace settlement, he offered impossible terms: "On this condition I will make a treaty with you, that I gouge out all your right eyes, and thus put disgrace upon all Israel" (I Sam. 11:2). Thereupon, as a last resort, the people of Jabesh-gilead sent messengers across the Jordan to Gibeah with an appeal for aid. This would have been the logical place for them to turn. (1) The Gileadites were among the tribes that had been closely aligned with Ephraim (what we have referred to above as the Ephraim/Israel group) prior to the Philistines' inroads. (2) There may have existed some special kinship relationship between Gibeah and Jabesh-gilead, as suggested by the account of the tribal war with Benjamin (Judg. 21:8–12). (3) Word would have spread to Gilead that Saul had defeated the Philistines and expelled them from the Ephraimite hill country. Perhaps this new Israelite military leader would extend his protection to Gilead as well.

Saul acted immediately. Butchering a yoke of oxen, he sent pieces of the carcass with messengers throughout the countryside with a call to arms and a stern warning: "Whoever does not come out after Saul and Samuel [the reference to Samuel here is probably secondary], so shall it be done to his oxen!" (I Sam. 11:7). Not surprisingly, there was an ample muster of troops. They crossed the Jordan under Saul's leadership and he achieved with their help a second major victory of his career: first the Philistines expelled from the hill country, now the Ammonite siege of Jabesh lifted.

If the above interpretation is correct, Saul emerged on the scene as essentially the same type of leader as were Jephthah and Abimelech before him and David after him. All of these men entered the picture as self-styled military leaders, each with a private army which they used to establish themselves as protectors/ rulers in a given locale. Jephthah was an outcast from the Gileadites around whom "worthless fellows" collected and they raided together (Judg. 11). Later, when threatened by the Ammonites, the Gileadites appealed to Jephthah for help. Jephthah and his men came to their aid and defeated the Ammonites, but on the advance agreement that he would rule Gilead thereafter: "If you bring me home again to fight with the Ammonites, and Yahweh gives them over to me, I will be your head" (Judg. 11:9). Abimelech solicited funds from the people of Shechem with which he hired an army and established himself as "king" of that vicinity (Judg. 9:6). As it turned out, the Shechemites themselves were the ones who later brought about his downfall. David, as we shall see below, commanded a renegade army in the Judean Wilderness during his early career, with which he posed as "protector" of the local people, collected "presents" from them, conducted raids on their enemies, and eventually secured the status of "king" in Hebron.

At some point Saul was also proclaimed king, possibly as a follow-up to his initial Philistine victory. According to I Sam. 10:20–24, Saul was selected by lot at a popular assembly held at Mizpah under Samuel's supervision. Although there is no reason to doubt that such an assembly occurred, or that it was presided over by a reluctant Samuel, it must be kept in mind that the details of this account have been shaped by the interests of the compilers of Genesis-II Kings who wished to emphasize divine guidance and Samuel's role in the selection process. The idea of selecting a king by lot seems particularly far-fetched. Some initial opposition from Saul's countrymen is understandable, as would have been a more unified and enthusiastic confirmation of his kingship after the Jabesh-gilead victory.

The Extent of Saul's Kingdom

Saul's "kingdom" would have consisted initially of southern Ephraim/Benjamin, his own home area from which he had cleared the Philistines. After the Jabesh-gilead victory, his realm of influence—the area that he dominated militarily and where the people looked to him for protection—would have been expanded to cover essentially the territories of the Ephraim/Israel tribes. Israel (in the Ephraim/Israel tribal sense of the word) would remain the core of Saul's kingdom, moreover, in spite of the fact that before the end of his reign he also exerted significant influence among the clans and villages of the southern hill country (south of Jerusalem).

I Samuel 15 describes a raid led by Saul against the Amalekites in the Negeb. The editors of the story explain that this action was intended as punishment to the Amalekites because they had harassed the Israelites during the exodus from Egypt. Be that as it may, the Amalekites presented a constant problem for the clans and villages in the southern hill country (I Sam. 30:1–3), which raises the possibility that some of them may have appealed to Saul for protection against the Amalekites in the same way that the people of Jabesh-gilead had appealed to him for help against the Ammonites. We are told that the Kenites were given advance warning of the raid so that they could remove themselves from danger, and that, having defeated the Amalekites, Saul set up a victory stela (or a monument of some sort, a *massib)* in Carmel, a town southeast of Hebron. Probably the monument was intended as a sign of Saul's claim to political authority in the area. Later we hear of Saul moving freely with his army throughout the southern hill country in search of David, while the local people are pictured reporting to Saul from time to time on David's whereabouts (I Sam. 23:6–14; 24:1; 26:1).

Joshua's southern campaign reported in Josh. 10:29–43 invites attention at this point. Commentators have observed from time to time that the passage seems to preserve the memory of an actual campaign which involved certain key cities in the southern hill country and the Shephelah (Libnah, Lachish, Gezer, Eglon, Hebron, and Debir) but that the campaign does not fit very well in its present context. We read earlier in the same chapter, for example, how Joshua made a nonaggression pact with the Gibeonites and then came to their aid when they were attacked by a coalition of Amorite kings. Yet the territory that fell under attack during the campaign in question, supposedly conducted by Joshua, seems to have included Gibeon: "And Joshua defeated them from Kadesh-barnea to Gaza, and all the country of Goshen, as far as Gibeon" (v. 41). Also, one is surprised to find that Hebron, mentioned among the cities conquered during the campaign in question, is still in enemy hands four chapters later (Josh. 14:6–15).

Possibly we have here in Josh. 10:29–43 a misplaced report on Saul's military activities in southern Palestine. Certainly the summary of the conquests in 10:41—"from Kadesh-barnea to Gaza, and all the country of Goshen, as far as Gibeon"—fits better with what is reported otherwise about Saul than with what is said about Joshua. Note that Shur in I Sam. 15:7 was in the same region as Kadesh-barnea, and that Gilgal appears to be the base of operations in both I Samuel 15 and Joshua 10. Moreover, Saul is remembered specifically as having encroached on Gibeon. Actually Gibeon was one of several Hivite cities (including Chephirah, Beeroth, and Kiriath-jearim; see Josh. 9:17) that formed a wedge of non-Israelite towns along the Valley of Aijalon extending into the central hill country north and west of Jerusalem. (Note also the reference to Aijalon in the Michmash episode; I Sam. 14:31.) These cities, along with Jerusalem, formed a barrier between Ephraim/Israel in the north and the various tribes including Judah in the southern hill country. II Samuel 21:1–6 clearly implies that it was Saul who first brought these Hivite cities under Israelite domination "in his zeal for the people of Israel and Judah" (II Sam. 21:2).

It is of interest to note in this regard that several genealogical references connect Saul's family with Gibeon (I Chron. 8:33–40; 9:39–44), suggesting a close association of the two. Furthermore, Saul's hometown of Zela (probably to be identified with present-day Khirbet es-Salah) was in close geographical proximity to Gibeon (Josh. 18:25–28). It has been speculated, in fact, that Saul actually made Gibeon his capital city. There is no really tangible evidence to support such a view, however, and it would require that some of the references to Gibeah in the stories about Saul be interpreted as references to Gibeon.

The description in II Sam. 2:8–9 of the territorial domain inherited by Ish-bosheth at Saul's death, although Ish-bosheth was unable to secure control over all of it, is also relevant for determining the extent of Saul's kingdom and influence. (See Map 13.) According to this passage, Ish-bosheth was made king "over Gilead and the Ashurites and Jezreel and Ephraim and Benjamin and all Israel." One expects to find Gilead, Ephraim, Benjamin, and "all Israel" included. Jezreel comes as no surprise either, although Saul's influence there probably was confined to the southeastern end of the valley. The only unexpected item in the description, therefore, is the reference to the "Ashurites." The term usually refers to the Assyrians, which would be totally out of place in this context. Some ancient versions read "Asher," apparently in reference to the Galilean tribe of that name, while others read "Geshur," which

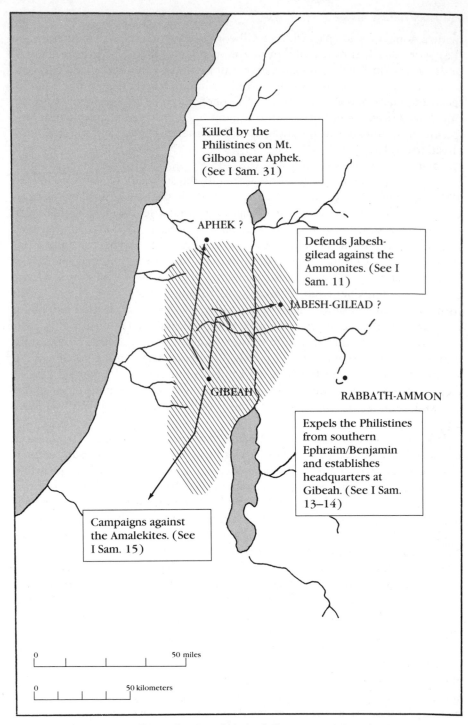

Killed by the
Philistines on Mt.
Gilboa near Aphek.
(See I Sam. 31)

APHEK ?

Defends Jabesh-
gilead against the
Ammonites. (See I
Sam. 11)

JABESH-GILEAD ?

GIBEAH

RABBATH-AMMON

Expels the Philistines
from southern
Ephraim/Benjamin
and establishes
headquarters at
Gibeah. (See I Sam.
13–14)

Campaigns against
the Amalekites. (See
I Sam. 15)

0   50 miles

0   50 kilometers

**MAP 13. Saul's Major Battles and the Approximate Extent
of His Kingdom**

was the name of a locale approximately east or northeast of the Sea of Galilee. "Geshur" would seem to make better historical sense, on the assumption that Saul expanded his influence beyond Gilead into the northern Transjordan. No texts associate Saul in any way with Galilee. And why would the tribe of Asher be singled out as belonging to Ish-bosheth's kingdom and the other Galilean tribes ignored? Note finally that the passage does not assign to Ish-bosheth any territory in the southern hill country, even though it seems clear that Saul's authority had been recognized there at least to some degree. Possibly this is to be explained on the grounds that the southern hill country fell quickly into David's hands after Saul's death.

In visualizing the extent of Saul's domain, one should not think in terms of a highly organized kingdom with precisely defined boundaries in any case. Loyalty to Saul (and later to Ish-bosheth) probably varied from region to region, with his strongest base of support being the Ephraim-Benjamin-Gilead zone. In peripheral areas Saul's authority would have consisted of little more than temporary forays during which he exercised control only as long as he or his troops were present, or as long as the local people needed to rely on him for protection against other threats.

Saul's Military Career

The continued warfare throughout Saul's reign, summarized in I Sam. 14: 47–48, is to be understood as the military activity necessary to maintain security within the realm identified above, and perhaps to expand it somewhat. Specifically, we are told:

> He fought against all his enemies on every side, against Moab, against the Ammonites, against Edom, against the kings [or "king," so some Hebrew manuscripts and the Greek] of Zobah, and against the Philistines; wherever he turned he put them to the worse. And he did valiantly, and smote the Amalekites, and delivered Israel out of the hands of those who plundered them.

This very positive assessment of Saul's military career appears somewhat unexpectedly among the materials in I-II Samuel, which otherwise have been edited from an essentially anti-Saulide slant. The contrast in itself suggests the general trustworthiness of the passage in question. Apparently military activities played an important role throughout Saul's reign and he was generally successful in this regard.

First among Saul's enemies, of course, were the Philistines. As discussed in Chapter 1, the Philistines were a subgroup of the Sea Peoples who make their first appearance in Egyptian documents from the early twelfth century (*ANET* 262–63). Having settled along the southwestern coast of Palestine, they eventually began to extend their influence and control into the central hill country. Probably they did not attempt any permanent occupation of the hill country, but were satisfied to establish outposts at various points and to undertake plundering raids from time to time (1 Sam. 10:5; 13:17; 14:1). Also, they apparently sought in some fashion to control the presence of weapons in that area (I Sam. 13:19–22). Saul's first major military accomplishment, as we have seen, was his expulsion of the Philistines from the north central hill country. Unfortunately this was only the beginning of his struggles with them. Conflicts with the Philistines continued throughout Saul's reign (see I Sam. 17:1–2; 18:20–30; 19:8) and Saul died in battle fighting them.

The battles with Zobah, Ammon, and Moab would have been related to the security of the Gileadite (and perhaps Geshurite) area. Zobah seems to have dominated southern Aram at the time, presumably with influence extending into the northern Transjordan. The Ammonites and the Moabites, of course, bordered Gilead on the east and south. Saul may have come into contact (and conflict) with the Edomites, on the other hand, in connection with his forays into the Negeb and the Judean Wilderness. The battles would have been frontier skirmishes for the most part, or temporary eruptions of violence resulting from plundering raids. In any case, one should hardly think in terms of fully mobilized warfare between firmly established nations with clearly defined boundaries. We know virtually nothing of the political structures of these various "nations" at the time, but probably they were not unlike Saul's Israel—newly emergent "kingdoms" with very loose political structures superimposed on a basically clan and tribal society.

Administrative Affairs

Command of the military forces during Saul's reign probably remained largely a family affair. Saul's son Jonathan and uncle Abner are presented performing leading roles, with Abner identified as commander of the army (I Sam. 14:50; 26:5; II Sam. 2:8). This is in spite of the fact that the stories about Saul's battles always depict Saul himself in command. Possibly Abner was placed in charge of the standing army at some point, while Saul continued to function in battle as general commander of the combined standing army plus mustered troops.

That Saul was supported by at least a rudimentary administrative and military officialdom seems indicated, but very little information on such matters can be gained from the biblical texts. Several times the texts refer to Saul's servants ("officials"), but little if any differentiation seems to be made between military and other types of servants (see I Sam. 18:5, 22, 30; 22:6; and so on). One such servant, Doeg the Edomite (or Aramean according to some ancient versions), is identified as "the chief of Saul's herdsmen" (I Sam. 21:7; see 22:9). However, one need not assume that Doeg's responsibilities were limited to, or even primarily related to, cattle-raising. Often in ancient times, as well as in modern, the name of an office does not correspond exactly to the actual responsibilities of the post (for example, a "chamberlain" in connection with British government or the papacy). It is tempting to speculate on the fact that Saul had an Edomite among his officials, but perhaps not too much should be made of that either in view of the heterogeneous character of Palestine's population and the fluid political situation of the period.

Saul's standing army and nascent administrative system required financial support. This would have come primarily in the form of "gifts" from those whom he protected (I Sam. 10:27; and compare I Sam. 25, where David attempts to extract such support from Nabal), from the spoils of warfare, and from raids (I Sam. 15:9). II Samuel 4:1–4 identifies two brothers from Beeroth as "captains of raiding bands" in the service of Ish-bosheth. Apparently they were leaders of hit-and-run squads operating for pillage and spoil. Such squads and actions seem to have been common features of the unstable times, even as policies of state. The Amalekites operated such bands (I Sam. 30:1) and, as we shall see, David and his men represented such a group while in the service of the Philistines (I Sam. 27:8–12). Joab led raiding forays for David even after the latter had become king at Hebron (II Sam. 3:22).

Taxes as such are not mentioned in connection with Saul's reign, although Samuel's tirade against kingship clearly denotes the ways that monarchs had of acquiring property and income through governmental policy (I Sam. 8:10–18). Although Samuel's speech reflects the subsequent course of the Israelite monarchy, it states what everyone in the ancient world knew: monarchy, taxation, and military conscription go hand in hand. Many of those who opposed Saul may have been antimonarchical for economic reasons.

The words attributed to Saul in his attempt to dissuade his inner circle of Benjaminite supporters of sympathy for David suggest that he had redistributed landholdings to them: "Hear now, you Benjaminites; will the son of Jesse [David] give every one of you fields and vineyards, will he make you all commanders of thousands and commanders of hundreds?" (I Sam. 22:7). The two "captains of raiding bands" in the service of Ish-bosheth mentioned above are identified as Benjaminite residents of Beeroth, one of the cities of the Hivite enclave from which the earlier population had been forced to flee: "For Beeroth also is reckoned to Benjamin; the Beerothites fled to Gittaim, and have been sojourners there to this day" (II Sam. 4:2–3). Saul's policy of land redistribution may have been the background of this Hivite displacement.

The biblical traditions preserve no detailed description of Saul's religious practices or policies. He is pictured throughout as a staunch Yahwist, however, and we have argued that he had special connections with the Shilonite priestly line. Clearly he fought his battles under the banner of Yahweh. We read of his erecting an altar to Yahweh in time of battle, for example, and of his extreme concern for sacrificial purity (I Sam. 14:31–35). I Samuel 28:3 notes the incongruity of Saul's visit to the witch of Endor, since he "had put the mediums and the wizards out of the land" (I Sam. 28:3, 9). Even Samuel's condemnations of Saul (I Sam. 13:13–14; 15:17–30), which reflect at least in part the anti-Saulide bias of later editors, never accuse him of infidelity to Yahweh but only of failure to follow all of Samuel's specific directives. To speak of a state religion under Saul would be inappropriate. Nonetheless, his reign and his pro-Yahwistic inclination must be seen as moving Yahwism nearer to center stage in Israelite cultic affairs.

Opposition to Saul

As one would expect for any political structure, there were those who opposed Saul's regime. David emerged as the leader of this oposition, and we will look more closely at his career in Chapter 5. At this point it is sufficient to note that David also came to the fore as a military hero, a Philistine fighter in the service of Saul. Later he departed Saul's court and operated as the commander of a renegade army along the fringes of the southern hill country. His soldiers represented various backgrounds.

> When his brothers and all his father's house heard it, they went down there to him. And every one who was in distress, and every one who was in debt, and every one who was discontented, gathered to him; and he became captain over them. And there were with him about four hundred men. (I Sam. 22:1b–3)

Among the "discontented" who joined David would have been, we may suppose, persons whom Saul had dispossessed of their lands. The land grants that he had made to his inner circle of Benjaminite supporters, and perhaps to others as well, had to be made at someone's expense. The favoritism which he apparently showed the Benjaminites would have had a negative effect of its own. And of course his encroachment upon non-Israelite city-states, such as Gibeon, won him especially bitter enemies (II Sam. 21:1–2).

Saul's Death and the Collapse of the Early Israelite Monarchy

Saul's Last Battle

Saul's career was ended as he had begun it, fighting against the Philistines. The circumstances that led up to his final battle with them remain vague—the passages that pertain to the incident are less concerned with the broader political situation than with describing David's activities and attempting to justify the fact that he was aligned with the Philistines at that point rather than with the Israelite army (I Sam. 28–31). The scene of the battle was the southeastern end of the Jezreel Valley, at the foot of Mt. Gilboa which juts out into the valley (I Sam. 31:1). This suggests that the battle was fought for control of the valley, or at least for the southeastern end of it where, as we observed in Chapter 3, there was some spillover of Manassites from the hill country. The Philistines apparently controlled much of the remainder of the valley. We are told that they camped at Shunem and then Aphek prior to the battle, for example, and took Saul's beheaded body to Beth-shean afterward. If Saul was attempting to press the Israelite claim to the southeastern end of the valley, this would have threatened the Philistines' access to Beth-shean.

The battle turned out to be a disaster for Saul and the Israelites. The Israelite army was routed and fled for cover on Mt. Gilboa (I Sam. 31:1). Saul and his three sons—Jonathan, Abinadab, and Malchishua—were all killed. Saul himself was mortally wounded, according to I Sam. 31:3–6, and then committed suicide by falling on his sword. II Samuel 1:1–16 provides a slightly different version, with an Amalekite claiming to have delivered the coup de grace at the wounded monarch's request. In any case, the bodies of Saul and his sons fell into the hands of the Philistines, who left them exposed on the wall of Beth-shean. Presumably they would have been left there to rot had not certain daring men from Jabesh-gilead, remembering no doubt that Saul had come to their city's aid at a crucial and desperate time, rescued the bodies in a nighttime raid and given them proper burial in Jabesh (I Sam. 31:11–13).

Something of Saul's popularity, heroism, and the significance of his reign is indicated by a lament recorded in II Sam. 1:17–27.

> From the blood of the slain,
>   from the fat of the mighty,
> the bow of Jonathan turned not back,
>   and the sword of Saul returned not empty.

Mt. Gilboa. This spur of the central hill country extends into the southeastern end of the Jezreel Valley. Saul and Jonathan were killed in battle with the Philistines at Mt. Gilboa. *(Robert Wright)*

Saul and Jonathan, beloved and lovely!
    In life and in death they were not divided;
they were swifter than eagles,
    they were stronger than lions.
Ye daughters of Israel, weep over Saul,
    who clothed you daintily in scarlet,
    who put ornaments of gold upon your apparel.
How are the mighty fallen
    in the midst of the battle!

                                        (II Sam. 1:22–25a)

These verses are attributed to David and a second stanza focuses on David's love for Jonathan (vs. 25b–27). Yet Davidic authorship seems unlikely (or at best self-serving) in view of the fact that David had thrown in his lot with the Philistines by the time of Saul's and Jonathan's deaths. Whoever the author, the words no doubt embodied the sentiment of many Israelites.

Abner and Ish-bosheth

The defeat at Gilboa left Saul's kingdom in disarray from which it never recovered. In addition to the fact that the Philistines (including David, who had gone over to their side) now had free run of the hill country, there was no one among Saul's descendants who could provide strong leadership. Abner, it turned out, took matters in hand. Orchestrating the transfer of the crown to Ish-bosheth and the transfer of the administration of the kingdom from Gibeah to Mahanaim in the Transjordan, he remained himself the real power behind the throne. David, in the meantime, who during the last years of Saul's reign has served as a Philistine mercenary and used his position to build support in the south, moved into Hebron with his private army and had himself proclaimed king over Judah (II Sam. 2:1–4).

The Bible tells us very little about Ish-bosheth—called Eshbaal in I Chron. 8:33 and 9:39. He is identified as a son of Saul in II Sam. 2:8, 12 but is never named among Saul's sons in other Samuel passages. Specifically, I Sam. 14:49 identifies Saul's sons as Jonathan, Ishvi, and Malchishua, while I Sam. 31:2 reports the death of "Jonathan and Abinadab and Malchishua, the sons of Saul." According to II Sam. 2:10, Ish-bosheth was "forty years old when he began to reign over Israel, and he reigned two years." The forty years is to be understood as a symbolic number, of course, and the two years at best a rough estimate. The fact that Ish-bosheth is not mentioned along with Saul's other sons even in connection with Saul's last battle suggests that he may in fact have been a grandson rather than a son, or in any case still a minor when Saul was killed. This would help explain also why he was so easily dominated by Abner (see II Sam. 2:8–9).

Ish-bosheth claimed authority over all the areas that Saul had ruled (see the comments above, p. 139, on II Sam. 2:9), but the kingdom was in shambles and he could not ensure the defense even of Gibeah. Thus the transfer of administration to Mahanaim would have been for security reasons. Mahanaim was in Gileadite territory, and the Gileadites, as we have seen, had special reasons for loyalty to Saul's house. No doubt Ish-bosheth could also count on the continued loyalty of many of his Benjaminite kinsmen, even though he had found it necessary to transfer the capital.

II Samuel 3:1 notes that "there was a long war between the house of Saul and the house of David; and David grew stronger and stronger, while the house of Saul became weaker and weaker." Only one battle is actually reported, which apparently began with some sort of ritual engagement at Gibeon between Israelite troops under Abner and David's troops under Joab (II Sam. 2:12–32). Before a truce was called, according to the report, nineteen of David's men had fallen, three hundred Benjaminites, and sixty of Abner's men. Three items are noteworthy about this encounter. First, the fact that it occurred at Gibeon suggests that David had taken the initiative by encroaching on Ish-bosheth's domain. Second, it illustrates the important role of family ties in political and military affairs at that time. Abner was Saul's uncle (I Chron. 8:33) or cousin (I Sam. 14:50), and the prominent Judeans mentioned—Joab, Abishai, and Asahel—were nephews of David, sons of his sister Zeruiah (I Sam. 26:6; II Sam. 2:18; I Chron. 2:13–16; see also II Sam. 21:11 for reference to another nephew of David). Abner killed Asahel during the battle which, as we shall see, would have significant later political consequences. Third, distinction is made in the account between the Benjaminites who fell in battle (accounting for most of the casualties) and Abner's men. Probably we have to do here with Benjaminite loyalists to the house of Saul who fought alongside Abner's professional soldiers.

Conflict between Abner and Ish-bosheth was perhaps inevitable. Abner was the real power behind the throne and Ish-bosheth must have feared that eventually he would take the throne itself. Thus, when Ish-bosheth accused Abner of relations with one of Saul's concubines, more was at stake than the concubine's reputation (II Sam. 3:7–11). Ish-bosheth, as Saul's successor, would have inherited the royal harem. Indeed, this would have been one of his symbols of office. By the same measure, he may have interpreted Abner's taking access to the harem as an initial step toward taking the crown also. Abner reacted angrily to the accusation, although apparently without actually denying it, and began negotiations with David toward shifting Israelite allegiance from Ish-bosheth to David.

Perhaps Abner was already beginning to realize by this time the inevitability of David's triumph and hoped to negotiate while he could still bargain from a position of strength. The success of the negotiations depended nevertheless on whether he could deal with two rather delicate matters. On the one hand, David stipulated as the first step of any arrangement that Michal, Saul's daughter whom he had married while still an officer in Saul's court, be returned to him (I Sam. 18:17–27; II Sam. 3:13). Such a decision would have to be made by Ish-bosheth, at least officially. Thus David sent messages to Ish-bosheth requesting Michal, and Ish-bosheth agreed to the request—probably on the advice of, or under pressure from, Abner, and certainly without knowledge of Abner's and David's intentions. The second barrier to the plan for shifting Israelite allegiance to David was the opposition to be expected from the staunch loyalists to the house of Saul, particularly the Benjaminites. In addition to the kinship connection with Saul, the Benjaminites had already suffered heavy casualties from David's men. It is not surprising, therefore, that II Sam. 3:17–19 has Abner giving the Benjaminites special attention as he conferred with the elders of Israel.

Apparently Abner was able to persuade the Benjaminites also, or was confident that he could orchestrate the shift of Israel's allegiance from Ish-bosheth in spite of their opposition. Thus he came to David at Hebron, sealed the agreement, and had already begun the return journey when Joab assassinated him (II Sam. 3:20–30). Joab claimed that this was vengeance for his brother Asahel, whom Abner had slain during the skirmish at Gibeon (II Sam. 2: 18–23). An additional factor must have been Joab's realization that Abner was about to become a very influential figure in David's administration and thus a challenge to him.

Ish-bosheth's days were numbered in spite of Abner's death. Possibly there was already significant momentum among the elders of Israel toward shifting their allegiance to David. The issue was forced when two brothers from Beeroth, the two "captains of raiding bands" in the service of Ish-bosheth mentioned above, brutally assassinated the king (II Sam. 4:1–4). Possibly taking advantages of their irregular contact with Ish-bosheth, they gained access to the royal quarters and decapitated him (II Sam. 4:5–7a; the original reading of v. 6 is uncertain). Then, no doubt expecting a reward from David, they hastened by night and delivered Ish-bosheth's head to him at Hebron (II Sam. 4:7b–8).

With both Abner and Ish-bosheth dead, representatives of the elders of Israel came themselves to David at Hebron and arranged a covenant which involved recognizing him as king over Israel as well as Judah. They were mindful, no doubt, that expediency favored their voluntary turnover of the kingdom rather than having David take it from them. This was the end of the early Israelite kingdom. David incorporated the Israelite constituency into his realm, borrowed some of the Israelite symbols such as the Ark, and apparently even used the name "Israel" for his kingdom. As we shall see in the next chapter, however, his was eventually a Jerusalem-based regime which by no means represented direct continuity with Saul's kingdom.

CHAPTER 5

David, King of Jerusalem

David founded a dynasty that was to rule from Jerusalem for over four centuries. Even after Jerusalem fell to the Babylonians in 586 B.C.E., which ended the long line of Davidic kings, many of the people of Jerusalem and Judah (including many scattered abroad at that time) continued to hope for a restoration of the days of old when the house of David was secure on the throne. Thus it is not surprising that David received so much attention in the biblical materials or that there was such an obvious effort on the part of the ancient Judean compilers of these materials to present him in a favorable light. The Genesis-II Kings account, compiled by Judean editors sometime after the fall of Jerusalem, devotes forty-two chapters to David and seeks to portray him as Yahweh's chosen, the true and righteous king. A second extended biblical account, I-II Chronicles, begins its coverage of Judean history with David and devotes twenty chapters to his reign. David as presented by the Chronicler is the ideal hero, God's man who can do no wrong. Finally, David is associated by tradition with the book of Psalms, where thirteen of the individual psalms are connected by their superscriptions with particular moments in his career.

David as Presented in the Biblical Materials

David in the Genesis-II Kings Account

The Genesis-II Kings account will be our primary source of information about David's career. Anticipated already in I Sam. 13:13–14 and 15:27–28, where Samuel proclaims that Yahweh has rejected Saul and selected another to rule over Israel, David first appears by name in I Samuel 16. From that point on, until Solomon gains the throne in I Kings 1–2, David dominates the account. We begin, therefore, with a summary of I Samuel 16–I Kings 2.

Summary of I Samuel 16–I Kings 2. Having denounced Saul a second time and proclaiming that Yahweh had chosen another to rule in Saul's stead, Samuel was sent by Yahweh to Bethlehem, to the house of Jesse, where he was to anoint this future ruler. Guided by Yahweh, Samuel anointed David, even though David was the youngest of Jesse's sons (I Sam. 16:1–13). Yahweh's Spirit "came mightily upon David from that day forward," while an evil spirit from Yahweh began to torment Saul. When a search was made throughout the land for a musician to play before Saul and soothe his tormented mind, David again was selected. Thus he came to Saul's court, where he entered service as Saul's personal musician and armor-bearer (I Sam. 16:14–23). On one occasion when the Israelite and Philistine armies were camped over against each other anticipating battle, Jesse sent David from Bethlehem to the battlefront with food for David's older brothers. When David arrived on the scene, a Philistine giant, Goliath, was challenging anyone from the Israelite camp to come out and face him in single combat. David accepted the challenge, killed Goliath, and became a hero. Saul sent to inquire who the young lad was who had killed the giant and "took him that day, and would not let him return to his father's house" (I Sam. 17:1–18:2).

As a member of Saul's court, David became a close friend of Jonathan, Saul's son. In fact, Jonathan gave David his own robe, armor, and weapons. Also Michal, Saul's oldest daughter, loved David. David continued to fight the Philistines with much success, to the extent that his fame as a military hero began to exceed that of Saul. As a result, Saul in jealousy attempted on more than one occasion to kill him. In connection with one such attempt, Saul promised to give Michal to David in marriage, with the understanding that David would give a hundred Philistine foreskins as the marriage present. David produced two hundred foreskins and married Michal (I Sam. 18:3–30).

Eventually the conflict between Saul and David became so great that David was forced to flee Saul's court. He was aided in his escape by Jonathan, Michal, Samuel, and Ahimelech of the priests of Nob (I Sam. 19:1–21:9). David went first to Achish, the Philistine king of Gath, and then to the vicinity of Adullam. There he was joined by kinsmen and others who were "on the run" for one reason or another, so that he became the commander of a renegade army. When Saul learned that David was in Keilah, one of the cities in the Adullam vicinity, and began preparations to march against the city, David moved with his men to the wilderness of Ziph. Finally, after several narrow escapes from Saul as he and his men roamed in that area, David returned to Achish and placed his army in Achish's service. Achish gave the city of Ziklag to David, from which base David and his men conducted raids against the Amalekites and other tribal groups in the Negeb (I Sam. 21:9–27:12).

David was still in the service of Achish when the Philistines routed Saul's army at Mt. Gilboa and killed Saul and his sons. David and his men did not actually fight in the battle, however, because the Philistines feared that they might switch sides during the fighting. Thus David returned to Ziklag with his army, where he found that the city had just been raided by the Amalekites. They overtook the Amalekite raiders, massacred them, and shared the spoil with some of the elders of Judah. The deaths of Saul and Jonathan were reported to David by an Amalekite who claimed to have delivered the coup de grace to Saul.

David executed the Amalekite and mourned Saul and Jonathan with a psalm (I Sam. 28–II Sam. 1).

Then David occupied Hebron and vicinity with his army, whereupon the men of Judah came and anointed him as their king. He sent messengers to the people of Jabesh-gilead indicating that they should take note of what had transpired. There was continued warfare between David's soldiers and those of Ish-bosheth, Saul's son now ruling at Mahanaim over the remnant of Saul's king-dom, with David becoming increasingly stronger. Six sons were born to David while he ruled from Hebron, including Amnon, Absalom, and Adonijah (II Sam. 2:1–3:5).

Abner began negotiations with David toward shifting the Israelite allegiance from Ish-bosheth to David. But when the negotiations were virtually com-pleted, Joab killed Abner. Then two men of Beeroth, "captains of raiding bands," assassinated Ish-bosheth. With both Abner and Ish-bosheth dead, the elders of Israel came to David at Hebron, made a covenant with him, and anointed him as their king (II Sam. 3:6–5:5).

Next David conquered Jerusalem and made it his capital. His reign was recognized internationally by Hiram king of Tyre. He took more wives and concubines, who bore him more sons and daughters. The Philistines began to attack when they heard that he had been made king of Israel, but he de-feated them also (II Sam. 5:6–25). Then he transferred the Ark from Kiriath-jearim (see I Sam. 7:1–2) to the house of Obed-edom, a Gittite, and from there to Jerusalem. David's ritual dance before the Ark was offensive to his wife Michal. David responded to her in anger, and she bore him no children (II Sam. 6).

Having been given rest by Yahweh from all his enemies and having built a palace for himself in Jerusalem, David proposed to build also a temple for Yahweh. Nathan the prophet, speaking for Yahweh, declined the proposal but promised that Yahweh would give David rest from all his enemies and establish his dynasty forever. David prayed to Yahweh for continued blessing.

David defeated the enemy on every side: the Philistines, the Moabites, the Zobahites, the Ammonites, the Amalekites, and the Edomites. And he reigned over all Israel and administered justice and equity to all his people (II Sam. 7–8). He restored Saul's family estate to Mephibosheth, a lame son of Jonathan, but placed Ziba, a former servant of Saul, in charge of the estate and specified that Mephibosheth was to remain in Jerusalem and eat at the king's table (II Sam. 9).

David's troops, now commanded in the field by Joab while David remained in Jerusalem, engaged in warfare with the Ammonites. These Ammonite wars were the context of battles with the Zobahites (Arameans) and of David's affair with Bathsheba. When Bathsheba became pregnant, David arranged for her husband's death and married her himself. The baby died, but Solomon was born to her later. Eventually the Ammonites were defeated (II Sam. 10–12).

Amnon raped Tamar, his half sister, and was killed by Absalom, her brother. Absalom was exiled to Geshur, but later allowed to return to Jerusalem, where eventually he was reconciled with David (II Sam. 13–14). Still later he led an uprising against David which was temporarily successful. David fled to Mahanaim in the Transjordan, and Absalom ruled in Jerusalem for a time. Absalom's army was defeated, Absalom killed, and David restored on the throne. Absalom's rebellion was followed by another less successful rebellion instigated by Sheba, a Benjaminite (II Sam. 15–20).

David executed Saul's male descendants in connection with a famine (II Sam. 21:1–14). There was further warfare with the Philistines (vs. 15–22). David delivered psalms of praise because Yahweh had delivered him out of the hands of his enemies and of Saul (II Sam. 22:1–23:7). Yahweh incited David to make a census of his realm and then punished David for doing so. The punishment consisted of three days of pestilence on the kingdom (II Sam. 24).

When David reached old age, was failing in health, and was no longer potent, Adonijah proceeded to assume the throne. Nathan brought the matter to Bathsheba's attention and together they influenced David to designate Solomon as his successor instead of Adonijah. Solomon was crowned in a ceremony orchestrated by Nathan and Zadok (I Kings 1–2).

Characteristics of the David Section of the Genesis-II Kings Account. Three observations that we have made about the nature of the Genesis-II Kings account need to be reemphasized and applied more specifically to this David section. (1) The Genesis-II Kings account is composite, and the various traditions that have been combined and intertwined to produce this David section can best be described, with some exceptions, as folk legends. Certainly they are not to be read as historical record. (2) Both the individual traditions that comprise this David section of the Genesis-II Kings account and the compilers' editorial contributions reflect a definite pro-Davidic and pro-Solomonic bias. (3) Not only the selection and the tone but also the arrangement of these materials has been determined to a significant degree by the theological interests of the late Judean compilers. Let us explore each of these three points in further detail.

1. The composite nature of the Genesis-II Kings presentation of David's career is apparent from the beginning. First we are told that David was brought to Saul's court as a musician to play before Saul and soothe his tormented mind. Once there, he became Saul's armor-bearer as well (I Sam. 16:14–23). But then the scene changes and we find David still at home in Bethlehem, from which he is sent to take food to his brothers serving in Saul's army. Having reached the battlefront, David accepts Goliath's challenge and kills the giant, whereupon Saul inquires who the lad is.

> When Saul saw David go forth against the Philistine, he said to Abner, the commander of the army, "Abner, whose son is this youth?" And Abner said, "As your soul lives, O king, I cannot tell." And the king said, "Inquire whose son the stripling is." And as David returned from the slaughter of the Philistine, Abner took him, and brought him before Saul with the head of the Philistine in his hand. And Saul said to him, "Whose son are you, young man?" And David answered, "I am the son of your servant Jesse the Bethlehemite." (I Sam. 17:55–58)

At least three details in the Goliath story suggest that originally it was told independently of the preceding story and of materials that follow in I-II Samuel: *(a)* If David previously had entered service as Saul's personal musician and armor-bearer, why then was he not already with Saul at the beginning of the Goliath episode rather than back home in Bethlehem? And why does Saul not know who David is? *(b)* I Samuel 17:54 states that David took Goliath's head to Jerusalem. According to II Sam. 5:6–10, however, Jerusalem would not yet have been in Israelite hands. *(c)* In contrast to this delightful story which relates how the lad David killed Goliath, II Sam. 21:19 credits another Bethlehemite, Elhanan, the son of Jaareoregin, with killing Goliath.

Conflicting items such as these are noticeable throughout the I Samuel 16–I Kings 2 presentation of David's career. They are to be attributed to the fact that this segment of the Genesis-II Kings account is, as the remainder of the account, composed of various originally independent traditions. The basic compositional units which we recognize in this David section of the Genesis-II Kings account are summarized in Chart V.

Folk themes, such as the lad killing the giant with a sling stone (I Sam. 17) and the young hero winning the hand of the king's daughter in marriage by overcoming impossible odds (I Sam. 18:20–29), remind us that we are dealing with largely legendary materials. This is particularly true of the collection of stories pertaining to David's rise to power. Admittedly, the other large block of material that comprises this David section of the Genesis-II Kings account (II Sam. 9–20; I Kings 1–2) is surprisingly free of obvious legendary elements and overt theological commentary. Indeed it gives the appearance of having been written by someone who was rather close to the royal family and who

---

CHART V: Basic Compositional Units of I Samuel 16–I Kings 2

I Sam. 16– II Sam. 5	A collection of stories pertaining to David's rise to power, from his anointment by Samuel to the establishment of his rule in Jerusalem
II Sam. 6:1–23	The continuation and conclusion of the Ark Narrative, the main part of which is to be found in I Sam. 4:1–7:2
II Sam. 7	A chapter essentially from the hands of the compilers of Genesis-II Kings which emphasizes Yahweh's affirmation of David and his dynasty
II Sam. 8:1–15	A summary of David's military accomplishments and administrative officials
II Sam. 9–20; I Kings 1–2	An essentially continuous narrative which describes various problems faced by David during his reign and explains how it happened that Solomon, rather than any of the older brothers, succeeded David to the throne
II Sam. 21–24	Miscellaneous materials relevant to David's reign

recorded their ups and downs dispassionately. Upon close examination, how-ever, one begins to notice items in even this source which are more suggestive of the storyteller's art than of historical record. The reader is allowed to listen in on private conversations, for example, and to witness bedroom scenes. This is not the sort of information that would have been readily available even to persons close to the royal court.

Included with the legends and stories are occasional miscellaneous items such as psalms, lists, and brief reports. Some of these have a strong claim to authenticity—for example, the list of David's officials in II Sam. 8:16–18. Oth-ers are less convincing, such as the psalms attributed to him in II Sam. 1: 19–27 and 22:2–23:7. Finally, certain key passages are essentially the product of the late compilers of the Genesis-II Kings account and are intended to convey what they regarded to be the significance of David's reign in Israel's history. Consider II Samuel 7, for example, where Nathan, in a style very similar to the farewell addresses of Moses, Joshua, and Samuel, pronounces Yahweh's blessing on David's kingdom and promises that the Davidic dynasty will last forever. In the same way that Joshua's farewell address concludes the era of conquest in the compilers' perception of Israel's past and Samuel's last address concludes the era of the great judges, so also Nathan's dynastic oracle informs the reader that the true king and the true dynasty are finally in place. In effect, Nathan's oracle expresses the same Davidic-Jerusalemite theology presupposed in Ps. 89 and 132. It was on the basis of this royal theology that the Davidic dynasty claimed perpetual right to the throne, and no doubt the roots of this theological claim are to be sought in David's reign. The full expression of it, however, such as one finds in Nathan's oracle and the psalms, probably belongs to a later day.

2. Actually the route by which David gained access to the combined crown of Israel and Judah and the process by which Solomon instead of one of David's older sons inherited the throne raised serious questions about the legitimacy of their respective reigns and, by extension, the legitimacy of the whole Davidic line. The issue was still very much alive in the exilic and early postexilic periods —the time of the final compilation of the Genesis-II Kings account. While the Judean compilers of this account would have hoped for a restoration of Jerusa-lem and the reunion of Israel and Judah under a revived Davidic dynasty, others of the day, the Samaritans in particular, held no such allegiance to either Jerusa-lem or the house of David. Accordingly, I Samuel 16–II Samuel 7 serves as an apology for David's usurpation of the throne and functions as authenticating tradition to legitimate both the Davidic dynasty and the preeminence of Jerusa-lem in the life of the people and the plan of Yahweh. This section opens with the story of David's divine election and concludes with Yahweh's promise that David's dynasty will rule securely in Jerusalem forever.

The concern to legitimize David's usurpation of the throne of Israel, thus displacing Saul's descendants, is especially obvious in the passages that empha-size Jonathan's deference to David. Consider the scene described in I Sam. 18:4, for example, where Jonathan "stripped himself of the robe that was upon him, and gave it to David, and his armor, and even his sword and his bow and his girdle." The text comes close to portraying Jonathan's deed as an act of abdication to any claim to the throne (see also I Sam. 23:15–18). While there may have existed a close relationship between David and Jonathan, one must suspect that this theme has been intentionally magnified in the traditions as we have received them in order to justify the fact that David and his descendants did in fact end up with the throne. Similarly, the passages that emphasize David's unwavering loyalty to Saul on the grounds that Saul was "Yahweh's anointed" (I Sam. 26; especially v. 9) anticipate that David will replace Saul in this capacity. In effect, therefore, these passages call for the same unqualified loyalty to David and his descendants that David is depicted giving to Saul.

3. Not only the selection and the tone of the material in this David section but also its arrangement has been determined to a certain degree by the views that the compilers of Genesis-II Kings wished to convey. II Samuel 8, which describes David's domain and provides a list of his cabinet officers, serves in effect as the center of their presentation of his career. What precedes, as noted above, tells how David replaced Saul, established his own rule, acquired and turned Jerusalem into the center for his kingdom, and received from Yahweh the dynastic blessing and promise. What follows (with the exception of II Sam. 20–24 which contains various miscellaneous items relevant to David's reign but not integrated into the story line) concerns the fate of the rule of David and how that rule was transferred to Solomon. Broadly speaking, then, we are presented first with a victorious David on the rise and then a David troubled by political and family problems; first a David under the blessing and then a David under the curse.

The fact that the materials in I Samuel 16–I Kings 2 are arranged in accordance with a theological perception of David's reign means that the resulting story line does not necessarily represent the actual chronological sequence of events. For example, David's wars with the Philistines are reported after his conquest of Jerusalem, and in that context seem intended to illustrate the military successes of the divinely chosen king now firmly established in the divinely chosen capital (II Sam. 5:17–25). One has to suspect, however, that the Philistines would have reacted to David's maneuvers before he conquered Jerusalem, and in fact the passage in question actually connects the beginning of the Philistine wars with David's acceptance of the crown of Israel rather than with his conquest of Jerusalem (see v. 17). In short, David probably had already had to deal with Philistine hostilities while he was ruling in Hebron.

Absalom's and Sheba's rebellions are reported near the end of the Genesis-II Kings presentation of David's career, thus leaving the impression that these incidents occurred fairly late in his reign, the time of "David under the curse." Yet it makes more sense to suppose that such challenges to David's authority would have occurred earlier, while he may have been less secure on the throne. Note also that when David, fleeing from Absalom, arrived in the Transjordan, he was greeted and aided by Shobi son of the Ammonite king Nahash. This is the sort of response one might expect before, but certainly not after, Nahash's death and David's ensuing war against the Ammonites (II Sam. 10:2–3; 17: 27–29).

A similar case can be made regarding David's execution of Saul's descendants, reported among the miscellaneous items at the end of II Samuel. Surely David would have had to deal with this potential threat early in his reign also. Three additional arguments may be marshaled for this position: *(a)* Probably there would not have been a long time lapse between Saul's offense against the Gibeonites and the famine which was attributed to the offense and served as the pretext of David's action (II Sam. 21:1–6). *(b)* The account of David's dealings with Mephibosheth presupposes that he was the only remaining descendant of Saul, the others presumably having already been executed (II Sam. 9; 21:7). *(c)* The arrangements regarding Mephibosheth, on the other hand, were already in place at the time of Absalom's rebellion (II Sam. 16:1–4).

The Chronicler's Presentation of David's Reign

The Chronicles account begins with Adam and follows the affairs of Judah through the fall of Jerusalem. Actually it carries the story a bit farther than does the Genesis-II Kings account, taking notice of Cyrus' decree to rebuild the Temple in Jerusalem after the Persians had replaced the Babylonians as the major Near Eastern power (in 538 B.C.E.). For the time from Adam through Saul, however, covered in I Chronicles 1–9, the Chronicler provides little more than a collection of genealogical lists, some of which provide data related to the period even after the exile. (See, for example, the list of royal descendants in I Chron. 3:17–24 and the list of returnees from exile in I Chron. 9.) Only occasionally are tidbits of nongenealogical information interspersed among these lists (see, for example, I Chron. 4:38–43; 5:23–26).

The material in I Chronicles 10 and following overlaps Samuel-Kings, often even verbally, beginning with Saul's death on Mt. Gilboa (compare, for example, I Chron. 10 with I Sam. 31). Clearly the Chronicler had access to the material of Samuel-Kings in essentially its present form and relied very heavily upon it. In fact, one might describe the Chronicles account of Israelite and Judean history as a more theologized version (a midrash) of that portion of the Genesis-II Kings account. The Chronicler, however, was more specifically interested in cultic and religious affairs than were the compilers of Genesis-II Kings, thus giving special attention to the life and organization of the Jerusalem Temple and its personnel. The work especially highlights the role of the Levites in the Jerusalem cult. The Chronicler also focuses in more narrowly on the Davidic dynasty and the kingdom of Judah than did the compilers of Genesis-II Kings, to the extent that the affairs of the northern Israelite kingdom which emerged after Solomon's death are virtually ignored.

Since the Chronicler's treatment depends so heavily on Samuel-Kings, it shares also in the limitations and difficulties of the latter for purposes of historical reconstruction. Moreover, comparison of parallel texts in Samuel-Kings and Chronicles reveals that the Chronicler often took extreme liberties with the Samuel-Kings material. Frequently numbers are exaggerated, miraculous features are introduced into the stories, religious aspects are emphasized, unedifying features about the prominent heroes are played down or bypassed, and the evils of antiheroes are stressed.

The Chronicler's tendentious use of the Samuel-Kings material is especially obvious in his treatment of David, who, for the Chronicler, is the great Israelite hero. There is no substantial description of the struggles between Saul and David, nor is David's early career covered in any significant fashion. It is hardly mentioned, for example, that David was in the service of the Philistines at the time of the battle of Gilboa, that Ish-bosheth ruled after Saul until assassinated, and that David was crowned first by the elders of Judah and only later by the Israelites. Instead, the Chronicler emphasizes that David received widespread support while at Ziklag, Mt. Gilboa, and Hebron, and leaves the reader to infer that the crown was passed on to David almost routinely immediately following Saul's death (I Chron. 10–12).

Perhaps the most characteristic feature of the Chronicler's presentation of David is that he credits David with being the real organizer of the Temple cult, its staff, and especially of the Levitical functionaries associated with the Temple and the Ark (I Chron. 15–16; 23–26). In fact, the Chronicler would have us suppose that David planned the entire construction of the Temple and passed along the plans and provisions to Solomon (I Chron. 28–29). This is in striking contrast to the Genesis-II Kings presentation, which allows David a much less significant role in the organization of the Jerusalem cult. To be sure, both II Samuel 6 and I Chronicles 15–16 testify that David brought the Ark to Jerusalem, and the stories in I Samuel stress David's musical capabilities (see I Sam. 16–18); but otherwise his role in setting up the primary features of Jerusalemite worship go unnoticed in Samuel. I Kings 6–7 clearly assigns to Solomon the planning and execution of Temple construction.

Finally, it is noticeable that none of the troubles of David's reign—the Bathsheba affair, Absalom's and Sheba's rebellions, the struggles between Adonijah and Solomon—are noted by the Chronicler. The transition to Solomon's rule is made under David's supervision and without incident (I Chron. 23:1; 29:22). In short, then, the Chronicler presents us with a highly idealized David who was a great warrior, who was the founder of the Temple with its associated religious orders and institutions, and whose reign was virtually free of internal conflicts from beginning to end.

The Chronicler clearly had access to the material in Samuel-II Kings, drew upon this heavily and selectively, but also introduced some material here and there which has no parallel in Samuel-Kings. Much of this supplementary material amounts to theological exposition. But occasionally there are items of substance which may have been derived from other sources which the Chronicler had at hand. In connection with David, for example, the Chronicler provides lists of:

> Men who came to David at Ziklag (I Chron. 12:1–7)

> Men who deserted Saul and joined David at the time of the battle at Mt. Gilboa (I Chron. 12:19–22)

> Fighting men who came to Hebron to crown David king (I Chron. 12:23–40)

> Levitical heads of families charged with attending the Ark and other cultic responsibilities (I Chron. 15:2–27; 23:3–26:32)

> Military officers, tribal chiefs, overseers of the king's treasuries and possessions, and so on (I Chron. 27)

In light of the obviously tendentious way in which the Chronicler used the Samuel-Kings materials, serious questions must be raised about the trustworthiness of these materials supplied in Chronicles but without parallels in Samuel-II Kings. It is not a question just of whether the Chronicler had access to other authentic sources no longer available today but of whether he also used whatever other sources he had at hand in the same tendentious fashion that he used the Samuel-Kings material. These lists which the Chronicler associates with David's reign may have been derived from authentic sources, for example, but sources which in fact had to do with a much later period of time than David's day.

David and the Psalms

David is associated by tradition with the book of Psalms, and in fact the superscriptions of seventy-three of the psalms (in the Masoretic Hebrew manuscripts) include the notation *ledawid.* This is usually translated "of David"—that is, with the inference that David composed these particular psalms. In thirteen of these "Davidic" psalms, moreover, the superscriptions report the circumstances under which David supposedly wrote or sang the psalm (Ps. 3; 7; 18; 34; 51–52; 54; 56–57; 59–60; 63; 142). If we do indeed have at hand psalms written by David, then this amounts to another valuable source of information about his life, and even his attitudes. Unfortunately the situation is not so simple.

In the first place, the preposition *le* of *ledawid* may be translated other ways ("for," "concerning," "dedicated to," and so on) which would not necessarily suggest authorship. The term *dawid,* on the other hand, which is not even necessarily to be taken as a proper noun, may refer to the Davidic dynasty in general rather than specifically to David himself (see Ezek. 34:23–24; 37: 24–25). Thus *ledawid* in the superscriptions of the psalms could mean simply that these particular psalms were connected in some way with the Davidic court, with the Jerusalem Temple (which was the Davidic chapel par excellence), with royal usage, or perhaps with a special royal collection of the psalms.

Second, while David may actually have had musical ability and probably did play some role in establishing the personnel and procedures of the Jerusalem cult (see I Sam. 16:14–22; Amos 6:5), it seems clear that his image as a musician and cultic innovator did not blossom until fairly late in Judean history and in the end bore little resemblance to the real David. We have already noted this as one of the ways in which the Chronicler's presentation of David differs from that of Genesis-II Kings. While the latter has very little to say about David's involvement with music or the cult, for the Chronicler this was the most important aspect of David's career. The final compilation of the Psalter belongs to the Chronicler's era or later, so it is not surprising that David is given pride of place in the editorial superscriptions to the psalms. Moreover, the later the version, the more numerous the psalms assigned to David. In fact, one of the Psalms manuscripts discovered among the Dead Sea Scrolls (11QPs^a) credits David with having written 4,050 psalms and contains previously unknown "autobiographical" psalms of David.

In short, the superscriptions which presuppose that David composed many of the psalms and seek to explain the circumstances under which he did so represent late speculative attempts to relate the feelings of trouble and distress reflected in the psalms to episodes in David's life. Even if it could be established that David wrote the *ledawid* psalms and that the superscriptions are authentic, the Psalter still would provide relatively little specific information about David's career. The psalms are poetry and generally speak in metaphorical, typical, and generalized language which provides few or no specific historical details.

Utilizing the Biblical Materials About David for Historical Reconstruction

While the Bible has much to say about David, it will be obvious from the preceding observations that none of the biblical material pertaining to him submits easily to critical historical inquiry. By the same measure, any attempt to describe the "historical" David will involve a great deal of subjective judgment, and our attempt below is no exception. It will be useful to identify in advance, therefore, some of the interpretative principles that we employ.

1. Our treatment of David will depend primarily on the Genesis-II Kings account. Certainly this account is to be given precedence over the Chronicler's presentation when the two parallel each other. But even items unique to the Chronicler will be regarded with extreme caution—especially where it appears that they were introduced to support the Chronicler's characteristic views.

2. While most of the traditions that comprise even the Genesis-II Kings presentation of David are folk legends from pro-Davidic Judean circles and with late editorial overlay, our treatment below presupposes that many, perhaps most, of these traditions are based ultimately on actual historical persons and events. This presupposition cannot be proved, and there are no extrabiblical sources from the period to serve as "outside control." There are no extrabiblical documents from the period that even mention David, for example; and the

archaeological information for David's reign is still essentially the same as that described for the early tribal period. Namely, while the relevant archaeological data are useful for gaining an understanding of the physical conditions and general life-style of Early Iron Age Palestine, the evidence collected thus far is not very useful for clarifying matters of historical detail. Several Iron I sites have been excavated that would have been included in David's kingdom (Jerusalem, for example). Yet it still would be difficult to establish with absolute certainty that any particular floor level, wall, city gate, or whatever actually dates specifically from his reign.

3. Presupposing that many of these folk traditions preserve a kernel of historical memory is only the first step. Attempting to separate the historical from the legendary and editorial overlay involves an even greater degree of subjectivity. We will attempt to explain as we proceed why and how we reach the particular conclusions that we do. In the final analysis, however, we must concede that the treatment of David which follows is simply "our best guess."

David in Saul's Court

David was a Judahite from Bethlehem. The Book of Ruth concludes with a genealogy (paralleled in I Chron. 2:9–20) that identifies Ruth, a Moabite, as his grandmother. His father, Jesse, is referred to both as a Bethlehemite (I Sam. 16:1, 18) and as an Ephrathite (I Sam. 17:12; see also Ruth 1:2). The frequent references to Jesse in the David materials may suggest that he was the head of a prominent Bethlehemite family, perhaps even a local chieftain.

The name Bethlehem ("temple of Lehem") would have derived from a local sanctuary, while Ephrathah presumably was the name of the dominant local clan. Whether there was any connection between the name Ephrathah as associated with Bethlehem and the same name that certain other passages clearly associate with Ephraim (Judg. 12:5; I Sam. 1:1; I Kings 11:26; Ps. 132:6) is less clear. Possibly the Ephrathites of Bethlehem were a subgroup of Ephraimite Ephrathites who had migrated south at some point. Note that the northerners in II Sam. 5:1 speak of David as their "bone and flesh." In any case, the notations in Gen. 35:19 and 48:7 which assume that the Ephrathah of Ephraim associated with Rachel's burial was identical with Ephrathah/Bethlehem is misleading. These were two different locales.

As seen above, we are presented with conflicting explanations as to how it happened that David came to Saul's court. Actually there are three separate stories, each of which focuses on a particular characteristic of what must be regarded as the legendary and ideal David. The first of the three stories (I Sam. 16:1–13) describes how David, as an innocent shepherd boy, was selected and anointed by Samuel to be Saul's successor. The emphasis here is on David the unpretentious lad "chosen of Yahweh" for greatness. In folkloric fashion, seven older brothers are passed over, young David is selected, and his career thrust upon him. The second story (I Sam. 16:14–23) depicts David as a musician called to Saul's court to soothe the king's nerves. This story corresponds of course to the tradition that associates David with Israel's cultic music. Finally, the third story (I Sam. 17) presents David as the giant killer, the naïve and unpromising lad who, because of his naïveté and simple faith, was able to "save the day" for Israel. Here again we recognize a very common folklore motif, including the ending of the story: David is to be rewarded with great riches, power, and the daughter of the king in marriage (see v. 25). The fact that II Sam. 21:19 attributes Goliath's death to a certain Elhanan is further warning that the story in I Samuel 17 is a folk tradition of doubtful historical value.

Probably David came to Saul's court as a young professional soldier—note that the second story cited above has him serving as Saul's armor-bearer (I Sam. 16:21). In any case, after joining Saul's service he made a name for himself as a gallant and successful warrior in skirmishes against the Philistines (I Sam. 18:5, 30; 19:8). Soon, we are told, his fame as a Philistine fighter began to surpass even that of Saul.

> As they were coming home, when David returned from slaying the Philistine, the women came out of all the cities of Israel, singing and dancing, to meet King Saul, with timbrels, with songs of joy, and with instruments of music. And the women sang to one another as they made merry,
> "Saul has slain his thousands,
> and David his ten thousands."
> (I Sam. 18:6–7)

In addition to his general popularity in Saul's court, David is pictured as having an intimate and favored relationship with Saul's own family (I Sam. 18:1–4, 20). We are told that a strong bond of friendship existed particularly between David and Jonathan, Saul's son and the heir apparent (I Sam. 18:1–4, 20; 23:16–18). In addition, Saul's daughter Michal is said to have loved David and was given to him in marriage (I Sam. 18:20–27). It is difficult to know how to assess the texts that emphasize this relationship. Presumably there is a kernel of truth in them, although one must suspect that the matter has been overplayed somewhat in an effort to legitimize David's usurpation of the throne. Namely, these texts seek to convince the reader that (1) David was innocent of any designs on the throne, (2) that Saul's own son and daughter were satisfied that David was to have the throne, and (3) David was practically a member of the family anyway.

It may well be also that Saul encouraged marriage between his daughter Michal and David. The manner in which the story is told in I Sam. 18:17–19, however, with the folkloric motif of the young man who acquires the king's daughter by performing a seemingly impossible deed and in spite of the monarch's machinations, suggests that it plays rather loose with the actual historical circumstances of the marriage. Possibly the marriage was arranged before David had become so exceedingly popular that Saul began to regard him as a threat. Such a marriage between the daughter of the house of a budding monarchy and the son of a prominent family in a region where the king's authority was still uncertain would have made good sense.

The stress in the biblical materials on David's military success, his popularity among the people, and his close relationship with Saul's family contrasts noticeably with the negative fashion in which Saul is depicted. On the one hand, we are presented with a humble, obedient, and even naïve but highly successful David. On the other hand, we encounter Saul as a melancholic paranoid who was suspicious of the success of his own soldier. To substantiate this, in good literary fashion but with doubtful historical basis, the narrators appeal to what Saul personally thought and felt (I Sam. 18:8–12), record his blundering attempts to kill David (I Sam. 18:10–11; 19:8–10) or to get him killed (I Sam. 18:17–29), and report the content of secret and private conversations (I Sam. 18:20–26; 19:1–6).

Here again one must suspect that the biblical traditions as they have been handed down to us rather overdo it. No doubt Saul did become jealous and greatly concerned as the young David's popularity increased. Saul himself had been hailed as king as a result of his military success, and the very concept of monarchy was not yet firmly established among the Israelites. Saul would have been well aware, therefore, that any exceedingly successful and popular military hero posed a threat, if not to his own hold on the throne, then certainly to Jonathan's chances of succeeding him. But while it is reasonable to suppose that Saul's jealousy and concern to ensure dynastic succession were factors in the Saul-David conflict, one senses that David's ambitions were also a contributory cause. This is suggested, if for no other reason, by the fact that the narrators of the stories in I-II Samuel seem so concerned to convince us otherwise.

Eventually David left Saul's court and organized a rebel army which operated along the fringes of the southern hill country. Again the narrators of the biblical account insist that it was Saul's blind jealousy which forced David to flee and emphasize that the escape was aided by Michal, Jonathan, Samuel, and the priests at Nob (I Sam. 19:11–23; 20; 21:1–9). But again one must wonder, as Saul apparently suspected, whether this was not a calculated move on David's part. If there is any historical basis to Samuel's denunciations of Saul (see I Sam. 13:8–15; 15:10–31), then these may have helped convince David that the time was ripe to withdraw from the court and begin to form a counterforce to Saul's reign.

David the Renegade

Having withdrawn from the royal court, David spent a period of time, the length of which cannot be determined, as a renegade, on the run from Saul. (See Map 14.) This period of his career is treated in I Sam. 19:11–II Sam. 1. Although the narratives that comprise these chapters do not necessarily represent the exact chronological sequence of events, they do seem to suggest the following four phases:

1. David escapes from Saul's court (I Sam. 19:11–21:15)

2. David hides in the vicinity of Adullam and is joined by others (I Sam. 22:1–23:14)

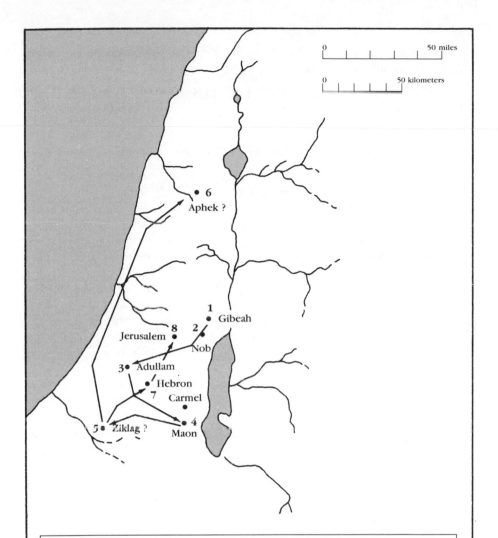

1. In Saul's court.

2. Escapes with the help of the priests of Nob.

3. David hides in the vicinity of Adullam. Others join him.

4. Saul learns David's position. David escapes to the "wilderness" area east of Carmel and Maon.

5. With Saul close on his trail, David goes over to Achish, the Philistine ruler of Gath. Achish assigns the city of Ziklag to David and his men.

6. David marches with the Philistines to Aphek, where they will defeat Saul and the Israelite army. Unsure of his loyalties, the Philistines do not allow David to join them in the battle.

7. With Saul and Jonathan dead, David and his men move into Hebron, where the Judahites crown him king. Later the remnant of Saul's Israelite kingdom accept David as their king also.

8. After ruling at Hebron for seven years, David conquers Jerusalem and makes it his capital.

MAP 14. David's Moves from Saul's Court to the Conquest of Jerusalem

3. David and his band roam at large in the wilderness east of Ziph, Carmel, and Maon (I Sam. 23:15–26:25)

4. David places himself and his army in the service of the Philistines (I Sam. 27–II Sam. 1)

Escape from Saul's Court

I Sam. 19:11–21:9 is composed of essentially four narratives that feature respectively Michal, Samuel, Jonathan, and Ahimelech of the priests of Nob, and describe how each of these persons aided David in his flight from Saul's court. The story of how Michal stalled Saul's soldiers while David escaped through a window (I Sam. 19:11–17) and the one about how David received provisions at Nob (I Sam. 21:1–9) are somewhat more convincing than the ones that involve Samuel and Jonathan (I Sam. 19:18–20:42). All four of the stories find their setting at Gibeah (present-day Jeba) or in the immediate vicinity. Ramah, Samuel's home (present-day er-Ram), was on the opposite side of the hill from Gibeah. Naioth (the exact meaning of which is uncertain) apparently was a camp of some sort at Ramah. Nob probably is to be identified with Mt. Scopus northeast of Jerusalem and only five or six miles south by southwest of Gibeah.

The follow-up narrative (I Sam. 21:10–15), which has David going over to the Philistines at this point, is obscure, probably a confusion of two separate traditions: the one about David and Ahimelech of Nob (note that the superscription to Ps. 34 has David playing the madman before Abimelech [= Ahimelech]) and the other about David's later alliance with the Philistines (I Sam. 27 and following). Our guess is that David slipped away from Gibeah with Michal's help, received provisions from Ahimelech of Nob without the latter realizing that he was "on the run," and headed straight for the tribal territory of Judah.

David in Adullam and Vicinity

Saul apparently did not pursue David immediately after the latter's flight from the court. In the meantime, David transferred his parents to Moab for their safety and secured himself at Adullam (Tell Sheikh Madhkur in the Shephelah; read "stronghold" rather than "cave" in I Sam. 22:1). There he was joined by individuals of various sorts—kinsmen, opponents of Saul, other persons "on the run" for one reason or another—so that soon he was in command of a small private army (I Sam. 22:1–2).

At least two religious functionaries also joined David's troop at this stage. One was the prophet Gad, a shadowy figure, who is pictured offering David advice about strategy (I Sam. 22:5) and who apparently remained with David throughout their careers (see II Sam. 24:11). Specifically, Gad convinced David to remove himself and his men from Adullam and camp in the forest of Hereth. (While the location of this forest is uncertain, it must have been in the same general vicinity. Possibly the name is preserved in that of present-day Kharas, approximately five miles southeast of Adullam / Tell Sheikh Madhkur.) The new campsite had a double advantage. It was less conspicuous—a forest rather than a known fortification—and it was in the territory of Judah, David's own tribe. Apparently Adullam was outside Judean territory (see I Sam. 22:5).

The other religious functionary who joined David at this stage was Abiathar, sole survivor of a ruthless massacre of the priests of Nob. As it turned out, David had been seen at Nob by Doeg, an Edomite in the service of King Saul. Doeg reported this to Saul, who jumped to the conclusion that the Nob priests were in conspiracy with David and ordered their execution (I Sam. 22:6–23).

Finally Saul learned that David was in the Adullam area as the result of an incident reported in I Sam. 23:1–5. Philistine raiders were robbing the threshing floors of the people of Keilah (present-day Khirbet Qila, also near Adullam), whereupon David and his men came and chased the Philistines away. This was a daring move, and the text suggests that some of David's men regarded it as bad judgment: "But David's men said to him, 'Behold, we are afraid here in Judah; how much more then if we go to Keilah against the armies of the Philistines?' " (v. 3). Having chased away the Philistine raiders, therefore, David now faced a double danger, especially if he and his men remained in Keilah. The Philistines could be expected to return in force; and Saul, who now knew David's whereabouts, began preparing a campaign against the city. Much depended upon whether David and his men could trust the people of Keilah.

> And Saul summoned all the people to war, to go down to Keilah, to besiege David and his men. David knew that Saul was plotting evil against him; and he said to Abiathar the priest, "Bring the ephod here." Then said David, . . . "Will the men of Keilah surrender me and my men into the hand of Saul?" And Yahweh said, "They will surrender you." Then David and his men, who were about six hundred, arose and departed from Keilah, and they went wherever they could go. When Saul was told that David had escaped from Keilah, he gave up the expedition. And David remained in the strongholds in the wilderness, in the hill country of the Wilderness of Ziph. And Saul sought him every day, but God did not give him into his hand. (I Sam. 23:8–14)

This text makes clear that David and his band could not rely upon the support of the citizens of Keilah and vicinity.

Roaming the Wilderness of Ziph

Fleeing Keilah, David and his men sought refuge in the barren southeastern slopes of the southern hill country, primarily the area between the villages of Ziph, Carmel, and Maon (present-day Tell Zif, Khirbet el-Kirmil, and Tell Ma'in) and the Dead Sea. This was on the southeastern fringe of Saul's area of influence. Saul had set up a monument for himself in Carmel (I Sam. 15:12) and, as we shall see below, persons such as Nabal of Maon seem to have recognized Saul's authority in the area. David's army is reported to have numbered six hundred fighting men by this time, but this seems excessive. It is difficult to see how he would have maintained such a number in this desolate "wilderness" region without support from the local people, which he obviously did not have, or without conducting successful raids, which would hardly have been possible with Saul in close pursuit. In fact, the stories that pertain to this phase of his career (I Sam. 23:15–26:25) reflect precisely these two themes: the lack of support David received from the local people in the areas where he and his men roamed and his narrow escapes from Saul.

Three of the stories about this period follow essentially the same pattern (I Sam. 23:19–29; 24; and 26). Each begins with the local people (Ziphites in two of the instances) reporting David's location to Saul. Then Saul arrives on the scene with a large army and it appears that David and his men surely will be captured. The three stories diverge from that point, but with essentially the same result in each case—Saul withdraws voluntarily, leaving David and his men at large. The story in I Sam. 23:19–29 has Saul withdrawing from the chase in order to deal with Philistine raiders elsewhere in his domain. The stories in I Sam. 24 and I Sam. 26 both describe scenes in which David declines opportunities to kill Saul and thus demonstrates his loyalty to "Yahweh's anointed," whereupon Saul confesses that he has misjudged David and withdraws. Probably these stories represent three versions of a single incident, in which case we regard the one in I Sam. 23:19–29 as the more convincing. The other two are more novelistic in their style, their scenarios as to how David spared Saul's life are hardly plausible, and their emphases on David's loyalty to Saul in his capacity as "Yahweh's anointed" sound too much like pro-Davidic propaganda.

The story about Nabal in I Sam. 25:1–42 further illustrates that the local inhabitants of the region looked primarily to Saul for protection and regarded David as a nuisance. In the story, Nabal, a Calebite rich in sheep and goats, lived in Maon but often grazed his flocks at nearby Carmel. On one occasion when Nabal was in Carmel for sheep-shearing, David sent ten men with the following message:

> I hear that you have shearers; now your shepherds have been with us, and we did them no harm, and they missed nothing, all the time they were in Carmel. . . . Therefore let my young men find favor in your eyes; for we come on a feast day. Pray, give whatever you have at hand to your servants and to your son David. (I Sam. 25:7–8)

In short, David suggested that payment was due in return for protection that he and his men had provided. Nabal responded with incredulity: "Who is David? Who is the son of Jesse? There are many servants nowadays who are breaking away from their masters" (I Sam. 25:10). David, upon receiving Nabal's reply, repeated the claim that he had been providing Nabal with a significant service and threatened to take drastic action.

> Now David had said, "Surely in vain have I guarded all that this fellow has in the wilderness, so that nothing was missed of all that belonged to him; and he has returned me evil for good. God do so to the enemies of David and more also, if

by morning I leave so much as one male of all who belong to him." (I Sam. 25:21–22)

As it turned out, Abigail, Nabal's wife, took matters into her own hands and sent David a caravan of supplies which included "two hundred loaves, and two skins of wine, and five sheep ready dressed, and five measures of parched grain, and a hundred clusters of raisins, and two hundred cakes of figs" (I Sam. 25:18). Now it was Nabal's turn to be angry, and he seems to have died a rather mysterious death soon thereafter: "His heart died within him, and he became as a stone. And about ten days later Yahweh smote Nabal; and he died" (I Sam. 25:37–38). The story ends with David marrying Abigail.

David took another wife from this area also, Ahinoam from Jezreel. The fact that her name was the same as that of one of Saul's wives (I Sam. 14:50) is probably only a coincidence, as is the coincidence that her village, Jezreel (compare Josh. 15:55–56), had the same name as the more prominent Jezreel of the Jezreel Valley.

David with the Philistines

Apparently realizing that he would not be able to elude Saul indefinitely, David took a drastic step. He and his band of followers entered the service of Achish, the Philistine king of Gath (I Sam. 27:1–4). Achish was no doubt familiar with David's recent activities and recognized the opportunity to formalize the split in Saul's ranks. As a vassal of the Philistine ruler, on the other hand, David secured what previously had eluded him, a stable base of operations beyond the reach of Saul. Specifically, Achish gave David the city of Ziklag, whose exact location is unknown, but clearly it was somewhere in the southern Shephelah or western Negeb—that is, on the frontier between Philistine territory and the southern hill country. Ziklag would remain crown property for the Davidic dynasty in years to come (I Sam. 27:5–7).

David's commitment to Achish was probably threefold. He would have been responsible for protecting this part of the Philistine frontier. In case of Philistine mobilization his troops would have been expected to fight under Philistine banners (see I Sam. 29:1–2). Finally, he would have been expected to engage in raids on the enemies of the Philistines, particularly the Judahite, Jerahmeelite, and Kenite villages in the nearby hill country and the Negeb. We are told that David remained in the service of Achish for a year and four months, presumably until the death of Saul on Mt. Gilboa (I Sam. 27:7), and that throughout that period he systematically deceived Achish by raiding farther south.

> Now David and his men went up, and made raids upon the Geshurites, the Girzites, and the Amalekites . . . as far as Shur, to the land of Egypt. . . . When Achish asked, "Against whom have you made a raid today?" David would say, "Against the Negeb of Judah," or "Against the Negeb of the Jerahmeelites," or, "Against the Negeb of the Kenites." And David saved neither man nor woman alive, to bring tidings to Gath, thinking, "Lest they should tell about us, and say, 'So David has

done.' " . . . And Achish trusted David, thinking, "He has made himself utterly abhorred by his people Israel; therefore he shall be my servant always." (I Sam. 27:8–12)

In short, this text claims that David never really preyed on his own people while serving the Philistines. The narrative in I Samuel 30 suggests that David used his vassal service to protect them and that on at least one occasion he shared the spoils of a victory with certain Judahite, Jerahmeelite, and Kenite villages. Only about half of the villages listed (see I Sam. 30: 27–31) can be located with any degree of certainty. Those which can be identified were situated south and southeast of Hebron.

When the Philistine troops massed at Aphek for a major confrontation with Saul, David and his troops were on hand with Achish ready to fight with the Philistines against the Israelites. The other Philistine rulers, however, were leery of "these Hebrews," fearing that in battle they might shift sides as had the Hebrews at the battle of Michmash (I Sam. 29:1–10; compare 14:21). Thus David was dismissed from the battlefield and saved from what could only have been an embarrassment, if not an impediment in his later rise to kingship over Israel.

From Philistine Vassal to King of Jerusalem

Saul emerged on the scene as a Philistine fighter, as we have seen in Chapter 4, and his kingdom consisted of a loosely defined and administered territory whose inhabitants looked to him for protection. With the Philistine victory at Mt. Gilboa and the deaths of Saul and his sons, the kingdom was left in a state of shock. No doubt the Philistines took full advantage of the situation, raiding and plundering the villages of the Ephraimite/Benjaminite hill country. Ishbosheth withdrew to Mahanaim in the Transjordan, presumably for security reasons, and this left the southern hill country completely beyond the range of his influence. There was nothing to prevent the Philistines, or more specifically their vassal David, from moving in.

David as King of Judah

After David had sufficiently and publicly lamented the deaths of Saul and Jonathan (II Sam. 1:17–27), he and his followers, "every one with his household," moved into and occupied the city of Hebron and its surrounding villages (II Sam. 2:1–3). Thus controlling Hebron, and with Bethlehem already a stronghold of the family of Jesse, David and his supporters were now firmly in command of the two major cities of the southern hill country. Under these circumstances, "the men of Judah came [to Hebron], and there they anointed David king over the house of Judah" (II Sam. 2:4).

Although none of the details of the occasion are reported, two observations should be made. First, the statement that it was "the men of Judah" who anointed David as king suggests that anointment at this stage, or at least in this context, symbolized a formal recognition of David's kingship by the people rather than a special form of divine designation as is presupposed in the stories about Samuel's anointment of both Saul and David (I Sam. 10:1; 16:1–13; see also I Kings 1:39; II Kings 11:12; 23:30). That being the case, one may speculate that the transaction involved some understanding (possibly even negotiations) regarding the rights and responsibilities of the parties involved (see I Sam. 10:25). Second, "Judah" at this stage is to be understood as Judah proper, an individual tribe composed of clans settled in the vicinity of Mt. Judah. The broader concept of "Greater Judah" (see Chapter 3) would be the consequence of David's rule in Hebron rather than the basis of its inauguration.

David is said to have ruled from Hebron seven years and six months (II Sam. 5:4–5; I Kings 2:11 rounds this off to an even seven years). During that time he expanded his authority to include all of the southern hill country and much of the surrounding Shephelah, Negeb, and Judean Wilderness. After Solomon's death this broader realm, "Greater Judah," would represent the ideal boundaries of the separate kingdom of Judah. Correspondingly, as we observed in Chapter 3, there is a tendency in the biblical genealogies to subsume under the tribe of Judah various other clans and tribes whose territories fell within these ideal boundaries.

Transfer of the Remnant of Saul's Kingdom

One may assume that, at least for a time, David maintained good relations with the Philistines, who now had the remnant of Saul's kingdom encircled on the west and north. Presumably David still enjoyed good relations with the Moabites as well. And perhaps it was during his Hebron period that David established an alliance with Nahash, the king of Ammon and an old enemy of Israel and Saul (I Sam. 11; II Sam. 10:1–2; 17:27). Shortly after Saul's death David contacted the people of Jabesh-gilead, commending them for their heroic gallantry in rescuing Saul's body and alerting them to the fact that the Judahites had anointed him king (II Sam. 2:4b–7). The implication was obvious. Perhaps they should consider shifting their allegiance to him as well. Note also that David's marriage to Maacah, daughter of Talmai king of Geshur, Absalom's mother, occurred during the Hebron phase of his career (II Sam. 3:3). If we read "Geshurites" rather than "Ashurites" in II Sam. 2:9, it would appear that David allied himself through marriage with this, another of the regions claimed by Ish-bosheth. Finally, the narrative in II Sam. 2:12–32 implies that David began to encroach on Benjaminite territory. All of these developments are summed up in the statement that follows the narrative: "There was a long war between the house of Saul and the house of David; and David grew stronger and stronger, while the house of Saul became weaker and weaker" (II Sam. 3:1).

Thus by the time Abner began negotiations with David regarding the transfer to him of Saul's kingdom, only a remnant of that kingdom remained. It was without effective leadership or defense and was virtually surrounded by David and others with whom David enjoyed good relations. Then, as a final blow, both Abner and Ish-bosheth were assassinated. Given these circumstances, it is not surprising that the "elders of Israel" came to David at Hebron and anointed him as their king also. II Samuel 5:3 reports the undertaking in a minimum of words: "King David made a covenant with them at Hebron before Yahweh, and they anointed David king over Israel." The terms of this covenant are not even hinted at, but one would assume that they deal with administrative issues, including military and civil matters. Again, the anointing is said to have been performed by the elders "before Yahweh," that is, probably in a Yahwistic shrine in Hebron. Both Israel and Judah appear to have remained separate political entities, so that the unity of the two states was represented by the person of the king.

The Philistines must have already sensed that David was outgrowing vassal status. Now that he had accepted kingship over Israel, with the responsibility of defending the Israelites, they appropriately regarded him as an enemy. The two Philistine skirmishes reported in II Sam. 5:17–25 probably belong to this period, that is, to the time shortly after "the Philistines heard that David had been anointed king over Israel" (v. 17).

The setting of the two skirmishes was the Valley of Rephaim, the upper branches of the Sorek Valley which descend from the hill country near Jerusalem to the plain below. This was a logical entrance to the hill country for the Philistines and an area that David would have to control if he was to keep them out of Israelite territory. The site of his first victory, Baal-perazim, is unknown, although Josh. 17:15 refers to "the land of the Perizzites and the Rephaim" in a context that suggests proximity to the hill country of Ephraim. This might suggest one of the northern branches of the Sorek valley system, northwest of Jerusalem. The second victory is placed northwest of Jerusalem, in any case. We are told that David chased the Philistines from Geba (possibly to be read "Gibeon") to Gezer (II Sam. 5:25).

David, King of Jerusalem

Surely the most important move of David's career was his conquest of Jerusalem and choice of this city as the capital of his domain. Jerusalem was one of the old Bronze Age cities, although not a particularly prominent one. The isolated notice in Judg. 1:8, which claims that the men of Judah took Jerusalem at some early stage, is to be discounted, or perhaps understood as a misplaced reference to David's conquest of the city. Otherwise everything seems to suggest that Jerusalem had remained independent of Israelite or Judean connections, and in fact was in Jebusite hands when David took it. The Jebusites were one of the various population groups that inhabited the hill country along with the clans of Israel and Judah. Their name was derived from Jebus, a place in the immediate vicinity of, but not actually identical with, the Jerusalem of David's day. Specifically, David's Jerusalem would have been confined to Ophel, the slope immediately south of the present-day Jerusalem Temple Mount.

II Samuel 5:6–9, which reports David's capture of Jerusalem and subsequent building program in the city, is not entirely clear because of the uncertainty of the meaning of two crucial terms. Usually *sinnor* in v. 8 is translated "water shaft" with the idea that it refers to a tunnel cut through the rock beneath the city wall to the Gihon spring outside the wall. Thus defenders of the city would have had access from inside the city wall to the spring, the city's main water source. David's men presumably would have discovered the tunnel, gained surprise entry to the city through it, and captured the place without any prolonged siege or assault. In other words, David would have gained an undamaged, populated, and fortified city, strategically located between Israel and Judah, ideal for his capital. "The Millo" in II Sam. 5:9b may refer to a system of retaining walls which enabled him to expand the city down the slopes of Ophel. Later he would construct a palace with the aid of Phoenician workmen.

Since Saul had incorporated Gibeon and the associated Hivite cities into his realm, Jerusalem represented the last alien town of consequence separating Israelite and Judean territory. Situated on the central north-south watershed, the city undoubtedly had been a disruptive feature for Saul's kingdom. By the same measure, Jerusalem became for David an ideal administrative center for both Israel and Judah. It was located in the frontier zone between the two and unencumbered by previous ties with either. Also, built on the southern spur of a mountain and surrounded on three sides by valleys, Jerusalem offered a defendable location with a good water source.

While Jerusalem's lack of previous connections with either Israel or Judah was one of its advantages—thus, for example, less grounds for jealousy between the two—David was rightly concerned that his Jerusalem-based administration be understood as heir to the political and cultic traditions of both Israel and Judah, and more specifically as a linear continuation of Saul's kingdom. His most obvious step to achieve this was the transfer of the Ark, the old religious symbol of the Shilonite cult and the Elide line, to Jerusalem, where it was placed in a special tent erected for that purpose (II Sam. 6:17). Probably this transfer occurred soon after David's conquest of Jerusalem; it implied David's role as the new protector of the "national" cult and symbolized Jerusalem's replacement of Shiloh as the new religious center.

In addition to transferring the Ark to Jerusalem, thus emphasizing the continuity between Ephraim/Israel and his now Jerusalem-based kingdom, David seems to have given a prominent role in his government to the Levites, thus emphasizing a Jerusalem-Judah connection. The evidence for this comes primarily from the Chronicler, and particularly suggestive in this regard is I Chron. 26:30–32 which assigns sweeping administrative responsibilities to certain Hebronite families.

> Of the Hebronites, Hashabiah and his brethren, one thousand seven hundred men of ability, had the oversight of Israel westward of the Jordan for all the work of Yahweh and for the service of the king. Of the Hebronites, Jerijah was chief of the Hebronites of whatever genealogy or fathers' houses. . . . King David appointed

him and his brethren, two thousand seven hundred men of ability, heads of fathers' houses, to have the oversight of the Reubenites, the Gadites, and the half-tribe of the Manassites for everything pertaining to God and for the affairs of the king. (I Chron. 26:30–32)

Admittedly the Chronicler is not an entirely trustworthy source, particularly in view of his tendency to idealize David and the Levites. Yet there are other bits of evidence to be taken into account as well.

1. As noted in Chapter 3, Levitical groups were in existence before the rise of the monarchy. Some had close connections with the south, especially Bethlehem, David's hometown (Judg. 17:7–8; 19).

2. Joshua 21:1–42, paralleled by I Chron. 6:54–81, provides a highly schematic list of Levitical cities. (See below, Maps 15 and 18.) The list conforms to a twelve-tribe scheme, with forty-eight cities distributed evenly among the various tribes. A close look at the actual locations of the cities, however, reveals that they are not distributed in schematic fashion but tend to be clustered in areas where David expanded his rule beyond the tribal territories of the Ephraim/Israel group and Judah. Possibly this present schematic list is based on an older authentic one which indicated the cities from which Levites administered recently annexed territories.

3. Genesis 49:5–7 depicts the Levites as fierce, zealous, and scattered among the tribes. Possibly this zealousness involved special loyalty to the Davidic regime, and their scattering was due at least in part to administrative purposes. This Genesis passage includes the Simeonites alongside the Levites in its characterization, while I Chron. 4:24–33 (see also II Chron. 15:9) suggests that some population movement also occurred among the Simeonites during David's reign.

4. As we shall see below, when Israel rebelled from the Davidic kingdom following Solomon's death, one of the first acts of Jeroboam I was to appoint new priests who were not Levites (I Kings 12:31). This would have been a reasonable move if the Levites were known to have a special loyalty to the Davidic regime.

These factors combined suggest to us that David made heavy use in his administration of Levites, an emerging priestly group from Judah, particularly from Bethlehem, David's own hometown, and Hebron, his first capital. As employees of the state, they would have comprised a stratum of the administration loyal and devoted to the person of the king upon whom their livelihood depended. Throughout the kingdom, but especially in non-Israelite and non-Judean areas annexed by David, they would have been a means for securing control and enforcing policies. Possibly the Simeonites were used in some similar fashion.

While David's transference of the Ark to Jerusalem and the heavy use of Levites in his administration suggested continuity with Saul's Israelite-Judean kingdom, his regime clearly represented a great deal more. Indeed, it was a quite new development for the clans and villages who earlier had looked to Saul, and the difference had largely to do with the role of Jerusalem.

In the first place, the fact that Jerusalem had been conquered by David and his professional army meant that it became, in effect, crown property, "the City of David." The Jerusalemites had not voluntarily anointed him their king following negotiations or with stipulations of any sort. He became their king and they his subjects by conquest. Moreover, this style of monarchy would have been in keeping with the traditions of the Jerusalemites. Jerusalem, being one of the old Bronze Age cities that survived into the Iron Age, would have had a long history of autocratic and hereditary rule. Other Palestinian cities with this heritage eventually fell to David also—Shechem, Megiddo, Hazor, and others. Thus, while the clans and villages of Ephraim/Israel and Judah remained an important constituency of David's kingdom, they ceased to be the vital center of his monarchy. His was a Jerusalem-based kingdom which took on more and more the character of one of the old Bronze Age city-states.

Moreover, in spite of the presence of the Ark and the administrative role assigned to the Levites, David seems to have retained the indigenous Jerusalem cult with its local priestly lines and allowed it to become, in effect, a major component of the national cult. Unfortunately the crucial passages that have most bearing on the identity of priestly officials under David are problematic. II Samuel 8:17 lists David's two main priests as "Zadok the son of Ahitub and Ahimelech the son of Abiathar." The account of Saul's massacre of the Nob priests in I Samuel 22 identifies Abiathar as the son of Ahimelech rather than the other way around, however, and identifies this priestly line as descendants of Ahitub. Finally, to take the problem a step farther back, I Sam. 14:3 connects Ahitub with the house of Eli. Supposedly, then, both of David's top priests, Zadok and Ahimelech (Abiathar), would have belonged to the Elide line. All of this seems most unlikely, particularly in view of the Ark Narrative which goes to such length to explain how the Elide line came to an end before the Ark found its way to Jerusalem.

The information provided in these texts is not necessarily incompatible of course. There may have been more than one Ahitub. Also Abiathar may have had both a father and a son named Ahimelech, although Abiathar himself was still active in David's old age (I Kings 1:7; 2:26). More likely, however, at least in our opinion, the texts of I Sam. 14:3 and II Sam. 8:17 have undergone some editorial tampering, probably intended precisely for the purpose of connecting David's two chief priests with the Elide line. In other words, we suspect that the reference to "Ahitub, Ichabod's brother" has been introduced secondarily into I Sam. 14:3, so that originally the passage would have read simply "Ahijah . . . son of Phinchas, son of Eli." II Samuel 8:17, on the other hand, would have read something like "Zadok and Abiathar the son of Ahimelech."

If these two passages are corrected accordingly, David's two chief priests would have been Zadok and Abiathar; and we are left to suppose that they represented local priestly families of Jerusalem and nearby Nob (Mt. Scopus, which overlooks Jerusalem on the northeast). That Zadok represented the indigenous Jerusalem priesthood is suggested by two other passages, both admittedly obscure, which associate with pre-Davidic Jerusalem persons whose names include *Zadok* as an element. Genesis 14:18–20 has Abraham paying a tithe to "Melchi*zedek* king of Salem." "Salem" here is probably an abbreviated form of "Jerusalem." Joshua 10:1–5 mentions an "Adoni-*zedek* king of Jerusalem." Abiathar had joined David much earlier, of course, in the aftermath of Saul's massacre of the Nob priests.

Dealing with Opposition

David's rise to power and his Jerusalem-based administration were not without opposition. Saul had been a popular ruler in many circles, especially among his Benjaminite kinsmen. There would have been those loyal to the Saulide family, therefore, who regarded David as a usurper. Also, the increasingly prominent role that Jerusalem played in David's kingdom would have resulted in a corresponding loss of influence and prestige for other cities and cultic centers—such as Shiloh, Gibeah, and Hebron. The administration of affairs from the new capital must have produced some sense of alienation on the part of the older Judahite and Ephraimite/Israelite power structures who had "anointed" David to begin with, while the official status of the Jerusalem-Nob priesthood will have had a similar effect in cultic affairs. Two items reported for David's reign must be understood in this context: the execution of Saul's descendants and the rebellions led by Absalom and Sheba. It is impossible to establish when in David's reign these developments occurred—indeed we do not even know how long his reign lasted. It would seem more likely that they occurred during the earlier years, however, while he was still in the process of securing the kingdom, rather than nearer the end of his reign as is implied by the present arrangement of the materials in II Samuel.

The Execution of Saul's Descendants

At some point David participated in the execution of several members of Saul's family. This was done, according to the narration in II Sam. 21:1–4, in an effort to remove bloodguilt and famine from the land; but obviously it also would have removed a potential threat to David's position on the throne. Saul, we are told, had attempted to annihilate the Gibeonites "in his zeal for the people of Israel and Judah" (II Sam. 21:1–2) and presumably in violation of a long-standing covenant relationship between Gibeon and the Israelites (see Josh. 9:3–21). This supposedly resulted in bloodguilt, which in turn was identified as the cause of the famine. Thus David, having consulted with the Gibeonites, ordered the ritual execution and public exposure of the corpses of seven of Saul's sons and grandsons. "The king took the two sons of Rizpah the daughter of Aiah [see II Sam. 3:7], whom she bore to Saul, . . . and the five sons of Michal the daughter of Saul . . .; and he gave them into the hands of the Gibeonites, and they hanged [impaled?] them on the mountain before Yahweh" (II Sam. 21:8–9).

Although most Hebrew manuscripts read "Michal" as the name of the second mother and thus associate five of the males with David's previously estranged wife, the name of the husband suggests that the second mother was Saul's daughter Merab (compare I Sam. 18:19 with II Sam. 21:8). It was Saul's concubine Rizpah who is said to have kept watch over the corpses for half a year, protecting the exposed remains from birds and beasts. Eventually David allowed the bones, along with the exhumed remains of Saul and Jonathan, to be interred in Saul's family tomb at Zela.

Perhaps at the time of these executions David also appropriated Saul's family estate. When the crippled son of Jonathan, Mephibosheth (called Meribbaal in I Chron. 8:34), turned up in Lo-debar, a place somewhere in the Transjordan, David restored the estate to Mephibosheth. Yet he required that Mephibosheth eat "at the king's table" from that time forward—that is, take up residence in Jerusalem, where his activities could be scrutinized. The property itself was placed in the custody of a certain Ziba, a servant of the house of Saul, who was to till the land and "bring in the produce, that your master's son [Mephibosheth] may have bread to eat" (II Sam. 9:1–13).

Absalom's Rebellion

Also probably early in his reign, but after having transferred the capital to Jerusalem, David was confronted with a rebellion led by his own son Absalom. This was followed in turn by a second rebellion led by a Benjaminite named Sheba. Absalom actually replaced David on the throne in Jerusalem for a brief period, while Sheba's rebellion was a less successful attempt to withdraw Ephraim/Israel from David's authority. Both suggest widespread unrest and discontent.

Absalom, born during David's rule at Hebron, was the son of Maacah, an Aramean princess from Geshur (II Sam. 3:3), and the only son of David explicitly said to have inherited royal blood from his mother's line. Like his father (I Sam. 16:12), Absalom was remembered for his beauty and the impact of his personality on the general populace (II Sam. 14:25). The account of Absalom's rebellion (II Sam. 15–19) is preceded by a narrative that describes how Amnon, Absalom's eldest half brother, raped Tamar, Absalom's sister. Absalom plotted revenge, had Amnon killed, and, fearing their father's wrath, fled into exile. Taking refuge with his grandfather in the kingdom of Geshur, Absalom remained absent from Jerusalem for three years until Joab intervened with David on Absalom's behalf. Initially David refused to see Absalom, but eventually the two were at least partially reconciled (II Sam. 14:28–33).

With Amnon dead, Absalom apparently was now David's oldest living son. Another older brother, Chileab (II Sam. 3:3), nowhere figures in the biblical narratives and may have died as a youngster. Thus Absalom began to play the role of the royal heir and to appeal to popular grievances.

> After this Absalom got himself a chariot and horses, and fifty men to run before him. And Absalom used to rise early and stand beside the way of the gate; and when

any man had a suit to come before the king for judgment, Absalom would call to him, and say, "From what city are you?" And when he said, "Your servant is of such and such a tribe in Israel," Absalom would say to him, "See, your claims are good and right; but there is no man deputed by the king to hear you." Absalom said moreover, "Oh that I were judge in the land! Then every man with a suit or cause might come to me, and I would give him justice." And whenever a man came near to do obeisance to him, he would put out his hand, and take hold of him, and kiss him. Thus Absalom did to all of Israel who came to the king for judgment; so Absalom stole the hearts of the men of Israel. (II Sam. 15:1–6)

The reference to "no man deputed by the king to hear you" implies grievances over David's administration, while the diverse elements that supported Absalom's conspiracy indicate that these grievances were widespread. Both Judeans and Israelites joined the movement. Moreover, Absalom's backers included some who might have been considered David's own close supporters. Among the latter, for example, were important members of David's administration, Ahithophel and a nephew, Amasa.

Absalom initiated the rebellion, according to the biblical account, by having himself proclaimed king in Hebron, the heartland of Judah and David's earlier capital. This was coordinated with proclamations of his kingship in other centers, particularly in Ephraim/Israel (II Sam. 15:7–12). The extent of southern support for the conspiracy as well as the increasing Israelite support in the north forced David to flee Jerusalem, accompanied by his royal forces and mercenaries. Otherwise there was danger of his being caught in the city by a pincer movement (II Sam. 15:13–31). Before leaving, however, David set up arrangements whereby the priests Zadok and Abiathar would remain behind and send him secret reports regarding developments. Also he left his counselor Hushai as a plant and pretended supporter of Absalom (II Sam. 15: 32–37; 17:15–22).

The biblical account reports various sentiments about David among the general populace, which represent the range of reactions one would expect. Ziba, the custodian of the royal lands previously held by Saul and now owned by Mephibosheth, is reported to have rushed to David's side and accused his master of expecting to be restored to the throne. David, on the spot, declared him the new owner of the Saulide estate. Shimei, a Benjaminite member of the house of Saul, cursed and threw stones at the fleeing king, denouncing him for shedding the blood of his predecessor's family (II Sam. 16:5–14; see II Sam. 21:1–6). Once across the Jordan and at Mahanaim, David was supported by various prominent persons in the Transjordan (II Sam. 17:27–29). These included Shobi, a son of Nahash the Ammonite king, Machir of Lo-debar who earlier had sheltered the young Mephibosheth (II Sam. 9:4), and Barzillai, a wealthy Gileadite whose name suggests that he may have been an Aramean (see II Sam. 19:31–38). David's forces were deployed under three field commanders: Joab and Abishai, the king's nephews, and Ittai a Gittite (II Sam. 18:1–3). The latter was apparently the head of a contingent of six hundred Philistine mercenaries who recently had arrived with their families from Gath (II Sam.

15:18–22). Absalom, on the other hand, appointed his cousin Amasa as the commander of his forces.

This review of the various persons and groups who supported Absalom and David respectively suggests the following: (1) Sectional interests, family ties, and personal animosities were still strong factors mitigating against the creation of a strong national state. (2) The wounds of the Davidic-Saulide conflict still festered. (3) David depended heavily upon foreign mercenaries and non-Israelites for his power base.

After occupying the capital, and on the advice of Ahithophel, Absalom made a public show of taking over David's harem. No doubt this was intended to emphasize his replacement of David and to demonstrate that the break was irrevocable (II Sam. 16:15–23). Ahithophel, of course, would have been particularly concerned to ensure that Absalom's policy left no room to abort the coup. David and Absalom were, after all, father and son, and might conceivably be reconciled again as they had after the Tamar affair. But for Ahithophel and other prominent persons like him who had chosen to side with Absalom, there could be no turning back. He had gambled both his career and his life on the success of the rebellion. By the same measure, it was a devastating blow to Ahithophel when Absalom rejected his advice in deference to that of Hushai, and failed to take best advantage of the military situation with a speedy attack on David's retreating forces (II Sam. 17:1–14). Instead, he wasted time rallying a large force and gave David's troops time to organize. Ahithophel, no doubt sensing that he would continue to be disregarded in the new government and that the rebellion was probably doomed to failure in any case, committed suicide (II Sam. 17:23).

The eventual encounter between David's and Absalom's forces took place, we are told, in Gilead in the forest of Ephraim (II Sam. 18:6). David's troops, with their prior deployment, would have had the advantage and were victorious. Absalom's forces, which seem to have consisted primarily of Israelites rather than Judeans, were severely beaten but were spared from slaughter by Joab. Joab killed Absalom, on the other hand, in spite of David's earlier admonition to "deal gently" with his son (II Sam. 18:5–16).

The fact that Absalom's rebellion had collapsed, leaving Israel and Judah without a monarch for the moment, did not mean that they were eager to reinstate David. The Israelites, and perhaps the Judahites as well, must certainly have considered the possibility of anointing another person as king. While discussions were still under way among the Israelites (II Sam. 19:8b–10), David, still in the Transjordan, sent a message to Zadok and Abiathar instructing them to encourage the elders of Judah to take the lead in restoring him to the throne since he was their flesh and bone. In addition, he promised to retain Amasa, who had commanded Absalom's army—a move probably intended to ease the fears of all those who had supported Absalom by signaling that they would receive clemency. Thus Judah rallied in support of David and came to meet him at Gilgal, situated near a crossing of the Jordan (II Sam. 19:11–15).

Once the Judeans had declared themselves in favor of David's reinstatement and begun the process of bringing him back to Jerusalem, the Israelites could delay their decision no longer. Their only choice was to support his return or to prepare for civil war—a war they would have little chance of winning. They decided to support his return, therefore, and sent their representatives to Gilgal as well.

The scene at Gilgal described in II Sam. 19:16–43 is further illustration of the disparate elements and internal tensions that characterized David's realm. The main contingent of Israelites appeared at Gilgal late, after David had been escorted across the Jordan primarily by Judeans. Israelite and Judean animosities surfaced immediately, with the Israelite representatives charging that the Judeans had acted precipitously and were being favored in spite of Israel's larger size. The Israelite representatives claimed, moreover, that it was they rather than the Judeans who had made the first moves toward restoring David to the throne (II Sam. 19:41–43). Also at Gilgal was Shimei, now repentant in the light of changed circumstances, offering his submission and support along with a thousand other Benjaminites. Even the lame Mephibosheth came to Gilgal to show his loyalty. David granted clemency to Shimei and restored half of Mephibosheth's estate (II Sam. 19:24–30).

This entire scenario, in which Israel and Judah act independently, suggests that the two groups, and perhaps the Benjaminites as a third (see II Sam. 19:16–17), still understood themselves as separate entities. Just as David earlier had been anointed separately by representatives of Judah and Israel (II Sam. 2:4; 5:3), the same thing may have happened with Absalom, with the Israelites anointing him after his arrival in Jerusalem (II Sam. 19:10). Now representatives of both Israel and Judah participated in David's reinstatement.

Sheba's Revolt

Obviously the Israelite support for David's return to power was neither enthusiastic nor unanimous. Sheba, another Benjaminite, was among those who opposed his return. Possibly while David was still meeting with Israelite and Judean leaders at Gilgal, Sheba was calling for a break with the house of David: "We have no portion in David, and we have no inheritance in the son of Jesse; every man to his tents, O Israel!" (II Sam. 20:1). Although the text goes on to say that "all the men of Israel withdrew from David, and followed Sheba," this is exaggeration no doubt, as is the statement in II Sam. 19:41 that asserts that "all the men of Israel" met David at Gilgal. The subsequent account of Sheba's venture suggests that his following was rather limited (see especially II Sam. 20:14, where he seems to have been supported only by his own clan).

After arriving back in Jerusalem, David moved quickly to put down Sheba's rebellion before it could mushroom: "lest he get himself fortified cities, and snatch away our eyes" (II Sam. 20:6b). David's original plan was for Amasa to muster Judean troops and deal with Sheba. Amasa delayed beyond the time that David had designated for the beginning of the campaign, however, possibly because of slow response on the part of the Judeans. Whatever the reason, by the time Amasa appeared on the scene with his troops David had already turned the affair over to his professional soldiers—specifically to Abishar, Joab, the Cherethites, and the Pelethites. Thereupon Joab killed Amasa, his temporary replacement as commander of the army, and pursued Sheba to Abel of Beth-maacah (Tell Abil, at the sources of the Jordan River in the extreme north of Palestine) with a combined force of professional troops and loyal volunteers (II Sam. 20:8–13). With their city under siege, the citizens of Abel decapitated Sheba and tossed his head over the wall to an awaiting Joab (II Sam. 20:14–22).

David's Wars and the Extent of His Kingdom

The summary of David's military activities provided in II Sam. 8:1–14 is reminiscent of the summary of Saul's conquests in I Sam. 14:47–48. Both kings are credited with sweeping victories and having subdued all their enemies on every side. David does seem to have been more successful than Saul in con-solidating and extending the frontiers of his domain. Also it appears that he played a somewhat more important role in international politics. Yet it is doubt-ful that the range of David's effective rule was ever extended to include even all of Palestine, and certainly there is no indication that he exerted any political influence beyond the immediately surrounding nations. Specifically, David's consolidation and expansion of his domain involved three aspects: (1) contain-ment of the Philistines, (2) extension of his frontiers beyond what Saul had ruled and annexation of the heretofore independent city-states within these frontiers, and (3) frontier wars and alliances with surrounding kingdoms.

Containment of the Philistines

David became popular as a Philistine fighter while still a professional soldier in Saul's court (I Sam. 17–18). Later when he had established his own kingdom at Hebron, and particularly after the elders of Israel anointed him as their king too, we find him again at war with the Philistines. His status had shifted from that of Philistine vassal to that of protector of Judah and Israel against the Philistines. This is the context of the wars reported in II Sam. 5:17–25 and probably most of the Philistine-related items reported in II Samuel 23. Perhaps there were frontier skirmishes later on as well, with the frontier being approxi-mately the Shephelah. The reference to Methegammah in the statement about David's defeat of the Philistines in II Sam. 8:1 is baffling. It is even unclear whether this should be translated as a place-name (see the parallel passage in I Chron. 18:1, which offers a different reading).

The Expansion of the Kingdom

The area of David's direct rule extended geographically beyond that ruled by Saul, the most obvious difference being that David's realm included the Jezreel Valley and Galilee. Also, David seems to have expanded the frontier in the Transjordan, although the situation there is less clear. Three texts come into consideration for determining the extent of David's direct rule: the account of David's census in II Samuel 24 (= I Chron. 21:1–27), the list of Levitical cities in Josh. 21:1–42 (= I Chron. 6:54–81), and the list of "unconquered cities" in Judg. 1:27–33.

The geographical coverage of the census is described in very general fashion, seems incomplete, and is not entirely intelligible. Beginning at the Arnon (present-day Wady Mujib) in the Transjordan, the surveyors are said to have proceeded northward to a point near Dan at the foot of Mt. Hermon and then westward across Upper Galilee approaching the Phoenician cities of Sidon and Tyre. A second arm of the survey is said to have covered the Negeb of Judah to Beer-sheba. Nothing is said of the heartland of the kingdom west of the Jordan. Perhaps the census, or at least the geographical description, pertained specifically to certain outlying territories that David incorporated secondarily into the kingdom.

We have already advanced a similar hypothesis regarding the Levitical city list. Although the list is highly schematic in its present form, the Levitical cities are clustered in areas that were outside the heartland of Israel and Judah yet probably inside the boundaries of David's direct rule. (See Map 15.) Finally, Judg. 1:27–33 lists cities that were incorporated into the Israelite monarchy at some point but whose indigenous, non-Israelite populations were allowed to remain in place. Several of these, like Jerusalem, were old Bronze Age city-states that had survived into the Iron Age—for example, Beth-shean, Taanach, Megiddo, Gezer, and Beth-shemesh. One thinks first of David's reign as the likely time when cities of this sort would have been incorporated under such circumstances. The only text that suggests otherwise is I Kings 9:16, where it is claimed that an Egyptian pharaoh captured and burned Gezer, annihilated the population, and gave the ruins to his daughter as dowry upon her marriage to Solomon. This seems to imply, although not necessarily, that Gezer did not become an Israelite possession until Solomon's reign.

It would be an overstatement of the evidence to claim that the account of the census, the Levitical city list, and the list of unconquered cities all presuppose essentially the same territorial boundaries, since the information provided in each case is not detailed or firm enough for close comparison. It is fair to say, however, that the three are compatible and that together they highlight what one suspects on other grounds to have been the territorial extent of David's direct rule. All three, for example, exclude Philistia.

Frontier Wars and Alliance Relationships

All three of the texts discussed above as relating to the extent of David's kingdom suggest expansion into Upper Galilee, approaching the Phoenician cities of Tyre and Sidon. During the census, for example, "they went around to Sidon, and came to the fortress of Tyre and to all the cities of the Hivites and Canaanites" (II Sam. 24:6–7). The only other information regarding

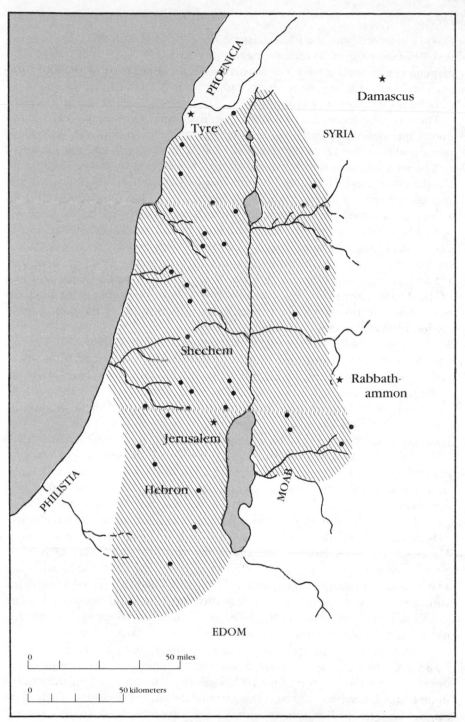

**MAP 15. The Approximate Extent of David's Kingdom
and Configuration of the Levitical Cities**

David's relations with the Phoenicians is the note in II Sam. 5:11 to the effect that "Hiram king of Tyre sent messengers to David, and cedar trees, also carpenters and masons who built David a house." One can only speculate as to whether there was any direct connection between David's encroachment on Phoenician territory and Hiram's gifts.

The meager information provided regarding David's dealing with Moab also invites speculation with no promise of satisfying results. On the one hand, there is the tradition that David himself was of Moabite ancestry and the statement that he took his parents to Moab for safety while he was on the run from Saul. On the other hand, II Sam. 8:2 reports that he defeated the Moabites and was particularly brutal to them. "And he defeated Moab, and measured them with a line, making them lie down on the ground; two lines he measured to be put to death, and one full line to be spared. And the Moabites became servants to David and brought tribute." Moab would refer here primarily to the tableland north of the Arnon. Moab proper, south of the Arnon, was never easily accessible to Israelite and Judean kings. Even if David conducted a campaign south of the Arnon with any success, he would hardly have been able to establish any permanent control. Note in this regard that Moab south of the Arnon is excluded from the census coverage.

The report that David slew eighteen thousand Edomites in the Valley of Salt and put garrisons throughout all Edom (II Sam. 8:13–14; read "Edomites" rather than "Syrians") is echoed in I Kings 11:15–16. "For when David was in Edom, and Joab the commander of the army went up to bury the slain, he slew every male in Edom (for Joab and all Israel remained there six months, until he had cut off every male in Edom)." Here again one recognizes hyperbole, especially if Edom is to be understood as it usually is depicted in modern biblical atlases—as an expansive nation south of Moab in the southern Transjordan. Actually "Edom" seems to have been a rather loose geographical designation, and in some biblical texts clearly refers to territory southwest of the Dead Sea (Num. 34:3; Josh. 15:1–4). A similar situation is reflected in the Edomite genealogies of Genesis 36 which include certain tribes that frequented this area —Kenizzites, Korahites, and Amalekites. Finally, while the location of the Valley of Salt remains uncertain, the Wady el-Milh (= "Valley of Salt" in Arabic), which lies roughly midway between Beer-sheba and the Dead Sea, is a very tempting candidate. In short, the Edom that David subjected and secured with garrisons was most likely the area southwest of the Dead Sea, along his own kingdom's southern frontier, inhabited by "Edomite" tribes such as the Kenezites and the Amalekites.

The Ammonites were a relatively small kingdom, actually a city-state centered in Rabbah (present-day Amman) which itself was situated at the edge of the desert on an upper branch of the Jabbok. Both Jephthah and Saul were called upon by the Gileadites to protect them from Ammonite oppression. Early in his reign, David formed an alliance with Nahash king of Rabbah which remained in effect until Nahash died. After Nahash was succeeded on the throne by his son Hanun, however, hostilities erupted between Jerusalem and Rabbah which seem to have continued off and on for some time. Usually Joab carried the fight to the Ammonites while David remained in Jerusalem. It was on one such occasion, for example, while Joab and his troops were ravaging the Ammonites and besieging Rabbah, that David is said to have had his affair with Bathsheba (II Sam. 11). Eventually Rabbah was taken, David was called to the scene in time to participate in the victory, and the Ammonites were consigned to forced labor (II Sam. 12:26–31).

Three passages come into primary consideration for understanding David's relations with the Arameans or Syrians—namely, II Sam. 10:6–19; 8:3–12; and I Kings 11:23–25. The first of these, II Sam. 10:6–19, places David's initial encounter with the Arameans in the context of the Ammonite wars.

> When the Ammonites saw that they had become odious to David, the Ammonites sent and hired the Syrians of Beth-rehob, and the Syrians of Zobah, twenty thousand foot soldiers, and the king of Maacah with a thousand men, and the men of Tob, twelve thousand men. (II Sam. 10:6)

Battle was joined before the gates of Rabbah, according to this passage, the Syrians fled, and the Ammonites retreated behind the city walls. Then Hadadezer (king of Zobah, although not actually identified as such in this passage) regrouped the Syrians, brought in reinforcements from "beyond the river," and deployed them at Helam (location unknown). David attacked the Syrians there and routed them a second time.

> And the Syrians fled before Israel; and David slew of the Syrians the men of seven hundred chariots, and forty thousand horsemen, and wounded Shobach the commander of their army, so that he died there. And when all the kings who were servants of Hadadezer saw that they had been defeated by Israel, they made peace with Israel, and became subject to them. So the Syrians feared to help the Ammonites any more. (II Sam. 10:18–19)

In short, David is credited with two victories over a Syrian mercenary army which had come to the aid of the Ammonites, the affair apparently ending with the Syrians retreating from the scene and establishing peaceful relations with Israel. The whole account seems quite reasonable, except for the excessive numbers of men said to have been involved in the battles and the final note which claims that the Syrians became subject to David at that point. This concluding note has the appearance of an editorial afterthought and does not follow naturally from the account. That the Arameans would have withdrawn from meddling in Transjordanian affairs after David twice defeated them in the field makes good sense. But that the Aramean cities themselves would have submitted to David's yoke without even attempting to defend their walls is another matter.

The second passage, II Sam. 8:3–12, reflects close parallels with II Sam. 10:6–19, but with some significant differences in the details and with even more excessive claims regarding the extent to which David became master of Aram as a result of two victories. Whereas II Sam. 10:6–19 has Hadadezer in charge of an army that includes Syrians from Beth-rehob and Zobah, II Sam. 8:3–11 identifies him as "Hadadezer the son of Rehob, king of Zobah." Instead of his bringing troops from "beyond the river" to reinforce and reassert Aramean strength in the Transjordan, this second passage has David attacking Hadadezer "as he went to restore his power at the river Euphrates." Again there are two battles, with Hadadezer receiving reinforcements for the second, and with David victorious in both. The reinforcements in the II Sam. 8:3–11 account, however, are Arameans from Damascus and we are told that after the second victory David "put garrisons in Aram of Damascus; and the Syrians became servants to David and brought tribute. And Yahweh gave victory to David wherever he went."

In short, vs. 3–6 of this second passage seem to represent a variant and somewhat garbled version of the scene described in II Sam. 10:6–10. The remaining verses, on the other hand, present distinctly new information. Verses 7–8 state that David took shields of gold which had been carried by servants of Hadadezer, as well as much bronze from two of Hadadezer's cities, Betah and Berothai. Verses 9–12 claim that Toi, king of Hamath and a long-standing enemy of Hadadezer, sent his son with gifts to congratulate David.

The third passage to be considered, I Kings 11:23–25, describes a situation in Damascus during Solomon's reign.

> God also raised up as an adversary to him [Solomon], Rezon the son of Eliada, who
> had fled from his master Hadadezer king of Zobah. And he gathered men about

Ammonite Head. This limestone head, possibly depicting an Ammonite ruler, was discovered in present-day Amman. *(Jordan Department of Antiquities)*

> him and became leader of a marauding band, after the slaughter by David; and they went to Damascus, and dwelt there, and made him king in Damascus. He was an adversary of Israel all the days of Solomon.

Here again David's defeat of Hadadezer is said to have had significant repercussions for Damascus.

The historical circumstances behind these three passages must, in our opinion, have been somewhat as follows:

1. The city-state of Zobah, which dominated southern Aram during Saul's reign, still represented a major power when David began his wars with the Ammonites. Hadadezer was the king of Zobah at that time. He dominated Damascus and probably considered Galilee and the northern Transjordan as belonging to his realm as well. The Ammonites called on him for protection against David and he gladly responded with troops from various Aramean cities.

2. David defeated Hadadezer decisively in two resulting battles, one before the gates of Rabbah and one at Helam, somewhere in the Transjordan. Subsequently Hadadezer withdrew from the Transjordan and exerted no further influence there. Hadadezer also lost control of Damascus at that time, although apparently not to David. The city fell into the hands of a marauding band led by Rezon son of Eliada. This does not necessarily conflict with II Sam. 8:6, which states that David placed garrisons in "Aram of Damascus"—that is, within some portion of the territory generally associated with Damascus.

3. David may actually have invaded the heartland of Hadadezer's realm at some point, although the only evidence for this is the rather ambiguous statement in II Sam. 8:7–8. Does this passage mean that he actually took Betah (read "Tibhath" with I Chron. 18:8) and Berothai; and where were these cities located? Regardless, there is no reason to suppose that David actually conquered Zobah or subjected Aram proper.

4. David also expanded his domain to include Galilee as far northward as the area near the Phoenician cities of Tyre and Sidon. In both cases, therefore, in the Transjordan and in Galilee, David expanded his kingdom at the expense of Hadadezer of Zobah. Naturally Toi of Hamath, a long-standing enemy of Hadadezer, was pleased with the turn of events. He sent his son to David with congratulations and gifts.

David's Administration

As observed in the previous chapter, one catches only glimpses of Saul's administrative structures and policies, which seem to have relied heavily upon family members and probably granted special prerogatives to the tribe of Benjamin. David apparently developed a somewhat more sophisticated and effective administration, although in his case also not many details are known. Several aspects have been mentioned already. (1) Jerusalem became the administrative, military, and cultic center of the kingdom. (2) Correspondingly, there was a tendency toward autocratic government in line with the traditions of the old

Bronze Age cities. David's kingdom was to become, if not during his own reign then certainly under Solomon, an extended Jerusalemite city-state. (3) David depended heavily in his government on groups whose allegiance would have been directed more toward the king than toward clan and tribal structures. For the military, he made heavy use of foreign mercenaries, including Philistine units. The national cult was in the hands of the indigenous priestly lines of Jerusalem and nearby Nob. For the general administration of government policies throughout his realm, but especially in outlying territories, he probably relied heavily on the Levites, who were themselves from his own home area and were paid off in land grants in the areas where they were stationed.

II Samuel 8:15–18 (= I Chron. 18:14–17) and II Sam. 20:23–26 are variant versions of a list of high officials under David (see Chart VI). "Ahimelech the son of Abiathar" in the II Sam. 8:15–18 version should be corrected to "Abiathar the son of Ahimelech," thus bringing it into line with I Sam. 22:20 and

---

CHART VI. High Officials Under David

II Sam. 8:16–18 (= I Chron. 18:15–17)

Over the army	Joab, son of Zeruiah
Recorder	Jehoshaphat, son of Ahilud
Priests	Zadok, son of Ahitub; Ahimelech, son of Abiathar
Secretary	Seraiah (Shavsha in I Chron. 18:16)
Over the Cherethites and the Pelethites	Benaiah, son of Jehoiada
Priests	David's sons (I Chron. 18:17 identifies David's sons as "chief officials in the service of the king")

II Sam. 20:23–26

Over the army of Israel	Joab
Over the Cherethites and the Pelethites	Benaiah, son of Jehoiada
Over the forced labor	Adoram
Recorder	Jehoshaphat, son of Ahilud
Secretary	Sheva
Priests	Zadok and Abiathar
David's priest	Ira the Jairite

---

the corresponding entry in the II Sam. 20:23–26 version. Also "Seraiah," "Shavsha," and "Sheva" are to be understood as variations of the name of the same secretary rather than as different persons. Otherwise the only significant differences between the two versions of the list are that the II Sam. 8:16–18 version identifies David's sons as priests (or "chief officials" in I Chron. 18:17), while the II Sam. 20:23–26 version includes Adoram, who was in charge of forced labor, and Ira, who served as David's personal priest.

Presumably these officials represented the basic functions of David's administration. The priests were in charge of religious affairs. The "recorder" would have been responsible for state records and documents both economic and administrative, while the secretary probably handled the routine activities of the king and court and perhaps diplomatic correspondence as well. Joab clearly was chief commander over the whole military, a position that he was not prepared to share earlier with either Abner or Amasa. The Cherethites and the Pelethites appear to have been royal mercenaries, members of the king's personal forces under their own commander. The names of these two mercenary groups remain unexplained. Perhaps they denote Cretans and Philistines, the former perhaps also to be associated with the Sea Peoples (see I Sam. 30:14). II Samuel 15:18 includes Gittites also among David's mercenaries. The "forced labor" over which Adoram had charge would have been conscripted for public and royal projects (see II Sam. 12:31; Judg. 1:28, 30, 33, 35).

Other officials are mentioned in various other texts, but seem to have had a lower or different status. Nathan and Gad functioned as prophets at the court (II Sam. 12; 24:11) and certainly Nathan had great influence on state affairs as his role in Solomon's coup demonstrates. II Samuel 23:8–39 refers to "the three" and "the thirty" as special groups, apparently military in function, who served with David at least during his earliest days in the south. The intended meaning of these terms is unclear. They may have referred to secondary levels of military leaders who functioned below the king and commander of the army.

The preceding observations about David's administration are based on the Genesis–II Kings account. The Chronicler duplicates most of the passages involved, and then adds a whole section of supplementary material pertaining to David's administration, his plans for the Temple, and the transfer of the crown to Solomon (I Chron. 22–29). If one could use this supplementary material with confidence, then a great deal more could be deduced about the persons, groups, and offices that comprised David's government.

Unfortunately this material cannot be used with confidence, even though some of the items included are corroborated by the Genesis–II Kings account and others may have been derived ultimately from authentic records. Consider, for example, the short list provided in I Chron. 27:32–34, which might be characterized as David's "cabinet."

> Jonathan, David's uncle, was a counselor, being a man of understanding and a scribe; he and Jehiel the son of Hachmoni attended the king's sons. Ahithophel was

the king's counselor, and Hushai the Archite was the king's friend. Ahithophel was succeeded by Jehoiada the son of Benaiah, and Abiathar. Joab was commander of the king's army.

Ahithophel, Hushai, Abiathar, and Joab are all well known from the Genesis-II Kings account, of course, and Ahithophel's role as an honored adviser to the king is emphasized in II Sam. 16:23: "Now in those days the counsel which Ahithophel gave was as if one consulted the oracle of God; so was all the counsel of Ahithophel esteemed, both by David and by Absalom." The reference to "Jehoiada the son of Benaiah" should be corrected to read "Benaiah the son of Jehoiada," thus bringing it into line with the lists of David's officials in II Sam. 8:16–18 (= I Chron. 18:15–17) and 20:23–26 discussed above (see also II Sam. 23:20 and I Chron. 11:22). Jonathan, introduced here as David's uncle, is probably to be identified with the Jonathan introduced in II Sam. 21:21 as the son of Shimei, David's brother and thus as David's nephew. This leaves Jehiel, known only to the Chronicler.

It is quite possible that Jehiel was an important person in David's court whose name and role the Chronicler derived from some other source or sources. The same may be true for many of the persons and groups introduced in I Chronicles 22–29. Be that as it may, it is still difficult to generate confidence in the elaborate cultic and administrative structure which the Chronicler attributes in these chapters to David. On the one hand, much of the detail seems garbled, such as "Jehoiada the son of Benaiah" rather than the other way around. On the other hand, the overall cultic and administrative structures propounded seem artificially schematic (note the constant use of twelve and multiples of twelve) and ideal (note the effort to organize the hodgepodge of data in accordance with the twelve-tribe scheme).

CHAPTER 6

The Reign of Solomon

Solomon's reign was "the golden age" of Israelite and Judean history—or at least that is what one would conclude from a casual reading of the Bible. The compilers of Genesis-II Kings depicted Solomon as an exceedingly wise, exceptionally wealthy, and extremely powerful ruler whose empire stretched from the Euphrates River to the Egyptian frontier. The Chronicler pressed these claims even further, neutralizing all negative aspects of Solomon's reign and elaborating on his role as Temple builder and cofounder with David of the Jerusalem cult. The superscriptions to the books of Proverbs, Ecclesiastes, and Song of Songs appear to credit him for their wisdom. Not surprisingly, Solomon's reign came to be regarded as the epitome of splendor, opulence, and wise government (see Luke 12:27).

A more careful examination of the biblical texts, however, probing beneath the sweeping claims and generalizations, reveals certain ironies about Solomon. We learn, for example, that the "wealthy" Solomon developed "cash flow" problems which required him to concede twenty cities in Galilee to the Phoenician king of Tyre (I Kings 9:10–14). The "powerful" Solomon who supposedly "ruled over all the kingdoms from the Euphrates to the land of the Philistines and to the border of Egypt" (I Kings 4:21), was troubled by adversaries much nearer home—Hadad of Edom, Rezon of Damascus, and Jeroboam of Ephraim (I Kings 11:14–40). The "wise" Solomon apparently so exploited his people through forced labor and other despotic practices that the bulk of the kingdom chose to break away from Jerusalem at his death rather than to continue under his policies (I Kings 12:1–20).

Solomon's reign is the earliest point where a fairly good case can be made for a correlation between a specific item in biblical history and the archaeological record. Namely, I Kings 9:15–19 mentions several cities that Solomon built (or fortified), including Hazor, Megiddo, and Gezer. Archaeological excavations at the sites of all three of these ancient cities have revealed strata of building and fortification remains which can be dated approximately to Solomon's reign and which do in fact suggest—by their large scale and similar design —a centralized, royally sponsored building program. Thus we seem to have at hand material evidence of Solomon's accomplishments as a builder. This same evidence, however, illustrates that his accomplishments in this regard were rather modest, certainly when compared to the works of the monarchs of the great empires of Mesopotamia and Egypt, but even when compared with the building remains of the later Omride period of Israel's history.

When all of this is taken into account, a much more subdued and, in our opinion, realistic portrait of Solomon begins to emerge. Before attempting any observations about this more realistic Solomon, let us examine the biblical materials pertaining to his reign.

The Genesis-II Kings Presentation of Solomon's Reign

While the Genesis-II Kings presentations of Saul and David are composed for the most part of numerous, previously independent folk legends that have been combined and superimposed with an editorial veneer, its presentation of Solomon is more thoroughly editorial. I Kings 1–2 provides the transition from David's reign to Solomon. Then, for the next nine chapters, until Solomon's reign is concluded at the end of I Kings 11, the narrator or narrators expound on Solomon's piety, wisdom, wealth, and international prestige. Various items are incorporated into the exposition by way of illustration—occasional stories (I Kings 3:16–28; 10:1–10, 13), descriptions (I Kings 6; 7:13–51), lists (I Kings 4:1–19), and so on. But these items are not always well integrated into the narration or interrelated with each other, which leaves the impression in some places of a disjointed assemblage of "odds and ends." Because it tends to be more exposition with illustrating odds and ends than story line, it is difficult to summarize the Solomon section of the Genesis-II Kings. The main sequence of events as narrated is essentially the following.

Summary of I Kings 1–11

When David grew old, was failing in health and no longer potent, Adonijah proceeded to exalt himself as king. This move was supported by Joab the chief commander of the army and Abiathar one of the two chief priests, but not by Nathan the prophet, Zadok the other chief priest, or Benaiah who commanded the Cherethite and Pelethite mercenaries. Nathan reported the matter to Bathsheba and together they influenced David to designate Solomon as his successor instead of Adonijah. Solomon was crowned in a surprise ceremony orchestrated by Nathan, Zadok, and Benaiah.

Before dying, David instructed Solomon to deal favorably with the descendants of Barzillai who had come to his aid at the time of Absalom's rebellion, but to execute Shimei the Benjaminite who had supported the rebellion and Joab the infamous commander of David's army. Solomon did as instructed, although he waited until there was some provocation before ordering the executions. Also he executed Adonijah and exiled Abiathar to Anathoth, a village near Jerusalem. The provocation in the case of Joab, Adonijah, and Abiathar was that

Adonijah requested a maiden from David's harem for his wife (actually the same Shunammite maiden who had been brought to the court to assist David in overcoming his impotency). Solomon interpreted this as a calculated move on Adonijah's part to recover the crown (I Kings 1:1–2:46a).

"So the kingdom was established in the hand of Solomon," and his royal status was recognized internationally. He entered into a marriage alliance with the pharaoh of Egypt and brought the pharaoh's daughter to live in Jerusalem.

Still no temple had been built for Yahweh in Jerusalem, so the people sacrificed at high places. Solomon was a pious king and went to the great high place at Gibeon to offer a thousand burnt offerings. Yahweh appeared to him in a dream there and called on him to "Ask what I shall give you." Solomon requested "an understanding mind to govern . . . , that I may discern between good and evil; for who is able to govern this thy great people?" This request pleased Yahweh, who granted it and promised riches and honor as well. Solomon awoke and returned to Jerusalem, where his ability as a wise judge was manifested. Namely, he offered wise judgment in a case that involved two prostitutes, both of whom claimed to be the mother of the same child (I Kings 2:46b–3:28).

Solomon's high officials are listed next (I Kings 4:1–6) and also the twelve officers in charge of providing food for the king's table and his household (I Kings 4:7–19). There follow sweeping claims regarding the extent of Solomon's realm, the splendor of his court, and his international renown as a wise king:

> Solomon ruled over all the kingdoms from the Euphrates to the land of the Philistines and to the border of Egypt; they brought tribute and served Solomon all the days of his life.
>
> Solomon's provision for one day was thirty cors of fine flour, and sixty cors of meal, ten fat oxen, and twenty pasture-fed cattle, a hundred sheep, besides harts, gazelles, roebucks, and fatted fowl. For he had dominion over all the region west of the Euphrates from Tiphsah to Gaza, over all the kings west of the Euphrates; and he had peace on all sides round about him. . . . Solomon also had forty thousand stalls of horses for his chariots, and twelve thousand horsemen. . . .
>
> And God gave Solomon wisdom and understanding beyond measure, and largeness of mind like the sand on the seashore, so that Solomon's wisdom surpassed the wisdom of all the people of the east, and all the wisdom of Egypt. For he was wiser than all other men, . . . and his fame was in all the nations round about. He also uttered three thousand proverbs; and his songs were a thousand and five. . . . And men came from all peoples to hear the wisdom of Solomon. (I Kings 4:21–34)

Solomon began preparations for building the Temple. Hiram king of Tyre agreed to supply building materials and skilled workmen, while Solomon raised a levy of forced labor for the project. Construction began in the fourth year of Solomon's reign, which was the four hundred and eightieth year after the people of Israel had come out of the land of Egypt. There is an elaborate description of the Temple, which itself was completed in seven years (I Kings 5–6). Thirteen years were required to build Solomon's palace and associated royal buildings (including a house for the pharaoh's daughter), which are described in less detail (I Kings 7:1–12). In addition, Solomon engaged a bronzesmith from Tyre, also named Hiram, to cast bronze fixtures and furnishings for the Temple (I Kings 7:13–50). When all the work was completed, Solomon stored the things that David had dedicated (silver, gold, and vessels) in the treasuries of the Temple (I Kings 7:51).

Then Solomon assembled all the dignitaries of his realm in Jerusalem and dedicated the Temple to Yahweh. The dedication ceremony included (1) a ritual transfer of the Ark into the Temple; (2) a long prayer by Solomon in which he called upon Yahweh to reconfirm his promise to David of a permanent dynasty, to bless the Temple with his special presence, and to forgive the people when they repented of their wrongdoings; (3) elaborate sacrifices and peace offerings; and (4) a great feast. When all the people had returned to their homes, Yahweh appeared to Solomon a second time and assured him that his prayer would be answered, depending on the king's faithfulness.

Several items are appended at this point which pertain in one way or another to the completion of the building program. Solomon gave twenty cities to Hiram king of Tyre in payment for the latter's contributions to the various projects. There is a clarification of Solomon's policies regarding forced labor. The pharaoh's daughter was moved to her own house. Solomon built the Millo. With the Temple and altar in place, Solomon began a schedule (three times a year) of burnt offerings and peace offerings (I Kings 9:10–25).

Finally, there is a series of items that further illustrate Solomon's wealth, wisdom, and international prestige. He built a fleet of ships at Ezion-geber and engaged in a shipping venture with the Phoenician king (I Kings 9:26–28; 10:11–12, 22). The queen of Sheba, hearing of Solomon's fame, came to test his wisdom. They exchanged costly gifts (I Kings 10:1–13). Solomon had an abundance of silver and gold as well as a huge chariotry with imported horses and chariots. "And the whole earth sought the presence of Solomon to hear his wisdom, which God had put into his mind. Every one of them brought his present, articles of silver and gold, garments, myrrh, spices, horses, and mules, so much year by year" (I Kings 10:14–25).

But Solomon loved many foreign women. In addition to the pharaoh's daughter, he had Moabite, Ammonite, Edomite, Sidonian, and Hittite women—totaling seven hundred wives-princesses and three hundred concubines—and these women turned his heart after other gods. Indeed, he built sanctuaries for Chemosh and Milcom, the gods of the Moabites and the Ammonites respectively, on the mountain ridge east of Jerusalem (I Kings 11:1–13). Thus Yahweh became angry with Solomon and sent adversaries. Three of these adversaries are named: Hadad of Edom (I Kings 11:14–22), Rezon of Damascus (I Kings 11:23–25), and Jeroboam of Ephraim (I Kings 11:26–40). Jeroboam was an able and industrious young man whom Solomon placed in charge of the forced labor of the house of Joseph. Ahijah, a prophet from Shiloh, confronted Jeroboam on one occasion, announced that Solomon's kingdom would be torn apart in the future, and predicted that Jeroboam would receive the major portion of it. Jeroboam escaped to Egypt, where he remained until Solomon died.

Solomon's reign lasted forty years and he was buried in Jerusalem.

Composition and Structure

This Genesis-II Kings presentation of Solomon is characterized throughout by editorial exaggeration. A cautious historian might be inclined to ignore it altogether if there were any other more convincing sources of information available. Unfortunately there are none. If we are to catch any glimpse of the "historical" Solomon, it will have to come primarily from the materials included in I Kings 1–11 and so thoroughly editorialized in these eleven chapters. As a first step in that direction, it is necessary to distinguish and evaluate some of the different kinds of material involved.

First, of course, there is the account in I Kings 1–2 that describes the palace intrigue surrounding Solomon's accession to the throne. This account concludes the narrative of David's rule in Jerusalem and of the troubles which plagued his reign, discussed in Chapter 5. As we observed there, this narrative invites more confidence as a source for historical information than much of the other material pertaining to David; yet it also has certain novelistic features more suggestive of a storyteller's skill than of pure historical record. Moreover, especially as we reach the conclusion of this narrative, its propagandistic intention becomes increasingly obvious. Namely, it explains how it happened that Solomon, who was not one of David's older sons in line for the crown, made it to the throne nevertheless, and seeks to justify Solomon's palace coup and subsequent executions. It was David himself, the narrator assures us, who designated Solomon as his successor and who instructed Solomon to execute Joab and Shimei. Adonijah's execution was his own fault. His request for the Shunammite maiden demonstrated that he still had designs on the throne.

A second large block of material consists of detailed descriptions of Solomon's cultic activities: the theophany at Gibeon (I Kings 3:2–15), his building program in Jerusalem with primary attention given to the Temple and its furnishings (I Kings 5–7), the dedication ceremony (I Kings 8), and Yahweh's second theophany (I Kings 9:1–9). The interests and intentions of the Judahite editors of the Genesis-II Kings account are very obvious in this block of material. Namely, these descriptions of Solomon's cultic activities emphasize that (1) Jerusalem is the appropriate center of Yahweh worship, (2) a new age in history was inaugurated when Solomon began work on the Temple, 480 years after the exodus from Egypt, (3) Solomon himself, who erected and dedicated the Temple, was a pious and righteous king who ruled at a time when Israel had peace on all sides and dwelt in safety, (4) Yahweh confirmed the dedication of the Temple, with the promise of his special presence in years to come, and (5) Yahweh also reconfirmed in connection with the dedication his commitment to the permanence of the Davidic dynasty.

Yet there is also a note of qualification in Solomon's long prayer and Yahweh's response. Solomon raises the possibility that the people might sin in future years, so that Yahweh would give them into the hand of an enemy who in turn would carry them captive into a foreign land:

> If they sin against thee—for there is no man who does not sin—and thou art angry with them, and dost give them to an enemy, so that they are carried away captive to the land of the enemy, far off or near; yet if they lay it to heart in the land to which they have been carried captive, and repent, and make supplication to thee in the land of their captors, . . . then hear thou in heaven thy dwelling place their prayer and their supplication, and maintain their cause and forgive thy people . . . (I Kings 8:46–50)

Yahweh's response to Solomon's prayer included a warning that unfaithfulness would indeed result in an end to Jerusalem with its Temple, foreign captivity for its people, and even an end to the Davidic dynasty:

> And as for you, if you will walk before me, as David your father walked, with integrity of heart and uprightness, doing according to all that I have commanded you, and keeping my statutes and my ordinances, then I will establish your royal throne over Israel for ever, as I promised David your father. . . . But if you turn aside from following me, you or your children, and do not keep my commandments and my statutes which I have set before you, but go and serve other gods and worship them, then I will cut off Israel from the land which I have given them; and the house which I have consecrated for my name I will cast out of my sight; and Israel will become a proverb and a byword among all peoples. (I Kings 9:4–7)

In short, these passages anticipate, interpret theologically, and offer hope in the face of circumstances which for Solomon's day were still in the distant future but which for the compilers of Genesis-II Kings were recent past—that is, the Babylonian capture of Jerusalem, exile of many of its people, the destruction of the Temple, and the end of the Davidic line. This happened, the compilers want us to understand, because the rulers who followed Solomon, and even he himself in his later years, were unfaithful to Yahweh and led the people astray. But theirs was also a message of hope, if the exilic community would repent: "if they lay it to heart in the land to which they have been carried captive, and repent."

Although these passages which focus on Solomon's cultic activities clearly were formulated long after Solomon's day and address theological concerns of the exilic community, they may include some elements of authentic historical memory. There is no reason to doubt that Gibeon was an important worship center during Solomon's reign, for example, or that Solomon himself worshiped there. The description of the Temple and its furnishings also seems realistic enough, if not entirely understandable at every point. The Temple remained standing until the sixth century B.C.E. If the description is misleading in any way, therefore, possibly it tends (1) to depict the Temple as it existed after four centuries of use (and perhaps after numerous modifications) rather than as it was when Solomon first built it, and (2) to exaggerate the richness of the original furnishings.

The report of Yahweh's appearance to Solomon in a dream while he slept in the Gibeon sanctuary finds close parallels in stories associated with other kings of the ancient world (see, for example, Herodotus, *Histories* II.141, and below, p. 349). The historicity of the "pharaoh's daughter," mentioned four different times (I Kings 3:1–2; 9:16, 24; 11:1), is doubtful on similar grounds. She also turns up fairly regularly in Arabic lore. The story about Solomon's wise judgment of the two prostitutes and the one about the visit of the queen of Sheba probably are just that and nothing more—good stories which emerged long after Solomon's day and play on the theme of his wisdom and wealth. Any attempt to identify the pharaoh who gave his daughter to Solomon in marriage or speculation on the political and commercial implications of the queen of Sheba's visit simply misunderstands the fanciful nature of the material. The same goes for the sweeping editorial claims regarding Solomon's daily food supply (ten oxen, twenty cattle, a hundred sheep, and on and on), the broad expanse of his dominion (from the Euphrates to the Egyptian frontier), his forty thousand stalls of horses, his three thousand proverbs, and so on. All of this belongs to the idealized Solomon of legend.

Some of the items included in the Genesis–II Kings treatment of Solomon have a more authentic ring, however, suggested if for no other reasons than that (1) they supply details of a sort not characteristic of folk legends or editorial

The Gibeon Pool. The pool of Gibeon, possibly this one, excavated at el-Jib, was the scene of a skirmish between David's men and the remnant of Saul's army after the latter's death. (*J. B. Pritchard*)

hyperbole and (2) they point to a Solomonic reign of more modest and realistic proportions than the editors of the Genesis-II Kings account wished to convey. Belonging to this category are the lists of Solomon's high officials (I Kings 4:1–6), of the officers in charge of providing food for his household (I Kings 4:7–19), and of the cities he built (fortified) with forced labor (I Kings 9: 15–19). Also to be considered in this regard are the occasional items that provide some specific detail about his international involvements: his dealings with Hiram the king of Tyre, particularly the shipping venture (I Kings 9: 26–28; 10:11–12, 22); the sources and costs of his horses and chariots, although not the excessive size of the chariotry attributed to him (I Kings 10:28–29); and the conflicts with Hadad of Edom and Rezon of Damascus (I Kings 11:14–25). Finally, the episode involving Jeroboam of Ephraim (I Kings 11:26–40) must be taken very seriously, since it conflicts so obviously with the portrait of Solomon that the compilers of Genesis-II Kings wished to convey and since it anticipates the rebellion that occurred at Solomon's death (see I Kings 12: 1–20).

The conflict noted at the beginning of this chapter between the sweeping claims about Solomon's wisdom, wealth, and power, on the one hand, and bits of information that seem to undercut these claims, on the other, was noticeable also to the compilers of Genesis-II Kings. They dealt with this conflict by distinguishing between the first and main part of Solomon's reign, during which they depict him as the faithful ruler who achieved "the golden age" (I Kings 3–10), and his last years during which they depict him as one led astray by foreign women. Accordingly, the negative items reported for Solomon's reign —such as Jeroboam's opposition to the forced-labor policies and his escape to Egypt—are all placed in the last years. We have encountered the same pattern in connection with David—David under the blessing followed by David under the curse—and will see it later in the biblical presentations of other Judean kings. Needless to say, this is an artificial arrangement of the material.

Also artificial and schematic are the chronological notations provided. The Temple, we are told, was begun in the fourth year of Solomon's forty-year reign, which was also the four hundred and eightieth year after the exodus from Egypt. Solomon's building projects required exactly half of his reign, twenty years, and seven years of that time were devoted to the building of the Temple (I Kings 6:1, 37–38; 7:1; 11:42). These are symbolic numbers—four, forty, multiples of forty, and seven—not to be taken literally. Moses is said to have lived for a hundred and twenty years, which were divided into three forty-year periods. Many of the judges served for forty years and were separated by forty-year intervals of peace. David ruled for forty years, seven of which he resided at Hebron, and on and on. Actually there is no way of knowing how long either David's or Solomon's reign lasted. It does appear, for reasons that will be discussed in Chapter 7, that Solomon's reign ended approximately in 925 B.C.E.

The compilers of Genesis-II Kings concluded their presentation of Solomon's reign with reference to a source from which, presumably, they derived some of their material. "Now the rest of the acts of Solomon, and all that he did, and his wisdom, are they not written in the book of the acts of Solomon?" (I Kings 11:41). This pattern will be repeated for each of the later Israelite and Judean kings. That is, for the "rest of the acts" of each of the Israelite kings the reader will be referred to "the Book of the Chronicles of the Kings of Israel" and for the "rest of the acts" of each of the Judean kings to "the Book of the Chronicles of the Kings of Judah" (I Kings 14:19, 29; 15:7, 23, 31; and so on). These books of "Chronicles" of the kings of Israel and Judah are not to be confused with the canonical books of I-II Chronicles, of course, which refer the reader to still other sources, such as "the Chronicles of Samuel the seer," "the Chronicles of Nathan the prophet," and "the Chronicles of Gad the seer" (I Chron. 29:29). Scholars have generally supposed, although it cannot be proved, that the books of "Chronicles" to which the compilers of Genesis-II Kings referred were annalistic-like accounts based ultimately on court records. That this was the case as well with "the book of the acts of Solomon," "the Chronicles of Samuel the Seer," "the Chronicles of Nathan the prophet," and so on, seems less likely. In any case, it is impossible to determine which material in the Genesis-II Kings presentation of Solomon was derived from "the book of the acts of Solomon."

Other Biblical Sources Pertaining to Solomon

The Chronicler's Presentation of Solomon

The Chronicler's treatment of Solomon (II Chron. 1–9) follows the same pattern as his treatment of David. Namely, it depends heavily upon, and largely reproduces, the corresponding section of the Genesis-II Kings account but modifies the latter in a noticeably tendentious fashion.

1. The questionable circumstances surrounding Solomon's accession to the throne disappear in the Chronicler's version. David designates Solomon as his successor and actually crowns him even before assigning the Levites their special responsibilities (I Chron. 23:1). Later, after completing his total organization of the cultic and civil administration and as he approaches death, David turns the throne over to Solomon, who receives unanimous approval.

> And they made Solomon the son of David king the second time, and they anointed him as prince for Yahweh, and Zadok as priest. Then Solomon sat on the throne of Yahweh as king instead of David his father; and he prospered, and all Israel obeyed him. All the leaders and the mighty men, and also all the sons of King David, pledged their allegiance to King Solomon." (I Chron. 29:22b–24)

2. When describing the actual reign of Solomon, the Chronicler omits or recasts any items that might be taken to suggest less than ideal circumstances. Thus, for example, the brief report in I Kings 9:10–14 about Solomon's concession of twenty cities to Hiram of Tyre is turned around to suggest that it was the Phoenician king who gave the cities to Solomon (II Chron. 8:1–2). We hear

nothing of the troubles with Hadad of Edom or Rezon of Damascus. There is silence as well about Jeroboam's role in Solomon's forced-labor program and Ahijah's prediction that Jeroboam would receive twelve parts of the kingdom (although Jeroboam's escape to Egypt will be presupposed later in the Chronicler's account; II Chron. 10:2–3).

3. The Chronicler assigns even greater prominence to Solomon's cultic activities than does the Genesis-II Kings account and elaborates on the details of the ceremonies. Of the nine chapters that the Chronicler devotes to Solomon, six have to do with the building and dedication of the Temple. Occasionally the Chronicler introduces supernatural elements into the ceremonies, as at the end of Solomon's prayer:

> Fire came down from heaven and consumed the burnt offering and the sacrifices, and the glory of Yahweh filled the temple. And the priests could not enter the house of Yahweh, because the glory of Yahweh filled Yahweh's house. When all the children of Israel saw the fire come down and the glory of Yahweh upon the temple, they bowed down. (II Chron. 7:1–3)

Most of the Chronicler's elaboration of the ceremonies, however, has to do with the various orders of Levites who are depicted fulfilling the cultic functions which, according to the Chronicler, David had assigned them.

Solomon and the "Wisdom" Books

In the same way that David, known as the patron of Israel's cultic music, came to be credited with many psalms that he did not compose, so also Solomon, remembered as the wise king with many wives, came to be associated with books pertaining to wisdom and love that were written or compiled long after his day. Specifically, Solomon is associated with the books of Proverbs, Ecclesiastes, Song of Songs, and Wisdom of Solomon. Two questions arise: How did Solomon come to be associated with wisdom in the first place? What was his connection, if any, with these particular books?

The collection and transmission of instructional and proverbial literature, the sort of thing one finds in the biblical books of Ecclesiastes and Proverbs, appear to have been largely a royal endeavor in the ancient Middle East. The king— or pharaoh, since our best examples come from Egypt—was the patron, while the actual literary activity was conducted by royal scribes. Solomon, as the monarch of a kingdom that now was reaching some maturity, would have begun to engage in the various royal pursuits of the day—building programs, international commerce, and also, one may presume, the patronage of learning and literature. Whether Solomon actually wrote any proverbs himself, or whether any of his own personal proverbs eventually made their way into the biblical books, is open to dispute, as is the corresponding question regarding David and the psalms. In any case, Solomon's primary association with "wisdom" would not have been originally in his own personal capacity as a composer of proverbs but in the fact that he encouraged instructional and proverbial literature in his court.

Correspondingly, Solomon's connection with the books of Ecclesiastes, Proverbs, and Wisdom of Solomon would be that (1) these books belong to a literary tradition which Solomon patronized and (2) some of the proverbs, wise sayings, and such which found their way into these books may actually date back to Solomon's day. This latter possibility seems more likely in the case of the book of Proverbs than Ecclesiastes or Wisdom of Solomon. Note the subtitles in the book of Proverbs which suggest that it incorporates older collections of proverbs, two of which are associated with Solomon (Prov. 10:1 and 25:1). The second of these subtitles reads "These also are proverbs of Solomon which the men of Hezekiah king of Judah copied." Presumably the compilers of the book of Proverbs drew on older collections which they in turn associated with Solomon.

Solomon's connection with the Song of Songs, a collection of love poetry, can be dismissed out of hand. Since Solomon was said to have had many wives, it was natural to fantasize that he must have been a great lover. Thus it seemed reasonable for the compilers of Song of Songs, or a later copyist, to identify the male character in the love poetry as Solomon.

The preceding discussion of the biblical materials pertaining to Solomon leads to three conclusions. First, the Genesis-II Kings account must serve as our primary source of information about his reign, as it has for the earlier periods of biblical history. The Chronicler's account is of no significant help. Nor is there anything of consequence to be learned about Solomon from any of the other biblical sources. Second, the Genesis-II Kings presentation of Solomon's reign consists largely of extended descriptions of Solomon's cultic activities and sweeping, generalized claims regarding his great wisdom, wealth, and international prestige. Third, which will become more apparent below, when one attempts to probe beneath these sweeping, generalized claims for specific information about Solomon's reign, the results are disappointing and the meager information derived simply does not support the sweeping claims.

If we read between the lines, it seems obvious that Solomon inherited a kingdom from David that was by no means unified in spirit. Perhaps the fact that Solomon was able to hold the kingdom together throughout his reign was one of his major accomplishments. Apparently the trend that was begun under David toward an autocratic, Jerusalem-based monarchy reached full development under Solomon. Solomon was probably an unusually wealthy and powerful ruler by the standards of Early Iron Age Palestine. Yet viewed in the broader context of the ancient Middle East, he is to be regarded more as a local ruler over an expanded city-state than as a world class emperor. He engaged in the normal royal pursuits of his day—building programs, commercial ventures, patronage of instructional and proverbial literature. Whether he was such a wise ruler would have been a matter of opinion even in his own day. Most of his constituency apparently thought not, since they chose to rebel at his death rather than to continue under his policies.

Solomon's Accession to the Throne

Allowing for the fact that the account of Solomon's accession to the throne is the work of a storyteller with pro-Solomonic inclinations, we nevertheless can draw certain basic conclusions from this material. The overriding conclusion, of course, is that Solomon was not the heir apparent but gained the throne by a surprise palace coup. The coup occurred after David had reached old age and was no longer effective as a ruler. Thus it was not really David whom Solomon displaced, but Adonijah. The narrative presupposes that Adonijah had already begun to function as king to some degree but that his support was not unanimous.

> Now Adonijah the son of Haggith exalted himself, saying, "I will be king"; and he prepared for himself chariots and horsemen, and fifty men to run before him. His father had never at any time displeased him by asking, "Why have you done thus and so?" He was also a very handsome man; and he was born next after Absalom. He conferred with Joab the son of Zeruiah and with Abiathar the priest; and they followed Adonijah and helped him. But Zadok the priest, and Benaiah the son of Jehoiada, and Nathan the prophet, and Shimei, and Rei, and David's mighty men were not with Adonijah. (I Kings 1:5–8)

It perhaps is significant to note that Adonijah and Solomon were each supported by a leading priest and a leading military figure, and that in both instances the one who had been with David the longest supported Adonijah. Joab, of course, was the commander of the army who had killed both Abner and Amasa when it appeared that they might pose a challenge to his supreme command. Abiathar, from the priests of Nob, had joined David when they both were fugitives from Saul.

It is useless to speculate on the reason for the division within the court between those who supported Adonijah's move and those who did not. At least three possibilities present themselves: (1) There may have been some ideological difference between the two parties. (2) Those who "were not with Adonijah" may have felt that it was premature for Adonijah to begin to play the role of king while David was still alive. (3) Adonijah may have turned only to Joab and Abiathar for support and ignored the others. Fearful that they would have a diminished role in his new administration, therefore, they may have organized against him.

It is also useless to speculate on whether David actually had promised Bathsheba that her son Solomon would inherit the throne, whether she and Nathan simply convinced David that he had made such a promise, or whether the whole bedroom scene described in I Kings 1:11–37 is the storyteller's fiction designed to authenticate Solomon's coup by explaining that it had David's approval. The same kind of uncertainty surrounds the report of David's last instructions to Solomon which claims that David himself approved the executions of Joab and Shimei.

In any case, David's commands and instructions presumably were all given behind the scenes and reported by those who supported the coup, rather than announced publicly by the old man himself. Moreover, Solomon's hasty coronation seems to have been conducted in semisecrecy, with only a select and controlled audience, and without any consultation with, or participation of, the elders of Israel or Judah.

> So Zadok the priest, Nathan the prophet, and Benaiah the son of Jehoiada, and the Cherethites and the Pelethites, went down and caused Solomon to ride on King David's mule, and brought him to Gihon. There Zadok the priest took the horn of oil from the tent, and anointed Solomon. Then they blew the trumpet; and all the people said, "Long live King Solomon!" And all the people went up after him, playing on pipes, and rejoicing with great joy, so that the earth was split by their noise. (I Kings 1:38–40)

Probably Saul, certainly David, and even Absalom, had been crowned in public ceremonies with some semblance of representative participation, including strong support from outside Jerusalem. Solomon's coronation was an act of appointees to office with the acclamation of a Jerusalem crowd.

Finally, we learn from the opening chapters of the book of I Kings that Solomon removed Adonijah and his two prominent supporters from the scene following David's death. The official explanation again presupposed an incident that occurred in private and involved Bathsheba. Adonijah supposedly came to Bathsheba with a rather precipitous and daring request: "And he said, 'Pray ask King Solomon—he will not refuse you—to give me Abishag the Shunammite as my wife' " (I Kings 2:17). Abishag was the young maiden who had been brought in to comfort David in his old age and now resided in the royal harem. Taking access to the king's harem may have been regarded as a symbolic action, on the other hand, perhaps tantamount to claiming the crown itself. We have seen, for example, that Absalom made a public show of entering the harem when he seized Jerusalem (II Sam. 16:21). Whatever the actual implications, Solomon accused Adonijah of still having designs on the crown and sent Benaiah to execute both him and Joab.

Abiathar, on the other hand, was exiled to his estate at the village of Anathoth a short distance northeast of Jerusalem. Anathoth was situated just beyond the Mt. Scopus ridge, in fact, which further supports the view that the Nob sanctuary, with which Abiathar was associated before he joined David, was on Mt. Scopus. The editors of the Genesis-II Kings account (or perhaps a later copyist) connected the Nob priests with the Elide line and interpreted Abiathar's exile as the fulfillment of predictions that the Elide line would come to a disastrous end (compare I Sam. 2:27–36; 14:3; 22:20; I Kings 2:27). But this is an artificial connection, as was observed and explained in Chapter 5.

Solomon and the Cult

The "Great High Place" at Gibeon

Solomon's sacrifices at the high place at Gibeon and his patronage of foreign gods in Jerusalem presented a theological problem for the compilers of Genesis-II Kings. Such acts were inappropriate for the builder of Yahweh's Temple and the king whom Yahweh blessed above all others. They resolved the problem by placing the Gibeon incident at the beginning of Solomon's reign, before the Temple would have been available for worship, and by placing Solomon's involvement with foreign cults at the end of his reign after he supposedly had fallen under the influence of foreign wives. This is an artificial and anachronistic arrangement; sacrifices elsewhere than at the Jerusalem Temple and royal patronage of foreign gods probably would not have been regarded as religious apostasy in Solomon's day. Yahweh had emerged as the national god of the kingdom already under Saul and David. This was formalized by Solomon when he included a Temple dedicated to Yahweh in the royal building complex at Jerusalem. But the concept of exclusive Yahwistic monotheism was still many years, even centuries, in the future. Given the religious perceptions and practices of Solomon's day, plus the still heterogeneous character of the population that he ruled, it would have been regarded as altogether appropriate for him to provide shrines in Jerusalem for other persons of the court (not just wives) who looked to other gods. Moreover, the Gibeon high place may have had its own special role in the Yahwistic cult.

According to I Sam. 7:1 and II Sam. 6:2–3 (from the so-called Ark Narrative discussed in Chapter 4), the Ark resided for a time at Gibeah ("the hill") in the vicinity of Kiriath-jearim before David brought it to Jerusalem. We suggested above that this Gibeah/"hill" may have been Nebi Samwil, a very prominent hill situated between the sites of ancient Kiriath-jearim and Gibeon. Now we hear of Solomon going to "the great high place" at Gibeon to offer sacrifices (I Kings 3:4). The Gibeon sanctuary would not necessarily have been in the village itself but more likely, it seems to us, on Nebi Samwil which overlooked the village. In other words, Solomon may have continued to worship at the same place where the Ark had resided before David transferred it to Jerusalem. (According to the Chronicler, in fact, the "tent of meeting" was still there when Solomon went to offer his sacrifices. See II Chron. 1:6.)

Construction of the Temple

Solomon's construction of the Temple is given pride of place among his accomplishments by the compilers of Genesis-II Kings and by the Chronicler. Actually the Temple was but part of a more extensive royal complex constructed by Solomon, and by no means the largest building in the complex. The Temple was built in tripartite form, with the dimensions provided for the three main sections requiring a total space of 70 cubits long by 20 cubits wide by 30 cubits high. Calculated on the basis of a royal cubit of twenty-one inches, this would be approximately 122 by 35 by 52 feet. Such a building obviously was not intended for the use of the general public but as a "house" for Yahweh (I Kings 6:1) and a royal chapel for the king and senior priests. A precise plan cannot be reconstructed in spite of the detail of the biblical description. It is unclear from the various dimensions provided, for example, how to allow for the width of the walls.

Two cherubim, winged guardian figures, each with a wingspan of some 20 feet, were placed in the inner sanctuary. The Ark itself was deposited beneath their wings. Flanking the entrance to the Temple were two freestanding, highly decorated columns which with their bronze capitals stood 23 cubits (or about 40 feet) high. These bore the names, still unexplainable, Jachin and Boaz. The general worship of the people and public cultic activity would have taken place in the courtyard where were situated the altar of sacrifice and an enormous laver, the "molten sea" (I Kings 8:62–64; for some reason the account omits any description of the altar).

The tripartite Temple plan as well as the decorations and furnishings appears to have been typical of the day and eclectic—that is, the various features find parallels from Egypt to Mesopotamia. This is what one would expect, of course, for a sacred precinct constructed and decorated by Phoenician craftsmen. Sanctuaries from approximately the same period and with comparable plans have been uncovered at Tell Tainat, Samal, and Hamath in Syria. The cherubim would be comparable to the sphinx-like guardian creatures that decorated Assyrian palaces and that are depicted in ivory carvings discovered among the ruins at Megiddo and Samaria.

Development of the Royal Zion Theology

Nathan's oracle in II Sam. 7:8–17, the psalm attributed to David in II Sam. 23:1–7, Solomon's prayer in I Kings 8:46–53 with Yahweh's response in 9:2–9, and a number of the psalms in the book of Psalms (such as Ps. 89 and 132) reflect what may be referred to as "royal Zion theology." The essence of this theology was the related claims (1) that Yahweh chose Jerusalem as the place of his own special presence and as the chief city of his people and (2) that Yahweh designated David and David's descendants to rule from Jerusalem in perpetuity. Secondary elements included (3) the cultic centrality of the Jerusalem Temple, (4) the special intermediary role of the Davidic king between Yahweh and the people, and (5) the qualification that Yahweh's protection of Jerusalem and the continuance of the Davidic dynasty depended on the faithfulness of the king and people to Yahweh.

Several of the psalms depict Jerusalem, particularly the Temple Mount, as a cosmic mountain where Yahweh himself actually reigned as king over all of his created order. Thus in a very special way he protected his city against its enemies (Ps. 46; 48; 76). Also there emerged the concept of a special covenant relationship between Yahweh and the Davidic rulers (II Sam. 23:5; Ps. 89:19–37). The king might even be referred to as "the son of God" (II Sam. 7:14; Ps. 2:7). As the representative of Yahweh and the embodiment of the community, the person of the king was a channel of Yahweh's blessings and the source of the life and fertility for the people (II Sam. 23:2–4; Ps. 72).

While this royal Zion theology may have already begun to emerge under David, the elaborated form summarized above and reflected in the passages cited will have developed over time. Probably it was under Solomon that this royal theology received its first clear and strong articulation. This seems likely on at least three grounds: (1) Solomon was the first of the Davidic kings whose claim to the throne was based purely on the dynastic principle. David was crowned by the people of Judah and Israel in ceremonies that involved covenant arrangements and he claimed Jerusalem by conquest. But Solomon's claim to authority over the land was in effect the royal Zion theology. Yahweh had chosen David and his descendants to rule, and David had chosen Solomon to be his successor. (2) The Jerusalem Temple, built by Solomon, is a prominent element in the Zion theology. (3) The passages listed above, although composed long after Solomon's day, seem to point particularly to him as the focus of the dynastic promise. Note, for example, the wording of Nathan's oracle:

> Moreover Yahweh declares to you that Yahweh will make you a house. When your days are fulfilled and you lie down with your fathers, I will raise up your offspring after you, who shall come forth from your body, and I will establish his kingdom. He shall build a house for my name, and I will establish the throne of his kingdom for ever. (II Sam. 7:11b–13)

Solomon's Administration

The occasional items of information provided regarding Solomon's administrative arrangements suggest an increase in bureaucracy over David's arrangements. This is only suggestive, however. The information provided is not adequate to reconstruct either David's or Solomon's administrative system in any comprehensive fashion. The following texts, or groups of texts, are relevant to Solomon's administration: (1) the list in I Kings 4:1–6 of Solomon's "high officials"; (2) the list in 4:7–19 of the twelve (or thirteen?) officers *(nissabim)* "over all Israel, who provided food for the king and his household"; (3) the

Ivory Cherub. Winged sphinx or cherub, discovered with other such ivory carvings among the ruins at Sebastiyeh (biblical Samaria). Although dating from somewhat later than Solomon's day, it illustrates one of the decorative motifs of Solomon's Temple. *(Israel Museum)*

several texts pertaining to Solomon's practice of extracting "forced labor" for his construction projects; and (4) the account of the Shechem assembly where Rehoboam is called on to decide whether he will continue Solomon's harsh policies (I Kings 12:1–20).

Solomon's "High Officials"

The list of Solomon's high officials *(sarim)* recorded in I Kings 4:1–6 (see Chart VII) corresponds to the list of David's chief officers provided in three versions (II Sam. 8:16–18; 20:23–26; I Chron. 18:15–17; compare Chart VI, above). In effect, these lists represent the "cabinet," the inner circle of advisers and chief administrators of David and Solomon respectively.

The entry for Zadok and Abiathar as priests in Solomon's list probably is a secondary scribal addition intended to take into account that Zadok and Abiathar were in fact the chief priests at the very beginning of Solomon's reign. But this would not have applied after Abiathar was exiled to Anathoth and after the sons of Zadok and Nathan assumed office. Presuming this entry to be secondary, the original list seems to have represented the situation later in Solomon's reign, after both Abiathar and Zadok had passed from the scene.

Two further observations are to be made: (1) Benaiah and Nathan apparently were rewarded for their role in securing the throne for Solomon. Benaiah has taken Joab's place as supreme commander over the military and two of Nathan's sons hold "cabinet positions." (2) The chief administrative offices are becoming hereditary.

Officers "Who Provided for the King"

The officers over whom Azariah had charge presumably were the twelve *nissabim* listed in I Kings 4:7–19 "who provided food for the king and his household" (see Chart VIII). Unfortunately there are so many uncertainties

---

CHART VII. Solomon's High Officials (I Kings 4:1–6)

The priest	Azariah the son of Zadok
Secretaries	Elihoreph and Ahijah the sons of Shisha
Over the army	Benaiah the son of Jehoiada
Priests	Zadok and Abiathar (?)
Over the officers	Azariah the son of Nathan
Priest and king's friend	Zabud the son of Nathan
Over the palace	Ahishar
Over the forced labor	Adoniram the son of Abda

CHART VIII: Officers Who Provided for the King (I Kings 4:7–19)

Ben-hur	In the hill country of Ephraim
Ben-deker	In Makaz, Shaalbim, Beth-shemesh, and Elon-beth-hanan
Ben-hesed	In Arubboth (to him belonged Socoh and all the land of Hepher)
Ben-abinadab	In all Naphath-dor (he had Taphath the daughter of Solomon as his wife)
Baana, son of Ahilud	In Taanach, Megiddo, and all Beth-shean . . . and from Beth-shean to Abel-meholah, as far as the other side of Jokmeam
Ben-geber	In Ramoth-gilead (he had the villages of Jair the son of Manasseh, which are in Gilead, and he had the region of Argob, which is in Bashan, sixty great cities with walls and bronze bars)
Ahinadab, son of Iddo	In Mahanaim
Ahimaaz	In Naphtali (he had taken Basemath the daughter of Solomon as his wife)
Baana, son of Hushai	In Asher and Bealoth
Jehoshaphat, son of Paruah	In Issachar
Shimei, son of Ela	In Benjamin
Geber, son of Uri	In the land of Gilead, the country of Sihon king of the Amorites and of Og king of Bashan

"And there was one officer in the land [of Judah]"

surrounding this list that it becomes virtually useless as a source of historical information: (1) Several of the place-names cannot be located with any degree of certainty—for example, Shaalbim, Arubboth, the land of Hepher, Abel-meholah, Jokmeam, the villages of Jair, the region of Argob. (2) The place-names are of different sorts—some are cities (Beth-shemesh, Taanach, Megiddo); some are geographical areas (all the land of Hepher, the region of Argob); some are tribal designations (Naphtali, Asher, Issachar). (3) The place-names, to the extent that they can be located geographically, seem to have been scattered throughout Solomon's kingdom. Yet there is nothing to suggest that they represented any kind of district system that incorporated the whole kingdom. On the contrary, given the strange assortment of place-names and the seemingly haphazard way they are scattered, it is difficult to reconstruct even a hypothetical district system which they might have represented. (4) There seem to be contradictions within the list, or at least overlapping assignments.

Thus Ramoth-gilead and other villages in that vicinity are assigned to Ben-geber, while the land of Gilead is assigned to Geber son of Uri. (5) The list seems to have received secondary scribal notations, such as the notation that equates the land of Gilead with "the country of Sihon king of the Amorites and of Og king of Bashan." But it is impossible to establish with certainty which elements are secondary and which are not. What should be said about the final note, for example, which introduces "one officer in the land" and thus brings the total number of officers to thirteen, in conflict with the introductory statement (compare I Kings 4:7 with 4:19)? And if this final note is taken as part of the original list rather than a later scribal addition, what about the reading "of Judah" which is found only in certain Greek manuscripts?

Finally, (6) it is unclear exactly what these officers did. Their function is described as twofold: *(a)* to supply provisions on a rotating monthly basis for the royal court and *(b)* to provide barley and straw for the horses of Solomon's chariotry (I Kings 4:7, 27–28). But how did they collect the produce? Were they in effect tax collectors who assessed the citizens in their assigned cities/areas? Or were they in charge of crown properties scattered throughout the kingdom, thus serving in a capacity similar to that of Ziba, whom David placed in charge of Saul's estate, and to that of the stewards who, according to the Chronicler, managed David's own properties (I Chron. 27:25–31)? Presumably Solomon had some means of doing both, collecting taxes as well as managing the royal estates.

Forced Labor

Already under David there was an official in charge of forced labor (II Sam. 20:24). Under Solomon the employment of forced-labor gangs seems to have become a much more significant policy of state. Moreover, while David was active and successful in military affairs, thus producing foreign prisoners for his labor gangs, Solomon seems to have placed this burden on his own subjects. Solomon's preparations for his building program are reported as follows:

> King Solomon raised a levy of forced labor out of all Israel; and the levy numbered thirty thousand men. And he sent them to Lebanon, ten thousand a month in relays; they would be a month in Lebanon and two months at home; Adoniram was in charge of the levy. Solomon also had seventy thousand burden-bearers and eighty thousand hewers of stone in the hill country, besides Solomon's three thousand three hundred chief officers who were over the work, who had charge of the people who carried on the work. (I Kings 5:13–16)

The figures provided in this passage must be regarded as editorial exaggerations. Also attributable to the compilers of Genesis-II Kings is the statement in I Kings 9:15–23 that seeks to clarify that only foreigners had to serve in the labor gangs:

> All the people who were left of the Amorites, the Hittites, the Perizzites, the Hivites, and the Jebusites, who were not of the people of Israel—their descendants

who were left after them in the land, whom the people of Israel were unable to destroy utterly—these Solomon made a forced levy of slaves, and so they are to this day. But of the people of Israel Solomon made no slaves; they were the soldiers, they were his officials, his commanders, his captains, his chariot commanders and his horsemen. (I Kings 9:20–22)

In addition to the fact that this comment presupposes the late editors' idealized view of Israel's origins (see Chapters 2 and 3), it is contradicted by the Jeroboam-Ahijah affair described in I Kings 11:26–40. Specifically, Jeroboam is introduced as an Ephraimite officer whom Solomon had placed in charge "over all the forced labor of the house of Joseph." The "house of Joseph" would be essentially the Ephraim/Israel group of tribes which are prominent in the narratives of the Book of Judges and which were the core of Saul's kingdom. In short, while there quite likely will have been exemptions to Solomon's forced-labor program and to whatever other means he had of extracting wealth from his kingdom—relatives and friends of the king if no one else—there certainly was no blanket exemption that extended to Ephraim/Israel.

Solomon the Builder

As indicated above, the Temple was only part of a more extensive building program that Solomon conducted in Jerusalem and elsewhere. Specifically, his building projects in Jerusalem included repair and probably expansion of the city walls, further work on the Millo, a royal palace-governmental complex (which included the Yahweh Temple), and shrines for certain other gods (I Kings 3:1; 7:1–8; 9:15, 24; 11:7–8, 27). (See Map 16.)

Bronze Age Jerusalem and the Early Iron Age city that David had conquered probably was confined to Ophel, the slope that extends south of what is known today as the Temple Mount or the Haram es-Sharif. Apparently Solomon built the palace-governmental complex on the Temple Mount itself, which means that the city was expanded northward. Actually David may have already done some building there, as he apparently had already begun work on the Millo (II Sam. 5:9). If so, and if Solomon expanded the city wall northward to include the newly built up area on the Temple Mount, perhaps this is what is meant when we are told in I Kings 11:27 that Solomon "closed up the breach of the city of David his father."

Since the Temple was included in the palace-governmental complex situated on what is known today (for that reason) as the Temple Mount, and in view of the fact that many of the psalms associate the Temple so closely with Mt. Zion, it is tempting to conclude that ancient Mt. Zion and the so-called Temple Mount are one and the same. Be that as it may, the name Mt. Zion has been associated since the Roman period with another hill which overlooks Ophel from the west.

Outside Jerusalem, Solomon is reported as having built Hazor, Megiddo, Gezer, Lower Beth-horon, Baalath, and "Tamar in the wilderness, in the land [of Judah]," as well as unnamed store-cities and cities for his horses and chariots

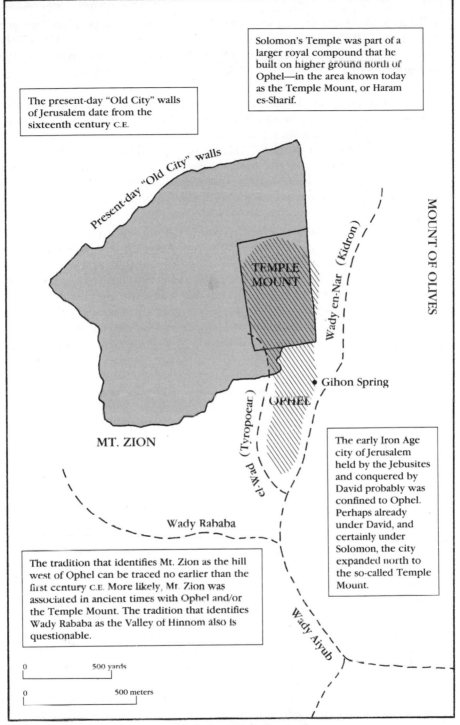

Solomon's Temple was part of a larger royal compound that he built on higher ground north of Ophel—in the area known today as the Temple Mount, or Haram es-Sharif.

The present-day "Old City" walls of Jerusalem date from the sixteenth century C.E.

Present-day "Old City" walls

MOUNT OF OLIVES

Wady en-Nar (Kidron)

TEMPLE MOUNT

Gihon Spring

el-Wad (Tyropoean)

OPHEL

MT. ZION

The early Iron Age city of Jerusalem held by the Jebusites and conquered by David probably was confined to Ophel. Perhaps already under David, and certainly under Solomon, the city expanded north to the so-called Temple Mount.

Wady Rababa

The tradition that identifies Mt. Zion as the hill west of Ophel can be traced no earlier than the first century C.E. More likely, Mt. Zion was associated in ancient times with Ophel and/or the Temple Mount. The tradition that identifies Wady Rababa as the Valley of Hinnom also is questionable.

Wady Aiyub

0   500 yards

0   500 meters

MAP 16. Solomon's Jerusalem

(I Kings 9:15–19). The first four of the named cities can be identified with present-day Tell el-Qedah, Tell el-Mutesellim, Tell Jezer, and Beit 'Ur et-Tahta respectively. Baalath and Baalah are variant forms of a common name used for several different places in ancient Palestine. Since it is mentioned with Lower Beth-horon in this context, one thinks of the Baalah near (or identical with) Kiriath-jearim (see Josh. 15:9–10). Tamar (meaning "palm tree") probably was located somewhere in the Judean Wilderness, although the qualifier "of Judah" is not supplied in the Hebrew (Masoretic) manuscripts. Note that the parallel passage in II Chron. 8:1–4 reads "Tadmor in the wilderness" (Tadmor usually identified with Palmyra in the Syrian desert) and has Solomon conquering Hamath-zobah and building his store-cities in that vicinity. This is that same fanciful passage which has Hiram giving Solomon the twenty cities rather than the other way around.

In regard to the four cities mentioned in the I Kings version that can be located with confidence, four observations are to be made. (1) None of these were entirely new cities founded by Solomon. In each case he was building on, or refortifying, a site that had been occupied earlier. (2) Each of these cities was strategically located to control traffic (military and commercial) through Solomon's realm (see below, Map 16). Hazor, in northern Palestine, was situated at the juncture of the main roads to Hamath and Damascus and at the place where the road to Damascus crossed the Jordan. Megiddo guarded the pass through which the coastal highway, or "the Way of the Sea," crossed from the Sharon Plain into the Jezreel Valley. Gezer and Beth-horon dominated the most direct approaches to Jerusalem from the west. (3) Excavations at three of these cities—Hazor, Megiddo, and Gezer—have produced remains approximately from the time of Solomon which are suggestive of royal building projects.

The archaeological record from these three cities is complex and much debated. That all three cities experienced a flurry of activity approximately during the tenth century, including building programs of more than local significance, seems certain. The debate centers on the precise stratigraphy of the three sites and the question of exactly which city walls, gates, and internal buildings are to be attributed to Solomon.

The situation seems most straightforward at Hazor (stratum X) where the excavators identified as Solomonic a casemate fortification wall with a four-entry gate defending an area of approximately 6.5 acres. A "casemate" wall is a double wall construction, two walls running parallel and connected by partitions at regular intervals. The "four-entry" gate is constructed so that those entering actually pass through a sequence of four entrys flanked by recessed cubicles. Similar casemate walls and four-entry gates have been discovered at Gezer and Megiddo. However, the stratigraphy at these latter two sites is less certain. At Megiddo, for example, where the casemate wall seems to have encircled the crest of the whole tell, approximately thirteen acres, it is uncertain whether the casemate wall actually belonged to the same building phase as the four-entry gate. Most scholars are inclined to believe that it does, in view of the fact that the same combination existed at Hazor and Gezer. Taking the same line of argument a step farther, it seems reasonable to assign all three fortification systems and associated buildings to Solomon.

While the dimensions of the casemate walls and four-entry gates at Hazor, Gezer, and Megiddo are not exactly the same, they are close enough to suggest a centralized building program. Some have suspected, in fact, that the same architect directed all three projects. The stones are large and well hewn. No doubt these three fortified cities were impressive for Palestine in the tenth century B.C.E.

I Kings 9:19, which speaks of Solomon's "store-cities," "cities for his chariots," and "cities for his horsemen," sounds like editorial generalization, although one would presume in any case that Solomon had storage depots and military units distributed throughout the land both for normal operations and in case of military emergencies.

Solomon's Involvement with Commerce

The passages that shed light on Solomon's commercial involvements were not intended primarily for that purpose but rather to emphasize and illustrate the luxury and wealth of his court. The reader is to understand that silver, gold, and exotic goods flowed into Jerusalem from all corners of the world: tribute from merchants and governors; presents from other rulers, such as the queen of Sheba; shiploads of gold, silver, precious stones, and exotica from Ophir; the finest horses and chariots from Que and Egypt. As with the whole Genesis-II Kings presentation of Solomon, it is difficult to know where realistic description ends and exaggeration begins. Moreover, the very passages that provide details to support the sweeping claims are beset with textual problems that preclude confident interpretation.

Overland Commerce

Solomon's main asset, as far as the potential for deriving profit from commerce was concerned, was the geographical position of his kingdom. As observed in Chapter 1, two international thoroughfares passed through Palestine: (1) "the Way of the Sea," which originated in Egypt, passed through the coastal plain until it turned inward at the Carmel ridge through the Megiddo pass into the Jezreel Valley, and joined at that point the main roads to the northern Transjordan, the Aramean cities of Damascus and Hamath, and the Phoenician coast; and (2) a north-south route through the Transjordan which connected western Arabia and the Red Sea, specifically the Gulf of Aqabah, with Damascus. A considerable stretch of "the Way of the Sea" fell within Solomon's territory and he would have been able to control the traffic along this stretch from cities such as Gezer, Megiddo, and Hazor. He would have controlled a somewhat smaller segment of the Transjordanian highway as well as numerous secondary routes. One of the important secondary routes, as we shall see below, was the overland connection between Ezion-geber at the northern end of the Gulf of Aqabah and Phoenician ports on the Mediterranean.

There would have been ways for Solomon to derive profit from commercial traffic through his realm without actually undertaking commercial ventures of his own—by imposing customs duties, for example, and by taxing transit traffic. One is tempted to read this sort of thing between the lines of I Kings 10:14–15, which states literally: "And the weight of gold which came to Solomon in one year was six hundred and sixty-six talents of gold beside that from the men of the merchants and the traffic of the traders and all the kings of the evening [west?] and the governors of the land." However, the exact meaning of this text is unclear and the income seems exaggerated beyond belief. Typical of the sweeping and generalized editorial statements of this Solomon section of Genesis-II Kings, the terminology is vague and the description based on later fantasies about Jerusalem's "golden age." Who were "the men of the merchants" or "the kings of the evening"? The term translated "governors of the land" *(pahoth ha'aretz)* derives from the later political vocabulary of the period of Assyrian domination in Palestine.

The one passage sometimes interpreted to mean that Solomon had his own merchants who engaged in overland commerce also is more ambiguous than one would have hoped. Literally, I Kings 10:28–29 reads:

> And Solomon's trade in horses was from Egypt, and from Que [Asia Minor] the merchants of the king took—from Que for a price. And a chariot went up and came out from Egypt for six hundred silver shekels, and a horse for one hundred fifty, and thus to all the kings of the Hittites, and to the kings of Aram, by their hand they delivered.

This passage is sometimes interpreted to mean that Solomon's merchants were middlemen, enjoying somewhat of a monopoly, in the horse and chariot trade between Egypt and Asia Minor. Yet the whole passage is ambiguous at best, and it may be saying nothing more than that Solomon imported his horses and chariots from Egypt and Que, paying the same standard price for them as did the kings of the Hittites and of Aram. No doubt the commerce that passed along the highways through Solomon's kingdom did involve some trade in horses and chariots. But to suppose that Solomon's merchants became deeply involved in this particular business is difficult to imagine since the Israelites heretofore had such little experience with either horses or chariots. David is said to have hamstrung horses taken in war (II Sam. 8:4). Also, it makes no sense for the Hittite or Aramean kings to have received horses from Que via Israel, since they were located much nearer to the Cilician source.

A Shipping Venture with the Phoenicians

The Phoenicians, whose merchant ships dominated the Mediterranean at the time, naturally wished to open new trading markets along the Arabian and

African coasts. The Red Sea gulf was the only viable sea route to these ports. Thus they apparently allowed Solomon some participation in the Red Sea trade in return for transit permission through his kingdom and access to the gulf. Solomon's involvement in the shipping venture is reported briefly in three slightly different versions. First we are told that Solomon himself built a fleet of ships at Ezion-geber and sent them out with Phoenician seamen to Ophir, from which they brought great amounts of gold (I Kings 9:26–28). A few verses later we read that the fleet belonged to the Phoenician king Hiram and that they returned with almug wood and precious stones as well as gold (I Kings 10: 11–12). Finally it is explained that Solomon had a fleet of ships which went out with Hiram's ships, and that they returned every three years bringing gold, silver, ivory, apes, and peacocks (I Kings 10:22).

Regardless of who actually owned the fleet or fleets, it is clear that both Hiram and Solomon made crucial contributions to the viability of the venture. Hiram provided the maritime knowledge—shipbuilders to direct the construction of the fleet at Ezion-geber, sailors to command the ships at sea, and merchants experienced in opening markets on distant shores. Solomon provided access to the Red Sea (perhaps not without difficulty, as we shall see below), laborers and supplies for the shipbuilding, and inexperienced sailors.

The exact location of Ezion-geber and even the general locale of Ophir are unknown. One suspects that the description of costly goods imported is a bit exaggerated and wishes to know what sort of trade items Solomon exported in

Phoenician Ship. This fragmentary relief from Nineveh shows a Phoenician ship at sea, being rowed by her crew. Solomon's shipping ventures (I Kings 9:26–28; 10:11–12, 22) involved Phoenician sailors and ships such as this in operations in the Red Sea. *(The British Museum)*

exchange. No ancient texts, biblical or otherwise, suggest that Solomon had mines. This is pure speculation of recent vintage.

The Extent of Solomon's Kingdom

Solomon's kingdom will have consisted of the bulk of western Palestine—but excluding most of the Mediterranean coast which would have been in the hands of the Philistines and the Phoenicians—and a large segment of the northern Transjordan. (See Map 17.) This is indicated on three grounds: (1) It is essentially the area indicated above which Solomon would have inherited from David, and there is nothing to indicate how he would have expanded the kingdom. Even the sweeping editorial claims about his wealth and power do not credit him with military conquests. (2) Although some of the locations are uncertain, it is clear that the cities/areas from which his twelve officers collected produce and the cities which he fortified all fell within the realm indicated above. (3) Information that can be gleaned about Solomon's international relations further confirms that this was his realm of authority.

The claim in I Kings 4:24, "For he [Solomon] had dominion over all the region west of the Euphrates from Tiphsah to Gaza, over all the kings west of the Euphrates," finds no support in the few details provided about his international relations. As we observed in Chapter 5, there is nothing to suggest that David ever subjected the Philistines; and certainly there is nothing to suggest that Solomon did. On the contrary, one of Solomon's purposes in fortifying Gezer would have been to secure his western frontier against Philistine encroachment. His northeastern frontier, on the other hand, fell short of Damascus. Earlier one of the cities of Hadadezer of Zobah, Damascus had fallen into the hands of Rezon, who in turn "was an adversary of Israel all the days of Solomon, doing mischief as Hadad did; and he abhorred Israel, and reigned over Syria" (I Kings 11:25).

Hadad was an Edomite prince who had been taken as a child to Egypt for safety during the years of warfare between David and the Edomites. Returning to his homeland after David's death, Hadad also gave Solomon problems of some sort (I Kings 11:14–22). Although no details are supplied, one suspects that he preyed on Solomon's caravans moving to and from Ezion-geber. Solomon's relations with the Moabites and the Ammonites apparently were peaceful and secured by his marriage to Moabite and Ammonite princesses. Possibly Jerusalem represented the stronger partner in these marriage alliances. But there is no clear evidence of this; and in any case Solomon's patronage of Moabite and Ammonite cults in Jerusalem suggests that Moab and Ammon were regarded as autonomous kingdoms.

The Phoenician cities were strong at the time, particularly Tyre under Hiram who had ascended the throne during David's reign. Both David and Solomon benefited from the more advanced technology and craftsmanship of the Phoenicians. As seen above, the joint shipping venture was really a Phoenician undertaking in which Solomon was allowed to participate because he controlled access

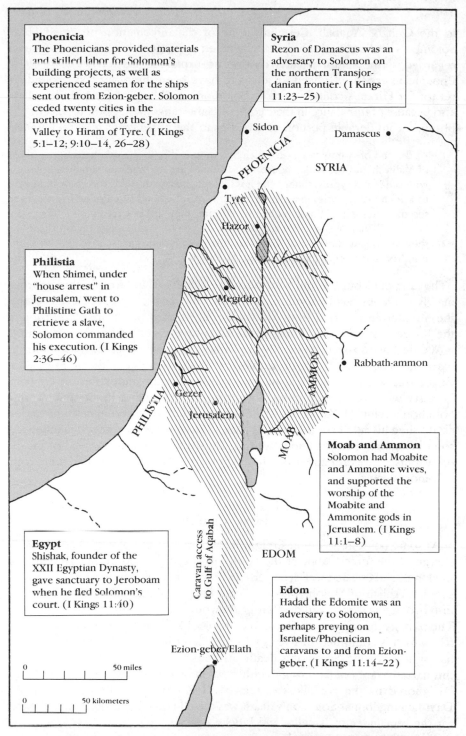

Phoenicia
The Phoenicians provided materials and skilled labor for Solomon's building projects, as well as experienced seamen for the ships sent out from Ezion-geber. Solomon ceded twenty cities in the northwestern end of the Jezreel Valley to Hiram of Tyre. (I Kings 5:1–12; 9:10–14, 26–28)

Syria
Rezon of Damascus was an adversary to Solomon on the northern Transjordanian frontier. (I Kings 11:23–25)

Philistia
When Shimei, under "house arrest" in Jerusalem, went to Philistine Gath to retrieve a slave, Solomon commanded his execution. (I Kings 2:36–46)

Egypt
Shishak, founder of the XXII Egyptian Dynasty, gave sanctuary to Jeroboam when he fled Solomon's court. (I Kings 11:40)

Moab and Ammon
Solomon had Moabite and Ammonite wives, and supported the worship of the Moabite and Ammonite gods in Jerusalem. (I Kings 11:1–8)

Edom
Hadad the Edomite was an adversary to Solomon, perhaps preying on Israelite/Phoenician caravans to and from Ezion-geber. (I Kings 11:14–22)

Sidon

Damascus

PHOENICIA

SYRIA

Tyre

Hazor

Megiddo

AMMON

Rabbath-ammon

Gezer

Jerusalem

PHILISTIA

MOAB

Caravan access to Gulf of Aqabah

EDOM

Ezion-geber/Elath

0   50 miles

0   50 kilometers

MAP 17. The Approximate Extent of Solomon's Kingdom

to the Gulf of Aqabah. Certainly none of the information provided about Solomon's dealings with Hiram can be taken to suggest that Solomon was ever regarded as the senior partner or that he expanded his territorial realm at Phoenician expense. Indeed, it seems to have been the other way around. In return for Hiram's contributions to Solomon's building program and perhaps also because of imbalance in their commercial arrangements, Solomon ceded to Hiram a considerable portion of territory in the northwestern Jezreel Valley.

> At the end of twenty years, in which Solomon had built the two houses, the house of Yahweh and the king's house, and Hiram king of Tyre had supplied Solomon with cedar and cypress timber and gold, as much as he desired, King Solomon gave to Hiram twenty cities in the land of Galilee. But when Hiram came from Tyre to see the cities which Solomon had given him, they did not please him. Therefore he said, "What kind of cities are these which you have given me, my brother?" So they are called the land of Cabul to this day. Hiram had sent to the king one hundred and twenty talents of gold. (I Kings 9:10–14)

"The land of Cabul" would have been the vicinity of the town Cabul approximately ten miles east by southeast of Acco. One must conclude, therefore, that the Mediterranean coast from Mt. Carmel northward plus a sizable portion of the Jezreel Valley was in Phoenician hands by the end of Solomon's reign.

We decline to speculate on which pharaoh gave his daughter to Solomon in marriage, since we regard the whole "pharaoh's daughter" theme as suspect. Egypt was weak at the time in any case, especially under the Twenty-first Dynasty which gave way to the Twenty-second, founded by Shishak, during Solomon's reign (I Kings 11:40). Shishak, a Libyan mercenary commander, established his rule first in Lower Egypt and from there expanded his influence, soon bringing all Egypt under control. Bubastis became the capital of his dynasty. Shishak was already strong in Egypt by the time Jeroboam fled there from Solomon's court.

Internal Conflict

At some point in Solomon's reign, Jeroboam, whom Solomon had placed in charge of the forced labor of the house of Joseph, "lifted up his hand against the king" and escaped to Egypt. Jeroboam was encouraged, we are told, by the prophet Ahijah of Shiloh, who predicted that the kingdom would be divided into two unequal parts and that Jeroboam would become king of the larger part. The passage that reports the incident, I Kings 11:26–40, begins a longer narrative which is continued in I Kings 12 and describes how the kingdom did in fact split following Solomon's death. Although the circumstances reported in this narrative are not flattering to either Solomon or Rehoboam, they could not be ignored by the compilers of Genesis-II Kings, since the collapse of the Davidic kingdom at Solomon's death was a well-known and determinative fact for the remainder of Israelite and Judean history.

We will look more closely at this narrative in the next chapter. For the moment it is sufficient to cite the Jeroboam incident as evidence of discontent among Solomon's subjects and to note that the friction in this particular case centered again on the Ephraimites who had dominated the old Ephraim/Israel tribal group and represented the core of Saul's kingdom. Jeroboam was an Ephraimite. He had been placed in charge over the forced labor of the house of Joseph, which was essentially the old Ephraim/Israel tribal group. The prophet Ahijah was from Shiloh, the Elide sanctuary that had enjoyed prominence under Saul.

CHAPTER 7

Separate Kingdoms

The Jerusalem-based kingdom established by David and held together by Solomon split apart following Solomon's death. In its place emerged two small kingdoms which would exist alongside each other for some two hundred years. The northern kingdom, which reverted to the name Israel and sometimes Ephraim, was centered in the hill country north of Jerusalem. The southern kingdom, which took the name Judah, was centered in the southern hill country encompassing Jerusalem and extending southward to the Negeb. Our task in the next five chapters is to recount the unfolding, parallel, and intertwined historical developments in the two kingdoms (see Chart IX).

Sources of Information

Our primary source of information for the period of the separate kingdoms is, as it has been for the preceding periods, the composite Genesis-II Kings account. Specifically, I Kings 12–II Kings 25 covers from Solomon's death to the time of the Babylonian exile. This is paralleled and partially duplicated by II Chronicles 10–36. Further information is derived from certain of the prophetical books, such as Isaiah and Jeremiah, and occasional nonbiblical documents.

Continuation of the Genesis-II Kings Account

The Genesis-II Kings treatment of the separate kingdoms follows a set pattern throughout. The kings of both Israel and Judah are introduced each in turn, in chronological order according to their respective accessions to the throne, regardless of which kingdom they represent. Brief notes are provided for each king which give certain specifics about his reign—family connections, building activities, length of reign, and so forth. These notations are generally believed to have been derived from the two sources cited by the compilers—"the Book of the Chronicles of the Kings of Israel" and "the Book of the Chronicles of the Kings of Judah." No longer available, these two sources may have been based in turn on official court records. Supplementing the brief notes about the deeds of each king is an evaluation of his reign and interpretative statements that explain theologically the overall flow of events. The presentation of Abijam's reign is typical:

> Now in the eighteenth year of King Jeroboam the son of Nebat, Abijam began to reign over Judah. He reigned for three years in Jerusalem. His mother's name was Maacah the daughter of Abishalom. And he walked in all the sins which his father did before him; and his heart was not wholly true to Yahweh his God, as the heart of David his father. Nevertheless for David's sake Yahweh his God gave him a lamp in Jerusalem, setting up his son after him, and establishing Jerusalem; because David did what was right in the eyes of Yahweh, and did not turn aside from anything that he commanded him all the days of his life, except in the matter of Uriah the Hittite. Now there was war between Rehoboam and Jeroboam all the days of his life. The rest of the acts of Abijam, and all that he did, are they not written in the Book of the Chronicles of the Kings of Judah? And there was war between Abijam and Jeroboam. And Abijam slept with his fathers; and they buried him in the city of David. And Asa his son reigned in his stead. (I Kings 15:1–8)

Occasionally there are extended interpretative passages such as II Kings 17.

The notations, evaluations, and interpretative passages described above represent the basic framework of I Kings 12–II Kings 25. Narratives of essentially two sorts have been inserted into this framework where the compilers considered them pertinent or illustrative. (1) Some of the narratives focus on key events, usually with a noticeable intention to provide a specific theological or political interpretation of the events. Examples of such narratives are the account of the assembly at Shechem (I Kings 12:1–19) and the story of the coup led by Jehu (II Kings 9:1–10:27). (2) Other narratives feature the prophets and emphasize their role in Israelite and Judean life. Examples of such prophetic narratives are the stories about Elijah and Elisha (I Kings 17–19; 21; II Kings 2; 3:4–8:15; 13:14–21).

Obviously then, I Kings 12–II Kings 25 provides a wealth of useful historical information that will serve as a reasonably secure basis for reconstructing the main features of the history of the separate kingdoms. Certainly it places the modern historian in a better position for dealing with Israel and Judah during this period than for any of the previous periods or for most of the other Near Eastern kingdoms and empires of the day. Still, this biblical account has its limitations as far as the historian's purposes are concerned and must be approached with reasonable caution.

Selectivity of the Information Provided. The information provided in I Kings 12–II Kings 25 is very selective—the names of the kings, basic chronological data about their reigns, a few notes about their wars and building activities, stories about the exploits of certain prophets, and so forth. Even the compilers of this material were conscious of their selectivity and for further information refer the reader again and again to "the Book of the Chronicles of the Kings of Israel" and "the Book of the Chronicles of the Kings of Judah." Modern historians,

CHART IX. Overview of the Kings and History of Israel and Judah

Solomon's death, the Shechem assembly, and the separation of the two kingdoms occurred approximately in 925 B.C.E. Israel and Judah existed alongside each other for approximately two hundred years, until the fall of Samaria, the Israelite capital, in 722 B.C.E. The Davidic kingdom of Judah survived 135 years longer, until the destruction of Jerusalem in 586 B.C.E.

Judah	Israel		
Rehoboam (924–907)	Jeroboam I (924–903)		Separation left the two kingdoms weak. Hostilities between them over the next half century drained their strength even further. Effective domain of Israel and Judah combined probably consisted of little more than the hill country west of the Jordan.
Abijam (Abijah) (907–906)		Four decades of hostilities between the two kingdoms (924–885 B.C.E.)	
Asa (905–874)			
	Nadab (903–902)		
	Baasha (902–886)		
	Elah (886–885)		
	Omri (885–873)		Under the Omride rulers Israel emerged as a strong kingdom and enjoyed a period of international prestige and internal prosperity which at least rivaled, and probably exceeded, that of Solomon. Judah under Jehoshaphat, was a close ally of Israel— possibly little more than a vassal.
Jehoshaphat (874–850)			
	Ahab (873–851)	The Omride Era (885–843 B.C.E.)	
	Ahaziah (851–849)		
Jehoram (850–843)			
	Jehoram (849–843)		
Ahaziah (843)			
Athaliah (843–837)	Jehu (843–816)		Related palace coups brought new rulers to the throne of both Israel and Judah and initiated a period of mutual weakness. Kings Hazael and Ben-hadad of Damascus made deep inroads into Israelite and Judean territory. Both Israel and Judah enjoyed a brief period of recovery during the reign of Jeroboam II.
Joash (Jehoash) (837–?)			
Amaziah (?–?)	Jehoahaz (816–800)	The Jehu Dynasty (843–745 B.C.E.)	
Uzziah (Azariah) (?–?)	Joash (800–785)		
Jotham (?–742)	Jeroboam II (785–745)		

	Zechariah (745)		Assyrian kings had threatened Syria-Palestine already during the mid-ninth century. Now Assyria turned its attention again to the west and, under Tiglath-pileser III (744–727), secured a firm grip on both Israel and Judah. Attempts to throw off the Assyrian yoke resulted in the annihilation of the northern kingdom. Judah continued to survive as an Assyrian vassal through the reign of Ashurbanipal (668–627), at which time a close alliance relationship existed between Assyria and Egypt, with Egypt gradually assuming dominance in Syria-Palestine.
	Shallum (745)		
Jehoahaz I (Ahaz) (742–727)	Menahem (745–736)		
	Pekahiah (736–735)		
	Pekah (735–732)	Assyrian domination (745–627 B.C.E.)	
	Hoshea (732–723)		
Hezekiah (727–698)	Fall of Samaria (722)		
Manasseh (697–642)			
Amon (642–640)			
Josiah (639–609)			
		Egyptian supremacy (627–605 B.C.E.)	Following the death of Ashurbanipal, Egypt became the dominant power in Syria-Palestine.
Jehoahaz II (609)			After the battle of Carchemish in 605, the Babylonians became masters of Syria-Palestine. Judean rebellions led eventually to the destruction of Jerusalem and the end of the Davidic kingdom of Jerusalem.
Jehoiakim (608–598)			
Jehoiachin (598–597)		Babylonian domination (605–586 B.C.E.)	
Zedekiah (597–586)			
Destruction of Jerusalem (586)			

aware that factors pertaining to economics, sociology, international politics, and the like must have had considerable bearing on the history of the two kingdoms, are given hardly enough information about those sorts of things even to specu-late. Moreover, the fact that I Kings 12–II Kings 25 focuses so specifically on Israelite and Judean history leaves the mistaken impression that Israel and Judah were the only kingdoms of consequence in Palestine at the time. One is tempted to think of Phoenicia, Philistia, Ammon, Moab, and Edom as having been marginal kingdoms by comparison, reduced to narrow strips of territory along the sea coast and the desert fringe. This may have been the case at times when Israel and Judah were strong (for example, under the Omrides). At other times, however, the domains of the Israelite and Judean kings were reduced to little more than an embattled foothold in the central hill country.

Theological Perspectives of the Compilers. As is the case throughout the Genesis-II Kings account, the theological perspectives of the compilers influenced their selection and arrangement of the materials pertaining to the separate kingdoms. Two working principles are especially noticeable. (1) The compilers clearly held the view that the security and prosperity of the kingdoms at any given time depended upon the religious fidelity of the current king. Accordingly, they tended to make rather much of the successes and to play down the failures of those kings whom they judged to be faithful, while deemphasizing the successes and magnifying the failures of those judged to be unfaithful. (2) Their primary criterion for evaluating each king's faithfulness was the extent to which he was loyal to the royal cult in Jerusalem and used his powers to eradicate worship of any sort, Yahwistic or otherwise, at sanctuaries outside that city. Thus the kings of Israel, who naturally rejected the Temple and worship in Jerusalem, were one and all judged to be unfaithful. As it turned out, most of the Judean kings had to be condemned as well, in varying degrees, because the principle itself was anachronistic. The idea that the Jerusalemite sanctuary and priesthood had exclusive claims on matters of Yahwistic worship apparently did not emerge even in Judah until the late eighth century.

The imbalance of attention given to Omri and Josiah in the Kings treatment of the separate kingdoms is a prime example of these two principles at work. Omri, a northern king and founder of what was considered to be an exceedingly evil dynasty, is allowed only thirteen verses, most of which have to do with events prior to his actual reign (I Kings 16:16–28). If one compares this with the lengthy treatment of the Judean king Josiah, who was regarded by the compilers to be a truly faithful king and credited with a royal program designed to destroy all sanctuaries outside Jerusalem, one might get the impression that Israel was a minor kingdom of little international consequence under Omri, while Judah under Josiah played a leading role in international affairs. Actually the situation was exactly the reverse, as we shall see in later chapters.

The Compilers' Use of Their Sources. The narratives interspersed throughout I Kings 12–II Kings 25 have their own individual theological (and sometimes propagandistic) intentions which the historian must also take into consideration. A more serious problem with the narratives, however, is that the compilers seem to have placed some of them out of proper historical context. This is particularly obvious with the Elisha narratives which appear in the context of the reign of Jehoram but which presuppose the sociopolitical circumstances of the later period of the Jehu dynasty. The same is probably true, as we shall see, of the three battle accounts in I Kings 20 and 22:1–38. It is easy to see how the compilers could have mistaken the appropriate context, since it is one of the characteristics of the narratives involved that they provide few specific political details and rarely refer to the kings of Israel by name.

The compilers may also have misunderstood their sources and created unnecessary problems for modern historians in connection with certain kings who had identical or similar names. At one point we are presented with contemporary Israelite and Judean kings, both named Jehoram, both descended from Omri, both reigning approximately the same number of years, and both meeting their death about the same time. Israel and Judah were very closely aligned at the time politically, which raises the possibility that Jehoram of Judah and Jehoram of Israel were in fact the same person—a single ruler over both kingdoms. Assuming that the official records of the Israelite and Judean kings were kept separately, one can see how later editors might have inferred that the Jehoram who appeared in the Judean records was distinct from the Jehoram who appeared in the Israelite records and treated them as separate kings.

Continuation of the Chronicler's History

Our second source of information for the period of the separate kingdoms is the Chronicler's history, specifically II Chronicles 10–36. As was the case with the Chronicler's treatment of David and Solomon, however, much of the Chronicler's material is found already in I-II Kings. Moreover, as we have observed, the Chronicler occasionally "adjusts" and elaborates on this material so that it will serve his theological purposes more effectively. Compare, for example, II Chron. 20:35–37 with I Kings 22:47–50 and note that the details of the account of Jehoshaphat's shipping venture as presented in I Kings have been conspicuously revised by the Chronicler, so that the failure of the venture is attributable to Jehoshaphat's alliance with the unfaithful king of Israel.

Apparently the Chronicler had access to other ancient sources also, in addition to the I-II Kings materials; and one must presume that he likewise "adjusted" the information derived from these other sources. Examples of supplemental material provided by the Chronicler are the report that Jehoshaphat had garrisons "in the cities of Ephraim which Asa his father had taken" (II Chron. 17:2) and the account of Yahweh's miraculous protection of Judah when Jehoshaphat was attacked by Moabites, Ammonites, and Meunites (II Chron. 20). Obviously these supplementary materials must be used with extreme caution, especially where it is apparent that the Chronicler's political or theological interests are involved. For example, the claim that Jehoshaphat placed garrisons "in the cities of Ephraim" appears to be part of the Chronicler's effort to present Jehoshaphat as a strong ruler, at least comparable to his Israelite contemporary Ahab. The very way in which the battle and victory are reported in II Chronicles 20—without Jehoshaphat and his army even having to take the field—marks the narrative as pious fiction. But is the account totally fictitious? Did the Moabites, the Ammonites, and the Meunites actually attempt to invade Judah during Jehoshaphat's reign and perhaps meet with some disaster? There is no way to know with certainty.

One other disadvantage with using the Chronicler's account as a source for reconstructing the history of the period of the separate kingdoms is that the Chronicler was interested almost exclusively in the southern kingdom, the Judean monarchs, and the Temple and cult in Jerusalem. Matters pertaining to the northern kingdom are mentioned only insofar as they have some bearing on Judean affairs.

Other Biblical Sources

Other biblical sources also provide data relevant to the history of the period of the separate kingdoms. For example, the prophetical books of Amos, Hosea, Micah, Isaiah, and Jeremiah provide considerable insight into the life and times of the eighth and seventh centuries B.C.E. All of these prophets addressed the political situation of their day and sought to persuade their countrymen of what they regarded to be the divine course of affairs. Thus one catches frequent glimpses in their pronouncements, even if only indirectly, of the inner dynamics of Israelite and Judean politics. Indeed, some of these prophets, particularly Isaiah and Jeremiah, were themselves overtly involved in politics. The prophets' scathing denunciations of the religiosity, the economic injustices, and the religious and civil leadership of their day provide insight into sociocultural matters —at least from the prophets' perspectives. The prophetic oracles against foreign nations extend the historian's vision beyond domestic to international affairs.

Other Ancient Texts

One of the truly exciting developments of modern times has been the recovery of literally thousands of texts from the various peoples of the Middle East and the decipherment of many of their ancient languages. As we noted above, the name "Israel" appears in one of these texts (the Merneptah Stela) from the end of the thirteenth century. There are no further such references in these documents to Israel (or Judah) until the end of the tenth century—that is, until the period of the separate kingdoms. From that time forward, numerous nonbiblical documents in several languages begin to come into consideration as directly relevant for understanding Israelite and Judean history.

First among these, chronologically, is the report of Pharaoh Sheshonk's campaign into Syria-Palestine recorded on a pylon of the Egyptian temple of Aton at Karnak, the site of ancient Thebes. This campaign is reported also in I Kings 14:25–27 (paralleled in II Chron. 12:1–12), where Sheshonk is called Shishak. A memorial inscription, written in Moabite and discovered near the site of ancient Dibon, recounts the deeds of King Mesha who ruled Moab during the ninth century. He is mentioned in II Kings 3:4–27 and his inscription refers to Omri king of Israel.

Royal Assyrian inscriptions and records, written in Akkadian cuneiform, have been discovered at dozens of sites in the Middle East. Some of these, from the ninth to the seventh century, report Assyrian activities that have direct connection with Israelite and Judean history and often make specific references to Israelite and Judean kings. After the decline of Assyria in the late seventh century, Babylonia became the dominant power in the Middle East. Accordingly, some of the royal Babylonian records from the late seventh and sixth centuries pertain to Babylonian-Judean relationships and provide the first precisely established date in biblical history, the Babylonian capture of Jerusalem on 15 or 16 March 597 B.C.E.

From sites in Palestine have come a number of nonbiblical texts—inscriptions, ostraca (inscribed potsherds), seals, and seal impressions. Among these are the Siloam tunnel inscription from Jerusalem which describes how the tunnel was built, apparently during the reign of Hezekiah (727–698 B.C.E.; see II Kings 20:20; II Chron. 32:30); the Samaria ostraca, which are administrative records of some sort, apparently from the reigns of two or more kings of the Jehu dynasty; the Arad and Lachish ostraca, which include communications sent to the commanders of these two fortifications during the seventh and sixth centuries; and various seals with names that sometimes can be associated with persons known from the biblical texts.

Lachish Ostracon. Ostraca (potsherds used in ancient times for writing) occasionally are found among the ruins of ancient Palestinian cities and provide valuable bits of information. The one above was discovered at Lachish and mentions the divine name YHWH (see Text XVI). *(The British Museum)*

All of these recently recovered nonbiblical items come as a mixed blessing. Obviously they shed much new and needed light on biblical history. They are especially helpful in establishing a chronological framework for the period of the separate kingdoms. At the same time, as we shall see below, they raise a multitude of tantalizing new questions and issues, many of which also have to do with chronology.

Archaeological Remains

The period of the separate kingdoms corresponds to the Late Iron (or Iron II) Age of Palestinian archaeology. A number of Iron II sites have been excavated and the results provide insight into the material culture of the day—size and layout of towns, domestic architecture, pottery forms, fortifications, and so on. One also gets some indication of general trends in national security and prosperity. Israel seems to have enjoyed its heyday during the ninth century, for example, as suggested by the impressive buildings, city walls, and water supply systems at Samaria, Megiddo, and Hazor. Less impressive building and fortification remains from the eighth, seventh, and sixth centuries, along with occasional indications of general city destructions, suggest economic decline and national insecurity. The ninth-century remains correspond, no doubt, to the Omride period when Israel's prosperity surpassed that of Solomon's day. Accordingly, the eighth-, seventh-, and sixth-century remains would represent post-Omride decline hastened on by Syrian, Assyrian, and Babylonian invasions.

More specific connections between the artifactual evidence and written records occasionally present themselves with varying degrees of likelihood. Thus the first two building phases of the royal citadel at Samaria can be attributed with a reasonable degree of certainty to Omri and Ahab respectively. It seems reasonable as well to attribute the Gihon-Siloam water tunnel at Jerusalem to Hezekiah. With less certainty one might associate the phasing out of the Arad temple with Hezekiah's or Josiah's cultic policies, the destruction of Lachish III with Sennacherib's invasion, and so on. In the final analysis, however, connections of this sort must remain hypothetical. Because of their very nature, nonliterary artifactual remains are much more useful for dealing with the general material culture of a period than with specific historical issues.

Establishing a Chronological Framework

The first securely dated event in Israelite and Judean history is the surrender of Jerusalem to Nebuchadrezzar's army reported in II Kings 24:10–17 and in a Babylonian chronicle. The Babylonian Chronicle reports the event as follows:

> Year 7, month Kislimu: The king of Akkad moved his army into Hatti land, laid siege to the city of Judah and the king took the city on the second day of the month Addaru. He appointed in it a king of his liking, took heavy booty from it and brought it into Babylon. (*ANET* 564)

The second day of Addaru in the seventh year of Nebuchadrezzar would have been 15 or 16 March 597 B.C.E. The uncertainty as to the specific day has to do with the fact that the Babylonians calculated their days from evening to evening rather than from midnight to midnight. In other words, one must presume from the chronicle that Jerusalem fell sometime between sundown 15 March and sundown 16 March.

With the exception of this date, the chronology provided in Chart IX, above, must be considered approximate. The range of error in the case of some kings may be as much as ten years, in other cases (Josiah and the later Judean kings, for example) no more than one or two years. The difficulties in establishing a chronological framework for the separate kingdoms result not so much from the absence of chronological information as from the fact that much of the information available is suspect, unclear, and simply does not "add up."

I-II Kings provides for each of the Israelite and Judean monarchs (1) a synchronistic date (that is, each king's accession to the throne is dated in relation to the reign of his contemporary on the throne of the other kingdom) and (2) the length of the king's reign. Occasionally the Chronicler adds further chronological data. Compare the following excerpts pertaining to Asa of Judah and Baasha of Israel.

> In the third year of Asa king of Judah, Baasha the son of Ahijah began to reign over all Israel at Tirzah, and reigned twenty-four years. (I Kings 15:33)

> In the twenty-sixth year of Asa king of Judah, Elah the son of Baasha began to reign over Israel in Tirzah, and reigned two years. But his servant Zimri, commander of half his chariots, conspired against him. . . . Zimri came in and struck him down and killed him, in the twenty-seventh year of Asa king of Judah, and reigned in his stead. (I Kings 16:8–10)

> In the twenty-seventh year of Asa king of Judah, Zimri reigned seven days in Tirzah. (I Kings 16:15)

> In the thirty-sixth year of the reign of Asa, Baasha king of Israel went up against Judah, and built Ramah. (II Chron. 16:1)

Obviously one can calculate only relative dates from information of this sort. Fortunately the Assyrian and Babylonian records provide dates calculable in terms of the Gregorian calendar, and occasionally cross references can be made between these records and the biblical accounts. It can be established, for example, that:

> Ahab was on the throne in Israel during Shalmaneser III's western campaign of 853 B.C.E.

> Jehu was on the throne at the time of Shalmaneser III's 841 B.C.E. campaign.

> Jehoash's reign overlapped with that of Adad-nirari III (810–783 B.C.E.) and Jehoash paid tribute to Adad-nirari sometime between 806 and 796 (most probably in 796 B.C.E.). And so on.

As indicated above, however, some of the chronological information available in the biblical texts is suspect and numerous difficulties arise when one attempts to work out specific dates for the Israelite and Judean kings on the basis of this information. (1) The chronological figures provided in I-II Kings are integral to the overall chronological structure of Genesis-II Kings which, as we saw in Chapter 2, presupposes an artificially schematic view of history. Even if these figures were derived originally from official records, therefore, some of them may have been adjusted to fit the requirements of the compiler's chronological schema. (2) Apparently these figures were somewhat fluid during the process of transmission, in any case, as is evidenced by the numerous variant readings in the different manuscripts and versions. Discrepancies are especially pronounced between the various Hebrew and Greek manuscripts. (3) There are internal discrepancies, moreover, in each of the manuscript traditions and versions. According to the passages quoted above from the standard Hebrew (Masoretic) tradition of Kings and Chronicles, for example, Baasha should have already been dead for ten years when he began building at Ramah (compare I Kings 16:8 with II Chron. 16:1). (4) The biblical figures require more time than the occasional "benchmarks" provided by the Mesopotamian records allow. We learn from the Assyrian records, for example, that Menahem paid tribute to Tiglath-pileser III in 737 B.C.E. and that Hoshea was placed on the throne in Samaria in 732 B.C.E. In other words, the Assyrian records allow a maximum of six years between the end of Menahem's reign and the beginning of Hoshea's. Yet II Kings credits Pekahiah and Pekah, who ruled between Menahem and Hoshea, with regnal periods totaling twenty-two years.

In addition to the difficulties that emerge from the available information, there are several crucial unknowns. What kind of calendar or calendars were in use in the two kingdoms? In other words, would a normal full year have been calculated from fall to fall or spring to spring? What method or methods were used to reckon the length of a king's reign? When a king died in midyear, for example, was the incomplete year ascribed to his reign, to his successor's reign, or to both? Were there coregencies or joint rules other than the one recorded for Uzziah and Jotham in II Kings 15:5? If so, how are they calculated in the biblical figures? To what extent have accidental errors and changes been introduced into the biblical figures during the process of transmission, or intentional changes introduced in an effort to clear up apparent inconsistencies?

By juggling the various possibilities and combinations of possibilities with respect to calendars, reckoning methods, and hypothetical coregencies, one can produce a chronology for the Israelite and Judean kings in which almost all the figures in any manuscript tradition fit together rather nicely. We have little confidence in the results of such endeavors, however, primarily because they overlook the schematic nature of the whole Genesis-II Kings chronology and the fact that the biblical figures for the synchronisms and regnal periods obviously were somewhat fluid during the process of transmission.

Accordingly, we offer only approximate dates for the Israelite and Judean kings. These approximations are based primarily on the regnal periods recorded in the Hebrew (Masoretic) version of I-II Kings calculated in accordance with an antedating reckoning system. That is, the length of reign recorded for each king is presumed to include the year in which he ascended the throne and in some cases the year in which his successor ascended the throne as well. When the biblical figures interpreted in this fashion simply do not "add up," however, or where the Mesopotamian records seem to require it, we have chosen to adjust the figures rather than to force an artificial harmony by proposing coregencies, shifting in midstream to another reckoning system, or the like. The main points of adjustment are as follows:

1. The regnal periods recorded for the early decades of the separate kingdoms are especially problematic. Moreover, the Lucianic recension of the Greek Old Testament preserves a pattern of synchronisms for the kings of the Omride

period which departs radically from those of the Hebrew manuscripts. The main difference is that the Lucianic version dates the kings of Judah earlier in relation to the kings of Israel. We suspect that the Lucianic recension preserves the more ancient tradition and have used its synchronisms to adjust the regnal periods which, as indicated above, must be adjusted in any case. The actual results are that Asa of Judah's reign is reduced from the forty-one years credited to him to thirty-one years, while the Omri-Tibni episode is confined to two years and dated to the twentieth/twenty-first year of Asa rather than his thirty-first year.

2. Our chronology for the period from Jehu's coup to Tiglath-pileser's invasions of Syria-Palestine gives precedence to the regnal periods recorded for the kings of Israel. The regnal periods assigned to the Judean kings for this period, particularly Jehoash, Amaziah, and Uzziah, are impossibly long. There may have been at least one coregency during this period, which raises the possibility that one or more of the excessively long Judean reigns overlapped. Actually, however, the wording of the very text that suggests the coregency of Uzziah and Jotham (II Kings 15:5–7, 32–33) seems to make a clear chronological distinction between the two reigns involved.

3. Tiglath-pileser received tribute from Menahem of Israel in 737 B.C.E. He placed Hoshea on the throne of Israel in 732 B.C.E. This means that the two years of rule in Samaria ascribed to Pekahiah plus the twenty years ascribed to Pekah are impossible. Accordingly, we have reduced the lengths of their reigns to two years and four years respectively.

The Shechem Assembly and Its Aftermath

Having reviewed the sources of information available for the history of the separate kingdoms and noted certain problems involved in their use, let us turn now to the events that unfolded immediately following Solomon's death. Rehoboam, Solomon's son and the offspring of Naamah an Ammonite (I Kings 14:21), was the heir designate. Presumably the Jerusalemites confirmed him as their new king without hesitation; the Bible simply does not report the matter. Jerusalem was the personal domain of the Davidic dynasty, of course, having been conquered by David. Officials there would have been appointed by and owed allegiance to the Davidic family, while the royal Zion theology perpetrated under David and Solomon called for an eternal rule of the Davidic dynasty over Jerusalem. Judah may have been inclined toward loyalty to the Davidic family also. After all, the dynasty was Judean in origin.

Rehoboam's confirmation obviously was not a matter of course in the north, however, since we read of Rehoboam making a journey to Shechem and appearing before "the assembly of Israel" there (I Kings 12). Why was this journey necessary? David had been confirmed by "all the tribes of Israel," with the elders of Israel coming to him at Hebron for that purpose (II Sam. 5:1–3). There is no indication, on the other hand, that Solomon went to Shechem for any sort of "double crowning" or that this would have been a normal expectation for his successors. Apparently there were pressing political reasons for Rehoboam to go to the north to negotiate the matter of kingship. Probably the people of the north had already given signals of disloyalty to Jerusalem and the Davidic dynasty. One clear signal would have been their failure to send representatives to Jerusalem affirming their support of Rehoboam in the first place.

The Constituency of the Shechem Assembly

The assembly of Shechem probably was an "ad hoc" convocation of voices that represented two not entirely distinct but essentially different groups. On the one hand, there would have been representatives of the old cities such as Megiddo, Tirzah, and Shechem, which had been brought under Jerusalem's domination by David and held by Solomon. These old cities had a history of being ruled by others, notably by the Egyptians. The foreign rule normally had been rather loose, however, allowing a degree of local autonomy. Such cities could not have been expected to remain in submission to an autocratic king in Jerusalem unless this was to their advantage or could not be avoided.

Shechem in particular was an important city with ancient traditions and no doubt much pride. Contrary to the implications of Judg. 8:30–35 and Joshua 24, which represent late editorial elements, Shechem seems not to have succumbed to Israelite domination during premonarchical times (see p. 116, above). One wonders, in fact, whether the account of the Shechem assembly reported in Joshua 24 might not have as its actual historical basis the same post-Solomonic assembly reported in I Kings 12, the event having been retrojected back to the period of the "conquest." If Judg. 8:30–35 and Joshua 24 are to be taken as authentic evidence of Israelite involvement in cultic activity at Shechem prior to the time of the monarchy, the cult probably would not have been that of the Baal/El-berith temple in the city but of another sacred place, the oak of Moreh (Gen. 12:6), somewhere outside the city.

Others among those who confronted Rehoboam at Shechem would have represented the sentiments of the clans, tribes, and small villages of the northern hill country—that is, essentially the constituency of the old Ephraim/Israel tribal group. These would have had special reasons for disenchantment with the house of David, beyond Solomon's harsh treatment of his subjects. In the first place, the Davidic dynasty, whose kingdom had emerged from Judah and been grounded primarily in Jerusalem, had displaced the house of Saul, whose kingdom was centered primarily in Ephraim/Israel. Second, the cultic places and priestly lines of Ephraim/Israel apparently had been deemphasized under David and Solomon in deference to those of Jerusalem. Indeed, as we have seen, there may have been a deliberate effort to co-opt some of the old Ephraimite/Israelite cultic relics, priests, and traditions to support the cultic primacy of Jerusalem. The Ark had been taken to Jerusalem. Jerusalemite court propaganda emphasized that Samuel, a Benjaminite prophet, had anointed David to rule in place of Saul. Especially the old sanctuary at Shiloh and its priesthood had been eclipsed by the Jerusalem cult. It is not at all surprising, therefore, that a Shilonite, Ahijah, is credited with predicting and helping to precipitate the north's break with Jerusalem (I Kings 11:29–39).

Alone, these small clans and villages, representative of the old Ephraimite/Israelite interests, would have been powerless to challenge Rehoboam. In cooperation with the large cities such as Shechem, however, they were in a position to resist. The extent to which the Shechem assembly was broadly representative is unclear. Which major cities other than Shechem actually participated? Were representatives of the Galilean tribes present? Nothing is said of these groups, but they can be expected to have followed the lead of Shechem and Ephraim/Israel.

The Secession of the North

Whatever chances Rehoboam had of holding together the Davidic state were dashed at Shechem. He was confronted with the demand that he alter Solomon's harsh policies: "Your father made our yoke heavy. Now therefore lighten the hard service of your father and his heavy yoke upon us, and we will serve you" (I Kings 12:4). Following the advice of his younger and perhaps lesser experienced advisers, Rehoboam chose not to negotiate but to threaten even more repressive measures: "My father made your yoke heavy, but I will add to your yoke; my father chastised you with whips, but I will chastise you with scorpions (I Kings 12:14). In response to this recalcitrant attitude and the deterioration of negotiations, the northerners raised the old cry of rebellion that had rung through the hills of Israel already during David's reign:

> What portion have we in David?
>   We have no inheritance in the son of Jesse.
> To your tents, O Israel!
>   Look now to your own house, David.
>   (I Kings 12:16; see II Sam. 20:1)

To handle matters, Rehoboam delegated Adoram, probably identical with Adoniram who had begun service as state supervisor of compulsory labor under David (II Sam. 20:24; I Kings 4:6; 12:17–18). No doubt Adoram had long experience in dealing with subject peoples, and for the northerners he embodied the policies of state which they had sought redressed. The rebels stoned Adoram to death and Rehoboam fled to Jerusalem in his chariot (I Kings 12:17–18).

Back in Jerusalem, Rehoboam is said to have assembled an army of Judeans and Benjaminites, but then decided against any immediate military attempt to recover the northern territories. The biblical account states that this decision was made on the advice of Shemaiah, a "man of God" (I Kings 12:21–24). Rehoboam may have realized as well that even Judah and the other southern territories were not entirely secure in his hands.

The Role of the Tribe of Benjamin

The Benjaminites, settled in the hill country immediately north of Jerusalem, were caught in between. On the one hand, they had been part of the old Ephraim/Israel coalition. Indeed, Saul himself was a Benjaminite whose power base included Ephraim. We have noted some indications, on the other hand, that suggest occasional conflicts between the Ephraimites and the Benjaminites during premonarchical times. Also, since the Benjaminites were situated in such close proximity to Jerusalem they could expect to suffer first and most from any Jerusalemite military action directed against the north.

The biblical account of the Shechem assembly does not indicate whether Benjaminites were represented, as they had been in the original negotiations between Israel and David (II Sam. 3:17–19), or, if they were present, what role they played. According to I Kings 12:21, which seems, however, to contradict the preceding verse, at least some Benjaminites remained loyal to Rehoboam. In any case, the tiny tribal territory of Benjamin became a frontier between the two kingdoms and thus the scene of intermittent warfare during the coming decades.

Jeroboam's Involvement in the Rebellion

The north apparently never gave any consideration to reverting to a non-monarchical form of government. Kingship had become an established tradition. Not surprisingly, the rebel kingdom took the old name "Israel," and Jeroboam, the Ephraimite from Zeredah who earlier had fled to Egypt in opposition to Solomon's forced-labor policies, was selected as the first king. The course of Jeroboam's earlier career, his role, if any, in the negotiations at Shechem, and the details of his rise to kingship are impossible to determine. The problem is not so much a lack of information as the fact that the Hebrew and Greek versions of the pertinent biblical passage (I Kings 11:26–12:33) differ significantly.

According to the Hebrew version, Jeroboam was one of Solomon's officials who had been given "charge over all the forced labor of the house of Joseph." Yet he "lifted up his hand against the king" and then was confronted by the prophet Ahijah from Shiloh, who predicted that Jeroboam himself would become king over the northern tribes. Specifically, we are told that Ahijah dramatized the forthcoming split of Solomon's kingdom by tearing Jeroboam's garment into twelve parts (representing the twelve tribes) and presenting him with ten of these. When Solomon sought to kill Jeroboam, the latter took refuge with Pharaoh Shishak in Egypt. Later, following Solomon's death, Jeroboam returned and presumably participated in the Shechem assembly—although there seems to be some internal contradiction in the Hebrew version on this latter score (compare I Kings 12:3, 12 with 12:20).

The Greek version duplicates most of the Hebrew account but then adds a supplement that reiterates some of the Hebrew version and expands upon it. Jeroboam, we are told, was the son of a harlot named Sarira. As Solomon's "lash master" over the levies of the house of Joseph, he built the city of Sarira (= Zeredah?) for the king. He possessed three hundred chariots, built the Millo, and fortified the city of David, but aspired to the kingship. When Solomon sought to kill Jeroboam, he fled to Shishak the king of Egypt. In Egypt, he married the sister-in-law of the pharaoh, who bore him a son, Abia (Abijah). At Solomon's death, Jeroboam returned to Sarira and fortified the city. When his son became ill, Jeroboam's wife visited the prophet Ahijah of Shiloh, who pronounced doom upon Jeroboam's family. It was Jeroboam, according to the Greek version, who assembled the tribes in Shechem; and it was at the Shechem assembly, before the negotiations with Rehoboam had begun, that the prophet Shemaiah (rather than Ahijah) tore a new garment into twelve pieces and presented ten of these to Jeroboam.

While the Hebrew and Greek versions thus present us with two differing accounts of Jeroboam's early career and rise to kingship, both support the following scenario: (1) Jeroboam, probably from an important and established family, was, in his early career, an official in the Solomonic bureaucracy. Specifically, he was an overseer of some sort in connection with forced laborers drafted from northern (Israelite) territory. (2) At some point, however, he defied Solomon with a mutinous act which is specified only as "lifting his hand against the king." This does not necessarily mean that Jeroboam proposed to overthrow the monarchy or to have himself crowned king. He may have simply protested Solomon's treatment of his Israelite subjects, a protest that eventually could have led to Jeroboam's fortifying his own hometown against Solomon. (3) Jeroboam thus gave expression to widespread anti-Solomonic sentiment and would have received the support of various disaffected groups. Among these, no doubt, were religious and prophetic figures such as Ahijah of Shiloh. Moreover, the very fact that a "wanted" governmental official such as Jeroboam could flee the country may suggest complicity on the part of other high-level officials. (4) The pharaoh who gave Jeroboam shelter in Egypt was Shishak, the founder of the Twenty-second Dynasty. (5) When the negotiations with Rehoboam failed and full-scale rebellion developed, it was only natural that attention should turn to Jeroboam. What role he or his supporters played in the Shechem assembly cannot be determined.

Differences Between the Two Kingdoms

Territorial Size and Strength

There now were two kingdoms, Israel in the north and Judah in the south, where formerly one had existed. From a casual reading of I-II Kings and II Chronicles, one might get the idea that these two kingdoms were roughly equal in size and strength, or perhaps even infer that Judah was the superior power and Israel only a breakaway fragment. Actually the reverse was the case. In many ways—including size, geographical position, and military strength—Israel was the dominant kingdom.

Not only did the northern kingdom encompass more territory than the southern kingdom (ten tribes over against two, according to the twelve-tribe scheme), this territory was more strategically located in relation to the main international communication routes. Traffic along the major coastal road, "the Way of the Sea," could bypass Judah altogether but had to negotiate through at least a corner of the hill country of Israel. Usually this traffic crossed the Mt. Carmel ridge at Megiddo or passed farther to the southeast through the Dothan plain. Also there was little east-west traffic through Judah, since the Dead Sea formed a barrier along the eastern side. For Israel, on the other hand, the Dothan plain and the Shechem pass were major east-west thoroughfares.

To the extent that the Israelites held the Sharon and Jezreel plains, Galilee, and the northern Transjordan, they had direct access to the Mediterranean Sea, close communication with Phoenicia and Damascus, and control of the north-south trade route through Transjordan. This access and control allowed Israel to share in and profit from international trade much more so than Judah. Accordingly, largely because of its more strategic geographical position, the northern kingdom included more cities of significant size.

Regarding the relative military strength of the two kingdoms, we have seen that Rehoboam backed down from making any immediate move to recover control of the northern territories. Subsequent skirmishes initiated by Judah during the early period of the separate kingdoms were never serious threats to Israel but merely attempts on the part of the Judean kings to establish a buffer zone of reasonable depth north of Jerusalem. Later, in the ninth and eighth centuries when Israel and Judah established a cooperative alliance, Israel was clearly the dominant partner. On one occasion when the Judean king Amaziah challenged his northern counterpart Jehoash "to look each other in the face," Jehoash scoffed at the idea that Amaziah would consider himself an equal, and then proceeded to crush the Judean army (II Kings 14:8–14).

Perhaps the Judeans occasionally liked to think of Israel as a breakaway fragment, and certainly the compilers of Genesis-II Kings did so; but the people of the north no doubt saw it quite the other way around. For them, the Davidic-Solomonic years represented an unfortunate episode in "Israelite" history and Judah was the fragment state.

Instability of the Northern Kingdom

In comparison with Judah, where the Davidic family remained in power for more than three centuries except for one brief interlude, Israelite political life appears to have been extremely unstable. We will see that the situation may not always have been as stable even in Judah as the biblical records seem to imply. Nevertheless, of the two kingdoms, it is clear that Israel had a far more turbulent political history. Seven of its kings were assassinated (eight if we count the pretender Zimri), and each time the assassination resulted in a dynastic change. There were several reasons for this political instability.

No doubt the plurality and diversity of the people who made up the northern kingdom were contributing factors to its instability. As noted above, Israel included several cities of reasonable size. These, with their more cosmopolitan inhabitants and their own cultic centers, self-interests, and pride existed side by side with the little villages of the hill country, Transjordan, and Galilee. The latter also had their self-interests and pride of course, not to mention their own political and cultic traditions grounded in the clan structure. The economic base of both city and village was agriculture and small handcraft industries. Yet the economy of the cities incorporated other components as well, such as income from trade and from services rendered to the central government. Any ruler would have been hard pressed to satisfy both of these diverse groups.

Israel's location astride the main Syro-Palestinian trade routes meant that the kingdom was particularly vulnerable to outside influences, including military pressures from other nations wishing to control the trade routes. This was another contributing factor to instability in the north. Struggles between Egyptian and Mesopotamian powers quickly drew Israel, much more so than Judah, into the maelstrom of international politics and meant that foreign governments exerted enormous influence on Israel's domestic affairs.

Still another cause of instability in Israel was the fact that there existed no generally accepted royal theology that could help sustain a dynasty on the throne during difficult times—through the reign of a weak king, for example, or one whose policies met with widespread disfavor among the populace. No doubt the northern kings attempted to develop something similar to the royal Zion theology of Jerusalem. This was never successfully achieved, however, and would have been difficult, since each ruling family, beginning with Jeroboam, had come to power by rejecting the dynastic claims of their predecessors.

Finally, political activism on the part of the Yahwistic prophets must be mentioned among the contributing factors to instability in the north. Admittedly, the importance of their political involvement may have been overemphasized somewhat by the compilers of the books of Kings and Chronicles. Nevertheless it is clear that the prophets did play some particular role as "king rejecters" and "king makers" in the history of the northern kingdom, and one of the practical results of this role seems to be that they were a constant source of antiroyal subversion.

These latter two factors, the absence of a sustaining royal theology in the north and the political involvement of Yahwistic prophets, require further comment.

Absence of a Sustaining Royal Theology

The people of the north obviously did not accept the royal Zion theology which emerged in Jerusalem and claimed that Yahweh had granted the exclusive right to rule his people to a Judean dynasty founded by David and centered in Jerusalem. On the contrary, the voices at the Shechem assembly made it clear that they were thoroughly disenchanted with Solomon's policies and felt no binding theological commitment to either the house of David or the city of

Jerusalem. This does not mean, as is sometimes supposed, that the people of the northern kingdom possessed a special political ideology of their own which rejected in principle the very concept of dynastic rule. Actually, the northern cities already had a well-established tradition of dynastic kingship, and even the clans and villages of Ephraim/Israel had accepted some sort of dynastic concept in the cases of Abimelech and Saul. Nor is there any reason to suppose that the concept of dynastic rule would have been considered an encroachment on Yahweh's kingship or incompatible with the view that he delegated this authority to individuals confirmed by prophetic word. The royal Zion theology itself illustrates how these two concepts could be combined in the view that Yahweh delegated his authority by the word of a prophet to a permanently ruling family rather than to a single individual.

The action of the Shechem assembly and the subsequent history of the northern kingdom demonstrate, on the other hand, that while the people of the north did not necessarily reject the dynastic concept in principle, neither did the population at large have any strong commitment to the dynastic principle, or at least never to any particular dynasty. The assembly dismissed any obligations to Rehoboam, who came with unquestionable hereditary credentials and opted instead for Jeroboam, who had made a name for himself opposing the royal family and who had been proclaimed by the prophet Ahijah as Yahweh's "next man."

A similar pattern would repeat itself again and again in the northern kingdom for the next two centuries: the old king would die; he would be succeeded on the throne by his son; the son would then be assassinated and the entire royal family annihilated; the assassin would become the new king. Usually the assassin, the new king, would be supported in his seizure of the throne by the military or some element in the military and usually there is some indication that he received prophetic support. When Israel eventually fell to the Assyrians in 722 B.C.E., only two of its royal families, those of Omri and Jehu, had been able to hold the throne through a second generation.

With the Omrides, prophetic opposition led by Elijah surfaced already in the second generation—that is, during Ahab's reign. Ahab was sufficiently strong to withstand opposition, but within a decade of his death the family line was eliminated by Jehu, who himself was supported by the prophet Elisha. The Jehu dynasty lasted then until the fifth generation, although during most of this time Israel was subject to Damascus. Once the kingdom began to recover, particularly under Jeroboam II, Yahwistic prophets, including Amos and Hosea, began to oppose the Jehu dynasty also. When Jeroboam II died and his son Zechariah attempted to ascend the throne, he was assassinated. Never again after Jeroboam II was a son able successfully to follow his father to the throne of Israel.

The Role of the Prophets in Northern Politics

Conflict between prophet and king is a recurring theme in the biblical materials pertaining to the northern kingdom. The compilers of Genesis-II Kings attribute this to apostasy on the part of the kings. Jeroboam I, it is claimed, led the whole kingdom astray when he instituted places and procedures of worship in competition with the Jerusalemite cult. The northern kings are charged further with supporting the worship of Baal in varying degrees.

Admittedly some of the prophets—Amos, for example—did specifically oppose the cultic practices at certain of the northern sanctuaries, including the royal sanctuaries at Bethel and Samaria. Nevertheless, the charge that Jeroboam committed religious apostasy when he revived the northern cults must be attributed largely to the Judean bias of the biblical compilers. The second charge, that the northern kings supported Baal worship in varying degrees, has more historical basis but surely represents an oversimplification. There does seem, especially under the Omrides, to have been some competition and conflict between the supporters of Yahwism and Baalism, with each side vying for support from the royal family. However, the issues will have been more complex than merely a religious clash between the worshipers of two different deities. Indeed, most of the people of Israel and Judah at that time probably saw nothing wrong with worshiping more than one god. Yahwism versus Baalism would have been but "the tip of an iceberg," an obvious embodiment of a much more complex and deeply rooted fracture within the pluralistic kingdom.

Possibly another aspect of this fracture was tension between the inhabitants of the larger cities on the one hand, such as Shechem and Samaria where the royal family resided, and the rural folk on the other, who may have been more firmly rooted in clan and tribal structures, particularly those who looked back to premonarchical Ephraim/Israel as their heritage. Since the prophets seem to have been strongest in their opposition when the monarchy itself was strongest, it may be that they functioned as a sort of check and balance over and against the kings and the centralization of power. In any case, we probably can assume some mutuality between the conservative stance and revolutionary actions of the Yahwistic prophets and the old clan/village/tribal interests and religious affiliation.

Four Decades of Hostilities Between the Kingdoms

The first four decades of the period of the separate kingdoms were a time of hostilities between Israel and Judah. These hostilities consisted primarily of border skirmishes fought on Benjaminite terrain. During the same four decades, and not unrelated to the hostilities, both Israel and Judah lost territory to surrounding kingdoms. (See Chart X for rulers of Israel and Judah during this period.)

Rehoboam, Abijam, and Asa of Judah

Rehoboam. Although reported to have already been forty-one years old when he became king, Rehoboam, the son of Naamah an Ammonite, is credited with a reign of seventeen years (I Kings 14:21). I Kings provides few specifics about

CHART X. From Solomon's Death to the Assassination of Elah

Judah	*Israel*	
Rehoboam (924–907)	Jeroboam I (924–903)	Shishak of Egypt invades in the 5th year of Rehoboam
Abijam (Abijah) (907–906)		
Asa (905–874)	Nadab (903–902)	Ben-hadad of Damascus, son of Tabrimmon, a contemporary of Asa and Baasha
	Baasha (902–886)	
	Elah (886–885)	

his reign except for the account of his actions in connection with the northern rebellion, the report of Shishak's invasion (I Kings 14:25–28), and the note that there was constant warfare between Rehoboam and Jeroboam. The Chronicler adds two other noteworthy items: a list of fifteen "cities of defense" which Rehoboam built in Judah (II Chron. 11:5–12), and the observation that Rehoboam "distributed some of his sons through all the districts of Judah and Benjamin, in all the fortified cities; and he gave them abundant provisions, and procured wives for them" (II Chron. 11:23).

Although these latter two items are included only by the Chronicler, we are inclined to regard them as authentic for three reasons: (1) The city list is more detailed than editorial fiction would have required. (2) Neither this list nor the report that Rehoboam distributed his sons around the kingdom in fortified cities serves any obviously ulterior motive in the Chronicler's work. (3) On the contrary, these two items make sense when understood as a coordinated move on Rehoboam's part to secure the territory that still remained under his control.

One need not assume that the clans/villages of the southern hill country, except possibly for Judah, were any more strongly committed to the Davidic dynasty than the people of the north had been. No doubt there were those even among the Judahite clans and villages who felt no strong loyalty to the royal family or to Jerusalem. It is noteworthy, on the other hand, that when Rehoboam's "cities of defense" are plotted on the map, they turn out to have been scattered throughout the southern hill country rather than along what would have been the kingdom's frontier. (See Map 18.) This suggests that they were not intended solely, if at all, as defense against foreign invaders. On the contrary, placing loyal family members at key places throughout the realm, particularly in fortified cities with abundant supplies and with the procurement of local wives, may have been a move on Rehoboam's part to strengthen the Davidic-Jerusalem hold on the southern hill country, lest it follow the actions of the rebel north. Even the Chronicler seems to connect the fortified cities with internal security: "So he held Judah and Benjamin" (II Chron. 11:12b).

We have taken the position above that it was David who established the

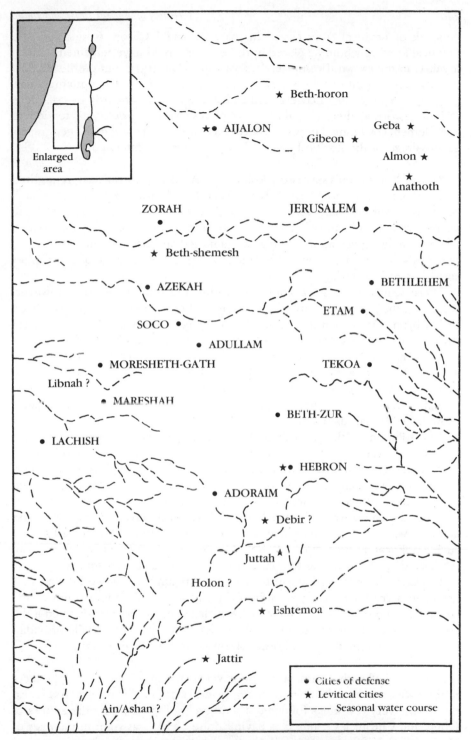

★ Beth-horon

★● AIJALON   Geba ★

Gibeon ★

Almon ★

★
Anathoth

ZORAH   JERUSALEM ●
●

★ Beth-shemesh

● AZEKAH   ● BETHLEHEM

ETAM ●

SOCO ●

● ADULLAM

● MORESHETH-GATH   TEKOA ●

Libnah ?

● MARESHAH

● BETH-ZUR

● LACHISH

★● HEBRON

● ADORAIM

★ Debir ?

Juttah ★

Holon ?

★ Eshtemoa

★ Jattir

● Cities of defense
★ Levitical cities
----- Seasonal water course

Ain/Ashan ?

MAP 18. Rehoboam's Cities of Defense

Enlarged
area

network of Levitical cities (listed in Josh. 21 and I Chron. 6) and that the Levitical families whom he placed in these cities would have remained staunch loyalists to the crown. Presumably Rehoboam could still count on the support of these Levitical cities, which, however, tended to be located in outlying areas, possibly territories that David added to his kingdom secondarily by conquest. It is noteworthy, therefore, that Rehoboam's "cities of defense" tended to complement (by filling the space in between) rather than overlap the geographical coverage of the Levitical cities. No doubt this was intended.

Abijam. Rehoboam's successor, Abijam (= Abijah in Chronicles), is credited with a reign of only three years (I Kings 15:1–8; II Chron. 13:1–21). This short reign, plus the unusually long reign ascribed to his successor Asa (forty-one years), who in turn was remembered for having taken action against the queen mother, invites speculation: (1) that Abijam died an early, untimely death; (2) that Asa was still a minor when he became king; and (3) that the queen mother served as regent during Asa's early years.

There seems to be some confusion within the biblical records, however, regarding the precise identity of this queen mother. I Kings 15:9–10, paralleled by II Chron. 15:16, identifies her as Maacah daughter of Abishalom. One might presume that Maacah was Asa's mother and Abijam's wife, therefore, except that I Kings 15:2 records this same Maacah as Abijam's mother. II Chronicles 11:20–22 elaborates further that Maacah was Rehoboam's favorite wife and that he passed over other sons to designate her son Abijam as crown prince. Finally, complicating matters all the more, II Chron. 13:2 records the name of Abijam's mother as Micaiah daughter of Uriel of Gibeah.

Any solution to this genealogical problem must be conjectural and take liberties with the biblical text. Two obvious possibilities present themselves: (1) Micaiah daughter of Uriel and Maacah daughter of Abishalom were two different persons who have become confused. It was the former whom Rehoboam favored over all his other wives; the latter was Abijam's wife and the mother of Asa. (2) There was only one Micaiah/Maacah involved. Abijam and Asa actually were brothers rather than father and son. Micaiah/Maacah had gained such a political position during Rehoboam's reign that even when her first son, Abijam, died she was able to secure the throne for a second son, Asa.

The Chronicler would have us believe that Abijam was a powerful king who achieved a crushing victory over Jeroboam of Israel. Yet the account of the battle (II Chron. 13:3–20) is typical Chronicler midrash. Moreover, even if the story is based on an actual historical incident, the few real details provided indicate that the battle was a border skirmish at most (see below).

Asa. Credited with a reign of forty-one years (which our chronology reduces to thirty-one years) and with performing several acts of cultic reform, Asa is also one of the very few kings following David and Solomon whom the editors of Kings and Chronicles counted as having done "what was right in the eyes of Yahweh" (I Kings 15:11–15; II Chron. 14:2). Maacah may have served as regent during Asa's early years, as indicated above, and the biblical editors saw it as significant that he eventually removed her from being the queen mother, "because she had an abominable image made for Asherah."

Among the other reforming acts credited to Asa in I Kings were that (1) he put away the male cult prostitutes from the land; (2) he removed all the idols his father had made; and (3) he brought the votive gifts of his father and his own votive gifts into the Temple of Yahweh. On the negative side, the editors of I Kings report that the local cultic shrines were not taken away (I Kings 15:14a). We are told that in his old age Asa was diseased in his feet (perhaps a euphemism for genitals as elsewhere in the Bible; I Kings 15:23b).

The Chronicler introduces further information, mostly negative, about Asa's reign. Also, in an obvious effort to deal with the theological problem of a cult-reforming king who nevertheless did evil and suffered tragedy, he reverts to the pattern which we have observed already in connection with David and Solomon. Namely, the Chronicler places all the negative aspects of Asa's reign in his last years, indicating that these occurred after a long and successful reign and were brought on by the king's unfaithfulness to Yahweh in his old age.

Specifically, the Chronicler allows Asa thirty-five good years, during which he is presented as an active cultic reformer with successes on every side—major building activities, a huge army, and victory over Zerah the Ethiopian (II Chron. 14–15). But then, during his last six years, Asa became an evil king whose rule turned sour. The turning point apparently was when, in the thirty-sixth year of his reign, Asa appealed to Ben hadad of Syria for help against Israel (I Kings 15:16–22; II Chron. 16:1–10), a move which the Chronicler clearly regarded as a breach of faith in Yahweh. Asa supposedly was confronted at that time by a prophet, Hanani the seer (II Chron. 16:7–10), just as earlier he had been confronted by the prophet Azariah (II Chron. 15:1–7). This second time, however, Asa responded negatively, put Hanani in stocks, and inflicted cruelties on the people in general (II Chron. 16:7–10). Eventually, in his thirty-ninth year when he was afflicted in his feet, Asa went so far as to consult physicians rather than Yahweh (II Chron. 16:11–12).

Not only is this an artificial literary pattern which we will encounter again in the Chronicler's work (compare the treatment of Jehoshaphat, for example), the Chronicler's contention that Baasha's attack did not occur until after Asa's thirty-five good years is far out of line with the chronological data provided in I-II Kings. According to the latter, as we have seen, Baasha would have died in Asa's twenty-sixth year—ten years before the attack (I Kings 16:8–10, 15).

Jeroboam, Nadab, Baasha, and Elah of Israel

I Kings provides only minimal information about the first four decades of the northern kingdom. Moreover, much of the space devoted to affairs in Israel during this early period has to do with Jeroboam's religious activities, which, not surprisingly, are seen in a very negative light by the Judean compilers. The

Chronicler ignores the first four Israelite kings completely except where they are directly involved with the Judean kings.

Jeroboam's Cultic Reformation. As observed earlier, the northern rejection of Rehoboam implied also a rejection of the royal Zion theology centered in the Jerusalem cult. Jeroboam followed through on this implication by renovating and upgrading the ancient sanctuaries at Bethel and Dan (erecting calf or bull images at both places), installing new priests in some of the northern sanctuaries, and perhaps revising the cultic calendar (I Kings 12:26–33). To the Judean compilers of I-II Kings, who lived long after the northern kingdom was no more, Jeroboam's actions were rank apostasy. Jeroboam and his contemporaries saw it, no doubt, as cultic reform and renewal, a movement back to old traditions uncontaminated by the ideas of the Jerusalemite and Davidic ideologies.

Both Bethel and Dan were old sanctuaries. Bethel, as we have seen in earlier chapters of this volume, figures prominently in the patriarchal stories (Gen. 12:8; 28:18–22; 35:1–15) and had associations with Samuel (I Sam. 7:16). Dan claimed a priestly line which traced its ancestry back to Moses (Judg. 18:30). The golden calves set up by Jeroboam probably were not intended as idol-gods any more than were the cherubim and the Ark in Solomon's Temple. They, like the cherubim and the Ark, would have served as symbols of the divine presence or pedestals on which the deity stood or sat invisibly. The difference between the Ark-cherubim and the bull images was primarily one of religious iconography rather than theology.

Naturally the separation of the kingdoms would have called for a change in priestly personnel in the northern shrines, if nothing more than an ousting of priests who had been installed in office by David and Solomon and/or who had pro-Davidic leanings. It is perhaps significant in this regard that Jeroboam is said to have installed priests who were not "Levites" (I Kings 12:31). If, as proposed in Chapter 5, the early Levites were particularly loyal to David, who had placed them at key places throughout the kingdom, then Jeroboam would have been a fool not to remove them from the sanctuaries now within his realm. One can imagine that there were many refugees from the north returning to the south after the partition—people who for various reasons were closely identified with the administration of David and Solomon (see II Chron. 11:13–17; 13:9; 15:9).

Jeroboam's cultic reformation apparently was oriented to Aaronite priestly lines, traditions, and iconography. This is suggested by the parallels between the way Aaron is depicted in Exodus 32 and Leviticus 10 and the way Jeroboam is depicted in I Kings 12. Both Aaron and Jeroboam are said to have constructed a golden calf on advice from the people (Ex. 32:1–4; I Kings 12:28a); both proclaim that the god worshiped was the one who had brought Israel up out of the land of Egypt (Ex. 32:4; I Kings 12:26–33); and both Aaron and Jeroboam have two sons with essentially the same names—Nadab and Abihu/Abijah (Lev. 10; I Kings 14:1, 20). At an earlier stage, the tradition or traditions behind these related passages in Exodus-Leviticus and I Kings may have presented both Aaron and Jeroboam in a favorable light. The passages as they stand now, however,

Bull Statuette. Although of bronze, rather than gold, and presumably smaller (about 5 inches high) than the golden calves erected by Jeroboam I at Dan and Bethel, this statuette nevertheless gives an idea of how Jeroboam's calves may have looked. *(Israel Museum)*

clearly show the imprint of anti-Aaronite circles which were hostile to both. As the likely source for such hostility, one thinks first of southern, Jerusalemite, cultic circles committed to Zadokite and Levitic priestly interests.

While Jeroboam's cultic moves probably are to be understood as an intentional effort to revive Aaronite traditions and priestly interests in certain of the old northern sanctuaries, especially Bethel, he seems to have passed over the Elide sanctuary at Shiloh. This is noteworthy especially in view of the tradition that it was a Shilonite prophet, Ahijah, who had predicted Jeroboam's rise to power. Actually there may have been little left at Shiloh to revive after the Davidic-Solomonic era—although there is no clear evidence, either biblical or archaeological, to conclude that the Shiloh sanctuary had been destroyed during the Philistine wars. With the end of the kingdom of Saul, whom they had supported, and the transfer of the Ark to Jerusalem, the Elide priestly line simply fades into the background. If Ahijah hoped for a revival of the Shiloh cultic center, he was disappointed. We hear of him last when, as a blind old man, he predicts the downfall of Jeroboam's dynasty.

Bethel and Dan were also frontier sanctuaries, possibly intended to mark the northern and southern limits of the newly established Israelite kingdom. Consequently they changed hands from time to time, Bethel perhaps falling occasionally into Judean hands and Dan into Syrian hands (for example, during the military conflict between Asa, Baasha, and Ben-hadad, which will be discussed below). Jeroboam's rebuilding of Penuel in the Transjordan (I Kings 12:25) represented the renovation of another old sanctuary (see Gen. 32:22–30) and affirmed Israelite control over Gileadite territory. Gilead, of course, had been aligned with Ephraim/Israel during the days of the Judges and had belonged to Saul's kingdom.

Shechem itself was another old sanctuary center that received new life under Jeroboam. Archaeological excavations at Shechem (Tell Balata in present-day Nablus) have revealed a major Bronze Age temple which went through several building phases and continued in use into the Early Iron Age. Possibly this was the temple of Baal-berith mentioned in Judg. 9:4. One is tempted to attribute the last destruction of this temple, during the twelfth century, to Abimelech (Judg. 9:46–49), but this of course cannot be established with absolute certainty. Nothing like a temple has been found in the less imposing remains from the later Iron Age. However, there must have been some continuation of the city's old religious traditions.

Political Life in Israel. I Kings 12:25 indicates that Jeroboam dwelt in Shechem and then went out from there and built Penuel. Tirzah, a few miles northeast of Shechem, is mentioned as the royal residence in I Kings 14:17, however, and apparently served as the capital until Omri moved to Samaria. Actually Tirzah may have been the seat of government from the beginning, with such texts as I Kings 12:25 meaning only that the kings resided in various cities such as Shechem and Penuel while overseeing construction work (compare I Kings 15:17 and 21).

The dynastic instability in Israel is well illustrated by the first four kings. Two of these kings (Jeroboam and Baasha) were usurpers for all practical purposes. Emerging with prophetic and, one would assume, popular support, they seized the throne in spite of the credentials of their predecessors and ruled until their natural deaths. They are credited with reigns of twenty-two and twenty-four years respectively. The other two, Nadab and Elah, sons of Jeroboam and Baasha respectively, ascended the throne by virtue of dynastic inheritance but quickly were assassinated and their families massacred.

Nadab had ruled only two years when he was assassinated by Baasha from the tribe of Issachar. Baasha's coup occurred, we are told, while "all Israel" (the generally mustered army?) was laying siege to Gibbethon of the Philistines. This suggests that the coup was supported, if not initiated, by the troops in the field. Elah, on the other hand, was still in his second year of reign when Zimri, a commander in the Israelite chariot corps, rose up against him. Zimri immediately encountered serious difficulties of his own, as we shall see below.

Jeroboam had been designated for the throne and subsequently was denounced by the prophet Ahijah of Shiloh. Baasha was first supported, it seems, and then denounced by the prophet Jehu son of Hanani (I Kings 16:1–14). Both prophetic denunciations, although perhaps heavily edited in their present forms, are violent pronouncements of judgment which call for regicide and massacre of the reigning families without benefit of burial: "Any one belonging to . . . who dies in the city the dogs shall eat; and any one who dies in the open country the birds of the air shall eat." No doubt these daring and stern pronouncements contributed to, if they did not trigger, the ensuing conspiracies (compare I Kings 14:10–16; 15:27; 16:1–4, 9).

Shishak's Invasion

In the fifth year of the reign of Rehoboam and Jeroboam, according to I Kings 14:25–28 and II Chron. 12:1–12, Pharaoh Shishak of the Twenty-second Dynasty of Egypt invaded Palestine. Rehoboam offered no resistance, according to the biblical account. In fact, the Chronicler describes Shishak's invasion as divine punishment for Rehoboam's apostasy and has the prophet Shemaiah instructing Rehoboam to submit.

Although his capital was Bubastis in the Nile Delta, Thebes was still an important city in Shishak's day. Thus, following the lead of the great pharaohs of the Nineteenth and Twentieth Dynasties, Shishak expanded the great Theban temple of Amon and adorned a section of its wall with an inscription recording his military exploits. Much of the inscription consists of a list of distant places which Shishak claims to have conquered. Of the names in the list that are still legible, only about twenty can be identified geographically with reasonable certainty. Moreover, while there is no doubt that the inscription pertains to a Palestinian campaign, it is less clear that the place-names are listed in any consistent geographical order. Attempts to read the list as an itinerary of Shishak's Palestinian campaign, for example, require that some of the names be shifted around and the text read in boustrophedonic fashion ("as the ox goes," that is, in one direction, then in the opposite direction).

Contrary to what one might suppose from the biblical record, analysis of the place-names recorded in the inscription indicates that the northern kingdom rather than Judah received the main thrust of Shishak's campaign. Indeed, Shishak seems virtually to have bypassed Judah, presumably because Rehoboam chose to ransom the kingdom with the Temple treasury. Among the northern cities that appear on the list is Megiddo; and a fragment of another of Shishak's inscriptions, a stela, has been discovered at the site of this ancient city.

Shishak's invasion was probably a *Blitzkrieg* affair intended to give stature to his regime, collect booty, and perhaps reassert Egyptian influence on Arabian trade. No doubt he wreaked havoc in the area and demonstrated how vulnerable the Palestinian kingdoms were to outside invasion. Shishak's campaign probably had little lasting impact, however, certainly not in terms of continuing Egyptian domination of Palestine. Destruction layers at numerous sites—Gezer, Megiddo, and Beth-shean, for example—have been interpreted as related to

Shishak's invasion, but one can never be very sure of such associations. Actually many of the cities that fell to Shishak may have submitted without a fight, as had Jerusalem.

The Chronicler reports one further international incident during this period —a battle between Asa and Zerah of Ethiopia (II Chron. 14:9–15). This is another of the Chronicler's stories that may be based on some historical event but that is presented in such midrashic form that the historian hardly knows what to do with it. Zerah is unknown from any other ancient source. The figures— one million men and three hundred chariots—are as weird as they are exaggerated. Whatever Zerah's Ethiopian connection, the incident seems at most to have involved frontier raiding between Judah and certain inhabitants of the western Negeb.

Hostilities Between the Two Kingdoms

When I Kings 14:30 reports that "there was war between Rehoboam and Jeroboam continually," this does not necessarily mean that there was constant open warfare between the two kings. More likely one should think in terms of a general state of hostilities with occasional frontier skirmishes. I Kings 12: 21–33 suggests that Rehoboam put aside any thought of recovering the north, while Jeroboam's policies were designed to halt religious traffic between his newly established kingdom and Jerusalem, with no apparent thought of invading Judah. After all, both kings had Shishak to deal with, first his invasion and then their recovery. At the most, then, we can presume that minor skirmishes occurred along the frontier between the two kingdoms—which itself was probably an ill-defined zone between Bethel and Jerusalem.

The same condition would have continued during Abijam's brief rule, even though the Chronicler recounts a major battle between Abijam and Jeroboam which supposedly ended in an overwhelming Judean victory (II Chron. 13). If there is any historical kernel to the Chronicler's story about the battle, it probably concerned a border skirmish around Bethel, Jeshanah, and Ephron, the latter two places probably near or just north of Bethel. Moreover, this would have been only a temporary Judean success. Note that Asa, who followed Abijam, was hard pressed to defend a frontier in the area of Mizpah and Geba —only about ten miles north of Jerusalem (I Kings 15:22).

The account of the military conflict between Asa and Baasha, which came to involve also King Ben-hadad of Damascus, has a much more authentic ring and represents a step beyond border skirmish (I Kings 15:16–22; II Chron. 16:1–6). Baasha initiated the incident, we are told, when he undertook to fortify Ramah (present-day er-Ram), "that he might permit no one to go out or come in to Asa king of Judah" (I Kings 15:17). This was not just an attempt to halt religious traffic between Israel and Jerusalem, which had been Jeroboam's concern and which the Chronicler would have us believe reached mammoth portions under Asa (II Chron. 15:9–10). A military garrison based at a fortified Ramah could also control commercial traffic into Jerusalem from the west, via the Aijalon

Valley, and would pose a constant threat to the Judean capital itself. Asa was fully aware that, with Israelite forces in Ramah, troubles were at Jerusalem's door. (See Map 19.)

Asa appealed to Ben-hadad of Syria, therefore, who at that point was allied with Baasha. The Judean king wanted Ben-hadad to (1) break the Syro-Israelite alliance and (2) apply military pressure to Israel's northern flank, thus forcing Baasha to withdraw troops from the Judah-Israel frontier. Encouraged by gifts, Ben-hadad broke with Baasha, moved on Israel's northern frontier, and "conquered Ijon, Dan, Abel-beth-maacah, and all Chinneroth, with all the land of Naphtali" (I Kings 15:20). The three towns noted here were all located along the upper reaches of the Jordan River between the southern slopes of the Lebanon and Anti-Lebanon mountains. Meanwhile Asa pushed northward from Jerusalem, dismantled Ramah, and used the building materials to fortify Mizpah and Geba. These two sites, probably to be identified with present-day Tell en-Nasbeh and Jeba, would have been obvious positions for fortification. Mizpah protected Jerusalem from Israelite advancement along the main north-south "watershed road" through the central hill country and also guarded the route leading westward to the Mediterranean Sea. Geba guarded the only easy crossing of the Wady es-Suweinit northeast of Jerusalem—that is, the second main route by which an army would have advanced on Jerusalem from the north (compare Isa. 10:27b–32; see above, Map 12).

The affair between Asa, Baasha, and Ben-hadad raises the issue of the overall territorial extent of the two kingdoms during this early phase of mutual hostilities and their relationships with neighboring states. The domain of the first three Judean kings apparently consisted, for all practical purposes, of Jerusalem, the surrounding vicinity, and the southern hill country. The spread of the Levitical cities, augmented now by Rehoboam's "cities of defense," is perhaps the best indication here. Also it is noteworthy that Asa's battle with Zerah the Ethiopian was placed near Mareshah, less than thirty miles southwest of Jerusalem. The sanctuary cities of Dan and Bethel represented the approximate northern and southern limits of the northern kingdom, while Penuel across the Jordan represented Israel's claim to at least a foothold in the Transjordan, no doubt the settlement area of the clans/villages that had been associated with the Ephraim/Israel tribal configuration of pre-Davidic times.

The Philistines, who apparently had remained independent under the shadow of David and Solomon, reemerge now as a constant threat. Two texts refer to battles between the Israelites and the Philistines at Gibbethon on the Philistine frontier (I Kings 15:27; 16:15). Northern Moab, the rolling plains surrounding Medeba, would be conquered by Omri during the coming years, which confirms that it was not under Israelite or Judean control at this point.

When Asa of Judah sought the aid of Ben-hadad of Syria against Baasha of Israel he alluded to a prior treaty between his own father and Ben-hadad's father. If this statement is to be taken literally and in the light of what we know about Davidic-Solomonic times, one must assume several reversals in the foreign relations between Judah and Damascus—namely, a state of hostility be-

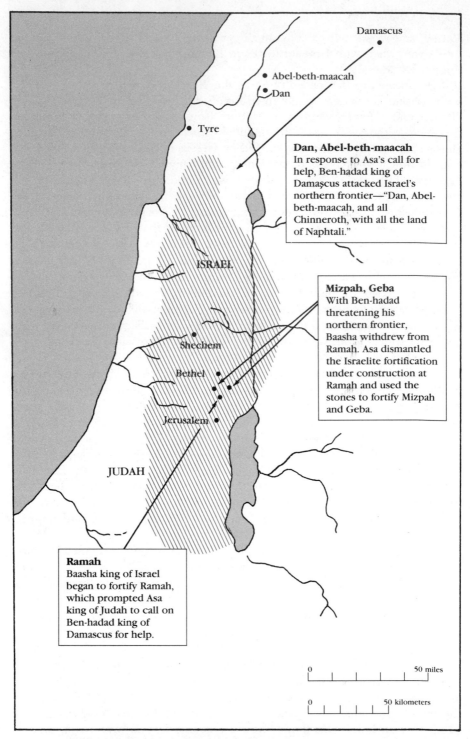

Damascus

Abel-beth-maacah

Dan

Tyre

Dan, Abel-beth-maacah
In response to Asa's call for help, Ben-hadad king of Damascus attacked Israel's northern frontier—"Dan, Abel-beth-maacah, and all Chinneroth, with all the land of Naphtali."

ISRAEL

Mizpah, Geba
With Ben-hadad threatening his northern frontier, Baasha withdrew from Ramah. Asa dismantled the Israelite fortification under construction at Ramah and used the stones to fortify Mizpah and Geba.

Shechem

Bethel

Jerusalem

JUDAH

Ramah
Baasha king of Israel began to fortify Ramah, which prompted Asa king of Judah to call on Ben-hadad king of Damascus for help.

0   50 miles

0   50 kilometers

MAP 19. Israel and Judah at the Time of Asa and Baasha

tween Rezon and Solomon (I Kings 11:23–25), followed by a Jerusalem-Damascus alliance negotiated by Abijam and Tabrimmon (the fathers of Asa and Ben hadad), a collapse of this alliance in deference to an Israel-Damascus alliance which was in effect when Baasha began to build Ramah, and now a reinstatement of the Jerusalem-Damascus pact (I Kings 15:19; II Chron. 16:3). But perhaps the references to "my father" and "your father" in I Kings 15:19 should be taken as no more than formulaic language, in which case the following, less dramatic, scenario presents itself. Rezon, Solomon's old enemy, would have been pleased, no doubt, with the course of affairs following Solomon's death. Indeed, he may have encouraged the rebellion that broke out at Shechem and stood ready to come to the aid of the rebel kingdom had Rehoboam decided to move militarily against Israel. It was in this context that the Syro-Israelite alliance would have been formed, and we may suppose that the alliance provided the basis for good relations between Israel and Damascus through the early years of Baasha's reign. Under Baasha, however, the situation began to change. Israel was on its feet now and posed potentially a more serious threat to Damascus than did Judah. Thus, when Asa offered to pay Ben-hadad to apply pressure on Israel's northern frontier, Ben-hadad agreed. It was a policy in his own best interests.

CHAPTER 8

The Omride Era

Zimri, commander of half the Israelite chariotry, assassinated Elah of the house of Baasha about 886 B.C.E. This was the second occasion on which an Israelite king succeeded his father to the throne in accordance with dynastic inheritance only to be assassinated within a year or so. As it turned out, Zimri himself was unable to hold the throne. Thus there ensued a period of political disturbance which may have reached civil war proportions and from which Omri emerged as the new king.

Omri's accession to the throne of Israel introduced a new era for both kingdoms which lasted approximately four decades (see Chart XI). Specifically, Israel and Judah entered into close alliance and together enjoyed a time of prosperity which probably surpassed that of the earlier days of David and Solomon. Omri himself must be recognized as the chief architect of the policies that characterized the era. It was under Omri's son Ahab, however, and Jehoshaphat who ruled Judah roughly contemporary with Ahab, that these policies came to fruition and the two kingdoms enjoyed the best years. The situation declined rapidly after the deaths of Ahab and Jehoshaphat and the era came to an abrupt end about 843 B.C.E. with the massacre of both royal families, now interrelated by marriage.

The Omrides were the first northern kings to accomplish dynastic succession, which they were able to do for three generations. Omri and Ahab were the first individuals in Israelite and Judean history to be mentioned in nonbiblical documents from the ancient Middle East. Long after the Omrides had passed from the scene, in fact, Israel was still referred to in the Assyrian records as "the land of Omri."

The Sources and Their Problems

Information about the Omride era is derived primarily from four sources: (1) the Genesis-II Kings account, of which I Kings 16:15–II Kings 8:27 pertains to the Omride period; (2) the Chronicler's account, specifically II Chron. 17–20; (3) royal inscriptions from King Mesha of Moab and Shalmaneser III of

Assyria; and (4) archaeology, the artifactual record at certain key Palestinian sites.

The Omride Era as Presented in I-II Kings

In terms of its literary structure, the I-II Kings presentation of the Omride era consists of the usual summations of the kings' reigns, a number of prophetical narratives which the compilers introduced into the summaries at points where they regarded them as relevant, and the account of Jehu's coup (II Kings 9:1–10:31) with which they concluded their treatment of the Omride era.

The Summations of the Kings' Reigns. The perspective of the compilers is to be seen most clearly in their summations of the reigns of the individual kings (I Kings 16:21–34; 22:39–53; II Kings 1:1, 17–18; 3:1–3; 8:16–29). The most important point to be made about the Omrides, in their opinion, especially Ahab, was that these rulers patronized Baalism to an unprecedented degree. The very idea that the Omrides might have been successful monarchs conflicted with one of the main theological principles which the compilers wished to illustrate in Genesis-II Kings—that Yahweh granted success only to those rulers who remained faithful to him and gave exclusive support to the Yahwistic cult in Jerusalem. No achievements are recorded for the Omrides, therefore, except for the notations that Omri founded the city of Samaria (I Kings 16:24) and that Ahab's acts included "the ivory house which he built, and all the cities that he

---

CHART XI. The Omride Era

Judah	*Israel*	*Damascus*	*Assyria*
Asa (905–874)		Ben-hadad (?–?)	
	Nadab (903–902)		
	Baasha (902–886)		
	Elah (886–885)		
	Omri (885–873)		Ashurnasirpal
Jehoshaphat	Ahab (873–851)		(883–859)
(874–850)			
		Hadadezer (?–?)	Shalmaneser III*
	Ahaziah (851–849)		(858–824)
Jehoram (850–843)	Jehoram (849–843)		
Ahaziah (843)	Jehu (843–816)	Hazael (ca. 843–?)	
Athaliah (843–837)			

*Shalmaneser conducted military campaigns toward Syria-Palestine in 853, 849, 848, 845, 841, and 838 B.C.E. His inscriptions mention Ahab and Hadadezer in connection with the 853 campaign, Jehu and Hazael in connection with the 841 campaign. All dates for the Judean and Israelite kings are approximate.

built" (I Kings 22:39). One would conclude from their summation of Jehoshaphat's reign that he too was a second-rate ruler with no successes worthy of mention. He is reported only to have continued Asa's policies regarding cultic matters, "made peace with the king of Israel," and failed in a maritime venture (I Kings 22:41–50).

The Prophetical Narratives. Actually most of the material in the Omride section of I-II Kings consists of narratives that apparently circulated independently before having been incorporated into the Genesis-II Kings account and that, at least in their present form, focus on the deeds of Yahwistic prophets. These prophetical narratives may be classified into the following groupings (see also Chart XII):

The Elijah Stories (I Kings 17–19; II Kings 1:2–16)

The Stories of the Three Battles with Ben-hadad (I Kings 20; 22:1–38)

The Naboth Vineyard Story (I Kings 21)

The Elisha Stories (II Kings 2; 4:1–8:15)

The Story of Jehoram's Moabite Campaign (II Kings 3:4–27)

These prophetical narratives, especially the Elijah and Elisha stories, abound with folk themes and describe miraculous circumstances that modern historians find difficult to accept—the jar of meal and the cruse of oil that never emptied (I Kings 17:8–16); fire from above which consumed Elijah's offering, the wood and stone of the altar, and even the dust and water surrounding the altar (I Kings 18:30–40); the Syrian general whose leprosy was cured when he bathed in the Jordan (II Kings 5); and so on. Since they are primarily interested in the deeds of the prophets, moreover, these same narratives provide few tangible details that are not related directly to the prophets' actions. The king or kings of Israel rarely are identified by name in the Elisha stories and in the stories of the three battles with Ben-hadad, for example; and they probably were entirely anonymous at an earlier stage of the transmission of these materials. For the historian's purposes, therefore, perhaps the most we can expect to learn from these prophetical narratives is something of the general social, religious, and political circumstances of the day and age from which they come. It is particularly noteworthy in this regard, as we shall see below, that the narrative groupings do not all presuppose the same background circumstances. The Elijah stories, for example, presuppose a time in which the kings of Israel ruled supreme from Samaria, the royal family was closely associated with Baalism, and there was sharp conflict between the royal family and the Yahwistic prophets. The Elisha stories and the stories of the three battles with Ben-hadad, on the other hand, depict the kings of Israel as international weaklings hard pressed to defend Samaria from the Syrians, yet strong supporters of Yahwism and on good terms with the Yahwistic prophets.

Some of these prophetical narratives show evidence of having been modified and expanded during the process of transmission from ancient times to the present. This is particularly true of the stories of the three battles with Ben-hadad and the story of Jehoram's Moabite campaign. Close analysis reveals essentially three stages in the process of their transmission. (1) At the first stage, these narratives appear to have been straightforward battle reports: three battles in which the king of Israel challenged Ben-hadad of Syria, and one in which Jehoram attempted to restore Israelite control over Moab. (2) Later these battle reports were expanded to give Yahwistic prophets center stage. An anonymous prophet predicts success for the king of Israel's challenge to Syria, provides the strategy for the first two battles, and then (another prophet?) denounces the king of Israel for allowing Ben-hadad to live and predicts that the king of Israel will pay with his own life (I Kings 20:13–43). The prophet Micaiah repeats this prediction as the king of Israel makes ready for the third battle against Syria, and the prediction is fulfilled when the king of Israel is killed in the third battle (I Kings 22:13–36). As Jehoram's army approaches Moab, they find themselves without water and thus facing certain defeat. Elisha enters the story at that point and saves the day (II Kings 3:9–27). (3) Finally, probably after these narratives had found their way into Judean hands, the two battle stories that involved the king of Judah were modified still further. Specifically, the king of Judah who appears in the third of the stories of the three battles with Ben-hadad (that is, the story of the Ramoth-gilead campaign; I Kings 22:1–38) and in the story of Jehoram's Moabite campaign (II Kings 3:4–27) was identified as Jehoshaphat and both stories expanded to emphasize Jehoshaphat's loyalty to Yahwism.

There is reason to doubt that some of these prophetical narratives pertain to the Omride period at all. We have indicated that the Elisha stories and the stories of the three battles with Ben-hadad presuppose social, religious, and political circumstances different from the Elijah stories. This contrast will become even more apparent as we explore the other sources of information for the Omride era. The best explanation for this situation, in our opinion, is that the stories of the three battles with Ben-hadad and the Elisha stories actually pertain to circumstances and events of a later period. We will return to this matter below.

The Naboth vineyard story is of a character different from the other narratives discussed above. In contrast to the Elijah stories, for example, which presuppose that the reader will be familiar with Elijah, Ahab, and Jezebel, the Naboth vineyard story carefully introduces each of these figures as if they belong to a distant time and place. Also, the Naboth affair as recounted in this story does not square exactly with a reference to the incident in the account of Jehu's coup. According to the latter account, after assassinating Jehoram, Jehu said to Bidkar his aid:

> Take him up, and cast him on the plot of ground belonging to Naboth the Jez-reelite; for remember, when you and I rode side by side behind Ahab his father, how Yahweh uttered this oracle against him: "As surely as I saw yesterday the blood of Naboth and the blood of his sons—says Yahweh—I will requite you on this plot

CHART XII. Prophetical Narratives Associated with the Omride Era

The Elijah Stories (I Kings 17–19; II Kings 1:2–16)—A recounting of the deeds of Elijah from Tishbi (in the northern Transjordan), who opposed, among other things, Omride patronage of Baalism. Ahab is depicted as an autocratic ruler; but Jezebel is the chief villain in the stories because of her active support of Baalism and persecution of the Yahwistic prophets. These are folk stories which abound with miraculous scenes.

The Stories of the Three Battles with Ben-hadad (I Kings 20; 22:1–38)—A recounting of a sequence of three battles between a king of Israel and Ben-hadad of Damascus. The first account describes how the king of Israel successfully defended Samaria against Ben-hadad's attack (20:1–25). The second describes how the king of Israel and his pitifully small army defeated Ben-hadad's army at Aphek (20:26–43). The third describes a campaign initiated by the king of Israel to restore Israelite control over Ramoth-gilead (22:1–38). These narratives show evidence of having been modified during the process of transmission. At an earlier stage of their telling, both the king of Israel and the king of Judah (who appears only in the third battle) probably were anonymous. In their present form, and in keeping with their present context, the two kings are identified as Ahab and Jehoshaphat respectively. Both identifications are problematic. Actually these three accounts seem to belong to the same setting as the Elisha stories—that is, to the later period of the Jehu dynasty.

The Naboth Vineyard Story (I Kings 21)—While most of the Elijah stories are typical folk tales, the Naboth vineyard story seems to be more on the order of historical fiction. The three most colorful characters of the Omride period and one of the most memorable events of the era have been worked together into a story which probably bears little resemblance to the actual circumstances of the Naboth incident. Note that the account of Jehu's coup seems to place the Naboth incident soon before the coup—that is, during Jehoram's reign (II Kings 9:25–26).

The Elisha Stories (II Kings 2; 4:1–8:15)—A recounting of the deeds of another Yahwistic prophet from the Transjordan (Abel-meholah) who was the recognized successor to Elijah. Elisha is remembered for the same sort of miraculous deeds as Elijah. In fact, some of the same deeds are credited to both. Yet these Elisha stories reflect a situation quite different from the Elijah stories. Namely, the Elisha stories presuppose close, positive relations between the "king of Israel" and the Yahwist Elisha. There are no references to Jezebel or to a Yahwism-Baalism conflict. Also, these stories presuppose a political situation in which the king of Israel is dominated by Ben-hadad of Damascus. The compilers of Genesis-II Kings placed these Elisha stories in the context of the reign of Jehoram of Israel, which implies that Jehoram was the "king of Israel" who figures in them. More likely, they belong to the post-Omride period and the anonymous king of Israel who appears in them was one of the rulers of the Jehu dynasty. Note that a concluding story which reports Elisha's death does in fact appear in this latter context —that is, during the reign of Joash, Jehu's grandson (II Kings 13:14–19).

The Story of Jehoram's Moabite Campaign (II Kings 3:4–27)—This narrative shows striking similarities to the third of the stories about the three battles with Ben-hadad—that is, the story of the Ramoth-gilead campaign (I Kings 22:1–38). (1) It seems to have undergone modifications during the process of transmission. Specifically, the story has been recast to give a Yahwistic prophet (Elisha in this case) and the king of Judah a prominent role. (2) The king of Judah has been identified, again secondarily and probably incorrectly, as Jehoshaphat. (3) Finally, the story as it stands now emphasizes Jehoshaphat's piety in contrast to that of Jehoram—specifically Jehoshaphat is depicted again, as in the Ramoth-gilead story, insisting that a Yahwistic prophet be consulted before proceeding with the campaign.

> of ground." Now therefore take him up and cast him on the plot of ground, in accordance with the word of Yahweh. (II Kings 9:25–26)

The phrase "when you and I rode side by side behind Ahab his father" probably is to be seen as a secondary editorial gloss intended to shift the time of the Naboth incident from "yesterday" to an earlier occasion during Ahab's reign. In other words, the account of Jehu's coup originally implied that the Naboth affair occurred shortly before Jehu's coup, and this phrase was introduced by the compilers of Genesis-II Kings to bring the account into line with the Naboth vineyard story.

Actually it is the Naboth vineyard story that probably is misleading. This story can best be described, in our opinion, as historical fiction. It is based on a historical incident of royal injustice that occurred in Jezreel (possibly touching off Jehu's coup), but the incident has been fictionalized by the introduction of the three most colorful characters of the Omride era (Ahab, Jezebel, and Elijah). The present form of the story probably bears little resemblance to the actual historical circumstances of the Naboth affair.

The Account of Jehu's Coup. The compilers of Genesis-II Kings concluded their presentation of the Omride era with an extended account of how Jehu, designated by Elisha to be Israel's next king, assassinated Jehoram and Jezebel, wiped out the remainder of the Omride family (including Ahaziah of Judah, who had come to visit Jehoram at the time), and seized the throne of Israel for himself (II Kings 9:1–10:27). This account, as did the other narratives discussed above, probably circulated independently before being included in the Genesis-II Kings corpus. Probably it dates from about the time of Jeroboam II, when the Jehu dynasty itself was facing opposition and standing accused of Jehu's bloody coup (see Hos. 1:4–5). Thus the account seeks to justify the massacre by emphasizing that Jehu was acting in behalf of Yahweh.

The Omride Era According to the Chronicler

The Chronicler, having no interest in Israelite affairs, mentions the Omrides only when they figure in the treatment of Jehoshaphat: (1) The first deed that the Chronicler records for Jehoshaphat is that he "strengthened himself against Israel" (II Chron. 17:1). (2) The third of the stories of the three battles with Ben-hadad (that is, the account of the Ramoth-gilead campaign in I Kings 22:1–38) is repeated but is expanded to give it a different context (a wedding feast), to emphasize Jehoshaphat's riches and honor, and to censure Jehoshaphat for having dealings with the wicked Israelite king (II Chron. 18:1–19:3). (3) The brief report of Jehoshaphat's unsuccessful maritime venture in I Kings 22:47–50 is repeated also, but restated to say that Jehoshaphat *did* take Ahaziah on as a partner in the venture and that this in itself was the reason that the venture failed (II Chron. 20:35–37). (4) Jehoram, who succeeded Jehoshaphat to the throne of Judah, is depicted as a wicked king whose wickedness derived from his Omride connection: "And he walked in the way of the kings of Israel, as the house of Ahab had done; for the daughter of Ahab was his wife" (II Chron. 21:6).

Otherwise the Chronicler elaborates extensively on the reigns of both Jehoshaphat and Jehoram, depicting the former as one of the truly great kings of Judah and the latter as totally unsuccessful. Jehoshaphat, we are told, was loyal to Yahweh—walking "in the earlier ways of his father" Asa (II Chron. 17:3). He sent princes and Levites to teach "in Judah, having the book of the law of Yahweh with them" (17:9). He had "great riches and honor" (II Chron. 17:5; 18:1), built fortresses and store-cities, and had abundant stores in the cities (II Chron. 17:12–13a). His impressive wealth came not only from Judean tribute (II Chron. 17:5) but also from surrounding peoples (Philistines, Arabs; II Chron. 17:11). He appointed judges throughout the land with instructions to judge "not for man but for Yahweh" (II Chron. 19:4–7), and designated certain priests and Levites in Jerusalem to make decisions in disputed cases (II Chron. 19:8–11). "He had soldiers, mighty men of valor, in Jerusalem" numbering some 1,160,000 (II Chron. 17:13b–19), plus soldiers garrisoned at fortified cities throughout the land (II Chron. 17:2, 19).

These mighty men of valor, however, seem to fade into the background in the one battle scene reported by the Chronicler for Jehoshaphat's reign (that is, aside from the Chronicler's revised rendition of the Ramoth-gilead campaign). Jehoshaphat, we are told, overwhelmed with great fear when a coalition of Ammonites, Moabites, and men from Mt. Seir marched on Jerusalem, assembled all Judah for fasting and prayer to Yahweh. The day was saved, as it turned out, without any need of an army. Yahweh set an ambush against the enemy so that they began to fight among themselves and completely destroyed each other. None escaped (II Chron. 20:24). Clearly the Chronicler had led us deep into the realm of midrash.

Royal Inscriptions of Moab and Assyria

The Mesha Inscription. Also called the Moabite Stone, this commerative stela was discovered in 1868 near the ruins of ancient Dibon (present-day Dhiban, east of the Dead Sea). Unfortunately the stela was broken to pieces soon after its discovery, but later was reconstructed almost completely and the inscription translated with few uncertainties (see below, Text IV). One learns from the content of the inscription that the stela was commissioned by King Mesha of Moab, apparently late in his reign and in connection with the dedication of a sanctuary to the Moabite god Chemosh. The text, looking back over Mesha's career, reports what he regarded to be the main accomplishments of his reign. He was especially proud of having brought Israelite dominance over Moab to an end and of recovering from Israel the Moabite territory north of the Arnon —that is, the plains surrounding the ancient city of Medeba.

Shalmaneser's Inscriptions. Inscriptions from the reign of Shalmaneser III (858–824 B.C.E.) record military campaigns into Syria-Palestine for his sixth, tenth, eleventh, fourteenth, eighteenth, and twenty-first regnal years. It is possible, with the Assyrian Eponym *(limmu)* lists to calculate the dates of these campaigns to 853, 849, 848, 845, 841, and 838 B.C.E. respectively. The first campaign (853 B.C.E.) is described in some detail in the so-called Monolith Inscription, engraved on a stela with the figure of Shalmaneser in relief, also discovered in the mid-1800s (at Kurkh in present-day Iraq; see Text III). We learn from the Monolith Inscription that a coalition of Syro-Palestinian kings defended against Shalmaneser and apparently halted his march in the vicinity of Qarqar, a city on the Orontes River. "Ahab the Israelite" is listed among the defending kings and credited with deploying two thousand chariots in the battle. (See Map 20.)

The Monolith Inscription, composed fairly early in Shalmaneser's reign, does not cover his later western campaigns. For these we must turn to the so-called Bull Inscription and Black Obelisk (both discovered at Nimrud, ancient Calah, in 1845), which record Shalmaneser's deeds through his eighteenth and thirty-first years respectively. The entries in these two inscriptions for Shalmaneser's next three western campaigns (849, 848, and 845 B.C.E.) are brief. Apparently Shalmaneser was met again on each of these three campaigns by the Syro-Palestinian kings, and while he claims to have achieved crushing victories, this seems unlikely, since he always turned back at the Orontes River rather than pushing on farther. Hadadezer of Damascus is mentioned by name in connection with the campaigns of 849, 848, and 845 B.C.E., but we can only speculate as to whether Jehoram, who would have been on the throne in Samaria during those years, continued to support the resistance.

The Black Obelisk provides our fullest report of Shalmaneser's 841 campaign (see Text V). Apparently he reached Damascus with no serious opposition this time, besieged the city (but does not claim actually to have taken it), and then marched into northern Palestine, where he collected tribute from Jehu. The Black Obelisk is also our source for Shalmaneser's 838 B.C.E. campaign, which of course takes us still farther beyond the Omride era.

Archaeological Evidence. Corresponding to the extrabiblical records which indicate that the Omrides played a significant role in internal affairs, the artifactual remains at key northern sites suggest an extensive post-Solomonic building phase, which must be dated approximately to the Omride era and no doubt is to be attributed to them. Chief among the sites to be considered in this regard are Samaria, Megiddo, and Hazor.

TEXT III. Excerpts from the Monolith Inscription

Assur, the great lord, king of all of the great gods; Anu, king of the Igigi and Anunnaki, the lord of lands; Enlil (Bel), father of the gods, who decrees destiny, who establishes the bounds of heaven and earth; Ea, the wise, king of the Apsu, endowed with wisdom; the god Nanir, (illuminator) of heaven and earth; the hero god, Shamash, judge of the four regions (of the world), who leads mankind aright; Ishtar, lady of conflict and battle, whose delight is warfare, (ye) great gods, who love my kingship, who have made great my rule, power, and sway, who have established for me an honored, an exalted name, far above that of all other lords!

Shalmaneser, king of all peoples, prince, priest of Assur, mighty king, king of Assyria, king of all of the four regions (of the world), Sun of all peoples, ruler of all lands, king, sought out by the gods, favorite of Enlil (Bel), vigilant viceroy of Assur, honored prince, who finds (his way among) the most difficult paths, who treads the summits of mountains and highlands far and near, who receives the tribute and gifts of all regions, who opens up trails, north and south (above and below), at whose mighty battle onset the regions (of earth) feel themselves threatened, at the vigor of whose bravery the lands are shaken to their foundations; mighty hero, who goes about, trusting in Assur (and) Shamash, his divine allies, who is without a rival among the princes of the four regions (of earth); the king of lands, the heroic, who advances over difficult roads, traverses mountains and seas; son of Assur-nasir-pal, prefect of Enlil (Bel), priest of Assur, whose priesthood was pleasing to the gods, at whose feet all lands bowed in submission; glorious offspring of Tukulti-Urta, who slew every foe of his, and overwhelmed them like a hurricane (deluge). . . .

In the eponym year bearing my own name, on the thirteenth of Airu, from [Nineveh] I departed. I crossed the Tigris, I marched across the lands of Hasamu (and) Dihnunu. I drew near to Til-bursip, the stronghold of Ahuni, son of Adini. Ahuni, son of Adini, trusted in the mass of his armies, and came out against me. I accomplished his overthrow. In [his city] I shut him up. . . .

In the year of Daian-Assur, in the month of Airu, the fourteenth day, I departed from Nineveh, . . . In (goat)-skin boats I crossed the Euphrates the second time, at its flood. The tribute of the kings on that side of the Euphrates,—of Sangara of Carchemish, of Kundashpi of Kumuhu (Commagene), of Arame son of Guzi, of Lalli the Milidean, of Haiana son of Gabari, of Kalparuda of Hattina, of Kalparuda of Gurgum,—silver, gold lead, copper, vessels of copper, at Ina-Assur-uttir-asbat, on that side of the Euphrates, on the river Sagur, which the people of Hatti call Pitru, there I received (it). From the Euphrates I departed, I drew near to Halman (Aleppo). They were afraid to fight with (me), they seized my feet. Silver, gold, as their tribute I received. I offered sacrifices before the god Adad of Halman. From Halman

I departed. To the cities of Irhuleni, the Hamathite, I drew near. The cities of Adennu, Barga, Argana, his royal cities, I captured. His spoil, his property, the goods of his palaces, I brought out. I set fire to his palaces. From Argana I departed. To Karkar I drew near.

Karkar, his royal city, I destroyed, I devastated, I burned with fire. 1,200 chariots, 1,200 cavalry, 20,000 soldiers, of Hadad-ezer, of Aram; 700 chariots, 700 cavalry, 10,000 soldiers of Irhuleni of Hamath, 2,000 chariots, 10,000 soldiers of Ahab, the Israelite, 500 soldiers of the Gueans, 1,000 soldiers of the Musreans, 10 chariots, 10,000 soldiers of the Irkanateans, 200 soldiers of Matinuba'il, the Arvadite, 200 soldiers of the Usanateans, 30 chariots, [ ],000 soldiers of Adunu-ba'il, the Shianean, 1,000 camels of Gindibu', the Arabian, [ ],000 soldiers [of] Ba'sa, son of Ruhubi, the Ammonite,—these twelve kings he brought to his support; to offer battle and fight, they came against me. (Trusting) in the exalted might which Assur, the lord, had given (me), in the mighty weapons, which Nergal, who goes before me, had presented (to me), I battled with them. From Karkar, as far as the city of Gilzau, I routed them. 14,000 of their warriors I slew with the sword. Like Adad, I rained destruction upon them. I scattered their corpses far and wide, (and) covered the face of the desolate plain with their widespreading armies. With (my) weapons I made their blood to flow down the valleys of the land. The plain was too small to let their bodies fall, the wide countryside was used up in burying them. With their bodies I spanned the Arantu (Orontes) as with a bridge. In that battle I took from them their chariots, their cavalry, their horses, broken to the yoke. (*ARAB* I, §§595–96, 601, 610–11) (See photograph on p. 261.)

Conflicts in the Sources

The General Political Circumstances of the Omride Period. One would conclude from the summations of the reigns of the Omride kings, the Elijah stories, the account of Jehu's coup, the Mesha Inscription, and the Assyrian records that the Omrides (particularly Omri and Ahab) were powerful kings who ruled over an independent kingdom. (1) The summary notes speak of their extensive building activities, marriage alliance with Phoenicia, and domination of Moab (see I Kings 16:24, 31; 22:39; II Kings 3:4). (2) The Elijah stories depict Ahab as an autocratic king in full control of his kingdom. (3) The Mesha Inscription confirms that Omri and Ahab dominated Moab. (4) The Assyrian records witness to the fact that Israel was a military power of some consequence under Ahab. (5) The account of Jehu's coup presupposes that the Omrides still controlled much of the Transjordan at the end of Jehoram's reign. We are told, namely, that Jehu made his move when the Israelite army was "on guard" at Ramoth-gilead, defending against Syrian encroachment (II Kings 9:14b). Thus Israel's holdings in the Transjordan presumably still extended as far north as

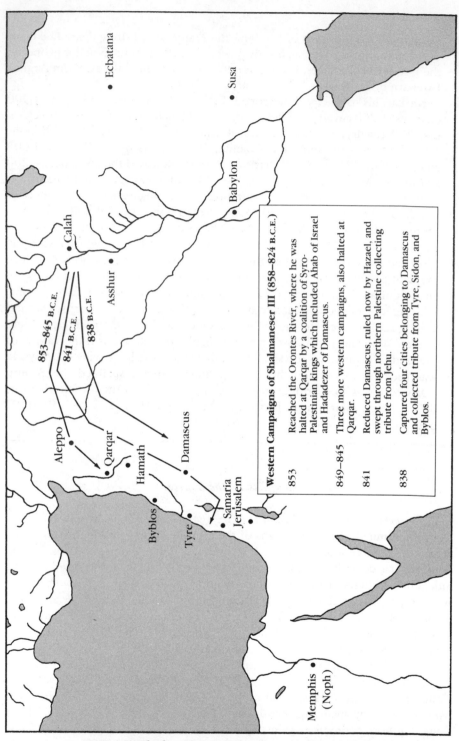

Western Campaigns of Shalmaneser III (858–824 B.C.E.)

853	Reached the Orontes River, where he was halted at Qarqar by a coalition of Syro-Palestinian kings which included Ahab of Israel and Hadadezer of Damascus.
849–845	Three more western campaigns, also halted at Qarqar.
841	Reduced Damascus, ruled now by Hazael, and swept through northern Palestine collecting tribute from Jehu.
838	Captured four cities belonging to Damascus and collected tribute from Tyre, Sidon, and Byblos.

MAP 20. Shalmaneser III's Western Campaigns

Monolith Inscription. The so-called Monolith Inscription (left), standing about 7 feet 2 inches high and dating from the reign of Shalmaneser III, depicts Shalmaneser himself in relief and lists Ahab of Israel among a coalition of Syro-Palestinian kings who defended against the invading Assyrian army at Qarqar (see Text III, p. 258). *(The British Museum)*

Black Obelisk. The so-called Black Obelisk (right), about 6½ feet high, records deeds of Shalmaneser III through the thirty-first year of his reign (see Text V, p. 286). On one of its panels (see inset), "Jehu son of Omri" bows before him. *(The British Museum)*

Ramoth-gilead (present-day Tell er-Remith). Conflict between king and prophet is another strong motif in the summary notes, the Elijah stories, and the account of Jehu's rebellion. All of these sources presuppose Baalistic leanings on the part of the Omrides and sharp conflict between the royal family and the Yahwistic prophets.

In contrast to these sources which presuppose that the Omrides were strong rulers over an autonomous kingdom and in hostile relations with the Yahwistic prophets, the stories of the three battles with Ben-hadad and the Elisha stories presuppose quite a different situation. Both of these narrative groups, associated by context with Ahab and Jehoram respectively, depict the king or kings of Israel as international weaklings, bullied by the Syrian king of Damascus, and often hard pressed to exercise authority outside the gates of Samaria. At the same time these narratives, especially the Elisha stories, presuppose a close supportive relationship between the "king of Israel" and the Yahwistic prophets.

Commentators and historians generally deal with this situation in either of two ways. Some conclude that the Omride era was a period of sharp contrasts. The Omrides had moments of greatness interspersed with moments of disaster; times when they dominated the surrounding nations interrupted by times when they could hardly defend their own royal city; periods of conflict with the Yahwistic prophets and other periods when they enjoyed the warm support of these Yahwistic champions. Others conclude, and it is our position, that the stories of the three battles with Ben-hadad (I Kings 20; 22:1–38) and the Elisha stories (II Kings 2; 4:1–8:15) do not pertain to the Omride period in the first place, but pertain to the following period of the Jehu dynasty when the conditions presupposed in these narratives did in fact apply. In short, we discount the narratives in question as valid sources of information for the Omride era but will draw upon them as sources for the Jehu period. Consequently, we view the Omride kings as strong rulers who were in full charge of the Israelite kingdom and, so far as we know, enjoyed friendly relations with Syria until late in Jehoram's reign.

The Sequence of Syrian Kings. Interrelated issues, also debated among historians, are the identity and the proper order of the kings of Damascus contemporary with the Omrides. Prior to the Omride period, we have encountered two Damascus kings: Rezon, Solomon's contemporary (I Kings 11:23–25), and Ben-hadad, the contemporary of Asa and Baasha (I Kings 15:18–20). The next mention of a king of Damascus in our sources occurs in connection with Ahab's last years. As seen above, the Monolith Inscription has Ahab fighting with Hadadezer of Damascus against Shalmaneser III in 853 B.C.E., a date that must have been near the end of Ahab's reign. According to the Black Obelisk, this Hadadezer was still on the scene in 845 but had been replaced by the usurper Hazael by 841 B.C.E. It seems clear from a Nimrud fragment, moreover, that Hazael followed immediately after Hadadezer, with no interim ruler.

> . . . Hadadezer perished. Hazael, a commoner, seized the throne, called up a numerous army and rose against me. I fought with him and defeated him, taking the chariots (?) of his camp. He disappeared to save his life. I marched as far as Damascus, his royal residence. . . . (*ANET* 280)

This information conflicts, of course, with the biblical stories of the three battles with Ben-hadad as well as with the Elisha stories, *if one assumes that these two narrative groups are in proper context.* That is, if the stories of the three battles with Ben-hadad actually pertain to the last years of Ahab (note that the king of Israel is killed in the third story) and the Elisha stories actually pertain to Jehoram's reign, then we have a Ben-hadad on the throne of Syria followed by Hazael (see especially II Kings 8:7–15) rather than a Hadadezer followed by Hazael.

Again historians part ways. Those who hold that the narratives in question are in proper historical context conclude that Ben-hadad and Hadadezer were the same person. Presumably the Assyrians knew him as Hadadezer, while the Israelites knew him as Ben-hadad. [For the purposes of clarity we have used Hebrew forms throughout this discussion. Actually the Akkadian form of "Hadadezer" used in Shalmaneser's inscriptions is "Adad-id-ri." The Aramaic form of "Ben-hadad" which appears in the Zakir and Melqart inscriptions (see below, p. 293) is "Barhadad."] Those inclined to believe that the narratives in question are not in proper historical context see the Ben-hadad/Hadadezer discrepancy as further evidence supporting that position. Indeed, the references to Ben-hadad in the stories of the three battles with Ben-hadad and in the Elisha stories serve as one of several clues that these narratives belong instead to the period of the Jehu dynasty. Hazael, as it turns out, was followed on the throne by a Ben-hadad who continued Hazael's policy of harassing Israel (II Kings 13:3–5, 14–25).

We will return to this matter below in our discussion of the Jehu dynasty. For the moment it is necessary only to make clear that we follow the second option indicated above and, accordingly, reconstruct the sequence of Damascus kings as follows:

Rezon	Solomon's contemporary
[Tabrimmon]	Whether Ben-hadad I was a commoner, or whether his father Tabrimmon ruled before him, is unclear.
Ben-hadad I	Son of Tabrimmon, contemporary of Asa and Baasha.
Hadadezer	Contemporary with Ahab's last years through most of Jehoram's reign.
[Ben-hadad]	
Hazael	Usurped the throne of Damascus sometime between 845 and 841 B.C.E.—that is, near the end of Jehoram's reign. It is possible that another Ben-hadad held the throne briefly between Hadadezer and Hazael (see II Kings 8:7–15), but unlikely in our opinion.

Ben-hadad II   Son of Hazael. Contemporary of Jehoahaz. This is probably the Ben-hadad of the Elisha stories and the three battle accounts in I Kings 20; 22:1–38.

Conflicting Chronologies in the Hebrew and Greek Manuscripts

Shalmaneser's records provide the first two secure "benchmarks" for developing a chronology of the Israelite and Judean kings. Specifically, we know from his records that Ahab was still on the throne in 853 B.C.E. and that Jehoram had been displaced by Jehu before or during 841 B.C.E. The chronological data provided in I-II Kings for the rulers of the Omride era are extremely problematic, on the other hand, to the extent that dates assigned to these kings will have to be largely guesswork. Three interrelated factors must be taken into account.

1. There are an unusually large number of textual variations in the manuscripts of I-II Kings for the chronological figures provided for the kings of the Omride period. Apparently these figures were rather "fluid" in the early stages of their transmission or they have been reworked from time to time.

2. Close examination of the variant readings of the different manuscript traditions reveals two distinct patterns of synchronisms for the Omride period, one dominating the Masoretic, or standard Hebrew, text (except for II Kings 1:17, which clashes with 3:1), the other dominating the Lucianic recension of the Greek. There are variant readings for the regnal periods also, but these differences are less pronounced.

3. The Masoretic figures (synchronisms and regnal periods) can be interpreted to fit together nicely if one hypothesizes that Omri and Tibni ruled simultaneously, perhaps over different parts of Israel, prior to the latter's "death" and further posits a coregency between Jehoshaphat and his son beginning with the former's seventeenth year. The Lucianic synchronisms clash with the story of Jehoram's Moabite campaign in II Kings 3:4–27, on the other hand, which, as we have seen, identifies Jehoshaphat as the king of Judah who marched with Jehoram on that occasion. According to the Lucianic synchronisms (and II Kings 1:17), Jehoshaphat would have died before Jehoram ascended the throne.

Obviously it is tempting to rely on the Masoretic figures. We are inclined not to do so, however, for three reasons. First, the brief report of Tibni's bid for the throne in I Kings 16:21–22 can hardly be taken to suggest that Tibni actually ruled a portion of Israel for four years anymore than there is any suggestion of a coregency between Jehoshaphat and his son Jehoram. Second, literary analysis of the story of the Moabite campaign of Jehoram of Israel in II Kings 3:4–27 suggests, as indicated above, that the king of Judah involved in the story has been identified only secondarily as Jehoshaphat. Third, the very fact that the Masoretic figures work out so nicely in spite of the obvious confusion in the Greek texts and allow for Jehoshaphat's appearance alongside Jehoram of Israel in II Kings 3 is a good warning, in our opinion, that they represent late scribal calculations intended to do just that.

In short, we suspect that the Lucianic texts preserve an earlier (pre-Masoretic revision) version of the synchronisms for the Omride period and thus regard the Lucianic figures as a better guide for reconstructing the relative chronology of the kings of the period. Accordingly, Jehoshaphat's reign does not overlap with that of Jehoram of Israel in our chronology.

Two further observations must be made regarding the chronology of the period. In order to allow enough time for the reigns of Ahaziah and Jehoram of Israel, one must conclude that Ahab was near the end of his reign in 853 B.C.E. when he fought against Shalmaneser at Qarqar, and that Jehu had not been on the throne long in 841 B.C.E. when Shalmaneser marched through northern Palestine and collected tribute from him. Mesha's statement that Omri's reign plus half the reign of his son (Ahab) amounted to forty years is not to be taken literally. "Forty years" is a round number, and excessive at that.

Israel at Its Zenith Under Omri and Ahab

Omri's Rise to Power

The circumstances of Elah's assassination, which is the only information provided about his reign, lead one to suspect that he was an inefficient or incompetent monarch not held in very high esteem by his compatriots. Although Israel's army was in the field at the time, fighting against the Philistines at Gibbethon, Elah was back at Tirzah "drinking himself drunk" in the house of one of his court officials. Moreover, Elah was assassinated by one of his own high-ranking professional soldiers, Zimri, commander of half the chariots. Possibly Zimri recognized that Elah did not have the full support of the people. Indeed, he may have been responding to popular sentiment voiced by the prophet Jehu son of Hanani (I Kings 16:7–10).

Zimri, having seized the throne, proceeded to massacre the royal family. When news of Zimri's coup reached Gibbethon, however, the troops proclaimed Omri, their field commander, as the new king and marched on Tirzah. Zimri soon recognized the futility of his position and committed suicide by burning the palace over himself. Tirzah fell to Omri, therefore, who now faced opposition from a certain Tibni the son of Ginath. The biblical account of this Omri-Tibni phase of the struggle for the throne provides the reader with just enough information to whet the appetite for more:

> Then the people of Israel were divided into two parts; half of the people followed Tibni the son of Ginath, to make him king, and half followed Omri. But the people who followed Omri overcame the people who followed Tibni the son of Ginath; so Tibni died, and Omri became king. (I Kings 16:21–22)

It is tempting to speculate about Tibni's background, the source and strength of his support, the tactics by which Omri's party overcame Tibni's party, and above all about the circumstances behind the curious statement, "So Tibni died." But there is very little basis for such speculation. It is not even certain that the statement, "So Tibni died," means that Tibni physically lost his life in connection with the struggle. Occasionally in ancient records, a ruler's loss of the throne is spoken of metaphorically as his "death."

We know very little about Omri, in spite of the fact that he is the earliest biblical character to be mentioned in ancient nonbiblical documents and also the first of the northern kings whose son and even two grandsons were able to follow him to the throne. We are informed that Jeroboam was an Ephraimite, for example, and that Baasha was from Issachar (I Kings 11:26; 15:27), but nothing is said of Omri's tribal origin. Possibly the village of Jezreel was his family home, since the Omrides apparently maintained an estate there in addition to the official residency at Samaria. If so, then it is tempting to speculate further that Omri was from the tribe of Issachar, which the Book of Joshua associates with the general vicinity of Jezreel. Yet we cannot assume that he represented any one of the traditional twelve tribes.

It is clear that Omri was a successful military figure. He was commanding Israel's army against the Philistines at Gibbethon when Zimri assassinated Elah, for example, and it was he who conquered Moab. Otherwise, the only specific item recorded for Omri's reign is that he established Samaria as the new capital of the northern kingdom. Much can be surmised, of course, about the Omride policies which introduced the new era of prosperity and international prestige. Yet it is difficult to distinguish Omri's contributions from those of Ahab. Probably the two construction phases at Samaria, if these are properly assigned (see below), represent the typical pattern—Omri made the beginning, but Ahab followed through in ways that far exceeded Omri's vision.

A New Capital at Samaria

Omri ruled from Tirzah during the first years of his reign, although the palace presumably had suffered considerable damage in connection with Zimri's aborted takeover. Then Omri purchased a site for the construction of a new capital which, according to I Kings 16:24, he named Samaria (Shomeron) after its previous owner Shemer. (Note Judg. 10:1, however, which presupposes the existence of an Ephraimite village named Shamir already during the time of the Judges. Was this the same place?) Samaria would serve as Israel's capital for the next century and a half, until the city and kingdom fell to the Assyrians in 722 B.C.E. Accordingly, the northern kingdom occasionally is referred to in the biblical materials as Samaria.

Tirzah, the old capital (or royal residency, and thus the seat of government), is to be identified with present-day Tell el-Far'ah, in the Wady Far'ah whose perennial springs flow eastward into the Jordan River. Stratum III of the ancient ruins excavated at the site probably represents the tenth- and early-ninth-century Israelite city. This stratum indicates a modest city with buildings that show evidence of numerous repairs and rebuilds. One of these buildings apparently was left unfinished, which has been interpreted to mean that Omri started to rebuild the city after its destruction but then aborted the plan, presumably when he turned attention to Samaria. Obviously this interpretation depends more on the biblical account than on the meager artifactual evidence.

The hill of Samaria (present-day Sebastiyeh) which Omri selected for his new capital, although not distinguished by its elevation, stood well isolated from the surrounding terrain. Thus its broad summit could be fortified to provide a formidable defense. Also, Samaria was much better located than Tirzah for international communication, particularly for contact with the north and west. Namely, Samaria was situated much nearer to the main north-south route through Palestine, "the Way of the Sea," and overlooked a valley (present-day Wady esh-Sha'air) which provided the most direct east-west route from the Mediterranean coast to the interior of the hill country at Shechem. The best north-south route connecting Shechem with the Jezreel Valley (via Dothan) also passed near Samaria. The fact that Omri is specifically stated as having "purchased" the site for his new capital may be significant as well. Presumably the whole city would have had the status of royal property, thus rendering Omride rule within the capital less dependent upon popular support than elsewhere in the kingdom.

The first two building phases at Samaria (Sebastiyeh strata I and II) probably represent the work of Omri and Ahab respectively. Stratum I, although not yet uncovered extensively, is represented by the remains of a modest palace on the summit of the hill. While this stratum I palace was still quite new, however, perhaps not even complete, work was begun on a second, more elegant, massive, and effectively defensive, palace compound (stratum II) which was to replace the first. Ivory inlay pieces, intricately carved and probably manufactured in Phoenicia, were discovered among the debris at the site. Although these were not found specifically in the stratum II context usually associated with Ahab, they do call to mind the reference to Ahab's "house of ivory" and suggest that this descriptive phrase had to do with the heavy use of ivory inlays in the palace decorations.

Omri and Ahab in International Politics

Omride international policies involved a system of negotiated alliances, combined with a buildup of military strength and territorial annexation, all conducted under the shadow of emerging Assyrian imperialism. (See Map 21.) Close relations with Phoenicia and Judah are indicated by the marriages between the royal families. Jezebel is identified in I Kings 16:31 as the daughter of Ethbaal king of the Sidonians. Josephus, writing in the first century C.E. and apparently following Menander of Ephesus, corrects this to "Ittobaal, the king of Tyre and Sidon" (*Ant.* VIII.316–18; *Contra Apion* I.116). Athaliah, on the other hand, the daughter of either Omri or Ahab (compare II Kings 8:18 with 8:26) was given in marriage to Jehoram son of Jehoshaphat. Thus disappeared, at least temporarily, the political hostilities between Israel and Judah which, since the separation of the kingdoms, would have hampered the free flow of trade. And once again, as in the days of Solomon, the overland trade routes

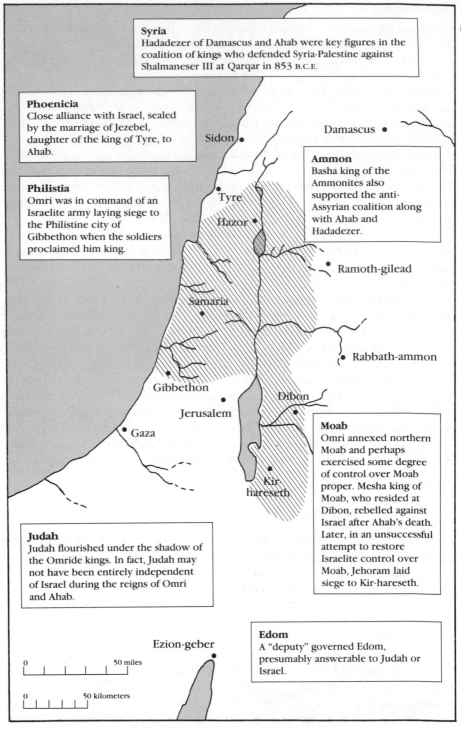

Syria
Hadadezer of Damascus and Ahab were key figures in the coalition of kings who defended Syria-Palestine against Shalmaneser III at Qarqar in 853 B.C.E.

Phoenicia
Close alliance with Israel, sealed by the marriage of Jezebel, daughter of the king of Tyre, to Ahab.

Philistia
Omri was in command of an Israelite army laying siege to the Philistine city of Gibbethon when the soldiers proclaimed him king.

Ammon
Basha king of the Ammonites also supported the anti-Assyrian coalition along with Ahab and Hadadezer.

Damascus •

Sidon •

Tyre •

Hazor •

• Ramoth-gilead

Samaria

• Rabbath-ammon

Gibbethon

Dibon •

Jerusalem

• Gaza

Moab
Omri annexed northern Moab and perhaps exercised some degree of control over Moab proper. Mesha king of Moab, who resided at Dibon, rebelled against Israel after Ahab's death. Later, in an unsuccessful attempt to restore Israelite control over Moab, Jehoram laid siege to Kir-haresteth.

Kir-haresteth

Judah
Judah flourished under the shadow of the Omride kings. In fact, Judah may not have been entirely independent of Israel during the reigns of Omri and Ahab.

Ezion-geber •

Edom
A "deputy" governed Edom, presumably answerable to Judah or Israel.

0   50 miles

0   50 kilometers

MAP 21. Omride International Affairs

passing through Israelite and Judean territory were connected with Phoenician ports.

Omri subjected Moab, we learn from the Moabite Stone, and the Moabites remained under Israelite domination through Ahab's reign (II Kings 1:1; 3: 4–5). Probably the actual military occupation was confined to the area north of the Arnon River where there were already "Israelite" elements among the population—Gadite clans which had ranged with their sheep and goats in this area as long as anyone could remember, and even certain villages which perhaps had survived from a half century earlier when this area was controlled by David and Solomon. Either Omri or Ahab fortified Jahaz, located somewhere in the general vicinity of Dibon and probably situated on one of the northern tributaries of the Arnon. A military garrison positioned in that vicinity (at the site of present-day el-Medeiyineh on Wady eth-Themed, for example) would have enabled them to maintain firm Israelite control over the rolling plateau north of the Arnon as well as control of the traffic, military or commercial, crossing the Arnon itself. Military strikes into the interior of Moab (between the Arnon and Zered canyons) would have been much more difficult, as illustrated by the narrative in II Kings 3:4–27. Note also that it is specifically the area north of the Arnon ("the land of Medeba") that Mesha claims to have recovered from Israel.

Assyrian imperialistic expansion westward had already begun with Ashurnasirpal II (883–859 B.C.E.), who ascended the throne in Assyria about the same time Omri came to power in Israel. Ashurnasirpal engaged in frequent sorties outside traditional Assyrian territory. These had several purposes, including the assertion of Assyrian claims along important trade routes, the establishment of Assyrian colonies, and the acquisition of tribute and luxury items. Also, there was a growing need for captives to swell the labor force at home where extensive construction was under way, such as Ashurnasirpal's new capital at Calah. Ashurnasirpal's armies reached the Mediterranean Sea as early as 875 B.C.E., at which time he received tribute from numerous cities, including Byblos, Sidon, and Tyre. This would have been near the end of Omri's reign.

Some two decades later (853 B.C.E.; near the end of Ahab's reign), Ashurnasirpal's successor, Shalmaneser III, conducted his first western campaign. Shalmaneser was met by a coalition of Syro-Palestinian kings, as we have seen, and apparently halted by them in the vicinity of Qarqar at the Orontes River. The Monolith Inscription records the opposing kings and their respective military contingents as follows:

Hadadezer of Damascus	1,200 chariots,	1,200 cavalry,	20,000 foot
Irhuleni of Hamath	700 chariots,	700 cavalry,	10,000 foot
Ahab the Israelite	2,000 chariots,		10,000 foot
from Que			500 foot
from Musri [Egypt]			1,000 foot
from Irqanata	10 chariots,		10,000 foot
Matinubalu of Arvad			200 foot
from Usanata			200 foot

Adunu-balu of Shian	30 chariots,	1[0?],000 foot
Gindibu of Arabia	1,000 camel riders	
Ba'sa of Ammon		[0?],000 foot

Note that "Ahab the Israelite" is credited with a larger chariot force than all of his allies combined, and even more than Shalmaneser himself claims to have deployed. Possibly there has been a scribal error, since "2,000" seems rather unreasonable. Nevertheless, even allowing for scribal error or exaggeration, it is clear that Israel represented one of the major military powers of Syria-Palestine during the latter part of Ahab's reign.

Judah, Moab, and Edom are not listed among the kingdoms that supported the coalition. The absence of Moab is not surprising, since we know that Moab was subject to Israel at the time; but why the absence of Judah and Edom? One possibility, of course, is that Judah and Edom chose not to participate since they were farther removed from the Assyrian threat. The Ammonites participated, however, and even some Arab groups who were also far removed. Another possibility to be considered, therefore, is that Judah and Edom, like Moab, were so closely aligned with Israel at the time that their soldiers were simply counted as belonging to Ahab.

Omri and Ahab as Builders

Both Omri and Ahab are remembered in I Kings for their building activities: Omri for founding and fortifying Samaria, and Ahab for building a temple of Baal in Samaria, an "ivory house," and other cities (I Kings 16:24, 32; 22:39). We have noted already that Sebastiyeh I and II probably represent Omri's and Ahab's building phases at Samaria. Among the other cities probably built (actually expanded) by Ahab were Megiddo and Hazor, both already discussed in connection with Solomon. At Megiddo, a solid wall 3.6 meters thick replaced Solomon's casemate wall. The so-called Megiddo stables, which probably were storage depots of some sort, also belong to the Omride phase, as does the impressive tunneled water system which allowed access to the water source from inside the city fortifications. At Hazor, where stratum VIII represents the Omride phase, the Solomonic city wall was also replaced with a more massive one which surrounded a larger area. One of the buildings of this phase measures 21.5 × 25 meters with walls two meters thick. A second building (20 × 13 meters) was constructed probably as a storeroom or warehouse. A water shaft similar to the one at Megiddo, although penetrating downward to groundwater level rather than to a spring, provided access to water from inside the city.

Huge capitals, proto-Aeolian in style, have been discovered from this period at all three sites—Samaria, Megiddo, and Hazor—as well as among roughly contemporary ruins in Judah (Ramat Rahel) and Moab (Medeibeh). These apparently were typical architectural features of the day and probably represent a general eastern Mediterranean style adapted and employed by Phoenician craftsmen. All three sites seem to represent royal administrative centers. Little evidence has been unearthed of the residential and market settlements which must have surrounded these royal complexes or of normal townships of the day. It has been suggested that these Omride constructions witness to a "royal city" concept according to which the king was isolated above and out of reach of the general citizenry. While this suggestion probably is an overinterpretation of the evidence, it is clear that these Omride constructions presupposed a great deal of wealth at the king's disposal and required a large labor force.

Yahwism and Baalism Under the Omrides

The compilers of Genesis-II Kings regarded Ahab as the most evil of all the kings who had ruled to his day.

> And as if it had been a light thing for him to walk in the sins of Jeroboam the son of Nebat, he took for wife Jezebel the daughter of Ethbaal king of the Sidonians, and went and served Baal, and worshiped him. He erected an altar for Baal in the house of Baal, which he built in Samaria. And Ahab made an Asherah. Ahab did more to provoke Yahweh, the God of Israel, to anger than all the kings of Israel who were before him. (I Kings 16:31–33)

The Elijah stories in I Kings 17–19 and the Naboth vineyard story seem to support this evaluation of Ahab, placing most of the blame on Jezebel. The Elijah story in II Kings 1 and the story of Jehoram's Moabite campaign in II Kings 3:4–27 depict Ahaziah and Jehoram as apostate kings also.

Several observations must be made as a warning against taking too literally the image of the Omride rulers and the perception of the Yahwism-Baalism conflict reflected in these sources. First, there are the anachronistic and pro-Judean perspectives of the compilers of Genesis-II Kings to be taken into account, particularly their tendency to project back into earlier times the con-

Proto-Aeolic Capital. The Omride kings rebuilt Megiddo and Hazor on a more impressive scale than had Solomon. This proto-aeolic capital is typical of the architectural style of the period. *(Oriental Institute)*

The Gateway from Hazor. This gateway, reconstructed from the remains at Hazor, also featured proto-aeolic capitals. Similar capitals have been discovered at Judean and Moabite sites. *(Israel Museum)*

cepts of exclusive Yahwism and the primacy of Jerusalem. It is doubtful in our opinion that even the most radical Yahwistic prophets of the ninth century B.C.E. would have been calling for the exclusive worship of Yahweh throughout the land, or even for the royal family. Second, as observed above, the Elijah stories are told from the perspective of the Yahwistic prophets and of groups that held these prophets in much awe. Thus they tend to oversimplify and exaggerate in their depiction of the Yahweh-Baal struggle. Third, as the Jehu dynasty began to lose popularity, there seems to have been an attempt to justify Jehu's coup and bloody massacre on the grounds that it was action taken in behalf of Yahweh. This apologetic theme is especially obvious in the account of Jehu's coup in II Kings 9:1–10:27. Finally, the emphasis on Jezebel as the aggressive champion of Baalism represents a tendency noticeable elsewhere in the Scriptures—namely, to see the queen, the queen mother, or foreign wives as the source of royal apostasy. (Compare the role of the foreign wives in the I Kings presentation of Solomon, for example, and of the queen mother in the presentation of Asa's reign; I Kings 11:1–8; 15:13.)

Nevertheless, while none of these sources can be regarded as entirely objective witnesses to the religious scene during the Omride period, together they point unmistakably to a serious Yahweh-Baal conflict which apparently surfaced during Ahab's reign and contributed to the eventual downfall of the dynasty. At the surface, the issue at stake probably was not whether Yahwism or Baalism would be practiced to the exclusion of the other, but whether Baalism as well as Yahwism would play a prominent role in the official cult of the kingdom. One presumes that the sanctuaries built (or revived) by Jeroboam I at Dan, Bethel, and Panuel were Yahwistic and, accordingly, that Israel's earlier kings had recognized Yahweh as the patron deity of the state. But quite a new situation seems to have developed with the Omrides. There is a new capital city, essentially private property of the royal family, and an impressive royal building complex under construction which will serve as the royal residence and administrative center of the land. In addition to, perhaps even instead of, a Yahwistic sanctuary, however, Ahab included in the new capital city a temple for Baal with all the associated furnishings. This was a new direction which, not surprisingly, brought protests from loyal Yahwists.

Moreover, the issue of whether Baalism would play a significant role in the official state cult probably was but "the tip of the iceberg," a polarizing issue symptomatic of a fracture that went to the very core of Israelite society. The protests against Baalism, we submit, were also a protest against the economic and social injustices which were attributed, correctly or not, to Omride policies.

One can ascertain only the faintest hints of social conditions during the Omride period. There was considerable prosperity, as we have already noted, especially in the better years during the reigns of Omri and Ahab. And certainly not all the wealth would have entered the royal treasury. Others in the kingdom will have benefited also from the active commerce made possible by the Omride successes in foreign policy, particularly the alliance of Phoenicia, Israel, and Judah. At the same time, the prosperity would not have spread to all. For most of the population of the land, certainly those in the rural villages, life must have continued at subsistence level. One of the results of Omride prosperity, therefore, would have been a substantial widening of the gap between the wealthy and the poor of the land.

In addition, the Omride rulers gained a reputation for self-serving high-handedness in their dealings with their subjects and as authors of unjust rules and regulations. This is illustrated by the Naboth vineyard story. While this story is probably historical fiction, authored long after the actual Naboth affair, it provides a glimpse of how the Omrides were remembered and typified in later years. Jezebel is depicted in the story using royal influence on local elders and nobles to pervert justice. More specifically, she employs the judicial system to destroy Naboth and allow the king to confiscate his family property in Jezreel. Micah 6:9–16 also recalls the Omride reputation for economic and social injustice. This latter text speaks of injustice, cheating, wicked scales, deceitful weights, violence, lies, and deceitful tongues, all of which it seems to equate with "the statutes of Omri, and all the works of the house of Ahab."

In short, the Yahweh-Baal struggle was only one aspect of a much more variegated rift that developed between the royal family and wealthy class on the one hand and the general population on the other. The former are to be associated primarily with the cities, such as Shechem and now Samaria, where autocratic rule was taken for granted and where foreign influences were strong. The latter are to be associated more with the rural villages where the old clan structures applied and where Yahwism found its strongest and more conservative adherents. It is easy to see how Ahab's association with Phoenician Baalism, particularly his marriage to a foreign, Baal-worshiping wife and construction of a Baal temple in the capital city, became symbolic of all that was disliked about the Omride dynasty.

Whether Ahab constructed the Baal temple merely as a gesture to his Phoenician queen, as Solomon had built sanctuaries for his foreign wives, or whether he actually intended to elevate Baalism in the national cult is uncertain. (Note that both of his sons, Aha*ziah* and *Jeho*ram, had Yahwistic names.) Regardless, prophetic groups led by Elijah began to call for destruction of the temple and annihilation of the royal family. The crown will have responded with repression, which explains the persecution of the Yahwistic prophets alluded to in the Elijah stories (see, for example, I Kings 18:4) as well as Elijah's enticement of the crowds to massacre the prophets of Baal (I Kings 18:40; 19:1–3).

Ahab's Death and the Beginning of Decline Under Ahaziah

The concluding summary of Ahab's reign in I Kings 22:39–40 states that Ahab "slept with his fathers" —a phrase normally used in the Genesis-II Kings account to refer to the burial of a person who died a natural death. This contrasts, of course, with the preceding and misplaced narrative (I Kings 22:1–38; the third of the stories of the three battles with Ben-hadad), which describes the death of an Israelite king in battle. Ahab was succeeded by his son Ahaziah, for whom we have only three items of information. We learn from I Kings 22:47–50 that Jehoshaphat refused Ahaziah's request that Israelite merchants be allowed to participate in a maritime expedition which the former sent out from Ezion-geber. The Elijah story in II Kings 1:2–16 recounts how Ahaziah suffered an injury from which he never recovered, thus explaining his unusually short reign. Finally, it seems clear from II Kings 1:1; 3:4–5 and the Mesha Inscription that King Mesha seized upon Ahab's death and Ahaziah's incapacitation as occasion to challenge Israelite domination of Moab and restore Moabite control over "the land of Medeba" (see Text IV, p. 283).

In short, Ahaziah's reign was characterized by inactivity and ineffectiveness as well as by its brevity. Thus began a sharp decline in Omride fortunes. Before tracing this decline through Jehoram's reign to Jehu's coup, let us review developments in Judah under Jehoshaphat, who was contemporary with Ahab and Ahaziah.

Jehoshaphat of Judah

Developments in Judah during the Omride era were closely related to developments in Israel, to the extent that Judah's history at this time is virtually a mirror image of Israelite history. Judah clearly benefited from the international security and economic revival that resulted from Omride military strength and international policies. The two royal families became related by marriage during Jehoshaphat's reign, moreover, so that eventually the separate status of the two kingdoms may have become more a matter of formality than of fact. Ahab's death, as we shall see, was also a turning point for Judah as it was for Israel.

Jehoshaphat in the Shadow of Ahab

Information about Jehoshaphat's reign comes from three biblical sources: the brief summary of his reign in I Kings 22:41–50; the two narratives in which he is featured as a pious Yahwist in contrast to the king of Israel (that is, the third of the stories of the three battles with Ben-hadad and the story of Jehoram's Moabite campaign); and the Chronicler's elaborate description of Jehoshaphat's power, wealth, and great deeds. The summary credits Jehoshaphat with very modest and not entirely successful accomplishments: some minor cultic reforms, peaceful relations with the king of Israel, and a maritime expedition which failed. The two narratives in question originally had nothing to do with Jehoshaphat, but illustrate in their present form how he was remembered by storytellers of later generations. He was remembered, namely, as a Judean king loyal to Yahweh but extremely deferential to the king of Israel. "I am as you are, my people as your people, my horses as your horses" (I Kings 22:4). Two themes thus emerge from both the summary and the two narratives—Jehoshaphat's strong Yahwistic leanings and his close supportive relations with the king

Mesha Inscription. The Mesha Inscription, discovered in 1868 and measuring some 44 inches in height, records the deeds of King Mesha of Moab, a contemporary of the Omride rulers of Israel (see Text IV, p. 283). *(The Louvre)*

of Israel. Both of these themes are magnified in II Chronicles where Jehoshaphat is depicted as an extremely successful monarch and energetic cultic reformer whose only flaw was that he became involved with the evil kings of Israel.

Clearly the Jehoshaphat who emerges from the I-II Kings materials does not measure up to the aggressive, strong and independent ruler one encounters in II Chronicles. Moreover, in the two instances where I-II Kings materials pertaining to Jehoshaphat are duplicated in II Chronicles, it is noticeable that these materials have been revised to support the image of Jehoshaphat that the Chronicler wished to convey.

The first of these instances involves the third of the stories of the three battles with Ben-hadad (compare I Kings 22:1–38 with II Chron. 18:1–19:3). The Chronicler's version follows I Kings virtually word for word, except that the Chronicler frames the narrative with a new introduction which emphasizes Jehoshaphat's great riches and honor, and with a second conclusion which has a Yahwistic prophet censure Jehoshaphat for giving military support to Israel.

> Now Jehoshaphat had great riches and honor; and he made a marriage alliance with Ahab. After some years he went down to Ahab in Samaria. And Ahab killed an abundance of sheep and oxen for him and for the people who were with him, and induced him to go up against Ramoth-gilead. . . .
> Jehoshaphat the king of Judah returned in safety to his house in Jerusalem. But Jehu the son of Hanani the seer went out to meet him, and said to King Jehoshaphat, "Should you help the wicked and love those who hate Yahweh? Because of this, wrath has gone out against you from Yahweh. Nevertheless some good is found in you, for you destroyed the Asherahs out of the land, and have set your heart to seek God." (II Chron. 18:1–2; 19:1–3)

The second passage that has been conspicuously revised in II Chronicles is the report of Jehoshaphat's unsuccessful maritime venture. According to I Kings, Jehoshaphat refused Ahaziah's request to participate in the venture. The Chronicler has Jehoshaphat granting Ahaziah's request, however, and then offers this as the reason that the venture failed.

> There was no king in Edom; a deputy was king. Jehoshaphat made ships of Tarshish to go to Ophir for gold; but they did not go, for the ships were wrecked at Ezion-geber. Then Ahaziah the son of Ahab said to Jehoshaphat, "Let my servants go with your servants in the ships," but Jehoshaphat was not willing. (I Kings 22:47–49)

> After this Jehoshaphat king of Judah joined with Ahaziah king of Israel, who did wickedly. He joined him in building ships to go to Tarshish, and they built the ships in Ezion-geber. Then Eliezer the son of Dodavahu of Mareshah prophesied against Jehoshaphat, saying, "Because you have joined with Ahaziah, Yahweh will destroy what you have made." And the ships were wrecked and were not able to go to Tarshish. (II Chron. 20:35–37)

Thus we are faced again with the same dilemma encountered earlier in connection with the Chronicler's work. Obviously the Chronicler's treatment of Jehoshaphat is not to be taken at face value. This is an ideal Jehoshaphat, a

Jehoshaphat re-created in accordance with a very distinctive theological perspective on Judah's history. Yet is the Chronicler's information to be disregarded altogether? Again, it is not just a question of whether the Chronicler had access to authentic sources unavailable to the compilers of I-II Kings but of whether information derived from such sources can be separated out from the Chronicler's imaginative editorial claims and whether, given the Chronicler's tendentious use of the Genesis-II Kings materials, this information has been distorted also.

Granting that the Chronicler may have preserved authentic information about Jehoshaphat's reign in addition to what can be gleaned from I-II Kings, the following items about Jehoshaphat present themselves for consideration.

> He built forts and store-cities and laid up provisions in cities throughout Judah. (II Chron. 17:12–13)

> He had soldiers and elite fighting men in Jerusalem (officers are named, with fighting units totaling over a million men) and also in the fortified cities throughout Judah. (II Chron. 17:2, 19)

> In the third year of his reign, he sent out five princes to teach in the cities of Judah; and with them nine Levites and two priests, Elishama and Jehoram. "And they taught in Judah, having the book of the law of Yahweh with them." (II Chron. 17:7–9)

> He appointed certain Levites, priests, and heads of families in Jerusalem to "give judgment for Yahweh and to decide disputed cases." Regarding "matters of Yahweh," they were answerable to Amariah the chief priest; in all the king's matters they were answerable to Zebadiah the governor of the house of Judah. Also he appointed judges throughout the land, particularly in the fortified cities. (II Chron. 19:5–11)

> He received presents and tribute from some of the Philistines and Arabs. (II Chron. 17:11)

Whatever the accuracy of these details, one receives the impression of a ruler who looked to the security of his kingdom in terms both of its defensive posture and of its central administrative control. Modern distinctions between church and state did not apply. Thus Jehoshaphat's administrative reforms were conducted in the name of, and largely through the mechanism of, the official Yahwistic cult.

Jehoshaphat's fortification of cities, buildup of a military force, and administrative reform would not have been incompatible with his establishment of peaceful relations with Ahab. On the contrary, as indicated above, it was the circumstances brought about by Omride military strength and foreign policies that enabled Jehoshaphat to do these things. Moreover, in spite of the Chronicler's efforts to convince the reader otherwise, one has to suspect that Jehoshaphat was at best a "junior partner" in the alliance with Ahab, sealed by the marriage of Athaliah, Ahab's sister (or daughter), to Jehoram, Jehoshaphat's son. This is suggested by at least two factors: (1) Judah goes unmentioned in the same nonbiblical records that witness to Israel's military strength and international prestige at the time of Ahab and Jehoshaphat. (2) Jehoshaphat came to be remembered by tradition as the Judean king who gave unqualified support to Israel—"I am as you are, my people as your people, my horses as your horses." Only after Ahab's death, when Mesha of Moab also began to challenge Omride authority, do we hear of Jehoshaphat taking a more independent stance. Namely, he refused Ahaziah's request to send Israelite merchants on the shipping expedition from Ezion-geber.

Jehoshaphat's Maritime Venture

The brief report in I Kings 22:47–49 of Jehoshaphat's ill-fated maritime expedition (preferred over the Chronicler's version of the incident for reasons given above) is open to two different interpretations. Since there has been no mention in the biblical materials of Israelite or Judean maritime activity in the Gulf of Aqabah since Solomon's day, one might conclude that this was an essentially new venture undertaken by Jehoshaphat. Once again, after three quarters of a century, a king of Jerusalem gained access to the Gulf of Aqabah and attempted to exploit the commercial advantage which this afforded. Yet it is difficult to believe that access would have been unavailable or the commercial advantage neglected earlier in the Omride period. With much of the Transjordan in Israelite hands; with Phoenicia, Israel, and Judah joined by marriage alliances; and with a "deputy" (answerable to whom?) in Edom—nothing would have been more natural than to revive the commercial arrangements that had been in effect during Solomon's day, whereby the Red Sea port was connected by overland routes through Judah and Israel to Phoenician ports on the Mediterranean. In fact, the alliance of Phoenicia, Israel, and Judah implied by the marriage of Jezebel to Ahab and Athaliah to Jehoram may have been essentially a commercial pact for this very purpose.

The other possibility, therefore, which seems more likely in our opinion, is that Jehoshaphat, rather than initiating a new shipping venture from Aqabah and refusing Ahaziah's permission to participate, had decided to seize the monopoly of a joint Phoenician, Israelite, and Judean shipping program which had already been under way for some time. Moreover, if Israel under Ahab had overshadowed and perhaps dominated Judah under Jehoshaphat, then Jehoshaphat's exclusion of Israelite merchants would have represented more than an economically motivated move. It would have been a signal asserting Judah's claim of independence from Omride domination.

The mention of an Edomite "deputy" in connection with Jehoshaphat's unsuccessful venture, plus a later statement in II Kings 8:20 to the effect that Edom rebelled against Judah during the reign of Jehoram (Jehoshaphat's son), could be taken to suggest that Jehoshaphat subjected Edom at some point. Yet the reference to the Edomite deputy is not introduced as an individual item about Jehoshaphat's reign, as if control of Edom was to be remembered among his deeds. Its purpose, rather, is to clarify how Jehoshaphat had thoroughfare across

Edomite territory to a port on the Gulf of Aqabah. Also the notation seems unnecessarily vague if its intention was to imply that Jehoshaphat himself controlled Edom through a deputy. Even the Chronicler apparently did not draw that conclusion or surely would have emphasized the point somewhere in the excessive claims about Jehoshaphat's greatness.

If, as suggested above, Israel dominated Judah as well as Moab during Ahab's reign, perhaps the Edomite deputy was also an Omride appointee. Ahab's death and Ahaziah's incapacitation would have left this deputy in a very insecure position. Possibly it was only then, therefore, if at all, that Jehoshaphat gained some degree of Judean authority over Edom. Another possibility, as we shall see below, is that Jehoram inherited control of Edom directly from Israel. One should not think in terms of total Judean (or Israelite) control over the whole of Edomite territory, in any case, but rather of some limited authority over the traditionally Edomite territory west of the Arabah—that part of Edom situated between Judah and the Gulf of Aqabah.

According to our chronology which depends on the Lucianic synchronisms, Jehoshaphat was a contemporary of Ahab and Ahaziah of Israel, but he would have died before Jehoram ascended the throne of Israel. This conflicts, we are well aware, with (1) the synchronisms provided in the traditional Hebrew (Masoretic) texts, which have Jehoshaphat still on the throne of Judah after Jehoram had ascended the throne of Israel, and (2) the story of Jehoram's Moabite campaign in II Kings 3:4–27 which *in its present form* has Jehoshaphat march with Jehoram against Moab. Our view on this matter, explained above, is that (1) the story did not involve Jehoshaphat originally, and (2) the Masoretic synchronisms also represent secondary editorial revision, intended to accommodate the story. Once the story had been modified to identify the "king of Judah" as Jehoshaphat and incorporated into the Genesis-II Kings corpus, then it was necessary also to revise the synchronisms so that Jehoshaphat would still be on the throne contemporary with Jehoram.

The Two Jehorams (?)

Jehoram (alternate form: Joram), son of Jehoshaphat and married to the Omride queen Athaliah, ascended the throne in Jerusalem during the brief reign of Ahaziah of Israel. Ahaziah, when he died, was also followed by a Jehoram, identified as "his brother" in some of the early versions of II Kings 1:17 but not in the Hebrew text: "So he died according to the word of Yahweh which Elijah had spoken. Jehoram [his brother] became king in his stead in the second year of Jehoram the son of Jehoshaphat, king of Judah, because Ahaziah had no son." For a time, therefore, some seven or eight years according to our chronology, both Israel and Judah were ruled by kings with the same name. Only one other throne change is reported to have occurred before Jehu's coup —namely, Jehoram of Judah is said to have been succeeded by his son Ahaziah shortly before the incident. Thus it was Jehoram king of Israel and Ahaziah king of Judah whom Jehu assassinated.

Who was this Jehoram who came to the throne in Samaria upon the earlier Ahaziah's death? One may assume that he was an Omride, and it is tempting to speculate with the early versions of II Kings 1:17 that he was Ahaziah's brother, another of Ahab's sons. However, the fact that we have two Jehorams on the throne at the same time, and for approximately the same length of time, raises the possibility that they were the same person—that is, that Ahaziah of Israel who died without any sons was succeeded on the throne in Samaria by his brother-in-law (married to Athaliah his sister) who was already king of Judah. If so, then once again for almost a decade, Israel and Judah would have been united under a single crown, a Judean king married to an Omride queen.

Obviously the compilers of Genesis-II Kings and the Chronicler did not understand it this way, and even report two different deaths for the two Jehorams (II Kings 8:24; 9:21–26; II Chron. 21:18–20). Yet it is easy to see how they might have misunderstood the records at their disposal, and several irregularities in their summations of the reigns suggest that they in fact did. (1) The text of II Kings 1:17, which reports Jehoram's accession to the throne of Israel, presents several variant readings—such as the insertion of "his brother" in some of the versions. (2) The usual references to "the Book of the Chronicles of the Kings of Israel" and "the Book of the Chronicles of the Kings of Judah" are absent for Jehoram of Israel and Ahaziah of Judah. (3) The Lucianic system of synchronisms for the Omride period does not include synchronisms for Jehoram and Ahaziah of Judah. All of this suggests that the ancient records for the period may not have required as many separate kings as the compilers of Genesis-II Kings inferred from them, and that even the early transmitters of the biblical texts sensed a degree of uncertainty about Jehoram of Israel's background.

In summary, there is reason to suspect that (1) only one Jehoram ruled both kingdoms, ascending the throne first in Jerusalem and later in Samaria. Thus (2) he was reported in different contexts in the official records—that is, his reign and deeds as king of Judah would have been recorded in the Judean records and his activities as king of Israel in the Israelite records. And (3) the compilers of Genesis-II Kings inferred incorrectly from these records (either directly or through intermediate sources such as "the Book of the Chronicles of the Kings of Judah" and "the Book of the Chronicles of the Kings of Israel") that Jehoram of Judah and Jehoram of Israel were two different persons.

This hypothesis would explain several other rather curious matters reported in Kings and Chronicles. For example, there is the passing observation in II Chron. 21:4 that Jehoram of Judah, once he was established on the throne, killed certain "princes of Israel" in addition to other sons of Jehoshaphat. It is understandable why a Judean king would have wanted to remove any other possible claimants to the Judean throne. But for what reason and on what authority would he have executed Israelite princes—unless he had inherited the throne of Israel also and needed to secure his position on it as well? The possibility emerges that Jehoram's dominion over Edom presupposed in II Kings 8:20 came with the Israelite rather than the Judean crown. If Jehu was

attempting to seize charge of a combined Israelite/Judean kingdom, it is understandable why he did not confine his massacre to the king and officials of Israel.
Finally, there are the related matters of the extremely brief reign of Ahaziah of
Judah (the one year ascribed to him in II Kings 8:26 could mean any length of
time up to a year) and his involvement in the events leading up to the massacre.
Ahaziah, we may suppose, to whom the throne in Jerusalem may have been
delegated already, would have come to Jezreel not simply to visit his wounded
father but to serve as coregent of Israel as well while his father recovered.

Whether Jehoram of Judah and Jehoram of Israel were the same person or
brothers-in-law, the years of his or their reign or reigns saw rapid decline for
both kingdoms. The summary of the reign of Jehoram of Judah in II Kings
8:16–24 reports that both Edom and Libnah revolted from Judah at that time.
Moab, on the other hand, under King Mesha, was already in open rebellion
against Israel. Mesha had succeeded his father as king of Moab approximately
midway in Ahab's reign, and his inscription presents this, Mesha's accession to
the throne, as the turning point in Israelite-Moabite relations. (See Text IV.)
Probably it was not until Ahab's death, however, during Ahaziah's weak reign,
that Mesha made his first moves to throw off the Israelite yoke (II Kings 1:1;
3:5). Specifically, Mesha's "rebellion" consisted of his refusal to pay the annual
tribute imposed by Omri and continued by Ahab, recovery of Moabite control
over northern Moab ("the land of Medeba," approximately from Heshbon to
the Arnon), and preparations to defend Moab against Israel's retaliatory attack
which could be expected as soon as an active ruler was established in Samaria.

In the process, Mesha took some limited military action against Israelite
settlements in the area north of the Arnon. Namely, he massacred the Israelite
population of two towns situated on the western slopes of northern Moab,
Ataroth and Nebo, and occupied Jahaz, near his own city of Dibon. The Israelite
population at Ataroth belonged to the tribe of Gad which had occupied the city
"always," in Mesha's estimation. At Nebo, where there was a Yahwistic cult
place, Mesha claims to have slaughtered seven thousand Israelites and dragged
away for presentation before Chemosh some sort of cultic object associated with
Yahweh. Both Ataroth and Nebo were resettled with Moabites, a measure
intended no doubt to ensure the defense of the Medeba plateau from any
Israelite retaliation from the northwest. Jahaz, which had been fortified by Omri
or Ahab to facilitate military and administrative control of the area north of the
Arnon, apparently was abandoned by the Israelites without a struggle. Mesha,
without any mention of military action, claims to have placed his own officials
in the city and attached it to the district of Dibon.

We hear nothing of any attempt on the part of Israel to restore control over
Moab until Jehoram's reign. And for Jehoram's unsuccessful attempt, we have
only the story of his Moabite campaign in II Kings 3:4–27 which is beset with
literary and interpretational problems. As indicated above, the parallels be-.
tween this narrative and the third of the stories of the three battles with Ben-
hadad (I Kings 22:1–38) are particularly striking—both narratives appear to
have been revised at some point to give a prominent role to the king of Judah

TEXT IV. The Mesha Inscription

I am Mesha, son of Chemosh[yatti] king of Moab, the Dibonite. My father reigned over Moab thirty years and I reigned after my father. And I built this high place to Chemosh at Qarhoh [. . .] because he saved me from all the kings and caused me to triumph over all my adversaries. Omri, king of Israel, humbled Moab many days because Chemosh was angry at his land. And his son succeeded him, and he also said, "I too will humble Moab." During my days he said this, but I have triumphed over him and over his house and Israel has perished for ever. Omri had occupied the whole land of Medeba and he dwelt in it during his days and half the days of his son, forty years, but Chemosh dwelt there in my days. And I built Baal-meon and I made in it a reservoir and I built Qaryaten.

And the men of Gad had dwelt in the land of Ataroth always and the king of Israel built Ataroth for them, but I fought against the town and took it. And I slew all the people of the town as satiation for Chemosh and Moab and I brought from there the *arel david* (the royal altar?) and I dragged it before Chemosh in Kerioth and I settled there men of Sharon and men of Maharith.

And Chemosh said to me, "Go, take Nebo from Israel." And I went by night and fought against it from the break of dawn until noon and I took it and I slew all seven-thousand men and boys and women and girls and maidservants because I had devoted them to Astar-Chemosh. And I took from there the [. . .] of Yahweh and I dragged them before Chemosh.

And the king of Israel built Jahaz and dwelt there while fighting me, but Chemosh drove him out before me. And I took from Moab two-hundred men, all of them noblemen, and established them in Jahaz; thus I took possession of it to attach it to (the district) of Dibon. And I built Qarhoh, the wall of the parkland and the wall of the citadel, and I built the gates and I built its towers and I built the king's house and I made both of its reservoirs for water inside the town. And there was no cistern in the town at Qarhoh, and I said to all the people, "Let each of you make a cistern for himself in his house." And I cut beams for Qarhoh with captives from Israel. And I built Aroer and I made the highway in the Arnon and I built Beth-bamoth, for it had been destroyed. And I built Bezer because it lay in ruins [. . . . . .] so men of Dibon, because all Dibon was loyal to me. And I ruled [. . .] one-hundred towns which I added to the land and I built [. . .] and Beth-diblathen and Beth-baal-meon and I placed there [. . . . . . .] the land.

And as far as Hauronen, there dwelt in it [. . . . . .]. Chemosh said to me, "Go down, fight against Hauronen." And I went down and I fought [. . . . . .]. Chemosh dwelt there in my time [. . . . . .]. (Compare *ANET* 320–21) (See photograph on p. 276.)

who is identified in turn as Jehoshaphat. Regardless of how one deals with the various uncertainties of this text, it is clear that Jehoram's attempt to restore control over Moab was unsuccessful. Apparently Jehoram marched on Moab from the southwest, around the southern end of the Dead Sea, and laid siege to Kir-hareseth (probably present-day Kerak). The city was about to fall, according to the narrative, when Mesha in desperation sacrificed his oldest son on the wall. "And there came great wrath upon Israel; and they withdrew from him and returned to their own land" (II Kings 3:27).

Shalmaneser remained a constant threat to Syria-Palestine, and Israel presumably continued to support the anti-Assyrian coalition which had already successfully defended against him once near the end of Ahab's reign and did so again in 849, 848, and 845 B.C.E. Israel's continued involvement in the coalition cannot be verified, however, since the entries in Shalmaneser's inscriptions for these latter three campaigns are unfortunately brief and identify only two of the opposing kings by name (Irhuleni of Hamath and Hadadezer of Damascus). Typical is the following entry in the Bull Inscription for Shalmaneser's tenth year (849 B.C.E.).

> At that time Hadadezer of Aram, Irhuleni of Hamath, together with twelve kings of the seacoast, trusted in each other's might and advanced against me, offering battle and combat. I fought with them, I defeated them. Their chariots, their cavalry, their weapons of war, I took from them. To save their lives they fled. (*ARAB* I, §652)

Jehu's Coup and the End of the Omrides in Israel

The Yahwistic prophets and their supporters who opposed the Omride dynasty were no match for Ahab. He was a powerful ruler over a kingdom enjoying unprecedented prosperity. After Ahab's death, however, when Omride fortunes began to take a turn for the worse, the royal family became increasingly vulnerable to their dissatisfied subjects and the opposing voices. Jehoram apparently sought to accommodate the Yahwists by removing the pillar or asherah of Baal which Ahab had installed (I Kings 16:33; II Kings 3:2). But by that time it was too late. The prophets were calling for blood, particularly the blood of Jezebel, now the queen mother. Again, as in the case of Ahijah the Shilonite, it was a Yahwistic prophet, Elisha, who instigated rebellion against the crown (II Kings 9:1–10; but see also I Kings 19:15–18). And again, as in the cases of Baasha and Zimri, it was a high military official who took matters in hand, assassinated the king, and wiped out the royal family.

The details of this turning point in Israelite and Judean history are described in the account of Jehu's coup (II Kings 8:25–10:27) which, although clearly written from a pro-Jehu perspective and perhaps overstating Jehu's Yahwistic zeal, does not wince from describing his bloody deeds. Israel's army was in the field at Ramoth-gilead defending against Syrian attack when Jehoram was wounded and returned to Jezreel to recover. This left Jehu, presumably Jehoram's "chief of staff," in charge of the army. Ahaziah, in the meantime, either

Jehoram's son (assuming one Jehoram) or the son of his brother-in-law (assuming two Jehorams), came to visit him at Jezreel, possibly to serve at least temporarily as coregent.

Jehu at that point, urged on by Elisha, who may have been prompted in turn by some royal injustice against the prominent Naboth family of Jezreel, hastened to Jezreel, where he assassinated both Jehoram and Jezebel. These two assassinations, and probably the more extensive massacre which followed, were conducted in accordance with the traditional prophetical malediction which called for death without burial. "Any one belonging to . . . who dies in the city the dogs shall eat; and any one of his who dies in the field the birds of the air shall eat" (see I Kings 14:11; 16:4; 21:24). Jehoram's body was left exposed for the animals and birds on the plot of ground belonging to Naboth, and Jezebel's body was devoured by dogs in the streets of Jezreel. Jezebel, we are told, faced death without flinching. No sackcloth and ashes or begging for mercy, she prepared to meet her murderer dressed like a queen, with eyes painted and head adorned. Then she addressed Jehu as a traitor: "You Zimri, murderer of your master." Holding her head aloof, this woman, no doubt now aged, played the role of queen to the very end (II Kings 9:30–37).

Ahaziah attempted to escape but was overtaken only a few miles away (near Ibleam), shot with an arrow, and continued on to Megiddo, where he died. Next, Jehu sent letters to Samaria giving notice of his actions and challenging the officials of the city to select another Omride as their king and prepare to defend the government.

> Now then, as soon as this letter comes to you, seeing your master's sons are with you, and there are with you chariots and horses, fortified cities also, and weapons, select the best and fittest of your master's sons and set him on his father's throne, and fight for your master's house. (II Kings 10:2–3)

The officials responded that they had no intentions of opposing Jehu, whereupon he sent further instructions with which they complied. "If you are on my side, and if you are ready to obey me, take the heads of your master's sons, and come to me at Jezreel tomorrow at this time" (II Kings 10:6). Finally, we are told, Jehu came himself to Samaria and made a great feast for all the prophets and worshipers of Baal. When all were assembled in the Baal temple and guards stationed at the doors, he gave the signal that all were to be killed. The account ends with his demolishing the pillar of Baal and the temple itself.

Jehu's seizure of the government would have occurred sometime between 845 B.C.E.—the year of Shalmaneser's fourth western campaign, at which time Hadadezer was still ruling in Damascus—and 841 B.C.E., the year of Shalmaneser's fifth western campaign, by which time Hazael had usurped the throne of Damascus and Jehu was already ruling in Samaria. Shalmaneser apparently met with no serious resistance during the 841 campaign. Thus he advanced all the way to Damascus, which apparently submitted to him, and then pushed into northern Palestine. Specifically, Shalmaneser claims in the Black Obelisk (*ANET* 280) to have reached the mountains of Hauran (in the northern Trans-

TEXT V. Excerpts from the Black Obelisk

Assur, the great lord, king of all of the great gods; Anu, king of the Igigi and Anunnaki, the lord of lands; Enlil (Bel), the exalted, father of the gods, the creator; Ea, king of the Deep (Apsu), who determines destiny; [Sin], king of the tiara, exalted in splendor; Adad, mighty, pre-eminent, lord of abundance (plenty); Shamash, judge of heaven and earth, director of all (things); Marduk, master of the gods, lord of law (omens); Urta, valiant (ruler) of the Igigi and the Anunnaki, the almighty god; Nergal, the ready (perfect), king of battle; Nusku, bearer of the shining scepter, the god who renders decisions; Ninlil, spouse of Bel, mother of the [great] gods; Ishtar, first in heaven and on earth, who fills full the measure of bravery;—the great [gods], who ordain destiny (destinies), who have made great my kingdom, (I invoke).

Shalmaneser, king of all peoples, lord, priest of Assur, mighty king, king of all the four regions (of the world), Sun of all peoples, despot of all lands; son of Assur-nasir-pal, the high priest, whose priesthood was acceptable to the gods and who brought in submission at his feet the totality of the countries (of earth); glorious offspring of Tukulti-Urta, who slew all of his foes and overwhelmed them like a hurricane (deluge). . . .

In my eleventh year of reign I crossed the Euphrates for the ninth time. Countless cities I captured. Against the cities of the land of Hamath, I descended. 89 cities I captured. Hadad-ezer of Aram (and) twelve kings of the land of Hatti stood by each other. I accomplished their overthrow. . . .

In my eighteenth year of reign I crossed the Euphrates for the sixteenth time. Hazael of Aram came forth to battle. 1,121 of his chariots, 470 of his cavalry, together with his camp, I captured from him. . . .

(from the reliefs)

Tribute of Sua, the Gilzanite. Silver, gold, lead, copper vessels, staves for the hand of the king, horses, camels, whose backs are two humps, I received from him.

Tribute of Iaua (Jehu), son of Omri. Silver, gold, a golden bowl, a golden beaker, golden goblets, pitchers of gold, lead, staves for the hand of the king, javelins, I received from him.

Tribute of the land of Musri. Camels, whose backs are two humps, a river-ox (buffalo), a *sakea,* a *susu,* elephants, monkeys, apes, I received from him.

Tribute of Marduk-apal-usur of Suhi. Silver, gold, pitchers of gold, ivory, javelins, *buia,* brightly colored (and) linen garments, I received from him.

Tribute of Karparunda, of Hattina. Silver, gold, lead, copper, copper vessels, ivory, cypress (timbers), I received from him. (*ARAB* I, §§555–56, 568, 589–93) (See photograph on p. 261.)

jordan), devastated that area, and to have erected a monument at Ba'li-ra'si ("Baal's Head"; probably the Mt. Carmel ridge where it reaches the Mediterranean at present-day Haifa). Also the Black Obelisk depicts Jehu in relief, bowing before Shalmaneser, with the following caption:

> Tribute of Iaua (Jehu), son of Omri. Silver, gold, a golden bowl, a golden beaker, golden goblets, pitchers of gold, lead, staves for the hand of the king, javelins, I received from him. (*ARAB* I, §590)

Three major events, therefore, occurred in rather close sequence (between 845 and 841 B.C.E.)—Hazael's usurpation of the throne in Damascus, his encroachment on Israel's territory in the northern Transjordan which occasioned Jehu's coup, and Shalmaneser's fifth western campaign during which he claims to have subdued Damascus and invaded Israelite territory. It is interesting, although historically doubtful, that both Elijah and Elisha are credited with playing some role in Hazael's as well as Jehu's rise to power (see I Kings 19:15–18; II Kings 8:7–15; 9:1–4).

Black Obelisk. On one of its panels "Jehu son of Omri" bows before Shalmaneser III. *(The British Museum)*

Rimah Inscription. The Rimah Inscription (51 inches high), discovered in 1967, reports the deeds of Adad-nirari III (see Text VI, p. 299). According to the inscription, Adad-nirari received tribute from Joash of Israel. *(British School of Archaeology in Iraq)*

CHAPTER 9

The Century
of the Jehu Dynasty

Jehu's coup marked the end of an era. Both kingdoms succumbed to Syrian domination soon after, and moments of national autonomy would be the exception rather than the rule during the remainder of their respective histories. Jehu's coup is also an important "benchmark" for chronological purposes. The incident can be dated fairly closely (shortly before or during 841 B.C.E.; 843 according to our chronology) and resulted in simultaneous throne changes in both kingdoms. As we shall see, while Jehu was securing his position in Samaria, Athaliah seized the throne in Jerusalem.

Jehu and his descendants would hold the throne in Samaria for approximately a century (until 745 B.C.E. according to our chronology). This record is less impressive than might appear when one considers that the first two rulers of the dynasty (Jehu and Jehoahaz) were largely at the mercy of Damascus and exercised little authority outside the gates of Samaria. Nevertheless, the era of the Jehu dynasty is the one period in the history of the separate kingdoms when royal assassinations and palace intrigue were more characteristic of Judah than of Israel. Three successive Judean rulers were assassinated—Athaliah, Joash, and Amaziah.

It will be useful to divide the century of the Jehu dynasty covered in this chapter into two parts. Roughly the first half century—the reigns of Jehu and Jehoahaz in Israel contemporary with Athaliah and Joash in Judah—was the time of severe Syrian oppression at the hands of Hazael and Ben-hadad of Damascus. At some point near the end of Jehoahaz's reign and/or early in the reign of Joash of Israel (the exact sequence of events is one of the issues to be explored below) the fortunes of Damascus took a turn for the worse. Thus the second half century of the Jehu dynasty—the reigns of Joash, Jeroboam II, and Zechariah in Israel, contemporary with Amaziah, Uzziah, and Jotham of Judah —represented a relatively brief moment of national restoration for Israel and Judah.

Sources of Information

The Biblical Materials

Although the Jehu dynasty held the throne of Israel twice as long as did the Omride dynasty, the compilers of Genesis-II Kings devoted less than half as much space to the Jehu era. This is not surprising, since it was not a very impressive period in the history of the two kingdoms, certainly not of Judah. Moreover, the circumstances of this era were problematic for the compilers' theological perspective, particularly the view that Yahweh gave success to those kings who were faithful to him and especially those who supported his cult in Jerusalem. Jehu, whose seizure of the throne had been encouraged by Yahwistic prophets and who began his reign with a purge of Baal worshipers, turned out to be powerless before Hazael. His great-grandson Jeroboam II, on the other hand, who was not remembered as a strong Yahwist, nevertheless was able to expand Israel's borders and clearly overshadowed his Judean contemporary, Uzziah.

Thus the section of the Genesis-II Kings corpus that has to do with the era of the Jehu dynasty—from the account of Jehu's coup (II Kings 9:1–10:27) through II Kings 15—consists of little more than brief summations of the individual kings' reigns. There is a relatively full report of how the child Joash survived Athaliah's purge of the royal family, displaced her on the throne, and later arranged for repairs of the Jerusalem Temple (II Kings 11:1–12:16) and of the conflict between Joash of Israel and Amaziah of Judah which resulted in the sack of Jerusalem (II Kings 14:8–14). Otherwise the only extended narrative in this section, comparable to the numerous prophetical narratives which the compilers introduced in the context of the reigns of the Omride kings, is the last of the Elisha stories which appears in connection with the reign of Joash of Israel (II Kings 13:14–21). As we observed in Chapter 8, however, some of the prophetical narratives associated by the compilers with Ahab and Jehoram actually belong to the period of the Jehu dynasty and thus must be taken into account in this chapter. This is true specifically of the earlier Elisha stories (II Kings 2; 4:1–8:15) and the stories of the three battles with Ben-hadad (I Kings 20; 22:1–38).

The Chronicler's presentation of the era of the Jehu dynasty (II Chron. 22:10–27:9) follows the now familiar pattern. The Israelite kings are ignored, except where they figure in Judean affairs. The information presented for the Judean kings essentially duplicates the summations that already appear in II Kings, but with expansions and modifications which often, but not always, reflect the Chronicler's particular interests and perspectives. The Levites are given an important role in the coronation ceremony for Joash of Judah, for example. There is a fuller account of Amaziah's victory over Edom. Finally, in the case of Joash, Amaziah, and Uzziah, there is the familiar pattern whereby a king's early years of rule, during which he supposedly was on good terms with the Yahwistic priests and prophets and led the kingdom to strength and prosperity, are contrasted with his later years when he turned against the Yahwistic leaders and met with various disasters.

Certain of the prophetical books come into consideration at this point in our survey of Israelite and Judean history. The superscriptions to the books of Amos and Hosea associate the early careers of these two prophets with the reigns of Jeroboam II and Uzziah, for example, and Isa. 1:1 places Isaiah's early career in the reigns of Uzziah and Jotham. Occasionally the oracles collected in these books contain rather specific references to the kings and the political circumstances of their reigns. Hosea 1, as we have seen, alludes to Jehu's bloody massacre of the Omrides and predicts that his dynasty will receive its own punishment. Amos' oracles uttered at Bethel also included a rather specific attack on Jeroboam II. For the most part, however, like the Elijah and Elisha stories, the oracles collected in these books provide only general background information about the social, economic, and religious circumstances of the day from which they come.

Royal Assyrian and Syrian Records

Also important, primarily for gaining an understanding of the broader political circumstances of the Middle East during the century of the Jehu dynasty, are certain royal inscriptions from Israel's neighbors. Shalmaneser's last western campaign, in 838 B.C.E. (early in Jehu's reign) is reported on the Black Obelisk described in Chapter 8. The relevant entry is as follows:

> In my twenty-first year of reign I crossed the Euphrates for the twenty-first time. I advanced against the cities of Hazael of Aram (? Damascus). Four of his cities I captured. The gifts of the Tyrians, Sidonians, and Gebalites, I received. (*ARAB* I, §578)

Assyria's threat to Syria-Palestine subsided for the next four decades, until the reign of Adad-nirari III (810–783 B.C.E.). According to the so-called Eponym (or *limmu*) List, Adad-nirari penetrated northern Syria, specifically Arpad and its vicinity, with a series of western campaigns during the years 805 to 803 B.C.E. It is unclear whether the campaign reported in this list for Adad-nirari's next year, 802 B.C.E., and summarized with the phrase "to the sea" reached the Mediterranean Sea or the Persian Gulf. Several years later, in any case, in 796 B.C.E., he marched west again and reached a place called Mansuate located somewhere in the Lebanese Bekaa Valley. (See Map 22.)

In addition to the Eponym List, four known inscriptions commemorate Adad-nirari's western campaigns, only two of which indicate penetration into southern Syria-Palestine. The first of these two is the inscription of the Saba'a Stela, discovered in the desert south of the Sinjar hills (in present-day Iraq) in 1905. Between the introduction and conclusion, which are typical of the royal Assyrian inscriptions, the following items are reported.

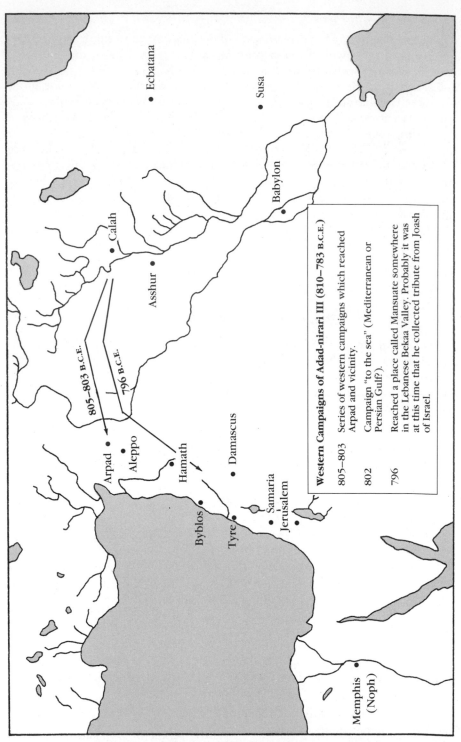

Western Campaigns of Adad-nirari III (810–783 B.C.E.)

805–803	Series of western campaigns which reached Arpad and vicinity.
802	Campaign "to the sea" (Mediterranean or Persian Gulf?).
796	Reached a place called Mansuate somewhere in the Lebanese Bekaa Valley. Probably it was at this time that he collected tribute from Joash of Israel.

MAP 22. Adad-nirari III's Western Campaigns

In (my) fifth year of reign, when I took my seat on the royal throne, in might, I mobilized (the forces of my) land, (to) the widespreading armies of Assyria, I gave the order to advance against Palashtu [Palestine]. The Euphrates I crossed at its flood. . . . [To march against Aram] I gave the command. Mari' [I shut up] in Damascus, [his royal city]. 100 talents of gold, 1,000 talents of silver . . . (*ARAB* I, §§734–35)

The second of the two inscriptions appears on the Rimah Stela discovered in 1967 during the excavations at al-Rimah in Iraq (see Text VI). After the usual introduction, Adad-nirari claims to have conquered "the land of Amurru and the Hatti land" in a single year. Lines 6–8 of this inscription, which shifts from first person to third person, repeats Adad-nirari's claim to have received tribute from Mari' of Damascus and makes the same claim regarding the rulers of Tyre, Sidon, and "Ia'asu (= Joash) of Samaria."

The crucial question that emerges for our purposes is when exactly Adad-nirari reached Damascus and collected tribute from Joash and other monarchs in that vicinity. At first glance, the reference to "(my) fifth year" in the Saba'a Inscription suggests Adad-nirari's earlier western campaigns, specifically the first of these in 805 B.C.E. It seems strange, however, if Adad-nirari actually penetrated as far as Damascus at that time, or during any of his earlier western campaigns, that the Eponym List reports activity only in northern Syria. It must be taken into account also that the Saba'a and Rimah inscriptions, like the Mesha Inscription, are summary texts which report Adad-nirari's deeds over a period of years. Accordingly, the reference to Adad-nirari's fifth year in the Saba'a Inscription probably should not be interpreted to mean that he did everything claimed in the inscription during his fifth year, but that this was the year in which he began his military career and/or, since these inscriptions summarize specifically his western campaigns, the year he began his conquest of the west. When these factors are taken into account, Adad-nirari's later (796 B.C.E.) western campaign emerges as the most likely occasion for him to have reduced Damascus and collected tribute from Joash of Israel. This was the only year, according to the Eponym List, that Adad-nirari reached southern Syria-Palestine.

During the interim of approximately four decades between Shalmaneser's last western campaigns (841 and 838 B.C.E.) and Adad-nirari's western ventures (805–803 and 796 B.C.E.) Hazael of Damascus dominated Syria-Palestine. The biblical materials witness to Hazael's imperialistic expansion in the direction of Israel, Philistia, and Judah as well as to the finally unsuccessful efforts of Ben-hadad, Hazael's son, to maintain control of Israel (II Kings 10:32–33; 13:3–25). Two inscriptions discovered in the vicinity of Aleppo witness to the extent of Hazael's domain in northern Syria and to Ben-hadad's equally unsuccessful efforts to maintain control there. The first of these, the so-called Melqart Stela discovered a few miles north of Aleppo in 1939 or soon before, presents a votive text dedicated by Ben-hadad to the Phoenician god Melqart.

A stela erected by Barhadad [= Ben-hadad], the son [of . . .], king of Aram, for his Lord Melqart, which he vowed to him and he heard his voice. (See *ANET* 655)

We cannot be absolutely certain that the Ben-hadad who erected this stela was Ben-hadad the son of Hazael, since there was more than one king of Damascus named Ben-hadad and a crucial portion of the text is so badly weathered that it can no longer be read. Ben-hadad the son of Hazael seems the most likely candidate, however, in view of the fact that the second inscription, discovered about twenty-five miles southeast of Aleppo in 1904, does identify its Ben-hadad as the son of Hazael. This latter inscription was erected by Zakir king of Hamath and Lu'ath, who had led several local kings in successful resistance against Ben-hadad and thus dedicated his inscription in thanksgiving to the god Ilu-Wer (see Text VII). Together the Melqart and Zakir inscriptions show Ben-hadad slowly loosing his grip on northern Syria.

Archaeology

It is possible, as indicated in the preceding chapter, to identify with some degree of certainty the Omride strata in certain key Palestinian sites. Evidences of city destructions at numerous sites approximately during the late eighth and early seventh centuries, on the other hand, can just as reasonably be attributed to Assyrian military activities in Palestine at that time. Thus the strata in between would represent the era of the Jehu dynasty. To be considered in this regard are Samaria/Sebastiyeh III-IV, Megiddo/Tell el-Mutesellim IV A, Tirzah/Tell el-Far'ah II, Hazor/Tell el-Qedah VII-V, Shechem/Tell Balata VIII-VII, Gezer/Tell Jezer VI, Lachish/Tell ed-Duweir IV, Arad/Tell Arad X-IX, and Beer-sheba/Tell es-Seba' II. In general, the major building structures of the Omride period remained in use, often repaired and occasionally expanded with less careful construction and masonry. There is little evidence of royal or public building programs, certainly nothing to compare with those of the Omride period.

A particularly interesting discovery among the ruins at Samaria are the so-called Samaria Ostraca—approximately sixty inscribed potsherds found in what appears to have been a storehouse and assigned by the excavators to stratum IV (see *ANET* 321). Typical are ostraca numbers 4 and 19 which bear the following inscriptions:

> In the ninth year, from Kozah to Gaddiyau, jar of old wine.
>
> In the tenth year, from Yazith, to Ahinoam, jar of fine oil.

Obviously these were records concerning dispatches of wine and oil; possibly tax records of some sort, or records of wine and oil shipments from royal estates to Samaria.

Mention should be made also of several seals and seal impressions from the period. One discovered at Megiddo, for example, identifies its owner as "Shema the servant of Jeroboam." The fact that he is referred to as a "servant" of Jeroboam would mean that he was a royal official under Jeroboam II.

"Shema the Servant of Jeroboam." Found in the ruins at Megiddo, this seal bears an inscription reading *"lshm' 'bd yrb'm"* ("belonging to Shema, servant of Jeroboam"). *(Israel Department of Antiquities and Museums)*

Chronological Uncertainties

It is established, on grounds indicated above, that Jehu came to the throne during or just before 841 B.C.E. and that Joash, his grandson, was on the throne by 796 B.C.E. The Jehu dynasty had already passed from the scene by 738 B.C.E., on the other hand, when Tiglath-pileser III began his western campaigns (see below). The regnal years recorded in II Kings for the rulers of the Jehu dynasty total 102 years and fit reasonably well into the parameters set by the Assyrian records (see Chart XIII).

The regnal periods assigned to the Judean rulers of this period present a host of difficulties, however. In the first place, the Judean rulers from Athaliah (who seized the throne of Judah at the time of Jehu's coup) to Hezekiah (who, as we shall see below, defended Judah against Sennacherib in 701 B.C.E.) are credited with more years than the time frame allows. The regnal periods ascribed to them are excessive also for the recorded synchronisms between their reigns and those of the kings of Israel. The forty-year reign ascribed to Joash is probably to be read as a symbolic figure, or estimate, in any case (compare the forty-year reigns ascribed to David and to Solomon).

Jotham apparently ruled as coregent with his father Uzziah for some time because of the latter's illness (II Kings 15:5). It is possible, therefore, that the regnal periods credited to Jotham and Uzziah overlapped. However, this does not seem to be the sense of II Kings 15:32–33, which records Jotham's sixteen years. Moreover, the unusually long reign ascribed to Uzziah, fifty-two years, is difficult to accommodate even if one counts the whole sixteen years credited to Jotham as coregency.

CHART XIII. The Century of the Jehu Dynasty

Regnal Periods Recorded for the Kings of Judah

Athaliah	7 years
Joash (Jehoash)	40 years
Amaziah	29 years
Uzziah (Azariah)	52 years
Jotham	16 years

Regnal Periods Recorded for the Jehu Dynasty

Jehu	28 years
Jehoahaz	17 years
Joash	16 years
Jeroboam II	41 years
Zechariah	6 months

Tentative Chronology

Judah	Israel	Damascus	Assyria
			Shalmaneser III
Athaliah	Jehu	Hazael	(858–824)
(843–837)	(843–816)	(ca. 843–?)	
Joash (Jehoash)			
(837–?)	Jehoahaz		Shamshi-Adad V
	(816–800)		(823–811)
		Ben-hadad	Adad-nirari III
Amaziah		(?–?)	(810–783)
(?–?)	Joash		
	(800–785)		Shalmaneser IV
Uzziah (Azariah)			(782–773)
(?–?)	Jeroboam II		
	(785–745)		Ashur-dan
Jotham			(772–756)
(?–742)			Ashur-nirari IV
	Zechariah		(753–745)
	(745)		

In short, the regnal periods provided in II Kings for the Judean kings contemporary with the Jehu dynasty, particularly those recorded for Joash and Uzziah, are, in our opinion, excessive. Thus our chronology for the period, which depends primarily on the figures provided for the Israelite kings, allows them somewhat shorter reigns of unspecified length. Also, we make no attempt to establish separate dates for Uzziah and Jotham. The overall result, in comparison to other chronologies for the period, is that we place Amaziah, Uzziah, and Jotham slightly earlier in relation to the kings of Israel. Specifically, we see Uzziah and Jotham as roughly contemporary with Jeroboam II.

Under Syrian Oppression and Recovery

Jehu, Jehoahaz, and Joash of Israel

Jehu. Israel's fortunes had declined rapidly during the years following the death of Ahab. Thus Jehu seized the throne of a kingdom already in trouble. Hazael was encroaching on Israelite territory in the northern Transjordan when Jehu made his move, and Shalmaneser's army swept through Syria-Palestine soon after (841 B.C.E.), devastating towns and requiring tribute from both Hazael and Jehu. Hosea 10:14 may allude to Shalmaneser's atrocities in the northern Transjordan at that time:

> Therefore the tumult of war shall arise among your people,
>   and all your fortresses shall be destroyed,
> as Shalman destroyed Beth-arbel on the day of battle;
>   mothers were dashed in pieces with their children.

Shalmaneser's 841 campaign and the one that followed in 838 B.C.E. served only to delay Hazael's aggression on Israelite territory. In those days, according to II Kings 10:32–33,

> Yahweh began to cut off parts of Israel. Hazael defeated them throughout the territory of Israel: from the Jordan eastward, all the land of Gilead, the Gadites, and the Reubenites, and the Manassites, from Aroer, which is by the valley of the Arnon, that is, Gilead and Bashan.

Hazael's invasion of the Transjordan was only the beginning. Later, perhaps already in Jehu's reign, Syrian armies would ravage the very heartland of Israelite territory west of the Jordan, conquer Gath, one of the prominent Philistine cities, and extort the Temple treasury from Jerusalem (II Kings 12: 17–18).

Jehu's coup meant an end to Israel's favorable relations with Phoenicia and Judah, which had been a key factor in the economic prosperity of the Omride period. His assassination of Jezebel would have strained relations with Phoenicia, to say the least; and we can hardly expect the Omride queen Athaliah to have had any positive dealings with this man who had massacred her family. Presumably Jehu could count on support for his new regime from conservative Yahwistic elements and others who had been discontented with the Omrides for one reason or another. At the same time, there will have been those in Israel also who had prospered under the Omrides and had little sympathy with the new regime.

The only deed attributed to Jehu in II Kings, aside from the circumstances of his seizure of the government and loss of territory to Hazael, is that he purged Israel of Baalism. Probably even in this regard Jehu is given more credit than he is due. Actually Jehoram had already taken some measures to reduce the prominence of Baalism in Samaria (compare II Kings 3:3 with 10:26), and there is ample evidence that Baalism remained strong in Israel during the remainder of the Jehu era ("Baal"-associated names in the Samaria Ostraca, for example). Nevertheless, it does appear that Jehu took some measures against Baalism, which also would have displeased some elements of the kingdom while ensuring him the support of others.

Jehoahaz. Syrian domination and harassment of Israel reached its extreme during the reign of Jehoahaz. II Kings 13:3 reports that Yahweh gave Israel "continually into the hand of Hazael king of Syria and into the hand of Ben-hadad the son of Hazael." Jehoahaz is described as possessing an army of no more than "fifty horsemen and ten chariots and ten thousand footmen; for the king of Syria had destroyed them and made them like the dust at threshing" (II Kings 13:7).

The Elisha stories (II Kings 2; 4:1–8:15) belong in this context and shed further light on Israel's dismal political situation. It would appear from these stories that Syrian raids into Israel were an ordinary occurrence and often involved the taking of slaves (II Kings 5:2). Israel's military tactic in response to such raids was simply to avoid the Syrians insofar as possible (II Kings 6:8–23). A letter from the Syrian king to the Israelite king requesting the aid of an Israelite prophet so frightened the Israelite king, we are told, that he tore his clothes. We hear of Samaria itself under siege on one occasion, and saved only by a miracle (II Kings 6:24–7:20). Elisha is depicted in these stories as a trusted adviser of the Israelite king and Israel's real champion in the struggle for survival under Syrian oppression. He used his miraculous powers as a man of God to thwart Syrian actions against Israel (II Kings 6:8–23), advised the king of Israel on matters of state, and could speak a word on others' behalf to the king or royal officials (II Kings 4:13).

Eventually the situation began to change, probably near the end of Jehoahaz' reign. Indeed, the "savior" mentioned in II Kings 13:4–5 may have been none other than Adad-nirari III, who was beginning his western campaigns about that time.

> Then Jehoahaz besought Yahweh, and Yahweh hearkened to him; for he saw the oppression of Israel, how the king of Syria oppressed them. (Therefore Yahweh gave Israel a savior, so that they escaped from the hand of the Syrians; and the people of Israel dwelt in their homes as formerly.)

Joash. As indicated above, the Rimah Stela identifies Joash among those who paid tribute to Adad-nirari III, probably in connection with the latter's last western campaign in 796 B.C.E. Two other items are reported for Joash in II Kings 13:14–14:14. He defeated Ben-hadad three times in battle and regained possession of Israelite cities that Hazael had seized. Also he defeated Amaziah of Judah near Beth-shemesh in a battle instigated by the Judean king, after which he proceeded to capture Jerusalem, tear down a large section of the city wall, take hostages, and loot the Temple and royal treasuries. We will return to this latter episode below in connection with Amaziah's reign. For the moment let

---

TEXT VI. The Rimah Stela of Adad-nirari III

(I, Adad-nirari) mobilized chariots, troops and camps, and ordered a campaign to the Hatti land. In a single year I made the land of Amurru and the Hatti land in its entirety kneel at my feet; I imposed tribute (and) regular tax for future days upon them.

I marched to the great sea where the sun sets, and erected a stele ("image") of my royal self in the city of Arvad which is in the middle of the sea. I went up the Lebanon mountains and cut down timbers: one hundred mature cedars, material needed for my palace (and) temples.

He received two thousand talents of silver, one thousand talents of copper, two thousand talents of iron, three thousand multi-coloured garments and (plain) linen garments as tribute from Mari' of the land of Damascus. He received the tribute of Joash of Samaria, of the Tyrians and of the Sidonians.

He received tribute from all the kings of the Na'iri land. (*Iraq* 35 [1973], 143) (See photograph on p. 288.)

---

us examine more closely the respective roles of Jehoahaz and Joash in Israel's recovery from Syrian oppression.

II Kings 13 consists of the summations of the reigns of Jehoahaz and Joash (13:1–9 and 13:10–13 respectively), followed by what amounts to an appendix to Joash's reign (13:14–25). This appendix consists, in turn, of the last of the Elisha stories (actually two episodes; 13:14–19 and 20–21) and some concluding summary notes about Syria's oppression of Israel and Joash's victories over Ben-hadad (13:22–25). A straightforward reading of the chapter invites the interpretation presented above—namely, that Israel received some relief from Syrian oppression before the end of Jehoahaz' reign but that it was Joash who actually defeated Ben-hadad in battle and recovered Israelite cities that had fallen into Syrian hands. At least three factors, however, suggest that this interpretation may be an oversimplification.

1. Actually the initial summations of the reigns of Jehoahaz and Joash (II Kings 13:1–9 and 10–13 respectively), read without reference to the appendix materials that follow, would seem to indicate that Ben-hadad had succeeded Hazael to the throne and that Israel had recovered its independence already before Jehoahaz' death. See especially 13:3–7 in the summation of Jehoahaz' reign and note that the summation of Joash's reign makes no reference to battles with Syria. It is specifically the appendix, in other words, which associates Israel's recovery from Syria (and also Ben-hadad's accession to the throne?; see especially vs. 24–25) with Joash's reign.

2. The theme of three battles, three Israelite victories over Syria, surfaces twice in the appendix. The Elisha story anticipates three battles in which the king of Israel will defeat the king of Syria (II Kings 13:17–19). Then it is explained in the concluding notes at the end of the appendix that "three times

Joash defeated him [Ben-hadad] and recovered the cities of Israel" (13:25). One is reminded of the stories of the three battles with Ben-hadad that appear in the context of Ahab's reign (I Kings 20; 22:1–38) but clearly do not belong there (see the discussion of these stories in Chapter 8). Several factors suggest, in fact, that these stories and the appendix to Joash's reign pertain to the same three battles. *(a)* The stories of the three battles assume a period in which Syria dominated Israel. The first of these stories begins, for example, with the Syrian king making exorbitant demands on Samaria which the king of Israel is reluctant to refuse. While it is difficult to imagine a Syrian king making such demands on Ahab, this squares very well with the situation of the early years of the Jehu dynasty. *(b)* Ben-hadad is the Syrian king defeated three times in the battle stories as well as in the appendix. *(c)* The battle stories locate Israel's main victory over Ben-hadad at Aphek, as does the Elisha story in the appendix. *(d)* Joash is said in the appendix to have recovered cities from Ben-hadad that Hazael had taken from Israel earlier. The same claim is made in the battle stories for the king of Israel after the victory at Aphek, and with surprisingly similar wording: "And Ben-hadad said to him, 'The cities which my father took from your father I will restore; and you may establish bazaars for yourself in Damascus, as my father did in Samaria' " (I Kings 20:34). *(e)* The king of Israel is killed in the third of the three battles, which would explain why the Elisha story anticipates only three victories and no more.

3. If the three battles mentioned in the appendix are the same three featured in the stories of the three battles with Ben-hadad, and if these stories preserve any accurate historical memory, then we must take into account certain factors that seem to point to Jehoahaz rather than to Joash as the king of Israel involved. *(a)* It was especially during Jehoahaz' reign, when Syrian oppression had reached its worst, that the conditions presupposed at the beginning of the three battle stories would have existed. Note in this regard the similarity between Israel's pitiful little army as described in the summation of Jehoahaz' reign and as described in the second of the battle stories (compare I Kings 20:27 with II Kings 13:7). *(b)* The king of Israel is killed in the third of the three battle stories, which means that the battles should be placed at the end of a king's reign. The end of Jehoahaz' reign, with Adad-nirari beginning his western campaigns, would have been a propitious time for Israel to challenge Syrian authority. By the end of Joash's reign, on the other hand, Israel apparently had already long since regained both independence from Damascus and domination over Jerusalem. *(c)* In the third of the three battle stories, the king of Israel leaves his son, the crown prince, in charge of Samaria while the king himself leads Israel's army against Ben-hadad at Ramoth-gilead. The son is identified by name—Joash. This would fit Jehoahaz, who was followed on the throne by Joash, but not Joash who was followed by Jeroboam.

Admittedly all of this is highly speculative, and there are counterarguments that cannot be ignored. The stories of the three battles show evidence of having undergone significant modifications during the process of transmission, for example, which serves as a warning in turn that they do not necessarily preserve accurate historical memory, certainly not in the details. This is especially true, as we have seen, of the third story which recounts the Ramoth-gilead campaign and concludes with the king of Israel's death (I Kings 22:29–38; see above, p. 253). It is possible that the ancient storytellers confused the circumstances of this third battle with those of an earlier conflict at Ramoth-gilead, the one in connection with which Jehoram was wounded and then assassinated (II Kings 8:28–29). Neither can it be ignored that the compilers of Genesis-II Kings (or whoever was responsible for the appendix to Joash's reign) clearly associated Elisha's death and the three victories over Ben-hadad with Joash rather than his father. Note also that it is recorded for both Jehoahaz and Joash that they "slept with the fathers," a phrase normally reserved for kings who died a natural death.

To summarize, it seems safe to conclude, at the very least, that circumstances occurring near the end of Jehoahaz' reign and the beginning of Joash's reign resulted in the recovery of Israelite independence from Damascus. If we dare to speculate further along the lines indicated above, the following scenario emerges.

1. Hazael established what amounted to a small empire in Syria-Palestine during the nearly four decades separating Shalmaneser's and Adad-nirari's western campaigns—that is, approximately the last four decades of the ninth century B.C.E.

2. Near the end of the century, by which time Ben-hadad had succeeded Hazael on the throne, Damascus began to lose its grip on the surrounding kingdoms. Adad-nirari's western campaign no doubt was a factor involved. Local rulers such as Zakir of Hamath and Jehoahaz of Samaria challenged Ben-hadad's authority and successfully defended against his attempts at reprisal. The three battle stories in I Kings 20 and 22:1–38 represent three stages in Jehoahaz' struggle to throw off the Syrian yoke.

3. The struggle began when Ben-hadad, perhaps in order to reaffirm his hegemony over Palestine, marched south with an army, established camp at Succoth in the Jordan Valley (read a proper name in I Kings 20:12 instead of "booths"), and sent demands to Samaria for tribute and hostages. The position of Ben-hadad's camp suggests that his action was directed against the various local kingdoms of Palestine, not just against Samaria. In other words, he may have sent similar demands to the Ammonites, the Moabites, and others.

4. Jehoahaz agreed to make the payment and send hostages, to which Ben-hadad responded with a new, even more exorbitant demand—he proposed to send Syrian officials into Samaria to confiscate what they chose and to make their own selections of hostages. Jehoahaz and the elders of Samaria decided to reject this new demand and attempt to defend their city. This they did and were successful.

5. The following spring Ben-hadad marched south again, this time against Israel in particular. Jehoahaz and the Israelite army met the Syrians at Aphek. The exact location of Aphek is unknown, but presumably this is the same Aphek that witnessed Saul's last battle with the Philistines—that is, situated at the northern end of the central hill country where its slopes give way to the Jezreel

Valley. Again Israel's army was victorious, in spite of overwhelming odds, and captured Ben-hadad himself. Jehoahaz allowed Ben-hadad to go free, but only after the latter agreed to relinquish all claims on Israel, return certain cities that Hazael had taken from Jehu, and allow Israelite merchants trading rights in Damascus.

6. The cities that Hazael had taken from Jehu were those located in the northern Transjordan (II Kings 10:32–33), and three years later Jehoahaz is heard complaining that one of these cities, Ramoth-gilead, was still in Syrian hands. This occasioned the Ramoth-gilead campaign in which, as the story stands now, Jehoahaz was killed.

7. Joash, the crown prince who had remained in Samaria while Jehoahaz conducted the Ramoth-gilead campaign, now ascended the throne. Joash may have continued hostilities with Ben-hadad, which would help explain why the compilers of Genesis-II Kings credited him with the victories. However, it is his father, Jehoahaz, who deserves the primary credit for successfully challenging Syrian authority.

Athaliah, Joash, and Amaziah of Judah

Athaliah. Athaliah came to Judah as the bride of Jehoram son of Jehoshaphat. When Jehoram ascended the throne, he took the precaution, according to II Chron. 21:4, of removing other possible claimants. Then when Jehoram himself died (or was assassinated, if he and Jehoram of Israel were the same person), and Ahaziah was assassinated, Athaliah herself seized the throne in Jerusalem. Again there was a purge of all others who might have some claim to the crown.

Nothing is recorded about Athaliah's reign except how she gained the throne and how she lost it. Supposedly Jehosheba, a daughter of Jehoram and sister of King Ahaziah, succeeded in hiding one of Ahaziah's sons, the remainder of whom were slain during Athaliah's purge. Jehosheba then cared for the child, Joash by name, until he was seven years old. At that point Jehoiada, a priest who was in on the secret, orchestrated a palace coup which resulted in the enthronement of Joash and the assassination of Athaliah.

The account of this episode in II Kings 11:4–20 provides a vivid glimpse of the personnel and ritual associated with the royal Judean palace and Temple, even if all the details are not entirely clear. The ritual of the young king's coronation and investiture included the crowning, the presentation of the testimony (Yahweh's promises to the Davidic line?), the proclamation, the anointment, the acclamation, and the enthronement (II Kings 11:12, 19). Along with the Temple officials and palace guard who participated in the coronation were others referred to collectively as "the people of the land." Encountered here for the first time in the Genesis-II Kings account, these would have been adult, landowning males, possibly but not necessarily representing a particular faction in the government. They would come to play an important role in southern politics.

The Chronicler's version of the episode follows the II Kings account with

TEXT VII. The Zakir Inscription

A stela set up by Zakir, king of Hamat and Lu'ath, for Ilu-Wer, [*his god*].

I am Zakir, king of Hamat and Lu'ath. A humble man I am. Be'elshamayn [*helped me*] and stood by me. Be'elshamayn made me king over Hatarikka (Hadrach).

Barhadad, the son of Hazael, king of Aram, united [seven of] a group of ten kings against me: Barhadad and his army; Bargush and his army; the king of Cilicia and his army; the king of 'Umq and his army; the king of Gurgum and his army; the king of Sam'al and his army; the king of Milidh and his army. [All these kings whom Barhadad united against me] were seven kings and their armies. All these kings laid siege to Hatarikka. They made a wall higher than the wall of Hatarikka. They made a moat deeper than its moat. But I lifted up my hand to Be'elshamayn, and Be'elshamayn heard me. Be'elshamayn [spoke] to me through seers and through *diviners*. Be'elshamayn [said to me]: Do not fear, for I made you king, and I shall stand by you and deliver you from all [these kings who] set up a siege against you. [*Be'elshamayn*] said to me: [*I shall destroy*] all these kings who set up [a siege against you and *made this moat*] and this *wall* which . . . .

I set up this stela before Ilu-Wer, and I wrote upon it my achievements [. . .]. Whoever shall remove (this record of) the achievements of Zakir, king of Hamat and Lu'ath, from this stela and whoever shall remove this stela from before Ilu-Wer and banish it from its [place] or whoever shall stretch forth his hand [to . . .], [may] Be'elshamayn and I [lu-Wer and . . .] and Shamash and Sahr [and . . .] and the Gods of Heaven [and the Gods] of Earth and Be'el- [. . . deprive him of h]ead and [. . . and] his root and [. . . , *and may*] the name of Zakir and the name of [*his house endure forever*]! (*ANET* 655–56)

only a few notable differences. For example, the Chronicler identifies Jehosheba as the wife of Jehoiada as well as the daughter of Jehoram. And it was the priests and the Levites who conducted the affair, according to the Chronicler, rather than the palace guard. Certain soldiers were involved, but their responsibility was to circulate through Judah and assemble the Levites and heads of families from all the cities. In the Chronicler's version, therefore, the displacement of Athaliah with Joash was a nationwide movement rather than an internal palace coup. Both II Kings and the Chronicler's version report that the crowd, after taking Athaliah out of the Yahweh Temple for execution, proceeded to the Baal temple, looted it, and killed the Baal priest.

Joash. Athaliah was executed in her seventh year of rule, according to the chronological data provided, and Joash was seven years old at the time. Who was this child whom Jehoiada presented as a royal heir and succeeded in placing

on the throne? Clearly the compilers of Genesis-II Kings were satisfied that
Joash was an authentic son of Ahaziah, presumably born the year of Ahaziah's
death. In view of the circumstances as described, however, one can hardly avoid
wondering whether Joash might have been an impostor whom Jehoiada used
to get rid of Athaliah and bring his own influence to bear on the nation.

On the one hand, there are the strange circumstances of the affair. Why
would it have been in the interest of Athaliah to kill her own grandchildren in
the first place? It seems they would have been her best justification for seizing
the throne and best insurance for holding it—that is, she would have posed as
regent in their behalf. And is it really likely, after the double purges of Jehoram
and Athaliah, not to mention the episode described in II Chron. 21:16–17
where it is said that Arabs and Philistines wiped out all of Jehoram's family
"except Jehoahaz [?], his youngest son," that anyone with a remote claim to the
crown had survived?

On the other hand, the priests and soldiers who participated in the coup, the
compilers of Genesis-II Kings, the Chronicler, and even we today ultimately are
dependent upon the word of Jehosheba and Jehoiada that Joash was in fact
Ahaziah's son. And both of these witnesses, of course, would have had good
reason to seek Athaliah's downfall. Jehosheba, a sister of Ahaziah, had lost
members of her family in Athaliah's purge. Jehoiada would have wanted a ruler
more favorably disposed toward Yahwism, and perhaps more susceptible to his
own influence. No doubt many other Temple and palace officials and much of
the population of Judah in general preferred to believe that Joash was an
authentic heir, or were prepared to accept him as such. Athaliah certainly had
no legitimate claim to the Judean throne; and as a foreigner with Baalistic
inclinations, she would hardly have been popular among her subjects.

Jehoiada in any case does seem to have exercised significant influence over
Joash. According to II Kings 12:2, Joash "did what was right in the eyes of
Yahweh all his days, because Jehoiada the priest instructed him." The Chroni-
cler expands on this, indicating that Jehoiada selected wives for the young king
and that Jehoiada's death brought to an end Joash's years of righteous rule.
Thereafter, according to the Chronicler, Joash fell under the influence of the
princes of Judah, rejected the words of Zechariah Jehoiada's son, and even had
Zechariah stoned (II Chron. 24:17–22).

A program of Temple repair is the main item reported for Joash's reign in
both Kings and Chronicles. Joash commanded that certain categories of funds
brought into the Temple be applied to repairs of the Yahweh Temple and left
the matter in the hands of the priests. By the twenty-third year of his reign,
however, no repairs had been made. Apparently the matter was handled haphaz-
ardly and, without any accountability, the collected funds had been misused or
embezzled. Thus Joash summoned Jehoiada and inaugurated new procedures
intended to reduce the graft and get the repairs under way. (1) All collected
funds were deposited in a secured box set beside the altar. (2) When the box
began to fill, the king's secretary and the high priest would open the box, count
the money, and place it in tied bags. (3) The bags were delivered then to the

workmen in charge of the repairs: "And they did not ask an accounting from the men into whose hand they delivered the money to pay out to the workmen, for they dealt honestly" (II Kings 12:15). The implication of the text seems to be that the contractors and overseers could be trusted better than the priests.

The other item reported for Joash's reign is Hazael's conquest of Gath and threat to sack Jerusalem. Joash chose to ransom the city with the Temple treasury rather than attempt to defend it.

> At that time Hazael king of Syria went up and fought against Gath, and took it. But when Hazael set his face to go up against Jerusalem, Jehoash king of Judah took all the votive gifts that Jehoshaphat and Jehoram and Ahaziah, his fathers, the kings of Judah, had dedicated, and his own votive gifts, and all the gold that was found in the treasuries of the house of Yahweh and of the king's house, and sent these to Hazael king of Syria. Then Hazael went away from Jerusalem. (II Kings 12: 17–18)

The Chronicler places the Syrian campaign immediately following the stoning of Jehoiada's son, reports that there was an actual battle in which Judah was defeated and Joash wounded, and explains that "his servants conspired against him because of the blood of the son(s) of Jehoiada the priest, and slew him on his bed" (II Chron. 24:25). II Kings also reports that he was assassinated by his servants (or "officials") but does not connect this with the Syrian conflict or with any action toward Jehoiada's son (II Kings 12:20–21).

Amaziah. Joash was succeeded on the throne by his son, Amaziah, who executed the assassins as soon as the royal power was "firmly in his hand" (II Kings 12:21; 14:5). It is tempting to speculate on the fuller circumstances of Joash's assassination and the nature of the challenge or challenges that Amaziah had to overcome before power was "firmly in his hand." Joash, as we have just observed, had been placed on the throne, strongly influenced (possibly dominated) throughout most of his reign, and finally killed by the inner circle of priests and officials in Jerusalem. Was Joash assassinated because he began to exert more independence and/or hold the priests and officials to closer accountability, as in the case of the funds collected for the Temple repair? Did Amaziah have to establish his authority over against powerful figures in the court, or come to terms with them? Were there other claimants to the throne—perhaps candidates who raised questions about Joash's legitimacy? Possibly the inner circle of leadership in Jerusalem knew all along that Joash was an impostor and allowed him to rule as a figurehead until he began asserting too much independence. Whatever the circumstances, it is obvious that palace intrigue was involved. Neither would Amaziah's position on the throne remain firm. After a reign presumably of reasonable length (he is credited with twenty-nine years), Amaziah too was assassinated.

Amaziah's reign overlapped the reigns of Jehoahaz and Joash of Israel, which means that he witnessed the decline of the power of Damascus under Benhadad. The local kingdoms of Syria-Palestine which had been dominated by

Damascus for several decades began to test their strength on each other. Joash
of Israel and Amaziah of Judah were no different. Amaziah defeated the Edomites in the Valley of Salt (possibly Wady el-Milh east of Beer-sheba) and chased
the fugitives to Sela, a huge rocky crag on the rugged slopes east of the Arabah
(probably as-Sil' south of Tafileh). Apparently the fugitives climbed to the top
of Sela and attempted to defend it. Somehow Amaziah's men were able to take
the position and, according to the Chronicler, threw ten thousand Edomites
from the summit to their deaths below (II Kings 14:7; II Chron. 25:11–12).
Defeating the Edomites meant renewed access to the Gulf of Aqabah. Thus we
are informed that "he [Amaziah? or Uzziah?] built Elath and restored it to
Judah, after the king [?] slept with his fathers" (II Kings 14:22).

Next Amaziah challenged Israel, which turned out to be a very unfortunate
move. II Kings states simply that he challenged Joash to battle, to which Joash
responded as follows:

> A thistle on Lebanon sent to a cedar on Lebanon, saying, "Give your daughter to
> my son for a wife"; and a wild beast of Lebanon passed by and trampled down the
> thistle. You have indeed smitten Edom, and your heart has lifted you up. Be content
> with your glory, and stay at home; for why should you provoke trouble so that you
> fall, you and Judah with you?" (II Kings 14:9–10)

Amaziah pressed the challenge, however, and a battle occurred which resulted
in overwhelming victory for Israel. Having routed the Judean army and captured Amaziah, Joash marched on Jerusalem, where he dismantled a large
section of the city wall, emptied the Temple treasury (which had already been
drained by Hazael not many years earlier), and took hostages back to Samaria.
The hostages would have included members of the royal family, certainly the
crown prince and any adult sons.

It is interesting to note that, although Amaziah was the one who supposedly
insisted on war, the battle actually occurred in traditionally Judean territory. We
are told, namely, that the two armies met near Beth-shemesh, which is in the
Shephelah, almost directly west of Jerusalem. The fact that the battle occurred
near Judah's western frontier is also problematic for the Chronicler's explanation that Amaziah was seeking redress of an incident that occurred in connection
with his Edomite campaign. Amaziah had hired one hundred thousand Israelite
soldiers for this campaign, according to the Chronicler, but then discharged
them before departure, presumably without pay. While Amaziah was fighting
the Edomites, therefore, the discharged Israelite soldiers looted some Judean
villages on their return home.

Whatever the specifics, the battle between Joash and Amaziah at Beth-
shemesh is to be understood in the context of the power vacuum that occurred
when Damascus lost its grip on the area. Joash had hopes, no doubt, of restoring
the situation that had obtained during the days of Omri and Ahab—that is, when
Israel was the major power in Palestine and overshadowed (possibly dominated) Judah. Amaziah had his own ambitions, however, which did not involve
any kind of secondary status or subjection to Israel. The location of the battle

may suggest that Joash had already moved to annex traditionally Judean territory west of Jerusalem. Thus Amaziah's call for war would have involved more than adventurism on his part and/or determination to hold Israel accountable for the actions of some renegade soldiers. It was his signal to Samaria that he intended to resist Israelite encroachment on Judean territory and to defend Judean independence.

Unfortunately for Judah, Amaziah had underestimated Israel's strength. Joash ridiculed his challenge, crushed the Judean army, and captured Jerusalem. In short, Joash reduced Judah to vassal status. This situation, a strong Israel dominating Judah, reminiscent of the early Omride period, probably continued through the reigns of Jeroboam II and Uzziah, the successors of Joash and Amaziah respectively.

One suspects that Amaziah's humiliation at the hands of Joash and subsequent submission to Samaria were primary factors leading to his assassination. In any case, the assassination had a broad base of support among the people of Judah.

> And they made a conspiracy against him in Jerusalem, and he fled to Lachish. But they sent after him to Lachish, and slew him there. And they brought him upon horses; and he was buried in Jerusalem with his fathers in the city of David. And all the people of Judah took Azariah [Uzziah], who was sixteen years old, and made him king instead of his father Amaziah. (II Kings 14:19–21)

This was no surprise murder while the king was sleeping, as had occurred with his predecessor. Amaziah knew that the conspiracy was developing and, probably recognizing that the plot had many supporters, sought to escape rather than attempt to crush it. Even in Lachish, where Amaziah must have hoped to find safety, he was powerless. Apparently the city officials turned him over to the conspirators with little or no hesitation.

National Restoration Under Jeroboam II and Uzziah

During the second half of the century of the Jehu dynasty, beginning with the reign of Joash of Israel (800–785 B.C.E.) but especially during that of Jeroboam II (785–745 B.C.E.), Israel enjoyed a period of national restoration and expansion. Judah, under Uzziah and Jotham, who were roughly contemporary with Jeroboam II, enjoyed a period of recovery as well, although overshadowed by, and possibly largely dependent upon, Israel. This time of national restoration for the two Hebrew kingdoms came to an end soon after the accession of Tiglath-pileser III to the throne over Assyria in 745 B.C.E. Tiglath-pileser soon conquered Syria-Palestine, as we shall see, and Assyria maintained a firm grip on the region for more than a century.

Israel Under Jeroboam

Jeroboam II "restored the border of Israel from the entrance of Hamath as far as the Sea of the Arabah" (II Kings 14:25). The "entrance of Hamath" refers generally to the Bekaa Valley, the corridor between the Lebanon and Anti-Lebanon mountains. The southern entrance to the corridor, to which this passage probably refers, would be approximately at the city of Dan. The Sea of the Arabah, on the other hand, is the Dead Sea. Jeroboam also restored Israelite control over much of the Transjordan, as presupposed by Amos 6: 13–14 and I Chron. 5:17.

Naturally Jeroboam and his administration took pride in having restored Israel's boundaries to what they had been in earlier times. And in fact this accomplishment is said in the II Kings summation of Jeroboam's reign (II Kings 14:23–29) to have been predicted by Jonah the son of Amittai—a prophet from Gath-hepher later to become the chief character of the fictitious book of Jonah. Amos obviously was less impressed, however, and made a wordplay on the name of two Transjordanian towns, Lo-debar (somewhere in Gilead near Maha-naim; see also II Sam. 9:4–5; 17:27) and Karnaim (Ashteroth-karnaim, some-where farther north in the Transjordan; see Gen. 14:5; I Macc. 5:26).

> You who rejoice in Lo-debar,
>   who say, "Have we not by our own strength
>   taken Karnaim for ourselves?"
> "For behold, I will raise up against you a nation,
>   O house of Israel," says Yahweh, the God of hosts;
> "and they shall oppress you from the entrance of Hamath
>   to the Brook of the Arabah."
>   (Amos 6:13–14)

I Chronicles 5:17 alludes to a census conducted in the Transjordan during Jeroboam's reign. Following genealogical material pertaining to Reubenite and Gadite clans settled in Gilead and Bashan, it is stated that "all of these were enrolled by genealogies in the days of Jotham king of Judah, and the days of Jeroboam king of Israel."

These passages which indicate that Jeroboam restored Israel's former fron-tiers do not prepare one, however, for the sweeping claim at the end of the II Kings summation of his reign:

> Now the rest of the acts of Jeroboam, and all that he did, and his might, how he fought, and how he recovered for Israel Damascus and Hamath, which had be-longed to Judah, are they not written in the Book of the Chronicles of the Kings of Israel? (II Kings 14:28)

Even if we interpret the references to "the entrance of Hamath" in II Kings 14:25 and Amos 6:14 as meaning the northern end of the corridor between the Lebanon and the Anti-Lebanon mountains, the boundaries implied still would not include Hamath. And Amos 1:3–5 obviously does not presuppose a Damas-cus subservient to Israel. In short, we must regard the claim that Jeroboam "recovered Damascus and Hamath" with the same reservations that we re-garded the sweeping editorial claims about Solomon's wealth and the extent of his realm. At the very most, one might suppose that the rulers of Hamath and

Damascus were willing to pay Jeroboam some nominal tribute and/or allow the Israelites commercial concessions in their cities rather that risk facing him in battle.

With Israel fully reestablished now, an autonomous kingdom with its former boundaries, the old conflict between prophet and king reemerged. Amos' oracles uttered at Bethel pronounce disaster ahead for the kingdom, and for the royal family in particular.

> Behold I am setting a plumb line
>   in the midst of my people Israel;
>   I will never again pass by them;
> the high places of Isaac shall be made desolate,
>   and the sanctuaries of Israel shall be laid waste,
>   and I will rise against the house of Jeroboam with the sword.
> (Amos 7:8–9)

The words of Amos relayed to Jeroboam by Amaziah the priest were more specific: "Jeroboam shall die by the sword, and Israel must go into exile away from his land" (Amos 7:11). Hosea recalls the "blood of Jezreel" and predicts that the Jehu dynasty will be punished for it:

> And Yahweh said to him, "Call his name Jezreel; for yet a little while, and I will punish the house of Jehu for the blood of Jezreel, and I will put an end to the kingdom of the house of Israel. And on that day, I will break the bow of Israel in the valley of Jezreel." (Hos. 1:4–5)

Given the complexities of the books of Amos and Hosea, one cannot necessarily assume that these are direct quotes from the two prophets. Also it would be misleading to suggest that Amos and/or Hosea was simply calling for a dynastic change. Other materials in both books point to a wide range of social and cultic ills attributed to the leadership of the day—for example, wealthy people who took advantage of the poor and priests who led their followers astray (see below). Also the pronouncements of forthcoming doom generally have to do with Israel in general rather than just the ruling dynasty.

Nevertheless it is noteworthy, especially in view of the role that previous prophets had played as initiators of dynastic change, that among the mix of oracles in Amos and Hosea are pronouncements that (1) remember Jehu's massacre of the Omrides at Jezreel as an affair deserving of divine punishment, (2) charge that the Jehu dynasty does not represent Yahweh (see especially Hos. 8:4), and (3) predict a terrible end for the dynasty. The account of Jehu's coup (II Kings 9:1–10:27), on the other hand, as suggested above, may have originated as a response from the royal family to counter such charges. Namely, it seeks to depict Jehu as a true champion of Yahwism and the Jezreel massacre as a prophetically inspired action.

The events following Jeroboam's death speak for themselves. Zechariah, Jeroboam's son, took the throne but was assassinated within six months. Never again in the northern kingdom was dynastic succession successfully accomplished. The northern kingdom would last only two chaotic decades more anyway.

Judah Under Uzziah and Jotham

Uzziah, who came to the throne as a teenager after the assassination of Amaziah his father, is also called Azariah. Possibly "Uzziah" was a throne name and Azariah his personal name, although the difference between the two forms is not so great in Hebrew as in English. Uzziah and his son Jotham were roughly contemporary with Jeroboam II, with Jotham probably outliving Jeroboam by a few years. One would assume from the presentation of their reigns in the Genesis-II Kings corpus that Uzziah and Jotham were very ordinary rulers overshadowed by, if not dominated by, Jeroboam. Jotham is credited with adding a new gate to the Temple compound in Jerusalem (II Kings 15:35). Otherwise, aside from the usual formulaic evaluations of their cultic fidelity, we learn only that Uzziah contracted leprosy and had to turn over the affairs of government to Jotham (II Kings 15:5).

Epitaph of Uzziah. The marble plaque bears the inscription *"lkh hyty tmy 'wzyh mlk yhwdh wl' lmpth"* ("here were brought the bones of Uzziah, King of Judah, and not to be moved"). Because he was a leper (see II Chron. 23:26), Uzziah may not have been buried in the royal necropolis. At some point, in any case, his remains were reburied, and this inscription marked the new burial spot. *(Israel Museum)*

Uzziah and Jotham are somewhat similar to Jehoshaphat, therefore, in that they ruled under the shadow of a powerful Israelite king, are passed over rather quickly by the compilers of Genesis-II Kings, but depicted by the Chronicler as majestic and powerful rulers in their own right (II Chron. 26–27). The Chronicler's effort to improve Uzziah's image is especially transparent. Moreover, as one could predict, the Chronicler emphasizes that Uzziah's accomplishments all occurred during the first part of his reign when he was on good terms with the Temple priests: "He set himself to seek God in the days of Zechariah, who instructed him in the fear of God; and as long as he sought Yahweh, God made him prosper" (II Chron. 26:5). The turning point occurred, according to the Chronicler, when Uzziah presumed to enter the Temple to burn incense on the altar. Challenged by the priests, who claimed this as a priestly prerogative, Uzziah became angry and broke out with leprosy (II Chron. 26:16–21).

The Chronicler's enumeration of the great deeds of Uzziah and Jotham probably represents a kernel of truth that is much exaggerated. Specifically, Uzziah is credited with building up Judah's army to 307,500 men; with victories over the Philistines, the Arabs, and the Meunites; with much building, including towers at key points on the walls of Jerusalem; and with extensive farms, vineyards, and herds throughout the land (II Chron. 26:6–15). Jotham is said to have done more building on the Jerusalem (Ophel) wall and at other places in Judah, and to have defeated the Meunites (II Chron. 27:3–6). The references to Ammonites in II Chron. 26:8 and 27:5 should be corrected to read "Meunites," which in Hebrew involves only reversing the first two consonants. One might expect Israel, which is known to have been expanding its territories in the Transjordan at that time, to come into conflict with the Ammonites; but not Judah. The Meunites, known also from Tiglath-pileser's inscriptions, apparently were a nomadic people who ranged to the southwest of Judah, from the vicinity of Wady esh-Shari'ah toward Sinai.

With the above correction, and allowing for exaggeration, the only item reported by the Chronicler for Uzziah and Jotham that raises serious doubts is the claim that Uzziah captured Philistine Gath, Jabneh, and Ashdod (II Chron. 26:6). The last activity reported in that general vicinity was Joash's defeat of Amaziah at Beth-shemesh. Possibly it was Joash and/or Jeroboam who went on to conquer the Philistine cities; and the Chronicler, who essentially ignores the existence of Israel during this period, has attributed the action to Uzziah.

Social and Religious Conditions

The prophetical literature and unimpressive archaeological remains provide some insight into the general economic, social, and religious conditions of the period of the Jehu dynasty. The Elisha stories, as we have seen, pertain to the early years of the dynasty—that is, to the latter part of the ninth century B.C.E. when Damascus dominated Syria-Palestine. While these stories have to do specifically with Israel, which was nearer to Damascus and thus more vulnerable to Syrian harassment, the situation in Judah would not have been much better.

This was a difficult time even for the royal family in Samaria, much less for villagers scattered throughout the land. Constant Syrian raids devastated the countryside, depleting the land of its agricultural produce and removing all accumulated wealth of any sort. There was famine, so severe that people searched desperately for wild herbs, vines, and gourds for food (II Kings 4:38–41). When a city dared to resist the Syrians and fell under siege, inflation and exorbitant prices prevailed (II Kings 6:24–25). One story tells of a widow about to lose her children to slavery because of debts (II Kings 4:1–7). We read of cannibalism even in Samaria, parents eating their children (II Kings 6:24–31).

With the Book of Amos, the scene shifts to the latter part of the period of the Jehu dynasty—that is, the mid-eighth century B.C.E. when Israel and Judah were enjoying better times. Here again, while Amos speaks primarily to conditions in Israel, similar conditions must have prevailed in Judah. In fact, as indicated above, Judah may not have been entirely independent from Israel—which would help explain why Amos, from the Judean town of Tekoa, directed so much of his message to Israelite affairs.

Still there were natural calamities, such as earthquake and famine, which Amos interprets as divine punishment and warnings of worse disasters to come (Amos 4:6–10; 7:1–9). Israel had recovered from the Syrians, however, refortified, and had expanded its territories (Amos 6:1–3, 8, 12–14). While most of the population consisted of poor peasant farmers who had barely survived the long years of Syrian oppression, a wealthy and privileged upper class had emerged in the process of national restoration which lived in stark contrast to the ordinary citizens. Amos uttered stern maledictions against this wealthy upper class which enjoyed its luxury while ignoring the dismal conditions of those around them.

> Woe to those who lie upon beds of ivory,
>   and stretch themselves upon their couches,
> and eat lambs from the flock,
>   and calves from the midst of the stall;
> who sing idle songs to the sound of the harp,
>   and like David invent for themselves instruments of music;
> who drink wine in bowls,
>   and anoint themselves with the finest oils,
> but are not grieved over the ruin of Joseph!
>
> (Amos 6:4–5)

Not only did this upper class enjoy great advantage over the poor, Amos accuses them of increasing this advantage by unjust means. He speaks of their "selling" the poor and placing exactions upon them—presumably references to debt slavery and excessive taxation (Amos 2:6b–7a; 5:11). Amos also condemns the abuse of the judicial process and those who profited thereby (Amos 5:10–12), especially the inhabitants of Samaria (Amos 3:9–11). In short, Amos' oracles presuppose a social and legal situation in which even the governmental and judicial officials, those allegedly committed to preserving justice, were the very ones contributing to what the prophet considered an ungodly social imbalance.

Yet Amos addressed a people—or at least a military and administrative officialdom—possessed of pride in its achievements (Amos 6:1–3, 12–14). Also he addressed a very religious people. Apparently expressions of piety were widespread and the main cultic centers, such as Bethel, Dan, Gilgal, and Beer-sheba, were visited regularly (Amos 3:14; 4:4–5; 5:4–7; 5:22–24). Israel's religious practices and cultic centers fell under Amos' stern condemnation, nevertheless. Amos proclaimed that Yahweh demanded justice and righteousness, not just feasts and sacrifices.

The superscription to the Book of Hosea indicates a rather long time span for this prophet's career—from as early as the reigns of Jeroboam and Uzziah to as late as that of Hezekiah. This long time span is suggested also by the contents of the book, where there is an allusion to the "sin of Jezreel" yet to be punished, along with references to Israel's political entanglements with Egypt and Assyria (Hos. 1:4–5; 5:13–14; 7:11–13; 8:8–10; 9:5–6; 11:10–11; 14:3). The former presupposes that the Jehu dynasty is still in power, while the latter suggests circumstances in foreign affairs after the end of the dynasty. On the whole, however, the Book of Hosea seems to reflect conditions of the third quarter of the eighth century, after the end of the Jehu dynasty when Israel was again in rapid decline.

CHAPTER 10

The Era of Assyrian Domination:
The End of the Kingdom of Israel

The Late Bronze Age in the Middle East was an era of empires. The disintegration of long-established cultures and powerful political centers occurring at the end of this age, in the thirteenth and twelfth centuries, inaugurated a lengthy period characterized by greatly reduced political entities—tribal groupings, city-states, and small kingdoms. This in turn was succeeded by a time of national states of limited size. The eighth century introduced what amounted to a new age of empires that lasted well into the first millennium C.E. Assyria, Babylonia, Persia, Macedonia, and Rome took their places, each in turn, as the head of major and far-flung international empires.

The first of these large empires was the Assyrian, whose age of extensive dominance may be said to have begun with the rule of Tiglath-pileser III (744–727 B.C.E.) and to have ended with the fall of the Assyrian capital at Nineveh in 612 B.C.E. Thus, for a little over a century the Assyrians, with their center of power on the upper Tigris River and its tributaries, dominated the life and politics of the Middle East. From about 732 B.C.E. onward, Assyria, for all practical purposes, was master over the Eastern Mediterranean Seaboard and thus over the kingdoms of Israel and Judah.

Israel ceased to exist as an independent kingdom quite early in the period of Assyrian domination. Its capital at Samaria was captured in 722 B.C.E., and Israelite territory was incorporated subsequently into the Assyrian provincial system. Judah maintained its national identity throughout this period but was almost completely dominated by Assyria.

Israelite and Judean history throughout the eighth and seventh centuries must be viewed, therefore, as the history of a small corner of the Assyrian empire. The course of events for both states was largely shaped by the ambitions and policies of Assyria, and most of their actions were largely reactions to the Assyrians.

Sources for the Period

II Kings 15:8 to 17:41 and II Chron. 28:1–15 are our primary biblical sources for this period of Israelite and Judean history. The latter, of course, because of its exclusive interest in Judean affairs, provides only incidental information on Israelite matters and then only when Israelite history impinged directly on that of Judah. For the last days of Israel, this was the case only in the reign of Ahaz.

We learn from the narrative in II Kings that four of Israel's final six rulers were assassinated, one died from nonviolent causes, and the other apparently ended life in Assyrian exile. More specifically, II Kings reports the following for the last years of Israel. (1) The dynasty of Jehu came to an end, after a rule of over a century, when Zechariah the son of Jeroboam II was assassinated (II Kings 15:8–12). (2) Zechariah's assassin and successor, Shallum, was killed by Menahem after a rule of only one month (II Kings 15:13–16). (3) Menahem ruled for ten years. At some point in his reign, the Assyrian king Pul (who bore the throne name Tiglath-pileser) confirmed Menahem's rule at the price of a rather heavy payment (II Kings 15:17–22). (4) Following Menahem's demise, his son Pekahiah was assassinated by Pekah after a rule of two years (II Kings 15:23–26). (5) Pekah, who is said to have reigned twenty years, was king over Israel when Tiglath-pileser conquered portions of Syria-Palestine and deported people from the area (II Kings 15:27–32). In reporting on Judean kings, the editors of II Kings provide additional information on Pekah, who is said, in alliance with the Syrian ruler Rezin, to have taken action against Judah during the reign of Jotham (II Kings 15:37) and to have attacked Jerusalem during the reign of Ahaz. The latter is said to have sent presents to Tiglath-pileser to secure the Assyrian king's aid against Israel and Syria (II Kings 16:5–9). (6) Pekah was killed and succeeded on the throne by Hoshea, who eventually was attacked by the Assyrians when they found treachery in him. Hoshea was captured, Samaria was taken, Israelites were deported, and foreigners were moved into the area, which was placed under direct Assyrian rule (II Kings 15:30; 17).

Other biblical material directly related to this period is found in the prophetical books of Hosea and Isaiah. Hosea appears to have been active during as well as after the last years of the Jehu dynasty and to have witnessed the troublesome conditions produced by the internal power struggles within Israel and by the westward advance of the Assyrians. Isaiah, a Judean prophet, functioned in Jerusalem throughout most of the last half of the eighth century. Many of his oracles were concerned with Israel and the international affairs of the time. Isaiah 7–8 provides important material independent of the II Kings narrative about the attack on Jerusalem by Pekah and Rezin, including the fact that Israel and Syria sought to depose Ahaz and replace him on the Jerusalem throne.

Assyrian inscriptions from this period—during the reigns of Tiglath-pileser III, Shalmaneser V, and Sargon II—are quite numerous, and several refer directly to Israelite rulers and to Assyrian policy toward Israel or to general Assyrian activity in the Eastern Mediterranean Seaboard. Included in these sources are materials of diverse form—letters addressed from Assyrian officials to the royal court, inscriptions commemorating military campaigns, and summary annals reporting the events of the various kings' rule. The Assyrian texts, however, present historians with a number of problems. For the second of these rulers, Shalmaneser V, we possess no historical texts and thus have no information from the Assyrian perspective on the final revolt of Israel. The inscriptions of Sargon II, however, do provide information about the disposition of the northern kingdom and its incorporation into the Assyrian empire. The most strategic Assyrian inscriptions for the period are those of Tiglath-pileser, but unfortunately most of these are fragmentary and problematic. Inscribed on stone slabs on the walls of his palace at Calah (Nimrud), his annals were removed by one of his successors and reused in a later palace. This plus the treatment the slabs received at the hands of their modern-day discoverers has left them severely damaged and disordered. Fortunately, other inscriptions of Tiglath-pileser, although again frequently fragmentary, supplement and make possible partial reconstruction of the events of his reign noted in the damaged annals. References in the Assyrian texts, in spite of their problems, provide a general chronology of the period.

In this and subsequent chapters, classical sources written in Greek or Latin become more relevant to the reconstruction of Near Eastern history. The most important of these are the writings of Herodotus and Josephus.

Herodotus, a fifth-century B.C.E. Greek historian, traveled throughout many Near Eastern countries collecting traditions and historical recollections. These were incorporated into the nine books of his *Histories,* which concern relations between the Greeks and the oriental kingdoms to the early years of the fifth century. Herodotus often supplies materials not found in other sources on various historical matters.

Josephus, a Jewish historian of the first century C.E., wrote three major works—*Jewish Antiquities, The Jewish War, Contra Apion*— and an autobiography. His *Antiquities* covers from the creation until the outbreak of the first Jewish revolt against Rome in 66 C.E. but consists primarily in a retelling of the biblical story. The *War* is a history of the Jews from the early second century B.C.E. until the time shortly after the first Jewish revolt, which ended in 70 C.E. To defend his role in the Jewish war with Rome, Josephus wrote his autobiography, actually an appendix for the *Antiquities,* which primarily describes and defends his actions as commander of the Jewish forces in Galilee. *Contra Apion* is a defense of Judaism against various pagan charges.

Four points should be noted about Josephus as a historical source. (1) Where his work and the biblical narrative overlap, he is fundamendally dependent on biblical materials. (2) At times, Josephus will supplement the biblical narrative. Sometimes his material is drawn from Jewish homiletical and midrashic traditions, and at other times it is drawn from ancient and reliable sources. This means that such supplemental material must be carefully evaluated in every particular case with regard to historical reliability. (3) For the postbiblical material, Josephus is frequently the only source we possess. (4) For the period of the first Jewish revolt, Josephus was an eyewitness and a participant in the events. Thus he possessed firsthand information. Even here, however, Josephus presents *his* version of events, a version colored and shaped by his viewpoints and his concerns.

Syria-Palestine and the Assyrian Empire

Before discussing the particular history of Israel and Judah during the eighth and seventh centuries, the time of Assyrian domination, we should survey the general outline of the Assyrian conquest of the Eastern Mediterranean Seaboard (see Chart XIV) and the empire's relationship to its conquered subjects.

The Assyrian Conquest of the Eastern Mediterranean Seaboard

Late in the tenth century, after almost two centuries in which Assyrian military conquests were almost nonexistent, Assyrian kings revived a policy of military campaigns beyond the borders of Assyria proper. During the ninth century and the first half of the eighth, however, Assyria was content to limit its direct rule to the territory east of the Euphrates, allowing the river to serve as the western boundary of Greater Assyria. Raids were conducted west of the Euphrates and trade colonies established in various places in the region, as we have noted earlier, but territories were not annexed. Ashurnasirpal II (883–859 B.C.E.), for example, carried out vicious but sporadic campaigns, occasionally penetrating into territory west of the Euphrates. His campaigns eventually carried him to the shores of the Mediterranean Sea. Kingdoms as far south as Tyre and Sidon paid him tribute (*ARI* II, §§586, 597). By the time of Shalmaneser III (858–824 B.C.E.), who reports that he crossed the Euphrates over twenty times, annual military campaigns became customary. Shalmaneser's campaigns were more systematic in their execution and more intent on establishing Assyrian domination than had been the case under his predecessors. Even southern Syria-Palestine was the object of Assyrian campaigns under Shalmaneser III and Adad-nirari III (810–783 B.C.E.). Most of the southern Syro-Palestinian states —Tyre, Sidon, Damascus, Israel, and Philistia—had paid tribute to Assyria by the end of Adad-nirari's reign (see *ANET* 281).

Eventually, under Tiglath-pileser III (744–727 B.C.E.), who came to the throne in the late spring of 745 B.C.E., a highly successful program of Assyrian expansion and consolidation was developed. This program included the relocation of conquered populations and the annexation of territories into the Assyrian provincial system, policies designed to ensure continued Assyrian domination of conquered areas. Before his death, Tiglath-pileser III had extended the Assyrian empire to include practically the whole of the Eastern Mediterranean Seaboard.

Two goals lay behind the new initiatives and policies of Tiglath-pileser III in the west. (1) He set out to reduce or eliminate Urartian influence in northern Syria and to consolidate Assyrian authority in this area. During the reigns of his three immediate predecessors, the kingdom of Urartu, to the north and northwest of Assyria proper, had expanded its presence and influence at Assyrian expense. That states in northern Syria had become vassals to Urartu is indicated by the fact that Tiglath-pileser's Eponym List notes that he fought Urartu in Arpad, in northern Syria, for three years early in his reign (743–740 B.C.E.).

CHART XIV. The Period of Assyrian Domination

Judah	*Israel*	*Assyria*
Jotham (?–742)	Zechariah and Shallum (745) Menahem (745–736)	Tiglath-pileser III (744–727) reports payment of tribute by Menahem probably in 738/7; he campaigns along the coast of the Eastern Mediterranean Seaboard and collects
Ahaz (Jehoahaz I) (742–727)	Pekahiah (736–735) Pekah (735–732) Hoshea (732–723)	tribute from Jehoahaz in 734 or shortly thereafter, conquers the interior of the seaboard and Damascus, and confirms Hoshea on the throne in 732. In the so-called Syro-Ephraimitic War, Rezin of Damascus and Pekah had sought to depose Jehoahaz prior to Tiglath-pileser's 734–732 campaigns.
Hezekiah (727–698)		Shalmaneser V (727–722) lays siege to Samaria, which fell in 722, about the time of his death.
	Fall of Samaria (722), after which the kingdom of Israel ceases to exist.	Sargon II (722–705) completes and reaffirms Assyrian control of Syria-Palestine with campaigns in 720, 716, and 712.
Manasseh (697–642)		Sennacherib (705–681) marches on Philistia and Judah in 701 and puts down a revolt in which Hezekiah plays a significant role.
		Esarhaddon (680–669) holds Syria-Palestine securely under control, collecting tribute from Manasseh. He conquered Memphis in 671 but died in a follow-up Egyptian campaign.
Amon (642–640)		Ashurbanipal (668–627) recovers Memphis and sacks Thebes in 663, but the Assyrian empire is confronted with numerous difficulties at the end of his reign.

Tiglath-pileser's immediate predecessor, Ashur-nirari IV (753–745 B.C.E.), had attempted to retain influence in northern Syria through treaty arrangements rather than through a strong Assyrian military presence (see his treaty with Mati'ilu of Arpad; *ANET* 532–33). This policy had obviously proven unsuccessful. Tiglath-pileser III chose to control the region directly through a strong military presence in the area. (2) The Assyrian king wanted not only to assure

Assyrian trade with the west but also to gain control of commerce on the Eastern Mediterranean Seaboard. By dominating the trade routes leading through northern Syria and into western Asia Minor, Urartu had deprived Assyria of such needed materials as metals, timber, and horses. The resulting shortages in Assyria had produced widespread insurrections in the homeland from about 760 B.C.E. Assyrian control over the trade routes from the west and the north was considered a necessity in order to secure needed supplies and satisfy Assyrian demands at home. Tiglath-pileser probably moved into southern Syria-Palestine in order to establish Assyrian control over the entire interregional trade along the Eastern Mediterranean Seaboard and to redirect the flow of western commerce into Assyria proper.

Tiglath-pileser III. Tiglath-pileser III (744–727) reorganized the Assyrian administrative bureaucracy and pursued an aggressive policy of control over the Phoenician and Palestinian seacoasts and trade routes. He was largely responsible for the resurgence of Assyrian strength in the mid-eighth century B.C.E. *(The British Museum)*

Tiglath-pileser III bequeathed to his successor an empire that included practically all of Mesopotamia and the mountainous region to the east and north, as well as eastern Anatolia, and much of the Eastern Mediterranean Seaboard. King Sargon II (722–705 B.C.E.) and his successors continued the process of Assyrian expansion by consolidating Assyrian hegemony to the border of Egypt. Assyrian control of the trade and commerce in the eastern Mediterranean was given an especially significant boost when Sargon succeeded in establishing suzerainty over the island of Cyprus (by 709 B.C.E.).

Naturally, the movement of Assyria into the Eastern Mediterranean Seaboard and its attempt to control the area's commerce precipitated a struggle between Egypt and Assyria for dominance in the area. While Tiglath-pileser was expanding westward, the Twenty-fifth (Ethiopian, or Nubian) Dynasty, headquartered in Upper Egypt, was seeking to dominate Lower Egypt and the Delta and to extend its influence in the eastern Mediterranean. Perhaps as early as the mid-eighth century, the Ethiopians/Egyptians were cooperating with powers in Syria-Palestine against Assyria, as they had a century earlier in the days of Shalmaneser III. The *Musr* in the Sefire Inscriptions, which date from this period, may refer to Egypt (see *ANET* 659–61). Competition between Assyria and Egypt greatly influenced the political and economic life of the Eastern Mediterranean Seaboard until well into the seventh century.

Assyrian Administrative Policies

Beginning with Tiglath-pileser III, a particular pattern in Assyria's dealings with subordinate and conquered peoples becomes noticeable. It is possible to distinguish three types of relationships between Assyria and its subjects, although it must be recognized that the distinction among the types should not be rigidly drawn or seen as consecutive stages. The Assyrians themselves did not use special terminology to differentiate among the types of relationships.

1. In some cases, relations with Assyria were based upon voluntary submission by local rulers. When the Assyrian army made its show of force in an area, many rulers chose not to offer opposition but to submit voluntarily to Assyrian overlordship and to become what might be called Assyrian satellites or puppet states. This meant that they accepted Assyrian authority, sent gifts, agreed to pay annual tribute, and supported Assyrian military as well as construction and other projects when called upon. The Assyrians interfered little or only minimally in the social, religious, and administrative life of such states so long as political allegiance was maintained, economic obligations fulfilled, and Assyrian interests respected. An intelligence system based on spying reports helped the Assyrians to keep informed of matters even in such satellite states (see II Kings 18:22).

2. When kingdoms, cities, or tribal groups refused to submit voluntarily or showed disloyalty to Assyrian authority, they were conquered by Assyrian forces. Payment of tribute and other requirements were imposed, and the Assyrians took on a significant role in the state's political, military, and diplomatic life. In these situations, Assyria assumed the role of overlord and the subdued state that of a vassal. Assyrian officials were stationed in the vassal states to oversee matters in which Assyrian interests might be involved and to send reports about local conditions to the royal Assyrian court. (For an example of such correspondence, see Text VIII.) In vassal states, members of the ruling family that had opposed the Assyrians occasionally were allowed to continue their rule, provided they were willing to offer allegiance to Assyria. The promise of such allegiance was usually expressed in the form of a vassal treaty.

3. Rebellions by vassals, usually signaled by failure to pay the regular tribute, were crushed mercilessly, and the rebel territory was reduced to the status of a province—that is, incorporated into the Assyrian provincial system and placed under the control of a military governor and a hierarchy of officials. The Assyrian monarch had traveling personnel who investigated and inspected the work of provincial officials and thus tended to oversee the overseers. As a further measure to maintain control over and stability in areas transformed into provinces, the Assyrians deported the "upper crust" and other elements of the population and settled them elsewhere in the empire. In turn, foreign populations from other countries were resettled in the new provinces. This mixing of

TEXT VIII. Correspondence of an Assyrian Official

To the king my lord your servant Qurdi-assur-lamur.

Concerning the people of Tyre, about whom the king said thus: "Reply. It is well with it?", all the wharves are occupied by the people. Its subjects (i.e. those of Tyre) who are within them (i.e. the wharves) enter and leave the warehouses, give and receive in barter, ascend and descend Mount Lebanon which is in front of it (i.e. of Tyre) as they will, and they have timber brought down here. I exact a tax on it from those who have timber brought down here. As to the tax-collectors who were over the wharves of Mount Lebanon, the people of Tyre attacked and killed them. I then appointed, when he came down to me, a tax-collector who had been in the warehouses of Sidon. The Sidonians then attacked him. Thereupon I sent the Itu'a contingent [a tribal group] to Mount Lebanon: they made the people jump around! Afterwards when the people had fled and the tax-collector had come out and I had sent him back into Sidon, I spoke to them in this manner: "Henceforth have timber brought down here, do your work upon it, but do not sell it to the Egyptians or to the Philistines. Otherwise I will not free you and you shall not go up the mountain."

Concerning the city of Kashpuna about which the king said: "Why do you delay their fortification?", while they had still sent no message from the palace I took hold of the affair myself and duly did the job. Afterwards, when they did send a scaled tablet, it did not come to me. Subsequently I tore away the surrounding rubbish at the side, from near to far, and I did indeed repair the great gate of the inner wall. It (i.e. Kashpuna) had collected . . . . -four soldiers at my disposal. Twenty of them I took under my control and they went with me: the royal officer who is chief of the garrison I appointed over them. I made thirty regular soldiers enter into the middle of Kashpuna: they will keep guard. The soldiers will relieve them by thirties.

As to what the king said, that is, "Cause ten households of the Iasubaeans to enter into Kashpuna," the water therein is 'strong' and people fall sick. When they have been duly equipped with their own water from Immiu I will cause them to enter . . . . . . into Kashpuna. (*Iraq* 17 [1955], 127–28)

populations through large-scale transplantations was intended primarily to reduce moves toward nationalistic resurgence.

This general pattern of political dominance was not a system rigidly followed, nor was it applied consistently throughout the empire. Local conditions and the political and economic needs of the Assyrians—that is, ad hoc considerations—often influenced the arrangement of relationships. Israel, for example, moved through three stages of domination very quickly: first submitting to Assyria voluntarily (by 738 B.C.E.), then being forcefully reduced to a vassal (in 732 B.C.E.), and shortly thereafter being incorporated in the Assyrian provincial system (722–720 B.C.E.). On the other hand, the Assyrians seemed very reluctant to reduce to provinces the territories and kingdoms in the southwestern tip of the Fertile Crescent: namely, the Phoenician and Philistine city-states, Judah, Ammon, Moab, Edom, and the Arabs. The Assyrians may have felt that it was advantageous to allow these regions to be governed as semi-independent states with some vested national interests. At least two geopolitical factors seem to have contributed to this situation. Some of these states—especially the Phoenician, Philistine, and Arab kingdoms—were important components in ancient Near Eastern trade. Since the Assyrians sought to control the commerce in the region, they certainly did not wish to diminish its importance or radically disrupt the relations on which it was based. These states were also border kingdoms and thus important as buffer zones. Egypt was on the horizon, to the south of Syria-Palestine, as a potential opponent, a persistent propagandist for revolt, and an Assyrian rival until the days of Ashurbanipal. Assyria must have been hesitant to annex territory directly adjoining Egyptian terrain.

The stakes were high for the Assyrian satellites and vassal kingdoms of Syria-Palestine. On the one hand, the Assyrian burden was heavy, financially and otherwise. This burden frequently led the states to participate in coordinated alliances and rebellion and to look southward, to Egypt, for hope and help. On the other hand, the horrendous disaster that accompanied the Assyrian suppression of an unsuccessful insurrection was an ever-present reality that tempered nationalistic enthusiasm. Assyrian rulers, who could take pride in their atrocities, were always to be feared. Once under the shadow of Assyrian power, practically every Syro-Palestinian kingdom developed pro- and anti-Assyrian parties. Such parties, of course, were not ideological adherents or opponents of Assyrian politics but merely divisions between those who called for defiance of Assyrian domination and for nationalistic resurgence and those who thought it best to swallow the bitter pill and continue submission and acquiescence to Assyrian rule.

Chronological Issues

The chronology of the Israelite kings and the sequence of events between 738 and 732 B.C.E. are extremely problematic, and the evidence is ambiguous. From Assyrian records we know that Tiglath-pileser III completed his first series of western campaigns in 738 B.C.E. During these initial western campaigns, he suppressed rebellions and established Assyrian provinces in northern Syria. Also at that time, as we have noted, he received tribute from several rulers in southern Syria-Palestine. An inscription recently discovered in Iran, which predates his previously known annals, reports on tribute that Tiglath-pileser received, probably in 737 B.C.E. Among the southern kings paying tribute at that time were Menahem of Israel, Rezin of Damascus, and Tubail of Tyre (*TNAS* 19 [= *BASOR* 206 (1972), 41]). (In Tiglath-pileser's annals, the king of Tyre is given as Hiram [see *ANET* 283]. Possibly the annals, although describing conditions in 738 B.C.E., were written later, after Hiram had succeeded Tubail.

Hiram was involved in Assyria's 734–732 B.C.E. campaigns [see ND 4301 + 4305 in *Iraq* 18 (1956), 123]).

In 734–732 B.C.E., Tiglath-pileser was again in the west suppressing a major revolt in southern Syria-Palestine. He first swept down the coast in 734 B.C.E. and followed this with campaigns against the interior, which concluded with the destruction of Damascus in 732 B.C.E. During or just after his campaign against Damascus, Tiglath-pileser III confirmed Hoshea on the throne in Samaria (*ANET* 284). Thus, any reconstruction of Israelite chronology must have Menahem on the Israelite throne in 738/7 B.C.E. and Hoshea ruling in 732 B.C.E. This provides us with two firm chronological points.

Two Israelite kings ruled in Samaria between Menahem and Hoshea and thus have to be placed sometime between 738/7 and 732 B.C.E. These were Pekahiah and Pekah. Pekahiah is assigned a rule of two years or parts thereof (II Kings 15:23). Pekah is said to have ruled twenty years (II Kings 15:27; see 16:1). It is, of course, impossible to fit a reign of twenty years in Samaria by Pekah into the firm chronology established on the basis of the Assyrian inscriptions. If Menahem died late in 737 or early in 736 B.C.E. and Pekahiah ruled for parts of two years, then Pekah would have come to the throne in Samaria sometime late in 736 or early in 735 B.C.E. This would have been prior to Tiglath-pileser III's 734–732 B.C.E. campaigns in Syria-Palestine during which Hoshea was placed on the Israelite throne. This seems in radical conflict with the twenty years assigned to Pekah in the Bible. This problem and the similarity of names have led some scholars to propose that Pekah and Pekahiah may have been the same person. An alternative explanation, which will be developed more fully below, is that Pekah was already ruling over a portion of Israelite territory before coming to the throne in Samaria and that the twenty years credited to him includes the earlier years of his partial rule.

Rezin's "Greater Syria"

While Assyria was the dominant Middle Eastern power throughout the period surveyed in this chapter and overshadowed politics far and wide, Israel and Judah also had to contend during the early part of this period—from the mid-eighth century until the fall of Damascus in 732 B.C.E.—with a less gigantic but more immediately neighboring power: namely, the Syrian kingdom of Damascus. The Syrian monarch at the time was the ambitious Rezin, who apparently had usurped the throne in Damascus, since the Assyrian inscriptions list Hadara rather than Damascus as his hometown (*ANET* 283). At any rate, Rezin and Damascus exerted significant influence among the local kingdoms of southern Syria-Palestine for more than a decade.

Rezin's direct involvement in Israelite and Judean affairs is clearly indicated in the biblical account of the so-called Syro-Ephraimite war (II Kings 16:5–9; II Chron. 28:16–21; Isa. 7–8). This combines with several other items of evidence to suggest (1) that Rezin had already begun to encroach on surrounding nations, especially Israel and Judah, as early as the reigns of Menahem of Israel and Jotham of Judah; (2) that his influence and territorial control had reached such an extensive level by the time of Pekahiah, Pekah, and Ahaz that it is possible to speak of a "Greater Syria"; and (3) that when Tiglath-pileser III began his western campaign in 734 B.C.E., Rezin was the leader of an anti-Assyrian movement supported by most of the nations of southern Syria-Palestine. Since the existence and policies of this coalition constitute the political background of the Syro-Ephraimite crisis, let us examine these three points in detail.

1. There is some evidence, admittedly open to different interpretations, to suggest that Rezin was already expanding southward and westward, exerting significant pressure among the Palestinian kingdoms, before and during the reign of Menahem. First, the oracle on Damascus in Amos 1:3–5 describes Syria as invading Gilead, traditionally Israelite territory in Transjordan. While this oracle cannot be dated precisely, the common tendency is to associate the opening chapters of Amos with the time of Jeroboam II or soon thereafter. Second, the note in II Kings 15:37 has Rezin *and Pekah* threatening Judah already in the reign of Jotham. Pekah could not yet have been on the throne in Samaria, given the chronological structures mentioned above. Although the note may be unhistorical, another possibility, anticipated above, is that Pekah was already ruling at that time over some portion of Israelite territory—that Pekah was a puppet ruler, subject to Rezin, over territory in the northern Transjordan or Galilee which Rezin had already wrenched away from Israel. Finally, there is the note in II Kings 16:6 to be taken into account. This text reads in Hebrew: "At that time Rezin the king of Syria recovered Elath for Syria, and drove the men of Judah from Elath; and the Syrians [or "Edomites," according to the Masoretic correction of the Hebrew] came to Elath, where they dwell to this day." The context would seem to place Rezin's seizure of Elath in Ahaz's reign. When one considers that the organization of the material in II Kings is often more theological than chronological, however, the possibility emerges that this action also occurred during the reign of Jotham.

Rezin's expansion of Syrian influence was not unlike that of his predecessor, Hazael, a century earlier (see above, pp. 293, 297), and for the same reasons. Hazael conquered much of Transjordan and probably all of Galilee and extended his influence into Philistine territory: that is, along the Mediterranean coast. At that time, both Israel and Judah suffered from Syrian oppression (II Kings 10:32–33; 12:17–18). Rezin seems to have been attempting to duplicate this earlier Syrian mini-empire.

2. However early Rezin began to expand his realm and exert influence on Israelite and Judean politics, it seems that he clearly established what might be called a "Greater Syria." Some of the evidence for this has been noted above (Amos 1:3–5; II Kings 15:37; 16:6). In addition, Isa 9:11–12 speaks of Israel's enemies eating up its territory—Syria from the east and Philistia from the west. After Assyria's triumph over Damascus in 732 B.C.E., Assyria brought to an end the Syrian kingdom. As part of the dismantlement of the state, Assyria incorpo-

rated Syrian territory into the Assyrian provincial system. In one of his inscriptions, Tiglath-pileser speaks of making provinces out of territory belonging to "the extended domain of the house of Hazael," territory which joined the house of Omri (*ANET* 283, revised in light of texts ND 4301 + 4305 and K 2649; see *Iraq* 18 [1956], 123 and *IEJ* 12 [1962], 116–18). II Kings 15:27 probably speaks of the same events when it describes the incorporation of (formerly) Israelite territory into the Assyrian empire. The places noted in this text are in Transjordan and Galilee, regions probably under Syrian control, the reason for their incorporation by Assyria. (The central coastal plain of Palestine, the region around Dor, between Phoenicia and Philistia, may also have been controlled by Syria, and this was the reason for its annexation by Assyria.) The extended domain of Syria ("Greater Syria") thus included large areas previously considered Israelite territory.

3. Rezin had put together a major coalition of states in Syria-Palestine to oppose Assyrian authority in the area, as Syria had done in the preceding century during the days of Shalmaneser III (see above, p. 269). The refusal of Israel under Menahem and of Judah under Ahaz to join forces with the anti-Assyrian movement, however, meant that a fully united front in Syria-Palestine had not been achieved by Rezin as was the case when such a coalition confronted Shalmaneser III.

Two factors may appear to call into question Rezin's leadership and even the existence of such an anti-Assyrian coalition. First, why did Rezin, if his Damascus kingdom was a power to be reckoned with, voluntarily send tribute to Tiglath-pileser III in 738 B.C.E.? Second, why did he not challenge Tiglath-pileser III when the Assyrian king marched his forces down the Philistine coast in 734 B.C.E.? The answer in the first instance is that a challenge to Tiglath-pileser III would have been more trouble than it was worth and that the payment of a nominal tribute under the circumstances was a cheap way to buy time. Assyria's threat to Rezin's emerging little empire was still fairly distant, even if one assumes that the Assyrians may have put on a show of force in Palestine to aid Menahem (see II Kings 15:19). Better to pay a nominal tribute voluntarily to a distant power than possibly have to deal with a wrathful Assyria bent on forcing submission. The 734 B.C.E. Assyrian campaign down the Mediterranean coast was a different matter. It was no longer a matter of nominal tribute to stave off a distant threat but a matter of submitting or not. Even though Rezin had not yet fully solidified his coalition, as evidenced by the continuing effort to force Judah's participation, Rezin refused to submit: he did not rush to meet Tiglath-pileser III in 734 B.C.E. with proper assurances of loyalty confirmed by tribute. Instead, he chose to fight, although not to attack. There are several indications, moreover, that Rezin was not alone in this regard—that is, that he and a coalition of states and rulers in Syria-Palestine strongly resisted Tiglath-pileser III for three years of hard conflict.

The evidence for this coalition is as follows. (*a*) Rezin's movement against Elath, probably in association with the Edomites (II Kings 16:6), suggests

Edomite and other Transjordanian support for Rezin. *(b)* In Isa 9:11–12, Syria is depicted attacking Israel from the east with Philistines attacking from the west, which suggests a Philistine-Syrian coalition. II Chronicles 28:18, which describes the Philistines invading Judean territory, could indicate Philistine pressure on Judah to join the coalition. *(c)* The so-called Syro-Ephraimite war, which we shall discuss further in this and the next chapter, was an attempt by Israel and Syria to force Judah into an anti-Assyrian coalition. *(d)* Mention is made in Tiglath-pileser's texts of his attacks and reprisals against several Syro-Palestinian states in 734–732 B.C.E. These include the Meunites to the south of Judah and Samsi, queen of Arabia (ND 400 [see *Iraq* 13 (1951), 24]; *ANET* 284). Hiram of Tyre, apparently a "son of Tubail," also cooperated with Rezin against Assyria, support noted in the Assyrian texts (ND 4301 + 4305; see *Iraq* 18 [1956], 123). *(e)* The nature of Tiglath-pileser's campaigns, first down the coast and then against the interior of Syria-Palestine, points to a coalition of coastal and internal powers in the area. The opposition to Assyria was not isolated but concerted opposition, and not opposition formed on the spur of the moment but opposition coordinated by Rezin, with his dreams of a united anti-Assyrian front led by "Greater Syria."

The Last Years of Israel

Having gained an overview of the general international circumstances, let us now focus attention specifically on political developments in the kingdom of Israel. Following the death of Jeroboam II, if not earlier, Israel began a rapid decline in its political situation from which it never recovered. Jeroboam's son and successor, Zechariah, reigned only a few months before being assassinated. Once more the old problem of dynastic insecurity surfaced in the north. Zechariah's was only the first in a series of assassinations. Never again was there a successful and lasting succession to the Israelite throne.

In addition to its monarchical instability, Israel was confronted on the one hand, as we have seen, with the looming Assyrian threat and on the other hand with a reinvigorated Damascus kingdom. No doubt there were strong pro-Assyrian and anti-Assyrian parties in Israel as well as pro-Syrian and anti-Syrian sentiments and factions. The anti-Assyrian party would have appealed to nationalistic hopes, urged cooperation with Rezin, and cast expectant glances in the direction of Egypt. Rezin's grandiose designs and anti-Assyrian program could not help but affect political and social matters in Israel and intensify conflict between the pro- and anti-Assyrian factions.

These three factors—the instability in leadership, the policies of Rezin, and the existence of pro- and anti-Assyrian parties—played their roles in the precipitous decline of the northern kingdom. A fourth element, sectional rivalry, developed, and competing claimants to the throne arose (see Isa. 8:14; 9:21 and Hos. 5:5, with their implications of competing realms in the north). All these contributed significantly to the downfall of Israel and its ultimate defeat at the hands of Assyria.

Shallum and Menahem

In an effort to obtain the throne, Shallum conspired against and slew Zechariah, the legitimate heir, and presumably the entire reigning house of Jehu. Zechariah had ruled for only six months (II Kings 15:8–10). His assassination and the extermination of the Jehu dynasty were probably encouraged by the prophetic denunciations of Amos (see Amos 7:10–17) and Hosea (Hos. 1:4–5), whose pronouncements of judgment on the royal house served as calls to action and assassination. Shallum assumed the kingship, but nothing is said in the II Kings account about the basis of his support, which proved to be insufficient to keep him in power. After one month he was slain by Menahem (II Kings 15:14). The Zechariah, Shallum, and Menahem affair has many parallels with the earlier episode of Elah, Zimri, and Omri, which brought an end to an earlier Israelite ruling family (I Kings 16:8–22; see above, pp. 265–266). In both cases, the ruling dynasty was eliminated by a usurper who could not hold the throne, and civil strife accompanied the struggle for power.

II Kings 15:16 notes that Menahem took some vicious action against Israelite citizens, either when taking over the throne or else following his accession: "At that time Menahem sacked Tiphsah and all who were in it and its territory from Tirzah on; because they did not open it to him, therefore he sacked it, and he ripped up all the women in it who were with child." Two problems about this text stand out: the identification of Tiphsah and the reason for Menahem's atrocity. The only Tiphsah known from antiquity was located on the Euphrates River, which clearly does not fit the geographical requirements of this text. Perhaps the Lucianic recension of the Greek of II Kings 15:16, which reads "Tappuah," should be followed. Tappuah was an Ephraimite town about fourteen miles southwest of Tirzah, the latter located in the territory of Manasseh (Josh. 17:8). It also has been hypothesized that "son of Jabesh" in describing Shallum (see II Kings 15:13–14) should be read "son of (the place) Jashib." Jashib was another Ephraimite village located in the general vicinity of Tirzah and only about two miles from Tappuah. If Shallum was from the Tappuah area, perhaps the local citizenry had supported him and opposed Menahem. This could explain why Menahem, once he gained the throne, treated them with such ferocity. Tribal rivalries between Ephraim and Manasseh may also have played a role (see Isa. 9:18–21).

Other than this reference to the trouble that he had establishing his reign, only one item is reported about Menahem (apart from his death notice). Both the biblical and Assyrian texts report that he submitted voluntarily to Tiglath-pileser III (= Pul) and, one assumes, remained a loyal subject until his death (II Kings 15:17–22; *ANET* 283). Menahem's name, as we have noted, appears both in a stela inscription (*TNAS* 19 [= *BASOR* 206 (1972), 41]) and in the annals of Tiglath-pileser III (*ANET* 283), in a list of rulers who sent tribute to the Assyrian king during or immediately following his 738 B.C.E. campaign in northern Syria, where he suppressed a rebellion that involved Hatrikka and other cities along the northeastern Mediterranean coast. Among the other southern Syro-Palestinian rulers offering tribute at the same time were the kings of Damascus (Rezin), Tyre, and Byblos and Zabibe, the queen of Arabia.

The biblical text suggests that Menahem submitted not only out of fear of the Assyrians but also because he needed Assyrian support "to confirm his hold of the royal power" (II Kings 15:19). In addition, II Kings 15:20b, with its statement that "the king of Assyria turned back, and did not stay there in the land," could imply that the Assyrian king or his army may have put in an appearance in Israelite territory itself. Tiglath-pileser's assessment of tribute was unusually high—a thousand talents—which Menahem collected by assessing the "wealthy men" of Israel fifty shekels of silver each. It has been estimated that this would have required about sixty thousand contributors. The unusually large assessment placed on Menahem by Tiglath-pileser III may have been in view of Menahem's incapability to hold the throne without Assyrian support and particularly in payment for the appearance of Assyrian troops in Israelite territory. The Assyrian kings often required what was called a *tamartu,* a spectacular gift for display, as an occasional or initial tribute. The annual or regular tribute, the *maddattu,* was much more modest.

Menahem died a natural death; "he slept with his fathers" (II Kings 15:22), the last Israelite king about whom this could be said.

Pekahiah

The son of Menahem, Pekahiah, ascended the throne in Samaria with dynastic credentials (II Kings 15:23–26). His rule was short-lived, for he was quickly assassinated by Pekah, who had the support of the anti-Assyrian faction and the advocates of cooperation with Syria. The burden of Assyrian tribute probably convinced many Israelites to support Pekah's coup and to favor Rezin's anti-Assyrian activities.

Pekah

II Kings 15:25 relates how Pekah conspired against Pekahiah and with a contingent of Gileadites assassinated the king in the citadel of the royal palace in Samaria. Pekah's revolt probably was either directly inspired or at least strongly supported by Rezin. This is suggested by several considerations. (1) The fact that men from Gilead, an area probably already under Syrian domination, as we have noted, participated in the takeover of the Israelite throne points to Syrian complicity. (2) Pekah and Rezin had already carried out cooperative actions against Judah during or just following the reign of Jotham (II Kings 15:37). (3) Pekah came to the throne in Samaria in 736/5 B.C.E., when anti-Assyrian fervor under Rezin's influence would have been at its peak in Syria-Palestine. (4) In the biblical statements about Pekah and Rezin, the latter is always mentioned first and seems definitely to have been the dominant figure in the Syro-Ephraimitic alliance against Ahaz (see, for example, Isa. 7:1).

Acting in partnership, Rezin and Pekah turned their efforts to the south and

Judah, hoping to increase the strength, proximity, and size of their coalition by including Judah in their program. Negotiations between Judah and Syria, even before Pekah secured the throne in Samaria, may have already taken place but with Ahaz refusing to join the movement. II Chronicles 28:7 suggests that at some point there was an unsuccessful attempt, apparently externally inspired, to remove Ahaz from the throne through assassination: "Zichri, a mighty man of Ephraim, slew Maaseiah the king's son and Azrikam the commander of the palace and Elkanah the next in authority to the king." Ahaz was also apparently under strong pressure from his own people to yield and join the coalition.

The Syro-Ephraimitic Siege of Jerusalem

Rezin and Pekah marched against Jerusalem to achieve through military force what they had not acquired through other means—a ruler in Judah who would join, support, and contribute to the anti-Assyrian coalition. This engagement, frequently called the Syro-Ephraimitic War, probably took place shortly after Pekah had usurped the throne and solidified his authority in Samaria. Numerous biblical texts (such as II Kings 15:29–30, 37; 16:5–9; Isa. 7:1–8:8; II Chron. 28:5–21), as well as several inscriptions of Tiglath-pileser III, are relevant and related either to the specifics of this invasion or to the events that constitute the larger background. As we learn from Isa. 7:6, the intention of Rezin and Pekah was to replace Ahaz on the Judean throne with a ruler who would support the anti-Assyrian fraternity. Ahaz had become king of Judah during the reign of Menahem. Menahem, of course, had remained submissive to Assyria throughout his reign, refusing to join the anti-Assyrian coalition. When Israel's policy toward Assyria changed with Pekah's assumption of the throne in Samaria, Pekah may have assumed that Judah would go along, since Judah basically had functioned for years as a vassal state to Israel. Ahaz refused to support the new Israelite policy, however, which could be seen from an Israelite perspective as the action of a renegade vassal. Thus Ahaz's dethronement would have been punitive action against a rebellious subordinate. Syria, Israel, and Tyre had agreed on a replacement for Ahaz, the unnamed "son of Tabeel" (Isa. 7:6), perhaps Hiram, a member of the ruling family of Tyre whose king Tubail (= Tabeel), as we have noted, had paid tribute to Assyria in 737 B.C.E. (If Jezebel was the wife of Ahab and the mother of Queen Athaliah [see I Kings 16:31; II Kings 8:16–18; but compare II Kings 8:26], then relatives of a Phoenician royal family had previously ruled over Judah. This may have been a factor in choosing to place a Tyrian ruler on the Jerusalem throne.) Widespread support for the Israelite-Syrian policy among the Judean population seemed to make the plan feasible.

The scheme of Rezin and Pekah was unsuccessful. Ahaz and Jerusalem held out against their efforts (this will be discussed further in the next chapter in the section on Ahaz). The anti-Assyrian coalition was demolished in Tiglath-pileser's three campaigns to the west.

Tiglath-pileser III's 734–732 B.C.E. Campaigns

Between 738 B.C.E. when he received the tribute of Rezin, Menahem, and other western rulers and 734 B.C.E. when he marched down the Mediterranean coast, Tiglath-pileser III was engaged in warfare against Urartu in the north and Media in the east and thus far from Palestine. When he had settled matters in these regions, the Assyrian king moved into southern Syria-Palestine, intent on securing control of the eastern Mediterranean commerce and on suppressing the anti-Assyrian coalition composed of many disloyal states that had shortly before offered him tacit submission only to organize opposition when his presence was elsewhere. In 734 B.C.E., Tiglath-pileser III's campaign took him, as his Eponymn List says, "against Philistia." (See Map 23.) Fragmentary texts mention military actions against Phoenician cities as well as the Philistine cities of Gaza, Ashkelon, and Gezer. In addition, he fought and defeated the Meunites in the northern Sinai and probably other groups in the area. His forces penetrated to "the city of the Brook of Egypt" (probably Wady Besor just south of Gaza), where he set up a stela indicating the southern boundary of the Assyrian empire. It was probably at this time that he "installed the Idibilu [apparently an Arabic tribe, possibly the Abdeel of Gen. 25:13] as a Warden of Marches on the border of Musur (Egypt)" (*ANET* 282, 284). The Idibilu tribesmen probably were made responsible and remunerated for supervision of the border region between Assyrian-dominated territory and Egypt. Land traffic and trade between Egypt and the areas to the north may also have been placed under their control. Such Assyrian association with nomadic Arab groups must have been seen as creating a loyal buffer at the southwestern boundaries of the empire.

Hanno, the king of Gaza, fled to Egypt before the city fell to the Assyrian forces but was later reinstated in office. Mitinti, king of Ashkelon, who initially offered submission and paid tribute, apparently died or was killed by the Assyrians, perhaps as late as 732 B.C.E. when Assyrian troops may have again been active in Philistia, and was replaced on the throne by his son Rukibtu. The coastal plain to the north of Philistia, at this time certainly not under Israelite but under Philistine, Phoenician, or, more likely, Syrian control, appears to have been made into an Assyrian province called Dor. Gaza was turned into an Assyrian port and custom station.

The Assyrian king's campaign down the southern Mediterranean coast and against powers on the border of Egypt was not only a movement to acquire control of the maritime commerce and the seaports in the region but also a restraining action against possible Egyptian support for the anti-Assyrian coalition. (Egypt, it should be recalled, had participated in the earlier anti-Assyrian coalition of Eastern Mediterranean Seaboard states that had opposed Shalmaneser III and may have had treaty contacts with Syro-Palestinian states at the time prior to Tiglath-pileser III's rule; see above, p. 269. For Assyrian efforts to control commerce between the Seaboard and Egypt, see above, Text VIII.)

In 733–732 B.C.E., Tiglath-pileser III turned his attention inland and success-

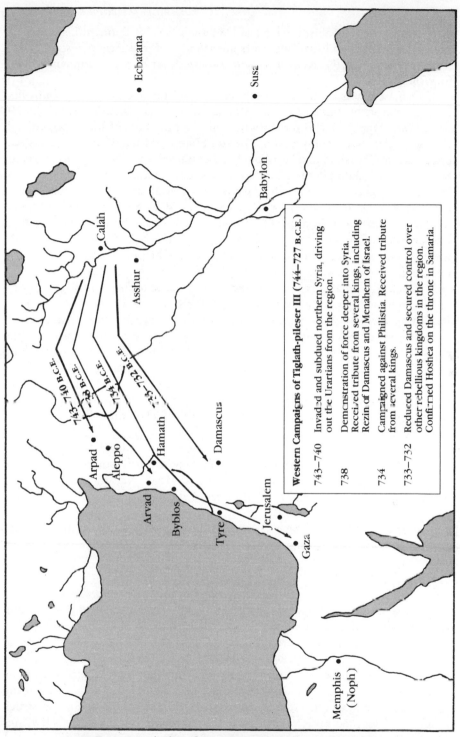

Western Campaigns of Tiglath-pileser III (744–727 B.C.E.)

743–740	Invaded and subdued northern Syria, driving out the Urartians from the region.
738	Demonstration of force deeper into Syria. Received tribute from several kings, including Rezin of Damascus and Menahem of Israel.
734	Campaigned against Philistia. Received tribute from several kings.
733–732	Reduced Damascus and secured control over other rebellious kingdoms in the region. Confirmed Hoshea on the throne in Samaria.

MAP 23. Tiglath-pileser III's Western Campaigns

fully campaigned "against the land of Damascus," as his Eponym List notes for both years. Rezin and his supporters apparently offered strong resistance but were no match for the Assyrians. The consequences of these campaigns were fourfold.

1. Damascus was destroyed, Rezin killed, and territory that was controlled by Syria was incorporated into the Assyrian provincial system (II Kings 15:29; 16:9). (See Map 24.) This territory became the provinces of Megiddo, Gilead, Karnaim, Damascus, and perhaps Dor and Hauran. Much of these regions had once been under Israelite control but had been taken over earlier into "Greater Syria" or, as Tiglath-pileser III called it, "the extended domain of the house of Hazael" (see above, p. 325). The Assyrian incorporation of this former Israelite territory is noted in II Kings 15:29, a text which does not claim, however, that the places were taken from Israel: "In the days of Pekah king of Israel Tiglath-pileser king of Assyria came and captured Ijon, Abel-beth-maacah, Janoah, Kedesh, Hazor, Gilead, and Galilee, all the land of Naphtali; and he carried the people captive to Assyria" (compare I Kings 15:20; see I Chron. 5:26).

2. Israel, which had already been reduced by Rezin to the central hill country of Mt. Ephraim, does not seem to have suffered severely from Tiglath-pileser III's campaign, although apparently there was some deportation of Israelites. A state of vassaldom was imposed on the kingdom and a new ruler placed on the throne. The Assyrian king reports that the Israelites "overthrew their king Pekah" and that he recognized Hoshea as his replacement (*ANET* 284). II Kings 15:30, however, says that Hoshea conspired against Pekah and assassinated him. At any rate, the pro-Assyrian party in Samaria seems to have gained the upper hand and to have removed Pekah in the nick of time. Hoshea became the new king in Samaria.

3. Many of the kingdoms in southern Transjordan submitted or were restored to Assyrian control. References are made in Assyrian inscriptions to the receipt of tribute from Sanipu of Ammon, Salamanu of Moab, Kaushmalaku of Edom, and Samsi queen of Arabia, the last offering stiff resistance to Assyria before capitulating (*ANET* 282, 284).

4. Judah had now become a satellite of Assyria, with all the responsibilities and obligations appertaining to such a status.

Hoshea and the Fall of Samaria

Hoshea, assigned a reign of nine years, began his rule at some point during the campaigns of Tiglath-pileser III against Damascus in 733–732 B.C.E. but probably late during this period (II Kings 17:1). The exact circumstances of Hoshea's displacement of Pekah are unclear. As we have noted, Tiglath-pileser III reports that the people "overthrew their king Pekah and I placed Hoshea as king over them" (*ANET* 284), while the biblical text says that "Hoshea the son of Elah made a conspiracy against Pekah the son of Remaliah, and struck him down [deposed him?], and slew him, and reigned in his stead" (II Kings 15:30). Whatever the exact course of action that brought Hoshea to the throne

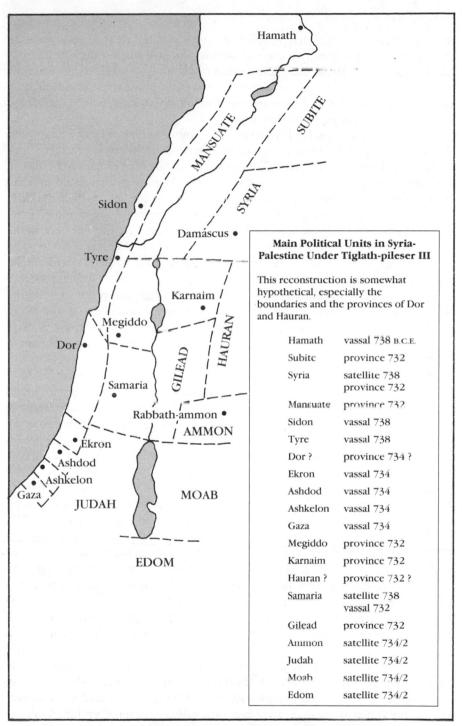

Main Political Units in Syria-Palestine Under Tiglath-pileser III

This reconstruction is somewhat hypothetical, especially the boundaries and the provinces of Dor and Hauran.

Hamath	vassal 738 B.C.E.
Subite	province 732
Syria	satellite 738 province 732
Mansuate	province 732
Sidon	vassal 738
Tyre	vassal 738
Dor ?	province 734 ?
Ekron	vassal 734
Ashdod	vassal 734
Ashkelon	vassal 734
Gaza	vassal 734
Megiddo	province 732
Karnaim	province 732
Hauran ?	province 732 ?
Samaria	satellite 738 vassal 732
Gilead	province 732
Ammon	satellite 734/2
Judah	satellite 734/2
Moab	satellite 734/2
Edom	satellite 734/2

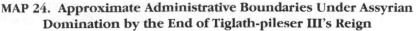

MAP 24. Approximate Administrative Boundaries Under Assyrian Domination by the End of Tiglath-pileser III's Reign

may have been, it is clear that his rise to power was based on the need to placate the Assyrians and to avoid their march against Samaria when it became obvious that Damascus and Rezin were going to fall to Tiglath-pileser III. Israel was now an Assyrian vassal. Hoshea's loyalty to Assyria early in his reign is indicated by the fact that in 731 B.C.E. he sent tribute to the Assyrian king, who was engaged at the time in a campaign in Babylonia.

Hoshea's kingdom probably consisted of no more than the city of Samaria and the surrounding Ephraimite hill country. Former Israelite territories in Transjordan, the Jezreel Valley, and Galilee had been taken over earlier by Rezin, probably during the reign of Menahem, and were now incorporated into the Assyrian provincial system as a consequence of Rezin's rebellion. This reduced status of the northern kingdom is reflected in the terminology of the prophet Hosea. He refers to Ephraim more than three dozen times, but not once in the earliest material of the book found in Hosea 1–3. These chapters seem to come from the last years of the Jehu dynasty and thus prior to Syria's widespread takeover of Israelite territory (see Hos. 1:4–5). The words of Amos, probably a contemporary of the early Hosea, contain not a single reference to Ephraim. The use of the designation Ephraim in Hosea's preaching following the fall of the Jehu dynasty (Hos. 4–14) suggests a period when Ephraim was the primary territory ruled over by the kings of Samaria (note the references to Ephraim in Isa. 7:2–17).

Hoshea paid tribute to Tiglath-pileser III's successor, Shalmaneser V (727–722 B.C.E.), but under what conditions remains unclear. II Kings 17:3 says "against him [Hoshea] came up Shalmaneser king of Assyria; and Hoshea became his vassal, and paid him tribute." This text could be interpreted to imply that Shalmaneser V had to force Hoshea's submission, but it probably means no more than that when there was a new Assyrian monarch on the throne, Hoshea voluntarily submitted to the new ruler.

Eventually Hoshea rebelled against the Assyrians: "But the king of Assyria found treachery in Hoshea; for he had sent messengers to So, king of Egypt, and offered no tribute to the king of Assyria, as he had done year by year" (II Kings 17:4). Why Hoshea revolted and adopted a fatal policy of anti-Assyrianism at this time remains a mystery. We possess no historical inscriptions or archival records from the reign of Shalmaneser V that could shed light on matters from the Assyrian perspective. Two conclusions seem in order: (1) Hoshea's revolt was part of a larger anti-Assyrian rebellion in Syria-Palestine and (2) the Israelite king was relying upon the propaganda and assistance of Egypt. Evidence to support these two conclusions, while not overwhelming, is substantial.

1. The evidence suggesting that Hoshea's revolt was part of a larger movement of anti-Assyrian sentiment is fourfold. *(a)* In *Ant.* IX.283–84, Josephus, claiming reliance upon the Greek author Menander, who is said to be dependent upon Tyrian archives, reports that during Shalmaneser V's reign Phoenicia was involved in revolt. The rebellion was suppressed by the Assyrian king, we are told, who "came with an army and invaded all Phoenicia and, after making

a treaty of peace with all (its cities), withdrew from the land." *(b)* Some of the oracles against foreign nations in Isaiah may stem from this period and suggest anti-Assyrian actions. This is especially the case with Isa. 14:28–32:

> In the year that King Ahaz died [727 B.C.E.] came this oracle:
> "Rejoice not, O Philistia, all of you,
>   that the rod which smote you [Tiglath-pileser III; 744–727 B.C.E.] is broken,
> for from the serpent's root will come forth an adder,
>   and its fruit will be a flying serpent.
> And the first-born of the poor will feed,
>   and the needy lie down in safety;
> but I will kill your root with famine,
>   and your remnant I will slay.
> Wail, O gate; cry, O city;
>   melt in fear, O Philistia, all of you!
> For smoke comes out of the north,
>   and there is no straggler in his ranks."
> What will one answer the messengers of the nation?
> "Yahweh has founded Zion,
>   and in her the afflicted of his people find refuge."

This text can be interpreted to suggest that Philistia's "rejoicing" involved plans for participating in revolt, perhaps even attempts to enlist the participation of Judah. *(c)* When Shalmaneser V's successor, Sargon II (722–705 B.C.E.), finished the work of suppressing rebels in Syria-Palestine, several kingdoms were involved. While some of these may have initiated revolt at the time of Shalmaneser V's death, it is also possible that rebellion had already begun before the Assyrian ruler's death: that is, at the time of Israel's rebellion. *(d)* It would have made no sense for Hoshea, ruling over the small and insignificant Ephraimite state, to have undertaken revolt alone or with nothing more substantial than the promise of Egyptian aid.

2. Hoshea carried on negotiations for assistance from Egypt, and Israelite leadership was divided between pro-Assyrian and anti-Assyrian elements. Egypt was naturally regarded by the anti-Assyrian element as the best possibility for assistance against Assyria. This is indicated by many of the oracles in the Book of Hosea.

> Ephraim is like a dove,
>   silly and without sense,
>   calling to Egypt, going to Assyria.
>   (Hos. 7:11)

> Ephraim herds the wind,
>   and pursues the east wind all day long;
> they multiply falsehood and violence;
>   they make a bargain with Assyria,
>   and oil is carried to Egypt.
>   (Hos. 12:1)

II Kings 17:4 says that Hoshea "sent messengers to So, king of Egypt." No Egyptian pharaoh by this name is known. Two possible explanations present themselves. *(a)* "So" may refer to the city of Sais rather than to a specific pharaoh. During the 720s an independent monarchy had been set up in Sais by Pharaoh Tefnakht (about 727–720 B.C.E.), founder of the Twenty-fourth Dynasty. According to this explanation, messengers would have been sent by Hoshea to the Egyptian ruler at Sais rather than to a pharaoh named So. *(b)* "So" may be an abbreviation of the name Osorkon (IV; about 730–715 B.C.E.), the last ruler of the Twenty-second Dynasty. At any rate, and regardless of the exact referent of "So, king of Egypt," an Israelite appeal was made to some authority in Egypt, which at the time was governed by several competing families (dynasties) located at various places.

When Shalmaneser V moved to quell the Israelite revolt, he was somehow able to seize Hoshea, so he "shut him up, and bound him in prison" (II Kings 17:4). Possibly Hoshea had appeared voluntarily before the Assyrian king to seek a settlement. The revolt and Israelite resistance did not end with Hoshea's arrest, however, which shows that the anti-Assyrian policy of the king was strongly supported by the general population. Samaria was besieged for three years (or parts thereof) before finally being captured (II Kings 17:5; 18:9–10). The biblical text attributes the capture of the city to Shalmaneser. A statement in the Babylonian Chronicles does also (*ABC* 73), although no records of Shalmaneser V survive to authenticate this.

Shalmaneser V seems to have died shortly after the conquest of Samaria or during its siege, and it was left to his successor, Sargon II, to carry out the Assyrian program for the region. However, Sargon II, whose claim to the throne may have been in question, was confronted with troubles elsewhere— first in Assyria and then in southern Mesopotamia—until 720 B.C.E. To aid in suppressing these troubles, the bulk of the Assyrian army was probably withdrawn from the west, where the rebellion apparently was renewed and expanded. Only in 720 B.C.E. was Sargon free to conduct a western campaign and put matters in order in Syria-Palestine.

During this 720 B.C.E. campaign to the west, Sargon II undertook a number of activities (*ANET* 284–86). (1) Ilubi'di (or Ia'ubidi) of Hamath and his allies were defeated near Qarqar and the rebel would-be king was flayed alive. (2) To the extent necessary, the cities of Arpad, Simirra, Damascus, and Samaria were recaptured. (3) The Assyrian king reconquered and subdued Gaza, where Hanno, the problematic vassal whom Tiglath-pileser III had dealt with in 734 B.C.E., was again causing trouble. (4) Sargon defeated an Egyptian force under Re'u, "the turtan of Egypt," probably dispatched by either Tefnakht or Bocchoris (about 720–715 B.C.E.) reigning in Sais or Osorkon IV reigning in Bubastis, and destroyed "the city of the Brook of Egypt." If the wall reliefs in Room Five of Sargon's palace at Dur-Sharrukin (Khorsabad) relate to this campaign, they could suggest that the Egyptian and Assyrian armies met at Gabbutunu (Gibbethon) in Palestine, which would indicate an advance by the Egyptians into Assyrian-claimed territory. Either at this time or later in 716 B.C.E., Sargon II established a military colony on the border of Egypt south of the Gaza region. (5) The Philistine cities of Gibbethon and Ekron may have been captured on this campaign. (6) Most important for Israelite history, Sargon II carried out the final disposition of Samaria.

The Assyrian Province of Samerina

The activity of Sargon II in Syria-Palestine during 720 B.C.E. brought an end to the northern kingdom of Israel. The territory ruled by Hoshea was incorporated into the Assyrian provincial system.

Deportation and Resettlement

The inscriptions of Sargon II provide us with a number of statements about the Assyrian treatment of Samaria (see Text IX). Several features of Assyrian administration and the treatment of rebellious states are reflected in these texts.

1. The city of Samaria was rebuilt; Sargon claims that it was better than it had been. The restoration of the capital city was part of the effort to return the area to economic and social health so that the population could "assume their social positions": that is, their normal life-styles and occupations.

2. The area was organized as a province with an appointed governor. Those living in the province were classified as Assyrian citizens and were required to contribute to the state treasury: that is, pay taxes. For Samaria the provincial assessment was the same as had been required of Hoshea as tribute. The Assyrian texts make no distinction between the native population that remained in the area and those resettled there, and probably there were no economic or social distinctions between the two groups. New settlers would, of course, have been provided with land and property, perhaps that of those who had been deported.

3. Segments of the surviving military were absorbed into the Assyrian army. Sargon II notes that he formed a contingent of fifty chariots (a variant version says two hundred) from Samaria, which then became a component in the Assyrian chariot corps.

4. A significant portion of the population was deported, along with the cultic symbols of the Israelite deity. One of the goals of deportation, in addition to punishment for rebellion, was to remove those in leadership and thus to lessen the likelihood of nationalistic uprisings in the future. A second goal was to supply populations for use in other areas of the empire. Deportees were utilized in various ways by the Assyrians—as settlers in sparsely populated areas, especially in depopulated urban centers and in rural areas needing agricultural improvements, as skilled workers in various crafts, and as general laborers throughout the empire. According to II Kings 17:6 (= 18:11), the Israelites were resettled "in Halah, and on the Habor, the river of Gozan, and in the cities of the Medes."

5. Foreign populations were resettled in Samaria. According to II Kings

TEXT IX. Sargon's Descriptions of the Capture and Resettlement of Samaria

I besieged and conquered Samaria, led away as booty 27,290 inhabitants of it. I formed from among them a contingent of 50 chariots and made the remaining population assume their social positions. I installed over them an officer of mine and imposed upon them the tribute of the former king. (*ANET* 284–85)

The town I rebuilt better than it was before and settled therein people from countries which I myself had conquered. I placed an officer of mine as governor over them and imposed upon them tribute as is customary for Assyrian citizens. (*ANET* 284)

Ia'ubidi from Hamath, a commoner without claim to the throne, a cursed Hittite, schemed to become king of Hamath, induced the cities Arvad, Simirra, Damascus and Samaria to desert me, made them collaborate and fitted out an army. I called up the masses of the soldiers of Ashur and besieged him and his warriors in Qarqar, his favorite city. I conquered it and burnt it. Himself I flayed; the rebels I killed in their cities and established again peace and harmony. (*ANET* 285)

[The man of Sa]maria, who with a king [hostile to] me had consorted not to do service and not to bring tribute—and they did battle: in the strength of the great gods, my lords I clashed with them, [2]7,280 people with their chariots and the gods they trust, as spoil I counted, 200 chariots (as) my royal muster I mustered from among them. The rest of them I caused to take their dwelling in the midst of Assyria. The city of Samaria I restored, and greater than before I caused it to become. People of lands conquered by my two hands I brought within it; my officer as prefect over them I placed, and together with the people of Assyria I counted them. (*Iraq* 16 [1954], 180)

The tribes of Tamud, Ibadid, Marsimanu and Haiapa, distant Arabs, who inhabit the desert, who know neither high nor low officials, and who had not brought their tribute to any king—with the weapon of the god Assur, my lord, I struck them down [in 716 B.C.E.], the remnant of them I deported and settled them in Samaria. (*ARAB* II, §17; compare *ANET* 286)

17:24 (see 18:34), Samaria was resettled with people from Babylon (where the Assyrians had constant trouble with the Chaldeans), Cuthah (generally identified with Tell Ibrahaim northeast of Babylon), Avva (site unknown), Hamath (in northern Syria; it had been one of Sargon's primary objectives in his 720 B.C.E. campaign), and Sepharvaim (listed among the Syrian cities noted in II Kings 18:34 and 19:13; see Ezek. 47:16, where it is spelled Sibriam and located on the border between Damascus and Hamath). Samaria continued to be the recipient of new settlers for several years. After a campaign in 716 B.C.E. in which Sargon II received gifts from Egypt and Queen Samsi of Arabia, he settled "distant Arabs" in Samaria. Further transfer of population may have occurred in the region after 712 B.C.E., when Sargon II had to campaign against Ashdod, where a usurper had seized the throne and was attempting to stir up rebellion in the surrounding kingdoms. According to Ezra 4:2, 10, Samaria received further settlers as late as the reigns of Esarhaddon (680–669 B.C.E.) and Ashurbanipal (668–627 B.C.E.). (Osnapper is generally identified with Ashurbanipal, since it was he who captured Susa/Elam in 646 B.C.E.)

Of Lions and Priests

II Kings 17:7–41 contains a judgmental, editorial explanation of why the northern kingdom fell (vs. 7–23, 34b–40) and a narrative describing conditions after the settlement of foreigners in the region (vs. 24–34a, 41). The theological explanation of Israel's downfall blames the people for apostasy and for failure to pay heed to the prophets. The narrative describing conditions in the province after resettlement is characterized by folkloristic features: all the native people were carried away, the newcomers were plagued with fierce animals (lions) because they did not know the law of the god of the land, and a single priest was returned to teach the citizens of the province and thus ward off the attacks of lions. (On lions as instruments of judgment, see I Kings 13:24–28; 20:36.) Such features in the narrative obviously cannot be the basis for historical reconstruction. What does seem to have been characteristic of the religious situation in Samerina are the following:

1. It should not be assumed that either Yahwism, the priesthood, or cultic places for the worship of Yahweh disappeared from the north. The Yahwistic temple in Samaria almost certainly would have been destroyed but could have been rebuilt. The sanctuary places south of Samaria, such as Bethel, Mizpah, and Gilgal, may have been little disturbed by the campaigns of Shalmaneser V and Sargon II, which centered on the capital city. The sanctuary at Bethel, later destroyed by Josiah, had presumably continued in use throughout the eighth and seventh centuries (II Kings 23:15).

2. The new settlers brought their own gods, religious traditions, and customs to their new home. At the same time they would have joined, at least to some extent, in the worship of Yahweh, the god of the land in which they now lived. Also, in such an Assyrian province as Samerina, official Assyrian religion certainly would have been given a prominent role.

3. Some of the northern population may have fled south to avoid deportation. Many northern traditions may have been brought south also, eventually to find their way into the Hebrew Scriptures. Among such traditions may have been some form of the royal annals and prophetical narratives such as the Elijah and Elisha stories.

CHAPTER 11

The Era of Assyrian Domination:
Judean History from Ahaz to Amon

For well over a century Judean life and politics were inexorably intertwined with those of Assyria. In 734 B.C.E. or shortly thereafter, Ahaz paid tribute to Tiglath-pileser III and from then until the decline of Assyria in the last quarter of the seventh century, Judah existed as one among many small powers dominated by Assyria. Unlike Israel, Judah seems to have offered no major resistance to Assyria during the reigns of Tiglath-pileser III (744–727 B.C.E.), Shalmaneser V (727–722 B.C.E.), and Sargon II (722–705 B.C.E.). For a time, during the early years of Sennacherib (705–681 B.C.E.), the aggressive Judean king Hezekiah participated in a widespread revolt against Assyrian rule. The revolt, although well planned, was quickly suppressed in Syria-Palestine by Assyria (in 701 B.C.E.). The failure of Hezekiah's rebellion inaugurated a long period of Judean submission and vassaldom to Assyria during the lengthy reign of Manasseh (697–642 B.C.E.) and his successors.

Throughout this period, extending from the final decades of the eighth century to the final decades of the seventh century, the relationship between Assyria and Egypt was highly significant for all of southern Syria-Palestine, including the state of Judah. Three dynasties, the Twenty-third, Twenty-fourth, and Twenty-fifth, struggled for control of Egypt during this period. The Twenty-fifth (Ethiopian, or Nubian) Dynasty eventually came to prominence. A non-native family whose primary support was in Upper Egypt, the Twenty-fifth Dynasty sought to compete with Assyria for control of the commerce on the Eastern Mediterranean Seaboard and therefore for influence over the southern Syro-Palestinian states. Thus the period of ascendancy for this dynasty, which was finally broken in 664/3 B.C.E., was a time of conflict between Assyria and Egypt. With the rise of the Twenty-sixth Dynasty to prominence, after 663 B.C.E., friendly and cooperative relationships developed between Egypt and Assyria and eventually produced their shared control of the states of southern Syria-Palestine. Accordingly Judean politics came to be dominated by this Assyrian-Egyptian alliance.

The biblical material for the reigns of the Judean kings of this period—Ahaz, Hezekiah, Manasseh, and Amon—is rather extensive although beset by numerous problems for interpreters. II Kings 16–21 (paralleled by Isa. 36–39) and II Chronicles 28–33 contain the biblical narratives about this period. In addition to these sources, much of the material in Isaiah 1–35 originated during the reigns of Ahaz and Hezekiah. Isaiah, whose career spanned the reigns of Uzziah, Jotham, Ahaz, and Hezekiah (Isa. 1:1), was significantly involved in Judean politics. Thus the material in Isaiah 1–35 that can be related to events and conditions during the prophet's career provides useful information for the historian.

The presentation of the material on Ahaz, Hezekiah, and Manasseh in Kings is strongly influenced by an editorial scheme in which the reign of a bad king is made to alternate with that of a good king. The rulers are represented as the epitome of either evil (Ahaz and Manasseh; see II Kings 16:2b–4 and 21:2, 9) or good (Hezekiah and, later, Josiah; see II Kings 18:3–5; 22:2; 23:2–5). This rigid pattern probably has affected not only the method of depicting the monarchs but also what has been told about them. Anything good known about Ahaz and Manasseh would have been omitted by the editors and anything bad about Hezekiah omitted or toned down. In the case of both the good and the bad rulers, the editors have presented us with idealized portraits. The nature of the particular biblical traditions about Ahaz, Hezekiah, and Manasseh will require more detailed comment when we discuss their individual reigns.

During the reigns of Ahaz, Hezekiah, Manasseh, and Amon in Judah, the Assyrian empire was ruled over by six kings—Tiglath-pileser III, Shalmaneser V, Sargon II, Sennacherib, Esarhaddon, and Ashurbanipal. As was noted in Chapter 10, we possess historical inscriptions from all of these rulers except Shalmaneser V. The inscriptions of Tiglath-pileser, while abundant, are very fragmentary. Those of Sargon II and Sennacherib provide a reasonably full depiction of their reigns in chronological order. The inscriptional material for Esarhaddon and Ashurbanipal is abundant, but the inscriptions of Esarhaddon do not present the events of his reign chronologically, while those of Ashurbanipal, in addition to not always following a chronological scheme, were edited and re-edited on several occasions. In spite of these problems, the Assyrian records augment greatly the biblical materials and are especially important for providing background information on the lengthy rule of Manasseh.

Egyptian involvement in Syro-Palestinian affairs during the last centuries of the Davidic kingdom is noted not only in Akkadian and Egyptian sources from ancient times but also in the works of Herodotus and other authors from the classical period.

Ahaz (Jehoahaz I)

According to II Kings 16:2, Ahaz, or Jehoahaz as his full name is indicated in one of Tiglath-pileser III's inscriptions (*ANET* 282), was the son of King Jotham. He is said to have succeeded to the throne at the age of twenty. (Ahaz is one of only two Judean kings whose mother's name is not given in the regnal formulations, the other being Jehoram [see II Kings 8:17]). The mother of

Hezekiah and the wife of Ahaz was Abi the "daughter of Zechariah" (II Kings 18:2), who may have been the Israelite king of this name. If so, then this would be another case of intermarriage between the two kingdoms and could partially explain why Ahaz is said to have "walked in the way of the kings of Israel" (II Kings 16:3).

According to our chronology, which relies heavily on the regnal periods given in the biblical text for the period following Jotham's death, Ahaz' sixteen-year reign would have begun about 742 B.C.E. and ended about 727 B.C.E. In any case, he was on the Judean throne during the crisis with Assyria in 734–732 B.C.E. precipitated by Rezin and his supporters. The biblical descriptions of Ahaz' reign (II Kings 16; II Chron. 28; Isa. 7:1–8:15) focus on the events associated with this crisis. Before we discuss what can be known about his rule, a further word is in order about the biblical sources related to his reign.

Ahaz as Depicted in the Biblical Sources

II Kings 16, after the introductory formalities, begins its presentation of Ahaz with an enumeration of his evil deeds (vs. 2–4). This is followed by a statement regarding his troubles (vs. 5–6). According to vs. 7–9, Ahaz secured the help of Tiglath-pileser by sending him a bribe. The Assyrian king responded by attacking Damascus, carrying away its people, and killing Rezin. More lengthy coverage is given to Ahaz' visit to meet Tiglath-pileser in Damascus where he saw an altar, a copy of which was set up in the Jerusalem Temple (vs. 10–16). Further alterations in the Temple are noted (vs. 17–18) before the conclusion of his reign (vs. 19–20).

II Chronicles 28 makes Ahaz into an even more villainous ruler (vs. 1–4) punished by Yahweh who gives him into the hand of Syrians and Israelites (vs. 5–7). The latter are reported to have carried away 200,000 Judeans but were convinced, by prophetic intervention, to return them (vs. 8–15). Ahaz is said to have sent to Tiglath-pileser for help against the Edomites and the Philistines, although even the Assyrian king ended up oppressing Ahaz (vs. 16–21). The chapter concludes with a denunciation of Ahaz, reporting his worship of Syrian gods, alteration of Temple features, and establishment of altars throughout the city (vs. 22–25).

In Isa. 7:1–8:15, the focus is on the prophet's advice and encouragement given to Ahaz, the house of David, and Jerusalem in the context of the Syrian-Israelite move to involve Judah in the anti-Assyrian coalition and to replace Ahaz on the throne. The advice offered by the prophet makes no mention of any appeal to Assyria by Ahaz.

Ahaz and the Syro-Ephraimite Crisis

During Ahaz' reign, Judah was hard pressed on all sides by Rezin and his supporters in the anti-Assyrian coalition. (1) Rezin and Pekah seem to have encroached already on Judean territory even before Ahaz became king, as we noted in Chapter 10 (see II Kings 15:37). (2) The Edomites expanded in the Arabah and the Negeb and occupied the seaport city of Elath, apparently with Rezin's help (II Kings 16:6; II Chron. 28:16). (3) The Philistines made raids on the Shephelah and the Negeb, taking "Beth-shemesh, Aijalon, Gederoth, Soco with its villages, Timnah with its villages, and Gimzo with its villages; and they settled there" (II Chron. 28:18).

In addition to these external pressures, Ahaz ruled over a state in which much of the population favored joining the anti-Assyrian coalition. Encouraged by the prophet Isaiah, and supported apparently by the people of Jerusalem, Ahaz opposed such a move, although the Isaiah traditions indicate that he had doubts about whether joining or abstaining from the coalition was the better decision. The possible threat of internal action by his own subjects to remove him from the throne as they had earlier toppled Athaliah must have caused him enormous unease.

The external threats and internal distress of Ahaz' kingdom reached their climax in the move which Rezin and Pekah made against Jerusalem. Shortly after Pekah occupied the Israelite throne in Samaria, he and Rezin marched against Jerusalem when Ahaz continued his refusal to join their anti-Assyrian escapade. Their intent was to depose the uncooperative king and replace him with the unnamed son of Tabeel (Isa. 7:6), apparently a member of the royal house ruling in Tyre, a son or relative of King Tubail (= Tabeel). Since Tyre was one of the strong supporters of the anti-Assyrian coalition, the new ruler would have brought Judah into the group. The enthronement of this son of Tabeel would have involved not only the removal of Ahaz from power but also the slaughter of himself and his family. The consequences of being a deposed ruler were no doubt vivid to Ahaz, since the family of Menahem/Pekahiah had been removed by Pekah only a short time earlier. As we noted in Chapter 10, an incidental reference in the Chronicler's history (see II Chron. 28:7) suggests that an unsuccessful effort was made to assassinate Ahaz either before or during the Syro-Ephraimitic crisis. In fact, not only Ahaz' life but also the lives of the entire reigning line of David would have been at stake. This explains why the "house of David" was so involved in the Syro-Ephraimitic affair: "When the house of David was told, 'Syria is in league with Ephraim,' its heart and its people shook as the trees of the forest shake" (Isa. 7:2; see Isa. 7:13, 17). The prophet Isaiah in offering encouragement to Ahaz in following his independent path did so by assuring him that, if the king acted in faith and relied upon Yahweh, the still unborn son of the royal family could function as a sign (see II Kings 15:16 for reference to Menahem's slaughter of pregnant women). The child would not be threatened or slaughtered; in fact, the prophet promised, while the child was still in its infancy, the lands of Ephraim and Syria would be devastated (Isa. 7:10–16).

Many, if not the majority, within Judah itself supported participation with Rezin and Pekah in the anti-Assyrian movement. This would suggest that the general Judean population had no do-or-die commitment to the Davidic dynasty. Judean support for the anti-Assyrian alliance and thus lack of support for Ahaz are suggested in some of Isaiah's preaching:

> Yahweh spoke to me again: "Because this people have refused the waters of Shiloah that flow gently, and rejoice in Rezin and the son of Remaliah [Pekah]; therefore, behold, Yahweh is bringing up against them the waters of the River [Euphrates], mighty and many, the king of Assyria and all his glory." (Isa. 8:5–7; the final phrase is probably an editorial gloss)

The cities denounced by the prophet Micah in the first chapter of his book were probably towns in the prophet's neighborhood that opposed Ahaz' stand and that favored joining the anti-Assyrian coalition. Possibly many, both Judeans and Israelites, were accusing Ahaz of conspiracy and treason against Israel, since Pekah probably still considered himself Judah's overlord. Ahaz' failure to support Israelite state policy and the anti-Assyrian coalition could have been seen as conspiracy (see Isa. 8:11–15).

The prophet Isaiah advised Ahaz and Jerusalem not to panic in the light of the Syro-Ephraimitic threat, promising that the fire produced by Pekah and Rezin would be quickly extinguished by Assyria (Isa. 7:3–17; 8:1–4). The prophet thus recommended that Ahaz stay out of the Syrian-Assyrian fracas and, with faith in Yahweh to preserve his chosen (the Davidic) dynasty, merely defend Jerusalem against Syria and Israel, allowing Assyria to handle matters on its own. (Isaiah, as we noted earlier, does not mention payment to secure Assyria's aid as an option for Ahaz.) In fact, he seems to have promised Ahaz that if he followed an independent policy and allowed the Assyrians to handle Israel and Syria without joining their coalition, then Ahaz and the Davidic house would stand a chance of regaining the old territory of Israel and restoring the glorious state of the two kingdoms under Davidic rule (see Isa. 7:17; the last phrase "the king of Assyria" is a later interpretative addition).

Israelite and Syrian forces moved south (Isa. 10:27b–32?) and surrounded Jerusalem, laying the city under siege (II Kings 16:5). If the Judean population at large favored joining Rezin and Pekah, these two kings and their forces may have moved to Jerusalem reasonably unmolested (note that II Kings 16:5 speaks only about waging war on Jerusalem). The Chronicler, in dramatic and theological fashion, describes the encounter as a major war (II Chron. 28:5–15). The figures and descriptions, however, are suspect: Pekah slew 120,000 Judeans in one day, and the Israelites took 200,000 Judeans captive and brought them to Samaria (II Chron. 28:6, 8). That some looting occurred and some captives were taken back to Samaria would be the minimum that one would surmise.

Ahaz' unwillingness to capitulate to Syria and Israel must have been supported by the citizens of Jerusalem and whatever personal forces the king commanded. For him, the appearance of Tiglath-pileser III in Syria-Palestine in 734 B.C.E. must have been a godsend. Ahaz probably voluntarily offered submission to Tiglath-pileser III on the first available occasion. II Kings 16:7–9 reports on Ahaz' delivery of tribute to the Assyrian ruler put together by taking the gold and silver found in the Temple and the royal treasury.

Several factors suggest that Ahaz actually sent his gift to Tiglath-pileser III after the latter arrived in Philistia in 734 B.C.E. or perhaps even after the defeat of Damascus in 732 B.C.E., that is, Ahaz' payment was a response to the Assyrian presence in the area rather than vice versa. (1) Since Ahaz had never previously submitted personally to Assyrian overlordship, he was not a subject who could have expected help from the Assyrians. The Assyrian monarch was no international mercenary waiting to pick up a few shekels as payment for rescuing beleaguered states. (2) Judah was surrounded by members of the anti-Assyrian coalition and to have succeeded in sending an embassy carrying such a "present" destined for the Assyrian monarch through one of these nations seems highly unlikely. (3) Ahaz' gift is associated specifically with Tiglath-pileser's movement against Damascus which occurred in 733/2 B.C.E. (II Kings 16:9) rather than with the campaign against Philistia in 734 B.C.E. (which goes unmentioned in the Bible). (4) Tiglath-pileser III mentions Ahaz' contribution as if it was merely a routine presentation of tribute, not a special bribe (*ANET* 282; see II Chron. 28:20–21). The Assyrian king makes no reference to any special appeal from Ahaz. (5) We hear of no return of Judean territory seized, for example, by the Philistines, which might have been the case if Ahaz was treated by the Assyrians with any favoritism. (6) The wording of the Kings report of the sending of the gift (II Kings 16:7–8) uses terminology ("bribe" and the biblically unparalleled "your servant and your son") that would not have been used in official annals. The section is thus a literary construct of the biblical editors based on the knowledge that Ahaz paid tribute, but it is written so as to make Ahaz the villainous king who "invited" the Assyrian troubles.

Ahaz' Religious Practices

In addition to describing Ahaz' troubles with Rezin and Pekah, the compilers of Kings present Ahaz as an apostate king guilty of religious irregularities. How much of this is the product of theological bias remains uncertain; it should be noted that the prophet Isaiah nowhere condemns Ahaz for apostasy. The king is said to have sacrificed one of his sons (literally "made his son to pass through the fire"; II Kings 16:3), presumably to Yahweh, and to have introduced cultic and ritual innovations. Perhaps the sacrifice of his son was occasioned by the Syro-Ephraimitic siege of Jerusalem, and he took drastic action, as had Mesha the king of Moab under similar circumstances on an earlier occasion (II Kings 3:27).

According to II Kings 16:10–20, Ahaz introduced into the Temple a new altar copied after one that he had seen at Damascus when he went there to submit personally to Tiglath-pileser III. The reader is tempted to conclude, as the Kings account could suggest, that this was actually an Assyrian altar which had been installed in Damascus when the Assyrians took the city. Surely this would have been an odd time for Ahaz to be copying things Syrian. The most natural reading of the II Kings narrative, however, points to a Syrian altar. Moreover, the Chronicler clearly specifies that Ahaz worshiped Syrian gods and disassociates this aspect of his reign altogether from the Assyrian invasion (II Chron. 28:22–25). One could postulate from the Chronicler's account that Ahaz' borrowing from the Syrian cult occurred when Damascus was still enjoying success, before the Syro-Ephraimitic affair began, after which time he would hardly have been making trips to Damascus. The introduction of such an altar into the Temple seems not to have bothered the religious establishment. The priest Uriah, who supervised the construction of the new altar and cultic arrangements apparently without any protest (II Kings 16:10), is also known to have served as a witness to one of Isaiah's symbolic acts at the time of the Syro-Ephraimitic crisis (Isa. 8:2), that is, he appears to have been fully orthodox and Yahwistic.

Although there is evidence that the Assyrians sometimes required their vassals to practice Assyrian religion and thus, at least tacitly, to recognize the supremacy of the Assyrian gods over national deities, this does not seem to have been a factor in the case of Ahaz, since he was not an appointee of Tiglath-pileser III, and even after his submission to Assyria, Judah was a satellite state, not a vassal. One aspect of Ahaz' religious changes, however, is connected by the editors of Kings with Assyrian domination: "The covered way for the sabbath which had been built inside the palace, and the outer entrance for the king he removed from the house of Yahweh, because of the king of Assyria" (II Kings 16:18). What was at stake here is not clear and the text presents numerous problems. (The last phrase in the verse may simply be a late gloss.) It could be that these changes within the sacred precinct had nothing to do with cultic matters per se. Ahaz simply may have had to melt down the bronze these items contained in order to make his tribute payment to Assyria.

On the whole, to assume that Ahaz' cultic reforms and religious practices were significantly influenced by his position as an Assyrian subject would be misleading. Ahaz seems to have faced a desperate situation which persisted throughout his early reign. His kingdom, his life, and his family were all threatened. Texts frequently refer to his possible panic and distress (II Chron. 28:22; Isa. 7:4). Except for Amaziah's ill-conceived adventure (II Kings 14: 8–14), Ahaz' action may have been the first time a Judean king had dared to act independently of and contrary to Israelite policies since the days of Omri. In the midst of anti-Assyrian nations, for Ahaz to follow an independent policy was indeed an act of faith. Isaiah appears to have been a persistent counselor to the king, who generally seems to have listened to and followed the prophet's advice.

Hezekiah

Under Hezekiah, Ahaz' successor, Judah recovered to the extent that the country eventually became involved in at least one widespread rebellion against Assyria. Hezekiah's years were recalled as highly significant in the history of

Judah and he was remembered as one of only a few good kings. Few reigns in the history of Israel and Judah, however, present the historian with as many problems of interpretation and reconstruction as that of Hezekiah. The problems are related not only to the biblical glorification of the king and his reign but also to issues of a chronological and literary nature.

Hezekiah as Depicted in the Biblical Sources

The biblical narratives about Hezekiah are extensive. They include II Kings 18–20; II Chronicles 29–32; and Isaiah 36–39. The material in II Kings 18–20 may be divided into the following episodes and sections:

A. General summary and evaluation (II Kings 18:1–8).

B. Synchronism with Samaria's siege and capture (II Kings 18:9–12).

C. The invasion of Sennacherib, Hezekiah's capitulation, and payment of the penalty placed on him by the Assyrian king (II Kings 18:13–16).

D. The Assyrian Rabshakeh is sent by Sennacherib from Lachish with a large army to convince Jerusalem and Hezekiah to capitulate, but Hezekiah, after hearing of the speech about surrender, goes to the Temple to pray. Isaiah the prophet responds to the visit of Hezekiah's officials, assuring the king that he should not be afraid, since Sennacherib will hear a rumor and will return home, where he will be killed. The Rabshakeh returns to Sennacherib, who is now at Libnah. The Assyrian hears that Tirhakah, the king of Ethiopia, has set out to fight him (II Kings 18:17–19:9a).

E. Again messengers are sent to Hezekiah with a letter to convince him to capitulate, and again he goes to the Temple and again the prophet Isaiah responds, giving assurance to Hezekiah and delivering a speech against Sennacherib announcing his defeat and containing promises to Hezekiah that Jerusalem will be saved. The city is saved when 185,000 Assyrians are killed in the night by the angel of Yahweh (II Kings 19:9b–35).

F. Sennacherib departs, returns to Nineveh, and is killed by his sons (II Kings 19:36–37).

G. Hezekiah becomes ill but is promised fifteen additional years of rule by Isaiah, who treats the king's malady with a cake of figs (II Kings 20:1–11).

H. Hezekiah is visited by envoys of Merodach-baladan of Babylon who inspect Hezekiah's treasures and armory. Isaiah condemns Hezekiah for granting these visitors such privileges and announces that the possessions of the king and his sons shall be carried to exile in Babylon (II Kings 20:12–19).

I. Concluding summary (II Kings 20:20–21).

The material in the Book of Isaiah is similar, with the exception that the report in II Kings of Hezekiah's bribe of Sennacherib has no parallel in Isaiah and the thanksgiving prayer of Hezekiah in Isa. 38:9–20 has no parallel in II Kings.

As on other occasions, the Chronicler builds upon the material in Kings but deviates considerably. The following are the significant sections and episodes in the Chronicler's account found in II Chronicles 29–32:

A. Opening summary (II Chron. 29:1–2).

B. Hezekiah and the Levites carry out a major purification of the Temple and reinstitute proper worship (II Chron. 29:3–36).

C. Hezekiah holds a Passover in Jerusalem to which he invites all Israel from Beer-sheba to Dan, including the northern tribes, and some of the northerners attend (II Chron. 30).

D. Following the great Passover observance, the people move into the countryside and destroy the local shrines and cultic furniture (II Chron. 31:1).

E. Hezekiah regulates the various divisions of the priests and the Levites, and the people bring in many tithes and gifts, so that larger chambers have to be built to house them in the Temple (II Chron. 31:2–21).

F. After these reforming activities and the people's religious responses, Sennacherib invades Judah, but Hezekiah makes preparation, encourages the people, and responds to the demands of Sennacherib's messengers and the letters he sent. Hezekiah and Isaiah pray together and Yahweh sends an angel who kills the Assyrian mighty men. When Sennacherib returns home, he is killed by his sons (II Chron. 32:1–23).

G. Hezekiah becomes ill because of his pride. When he humbles himself, he and Jerusalem are spared (II Chron. 32:24–26).

H. A description of Hezekiah's wealth is followed by a cryptic reference to "the matter of the envoys of the princes of Babylon" (II Chron. 32: 27–31).

I. Concluding summary (II Chron. 32:32–33).

Noticeably, the account in II Chronicles focuses on Hezekiah's religious reforms (II Chron. 29:3–31:21) which II Kings notes explicitly only in its opening summary (II Kings 18:4). The Chronicler makes no reference to the fact that Hezekiah rebelled against Sennacherib (see II Kings 18:7b, 20) but merely states that the Assyrian king wanted to take over the cities of Judah, "thinking to win them for himself" (II Chron. 32:1). The Chronicler, like Isaiah, omits the account of Hezekiah's capitulation to Sennacherib (II Kings 18:13–16). At the same time, Hezekiah is presented as a courageous leader who encourages his people and keeps his faith, unlike the Hezekiah in II Kings who relies upon Isaiah for encouragement (compare II Chron. 32:6–8, 20 with II

Kings 19:1–2, 14). The Chronicler includes no speeches of Isaiah addressed either to Hezekiah (see II Kings 19:6–7, 20) or to Sennacherib (see II Kings 19:21–34) and no prayer of Hezekiah (see Isa. 38:9–20).

For the compilers of II Kings, Hezekiah's rule was a good reign sandwiched between those of two horrible monarchs. The compilers' verdict on Ahaz, strongly biased to fit their theological schematization, is harshly acrimonious: "He did not do what was right in the eyes of Yahweh his God, as his father David had done, but he walked in the way of the kings of Israel" (II Kings 16:2b–3a). Hezekiah's son, Manasseh, is described as even worse than his grandfather, for he "seduced them [the people] to do more evil than the nations had done whom Yahweh destroyed before the people of Israel" (II Kings 21:9). Both Ahaz and Manasseh are depicted in extremely negative terms in order to serve as villainous and apostate antiheroes against whom the heroes, Hezekiah and Josiah, can stand out more sharply. In contrast to his predecessor and successor, Hezekiah is depicted as the ideal king:

> He did what was right in the eyes of Yahweh, according to all that David his father had done. . . . He trusted in Yahweh the God of Israel; so that there was none like him among all the kings of Judah after him, nor among those who were before him. For he held fast to Yahweh; he did not depart from following him, but kept the commandments which Yahweh commanded Moses. And Yahweh was with him; wherever he went forth, he prospered. (II Kings 18:3, 5–7)

This idealization of Hezekiah, which was intensified in other biblical traditions (see Isa. 36–39; II Chron. 29–32) and in postbiblical interpretations, has, no doubt, greatly influenced not only what the compilers of the Kings materials recorded about Hezekiah but also how they have reported his reign.

What can be said regarding the biblical traditions about Hezekiah now that we have examined their contents? (1) In all of these accounts, religious concerns take precedence over political concerns. In II Kings and Isaiah, the focus is on the Assyrian threat to the sacred city of Jerusalem, the town's miraculous deliverance, and Yahweh's fidelity to his promises. In II Chronicles, the emphasis is on the religious reforms of Hezekiah. (2) II Kings and the Book of Isaiah stress the role of the prophet Isaiah in the crisis, whereas II Chronicles focuses on the person of Hezekiah. (3) Even within II Kings, there appear to be duplicate accounts of the episode of Jerusalem's miraculous deliverance. II Kings 18:17–19:9a + 19:36–37 tells one version of the story and II Kings 19:9b–35 another version. (4) The episode of Jerusalem's miraculous deliverance in spite of great odds has many folkloric characteristics, and its themes appear in an Egyptian story, itself highly legendary, that also deals with the invasion of Sennacherib. In his history the Greek historian Herodotus (II.141) tells a version that he learned in Egypt. The story reported that when Sennacherib, the "king of the Arabians and Assyrians," marched against Egypt, the Egyptian ruler had no support from his military, since he had recently deprived the soldiers of their traditional land grants. In his predicament the ruler went to a temple, where he bewailed the potential calamities confronting him. While lamenting, he fell asleep and received a divine vision promising that the god would let the king suffer nothing disagreeable from the attack but would send messengers to aid him. Awaking, he gathered what followers he could and set out for Pelusium on the northern Egyptian border. When they arrived there, a horde of field mice invaded Sennacherib's camp and devoured the Assyrian forces' quivers and bows and the handles of their shields. On the morning of battle the Assyrians discovered that they were bereft of arms and many were slain. Herodotus reports that the salvation of the Egyptian ruler was commemorated by a statue of the king with a mouse in his hand and an inscription saying, "Whoever looks on me, let him revere the gods." The similarity of this legend to the biblical story or stories of the deliverance of Hezekiah and Jerusalem is obvious and raises problems for any interpretation that would accept all the details of the biblical account at face value, especially those about an extraordinary deliverance. (5) The account of the visit of Merodach-baladan's envoys to Jerusalem, in its present form and place in the text of II Kings, functions to prepare the reader for the coming narrative on the fall of Jerusalem and the Judean exile. The story has thus been shaped in the exilic period or later. The episode with which this story about the Babylonian envoys is concerned probably occurred in Hezekiah's career before his revolt against Sennacherib.

Chronological Difficulties

Both the beginning and the end of Hezekiah's reign as well as the synchronisms between his reign and those of Israelite and Assyrian kings present unusual chronological problems. His first year is correlated with the third year of Hoshea (II Kings 18:1), his fourth year with the beginning of the siege of Samaria by Shalmaneser V, and his sixth year with the fall of the city (II Kings 18:9–10), while his fourteenth year is correlated with Sennacherib's invasion (II Kings 18:13). Since Samaria fell in 722 B.C.E., or in the following year at the latest, and Sennacherib's invasion of Judah occurred in 701 B.C.E., we are given the following impossible synchronisms for Hezekiah's reign: his sixth year = 722 B.C.E., and his fourteenth year = 701 B.C.E. The chronology that we propose, which assigns his rule to 727–698 B.C.E., is based on the twenty-nine years assigned him in the notation on regnal years (II Kings 18:2) and calculated by moving backward from the certain date of the first Babylonian capture of Jerusalem (16 March 597 B.C.E.).

Hezekiah is said to have been twenty-five years old when he began his reign, although his father Ahaz is reported to have died at the age of thirty-six (II Kings 16:2; 18:2). To believe that Ahaz fathered a child at the age of eleven is a bit difficult. Undoubtedly some figures are wrong and we earlier (see above, p. 341) noted irregularities in the regnal statements about Ahaz. In addition, Hezekiah does not seem to have been Ahaz' oldest son. His father apparently sacrificed one of his sons (II Kings 16:3), and another was killed in the attempt to overthrow Ahaz (II Chron. 28:7). Though it is nowhere said that the king sacrificed his oldest son, this could be assumed, since to offer the firstborn rather than a younger son would have been a greater expression of religious devotion. This issue, in addition to the problem of the synchronisms, raises further doubt about the reliability of specific chronological references for Hezekiah.

In the narrative about Hezekiah's sickness (II Kings 20; Isa. 38), the king is promised an additional fifteen years of life (II Kings 20:6; Isa. 38:5). Since the narrative relates this episode to the time of Sennacherib's invasion, one would assume that Hezekiah should reign for fifteen years after 701 B.C.E. To extend his rule much beyond 700 B.C.E. is difficult, however, since it then would overlap with the regnal years assigned to Manasseh. Probably even the reference to Sennacherib's invasion in Hezekiah's fourteenth year in II Kings 18:13, which appears to be our firmest synchronism, should be disregarded. Since the "extension" of Hezekiah's life by fifteen years was assumed to have occurred in conjunction with Sennacherib's invasion and he ruled for twenty-nine years, the compilers logically assumed that Sennacherib's invasion occurred in his fourteenth year.

Sargon and Hezekiah

If the chronology proposed above for Hezekiah (727–698 B.C.E.) is correct, then Assyrian forces under Sargon campaigned in southern Syria-Palestine on three occasions during his reign. Sargon's campaign in 720 B.C.E., which we have noted formed the background for the creation of the Assyrian province of Samerina, had the purpose of subduing widespread rebellions in the western area of the empire which had broken out simultaneously with Merodach-baladan's uprising in Babylonia, supported by Elam (*ABC* 73–74). Assyrian opponents ranged throughout the area: Hamath, Damascus, and Arpad to the north of Judah and Gaza to the west. Whether Judah and Hezekiah became involved in any way in the rebellious western affairs cannot be determined. The only hint in presently known Assyrian texts which might suggest that Judah was involved is the single statement in a Sargon inscription, probably composed about 717 B.C.E., which refers to Sargon as "the subduer of the country Judah which is far away" (*ANET* 287). Such a reference may denote nothing more than that the state of Judah submitted to Sargon and continued as a satellite of Assyria, a condition dating from the days of Ahaz. The absence of any statements about Judah in Sargon's description of his 720 B.C.E. campaign suggests that if Judah participated in the revolts, it took a very secondary role, and that Hezekiah was quick to offer submission and pay the imposed tribute. A biblical text that might be related to a movement of Sargon against Jerusalem at the time is Isa. 10:27b–32, but even this is doubtful.

In 716 B.C.E., Sargon again campaigned near the Egyptian border. A gift of twelve big horses was received from "Shilkanni king of Egypt," perhaps Osorkon IV, the last ruler of the Delta-based Twenty-second Dynasty (*ANET* 286). Deportees were settled in the region of the city of the Brook of Egypt (Wady Besor) as part of an Assyrian military outpost and placed under the supervision of the sheikh of the city of Laban. The references in one of Sargon's fragmentary inscriptions (Nimrud Prism, Fragment D; see *Iraq* 16 [1954], 179) to his "opening the sealed harbor of Egypt" and his "mixing the Assyrians and Egyptians together" may denote actions taken in 716 B.C.E. to normalize relations in the area and stimulate trade between the two countries. The text would seem to suggest the establishment of a commercial center, perhaps for both land and sea trade, which was shared by Assyrians and Egyptians as an encouragement to trade between the two states. (Assyrian interest in Mediterranean commerce is further evidenced by the Assyrian dominance over Cyprus, which paid tribute to Sargon II in 709 B.C.E.; see *ANET* 284.) It was following this 716 B.C.E. campaign which also involved actions against several desert tribes that Arabs were resettled in Samaria. Again, there is no evidence of Hezekiah's participation in a revolt.

Judah's name appears in a Sargonic inscription describing Assyria's suppression of a revolt spearheaded by the Philistine city of Ashdod in 713–711 B.C.E. (*ANET* 286–87). Azuri, the reigning monarch in Ashdod, "schemed not to deliver tribute anymore and sent messages full of hostilities against Assyria to the kings living in his neighborhood." Sargon quickly deposed him and replaced him on the throne with Ahimiti, his younger brother, probably in 713 B.C.E. The latter was subsequently deposed by his subjects and replaced by a certain Yamani, who ceased the payment of tribute and attempted to stir up rebellion among neighboring cities and kingdoms. Sargon's inscription mentions some involvement by Judah, Edom, and Moab, but they appear to have been participants in the early planning stages of the rebellion and then to have withdrawn.

> Together with the rulers of Philistia, Judah, Edom, Moab and those who live on islands and bring tribute and *tamartu* gifts to my Lord Ashur—they [Ashdod and other Philistine cities] sent countless evil lies and unseemly speeches with their bribes to Pir'u, king of Egypt—a potentate, incapable to save them— to set him at enmity with me and asked him to be an ally. (*ANET* 287, modified)

This revolt led by Ashdod is the topic of Isaiah 20. According to this text, the prophet went about Jerusalem naked and barefoot for three years demonstrating his opposition to the revolt, but the account does not imply that Judah became seriously involved. The attempt to involve Egypt in the revolt is mentioned in both Isaiah 20 (note that the Ethiopians are particularly singled out) and Sargon's inscription. Appeals for assistance from Egypt, according to the Assyrian inscription, were made with requests and presents sent to "Pir'u of Egypt." This Pir'u (perhaps a title, the equivalent of "pharaoh") was one of the rulers vying for Egyptian hegemony. It may have been the Ethiopian (Nubian) ruler Shabako (716–702 B.C.E.) who appears to have invaded the Delta in 713 B.C.E. Ashdod may have based its revolt on expectations of help from this assertive Twenty-fifth (Ethiopian) Dynasty. The ringleader of the revolt, the usurper Yamani, fled to Egypt at the approach of the Assyrian army (in 712 B.C.E.) which was under the command of an Assyrian field marshal (the "tartan" or "commander in chief" of Isa. 20:1) rather than Sargon himself, who remained at home. The city of Ashdod was captured and an Assyrian victory stela set up to commemorate the conquest. The Egyptian leadership in the Delta refused aid to Yamani and he made his way south. Here he encountered the same reluctance of the rulers to involve themselves. In fact, he was eventually returned in fetters to the Assyrian monarch, apparently by Shabako, who at this stage was unwilling to oppose Assyria. Sargon says that he turned Ashdod into a province (*ANET* 286). What may have been involved was the appointment of an official Assyrian commissioner to function alongside the local vassal king who is mentioned later. Ashdod seems to have been joined in its revolt by other Philistine rulers. The depiction of the capture of Ekron and Gibbethon on a wall relief in Sargon's palace at Khorsabad may reflect events on this same campaign rather than an earlier one and thus the involvement of other Philistine cities in addition to Ashdod, Gath, and Asdudimmu noted in Sargonic texts.

With either the incorporation of Ashdod into the Assyrian provincial system or the appointment of a royal commissioner to function alongside the king, Judean territory was becoming more and more encircled by the representatives of Assyrian power and presence. To the north lay the province of Samerina, to the south were Arab groups as special Assyrian appointees as well as Assyrian military outposts on the border of Egypt, and now there was the establishment of a permanent presence to the immediate west in Ashdod.

Throughout the remainder of the reign of Sargon, no further Assyrian campaigns were conducted in Syria-Palestine. Peaceful conditions which prevailed between Assyria and Egypt, partially initiated by Sargon in 716 B.C.E. and furthered by continuing internal struggle for power within Egypt itself, brought political stability to Syria-Palestine for over a decade. The activities of the Assyrians in the region of Judah between 725 and 712 B.C.E., however, had probably impressed several lessons upon rulers such as Hezekiah. Among these must have been the recognition that unsuccessful revolts were costly enterprises, that unplanned, spur-of-the-moment rebellions were almost doomed from the beginning, and that help from Egypt could be counted upon only if that country possessed a stronger and better organized administration than had been the case with the Twenty-third and Twenty-fourth Dynasties.

Hezekiah's Revolt and Sennacherib's Invasion

Late in the eighth century, Sargon was confronted with major problems in the northeast. Renewed trouble with Urartu, led by Rusa I (about 733–714 B.C.E.), was suppressed when Sargon invaded the Urartian homeland. This was followed a few years later by an invasion of the barbarian Cimmerians at whose hands Sargon apparently fell in battle. The period following his death was the occasion for widespread revolt throughout the empire. In Syria-Palestine, Hezekiah was one of the prime movers behind rebellion.

Hezekiah's Preparations for Revolt. There are numerous indications both in the biblical traditions and in the archaeological evidence that Hezekiah had begun much earlier to mobilize his state and prepare for the revolt. Many of his preparations and programs may have been carried out in the years between Assyria's last western campaign in 712 B.C.E. and Sargon's death in 705 B.C.E.

Several biblical texts note the strengthening and reorganization of the Judean military: Hezekiah "made weapons and shields in abundance" (II Chron. 32:5); "he set combat commanders over the people" (II Chron. 32:6); he had "storehouses also for the yield of grain, wine, and oil; and stalls for all kinds of cattle, and sheepfolds" and "provided cities for himself" (II Chron. 32:28–29); he "built up all the wall [in Jerusalem] that was broken down, and raised towers upon it, and outside it he built another wall; and he strengthened the Millo in the city of David" (II Chron. 32:5); "he made the pool and the conduit and brought water into the city" (II Kings 20:20; see II Chron. 32:30; Isa. 22:11; Sirach 48:17); and "he planned with his officers and his mighty men to stop the water of the springs that were outside the city" (II Chron. 32:3). All of this activity, some of which may have been carried out before and some after the actual outbreak of rebellion, suggests a concerted effort to arm the nation, to prepare for war, and to plan for a siege of the capital city. (See Map 25.)

Archaeological evidence and nonbiblical texts support the picture of elaborate military planning and fortification by Hezekiah. Sennacherib's account of his campaign against Hezekiah, reported fully in two slightly different versions (see Text X), mentions taking forty-six strong and walled cities in Judah and that Hezekiah had not only regular but also irregular troops (national militia? foreign mercenaries?) under his command (*ANET* 288). The so-called Siloam tunnel in Jerusalem with its inscription describing the means of construction (*ANET* 321) can with reasonable certainty be ascribed to Hezekiah's preparations for the anticipated siege of Jerusalem. This tunnel carried the water from the spring Gihon under the old city of David (Ophel) to the western side of the mount. Hezekiah probably expanded the city westward by enclosing part of the western hill within the city's fortification (note the second wall mentioned in II Chron. 32:5), so that the main water reservoir was within the defensive perimeters of the city. On the basis of archaeological evidence, it has been speculated that there was a sizable increase in the population of Jerusalem during Hezekiah's reign, perhaps swelled by refugees from the north, although part of the increase may have occurred late in his reign after Assyrian reduction of his territory.

Special types of seal impressions on large storage jars have been unearthed at numerous Judean sites. The hundreds of examples discovered, almost totally at Judean sites, are of three types. Two of these show a four-winged scarab or beetlelike emblem, with one type slightly more stylized than the other. The third type shows a double-winged sun disk. All the impressions were made from a very limited number of no more than two dozens seals. Along with the impression of the winged emblem appears the Hebrew inscription *lmlk,* "of, to, or belonging to the king." In addition, one of four place-names occurs: Hebron, Socoh, Ziph, or *mmsht.* The jars on which these impressions appear are large four-handled storage jars. This artifactual evidence has been interpreted as

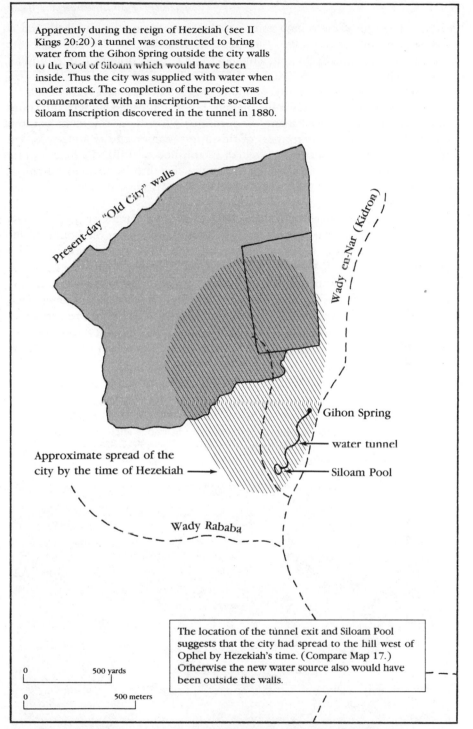

Apparently during the reign of Hezekiah (see II Kings 20:20) a tunnel was constructed to bring water from the Gihon Spring outside the city walls to the Pool of Siloam which would have been inside. Thus the city was supplied with water when under attack. The completion of the project was commemorated with an inscription—the so-called Siloam Inscription discovered in the tunnel in 1880.

Present-day "Old City" walls

Wady en-Nar (Kidron)

Gihon Spring

water tunnel

Approximate spread of the city by the time of Hezekiah

Siloam Pool

Wady Rababa

The location of the tunnel exit and Siloam Pool suggests that the city had spread to the hill west of Ophel by Hezekiah's time. (Compare Map 17.) Otherwise the new water source also would have been outside the walls.

0   500 yards

0   500 meters

MAP 25. Jerusalem at the Time of Hezekiah

follows. The use of these impressions was introduced under Hezekiah and is evidence for the administrative system used during his reign. The jars were part of a system of tax collection in kind and/or a royal storage program. The material collected in these containers was sent to four district centers for storage, redistribution, and administrative/military usage. These centers were Socoh for the Shephelah region, Ziph for the Negeb, Hebron for the southern hill country, and *mmsht* (= "government" = Jerusalem) for the northern Judean hill country. Assuming the correctness of this interpretation of the archaeological evidence, it demonstrates that Hezekiah established or utilized a highly organized administrative system oriented to the effective distribution and storage of goods for national usage. (Perhaps the Judean town lists in Josh. 15:21–62 come from and reflect the Judah of Hezekiah's day.)

In addition to Hezekiah's efforts to strengthen Judah's military preparedness and ability to withstand invasion and siege, he also carried out religious reforms related to his nationalistic ambitions. At what time Hezekiah instituted these reforms is uncertain; II Chron. 29:3 claims that he began reforms in the first month of his first year, but this seems highly unlikely. The account found in II Kings 18:4–6 supplies no date for and provides only a rather generalized account of Hezekiah's cultic reform. II Chronicles 29–31 gives the reform pride of place in what appears to be an idealized version emphasizing those elements and cultic groups (the Levites) with which the Chronicler was most in sympathy.

Royal Judean Stamp. The inscription reads *lmlk swkh* ("of [to, belonging to] the king, Socoh"). One of three different designs, the impression is stamped on a handle from a storage jar, which probably contained material gathered as part of Hezekiah's tax collection system or his program of military preparedness. Scientific analysis of the clay from hundreds of such inscribed jar handles indicate that they may have derived from a single manufacturing area. *(Israel Department of Antiquities and Museums)*

II Kings 18:4 reports that Hezekiah "removed the high places [local sanctuary places], and broke the pillars, and cut down the Asherah. And he broke in pieces the bronze serpent that Moses had made, for until those days the people of Israel had burned incense to it; it was called Nehushtan." This verse suggests that Hezekiah took actions to close Yahwistic places of worship outside Jerusalem and to remove some practices and artifacts from the Jerusalem Temple. The bronze serpent had played some role in previous Yahwistic practices. Numbers 21:6–9 with its reference to Moses' elevation of the bronze serpent in the wilderness seems to be a story justifying the use of such an image in Yahwism.

II Kings 18:22, placed on the lips of an Assyrian ambassador, makes the following reference to the cultic reforms of Hezekiah: "But if you say to me, 'We rely on Yahweh our God,' is it not he [Yahweh] whose high places and altars Hezekiah has removed, saying to Judah and to Jerusalem, 'You shall worship before this altar in Jerusalem'?" This description of Hezekiah's religious innovations clearly suggests a deliberate effort on the part of the Judean king to centralize worship in Jerusalem. Centralization of the cult would have been a drastic move, opposed by some, but intended to make the population dependent upon Jerusalem and thus upon Hezekiah and the capital city. By making the other cities religiously dependent upon the capital city, Hezekiah must have been seeking to tie their political and religious allegiance more firmly to himself, to the Davidic family which had almost been toppled at the time of his father, and to the state cause which he espoused. In addition, the religion of the state could be more adequately supervised and the capital city benefit from the economy associated with official religion.

II Chronicles 30:1 states that Hezekiah also sent letters throughout Ephraim and Manasseh inviting the population in these old Israelite territories now under Assyrian provincial administration to worship in Jerusalem. This move, idealistically reported in II Chron. 30:2–27, if historical, would have been an effort on Hezekiah's part to enlist in his cause the support of northern Yahwistic followers and at the same time an expression of his desire to restore the old kingdom under Davidic rule, an ideal no doubt fostered in many Yahwistic circles, given expression even by the prophet Isaiah himself (see Isa. 9:1–7), and now more theoretically possible since no native ruler reigned in the north. (A son of Hezekiah and future king, born about 710 B.C.E., was given the name Manasseh, a name with northern tribal associations.) Thus Hezekiah's religious and cultic innovations were part of his efforts to revive nationalistic inclinations and to rally the people to a nationalistic cause that would ultimately mean a clash with the Assyrians.

The final component in Hezekiah's plans for revolt and independence from Assyria was the coordination of his efforts with those of other rulers and the extension of his authority into territory of the noncooperating Philistine states. In Syria-Palestine, rebellion was supported by Luli king of Sidon; Sidqia, who had usurped the throne of Ashkelon; and the city of Ekron, which deposed its noncooperative king Padi and turned him over to Hezekiah. Judah moved to occupy the territory of the Philistine city of Gaza whose king, Sillibel, remained loyal to Assyria (II Kings 18:8; see I Chron. 4:39–43 which describes a movement of Judeans into this territory during the days of Hezekiah). In addition, Hezekiah may have seized and fortified the city of Gath. Judah at the time was undoubtedly the strongest power in southern Syria-Palestine.

In the east, Merodach-baladan had seized the throne of Babylon in 721 B.C.E. but had been forced by Sargon to flee to Elam in 710 B.C.E. when the latter assumed the Babylonian throne (*ABC* 75). Merodach-baladan, who had earlier sent envoys to Hezekiah (see II Kings 20:12–15), led a simultaneous revolt in southern Babylonia after 705 B.C.E. Major Anatolian provinces—Que, Til-Garimmu, Tabal, and Hilakku—rebelled as well, but we have no evidence that their action was overtly coordinated with the revolts in Syria-Palestine and southern Mesopotamia.

Egypt was a strong supporter, if not an instigator of the revolt. The Twenty-fifth (Ethiopian, or Nubian) Dynasty from Upper Egypt, having established a base of control in Lower Egypt and the Delta, was now in a position to act with concerted strength. How early the Twenty-fifth Dynasty became involved in the plans for rebellion cannot be determined, but Isaiah was strongly opposed to Judah's policy of negotiating with them for aid and to his country's reliance upon their promises.

> Woe to those who go down to Egypt for help
>   and rely on horses,
> who trust in chariots because they are many,
>   and in horsemen because they are very strong,
> but do not look to the Holy One of Israel
>   or consult Yahweh.
> And yet he is wise and brings disaster,
>   he does not call back his words,
> but will arise against the house of the evildoers,
>   and against the helpers of those who work iniquity.
> The Egyptians are men, and not God;
>   and their horses are flesh, and not spirit.
> When Yahweh stretches out his hand,
>   the helper will stumble, and he who is helped will fall,
>   and they will all perish together.
>
>   (Isa. 31:1–3)

Sennacherib's Invasion. On the basis of the Kings accounts and Sennacherib's inscriptions (*ANET* 287–88; *BASOR* 214 [1974], 26–28), the course of Hezekiah's encounter with the Assyrians and the campaign of Sennacherib can be reconstructed with some certainty (for the Assyrian account, see Text X; for Herodotus' account of the Egyptian version, see above, pp. 349–350). As we have noted, rebellion broke out in numerous regions following Sargon's death —in Anatolia, Babylonia, and Syria-Palestine. After Sennacherib had suppressed rebels led by Merodach-baladan in southern Mesopotamia (*ABC* 77), he turned his attention, in his third campaign, in 701 B.C.E., to the revolt in Syria-Palestine. The Assyrian monarch marched down the Phoenician coast into Philistia before he encountered any major opposition. Luli of Sidon had fled overseas and the cities under his influence submitted—Tyre, Akzib, Acco, and others. A new vassal king, Ethbaal, was installed on the throne in Sidon. Embassies of other kingdoms reaffirmed their loyalty. These included Arvad, Byblos, Ashdod, Ammon, Moab, and Edom. Garrisons of these vassal kingdoms were apparently required to accompany Sennacherib on his march southward.

Without mention of having captured the city of Ashkelon, Sennacherib claims to have taken prisoner and deported its king Sidqia and his family ("the gods of his father's house, himself, his wife, his sons, his daughters, his brothers, the seed of his father's house"). He replaced him on the throne with Sharruludari, the son of Rukibtu, the former ruler of the city. One suspects that Sidqia, who had been supported by the anti-Assyrian element of the population, was overthrown by his own subjects and turned over to Sennacherib once the cause had been assessed as hopeless.

Sennacherib then set out to reduce all the cities that had been under the influence of Sidqia—Beth-dagon, Joppa, Banai-Barqa, Azor—as well as those under the control of Hezekiah—Ekron, Eltekeh, Timnah, Lachish, Azekah, and others. Sennacherib claims eventually to have conquered forty-six strong walled cities that had been under Hezekiah's control.

Obviously Sennacherib intended eventually to conquer Jerusalem. While fighting against other Philistine and Judean strongholds, he sent forces and ambassadors to the Judean capital to propose that Hezekiah and the city capitulate. At Jerusalem, an earthwork was constructed around the city so that the Assyrian troops could molest people leaving the town. The Assyrian king could later speak of shutting up Hezekiah as "a prisoner in Jerusalem, his royal residence, like a bird in a cage" (*ANET* 288). The Rabshakeh, the official Assyrian spokesman, representing Sennacherib and probably utilizing Assyrian military intelligence reports, offered reasons why the Judean king and the city should surrender (II Kings 18:19–25; 19:9b–13). The text has the Assyrian diplomat develop a case based on five arguments. (1) Words and baseless confidence are no substitute for strategy and power. (2) Egypt, "that broken reed of a staff," cannot be leaned upon for support. (3) Hezekiah's Yahwism was ambivalent, since he had actually taken steps to suppress Yahwistic practices outside Jerusalem. (4) Jerusalem could not supply two thousand horsemen even if Assyria supplied the horses. (5) The Assyrian invasion of Judah had the sanction and word of Yahweh behind it. In the latter argument, there is probably a reference to the fact that the Assyrians had carried into exile the Yahwistic cult materials from Samaria (see the fourth item in Text IX, above) and thus could consult Yahweh and receive his word and/or a reference to the treaty ritual and oaths in which Hezekiah had participated in becoming a subject. Such treaties included curses and sanctions in the name of the subject's deity, so that the judgment of Yahweh was self-invoked upon Hezekiah should he not remain loyal to his Assyrian overlord. In addressing the city, the Rabshakeh proposed

TEXT X. Sennacherib's 701 Campaign to the West

In my third campaign I marched against Hatti. Luli, king of Sidon, whom the terror-inspiring glamor of my lordship had overwhelmed, fled far overseas and perished. The awe-inspiring splendor of the "Weapon" of Ashur, my lord, overwhelmed his strong cities such as Great Sidon, Little Sidon, Bit-Zitti, Zaribtu, Mahalliba, Ushu (i.e. the mainland settlement of Tyre), Akzib and Akko, all his fortress cities, walled and well provided with feed and water for his garrisons, and they bowed in submission to my feet. I installed Eth-ba'al upon the throne to be their king and imposed upon him tribute due to me as his overlord to be paid annually without interruption.

As to all the kings of Amurru—Menahem from Samsimuruna, Tuba'lu from Sidon, Abdili'ti from Arvad, Urumilki from Byblos, Mitinti from Ashdod, Buduili from Beth-Ammon, Kammusunadbi from Moab and Aiarammu from Edom, they brought sumptuous gifts and—fourfold—their heavy *tamartu*-presents to me and kissed my feet. Sidqia, however, king of Ashkelon, who did not bow to my yoke, I deported and sent to Assyria, his family-gods, himself, and his wife, his children, his brothers, all the male descendants of his family. I set Sharruludari, son of Rukibtu, their former king, over the inhabitants of Ashkelon and imposed upon him the payment of tribute and of *katru*-presents due to me as overlord—and he now pulls the straps of my yoke!

In the continuation of my campaign I besieged Beth-Dagon, Joppa, Banai-Barqa, Azuru, cities belonging to Sidqia who did not bow to my feet quickly enough; I conquered them and carried their spoils away. The officials, the patricians and the common people of Ekron—who had thrown Padi, their king, into fetters because he was loyal to his solemn oath sworn by the god Ashur, and had handed him over to Hezekiah, the Jew and he (Hezekiah) held him in prison, unlawfully, as if he (Padi) be an enemy—had become afraid and had called for help upon the kings of Egypt and the bowmen, the chariot-corps and the cavalry of the king of Ethiopia, an army beyond counting—and they actually had come to their assistance. In the plain of Eltekeh, their battle lines were drawn up against me and they sharpened their weapons. Upon a trust-inspiring oracle given by Ashur, my lord, I fought with them and inflicted a defeat upon them. In the mêlée of the battle, I personally captured alive the Egyptian charioteers with their princes and also the charioteers of the king of Ethiopia. I besieged Eltekeh and Timnah, conquered (them) and carried their spoils away. I assaulted Ekron and killed the officials and patricians who had committed the crime and hung their bodies on poles surrounding the city. The common citizens who were guilty of minor crimes, I considered prisoners of war. The rest of them, those who were not accused of crimes and misbehavior, I released. I made Padi, their king, come from Jerusalem and set him as their lord on the throne, imposing upon him the tribute due to me as overlord.

As to Hezekiah, the Jew, he did not submit to my yoke, I laid siege to 46 of his strong cities, walled forts and to the countless small villages in their vicinity, and conquered them by means of well-stamped earth-ramps, and battering-rams brought thus near to the walls combined with the attack by foot soldiers, using mines, breeches as well as sapper work. I drove out of them 200,150 people, young and old, male and female, horses, mules, donkeys, camels, big and small cattle beyond counting, and considered them booty. Himself I made a prisoner in Jerusalem, his royal residence, like a bird in a cage. I surrounded him with earthwork in order to molest those who were leaving his city's gate. His towns which I had plundered, I took away from his country and gave them over to Mitinti, king of Ashdod, Padi, king of Ekron, and Sillibel, king of Gaza. Thus I reduced his country, but I still increased the tribute and the *katru*-presents due to me as his overlord which I imposed later upon him beyond the former tribute, to be delivered annually. Hezekiah himself, whom the terror-inspiring splendor of my lordship had overwhelmed and whose irregular and elite troops which he had brought into Jerusalem, his royal residence, in order to strengthen it, had deserted him, did send me, later, to Nineveh, my lordly city, . . . (Oriental Institute Prism, *ANET* 287–88)

(In addition to the) 30 talents of gold, 800 talents of silver, there were gems (precious stones), antimony, jewels(?), great *sandu*-stones (carnelian?), ivory beds, house chairs of ivory, elephant's hides, ivory (elephant's tusks, teeth), maple, boxwood, colored woolen garments, garments of linen, violet and purple wool, vessels of copper, iron, bronze and lead, iron, chariots, shields, lances, armor, girdle daggers of iron, bows and arrows, spears, countless implements of war, together with his daughters, his palace women, his male and female musicians which he had them bring after me to Nineveh, my royal city. To pay tribute and to render servitude, he dispatched his messenger(s).

From the booty of those lands which I plundered, 10,000 bows, 10,000 shields I took therefrom and added them to my royal equipment. The rest, the heavy spoil of enemy captives, I divided like sheep among my whole camp (army) as well as my governors and the inhabitants of my large cities. (Rassam Cylinder, *ARAB* II, § 284)

---

that if Hezekiah was not willing to capitulate, then the population of the town should consider giving up the cause and turning over their king (II Kings 18:28–35), as had probably the people of Ashkelon.

With negotiations under way, and Isaiah offering encouragement to Hezekiah while denouncing the Assyrians and predicting that Jerusalem would not fall (II Kings 19:6–7, 20–34), an Egyptian army appeared on the scene. Sennacherib notes that the rebels had appealed to the kings of Egypt (apparently the native rulers in the Delta) and to the king of Ethiopia (apparently the ruling pharaoh of the Twenty-fifth Dynasty). At least one Egyptian force was dispatched, probably by the Ethiopian pharaoh, Shebitku (about 702–690 B.C.E.), under the command of Tirhakah (II Kings 19:9). Apparently both Egyptians and Ethiopians were involved in the battle. The Egyptian force clashed with the Assyrians near Eltekeh. Although Sennacherib claimed a great victory, the battle may have been far less than an overwhelming success and his victory less glorious than he claimed. He is rather vague about spoils taken and only reports that he "personally captured alive the Egyptian charioteers with their princes and also the charioteers of the king of Ethiopia" (*ANET* 287). Perhaps it was at this time or even before the battle that Hezekiah decided to capitulate, offer his confession, and make assurance of future loyalty. Padi, the king of Ekron, was released by Hezekiah and restored to his throne. With Hezekiah's capitulation, the Assyrian monarch imposed an indemnity on him.

Results and Aftermath of the Invasion. Before leaving Syria-Palestine, Sennacherib consolidated matters so as to preserve Assyrian interests in the area. The rulers in the rebellious kingdoms were replaced with loyal vassals. Ethbaal had been placed on the throne in Sidon, the usurper Sidqia was deported to Assyria and the son of a former ruler installed as a vassal, Padi was returned to Ekron, and Hezekiah was left on the Judean throne after agreeing that he had "done wrong" and was willing to bear whatever the king imposed on him (II Kings 18:14). That is, none of the kingdoms were transformed into Assyrian provinces as one would have expected. This was consistent with earlier Assyrian policy in which the seaport kingdoms and Judah along with Moab, Ammon, and Edom had been left as semi-independent kingdoms with kings from the ruling families or local populations. As we have seen, Assyria was always hesitant to take over directly the Phoenician and Philistine seaport kingdoms and probably saw Judah and the Transjordanian states as buffer kingdoms best left semi-independent. Hezekiah may have been left on the throne not only because he offered apologies, swore allegiance, and paid imposed fines and an increased tribute but also because there may have been no ready suitable candidate from his immediate family to take over the throne. His successor and son Manasseh, whose name given some few years earlier (about 710 B.C.E.) may reflect Hezekiah's territorial aspirations to take over the north, would have been a very young lad at the time.

Portions of Judean territory were removed from Hezekiah and given or returned to the Philistine rulers of Ashdod, Ekron, Gaza, and perhaps Ashkelon. Citizens were exiled; Sennacherib claims to have taken 200,150 persons as booty (*ANET* 288), but this figure seems highly exaggerated if it is understood as referring to persons actually deported. Sennacherib's inscriptions do note the dispersement of captives but do not stipulate their number (see above, Text X). The redistribution of territory and the possible assignment of portions of Hezekiah's territory to various Philistine rulers restored political equilibrium in the area, so that no ruler had a balance of power in his favor. Hezekiah paid three hundred talents of silver and thirty talents of gold as indemnity, according to the biblical text (II Kings 18:14), but even more according to the Assyrian texts.

Jerusalem's escape from Assyrian devastation was recalled in Hebrew tradition as a fulfillment of Isaiah's prophecy and was retold, like the Egyptian version of its battle with Sennacherib, in legendary form as a time of miraculous deliverance wrought by divine intervention. It may already have been celebrated as such by the Jerusalemites before the Assyrians had had time to disappear over the horizon. Before the dust of battle had settled, we seem to find the prophet Isaiah castigating the town's citizens for celebrating when, from the walls of Jerusalem, they could view the devastation that characterized western and southern Judah and the suburbs of Jerusalem.

> What do you mean that you have gone up,
>   all of you, to the housetops,
> you who are full of shoutings,
>   tumultuous city, exultant town?
> Your slain are not slain with the sword
>   or dead in battle.
> All your rulers have fled together,
>   without the bow they were captured.
> All of you who were found were captured,
>   though they had fled far away.
> Therefore I said:
> "Look away from me,
>   let me weep bitter tears;
> do not labor to comfort me
>   for the destruction of the daughter of my people."
>
> (Isa. 22:1–4)

> Your country lies desolate,
>   your cities are burned with fire;
> in your very presence
>   aliens devour your land;
>   it is desolate, as overthrown by aliens.
> And the daughter of Zion is left
>   like a booth in a vineyard,
> like a lodge in a cucumber field,
>   like a besieged city.
> If Yahweh of hosts
>   had not left us a few survivors,
> we should have been like Sodom,
> and become like Gomorrah.
>
> (Isa. 1:7–9)

Manasseh

The son of Hezekiah, Manasseh (697–642 B.C.E.), became king at the age of twelve and enjoyed the longest reign—fifty-five years—of any king in the history of Israel and Judah. Assuming the essential accuracy of the regnal periods recorded for the Judean kings of this period, Hezekiah would have died at the age of about fifty-four, only a few years after resubmitting to Assyrian vassalage. That Hezekiah was already forty-two years old when his successor was born seems a most unusual phenomenon. Whether Manasseh was the oldest or only (or the only surviving) son of Hezekiah (see II Kings 20:18), or whether Assyrian pressure was applied to bypass older sons because of previous or possible involvement in the recent rebellion, or whether he was chosen because he was considered to be a "safe" heir by the pro-Assyrian party in Judah cannot be determined. At any rate, his case is unusual.

The youthful Manasseh inherited a reduced and war-torn Judean state. Evidence from Assyrian inscriptions, archaeological data, and some indications in the biblical traditions provide a partial picture of the conditions he inherited (see above, Text X). (1) Sennacherib reports that he had conquered forty-six cities controlled by Hezekiah as well as countless small villages. Even if one allows for some Assyrian exaggeration and assumes that some of these cities were Philistine towns that Hezekiah had occupied temporarily, the devastation in western and southwestern Judah must have been enormous (see Isa. 1:4–9). (2) Sennacherib claims that 200,150 people in Hezekiah's kingdom were counted as Assyrian booty. This figure appears to be an exaggeration even if one assumes that the reference is to the total head count of the cities and villages that Sennacherib captured rather than to the actual deportees. No claim is made that all of these people were taken into exile or deported, but the population drain on the state must have been great. (3) Portions of Judean territory were removed from Hezekiah's control and turned over to the several Philistine kings. This must not only have disrupted the population in these areas, creating numerous refugees, but also have reduced state resources and income. (4) The tribute assigned to Hezekiah and increased as a consequence of the rebellion was a great economic burden for the impoverished state.

Little is known about the course of historical events in Judah during the more than half century that Manasseh ruled. The editors of the biblical traditions in Kings were content primarily to theologize about his reign. II Kings 21:1–18 provides only the bare minimum of facts—age at accession, length of reign, mother's name (v. 1)—and then begins to tick off in staccato fashion all his apostate ways (vs. 2–9), following this with a theologizing tirade—which begins with a condemnatory *because*—blaming the fall of Jerusalem and the end of Judah on his reign (vs. 10–15). One last swipe is taken in the description of his shedding innocent blood (v. 16) before he is laid to rest with the typical biblical formula for concluding the account of a king's reign (vs. 17–18). Since the compilers of the material laid on him the blame for the ultimate fall of Jerusalem, they could say nothing good about his reign.

The Chronicler's account differs somewhat. Beginning with a restatement of the material in Kings (II Chron. 33:1–9), the Chronicler reports that Manasseh was taken by the Assyrians to Babylon, from where he was released after praying to Yahweh for forgiveness. He subsequently became a religious reformer (vs.

9–10, 15–17). In addition, the Chronicler notes that the king carried out certain building and military projects (v. 16). Since the Chronicler has Manasseh repent, Judah's fall could not be blamed on him. The Chronicler seems to have found it unbelievable that a Judean king could be blessed with the longest reign in the state's history without being or becoming a crusading Yahwist.

Judah during the reign of Manasseh played no consequential role in international affairs. Although Manasseh's reign overlapped the reigns of three Assyrian kings, his name makes an appearance in their inscriptions only in lists. Such scarcity of nonbiblical data about him parallels the paucity of biblically supplied information. This lack of data means that to understand Manasseh's reign at all we must look at the larger history of the period and note where Manasseh is mentioned in nonbiblical texts and where Judean life impinged on that of the larger Assyrian world.

Pax Assyriaca

Three factors about Assyrian history during the period are noteworthy and form the backdrop for understanding Judean history. (1) During Manasseh's reign, Assyrian power was at its apogee. Compared with the eighth century, the first three quarters of the seventh century under the Pax Assyriaca were rather tranquil times in the Middle East. This does not mean that Assyria enjoyed an era completely free from troubles. It certainly did not. In the northwest, Anatolian regions were rebellious; in the east and southeast, Babylon, Elam, and the Arabs were constant troublemakers; and in the west and southwest, the Phoenician and Philistine states and the Ethiopian rulers of Egypt had to be dealt with. (2) During the seventh century, Assyria increasingly sought to control maritime commerce along the Eastern Mediterranean Seaboard. In many ways, this intensified Assyrian interest in and domination of the area. (3) Assyria was particularly involved with Egypt throughout this period, although the relationship between the two kingdoms varied from hostility during the time of the Twenty-fifth Dynasty when Egypt was controlled by Ethiopian rulers to friendship and mutual support after the Assyrian-backed native Egyptian Twenty-sixth Dynasty came to dominance.

The early years of Manasseh's rule apparently witnessed no renewed campaign of the Assyrian king Sennacherib into the Syro-Palestinian area. Sennacherib was involved for years with rebellions in Anatolia, Elam, and Babylon. Only in 696 B.C.E. was Sennacherib able to move against rebellious Anatolian provinces. Further campaigns in this area occurred after 689 B.C.E. Troubles with Babylonia finally culminated in Sennacherib's vicious destruction of the city of Babylon in 689 B.C.E. A single fragmentary inscription from his reign speaks of an Assyrian campaign against certain Arab rulers, but neither their location nor the nature of the trouble is clear. Sennacherib's rule came to an end when, according to the Babylonian Chronicles (*ABC* 81), he was killed by one of his sons in a rebellion (see II Kings 19:36–37). The short-lived fraternal civil war in Assyria which followed Sennacherib's murder was speedily squelched by the crown prince Esarhaddon apparently without any major repercussions throughout the empire.

Esarhaddon (680–669 B.C.E.) moved quickly to display his authority and Assyrian might in the west. The Ethiopian leaders in Egypt must actually have been, or were suspected of, stirring up trouble in Syria-Palestine. In 679 B.C.E., Esarhaddon plundered the city of Arsa on the Egyptian border, deporting its ruler Ashuli, who, along with his advisers, was displayed like a caged animal in Nineveh, the Assyrian capital (*ANET* 290). This expedition would have had two purposes. First, it reaffirmed Assyrian control over the Eastern Mediterranean Seaboard as far as the Brook of Egypt, which the Assyrians had claimed since Tiglath-pileser III had set up a victory stela there in 734 B.C.E. Second, it was a warning to the leaders of the Ethiopian dynasty to keep hands off Syria-Palestine and to confine itself to its borders. Egypt at the time was under the control of the aggressive Ethiopian king, Tirhakah (690–664 B.C.E.), who had participated, but apparently not as pharaoh, in the battle of Eltekeh in 701 B.C.E. (II Kings 19:9). Tirhakah may already have been intervening in Syro-Palestinian matters during the last years of Sennacherib.

Esarhaddon's show of force on the Egyptian border was followed by other actions which asserted Assyrian dominance in the eastern Mediterranean. Assyrian suzerainty over Cyprus was reestablished or reaffirmed (*ANET* 291). Campaigns were conducted against the Phoenician cities of Sidon and Tyre (*ANET* 290–91). Abdimilkutte the king of Sidon, along with his ally Sanduarri king of Kundi, was captured, decapitated, and his head paraded in triumph in Nineveh. His family, possessions, and many of his subjects were deported. In the vicinity of Sidon, Kar-Esarhaddon ("Port of Esarhaddon") was constructed as a commercial and administrative center, with an Assyrian commissioner appointed to oversee the region. Esarhaddon reports that he "called together all the kings of the country Hatti and from the seacoast and made them build a town on a new location, calling its name Kar-Esarhaddon" (*ANET* 291). Among these "kings of the country Hatti" would have been Manasseh, king of Judah.

The destruction of Sidon was followed by action against Tyre. A treaty between Baal king of Tyre and Esarhaddon was concluded (*ANET* 533–34). The treaty restricted Tyrian freedom, requiring that all Assyrian correspondence to the court had to be read in the presence of an Assyrian commissioner and giving Assyria possession of any Tyrian ships wrecked along the Eastern Mediterranean Seaboard.

Probably shortly after the affair with Baal of Tyre, Esarhaddon compelled "twenty-two kings of Hatti, the seashore and the islands" to "transport under terrible difficulties, to Nineveh, . . . as building material for my palace: big logs, long beams and thin boards from cedar and pine trees, products of the Sirara and Lebanon mountains, which had grown for a long time into tall and strong timber, also from their quarries in the mountains, statues of protective deities" (*ANET* 291). Among these kings forced to provide this corvée labor, Esarhaddon lists Manasseh of Judah.

Assyrian-Egyptian Rapprochement

Esarhaddon's campaigns in Syria-Palestine and his reordering of the life of the Phoenician cities were related to Assyria's attempt to gain complete control over the important sea commerce in the eastern Mediterranean. (See Map 26.) A clash with the other Mediterranean power in the area, namely, Egypt, became inevitable. In fact, two considerations suggest that Egyptian influence was a factor behind the Phoenician uprisings and that Egypt had encouraged and supported Sidon and Tyre. First, two fragmentary Assyrian texts probably from the early years of Esarhaddon refer to Egypt in association with Syro-Palestinian cities and suggest that a conspiracy was afoot. One text associates a "man of Egypt" with Sidon (*AGS* II, #109) and another connects Tirhakah with Tyre and Ashkelon, and mentions twenty-two unnamed kings, perhaps the western vassals of Assyria (Nahr El Kelb Stela; see *IAKA*, §67). Second, in 673 B.C.E. Esarhaddon invaded Egypt probably to stem Egyptian influence at its source. Since the campaign was a failure, it goes unmentioned in Assyrian texts. The later Babylonian Chronicles, however, report that "the army of Assyria was defeated in a bloody battle in Egypt" (*ANET* 302). Prayers of Esarhaddon to the sun-god Shamash which can be related to this campaign have the king inquiring about whether he would encounter the Egyptians at Ashkelon (*AGS* II, #69 and #70; for an English translation, see *BA* 29 [1966], 100). This suggests that the Ethiopian pharaoh was operative in southern Syria-Palestine and that Esarhaddon's invasion was a response to hostile actions initiated by Tirhakah. At any rate, Esarhaddon's invasion of Egypt represented a radical change in policy for the Assyrians who had previously been content with confining Egypt within its borders rather than invading the country itself. The Assyrians, however, seem never to have wanted to annex Egypt into their empire.

In his tenth year (671 B.C.E.), Esarhaddon again moved into Egypt. This time he was successful against Tirhakah. After fierce fighting, Memphis was taken. Tirhakah escaped to the south, but his wife, harem, brothers, and heir apparent were captured. The Assyrian king's goal was achieved temporarily: "All Ethiopians I deported from Egypt—leaving not even one to do homage" (*ANET* 293). By appointing various rulers throughout the land Esarhaddon sought to establish administrative order in Lower Egypt, which at the time was a patchwork of competing principalities (*ANET* 292). Many of these appointees were already ruling over various political entities. One of those affirmed in office was Neco I, ruler in Sais. Esarhaddon's actions not only sought to establish some form of Assyrian authority in the country but also to affirm in office many native Egyptians whose vested interests would produce greater support for Assyria than for the non-Egyptian Tirhakah. Two years later Esarhaddon set out again for Egypt to confront Tirhakah, who had moved back into the Delta region, but he fell sick on the way and died (*ANET* 303).

The new Assyrian king, Ashurbanipal (668–627 B.C.E.), was immediately confronted with problems in Egypt, where Tirhakah had reestablished himself

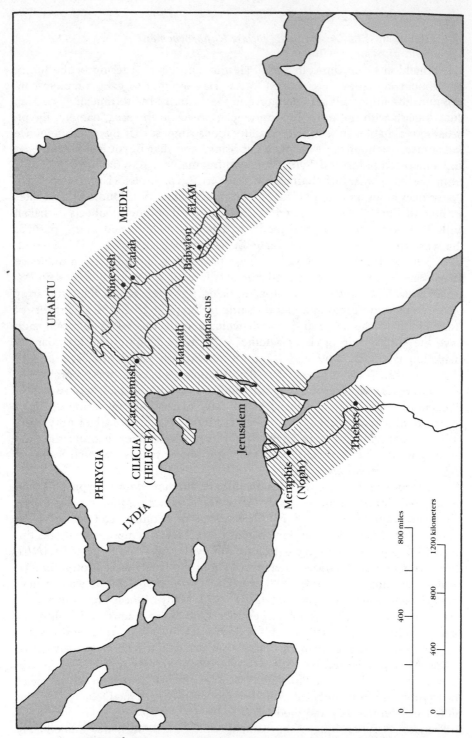

MAP 26. The Assyrian Empire at Its Greatest Extent

in Memphis and "turned against the kings and regents whom" Esarhaddon "had appointed in Egypt." Ashurbanipal dispatched his military commander to quell the revolt. The vassal kings in the west were mustered to the cause, required to provide troops as well as ships for transportation, and made to accompany the invading army (*ANET* 294). Among these vassals would have been Manasseh king of Judah (see Deut. 28:68). Ashurbanipal notes that Neco I and others whom his "father had appointed in Egypt and who had left their offices in the face of the uprising of Tirhakah and had scattered into the open country" were reinstalled. For some reason, many of these appointees subsequently sided temporarily with Tirhakah, but their plotting was discovered by the Assyrians (*ANET* 294). Although many of these appointees were punished for breaking faith with Assyria, Neco was given special treatment. Ashurbanipal reports the following about the status assigned him:

> From all of them, I had only mercy upon Necho and granted him life. I made a treaty with him protected by oaths which greatly surpassed those of the former treaty. I clad him in a garment with multicolored trimmings, placed a golden chain on him as the insigne of his kingship, put golden rings on his hands; I wrote my name upon an iron dagger to be worn in the girdle, the mounting of which was golden, and gave it to him. I presented him furthermore with chariots, horses and mules as means of transportation befitting his position as ruler. I sent with him and for his assistance, officers of mine as governors. I returned to him Sais as residence the place where my own father had appointed him king. Nabushezibanni (Psammetichus I), his son, I appointed for Athribis thus treating him with more friendliness and favor than my own father did. (*ANET* 295)

Thus began an alliance of kingdoms that was to last without interruption until the end of the Assyrian empire. This alliance eventually produced shared rule between Egypt and Assyria in Syria-Palestine and greatly influenced the course of Judean history throughout the seventh century.

Because of the importance of this Egyptian-Assyrian coalition for Judean history, three more factors about Egyptian history in the early decades of the Twenty-sixth (Saite) Dynasty should be noted.

1. Tirhakah's nephew, Tantamani (664–656 B.C.E.), assumed leadership in Upper Egypt and invaded the Delta (665/4 B.C.E.). The Delta cities all remained loyal to Assyria. Tantamani besieged the Assyrian forces in Memphis. Loyally supporting his Assyrian overlord, Neco I died in battle opposing Tantamani (Herodotus II.152). Neco's son, Psammetichus I, fled Egypt, taking refuge in Syria. From there, he accompanied the Assyrian troops on their return to Egypt. Ashurbanipal marched into the Delta, forced the retreat of Tantamani, retook Memphis, and looted and destroyed Thebes which was a stronghold for the Ethiopian ruler. (Nahum 3:8–10 recalls the impact made by the conquest of Thebes [called No-amon in Hebrew].) With the fall of Thebes, Ethiopian authority in the Delta was shattered. Ashurbanipal and the Assyrians could assume the role of liberators in Lower Egypt. Psammetichus I succeeded his father Neco I and enjoyed the good graces of Ashurbanipal. Ethiopian domi-

nance in Egypt was broken, and Egyptian meddling at Assyrian expense in Syro-Palestine was ended.

2. Gradually, Psammetichus I moved to extend his control over the other Egyptian rulers and eventually to unite the country under his rule. He laid claim to the kingship of all Egypt. The only reference in Assyrian texts indicating hostility toward Psammetichus I speaks of the breaking of his agreement reached with Ashurbanipal (*ARAB* II,§785). The agreement between the two had apparently called for the continued rule of various kinglets in the Delta whom Psammetichus I moved to dominate. In order to support his efforts toward unification, Psammetichus I utilized external mercenaries. Sometime after 664 B.C.E., Gyges the king of Lydia dispatched troops to Egypt to aid Psammetichus' cause. These along with freebooting Greek pirates may be the Hellenic (Ionian and Carian) mercenaries, "the bronze men from the sea," which Psammetichus I used in suppressing native rivals (Herodotus II.152). Judeans may also have served in his mercenary forces. The *Letter of Aristeas* (paragraph 13) speaks of Jews who had been sent to Egypt to help Psammetichus in his campaign against the king of the Ethiopians, apparently having been dispatched or carried there by Ashurbanipal in 664 B.C.E. One component of these Jewish troops was later settled as a border guard at Elephantine in Upper Egypt, probably after Psammetichus I's war with Libya in 655–654 B.C.E.

3. With the unification movement by Psammetichus I under way or successful, after a brief period of civil war and a short interlude when rule was shared by a council of twelve leaders (Herodotus II.147–150; Diodorus I.66.1–7), Assyrian forces seem to have been withdrawn from Egypt. There is no evidence that they were forced out or that hostile attitudes developed between Assyria and Egypt. Assyrian actions all along suggest that they were never really interested in occupying Egypt or in turning it into an Assyrian province. Their primary concern was to establish Assyrian dominance over the commerce of the Eastern Mediterranean Seaboard. The Twenty-sixth Dynasty apparently acceded to Assyrian hegemony in this area, and Ashurbanipal was willing to allow Psammetichus to govern his own country under terms similar to those established in his earlier treaty with Neco I.

Manasseh and Assyria

It is unfortunate that the biblical traditions tell us nothing about the participation and reaction of Manasseh and Judah to contemporary events of the day. The situation suggests that Manasseh, like Ahaz before him, was a loyal Assyrian subject. The political realities of the time left him with little choice. Probably during Manasseh's reign, Assyria controlled the economic, religious, and political life of Judah with a strong hand. During the eighth century, in the reigns of Ahaz and Hezekiah, Assyria had not intervened in Judah's internal life or regulated its affairs in any extreme fashion. Matters were probably completely different in the seventh century.

A number of factors contributed to these different modes of relationship between Judah and Assyria. All of them help to explain why Judah was far more strongly influenced and dominated by Assyria after the time of Hezekiah's revolt than before. (1) Ahaz had voluntarily submitted to Assyrian hegemony, turning Judah into an Assyrian satellite, and until the death of Sargon II in 705 B.C.E., Hezekiah appears not to have challenged the Assyrians seriously. On the other hand, Manasseh had come to the throne following a major rebellion by Judah which now would have been placed under more stringent controls. (2) Ahaz' submission to Assyria had come at a time when Assyrian strength under Tiglath-pileser was seriously challenged but not greatly threatened. Manasseh, however, came to the throne in the context of widespread and serious anti Assyrian rebellion in Syria-Palestine, Anatolia, and Babylonia. Sennacherib in 696 B.C.E. had just begun to take action against the Anatolian vassaldoms and provinces where revolt had ignited after 705 B.C.E., action that later proved to be less than completely successful. Thus it was not a time for the Assyrians to establish conditions in Syria-Palestine that might allow revolt, much less encourage it. (3) The accessions of both Ahaz and Hezekiah had occurred under Assyrian kings who were firmly secure in their rule. Sennacherib's control of parts of his empire was still in question at the time of Manasseh's accession. Where the Assyrians had the opportunity to exercise firm control, as in Judah, they would certainly have done so. (4) Following Hezekiah's defeat, Judah would have been treated as a vassal state rather than a mere satellite, as was the situation earlier. Vassal states were more firmly controlled than satellite states, and it is quite clear from the inscriptions of both Esarhaddon and Ashurbanipal that Manasseh was treated as a vassal. (5) Manasseh appears to have been handpicked by the Assyrians to succeed Hezekiah. Earlier we noted the issue of Manasseh's age at his accession. Older siblings or relatives must have been bypassed to place the youngster on the throne. This meant, of course, that Assyria, not Judah, was "calling the shots." Manasseh's youth would mean that others were running the government initially. This had to be the members of the Judean pro-Assyrian faction aided by Assyrian officials. Although there is no reference to the appointment of an Assyrian high commissioner in Judah after Hezekiah's revolt, the practice of doing so elsewhere could suggest that this was the case here. Such a commissioner would have served as adviser to the boy king. (6) During the early seventh century, Assyria was deeply involved in conflict with the Ethiopian leadership of Egypt. Imperial Assyrian troops and outposts dotted the terrain of southern Syria-Palestine. Thus during the early seventh century, at such sites as Tell Jemmeh, numerous Assyrian troops bivouacked within a short distance of the Judean capital. In the eighth century, this had not been done to the same degree. (7) In the seventh century, Esarhaddon exercised great caution about the accession of his son Ashurbanipal to the throne. Esarhaddon himself had secured the throne after his father's assassination but only after a fraternal struggle (*ANET* 289–90). In order to prevent a situation from developing in his own reign that could have produced his own assassination or the usurpation of the throne at his death, Esarhaddon made all his subjects submit to a special treaty (in 672 B.C.E.) pledging their fidelity and the suppression of any rebellious sentiments (*ANET* 534–41; see Text XI). This suggests an Assyrian supervision of subject states unparalleled in the eighth century as well as the requirement that vassal states hold firm lines against any seditious activity. (8) In his vassal treaty with subject states, Esarhaddon made his subject rulers swear to fear the god Ashur and to revere and respect Ashur as they did their own god (*ANET* 538, §§ 34–35).

All of these factors point to a powerful Assyrian influence in and over Judah from the days of Hezekiah's capitulation. This influence can be seen in a number of ways. (1) The negative assessment of Manasseh by the compilers of Kings suggests that he was probably a loyalist to the Assyrians throughout his reign. Submission to Assyria must have been judged by Manasseh to be the only policy in Judah's best interests. (2) The association of non-Yahwistic worship with Manasseh's reign probably means that during his rule Assyrian religion with its worship of the male god Ashur, Ishtar the queen of heaven, and astral deities ("the host of heaven") became a common feature of Judean cultic life, even intruding into the Jerusalem Temple itself. The imposition and encouragement of Assyrian religion was probably used as an important feature of imperial control and propaganda even within Judah. (3) Conflict between strict and syncretistic Yahwists and between those advocating anti-Assyrian and pro-Assyrian policies must have existed throughout the final years of Hezekiah's rule and all of Manasseh's reign. Oracles in Isaiah frequently refer to divisions and competing groups in Judah (Isa. 3:5), and II Kings 21:16 depicts Manasseh as carrying out suppressive policies. The king probably had no other choice with Assyrian troops in the neighborhood, Assyrian colloborators and informants in his midst, and Assyrian officials, if not an Assyrian commissioner, at his court. (4) Several oracles in Isaiah refer to the presence in Judah of "men of strange lips" and "people of an obscure speech," probably denoting the presence of Assyrians (Isa. 28:11–13; 33:19). These Assyrians, perhaps including merchants and other classes as well as governmental officials, would have ensured that Assyrian interests were well protected in Judah (see above, p. 320, and Text VIII). Yahweh had indeed fulfilled his threatening words offered initially to Ahaz: "Yahweh is bringing up against them [Pekah and Rezin and their sympathizers] the waters of the River [Euphrates], mighty and many, the king of Assyria and all his glory; and it will rise over all its channels and go over all its banks; and it will sweep on into Judah, it will overflow and pass on, reaching even to the neck; and its outspread wings will fill the breadth of your land" (Isa. 8:7–8). Revolutionary sentiments—both political and religious—must have boiled beneath the surface of Judean society awaiting the day when Assyrian officials no longer supervised Judean life.

> Your mind will muse on the terror:
>   "Where is he who counted, where is he who weighed the tribute?
>   Where is he who counted the towers?"

TEXT XI. Excerpts from Esarhaddon's Vassal Treaty

(This is) the treaty of Esarhaddon, king of the world, king of Assyria, son of Sennacherib, likewise king of the world, king of Assyria, with Ramataya, city-ruler of Urakazabanu, with his sons, grandsons, with all the people of Urakazabanu, (all the men under his command) young and old, from sunrise (east) to sunset (west), all those over whom Esarhaddon, king of Assyria, acts as king and lord; with you, your sons, your grandsons, all those who will live in the future after this treaty. . . .

(This is) the treaty which Esarhaddon, king of Assyria, has established with you before the great gods of heaven and earth, on behalf of the crown prince designate Ashurbanipal, the son of your lord Esarhaddon, king of Assyria, who has designated and appointed him for succession. When Esarhaddon, king of Assyria, departs from the living, you will seat the crown prince designate Ashurbanipal upon the royal throne, he will exercise the kingship and overlordship of Assyria over you. (If) you do not serve him in the open country and in the city, do not fight and even die on his behalf, do not always speak the full truth to him, do not always advise him well in full loyalty, do not smooth his way in every respect; if you remove him, and seat in his stead one of his brothers, younger or older, on the throne of Assyria, if you change or let anyone change the decree of Esarhaddon, king of Assyria, if you will not be subject to this crown prince designate Ashurbanipal, son of Esarhaddon, king of Assyria, your lord, so that he cannot exercise kingship and lordship over you . . .

If you do not always offer complete truth to the crown prince designate Ashurbanipal whom Esarhaddon, king of Assyria, has presented to you, as well as to the brothers by the mother of the crown prince designate Ashurbanipal, concerning whom Esarhaddon, king of Assyria, has established this treaty with you; if you do not treat them with proper loyalty, speak to them with a true heart, and serve them in the open country and in the city . . .

If any (of you) hears some wrong, evil, unseemly plan which is improper or detrimental to the crown prince designate Ashurbanipal, son of your lord Esarhaddon, king of Assyria, whether they be spoken by his enemy or his ally, by his brothers, by his sons, by his daughters, by his brothers, his father's brothers, his cousins, or any other member of his father's lineage, or by your own brothers, sons, or daughters, or by a prophet, an ecstatic, a dream-interpreter, or by any human being whatsoever, and conceals it, does not come and report it to the crown prince designate Ashurbanipal, son of Esarhaddon, king of Assyria . . .

If anyone instigates you to a revolt or rebellion against the crown prince designate Ashurbanipal, son of your lord Esarhaddon, king of Assyria, concerning whom he has established (this) treaty with you, in order to kill, harm and destroy him, and you, upon hearing such a thing from anybody, do not seize the instigators of the revolt, do not bring them before the crown prince designate Ashurbanipal, (and) if you, being able to seize and kill them, do not seize and kill them, do not eradicate their name and descendants from the country, or, being unable to seize and kill them, you do not inform the crown prince designate Ashurbanipal, do not stand by him and seize and kill the instigators of the revolt . . .

If you do not love the crown prince designate Ashurbanipal, son of your lord Esarhaddon, king of Assyria, as you do your own lives . . .

If you do not say and do not give orders to your sons, grandsons, to your offspring, to your descendants, who will live in the future after this treaty, saying: "Keep this treaty, do not sin against this treaty with you, lest you lose your lives, deliver your land to destruction, and your people to be deported . . ."

May Ashur, king of the gods, who determines the fates, decree for you an evil, unpropitious fate, and not grant you fatherhood, old age . . .

May Anu, king of the gods, rain upon all your houses disease, exhaustion, *di'u*-disease, sleeplessness, worries, ill health.

May Sin, the luminary of heaven and earth, clothe you in leprosy and (thus) not permit you to enter the presence of god and king; roam the open country as a wild ass or gazelle! . . .

May all the gods who are named in this treaty tablet reduce your soil in size to be as narrow as a brick, turn your soil into iron, so that no one may cut a furrow in it.

Just as rain does not fall from a copper sky, so may there come neither rain nor dew upon your fields and meadows, but let it rain burning coals in your land instead of dew. . . .

Just as this ewe is cut open and the flesh of its young placed in its mouth, so may he (Shamash?) make you eat in your hunger the flesh of your brothers, your sons, and your daughters.

Just as (these) yearlings and spring lambs, male and female, are cut open and their entrails are rolled around their feet, so may the entrails of your sons and daughters be rolled around your feet. (*ANET* 534–41)

> You will see no more the insolent people,
>   the people of an obscure speech which you cannot comprehend,
>   stammering in a tongue which you cannot understand.
>   (Isa. 33:18–19)

Manasseh in Babylon?

Scholars have labored long and hard to authenticate the tradition about Manasseh found in II Chron. 33:10–13 which reports that "the commanders of the army of the king of Assyria . . . took Manasseh with hooks and bound him with fetters of bronze and brought him to Babylon [!]." Attempts have been made to associate this episode with some known event: the rebellion of Sidon

Esarhaddon's Vassal Treaty. Fragments of several copies of a treaty which Esarhaddon made with his subject kingdoms have been unearthed by archaeologists. This clay tablet is one such copy. *(The British Museum)*

in 677/76 B.C.E. during the reign of Esarhaddon, the treaty-swearing conclave held in 672 B.C.E., the rebellion of Baal king of Tyre in 668/7 B.C.E. against Ashurbanipal (*ANET* 295–96), the period of major Assyrian trouble with the Arabs in the 640s (*ANET* 297–98), the rebellion in Babylon of Ashurbanipal's brother Shamash-shum-ukin in 652–648 B.C.E., or the troubles with Elam in 654–646 B.C.E. None of these efforts have been successful, and II Kings suggests that no major changes took place during Manasseh's reign; he was not, nor did he become, a Yahwistic reformer (II Chron. 33:12–13, 15–16; but note 33:22). The Chronicler's account may be based on an inherited tradition which told of Manasseh's conversion and even contained his presumed prayer of repentance (see the later "Prayer of Manasseh" in the Apocrypha). Such a tradition reflects what may have been a common Near Eastern folklore motif of the bad king who changes his course of action after some intervening significant event (see the books of Esther and Daniel and the Nabonidus text from Qumran).

Amon

Manasseh was succeeded on the throne by his twenty-two-year-old son Amon (642–640 B.C.E.) whose name has been associated frequently with the Egyptian sun-god Amun and who, according to our chronology, would have been born in the year that Ashurbanipal and his western vassals defeated the Egyptians (664/3 B.C.E.). Amon was assassinated after a two-year reign (II Kings 21: 19–26; II Chron. 33:21–25). The biblical text provides the historian with little information about his reign. He is said to have followed the syncretistic religious policies of his father. Amon was killed by his "servants," that is, royal officials. After his death, "the people of the land" intervened and executed those who had conspired against Amon. They then placed his eight-year-old son Josiah on the throne.

Nothing is known about the details of this court conspiracy or about the plans of the people of the land. Were these events inspired by groups who sought change in the cultic and religious life of Judah? Or was it an effort to stifle anti-Assyrian sentiments and preserve the status quo? Or was there some attempted palace coup by other and older sons of Manasseh who would have been forty-five years old when Amon was born? Or were the assassins inspired by a nationalistic surge which thought the time had come to be done with submission? The historian must simply admit that the course and cause of the events remain a mystery.

CHAPTER 12

The Last Years
of the Davidic Kingdom

The story of the final years of the Davidic state of Judah forms one subplot in a large drama that involved most of the kingdoms in the Middle East. The major actors in this drama were the three great Near Eastern powers of the day, Assyria, Babylon, and Egypt. Minor but important roles were played by the Cimmerians, the Medes, and the Scythians, and a host of other characters with their bit parts.

Chronologically, this drama covers the final four decades of the seventh (640–600 B.C.E.) and the first decade and a half of the sixth century (600–586 B.C.E.). Near the beginning of this period, Judah experienced a brief time of religious reform under King Josiah (639–609 B.C.E.). The Davidic state, however, was swiftly sucked into the maelstrom of international affairs from which it was never able to extricate itself. Of its last five Davidic kings, two met their deaths in direct connection with international struggles and the other three died in foreign exile.

Sources for the Period

In comparison with other epochs in Israelite and Judean history, the written source material for this period is abundant. This includes both biblical and nonbiblical texts. The biblical texts, still our primary source of information about the specifics of Judean history, include the accounts in II Kings and II Chronicles as well as several prophetical books.

The Accounts in II Kings and II Chronicles

At the end of this period, that is, with the fall of Jerusalem and with the Judean kings Jehoiachin and Zedekiah in exile, the account of Israelite and Judean history in II Kings draws to a close. As the compilers of I-II Kings moved in their narration to the reign of Josiah and the exile, they had moved to the period of their own day or of the recent past.

Josiah is depicted in II Kings as one of the most righteous rulers that either of the two kingdoms ever produced, and earlier events tend to be both depicted and interpreted in the light of events described during his reign. This has influenced the narratives and the content of Joshua-II Kings in various ways. (1) Many of the preceding reigns—for example, that of Manasseh (II Kings 21)— are depicted as more apostate and unproductive than was probably the case. By deprecating Manasseh, the editors sought to demonstrate the radically different character of Josiah's reign. This endeavor reflects a fairly common Near Eastern pattern in which predecessors are deprecated in order to demonstrate the greatness of the "good," current, or ideal ruler. (2) The reign of Josiah, or portions of it, are depicted as embodying the ideals and programs of the editors. That is, certain factors and impulses in Josiah's reign that became the religious commitments of the editorial compilers are now seen as the dominant characteristics of his reign. (3) The account of the division of the kingdom of Solomon has been made to focus on the apostate sanctuary at Bethel and anticipates the time when Josiah would destroy it (compare I Kings 13:1–10 with II Kings 23: 15–18). (4) Each of the kings of both kingdoms has been evaluated with the purification of the cult and the centralization of worship in Jerusalem, considered the hallmarks of Josiah's reign, as the criteria.

The above considerations point, first, to the enormous impact that the compilers' view of Josiah had on the editing of the Books of Kings. Josiah is given such high marks by the compilers of II Kings, and his death at Megiddo seems so completely out of step with the theological principle that otherwise pervades much of Joshua-II Kings—namely, that a leader's or king's faithfulness to Yahweh would be rewarded by Yahweh's protection and support—that many scholars think an original edition of Joshua-II Kings must have been compiled during Josiah's reign, before his untimely death and that later, after the fall of Judah, the account was expanded to cover the reigns of Jehoahaz II, Jehoiakim, Jehoiachin, and Zedekiah. Second, the portrait of Josiah in II Kings goes out of its way to depict Josiah as the ideal ruler who embodied and exemplified the religious commitments of the editors and, therefore, must be used with caution by the historian. (We shall note the Chronicler's portrayal of Josiah in the later discussion.)

The Prophetical Books

In addition to the prophetical Book of Nahum, which gloats over the fall of the Assyrian capital at Nineveh, the prophetical books of Jeremiah, Ezekiel, and Habakkuk relate to this period. The prophetical activity of both Jeremiah and Ezekiel spanned the last years of Judah and Jerusalem. The Book of Jeremiah, especially, provides important information on this period. Particularly useful are the prose sections of the book, which, interestingly enough, are cast in the same literary style as Deuteronomy and Joshua-II Kings. Jeremiah's career is said to have begun in the thirteenth year of Josiah (about 627 B.C.E.; Jer. 1:1–2). The specific dates scattered throughout the book, however, pick up with his famous Temple sermon (Jer. 7; 26) at the beginning of Jehoiakim's reign (608 B.C.E.).

Although some of the oracles in the early chapters of the book derive from the reign of Josiah, they do not refer to Judean events very explicitly and make no overt reference to Josiah's famous religious reform.

The Babylonian Chronicles

A major source of considerable usefulness for reconstructing the history of the period, in addition to the biblical materials, are the so-called Babylonian Chronicles (see Text XII). These chronicles do not represent a single document but rather a particular genre of literature. The chronicles present selective summaries of royal reigns, based apparently upon year-by-year records of events kept in Babylon. Only portions survive, but these include coverage of the years 626–623 and 616–594 B.C.E. That is, they cover much of the reigns of Nabopolassar (626–605 B.C.E.) and Nebuchadrezzar (605–562 B.C.E.). These texts provide the historian with incomparable data concerning the last days of Assyria and the struggles of Assyria, Babylonia, and Egypt. They also make possible the determination of the exact date of Nebuchadrezzar's first capture of Jerusalem.

Chronological Problems

In short, we have more useful information for reconstructing the last half century or so of Judah's history than we have had for any of the preceding periods. That still does not mean that we can reconstruct the whole story or that any reconstruction will be free of problems. For example, we really possess little material about Josiah's reign except for the extensive accounts in II Kings and II Chronicles of his religious reform. The information at hand is thus still very selective and sometimes contradictory. Even Josiah's death at Megiddo remains something of a mystery, and in their reports of his "reform" II Kings and II Chronicles differ notably, as we shall see.

This tantalizing situation—rather full and detailed information that almost fits nicely but not quite—is perhaps illustrated best by the chronological data. Both the account in II Kings and the Book of Jeremiah provide synchronisms between reigns of the Judean kings and Nebuchadrezzar. In addition, the Babylonian Chronicles allow for absolute dates for the first twelve years of Nebuchadrezzar's reign. There are two difficulties, however, which still prevent any calculation of absolute dates for the Judean kings of this period. (1) There are apparent, even though minor, discrepancies in the biblical dates given for the first and second captures of Jerusalem. II Kings 24:10–12; 25:8 and Jer. 52:12 place Judah's two defeats in Nebuchadrezzar's eighth and nineteenth years respectively. On the other hand, Jer. 52:28–30 reports two deportations (which apparently should have corresponded in time or followed the two defeats), but these are placed in Nebuchadrezzar's seventh and eighteenth years respectively. (2) Uncertainty exists as to whether Judean dates were calculated on the basis of a spring to spring (Nisan to Nisan) annual calendar, as were the regnal years

TEXT XII. Selections from the Babylonian Chronicles

In the month of Iyyar [626 B.C.E.] the Assyrian army had come down into Babylonia. On the 12th of the month of Tisri the Assyrian troops when they came against Babylon, on that same day the Babylonians, when they had gone out from Babylon, did battle against the Assyrian army and heavily defeated the Assyrian army, captured their spoil. For one year there was no king in the land. On the twenty-sixth day of the month of Marcheswan, Nabopolassar sat upon the throne in Babylon. (This was) the "beginning of reign" of Nabopolassar. In the month of Adar the gods of the land of Susa which the Assyrians had carried off and settled in Erech those gods Nabopolassar let return to the city of Susa. . . .

(In) the tenth year [616 B.C.E.], in the month of Iyyar, Nabopolassar called out the Babylonian army and marched up the bank of the river Euphrates. . . . In the month of Tisri the Egyptian army and the Assyrian army marched after the king of Akkad as far as the town of Qablinu but did not overtake the king of Akkad and then went back. In the month of Adar the Assyrian army and the Babylonian army attacked each other in the town of Badanu which is in the territory of the city of Arraphu and the Assyrian army broke off contact from the Babylonian army which defeated them heavily and threw them (back) to the river Zab. Their chariots and horses were captured and they took much spoil from them. Many of his (prisoners) they made to cross the river Tigris with them and (so) they brought them into Babylon. . . .

In the twenty-first year [605 B.C.E.] the king of Akkad stayed in his own land, Nebuchadrezzar his eldest son, the crown-prince, mustered (the Babylonian army) and took command of his troops; he marched to Carchemish which is on the bank of the Euphrates, and crossed the river (to go) against the Egyptian army which lay in Carchemish, ... fought with each other and the Egyptian army withdrew before him. He accomplished their defeat and to non-existence [beat?] them. As for the rest of the Egyptian army which had escaped from the defeat (so quickly that) no weapon had reached them, in the district of Hamath the Babylonian troops overtook and defeated them so that not a single man [escaped] to his own country. At that time Nebuchadrezzar conquered the whole area of the Hatti-country. For twenty-one years Nabopolassar had been king of Babylon. On the 8th of the month of Ab he died (lit. "the fates"); in the month of Elul Nebuchadrezzar returned to Babylon and on the first day of the month of Elul he sat on the royal throne in Babylon.

In the "accession year" [605/604 B.C.E.] Nebuchadrezzar went back again to the Hatti-land and until the month of Sebat marched unopposed through the Hatti-land; in the month of Sebat he took the heavy tribute of the Hatti-territory to Babylon. In the month of Nisan he took the hands of Bel and the son of Bel and celebrated the *akitu* (New Year) festival.

In the first year [604/603 B.C.E.] of Nebuchadrezzar in the month of Sivan he mustered his army and went to the Hatti-territory, he marched about unopposed in the Hatti-territory until the month of Kislev. All the kings of the Hatti-land came before him and he received their heavy tribute. He marched to the city of Askelon and captured it in the month of Kislev. He captured its king and plundered it and carried off [spoil from it . . . . .]. He turned the city into a mound and heaps of ruins and then in the month of Sebat he marched back to Babylon. . . .

In the fourth year [601/600 B.C.E.] the king of Akkad (Nebuchadrezzar) mustered his army and marched to the Hatti-land. In the Hatti-land they marched unopposed. In the month of Kislev he took the lead of his army and marched to Egypt. The king of Egypt heard (it) and mustered his army. In open battle they smote the breast (of) each other and inflicted great havoc on each other. The king of Akkad and his troops turned back and returned to Babylon.

In the fifth year [600/599 B.C.E.] the king of Akkad (stayed) in his own land and gathered together his chariots and horses in great numbers.

In the sixth year [599/598 B.C.E.] in the month of Kislev the king of Akkad mustered his army and marched to the Hatti-land. From the Hatti-land he sent out his companies, and scouring the desert they took much plunder from the Arabs, their possessions, animals, and gods. In the month of Adar the king returned to his own land.

In the seventh year [598/597 B.C.E.], the month of Kislev, the king of Akkad mustered his troops, marched to the Hatti-land, and encamped against (i e besieged) the city of Judah and on the second day of the month of Adar he seized the city and captured the king. He appointed there a king of his own choice (lit. heart), received its heavy tribute and sent (them) to Babylon. (*CCK* 51, 55–57, 67–69, 71–73)

for the king in Babylonian documents, or from a fall to fall (Tishri to Tishri) annual calendar.

The Collapse of Assyria and the Rise of Babylonia

After a rule of thirty-eight years, Ashurbanipal apparently abdicated the throne in 630 B.C.E. and/or else elevated his son Ashur-etil-ilani to the kingship of Assyria as coruler. Either Ashurbanipal's fear of a disputed succession, which eventuated anyway at his death (in 627 B.C.E.), or his physical and administrative ineffectiveness may have been reason for his action. He bequeathed to his successor an empire with many internal and external troubles but an empire far from being impotent. Since the annals of Ashurbanipal do not extend beyond 639 B.C.E., the last years of his rule are largely unknown. The king's activities in the 640s, however, suggest that he confronted diverse difficulties but did so with a remarkable amount of success. The revolt of his brother Shamash-shum-ukin, the king of Babylon, was suppressed in a vicious four-year war

(652/1–648 B.C.E.) that saw the destruction of the city of Babylon and the death of Shamash-shum-ukin. Troubles with Elam lasted almost a decade (654–646 B.C.E.) and terminated with the destruction of the Elamite capital at Susa in 646 B.C.E. Apparently some Elamites who had been deported as a consequence of these wars were resettled in Samaria following the fall of Susa (see Ezra 4:9–10). A series of campaigns, ending in about 642 B.C.E., were fought against the Arabs who had supported Babylon's earlier revolt. In 644 B.C.E., Ashurbanipal campaigned against Tyre and Usu (the mainland city) on the Mediterranean coast. Sarduri III (about 640–610 B.C.E.) of Urartu acknowledged Assyrian sovereignty in his territory, and Ashurbanipal received tribute from Kurash (Cyrus I) of Parsumash (Persia). All of this activity suggests that the Assyrian empire was still vigorous in Ashurbanipal's last years and that the terminal difficulties, involving fraternal claimants to the throne and civil war, set in after his death.

With the demise of Ashurbanipal in 627 B.C.E., an Assyrian military commander, Sin-shum-lishir, was proclaimed king in Babylon. His forces were defeated, however, and Sin-shar-ishkun, the brother of Ashur-etil-ilani, Ashurbanipal's son and successor on the Assyrian throne, had himself proclaimed king. Thus began a four-year period of civil strife (627–623 B.C.E.) which, when combined with external pressures upon the empire, proved to be overwhelming. Before we examine more closely the final years of the Assyrian kingdom, we need to look briefly at historical developments that impinged directly on the Assyrian empire itself and thus affected, however remotely, Judean life and history.

Cimmerians, Scythians, and Medes

Three groups of seminomadic peoples became major factors in the life of the Fertile Crescent beginning in the late eighth and early seventh centuries. The Cimmerians, barbarian groups from the north, entered Urartu late in the eighth century and defeated the Urartians who were ruled at the time by Argishti II (about 714–680 B.C.E.). Sargon II fought the Cimmerians in the province of Tabal in 706/5 B.C.E. and apparently died in battle against them. They eventually moved west, taking the city of Gordium in 696/5 B.C.E. They later invaded the kingdom of Lydia, where King Gyges, who had recently made contact with and received support from Ashurbanipal, defeated them in battle (about 663 B.C.E.). A few years later, a second wave of Cimmerians attacked Lydia (in about 657 B.C.E.). In about 644 B.C.E., King Gyges of Lydia died in battle against the Cimmerians, led by Lygdamis, and the capital city of Sardis was taken. Lygdamis and his followers then threatened the northwestern frontier of Assyria, but a temporary alliance was established between the Cimmerian leader and Ashurbanipal. After the death of Lygdamis in about 640 B.C.E., his son and successor, Sandakshatru, continued the challenge to Assyria in the northwest. Sardis was again overrun by groups of the Cimmerians (the Trereans and Lycians) in about

637 B.C.E. Shortly thereafter the threat and disturbances of the Cimmerian tribes were brought to a halt by another barbarian group.

This second nomadic group is generally referred to as the Scythians, although various tribes are included in this designation. The Scythians were Indo-Europeans from the Crimean region, who had moved into western Asia Minor just after the turn of the century. During the days of Esarhaddon, they had invaded Urartian territory. The Assyrian king entered an alliance with them at that time and married one of his daughters to a Scythian prince. Eventually the Scythian groups occupied an extensive but undefined area along an east-west axis reaching from Asia Minor to the Iranian plateau, from about the Halys River to northwestern Media, but not including Assyrian territory proper. The Scythians apparently also conducted wide-ranging raiding expeditions. Herodotus (I.104) speaks about the Scythians controlling all Asia, but he is probably noting only what might be called Upper Asia (see Herodotus I.95, 130; IV.1). In the 630s, the Scythians under Madyes defeated the Cimmerians, driving them out of Asia Minor. Following this victory, the Scythians spread eastward, where they encountered the Medes, and southward, into the Eastern Mediterranean Seaboard. The fourth-century C.E. Christian historian Eusebius declares that the Scythians, as early as 633 B.C.E., had reached as far as Palestine.

The Medes, a third group, centered in northwestern Iran, also consisted of a number of separate but associated tribes. In the reign of Esarhaddon they had begun to unite, eventually becoming under King Phraortes (about 647–624 B.C.E.) a formidable enemy of Assyria. Early in the reign of Phraortes' son and successor Cyaxares (about 623–584 B.C.E.), the Medes fought the Scythians under Madyes and were defeated but quickly recovered and played a significant role in the downfall of Assyria, as we shall see.

Egypt and Syria-Palestine

As we noted in Chapter 11, the establishment of the Twenty-sixth (Saite) Dynasty in Egypt led to a period of cooperative rapprochement between Assyria and Egypt. The treaty alliance between Assyria and the first rulers of the dynasty, Neco I and Psammetichus I, continued until the end of Assyrian rule. As Ashurbanipal became more and more involved with pressures in the north and east, Egypt became more dominant in Syria-Palestine. The expansion of Egyptian influence in the Eastern Mediterranean Seaboard probably occurred gradually at the start, beginning in the 640s after Psammetichus I was secure at home, and then expanded significantly in the last years of the Assyrian empire. Nothing in Near Eastern texts would suggest that during this period Egypt saw itself as a competitor to Assyria; everything points to a cooperative attitude between the two powers.

A number of factors indicate Egyptian dominance in Syria-Palestine throughout most of the second half of the seventh century. (1) Herodotus (II.157) reports that Psammetichus I took the city of Ashdod after a siege of twenty-nine years. (Possibly Herodotus mistook the twenty-ninth year of the king's reign for the length of the siege, which would mean that the capture of Ashdod occurred about 635 B.C.E.) The subjugation of Ashdod, which at the time may have been moving to assert its independence from Assyria, illustrates that Egypt was willing to fight the local kingdoms in order to assert its presence in the area. Also according to Herodotus, when the Scythians moved down the eastern Mediterranean coast, they encountered the Egyptians in Palestine. Specifically, Herodotus reports that when "they [the Scythians] were in the part of Syria called Palestine, Psammetichus king of Egypt met them and persuaded them with gifts and prayers to come no farther" (Herodotus I.105). Other classical sources report military engagements between the Egyptians and the Scythians undoubtedly referring to this same episode. This Egyptian encounter with the Scythians probably took place in Palestine in the late 630s or, more probably, the 620s. It would have been then that the Scythians plundered the temple of the "heavenly Aphrodite" at Ashkelon (Herodotus I.105). The Scythians seem to have withdrawn from the region soon thereafter, since no further encounter with the Egyptians is reported. Thus by the 620s, Egypt was clearly operating as the dominant military power in Palestine. (2) Egyptian campaigns in support of Assyria, reported in the Babylonian Chronicles and the Bible and to be discussed in more detail below, took Egyptian troops across the Euphrates River, which suggests sufficient Egyptian control in Syria-Palestine to operate freely throughout the region. It is apparent from these two sources that the Egyptians possessed major military outposts at Riblah, Carchemish, Haran, and probably Megiddo. Such military entrenchment implies military dominance in the area. (3) Three inscriptional sources indicate that Syro-Palestinian powers were allied to Egypt at this time through treaty arrangements. In an inscription of his fifty-second year (612 B.C.E.), Psammetichus I describes the Phoenician region in a manner that clearly indicates the subordination of the Phoenician cities: "Their chiefs were subjects of the (Egyptian) palace, with a royal courtier placed over them; and their taxes were assessed for the (pharaoh's) residence, as though it were in the land of Egypt" (*ARE* IV.493–94). The so-called Wady Brisa inscription set up by the Babylonian king Nebuchadrezzar describes the Lebanon area prior to his taking the territory as a region "over which a foreign enemy [no doubt Egypt] was ruling and robbing it of its riches" (*ANET* 307). In about 604/3 B.C.E., Adon the Philistine king of (probably) Ekron wrote to the Egyptian court requesting aid from the pharaoh. The form and content of his letter, discovered in Egypt, clearly indicate that Adon was a vassal with a treaty agreement with Egypt (see Text XIII). Finally, (4) statuary and other artifacts from the early Saite rulers have been found as far north as the traditional site of Arvad. This suggests Egyptian presence all along the coast.

Two general conclusions relative to Judean history may be drawn from the above evidence and will be discussed in detail later. (1) The Egyptians were in control of the *via maris,* the main highway running north-south through the Eastern Mediterranean Seaboard by the late 630s and early 620s. This probably would have remained the case until the Egyptians were driven out of Syria-

Palestine by the Babylonians after 609 B.C.E. In short, the main route through Palestine was in Egyptian hands during most, if not all, of the reign of Josiah (639–609 B.C.E.). (2) Judah never enjoyed a time of political independence during this period. The Assyrian control over Judah which had been exercised for about a century would have given way gradually to Egyptian dominance. Perhaps for a time Judah was subservient to both Assyria and Egypt, as is indicated in Jeremiah 2. At any rate, Judah, probably early in the reign of Josiah, became subordinate to Egypt and was part of "all that belonged to the king of Egypt from the Brook of Egypt to the river Euphrates" (II Kings 24:7).

The Rise of Babylon

For generations, Babylonia, in southern Mesopotamia, had been a trouble spot for Assyria. Sennacherib had destroyed the city of Babylon in 689 B.C.E. Esarhaddon subsequently ordered it rebuilt and repopulated. Continued struggles led to Babylon's further destruction in 648 B.C.E. By the time of Ashurbanipal's rule, Chaldean tribes controlled most of the region south of Babylon and constantly endangered and on occasion seized control of the city. With the death of Ashurbanipal in 627 B.C.E., the Babylonians moved to assert their independence and became entangled in the struggle for the Assyrian throne. This new Babylonian revolt can be seen essentially as the renewal of the struggles that had led to the city's destruction in 648 B.C.E.

As indicated above, with the demise of Ashurbanipal an Assyrian general named Sin-shum-lishir was proclaimed king of Babylon and ruled the southern province for about a year before his own death. Then Sin-shar-ishkun, the brother of Ashur-etil-ilani (630–623 B.C.E.) whom Ashurbanipal had designated as his own successor on the Assyrian throne, proclaimed himself and was recognized as king in Babylon for a short time (probably in late 627 or early 626 B.C.E.). Babylonia's future and that of the ancient Near East, however, actually lay with Nabopolassar, the king of the Marshland, who had himself proclaimed king of Babylonia in 626 B.C.E. Thus three rulers and three armies vied for authority of the area. Apparently Sin-shar-ishkun and Nabopolassar temporarily allied their efforts, with the former claiming the throne of Assyria and conceding Nabopolassar's claim to the throne of Babylonia. Nabopolassar emerged victorious. After defeating an Assyrian army sent to subdue him, he gained control of the city of Babylon and the whole southern region in November 626 B.C.E. (*ABC* 88). Seeking to gain support in the east, he returned to the Elamites the gods of Susa which had been taken by the Assyrians in 646 B.C.E. and held in the city of Uruk.

Sin-shar-ishkun gained the throne of Assyria in 623 B.C.E., on the other hand, Ashur-etil-ilani apparently having fallen in battle. Sin-shar-ishkun's agreement with Nabopolassar over shared rule soon lapsed and the two began their struggle with each other for dominance in Mesopotamia. Involvement of other powers in the Assyro-Babylonian civil war began to complicate matters further. The province of Der on the Elamite border rebelled (*ABC* 89), for example,

---

TEXT XIII. King Adon's Appeal to Pharaoh

To Lord of Kings Pharaoh, your servant Adon King of [Ekron. The welfare of my lord, Lord of Kings Pharaoh may the gods of] Heaven and Earth and Beelshmayin, [the great] god [seek exceedingly at all times, and may they lengthen the days of] Pharaoh like the days of (the) high heavens. That [I have written to Lord of Kings is to inform him that the forces] of the King of Babylon have come (and) reach[ed] Aphek . . . . . they have seized . . . for Lord of Kings Pharaoh knows that [your] servant . . . to send a force to rescue [me]. Do not abandon [me, for your servant did not violate the treaty of the Lord of Kings] and your servant preserved his good relations. And as for this commander . . . . a governor in the land. And as for the letter of Sindur . . . (*BA* 44 [1981], 36)

---

and Median attacks on Assyrian territory intensified. Phraortes the leader of the Medes was killed in battle, however, whereupon Cyaxares, Phraortes' son and successor, was immediately confronted and defeated by the Scythians under Madyes. Whether the Scythians at this time were supporting the Assyrians or merely acting on their own remains unknown, although the long history of reasonably friendly relations between the two suggests the former.

The loyalty to the Assyrian empire of many of its vassal states and cities is rather surprising at a time when civil struggle was so rampant. Nothing comparable to the widespread revolts early in Sennacherib's reign is evident. Even some cities in the province of Babylonia itself remained loyal to Sin-shar-ishkun until his death and the fall of Nineveh the capital, in 612 B.C.E. The existence of groups such as the Scythians and the Medes on the peripheries of the empire may have encouraged the continued alliance of vassal states and cities.

The Last Days of Assyria

When the extant Babylonian Chronicles resume, after a gap from 623 to early 616 B.C.E., they show Nabopolassar firmly in control of the region of Babylonia. After advancing up the Euphrates, the Babylonian king, however, was forced to withdraw before the combined Assyrian and Egyptian forces (*ABC* 91; see Text XII). In the year following (615 B.C.E.), Nabopolassar attacked Ashur, the old Assyrian capital, but was forced to flee the field and take refuge in the city of Takrit. After a ten-day siege the Assyrian army withdrew and Nabopolassar escaped (*ABC* 91).

For a time thereafter the Medes were the major threat to Assyria. The Scythians appear to have been neutral or even pro-Assyrian at this point. In 614 B.C.E., for example, the Medes attacked several metropolitan districts in Assyria and succeeded in taking Ashur. Nabopolassar and his troops arrived at Ashur after the city fell, but he and the Median Cyaxares sealed their anti-Assyrian opposition with a treaty alliance (*ABC* 93). In 612 B.C.E., Cyaxares and Nabopolassar captured the Assyrian capital at Nineveh, an event celebrated with eloquent boasting in the biblical Book of Nahum. The Assyrian monarch, Sin-shar-ishkun, apparently died in the flames of the city's destruction, and the remnants of the Assyrian army were forced to move westward where they could make contact with their Egyptian allies. In Haran, one hundred miles to the west, Ashur-uballit (612–609 B.C.E.), presumably a junior member of the royal family, became the last Assyrian ruler.

During the next two years, Nabopolassar sought to extend his control to include as much of Assyria as possible, especially the middle Euphrates region. This gave the Egyptians and the Assyrians on the upper Euphrates time to recoup somewhat (*ABC* 94–95).

In the autumn of 610 B.C.E., the Babylonians and the Umman-manda (apparently the Medes) took Haran, forcing the Assyrians and the Egyptians to abandon the area temporarily and to withdraw to the west bank of the Euphrates (*ABC* 95). (The term "Umman-manda," used in the Babylonian Chronicles, was an archaic expression revived by Babylonian scribes and employed primarily in reference to the Medes. In the description of the fall of Nineveh, Cyaxares is called king of the Umman-manda; *ABC* 94. At a late stage in the Assyrian struggles, Scythians and other groups may have been included in the designation.) In 609 B.C.E., Ashur-uballit and the Egyptian army, now under the command of the new pharaoh Neco II, counterattacked the Babylonians in Haran. Although they experienced some initial success evidenced in their victory over the Babylonian garrison, the broken Babylonian Chronicle suggests that the Assyro-Egyptian coalition encountered failure in the long run (*ABC* 96). The name of Ashur-uballit appears no more in the chronicles; the Assyrian empire was at an end. With this second battle of Haran, the issue shifted to a Babylonian-Egyptian struggle over the control of Syria-Palestine and for dominance along the Eastern Mediterranean Seaboard.

Judah and International Affairs

Two external factors must be emphasized in order to understand Judean history during the years of Assyria's collapse: (1) Judah was probably under Egyptian control during these years and (2), like many of the other Near Eastern states at that time, Judah was much affected by barbarian movements from the north.

As we indicated in a preceding section, Egypt under the Twenty-sixth Dynasty and Assyria under Ashurbanipal probably were cooperative allies. As Assyria became more and more preoccupied against Babylon, the Elamites, and others in the 640s, Egypt seemed to move into Syria-Palestine in partnership with Assyria. After the death of Ashurbanipal and the outbreak of fraternal struggle for the throne exacerbated by Nabopolassar's rebellion in southern Mesopotamia, Assyria was too preoccupied to control southern Syria-Palestine directly. This task fell to Egypt. (One broken text in the Babylonian Chronicles may be interpreted to suggest that either Ashur-etil-ilani or Sin-shar-ishkun conducted a campaign west of the Euphrates as late as 623 B.C.E. [*ABC* 89–90]. Otherwise Assyria was certainly not operative in force in the Eastern Mediterranean Seaboard after 627 B.C.E.)

Judah as an Egyptian Vassal

Several factors suggest that Judah was under Egyptian dominance and probably an Egyptian vassal throughout Josiah's reign.

1. References in Jeremiah 2 speak of Judah's submission to both Assyria and Egypt (see vs. 16–18 and 36–37). The country is depicted going to Egypt to drink the waters of the Nile and to Assyria to drink the waters of the Euphrates (Jer. 2:18). The condition depicted in these verses does not seem to be one in which a choice between Egypt and Assyria is demanded but rather a requirement of serving two masters. A date for this situation is suggested by the date of Jeremiah's call, namely, some time shortly after 627 B.C.E., the thirteenth year of Josiah's reign (Jer. 1:2; 25:3). The condition presupposed by Jeremiah 2 was one in which rule over Judah, and probably other nations in the region, was a hegemony shared between the Nile and Mesopotamian superpowers. (Does Isa. 19:19–25 with its emphasis on Egypt, Assyria, and Israel as cooperative powers belong to this same historical milieu?)

2. A Judah subservient to Egypt is suggested by the Egyptian campaigns and tactics described in the Babylonian Chronicles. The chronicle for 616 B.C.E., after a gap of seven years, reports that the Egyptian army with its Assyrian ally pursued Nabopolassar on the middle Euphrates (*ABC* 91; see Text XII). At least again in 610 B.C.E. and subsequently afterward, the Egyptian army was deep in Syrian territory. How early and how frequently such campaigns occurred cannot be determined. Two things, however, are clear. The 616 B.C.E. campaign, conducted so far from home, was certainly not Egypt's first foray in the area. Such an expedition and deployment of forces indicates a period of ever-increasing involvement in northern Syria prior to 616 B.C.E. In addition, the Egyptian army must have been reasonably certain of its dominance in an area prior to extending its supply lines to such an extent and thus exposing itself to possible attack from the rear. Egypt therefore must have been rather confident of its relationship to Syro-Palestinian states such as Judah; that is, Judah must have been in Egypt's camp and confidence.

3. In its efforts to aid the Assyrians and to halt the Babylonian movement into Syria, the Egyptians appear to have been in complete control of the main highways of the Eastern Mediterranean Seaboard. The most important southern segment of this international roadway was the *via maris* which passed along the western edge of traditional Judean territory and moved through the Jezreel Valley near Megiddo. This route joined other roads in Syria of which the most important north-south route passed through Riblah, Hamath, and Aleppo. The Egyptian presence in Carchemish and Haran, even farther to the

north, indicates control of the entire trade routes along the Eastern Mediterranean Seaboard and thus direct control over the region where the route passed through Palestine.

4. The employment of Judean troops in the Egyptian military and the presence of Greek mercenaries, apparently in the service of Egyptian pharaohs, in Palestine suggest Egyptian dominance in the area. The evidence of Judean forces in the Egyptian army is threefold. (*a*) We have already noted the presence of Jewish troops in Egypt in such military colonies as Elephantine (see above, p. 370). (*b*) Josephus provides a quote from the fourth-century Chaldean historian Berosus about Nebuchadrezzar's defeat of the Egyptians at Carchemish in 605 B.C.E. which indicates that Judean soldiers were fighting with Egypt in northern Syria. The young Babylonian crown prince had to depart Syria speedily upon receiving word of the death of his father. Berosus reports that "the prisoners—Jews, Phoenicians, Syrians, and those of Egyptian nationality— were consigned to some of his [Nebuchadrezzar's] friends, with orders to conduct them to Babylonia, along with the heavy troops and the rest of the spoils; while he himself, with a small escort, pushed across the desert to Babylon" (*Contra Apion* I. 136–37). Although this text indicates that Judean soldiers were fighting under Egyptian auspices far from their homeland in 605 B.C.E., and thus a few years after Josiah's reign, the same situation probably prevailed earlier as well. (*c*) As we noted previously, Greek mercenaries comprised a major part of the Egyptian army under Psammetichus I and his successors. Evidence of the presence of Greeks, probably in the service of the Egyptian pharaoh, shows up in Palestine during the last part of the seventh century. Several letters, unearthed from the site of ancient Arad in southern Judah, refer to Greeks (called Kittim) passing by the settlement and being furnished with supplies by Judean forces (see below, Text XVI). This situation would indicate that Judean forces were aligned with or subservient to Egypt in whose service such Hellenic mercenaries functioned. Excavation at Mesad Hashavyahu on the Palestinian coast south of Joppa has revealed evidence of a Greek settlement from the period, probably also a contingent of Psammetichus I's forces. In addition, an inscription found at the site indicates the presence of a Semitic, probably Judean, force under a commander there (see Text XIV).

This evidence suggests a situation in which contingents of Greek and Judean forces were employed by the Egyptians and stationed on the Mediterranean coast.

5. The final evidence suggesting that Judah under Josiah was subject to Egypt is found in the narratives of Kings. II Kings 24:7 reports in connection with Nebuchadrezzar's taking of Judah that "the king of Babylon had taken all that belonged to the king of Egypt from the Brook of Egypt to the river Euphrates." This implies Egypt's previous control over the entire Eastern Mediterranean Seaboard including Judah. Also to be taken into account is the fact that when Josiah was killed at Megiddo, the Egyptian pharaoh assumed the authority to appoint the next king over Judah. Specifically, Jehoahaz II, who ascended the

---

TEXT XIV. The Mesad Hashavyahu Letter

May the official, my lord, hear the plea of his servant. Your servant is working at the harvest. Your servant was in Hasar-Asam. Your servant did his reaping, finished, and stored (the grain) a few days ago before stopping. When your servant had finished his reaping and had stored it a few days ago, Hoshayahu ben Shabay came and took your servant's garment. When I had finished my reaping, at that time, a few days ago, he took your servant's garment. All my companions will testify for me, all who were reaping with me in the heat of the sun—they will testify for me that this is true. I am guiltless of an infraction. (So) please return my garment. If the official does (= you do) not consider it an obligation to return your servant's garment, then have pity upon him and return your servant's garment (from that motive). You must not remain silent when your servant is without his garment. (*HAHL* 20–21; partially restored)

---

throne while Neco II was in northern Syria, was deposed by the pharaoh when he returned to the area, Judah was forced to pay a penalty for its rash initiative, and a ruler selected by Egypt was placed in power (II Kings 23:28–35). All of this takes for granted that Judah was subservient to Egypt, even during Josiah's reign, and that no ruler could hold the Judean throne without Egyptian approval.

Judah and the Barbarian Movements

Judah, like most of the states in the Near East, was affected during the seventh century B.C.E. by the barbarian movements from the north. This is most clearly evident in the Book of Jeremiah. This prophet viewed affairs to the north as a seething caldron with evil boiling over its sides (Jer. 1:13–15). In his call vision, Jeremiah claimed to hear Yahweh "calling all the tribes of the kingdoms of the north . . . ; and they shall come and every one shall set his throne at the entrance of the gates of Jerusalem, against all its walls round about, and against all the cities of Judah" (Jer. 1:15). The enemy from the north whose coming the prophet proclaims in Jer. 4:5–6:30 must certainly be connected with the movements of the Scythian and associated groups.

Although the tribal groups did not overrun Judah as Jeremiah predicted, they did penetrate into the Palestinian area. The Egyptians battled and bribed them in Palestine itself but apparently affected their departure. The fact that Egypt was a cooperative ally of Assyria and that the Scythians were certainly not anti-Assyrian may have helped moderate their encounter. The most likely date, as we noted earlier, for the Scythian penetration to the border of Egypt was the early 620s, the period of Jeremiah's early preaching.

Josiah

Following the assassination of Amon, "the people of the land" placed Josiah the son of Amon, then an eight-year-old youngster, on the throne in Jerusalem. Josiah ruled for thirty-one years (639–609 B.C.E.). Unfortunately neither II Kings nor II Chronicles provides extensive details about his reign or about international affairs generally, except with regard to his religious reforms. For reasons indicated above, however, it is evident that Josiah's reign witnessed Judah's transition from an Assyrian vassal to a position of subservience to Egypt.

Egyptian policy in Syria-Palestine was far more politically laissez-faire in nature than had been Assyrian policy and was primarily commercial in operation. Egypt did not seem to have had any plans or desire to annex or subjugate completely Syro-Palestinian states, for example, and thus developed no provincial governmental system. This means that Egypt was probably little concerned with internal Syro-Palestinian affairs, such as religious practices and developments. Accordingly, while Judah under Josiah did not experience a period of complete freedom unhampered by foreign domination, internal affairs were certainly more under Judean control under Egyptian than Assyrian overlordship. As direct Assyrian control in Judah began to loosen, and was replaced with an Egyptian program far more benevolent in character and less oppressive in nature, Josiah was able to reform the Jerusalem and Judean cult. Before discussing the nature of this reform, we must examine the literary traditions about Josiah's reformation.

Literary and Chronological Matters

The account of Josiah's reign in II Kings notes the following episodes:

A. In Josiah's eighteenth year (622 B.C.E.), "the book of the law" was discovered in the Temple while repair work was being conducted (II Kings 22:3–7).

B. The book was read to the king; Huldah the prophetess was consulted about the work; and she responded with an oracle emphasizing its importance (II Kings 22:8–20).

C. The king assembled the elders of Judah and Jerusalem, and after reading the book, the king covenanted to obey its words (II Kings 23:1–3).

D. A purging of the Judean cult commenced, beginning with the Jerusalem Temple and extending from Geba to Beer-sheba (II Kings 23:4–14).

E. The temple at the northern shrine of Bethel was destroyed as well as other shrines in Samaria (II Kings 23:15–20).

CHART XV. The Last Days of the Davidic Kingdom

Judah	*Assyria*	*Egypt*	*Babylonia*
Manasseh (697–642)		Neco I (665–664)	
	Ashurbanipal (688–627)		
		Psammetichus I (664–610)	
	Cooperative alliance between Assyria and Egypt		
			Shamash-shum-ukin defeated (652/1–648)
Amon (642–640)			
Josiah (639–609)	Ashur-etil-ilani (630–623)		Sin-shum-lishir (627–626)
			Nabopolassar (626–605)
	Sin-shar-ishkun (623–612)		
	Fall of Ashur (614)		
	Fall of Nineveh (612)		
	Ashur-uballit (612–609)		
		Neco II (610–595)	
Jehoahaz II (609)			
Jehoiakim (608–598)			Victory at Carchemish (605)
			Nebuchadrezzar (605–562)
Jehoiachin (598–597) Surrender of Jerusalem (March 15/16, 597)			
Zedekiah (597–586)		Psammetichus II (595–589)	
		Apries (Hophra) (589–570)	
Capture of Jerusalem (586)			

F. The king followed the stipulations of the recently discovered law book and held the Passover as a pilgrim festival in Jerusalem (II Kings 23: 21–23).

G. Josiah met his death at Megiddo (II Kings 23:29–30).

On the other hand, II Chronicles presents the following course of events for Josiah's reign:

A. In his eighth year (631 B.C.E.), Josiah began to seek the God of David his father (II Chron. 34:3a).

B. In his twelfth year (627 B.C.E.), Josiah began to purge the cult throughout Judah and Jerusalem, even extending the purge into the tribal territories of Manasseh, Ephraim, Simeon, and Naphtali (II Chron. 34:3b–7).

C. In his eighteenth year (622 B.C.E.), "the book of the law of Yahweh given through Moses" was discovered in the Temple (II Chron. 34:8–18).

D. The book was read to the king; Huldah the prophetess was consulted about the work; and she responded with an oracle emphasizing its importance (II Chron. 34:19–28).

E. The king assembled the elders of Judah and Jerusalem, and after reading the book, he covenanted to obey the words of the book and involved the people of Jerusalem and Benjamin and Israel in the observance of its stipulations (II Chron. 34:29–33).

F. The king followed the stipulations of the law regarding Passover and also appointed priests (II Chron. 35:1–19).

G. Josiah met his death at Megiddo (II Chron. 35:20–27).

The primary differences in these narratives concern (1) whether Josiah's reform was conducted in clearly defined stages in Josiah's eighth, twelfth, and eighteenth years respectively, (2) the relationship of the reform to the law book, and (3) the geographical extent of the reform. The discussion that follows tends to rely on II Kings, which has the basic reform begin in Josiah's eighteenth year after the discovery of the book in the Temple. The Chronicler's material appears to be more tendentious than that of II Kings. It assumes, for example, that a king as good as Josiah must have become religious (II Chron. 34:3a) and initiated reform (34:3b) prior to his twenty-sixth year. Thus the Chronicler depicts the finding of the law book as a reward for the king's reforming activity already under way. Likewise, the Chronicler's depiction of the reformation as a widespread movement extending even into the north is so undetailed that it gives the impression of unhistorical generalization.

The Book of the Law

The identity of the law book, its place of origin, and its role in Josiah's reforms have been issues occupying scholars for generations and about which there can be few certainties. On one point there is general but not universal agreement: the content of the book of the law was identical or related in some way to portions of our present book of Deuteronomy. This conclusion is based on parallels between the content of the book and some of the specific actions embodied in Josiah's reform, which we shall note below.

It is highly unlikely that the book of Deuteronomy in its present form was the document discovered in the Temple. On the contrary, Deuteronomy apparently went through several stages of compilation, and the book as it stands now has been edited in the light of the later Babylonian exile (see Deut. 28:36–37 and chs. 29–30). While any attempt to delineate the history of the work's development necessarily involves speculation, we presuppose that the earliest corpus of the Deuteronomic material was compiled for the support of Hezekiah's reform program or as a consequence of this program. This early corpus would have consisted basically of the material found now in Deuteronomy 12–26. These chapters, it should be noted, are not presented in the form of a covenant or treaty between God and the people, nor are they shaped by covenant theology. Moreover, they are not explicitly presented as stemming from Moses. Stage one of the development of Deuteronomy, therefore, would have consisted of the essential content of Deuteronomy 12–26, which does not mention Moses and in which the term "covenant" occurs only once (Deut. 17:2) and could be omitted without any loss of meaning or continuity in the text. This form of Deuteronomy may have come from late in the eighth or early in the seventh century.

A second stage in the formation of the book of Deuteronomy would have been produced by the expansion of the original corpus by a radical Yahwistic and anti-Assyrian subculture during the reign of Manasseh or early in the reign of Josiah. This expansion is now reflected primarily in Deut. 4:44–11:32 + 28:1–35, 38–68. This expanded form of the book has two characteristics: (1) the material is presented as a series of farewell addresses that Moses delivered to Israel in Transjordan just before the conquest of the land and (2) the material has been patterned after the Assyrian treaty form (see Text XV), being formulated to give expression to a theology based on a covenant/treaty understanding of the relationship between Yahweh and his people. The group or groups who put together this expanded form of the law book may have had some association with both the royal court and the Temple, and it would have been Deuteronomy at this stage of development that was "discovered" during Josiah's reign, but there are no substantive reasons for assuming that Josiah himself was involved in the book's production.

This second edition of the Deuteronomic materials, while idealistic in many respects, was aptly formulated for use in an anti-Assyrian and pro-Yahwistic campaign and fitted the needs for reviving nationalistic religion and consciousness. It assumed the necessity and proclaimed the urgency of conquering the land, eradicating non-Yahwistic religion, centralizing control in Jerusalem, and yet placing the powers of the monarchy under certain limitations. While not speaking directly about Assyrian presence or the existence of Assyrian "civil

TEXT XV. Parallels Between Esarhaddon's Vassal Treaty and Deuteronomy

Esarhaddon's Treaty	*Deuteronomy*
§24. If you do not love the crown prince designate Ashurbanipal, son of your lord Esarhaddon, king of Assyria, as you do your own lives. . . .	*6:5*—You shall love Yahweh your God with all your heart, and with all your soul, and with all your might.
§25. If you do not say and do not give orders to your sons, grandsons, to your offspring, to your descendants, who will live in the future after this treaty. . . .	*6:7*—You shall teach [these words] diligently to your children, and shall talk of them when you sit in your house, and when you walk by the way, and when you lie down, and when you rise.
§37. May Ashur, the king of the gods, who determines the fates, decree for you an evil, unpropitious fate and not grant you fatherhood, old age.	*28:20*—Yahweh will send upon you curses, confusion, and frustration, in all that you undertake to do, until you are destroyed and perish quickly, on account of the evil of your doings.
§39. May Sin, the luminary of heaven and earth, clothe you in leprosy, and thus not permit you to enter the presence of God and king; roam the open country as a wild ass or gazelle!	*28:27*—Yahweh will smite you with the boils of Egypt, and with the ulcers and the scurvy and the itch, of which you cannot be healed.
§40. May Shamash, the light of heaven and earth, not give you a fair and equitable judgment, may he take away your eyesight; walk about in darkness!	*28:28–29*—Yahweh will smite you with madness and blindness and confusion of mind; and you shall grope at noonday, as the blind grope in darkness.
§41. May Ninurta, leader of the gods, fell you with his fierce arrow, and fill the plain with your corpses, give your flesh to eagles and vultures to feed upon.	*28:26*—And your dead body shall be food for all birds of the air, and for the beasts of the earth; and there shall be no one to frighten them away.
§42. May Venus, the brightest among the stars, let your wives lie in the embrace of your enemies before your very eyes, may your sons not	*28:30–32*—You shall betroth a wife, and another man shall lie with her; you shall build a house, and you shall not dwell in it; you shall plant a vine-

have authority over your house, may a foreign enemy divide your possessions.

yard, and you shall not use the fruit of it. . . . Your sons and your daughters shall be given to another people, while your eyes look on and fail with longing for them all the day; and it shall not be in the power of your hand to prevent it.

§47. May Adad, the canal inspector of heaven and earth, put an end (to vegetation) in your land, may he avoid your meadows, and hit your land with a severe destructive downpour, may locusts, which diminish the produce of the land, devour your crops, let there be no sound of the grinding stone or the oven in your houses, let barley rations to be ground disappear for you, so that they grind your bones, the bones of your sons and daughters instead of barley rations. . . . Mother shall bar the door to her daughter, may you eat in hunger the flesh of your children, may, through want and famine, one man eat the other's flesh, clothe himself in the other's skin, let dogs and pigs eat your flesh, and may your spirit have no one to take care of and pour libations to him.

28:47–54—Because you did not serve Yahweh your God with joyfulness and gladness of heart . . . therefore you shall serve your enemies whom Yahweh will send against you, in hunger and thirst, in nakedness, and in want of all things. . . . And you shall eat the offspring of your own body, the flesh of your sons and daughters, whom Yahweh has given you. . . . The man who is the most tender and delicately bred among you will grudge food to his brother, to the wife of his bosom, to the last of his children who remain to him.

§48. May Ishtar, the lady of battle, break your bow in a heavy battle, tie your arms, and have you crouch at the feet of your enemy.

28:25—Yahweh will cause you to be defeated before your enemies; you shall go out one way against them, and flee seven ways before them.

§49. May Nergal, the warrior among the gods, extinguish your life with his merciless dagger, may he plant carnage and pestilence among you.

28:21—Yahweh will make the pestilence cleave to you until he has consumed you off the land which you are entering.

§52. May Gula, the great physician, put illness and weariness (into your hearts), an unhealing sore in your

28:35—Yahweh will smite you on the knees and on the legs with grievous boils of which you cannot be

body, so that you bathe in (your own blood) as if in water.

§§63–64. May all the gods who are named in this treaty tablet reduce your soil in size to be as narrow as a brick, turn your soil into iron, so that no one may cut a furrow in it. Just as rain does not fall from a copper sky, so may there come neither rain nor dew upon your fields and meadows, but let it rain burning coals in your land, instead of dew.

§96. If you abandon Esarhaddon, king of Assyria, or the crown prince designate Ashurbanipal, and disperse right and left, may swords consume the one who goes to the right, and may swords consume the one too who goes to the left.

healed, from the sole of your foot to the crown of your head.

28:23–24—And the heavens over your head shall be brass, and the earth under you shall be iron. Yahweh will make the rain of your land powder and dust; from heaven it shall come down upon you until you are destroyed.

5:32—You shall be careful to do therefore as Yahweh your God has commanded you; you shall not turn aside to the right hand or to the left.

(*ANET* 534–41)

---

religion" in the land, it pointed in directions that would have left no doubt about how its laws should be applied in the context of seventh-century Judah. It insisted that Yahweh, not the Assyrian or some other ruler, should be the true overlord of the people.

Thus the book of Deuteronomy was formulated as not only a document of religious independence but also as a document of political independence. Assyrian political domination and religious influence lay at the root of many of its formulations. By 622 B.C.E., Assyrian presence in Palestine must have been minimal, if not nil. The Egyptians had filled the political vacuum, but the "anti-Assyrian" religious reforms could be carried out under Egyptian control and without such reforms representing a move for political autonomy.

Josiah's Reform

According to the report of II Kings 22:3–23:3, the book of the law was turned over to Shaphan the secretary by Hilkiah the high priest, who reported finding the book in the Temple. Shaphan then read the book to the King, who reacted strongly to its contents and sent a deputation to make inquiry "concerning the words of this book that has been found" (II Kings 22:13). The officials carried the book to Huldah the prophetess, who "dwelt in Jerusalem in the Second Quarter," or "New City," perhaps the refugee suburb of Jerusalem, and who was the wife of Shallum the "keeper of the wardrobe" (II Kings 22:14). Huldah is presented pronouncing a word from Yahweh (II Kings 22:15–20). The present account of her proclamation and its content seem to have been edited to conform with the subsequent course of Judean history. It might be presumed that her speech in the name of Yahweh declared that the curses for failure to implement the requirements of the book would fall upon the people unless a concerted effort was made to adhere to its teachings. The king then assembled the people, presented the contents of the book to them, and "made a covenant before Yahweh . . . to perform the words of this covenant that were written in this book; and all the people joined in the covenant" (II Kings 23:3).

Close analysis of the account in Kings of subsequent activity (II Kings 23: 4–24) suggests that the reform occurred in stages which the compilers have telescoped. The main focus and surely the initial stage had to do with the Temple in Jerusalem and with cult places in the immediate vicinity. The editors of the material noted a number of actions taken to purify worship. (It must be remembered, however, that the editors wanted to glorify Josiah's actions and thus may have exaggerated the non-Yahwistic features associated with earlier monarchs as well as the "purges" of Josiah.) The "idolatrous" priests whom the kings of Judah had appointed to officiate in non-Yahwistic worship were deposed (II Kings 23:5). It may be assumed that such worship was related to Assyrian cultic practices. The cultic artifacts associated with such worship were removed (II Kings 23:4a). The Asherah was taken from the Temple, burned, its ashes beaten to dust, and the dust thrown on the paupers' graves (II Kings 23:6). Quarters that had been constructed in the Temple area for male prostitutes where the women "wove hangings" (or "wove cubicles") for the Asherah were demolished (II Kings 23:7). Horses that former kings had dedicated to the sun and placed at the entrance to the Temple were removed and "the chariots of the sun" were burned (II Kings 23:11). Altars constructed on the roof and in the two courts of the Temple were pulled down and thrown into the Kidron (II Kings 23:12). Topheth, an installation in the valley of Hinnom for sacrificing or dedicating children as Molech offerings, is said to have been defiled (II Kings 23:10). Also defiled were the high places (altar shrines) on the mountain east of Jerusalem ("Mount of Olives") dedicated to Ashtoreth, Chemosh, and Milcom. Their pillars were broken, the Asherahs were cut down, and the sites strewn with human bones, rendering them unclean (II Kings 23:13–14).

The second stage of the reform involved an attempt to extend the purge throughout the land—"from Geba to Beer-sheba"—that is, throughout Judah proper (II Kings 23:8). What was involved in Josiah's purge of the cult at large in Judah is not entirely clear. II Kings 23:5 notes that the king deposed the idolatrous priests in Judah who had earlier functioned under royal patronage. Action must also have been taken against some Yahwistic establishments as well, since II Kings 23:8–9 notes that "he brought all the priests out of the cities of Judah, and defiled the high places where the priests had burned incense, from Geba to Beer-sheba. . . . However, the priests of the high places did not come up to the altar of Yahweh in Jerusalem, but they ate unleavened bread among their brethren." These verses suggest (1) that some attempt was made to put the local Yahwistic priests and their sanctuaries out of business by defiling the Yahwistic high places, but (2) that the attempt was not very successful. Apparently the reference in II Kings 23:8b to the destruction of "the high places of the gates that were at the entrance of the gate of Joshua the governor of the city, which were on one's left at the gate of the city" refers to the destruction of a particular high place, namely, the one at Beer-sheba.

The material in Deuteronomy 12 clearly emphasizes the restriction of the sacrificial cult to one sanctuary and makes provisions for certain changes that would result as a consequence. Destruction of other places of worship is decreed. Allowance is made, however, for priests in other shrines to come "to the place which Yahweh will choose" and there they "may minister in the name of Yahweh" their God (Deut. 18:6–7).

Surprising, however, is the fact that such a drastic move as the centralization of the cult as envisioned in Deuteronomy receives such little comment in the narrative about Josiah's reforms in II Kings. This becomes even more surprising in light of the fact that the editors of the material in Kings were committed to the theological concept of centralized worship in Jerusalem. The vagueness of II Kings on the centralization aspects perhaps suggests that the concept of centralized worship was regarded, even in Josiah's day, as a rather idealistic concept and that the royal attempt to enforce the program of centralization was compromised from the beginning.

The idea of centralization had already emerged, of course, in the days of Hezekiah. Thus when the Deuteronomic corpus was put into effect at the time of Josiah's reform, the concept was in the text awaiting enforcement. For Hezekiah, the move toward centralization was a defensive maneuver. He wished to associate Yahwism so closely and exclusively with Jerusalem that the people throughout the land would fight loyally to defend the royal city. Conditions were different under Josiah. The priests of Jerusalem would have had their own reasons for favoring centralization, and it was perhaps under their influence that the idea was written into the Deuteronomic materials from the beginning. Times were different now, however, and the need to strengthen national defense on the basis of a centralized place of worship was no longer at issue. Thus even if Josiah pushed the idea, it seems not to have met with overwhelming success.

II Kings 23:21–23 stipulates that Josiah enforced the observance of the Passover "as it is written in this book of the covenant." That is, he required that particular Passover to be held in Jerusalem (see Deut. 16:1–8). II Kings 23:23 notes, however, only that such a Passover was held in his eighteenth year, the year when the law book was found. If II Kings 23:9 refers to this same celebration, it suggests that even the rural Yahwistic priests did not participate in this centralized Passover observance. Josiah is said also to have banned wizards, mediums, and the like (II Kings 23:24). This again could have been based on Deuteronomic material but would have been a prohibition very difficult to enforce.

Judean Temple at Arad. Shown here after excavation, the entrance to the "holy of holies" of the Arad shrine is flanked by two stone altars, or incense stands. Hezekiah or Josiah may have closed down the sanctuary during his religious reforms. *(Arad Archaeological Expedition)*

Was there a third stage in Josiah's religious reform, namely, a movement beyond Jerusalem and the boundaries of Judah ("from Geba to Beer-sheba"; II Kings 23:8)? Both II Kings (23:15–20) and II Chronicles (34:6–7) suggest there was. It is highly doubtful, however, that Josiah extended Judean borders or purged religious cult places outside Judean territory except in the case of Bethel. Except for this case, the assertions in II Kings and II Chronicles that Josiah carried his reformation into old Israelite territory are highly general, sweeping statements which supply no specific details and appear to be later editorializing notations. The fact that in the later Persian provincial system, which generally followed the situation inherited from the Babylonians, Bethel was part of the province of Judah would suggest that Josiah expanded his kingdom a few miles northward from Geba to include the region around Bethel which was later left under Judean authority by the Babylonians. In the process, the old royal sanctuary at the site was destroyed and polluted.

Horned Altar from Beer-sheba. Unearthed in the excavations at Beer-sheba and reconstructed, the stones of the altar had been dismantled and reused in other construction. *(Institute of Archaeology, Tel Aviv University)*

The Death of Josiah

In 609 B.C.E., the new Egyptian pharaoh, Neco II (610–595 B.C.E.), marched north to aid the Assyrians and to confront the westward-advancing Babylonians. It was probably during the pharaoh's march to the north that Josiah was killed by Neco II at Megiddo. The Kings account is very vague about the circumstances of Josiah's death: "Pharaoh Neco king of Egypt went up to the king of Assyria to the river Euphrates. King Josiah went to meet him; and Pharaoh Neco slew him at Megiddo, when he saw him" (II Kings 23:29). What happened at Megiddo remains a mystery. The Chronicler (II Chron. 35:20–23) turns the meeting of the two monarchs into a military confrontation, the pharaoh into a Yahwistic preacher, and Josiah into a "second Ahab" who though disguised was accidentally killed in battle (see II Chron. 18:28–34). Any proposed scenario about why and how Josiah was killed at Megiddo must be based on speculation. Was it the result of some misunderstanding between the new pharaoh and the Judean king on their first meeting? Were some extenuating circumstances, some accidents of history, to blame? Did Josiah assume that something was to be gained by opposing Egypt and siding with Babylonia? The historian can simply not know. Both II Chronicles and II Kings agree on one thing: the Judean king was returned to the capital city and given a proper burial in Jerusalem (II Kings 23:30; II Chron. 35:24).

Jehoahaz II

With Josiah's death, "the people of the land" placed his son Jehoahaz on the throne (II Kings 23:30–31), bypassing the latter's elder brother in the succession (II Kings 23:36). The Judean "people of the land" were again attempting to dominate Jerusalem politics. Jehoahaz' mother was from Libnah, one of the major Judean cities, and this may have influenced their specific choice. The reign of Jehoahaz, who was also known in the Bible as Shallum (Jer. 22:11; I Chron. 3:15), lasted only three months, the period of Neco's stay in northern Syria. As it turned out, it was the Egyptian pharaoh, not "the people of the land," who had the last say. When Jehoahaz presented himself to Pharaoh Neco at Riblah, upon the latter's return from Haran, he was voluntarily recognizing what Josiah also had acknowledged, namely, Judah's subservience to Egypt. In spite of his submissive posture, the Judean king was placed in bonds and deprived of his rule. The pharaoh, nursing the Egyptian frustrations of continued lack of success against the Babylonians, probably was in no mood to put up with the rash actions of the Judean leaders who had appointed a successor of their own choosing and without his consent. A modest fine of one hundred talents of silver and a talent of gold was imposed on Judah, and Jehoahaz was taken into exile in Egypt, where he eventually died (II Kings 23:33–34). In Jerusalem, the prophet Jeremiah advised his countrymen not to lament Josiah but to lament Shallum (Jehoahaz):

> Weep not for him who is dead,
>   nor bemoan him;
> but weep bitterly for him who goes away,
>   for he shall return no more
>   to see his native land.
>   (Jer. 22:10; see Ezek. 19:1–4)

Jehoiakim

Neco took Eliakim, the older brother of Jehoahaz, and made him the Judean king, giving him the throne name Jehoiakim (II Kings 23:34). Egypt for the moment was still supreme in Syria-Palestine, "from the Brook of Egypt to the river Euphrates" (II Kings 24:7). Jehoiakim, along with Judean society at large, was clearly pro-Egyptian. To raise the special tribute placed on Judah, Jehoiakim did not raid the royal or Temple treasury but instead extracted the silver and gold from the people of the land in a special taxation (II Kings 23:35). Jehoiakim may already have ascended the throne in 609 but certainly no later than 608 B.C.E. For four years he remained a loyal Egyptian vassal.

In 606 B.C.E., the Egyptian army had overcome the Babylonian garrison at Kimuhu near Carchemish (*ABC* 98), but the Egyptian-Babylonian struggle was already tilting in favor of Babylon. A year later, in 605 B.C.E., the great encounter for dominance in the Eastern Mediterranean Seaboard between Babylonia and Egypt occurred at Carchemish (see Jer. 46:1–12). Nebuchadrezzar, the Babylonian crown prince, led his forces to an overwhelming victory. After futilely attempting to halt the Babylonians at Carchemish, the Egyptian army retreated, only to be defeated again in Hamath. The remnants of the Egyptian army were decimated while fleeing Syria for their homeland (*ABC* 99). As we noted earlier, Judean troops formed part of the Egyptian military fighting to halt Nebuchadrezzar's advance westward (*Contra Apion* I.136–37). From this time on, Nebuchadrezzar regarded himself as master of Syria-Palestine and could portray himself as a liberator freeing the region from Egyptian domination (see *ANET* 307).

Jehoiakim was Neco's man on the Judean throne, and he and most of the Judean population, even after Carchemish, probably hoped that the Egyptian pharaoh could secure the region against Babylonian dominance and resist any attempt on Nebuchadrezzar's part to push farther into the region than northern Syria. The prophet Jeremiah saw matters differently.

King Jehoiakim and the Prophet Jeremiah

Jeremiah may be seen not only as a prophet with his own particular perspectives on Judean life and international affairs but also as the spokesman of a minority position concerning the most appropriate foreign policy for the state. He represented those who felt that submission to Babylonia was the most advantageous policy Judah could take. In criticizing royal practices and state policies, Jeremiah was more than an isolated voice crying in the wilderness. Some members of his immediate family and his personal supporters probably were important and powerful figures in the political and cultic life of Judah.

The names of several members of Jeremiah's immediate family were also the names of leading Judean officials at the time. (It is impossible to know for sure whether an identical name refers to the same individual or to a different individual.) Jeremiah's father was named Hilkiah, the same name as the high priest at the time of the Josianic reform (Jer. 1:1; II Kings 22:4, 8). His uncle, Shallum, had the same name as the husband of the prophetess Huldah (Jer. 32:7; II Kings 22:14). Maaseiah, the son of Shallum (and Jeremiah's first cousin?), was a priestly official, the keeper of the threshold (Jer. 35:4). Zephaniah, another son of Shallum, was second to the high priest in the Temple hierarchy (Jer. 21:1; 37:3; 52:24).

In addition, Jeremiah was supported by several high-ranking government officials, many from the family of Shaphan, who possessed strong connections with the reform movement of Josiah. Ahikam, son of Shaphan and court official under Josiah, aided Jeremiah when he was arrested for treason (Jer. 26:24; II Kings 22:11, 14). Another son of Shaphan, Elasah, carried Jeremiah's correspondence to the exiles in Babylon (Jer. 29:3). Jeremiah's scroll was given a reading in the house of Gemariah, another son of Shaphan (Jer. 36:10–12). Elnathan son of Achbor, a prince in Jehoiakim's court, whose father was involved in Josiah's reform (II Kings 22:12, 14), was at least sympathetic to Jeremiah's preaching (Jer. 36:12, 25).

Jeremiah and Jehoiakim seldom seem to have held similar opinions about either Judean life or international affairs. Already "in the beginning of the reign of Jehoiakim" (between his accession and coronation?), Jeremiah had delivered his famous Temple sermon (Jer. 7; 26) warning that, unless repentance and strict adherence to the law were forthcoming, the Jerusalem Temple would become like the temple of Shiloh (Jer. 26:6). Just as Shiloh had once housed the Ark and functioned as an important sanctuary but now was an insignificant place, so would Jerusalem soon be. The implication of Jeremiah's sermon, given in Jeremiah 7 in a form strongly reminiscent of Deuteronomic perspectives and terminology, suggests that Jehoiakim was no strict Yahwist cut from the same cloth as his father. Jeremiah 7:31–32 and ch. 19 imply instead that the king had returned to the oldtime religion of pre-Josianic days.

Jeremiah was not alone in his evaluation of the situation. The prophet Uriah ben Shemaiah from Kiriath-jearim proclaimed a similar message. Both men angered governmental officials, who must have regarded their words as blasphemy and "un-Judean." In light of the people's reactions, Uriah fled to Egypt but was extradited by an Egyptian government friendly to Judah, returned to Jerusalem, executed on order of the king, and his body thrown into the pauper's graveyard (Jer. 26:20–23). Jeremiah was saved from an identical fate when prophetic precedent was appealed to—the case of the prophet Micah who had preached a similar message provoking King Hezekiah to heed his word and call on Yahweh for help, and Yahweh had changed his verdict (Jer. 26:16–19). The text notes also perhaps the more important factor in his escape from execution, namely, that Jeremiah was supported by Ahikam, the son of Shaphan the state secretary (Jer. 26:24; II Kings 22:3, 8).

The tensions between Jehoiakim and Jeremiah did not subside with the passage of time. In the fourth year of Jehoiakim (605 B.C.E.), the year of the battle of Carchemish, Jeremiah proclaimed that Yahweh would send for all the tribes of the north and for Nebuchadrezzar and would bring them against the land of Judah and utterly destroy it (Jer. 25). He predicted that "this whole land shall become a ruin and a waste, and these nations shall serve the king of Babylon seventy years" (Jer. 25:11). Seventy years was a common figure used in Near Eastern literature to speak of the period of a city's devastation or ruin (see Isa. 23:17 and below, p. 440). Yahweh's scourge at the hands of the Babylonians was to reach other nations as well, including Egypt (Jer. 25:15–26; 46:1–12). Clearly, Jeremiah saw Nebuchadrezzar as Yahweh's new man, as Yahweh's servant, to master the nations for the coming years (Jer. 25:9).

Jeremiah was barred from entering the Temple, possibly as a consequence of his earlier sermon delivered there. To make his oracles public, he engaged Baruch, a scribe, to write his words on a scroll and read them in the Temple (Jer. 36). The occasion for the reading was a public fast proclaimed in the fifth year of Jehoiakim, probably at the time of Nebuchadrezzar's attack on Ashkelon (*ABC* 100). After the reading, the scroll was taken and privately read to the king, who defiantly burned it and ordered that Jeremiah and Baruch be arrested. The two, having been earlier warned, had taken precaution and were already in hiding. A new scroll was produced containing Jeremiah's message but expanded to include a warning that Nebuchadrezzar would destroy Judah and specifying that Jehoiakim would meet a particularly terrible fate—death without burial.

Sometime in his reign, perhaps before the Babylonians completely took over Syria-Palestine, Jehoiakim began the construction of a new royal palace apparently with the use of conscripted labor. A recently published seal, probably from the late seventh century, contains the inscription: "Belonging to Palayahu who is over the compulsory labor." Whether the practice of using conscripted laborers on royal land and projects had continued throughout Judean history from the time of David and Solomon or was a renewed practice of Jehoiakim's reign cannot be determined. At any rate, Jeremiah denounced Jehoiakim in a scathing oracle:

> Woe to him who builds his house by unrighteousness,
>   and his upper rooms by injustice;
> who makes his neighbor serve him for nothing,
>   and does not give him his wages;
> who says, "I will build myself a great house
>   with spacious upper rooms,"
> and cuts out windows for it,
>   paneling it with cedar,
>   and painting it with vermilion.

> Do you think you are a king
>> because you compete in cedar?
> Did not your father [Josiah] eat and drink
>> and do justice and righteousness?
>> Then it was well with him.
> He judged the cause of the poor and needy;
>> then it was well. . . .
> But you have eyes and heart
>> only for your dishonest gain,
> for shedding innocent blood,
>> and for practicing oppression and violence.
>>>>>> (Jer. 22:13–17)

In his denunciations of Jehoiakim, Jeremiah seems clearly to have called for the assassination of the king and his family. Jeremiah 36:30 has the prophet announce an oracle of doom: "Therefore thus says Yahweh concerning Jehoiakim of Judah, He shall have none to sit upon the throne of David, and his dead body shall be cast out to the heat by day and the frost by night." Jeremiah 22:18–19 is even more explicit: "Therefore thus says Yahweh concerning Jehoiakim the son of Josiah, king of Judah: 'They shall not lament for him, saying, . . . "Ah lord!" or "Ah his majesty!" With the burial of an ass he shall be buried, dragged and cast forth beyond the gates of Jerusalem.' " Both of these announcements of judgment were proclaimed as rhetorical calls for assassination, but apparently there were no takers.

Judah as a Babylonian Vassal

In 604 B.C.E., following his victory at Carchemish, Nebuchadrezzar marched unopposed into Syria-Palestine and conquered the Philistine city of Ashkelon. This was perhaps the occasion for the national fast noted in Jer. 36:9 and for the lamenting oracle of Habakkuk on the growing power of the Chaldeans (Hab. 1–2). For the following two years, 603–602 B.C.E., the Babylonian texts are fragmentary, but Nebuchadrezzar seems to have continued to operate in Syria-Palestine and to secure his control there. Probably following the Babylonian capture of Ashkelon in 604 B.C.E. (see above, Text XII), Jehoiakim gave up his tenacious determination not to submit to the Babylonians and became Nebuchadrezzar's vassal. Apparently neither he nor the majority of his officials ever surrendered their confidence in Egypt, however, and remained loyal to Babylonia only long enough to pay annual tribute on three occasions (II Kings 24:1), probably in 603, 602, and 601 B.C.E.

If Jehoiakim transferred his allegiance from Neco II to Nebuchadrezzar sometime in 604/3 B.C.E., then it would have been about 600 B.C.E. that he decided to withhold tribute and challenge Nebuchadrezzar. From the Babylonian Chronicles it becomes obvious why Jehoiakim chose to pursue this action which otherwise appears irrational. The chronicles report the following:

Year 4 [601–600 B.C.E.]: The king of Akkad [Nebuchadrezzar] sent out his army and marched into Hatti land [Syria-Palestine]. They marched unopposed through Hatti land. In the month of Kislev he took the lead of his army and marched toward Egypt. The king of Egypt [Neco] heard of it and sent out his army; they clashed in an open battle and inflicted heavy losses on each other. The king of Akkad and his army turned back and returned to Babylon. (*ANET* 564; *ABC* 101)

The frank Babylonian report demonstrates that Nebuchadrezzar attempted to invade Egypt late in 601 B.C.E. but was either defeated or fought to a draw. This Egyptian-Babylonian battle also appears to be noted in Herodotus, who reports that "with his land army, he (Neco) met and defeated the Syrians (= Babylonians?) at Magdolus (= Migdol in Egypt?), taking the great Syrian city of Cadytis (= Gaza?) after the battle" (Herodotus II. 159). Jeremiah 47:1 also refers to the Egyptian capture of Gaza. Probably in late 601/early 600 B.C.E., Babylonia invaded Egypt, was severely defeated and repelled from Egypt, and Neco carried the conflict into Palestine, where he captured the city of Gaza. According to the Babylonian records, Nebuchadrezzar spent the year following his defeat in Babylon refurbishing his chariot forces (*ANET* 564; *ABC* 101; see above, Text XII). For the first time since 604 B.C.E., no Babylonian campaign was conducted in the direction of Syria-Palestine. Perhaps Jehoaiakim, encouraged by the pharaoh's showing and by the absence of the main Babylonian army, took the occasion to withhold tribute and thus to rebel.

Following their victory in 600/601 B.C.E. over the Babylonians, Neco and the Egyptians, while still attempting to foment rebellion in Syria-Palestine, were either unable or unwilling to reassert themselves further in land battles with Nebuchadrezzar. Neco turned his attention more to the sea. Perhaps recognizing that the Babylonians had control of the land area of the Eastern Mediterranean Seaboard, Neco sought a greater share of the naval commerce. A canal joining the Mediterranean and the Red Sea was begun, and large seagoing triremes were introduced into the Egyptian fleet. Thus, although an Egyptian victory triggered Jehoiakim's revolt, the Egyptians proved not to be a major support in the long run partly because of their naval preoccupation.

In the sixth year of his reign (599 B.C.E.), Nebuchadrezzar moved back into Syria-Palestine, but the period was spent in raids against Arab tribes in the desert (*ANET* 564; *ABC* 101; see above, Text XII). The main Babylonian forces took no direct action against the rebel Jehoiakim. II Kings 24:2 notes that "Yahweh sent against him bands of the Chaldeans, and bands of the Syrians, and bands of the Moabites, and bands of the Ammonites." Apparently Nebuchadrezzar contented himself for the moment with allowing the Jerusalem situation to be handled by auxiliary forces and the Babylonian (Chaldean) garrisons stationed in the region. Probably at this time Jeremiah had his famous encounter with the Rechabites (Jer. 35). The group had moved into Jerusalem "for fear of the army of the Chaldeans and the army of the Syrians" (Jer. 35:11). Jeremiah used the Rechabites as an object lesson for the people: they manifested a fidelity to their commitments that was in stark contrast to the unfaithfulness of Judah and Jerusalem.

In the following year, Nebuchadrezzar marched out with his main army. The Babylonian Chronicles report his suppression of the Judean revolt in the following terms:

> Year 7 [598–597 B.C.E.], month Kislev [18 Dec. 598–15 Jan. 597 B.C.E.]: The king of Akkad [Nebuchadrezzar] moved his army into Hatti land, laid siege to the city of Judah [Jerusalem] and on the second day of the month Adar he captured the city and seized its king. He appointed in it a king of his liking, took heavy booty from it and sent it to Babylon. (See *ANET* 564; *ABC* 102)

The second of Adar in Nebuchadrezzar's seventh year would correspond to either the 15th or the 16th of March 597 B.C.E. The uncertainty over the day is due to the fact that the Babylonians reckoned the day from dusk to dusk.

Jehoiachin

The king whom Nebuchadrezzar captured when Jerusalem surrendered was Jehoiachin (also called Jeconiah and Coniah), the eighteen-year-old son and successor of Jehoiakim. The biblical texts assign three months (II Kings 24:8) or three months and ten days to his reign (II Chron. 36:9). This means that he would have become king sometime early in December 598 B.C.E. before Nebuchadrezzar personally arrived on the scene in Jerusalem. There are diverse traditions about what happened to Jehoiakim. II Kings 24:6 reports that he slept with his fathers, thus implying that he died a natural death. II Chronicles 36:6, on the other hand, says that Nebuchadrezzar bound him in fetters to take him to Babylon. The Lucianic recension of the Greek for both II Kings 24:6 and II Chron. 36:8 reports that he was buried in the Garden of Uzzah, outside the wall of Jerusalem (see II Kings 21:18, 26). Finally, Josephus has Jehoiakim killed by Nebuchadrezzar after Jerusalem fell (*Ant.* X.96). II Kings 24:6 is probably the more reliable. Jehoiakim must have died in office, still anticipating the arrival of the Egyptians but "the king of Egypt did not come again out of his land" (II Kings 24:7).

After a reign of three months, upon the arrival of Nebuchadrezzar on the scene, "Jehoiachin the king of Judah gave himself up to the king of Babylon, himself, and his mother, and his servants, and his princes, and his palace officials" (II Kings 24:12). These and other leading citizens along with the Temple and royal treasures were carried away by Nebuchadrezzar to Babylon.

Zedekiah

The "king of his liking" whom Nebuchadrezzar placed on the Judean throne was Mattaniah, an uncle of Jehoiachin, who bore the throne name Zedekiah (II Kings 24:17). Zedekiah was probably subjected to a treaty and made to swear an oath of fidelity to the Babylonian ruler in the name of Yahweh (II Chron. 36:13; Ezek. 17:12–20), "that he would surely keep the country for him and attempt no uprising nor show friendliness to the Egyptians" (so Josephus, *Ant.*

X.102). He ascended the throne in 597 B.C.E. and his rule lasted for eleven years.

The capture of Jerusalem and the exile of Jehoiachin left the people stunned and polarized. There were those—perhaps a majority—who could not believe that this had really happened, that Jerusalem, Yahweh's city, had been taken. Yahweh had stepped in before, at the last moment, and saved the city during Hezekiah's reign. Moreover, the Zion theology proclaimed the inviolability of the city (Ps. 46; 48; 76). Surely the capture had been only a historical accident. In short, there were hopes, encouraged by prophetic announcements, that the whole bad dream would be reversed in the future and Jehoiachin and the exiles would return.

Feelings were partially polarized around the figures of Jehoiachin and Zedekiah. Dates are frequently given with references to Jehoaichin's exile (in the Book of Ezekiel; II Kings 25:27) suggesting that many still considered him the real king and looked forward to his release and reinstatement. Zedekiah had been put on the throne by a foreign monarch, not installed by his own people. On the other hand, Jehoiachin was considered totally unacceptable by Jeremiah (Jer. 22:24–30; referred to here as Coniah). Jeremiah and Judah were also divided over what course of action to take, whether to continue hoping in Egypt or to submit completely to the Babylonians. In all of this, Zedekiah seems to have lacked full control over his own people and to have vacillated in his actions or to have been forced into positions he would rather not have taken. In addition, many of the seasoned Judean diplomats and officials were in exile, no longer present to offer advice.

Judah Under Babylonian Hegemony

Little is known about international events during Zedekiah's reign. The account in II Kings moves directly from his accession to the outbreak of rebellion in his ninth year (II Kings 24:18–25:1). The Babylonian Chronicles are fragmentary for this period. Fortunately some material has been supplied in the books of Jeremiah and Ezekiel. Jeremiah 27–29, for example, which belongs primarily to the beginning of the reign of Zedekiah (Jer. 27:1; 28:1), provides some information about international affairs. (The reference to "the fifth month of the fourth year" in Jer. 28:1 probably is a calculation associated with a seven-year or sabbatical cycle [see Deut. 15] rather than the chronology of the reign of Zedekiah.)

In 597 B.C.E., after Nebuchadrezzar had quickly returned to Babylon, as was his custom after completing a campaign, a six-nation conclave was held in Jerusalem. Representatives from Edom, Moab, Ammon, Tyre, and Sidon gathered in the Judean capital to discuss possible plans and to coordinate strategy (Jer. 27:3). The absence of any representatives from Philistia suggests that this area was under strong Babylonian control. Apparently the Transjordanian and Phoenician ambassadors discussed with Zedekiah the prospects of a united revolt to take place two years later in conjunction with a simultaneous rebellion

being planned by states in the east that were subject to Babylon. Whether
Zedekiah initiated the meeting and what his stance on the planned rebellion was
remain unknown.

Jeremiah vigorously opposed the conclave and picketed the meeting wearing
thongs and yoke bars (Jer. 27:2). He denounced all plans for rebellion and
called upon all the nations and especially Zedekiah to remain loyal to Babylon,
threatening them with divine judgment if they did not serve Nebuchadrezzar.
Apparently the anti-Babylonian sentiment had the support of many religious
leaders, especially some of the prophets (Jer. 27:9, 16). Jeremiah, in his letter
to the exiles, which Zedekiah allowed him to send to Babylon with royal
emissaries, referred to the prophetical activity in Babylon which was apparently
aware of the movement underfoot (Jer. 29:8–9, 20–23). Jeremiah also responded to the attempt to have him arrested and the charge that he was a
madman (Jer. 29:24–28). In his letter Jeremiah advised the exiles not to place
any hopes in a speedy return but to settle down in their new locale and cause
no trouble (Jer. 29:4–7).

The prophet Hananiah spoke out in Jerusalem promising that the yoke of the
king of Babylon would be broken in two years and that King Jehoiachin and
the exiles would soon return home (Jer. 28:1–4). He seems to have placed his
faith in the planned forthcoming rebellion and proclaimed it as Yahweh's will.
According to Hananiah, the yoke of Babylon would be broken "from the neck
of all the nations" (Jer. 28:11). To symbolize his prophecy, Hananiah had
removed the yoke bars from Jeremiah and broken them (Jer. 28:10). Jeremiah
subsequently replaced these with iron yokes to symbolize that Nebuchadrezzar's
rule was a rule of iron (Jer. 28:12–14). Jeremiah prophesied Hananiah's death,
and apparently someone in Zedekiah's administration or in the pro-Babylonian
segment of the society saw to it that the prophecy was fulfilled, since "in that
same year, in the seventh month, the prophet Hananiah died" (Jer. 28:15–17).

In Nebuchadrezzar's ninth and tenth years (596/5, 595/4 B.C.E.), trouble
did break out in the east. Although the Babylonian Chronicles are fragmentary
at this point, they refer to a movement by the king of Elam against Nebuchadrezzar in the king's ninth year. Elam may have been influential earlier in
the call of the planning meeting held in Jerusalem to plot revolt in the west (see
Jer. 49:34–38). The Elamite advance was met by a Babylonian response and the
Elamites fled. In his tenth year Nebuchadrezzar remained most of the year in
Babylonia, where he had to put down a local rebellion which broke out in
December 595 B.C.E. and involved elements in his own army. Later in the year
he marched to the west and collected tribute (*ABC* 102). So far as is known,
none of the nations that sent representatives to the Jerusalem conference re-
belled during Babylonia's troubles in 596–594 B.C.E.

In Zedekiah's fourth year (594–593 B.C.E.), we hear of a trip of the Judean
king to Babylon (Jer. 51:59). Such a trip undoubtedly had a political purpose:
to offer to Nebuchadrezzar assurances of Judean loyalty in light of the recent
uprisings. On this occasion Jeremiah is said to have sent a letter (Jer. 51:60)

containing an oracle proclaiming the ultimate downfall of Babylon (Jer. 51: 1–58), with orders that the document be read and then thrown into the Euphrates (Jer. 51:61–64). Such an oracle makes sense as Jeremiah's response to the demoralized Judean exiles who had set their hopes on the success of the recently suppressed insurrection. All along, it seems, Jeremiah had viewed the exiles in a positive light, comparing them to good figs and those left in Palestine to bad figs (Jer. 24).

In Egypt, meanwhile, Psammetichus II (595–589 B.C.E.) had succeeded Neco II. Two events in this pharaoh's reign had enormous impact on Judean politics and tipped the scales toward a second revolt against Babylonia. (1) The pharaoh carried out a successful campaign against Nubia (Ethiopia). The Egyptian army marched south, apparently encountered no overwhelming opposition, and returned home victorious in 592 B.C.E. (Herodotus II.161; *AEL* III.84–86). The pharaoh sought to make the most of this victory to counter Egyptian lack of success against Babylonia. (2) In 591 B.C.E., shortly after the return from Nubia, Psammetichus II went on a victory tour of Palestine. This journey is reported in the so-called Rylands IX papyrus (*CDP* II.64–65). The following extract from the papyrus text describes the visit:

> In the fourth regnal year of Pharaoh Psamtek Neferibre they sent to the great temples of Upper and Lower Egypt, saying, "Pharaoh (Life, Prosperity, Health) is going to the Land of Palestine. Let the priests come with the bouquets of the gods of Egypt to take them to the Land of Palestine." And they sent to Teudjoy saying: "Let a priest come with the bouquet of Amun, in order to go to the Land of Palestine with Pharaoh." And the priests agreed and said to Pediese, the son of Essamtowy, "you are the one who, it is agreed, ought to go to the Land of Palestine with Pharaoh. There is no one here in the town who is able to go to the Land of Palestine except you. Behold, you must do it, you, a scribe of the House of Life; there is nothing they can ask you and you not be able to answer it, for you are a priest of Amun. It is only the priests of the great gods of Egypt that are going to the Land of Palestine with Pharaoh." And they persuaded Pediese to go to the Land of Palestine with Pharaoh and he made his preparations. So Pediese, son of Essamtowy, went to the Land of Palestine, and no one was with him save his servant and an hour-priest of Isis named Osirmose.

Two factors about this text are noteworthy and must be taken into consideration in its interpretation. First, the text presents the expedition to Palestine as if it was fundamentally a religious, festive occasion. Second, the focus in the narrative is on Pediese the priest and his fate and not on the larger historical issues. In the story's continuation, the account reports how Pediese returned to Egypt to find that he had been cheated out of his priestly income and was forced to appeal unsuccessfully to the pharaoh.

The visit of Psammetichus II to Palestine must, however, be seen as more than a triumphant religious procession. After all, at least some Babylonian troops were stationed in the area and the states of Syria-Palestine were committed to Nebuchadrezzar by treaty. Such a visit by a long-standing anti-Babylonian power could not help carrying political and military implications. Psammetichus' visit must have been seen as Egypt's reassertion, even if somewhat ceremonial, of its claims over Syria-Palestine.

The Judean Rebellion and the Fall of Jerusalem

Sometime very late in the 590s or early in the 580s, Judah rebelled against Babylon, a move presumably symbolized by Zedekiah's failure to render annual tribute (II Kings 24:20b). The account in II Kings offers no explanation for the rebellion, nor does it provide any clues about why the Judean political hierarchy thought it had a chance to succeed. In fact, this account moves quickly to the final days of the two-year Babylonian siege of Jerusalem.

Two factors must be seen as contributing causes to Zedekiah's revolt. (1) Nebuchadrezzar apparently had not put in an appearance in Syria-Palestine since 594 B.C.E. The Babylonian Chronicles report that in his eleventh year (594–593 B.C.E.) Nebuchadrezzar mustered his army and marched to Hatti (*ABC* 102), but they provide no details about this western campaign. As we have noted, even prior to this date, Nebuchadrezzar was fairly consistently occupied in the east. (2) Psammetichus II's triumph in Nubia must have stirred the hopes of Judean circles who still believed that Egypt could offer military salvation. Undoubtedly a large portion of the Judean leadership held this view. Likewise, the visit of Psammetichus II to Palestine and his "triumphant tour" in the area must have fed the fires of revolt. It is not out of the question that Psammetichus actually may have visited Jerusalem, conferred with Zedekiah,

Psammetichus II. After a successful military campaign against Nubia, Psammetichus II (595–589 B.C.E.) appeared in Palestine in 591 B.C.E. His visit undoubtedly contributed to the volatile political mix which gave rise to the Judean rebellion from Babylon about 590 B.C.E. (From J. B. Pritchard, *The Ancient Near East in Pictures,* Princeton University Press, 1969)

and entered into a treaty with him. (Ezekiel 8 has been interpreted in terms of such a visit, and the reference in v. 17 to putting "the branch to the nose" has been associated with the garlands of the Egyptian gods.) Ezekiel 17:15 clearly refers to Zedekiah's negotiations with Egypt over supplying him with horses and troops. It cannot be determined when this negotiation took place. If the date in Ezek. 8:1 is applicable to the whole section of chs. 8–19, then negotiations with Psammetichus II could certainly be alluded to in Ezek. 17:15.

It may have been these Egyptian negotiations, therefore, which led to the breaking of Zedekiah's treaty with Babylonia (Ezek. 17:13–21). At any rate, Zedekiah was clearly relying on Egyptian aid in his endeavors. Among the ostraca (inscribed potsherds) discovered at the site of ancient Lachish was a letter mentioning the visit to Egypt of Coniah son of Elnathan, a general in the Judean army (*ANET* 322; ostracon III; see below, Text XVI), possibly to conduct negotiations for assistance.

No evidence exists to suggest that Judah's uprising was coordinated with any country other than Egypt. Neither does there appear to have been any broad move of insurrection against Babylonia in Syria-Palestine at the time or a united anti-Babylonian front in Judah. Of the other states in the region, only Ammon (see Ezek. 21:18–23) and Tyre, which was subsequently placed under a thirteen-year siege by Nebuchadrezzar (Ezek. 26–28; 29:17–20; *Ant.* X.228), rebelled. Likewise, elements of the population, including Jeremiah and his followers and associates, strongly opposed rebellion. One of the Lachish ostraca can be interpreted to suggest that there was dissension and tension even in the military over the best attitude to take toward Babylonia (*ANET* 322; ostracon VI; see below, Text XVI).

Many episodes in the Book of Jeremiah concern events associated with the days of Jerusalem's siege and illustrate the diverse sentiments in the city. As Nebuchadrezzar approached the city, for example, Zedekiah is reported to have sent a delegation of nobles to Jeremiah to "inquire of Yahweh" (Jer. 21). Jeremiah responded very negatively, announcing that Yahweh would fight on the side of the Babylonians and recommending that the citizens surrender to the Chaldeans. Jeremiah 19:1–20:6 may belong to this same context. In Jeremiah 19, Jeremiah proclaimed in a symbolical act, and publicly, the same message that had been transmitted privately to Zedekiah's delegation. Thereupon, Pashhur, the priest who had been a member of the delegation, beat Jeremiah and had him put in stocks in the Upper Benjamin Gate of the Temple. When released the next day, Jeremiah reaffirmed his position that Judah would fall to the Babylonians and added that Pashhur and his family would die in exile.

While the siege of the city was under way, Apries (Hophra) (589–570 B.C.E.), the new Egyptian pharaoh, sent an Egyptian army into Palestine, causing the Babylonians to lift the siege temporarily (Jer. 37:1–10). It is impossible to know how seriously Apries took his commitment to Judah. Classical sources note that he fought against Tyre and Sidon and defeated the armies of Cyprus and Phoenicia (Herodotus II.161; Diodorus I.68.1). This would suggest that

Apries was more concerned with naval exploits and Mediterranean trade than with aiding landlocked Judah.

Apparently while the Egyptian army was on the scene and the Babylonian army temporarily withdrawn, Zedekiah sent yet another delegation to Jeremiah requesting that he pray for the people. Again the prophet responded negatively and offered his evaluation of Egyptian assistance: "Behold, Pharaoh's army which came to help you is about to return to Egypt, to its own land. And the Chaldeans shall come back and fight against this city; they shall take it and burn it with fire" (Jer. 37:7–8; see Ezek. 17:17).

Also while the Babylonian army was temporarily withdrawn, Jeremiah sought to leave the city for business reasons (perhaps to buy a plot of land in Anathoth; see Jer. 32). He was arrested again, charged with deserting to the Babylonians, beaten, and imprisoned (Jer. 37:11–15). While imprisoned in the house of Jonathan the secretary, he was summoned to Zedekiah for a private meeting. To the king he reaffirmed his negative assessment of the situation and appealed for release from prison. Zedekiah removed him to the court of the guard with orders that he be given a daily ration of bread as long as there was food in the city (Jer. 37:16–21).

Apparently no major encounter occurred between the Egyptians and the Babylonians. The former may simply have withdrawn from Palestine. The siege of Jerusalem was again taken up in earnest and the situation in the town became desperate. Among the Judean cities, only Jerusalem, Lachish, and Azekah remained in Judean hands (Jer. 34:7).

Jeremiah apparently continued his preaching throughout the Babylonian campaign against Judah (Jer. 38). A delegation went to Zedekiah urging the king to put the prophet to death, "for he is weakening the hands of the soldiers who are left in this city, and the hands of all the people, by speaking such words to them. For this man is not seeking the welfare of this people, but their harm" (Jer. 38:4). The king turned the prophet over to the accusers and Jeremiah this time was put into the cistern of Malchiah, the king's son, which was in the court of the guard. An Ethiopian in the royal service, Ebed-melech, appealed to the king for permission to draw Jeremiah out of the mire of the cistern. Following his rescue, Jeremiah remained in the court of the guard. Again the texts report a meeting between Zedekiah and Jeremiah. The prophet tried to talk Zedekiah into surrendering, and the king admitted that he was afraid to capitulate to the Babylonians lest they hand him over to the Judeans who had deserted to Nebuchadrezzar for fear they would abuse him. After Jeremiah described for the king the consequences to his family of their capture, Zedekiah begged the prophet not to divulge the contents of their conversation and Jeremiah agreed.

In Jeremiah 34 there are two oracles related to Zedekiah. In the first, Jeremiah predicts the fall of Jerusalem, but promises Zedekiah that he will die in peace after seeing the Babylonian king eye to eye and face to face (Jer. 34:1–5). In Jer. 34:8–22 he condemns the king and the princes for granting liberty to their slaves (so they would not have to feed them?) when the city was besieged but then reenslaving them as soon as the Babylonians moved away at the approach of the Egyptians.

As Jerusalem's situation became increasingly desperate and the city appeared doomed, Jeremiah seems to have shifted his preaching to pronouncements about the future. Of the city's impending ruin, he had no uncertainty, but he attempted to give hope for the more distant future. While still a prisoner in the court of the guard, for example, he reported on his earlier purchase of land in Anathoth (Jer. 32). The point he made was that, although Jerusalem would surely fall, things would someday surely return to normal: "Houses and fields and vineyards shall again be bought in this land" (Jer. 32:15). The same point is made in Jeremiah 33. The houses that had been dismantled for stones to strengthen the city defenses would be rebuilt.

After a two-year siege the people who were defending Jerusalem ran out of food. The wall was breached. Zedekiah with a military escort fled by night in the direction of Transjordan. The Babylonians gave chase and overtook them near Jericho. Zedekiah was captured and carried before Nebuchadrezzar, who was encamped at Riblah. There, sentence was passed, no doubt in terms of the treaty to which Zedekiah's and Yahweh's names had been earlier affixed: Zedekiah's sons were slaughtered before his eyes, he was blinded, bound in fetters, and taken to Babylon (II Kings 25:3–7; Jer. 52:5–11; 39:1–7).

CHAPTER 13

The Period
of Babylonian Domination

Babylonian troops, under the direction of Nebuzaradan the captain of the royal bodyguard, ravaged Jerusalem a few weeks after the city's capture (II Kings 25:8; Jer. 52:12). The Temple, the royal palace, and homes of citizens were burned. The city walls, already breached, were pulled down (II Kings 25:9–10; Jer. 52:13–14). The remaining vessels and treasures from the Temple, as well as reusable bronze, were carted away (II Kings 25:13–17; Jer. 52:17–23). The conquering army, no doubt, had already plundered the city. The top priests, some surviving royal officials and commanders, and provincial leaders were rounded up, escorted to Riblah, and there executed in the presence of Nebuchadrezzar (II Kings 25:18–21; Jer. 52:24–27). Many persons were led away into exile (II Kings 25:11–12). Indeed, "the pleasant land" was in ruins (Zech. 7:14).

Judah After the Fall of Jerusalem

The suppression of Judah's rebellion and the destruction of the city of Jerusalem were severe cultural and theological shocks for Judean society. The fall of the city and the exile of many of its citizens marked a watershed in Judean history and have left fissure marks radiating throughout the Hebrew Scriptures. The "day of judgment" heralded in prophetic pronouncements had not just dawned, it had burst on Judah with immense ferocity.

General Destruction in the Land

The immediate results of the Babylonian conquest of Judah are clear. Much of the country was destroyed by the foreign invaders. Archaeological excavations at many Judean sites show evidence of destruction which scholars have related to Nebuchadrezzar's campaigns. Evidence for destruction extends from Tell ed-Duweir (Lachish) in the west, to Arad in the south, to En-gedi in the east. This is not to suggest, however, that every Judean city was left in ruins. Primarily those cities which served as fortress towns would have been the most likely targets for the Babylonians. Cities north of Jerusalem, in the traditional territory of Benjamin, apparently did not suffer much destruction. These may have surrendered to the Babylonians early.

At the southern site of Arad, excavations have revealed a destroyed military fortress which included remains of a Yahwistic sanctuary whose usage seems to have been discontinued in the late seventh or early sixth century. To associate this discontinuation with the reform of either Hezekiah or Josiah is tempting. If this sanctuary was a royal installation in a military garrison, then it would have been more directly responsive to Josiah's program of cultic centralization than other local shrines. A second category of finds consists of over two hundred Hebrew and Aramaic ostraca, or inscribed potsherds, many in letter form and dating from the last years of Judah (see Text XVI). Most of the letters are addressed to a certain Eliashib, presumably the commander of the military garrison. The letters contain references, as we have noted, to Kittim, Hellenic mercenaries apparently in the service of the Egyptian pharaoh and stationed in the Palestinian area. In addition, the letters refer to the Jerusalem Temple and to Edomites in the area of Arad.

At the site of Tell ed-Duweir, generally identified with ancient Lachish, twenty-two inscribed ostraca were found belonging to the last years of Judah (see Text XVI). Apparently to be dated before Nebuchadrezzar's actual invasion, some refer to the preparations for battle, the use of fire signals, the employment of some code for communicating between towns, the sending of a delegation to Egypt, concern for the harvest, differences of opinion among the population over strategy and the forthcoming conflict, and the presence of prophets.

The destruction of the major Judean cities meant a disruption in the industry and economics of the country. Because soldiers profited from the spoils of war, plundering was the conqueror's privilege and the conquered's fate. Thus one must assume that much of the people's possessions became Babylonian spoils of war. Many cities, like Jerusalem, that had once been thriving centers were left as depleted, subsistence-level villages. The primary economy of the country was probably reduced to a purely agricultural base.

A fair percentage of the manpower and leadership was killed off. There is no way to estimate the number of casualties who died at the hands of Babylonian troops, but it certainly would have been a sizable portion of the population even though the Babylonians had no reputation for needless destruction and excessive killing. Nebuchadrezzar had taken a lenient attitude toward the country in 597 B.C.E., but no ancient ruler was very hospitable to a rebellious subject on the second military visit.

Judean Exiles

The biblical materials contain two parallel accounts of the Judean revolt, the fall of Jerusalem, and the deportation of Judeans: II Kings 24:18–25:21 and Jer. 52:1–30. These texts are identical, with one major exception. Jeremiah 52:

TEXT XVI. Lachish and Arad Letters

Lachish Letters

Your servant Hoshayahu (hereby) reports to my lord Ya'ush. May YHWH give you good news . . . . . And now, please explain to your servant the meaning of the letter which my lord sent to your servant yesterday evening. For your servant has been sick at heart ever since you sent (that letter) to your servant. In it my lord said: "Don't you know how to read a letter?" As (Y)HWH lives, no one has ever tried to read *me* a letter! Moreover, whenever any letter comes to me and I have read it, I can repeat it down to the smallest detail. Now your servant has received the following information: General Konyahu son of Elnatan has moved south in order to enter Egypt. He has sent (messengers) to take Hodavyahu son of Ahiyahu and his men from here. (Herewith) I am also sending to my lord the letter (which was in the custody) of Tobyahu, servant of the king, which was sent to Shallum son of Yada from the prophet and which begins "Beware." (*HAHL* 84–85; partially restored)

May YHWH give you good news at this time. And now, your servant has done everything my lord sent (word to do). I have written down everything you sent me (word to do). As regards what my lord said about Beth-HRPD, there is no one there. As for Semakyahu, Shemayahu has seized him and taken him up to the city. Your servant cannot send the witness there today. For if he comes around during the morning tour he will know that we are watching the Lachish (fire-)signals according to the code which my lord gave us, for we cannot see Azeqah. (*HAHL* 91)

To my lord Yaush. May YHWH make this time a good one for you. Who is your servant (but) a dog that my lord should have sent (him) the king's letter and those of the officials asking (me) to read them? The [officials'] statements are not good—they are of a kind to slacken your courage and to weaken that of the men . . . . . my lord. Won't you write to them as follows: "Why are you acting thus" . . . . As YHWH your God lives, ever since your servant read the letters he has not had [a moment's peace]. (*HAHL* 100; partially restored)

Arad Letters

To Elyashib. And now, give to the Kittim three *bat*-measures of wine and write down the date. From what is left of the first meal have one *homer*-measure(?) of meal loaded to make bread for them. Give (them) the wine from the craters. (*HAHL* 31)

To Elyashib. And now, give to the Kittim two *bat*-measures of wine for the four days, three hundred loaves of bread, and a full *homer*-measure of wine. Send (them) out tomorrow; don't wait. If there is any vinegar left, give (it) to them (also). (*HAHL* 33)

To Nahum. [And] now, go to the house of Elyashib son of Eshyahu and get from there one (*bat*-measure?) of oil and send (it) to Ziph right away. (*HAHL* 51)

To my lord Elyashib. May YHWH concern himself with your well-being. And now, give Shermaryahu a *letek*-measure(?) (of meal?) and to the Qerosite give a *homer*-measure(?) (of meal?). As regards the matter concerning which you gave me orders: everything is fine now: he is staying in the temple of YHWH. (*HAHL* 55)

To Elyashib . . . . king . . . . army . . . . servant . . . . from Arad fifty and from Qinah . . . . and send them to Ramat-nege[b unde]r Malkiyahu son of Qerabur. He is to hand them over to Elisha son of Yirmeyahu at Ramat-negeb lest anything happen to the city. This is an order from the king—a life and death matter for you. I have sent you this message to warn you now: These men (must be) with Elisha lest (the) Edom (ites) go there. (*HAHL* 59–60)

Your son Gemaryahu, as well as Nehemyahu, hereby send greetings to (you) Malkiyahu. I bless you to YHWH. And now, your servant has applied himself to what you ordered. I (hereby) write to my lord [everything that the man] wanted. [Eshyahu has co]me from you but [he has not given] them any men. You know [the reports from] Edom. I sent them to [my] lord [before] evening. Eshyahu is staying [in my house.] He tried to obtain the report [but I would not give (it to him).] The king of Judah should know [that] we [are unable] to send the . . . . . The evil which the Edo[mites have done] . . . (*HAHL* 64)

28–30, which provides figures and dates for the two exiles, disrupts the parallel with the account in Kings and contradicts the dates and figures in both II Kings 24:8–16 and 25:8–27 concerning the number of Judeans taken into exile. In addition, Jer. 52:30 speaks of a third deportation. The following illustrates the differences between the accounts:

	II KINGS	*JEREMIAH*
First Deportation	All Jerusalem, 10,000 captives (24:14)	3,023 Judeans (52:28)
	7,000 brought to Babylon, plus 1,000 craftsmen and smiths (24:16)	
	Eighth year of Nebuchadrezzar (24:12)	Seventh year of Nebuchadrezzar (52:28)

Second Deportation	The rest of the people left in the city and the deserters together with the rest of the multitude (25:11)	832 from Jerusalem (52:29)
	Nineteenth year of Nebuchadrezzar (25:8)	Eighteenth year of Nebuchadrezzar (52:29)
Third Deportation		745 Judeans in the twenty-third year of Nebuchadrezzar (52:30), making a total of 4,600

Various attempts have been made to harmonize or explain these figures, but none is completely satisfying. One approach is to assume that both accounts are talking about the same events in the statements on the first two deportations. The difference in the dates given would be due to the use of a different system of calendar reckoning in the two texts, one calculated from a spring and the other from an autumn new year. The difference in the head count would be due to a gradual stylization in the presentation: from Jeremiah's rather concrete count, to the round figures in Kings, to the assumption in II Chron. 36:17–21 that the entire population was deported. A second approach assumes that the figures in Jeremiah for the first two deportations refer to deportations that occurred in 599/98 and 587 B.C.E. before the actual captures of Jerusalem. The first group would have been Judeans captured in Nebuchadrezzar's seventh year when he was fighting the Arabs but at a time when Jerusalem was already in revolt (*ANET* 564; Jer. 49:28–33). The second group would have been Jerusalemites captured in the early stage of the two-year siege of Jerusalem during the second revolt, perhaps those seized before the Babylonian siege was temporarily lifted when an Egyptian army appeared on the scene (Jer. 37:5). This approach assumes that Jer. 52:28–30 represents a special source originally unconnected with the rest of Jeremiah 52 which seems otherwise to be based on II Kings 24:18–25:30. The account in Kings would then be a report of the main deportations after the city surrendered.

Under either circumstance, it must be assumed that sizable groups of Judeans were carried by Nebuchadrezzar into Babylonian exile. Such deportations frayed the total fabric of society, siphoning off many of the upper and artisan classes. At the same time, such deportations led to some redistribution of Judean property and wealth and thus benefited portions of the lower classes. Those left behind could occupy the land of those taken into exile (see Ezek. 11:15), and debtors may have been left suddenly without creditors to whom they were indebted.

Verification of Prophetic Proclamation

Judah, which had been ruled for over four centuries by Davidic kings, except for one short interlude, now saw the Davidic monarch led away into exile. The

Temple and sacred city lay in ruins. A particular theological reading of Judean history—namely, the prophetic and the Deuteronomic—could now point to the end of the kingdom and the destruction of the Temple as historical verification of its theology. The classical prophets and Deuteronomy had argued that the people's fortune and fate were determined by their fidelity or infidelity to God, and the former had proclaimed the fall of the state as a result of the people's immorality and apostasy. This understanding of history provided the means by which the people could now interpret their tragic conditions and understand their fate as a punishment from God rather than as an indication of Yahweh's weakness. Thus they could remain faithful to their God even in the midst of calamity and even look forward to the future with some hope and expectation. God had destroyed their nation and their Temple because of their religious infidelity, but this did not mean that Yahweh had deserted his people. This perspective became a dominant lens for viewing the traditions of the past and a dominant concern in the editing of these traditions. That this was not the only way in which to understand the historical conditions and the fall of Jerusalem is indicated by the statement of those who felt that it was Josiah's suppression of religious pluralism that had been the source of their trouble: "We will do everything that we have vowed, burn incense to the queen of heaven and pour out libations to her, as we did, both we and our fathers, our kings and our princes, in the cities of Judah and in the streets of Jerusalem; for then we had plenty of food, and prospered, and saw no evil" (Jer. 44:17). For many, the city's destruction probably led to a loss of faith in Yahwism or to a continuation and even intensification of syncretistic practices.

The Rule of Gedaliah

It is easy to paint a very dreary and dismal view of Judean life and to overemphasize the drastic and debilitating consequences of the fall of Jerusalem and the triumph of Babylonian forces. Various aspects of life certainly were greatly modified, but Babylonian policy was not overly oppressive. Judeans were not systematically tortured or annihilated. Unlike the Assyrians, over a century earlier, the Babylonians did not move into Judah, restore the capital city, and partially repopulate it with foreigners. Instead, only minimal actions seem to have been taken to make the region a viable political entity. Since earlier Assyrian military installations established in the area now came under Babylonian hegemony, Nebuchadrezzar did not need to establish new major military centers or to settle the area with soldiers or foreigners. Instead, a local administration was set up drawn from the local population.

The exact details of the political status of Judah immediately following the destruction of Jerusalem are unclear and disputed. We are told that Nebuchadrezzar "appointed over them" Gedaliah the son of Ahikam, the son of Shaphan (II Kings 25:22 and Jer. 40:7; many translations supply the title "governor" in these and other passages about Gedaliah but without textual warrant). To what office he was appointed we are not told, but two lines of evidence

Seal of Gedaliah. The inscription of this seal, found at Lachish, reads *lgdlyhw 'šr 'l hbyt* ("belonging to Gedaliah, who is over the House" [i.e., Lord Chamberlain]). Such seals were used for marking official documents and affixing one's "signature." *(The Wellcome Trust)*

Seal of Jaazaniah. The inscription reads *ly'znyhw 'bd hmlk* ("belonging to Jaazaniah, servant to the king"). The seal, from Mizpah (Tell en-Nasbeh), is adorned with the image of a fighting cock, the first known representation of the chicken in Palestine. From II Kings 25:23, we know of one Jaazaniah the Maachathite, who was an official under Gedaliah at Mizpah. Thus the seal inscription could suggest that Gedaliah was king over a Judean kingdom centered at Mizpah, following the fall of Jerusalem in 586 B.C.E. (From *Tell En-Nasbeh* by C. C. McCown, Palestine Institute of Pacific School of Religion/ASOR, 1947)

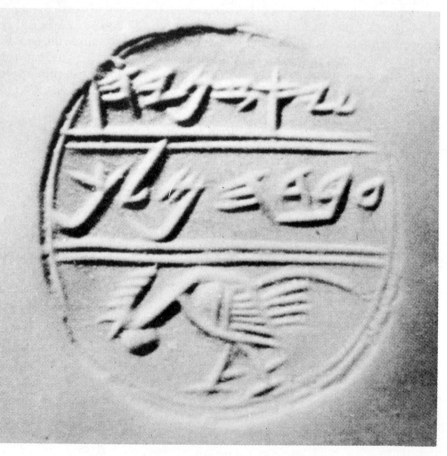

suggest that he was made king replacing Zedekiah on the throne. (1) The failure to mention any title whatever in the text suggests that the final editors of the Kings material did not wish to reveal his real title. The reason was probably that it would have required the admission that a non-Davidic person was appointed as king. (See II Kings 25:27–30 which reports the release of Jehoiachin from prison and where the possibility is held out for the continuation and restoration of the Davidic line.) (2) Two texts in Jeremiah 40–41 speak of "the king" in describing conditions after the fall of Jerusalem and these are best seen as references to Gedaliah. In the first, mention is made of "the king's daughters" at Mizpah (Jer. 41:10). The king's daughters would have been either the actual daughters of Gedaliah or the women at his court (perhaps women of Zedekiah's court whom Gedaliah had inherited as part of his new appointment?). The second text (Jer. 41:1) describes Ishmael as "one of the chief officers of the king," that is, as an officer of Gedaliah under whose authority he had earlier placed himself (Jer. 40:8). Here "the king" appears to be Gedaliah. If Gedaliah was made king, it would suggest that the Babylonians were following the old Assyrian policy of not incorporating the southern Palestinian states into their provincial system but allowing them limited independence as vassal states. Gedaliah would thus have been viewed as the successor to Zedekiah but simply not from the old ruling family. Since Gedaliah was not of the family of David, his appointment as king could have been deliberately suppressed by the compilers of the biblical text, thus explaining the absence of any reference to his exact office. The support given to Gedaliah by Jeremiah and the general population in Judah suggests that large segments of the population were willing to go along with a non-Davidic monarch just as had been the case at the time of Ahaz when the Davidic ruler was almost deposed and replaced by a son of Tabeel.

Gedaliah came from a prominent family. His grandfather, Shaphan, served as royal "secretary" and thus was a high governmental official under Josiah (II Kings 22:8). Shaphan's son, Gemariah, and his grandson, Micaiah, were prominent leaders at the time of Jehoiakim (Jer. 36:11–13). Another son, Elasah, was one of Zedekiah's envoys to Babylon (Jer. 29:3). Gedaliah's father, Ahikam, had supported the prophet Jeremiah when the latter was placed on trial for his inflammatory denunciation of Jerusalem's citizens and their confidence in the Temple and the city's inviolability (Jer. 26:24). A seal impression unearthed at Tell ed-Duweir reads, "Belonging to Gedaliah who is over the household." If this refers to the biblical Gedaliah, then it could suggest that even before the fall of Jerusalem he had held a prominent position in Judean administration. The choice of Gedaliah was no doubt based on his pro-Babylonian sentiments. Many in Judah, like the prophet Jeremiah, had favored submission and surrender to Babylonia rather than war (see Jer. 38:19), and Nebuchadrezzar now placed this group, the earlier minority opposition party, in charge of Judean affairs.

Gedaliah set up his administrative center or capital at Mizpah just north of Jerusalem but in the old territory of the tribe of Benjamin. Mizpah had been an important cultic center in premonarchical days, had special connections with

Samuel (Judg. 20:1–3; 21:1–8; I Sam. 7; 10:17), and its renown as a prominent place of worship continued into Maccabean times (I Macc. 3:46). The choice of Mizpah as the capital for Judah may partially have been determined by the fact that it, unlike Jerusalem, had not been destroyed in the war with Babylon. Mizpah probably continued as the capital of Judah for over a century, from the days of Gedaliah until Nehemiah's refortification of Jerusalem. In support of his cause, Gedaliah seems to have been provided with a contingent of Babylonian (Chaldean) troops or at least advisers (see II Kings 25:24–25 and Jer. 40:10; 41:3).

Nebuzaradan, the captain of the Babylonian bodyguard, had already taken some steps to normalize life in Judah. The poor in the land, "who owned nothing," were provided with vineyards and fields (Jer. 39:10; II Kings 25:12), that is, there was some redistribution of property to the benefit of previously landless classes. Pro-Babylonians like Jeremiah were given preferential treatment (see Jer. 39:11–14 and 40:1–5, although the details differ). Judeans were encouraged by Gedaliah to resume ordinary agricultural pursuits and live peacefully under Babylonian hegemony. Jews from neighboring areas—Moab, Ammon, Edom, and elsewhere—who had fled the country returned and submitted themselves to Gedaliah's authority (Jer. 40:10–12).

An Attempt at Davidic Restoration

Peaceful conditions, counseled by Gedaliah, did not materialize. Some Judean field commanders and their troops had survived the recent struggles. II Kings 25:22–24 and Jer. 40:7–13 imply their submission to Gedaliah and their continuation as a military force under his command. Ishmael, one of these commanders, was or claimed to be a member of the Davidic family, though perhaps not from the immediate ruling line (II Kings 25:25; Jer. 41:1). He apparently belonged to the Davidic family strand that went back to Elishama, a son of David (see II Sam. 5:16; I Chron. 3:8; 14:7). Ishmael submitted, at least temporarily, to the authority of Gedaliah (Jer. 40:8–10) and was placed in a position of authority (note that Jer. 41:1 refers to Ishmael as "one of the chief officers of the king" [Gedaliah]). At the instigation of Baalis, the Ammonite king, Ishmael and a contingent of his troops assassinated Gedaliah, his entire entourage, and the Babylonian contingent at Mizpah (II Kings 25:25–26; Jer. 40:13–41:3). The biblical text offers no rationale for these murders, but one must assume they were the act of nationalistic patriots who wished to reestablish an independent Judean state under a Davidic ruler with the support of a foreign monarch, the Ammonite king. After further killings, Ishmael and his force were opposed by other Judean officers, especially Johanan the son of Kareah (Jer. 41:11–14). The Judean population was in no mood to support the ambitions of a would-be Davidic messiah. Without the sympathy and support of the general population, which seems to have placed its hope in the non-Davidic Gedaliah (see Jer. 42:7–11), Ishmael's plans faltered and he took refuge in Ammon (Jer. 41:4–16). Fearful of Babylonian retaliation, many of the military leaders and general population fled to Egypt, carrying along the protesting prophet Jeremiah (Jer. 41:17–43:7).

Direct evidence about the status of affairs in Judah following Gedaliah's assassination is almost nonexistent. Jeremiah 52:30 reports a third Babylonian deportation of Judeans—745 persons were exiled in the twenty-third year of Nebuchadrezzar (581 B.C.E.). What precipitated this deportation is not discussed by Jeremiah. Many scholars, perhaps correctly, associate it with the Gedaliah affair, although II Kings 25:25 and Jer. 41:1 seem to imply that Gedaliah had been killed only shortly after the fall of Jerusalem. Josephus reports that Nebuchadrezzar was again in Syria-Palestine in 582/1 B.C.E.:

> The Deity revealed to the prophet [Jeremiah] that the king of Babylonia was about to march against the Egyptians, and He bade the prophet foretell to the people that Egypt would be taken and that the Babylonian king would kill some of them and would take the rest captive and carry them to Babylon. And so it happened; for in the fifth year after the sacking of Jerusalem, which was the twenty-third year of the reign of Nebuchadnezzar, Nebuchadnezzar marched against Coele-Syria and, after occupying it, made war both on the Moabites and the Ammanites. Then, after making these nations subject to him, he invaded Egypt in order to subdue it, and, having killed the king who was then reigning and appointed another, he again took captive the Jews who were in the country and carried them to Babylon. (*Ant.* X.180–82)

Josephus' account is suspected of being based on his desire to have Jeremiah's prophecies of Egypt's capture fulfilled literally (see Jer. 27:1–7; 44:30; 46: 13–24; 48:1–49:6). Certainly, Nebuchadrezzar did not invade Egypt and kill and replace the Egyptian pharaoh in 581 B.C.E., since Apries (Hophra), who had become pharaoh in 589 B.C.E., continued to reign until 570 B.C.E. If Josephus, however, does preserve the recollection of trouble in Syria-Palestine in 582/1 B.C.E. involving Moab and Ammon, then this may have been the setting for Ishmael's attempted coup or at least the background for Jeremiah's report that 745 Judeans were taken captive to Babylon in Nebuchadrezzar's twenty-third year. Egyptian influence may have been asserted in Syria-Palestine in support of anti-Babylonian uprisings. At any rate, Egypt seems to have been receptive to the Judeans fleeing Palestine for fear of Babylonian reprisal. At the time, Tyre on the coast was under Babylonian siege, a siege that lasted thirteen years (586–573 B.C.E.; *Ant.* X.228; *Contra Apion* I.156) and whose immediate lack of success may have stimulated hopes that Babylonia would prove not to be invincible. Also, efforts at revolt in Syria-Palestine in the mid-580s would have occurred while Nebuchadrezzar was preoccupied with matters in Asia Minor.

If Gedaliah was appointed king over Judah, his assassination may have brought this experiment in non-Davidic monarchy to an end. Perhaps it was at this time that Judah became a Babylonian province, but we know nothing of Judean politics for the period following Gedeliah's murder. If Judah was given provincial status, it would have had its own governor, perhaps a native Judean, appointed by the Babylonians.

Continuation of Cultic Life

The general perception gained from the books of II Kings and Ezra, the latter describing conditions in the later Jerusalem community, is that cultic activity ceased in Judah following the destruction of the Temple in Jerusalem. This perception has, however, probably been retrojected onto a situation that was actually quite different, although the details escape us.

In reporting the Gedaliah-Ishmael episode, the Book of Jeremiah notes that "eighty men arrived [at Mizpah] from Shechem and Shiloh and Samaria, with their beards shaved and their clothes torn, and their bodies gashed, bringing cereal offerings and incense to present at the temple of Yahweh" (Jer. 41:5). This text suggest two things: (1) Cultic worship continued in Judah during the "exilic" period and (2) Mizpah seems to have been one of the sites of such worship.

Cultic activity probably also continued at the site of the Temple in Jerusalem. Three factors support such a contention. (1) No reference is made to the destruction or desecration of the Jerusalem altar in conjunction with the Babylonian burning of the Temple (II Kings 25:9). Thus it may have remained in use. (2) The cultic laments in the book of Lamentations seem to presuppose worship at the site of the destroyed sanctuary and city. (3) When the Persians replaced the Babylonians as the dominant Near Eastern power, they returned the Temple vessels to Jerusalem. This makes more sense if one assumes that they were being returned for use in some ongoing cult.

The continuation of cultic activity, in Mizpah, Jerusalem, and perhaps elsewhere, would of course have required priests. We hear nothing in the books of II Kings and Jeremiah about the condition of the priesthood after the destruction of Jerusalem except the notice that Seraiah the chief priest, Zephaniah the second priest, and the three keepers of the threshold were put to death by Nebuchadrezzar at Riblah (II Kings 25:18–21; Jer. 52:24–27). At any rate, however, II Kings 25:18–21 suggests that the Jerusalem priestly hierarchy was decimated as a consequence of Babylonian action. Once the capital of the region shifted away from Jerusalem, the priesthood at the sanctuary at Mizpah or that region may have risen to greater prominence in Judah and even replaced in leadership the Zadokite line established under David and Solomon.

The Era of Babylonian Dominance

At the end of the seventh century, four major powers existed in the Near East —Babylonia, Egypt, Media, and Lydia. Babylonia, in spite of being the strongest of the four powers, was never able to dominate Near Eastern affairs as had the Assyrians earlier or as the Persians would later. The Medes, who had aided Babylonia in its conquests of Assyria, controlled the highlands north and east of the Mesopotamian plain. Most of the Fertile Crescent was in Babylonian hands, but the Medes largely controlled the eastern trade routes, forcing the Babylonians to turn their economic interests more to the west.

The Medes also expanded westward. Cyaxares had overrun the Urartian kingdom and extended his rule into Asia Minor. The growth of Median power led some Jews to suppose that the Medes might topple Babylonia (see Isa. 13:17; 21:2; Jer. 51:11). Nebuchadrezzar, however, remained on good terms with Media. Median expansion into Asia Minor eventually resulted in a clash with Lydia. About 585 B.C.E., the Babylonians served as mediators in Lydian-Median territorial disputes. A Babylonian officer and future king, Nabonidus, mediated a treaty of peace which established the River Halys as the boundary between the two kingdoms' spheres of influence (see Herodotus I.72).

In the eastern Mediterranean, Babylonia and Egypt vied for control of the area and its maritime commerce. The Babylonians seem never to have been as successful as the Assyrians in dominating this area. The Phoenician city of Tyre, for example, held out for thirteen years against Nebuchadrezzar's siege. What role Egypt may have played in the Babylonian-Phoenician struggle remains uncertain. Herodotus reports, as we have noted, that the Egyptian pharaoh Apries (Hophra) sent an army against Sidon and fought a naval battle with the Tyrians (Herodotus II.161). That Egypt fought against the Phoenician states while Tyre was under siege by Nebuchadrezzar, and thus in support of the Babylonians, seems highly unlikely. Perhaps Herodotus has confused his information. The Egyptian pharaoh may have aided the Phoenicians against the Babylonians as he had earlier offered some assistance to Judah. If Egypt attacked Phoenicia, it must have been before Tyre was placed under Babylonian siege.

We have noted earlier in this chapter that Babylonia had to deal with additional troubles in Syria-Palestine in the late 580s (see above, p. 425). These too may have been partially precipitated by Egypt. According to Ezek. 29:17–20, an oracle dated to April 571 B.C.E., Nebuchadrezzar received the spoils of Egypt as wages for his unprofitable siege of Tyre which ended with less than overwhelming success for the Babylonians. The Ezekiel text would suggest an invasion of Egypt. (In *Ant.* X.182, as we have noted, Josephus reports that Nebuchadrezzar in his twenty-third year did invade Egypt and replace the reigning pharaoh with another ruler.) Only fragmentary cuneiform evidence and late legendary stories can be mustered, however, to support Josephus' and Ezekiel's claim of a Babylonian invasion of Egypt. The following text, greatly restored, points to a military engagement between the two powers but does not unequivocally imply an invasion:

> In the 37th year, Nebuchadnezzar, king of Babylon marched against Egypt to deliver a battle. Amasis, of Egypt, called up his army . . . from the town Putu-Iaman . . . distant regions which are situated on islands amidst the sea . . . many . . . carrying weapons, horses and chariots . . . he called up to assist him . . . (*ANET* 308)

Unfortunately such a fragment is more tantalizing than informative. The thirty-seventh year of Nebuchadrezzar (568–567 B.C.E.) would have been shortly after Amasis (570–526 B.C.E.) had replaced Apries as pharaoh following a period of Egyptian civil war (Herodotus II.161–69). Whether Nebuchadrezzar took advantage of the civil strife to invade Egypt or even to remove Apries from the throne remains unknown.

Amasis brought Egypt to a period of great prosperity (Herodotus II.177). His predecessor had relied greatly on Greek mercenaries, earning him the epithet "Philhellene," and during his reign Greek merchants were widespread in Egypt. The city of Naucratis in the western Delta had become an international trading center where the Greeks had special prerogatives. Amasis took more direct control of matters both internally and externally than had Apries. Greek mercenaries and traders were brought under more disciplined control. Legal practices were reformed. Treaties were made with Croesus king of Lydia and Polycrates king of Samos in Asia Minor and friendly relations established with the Greek colony of Cyrene. The island of Cyprus, which had formerly been under Assyrian control, was conquered by Amasis and subjected to tribute (Herodotus I.77; II.177–82). Egyptian expansion and prosperity must have been partially at the expense of Babylonia.

The Babylonian kingdom, in spite of its inability to emulate the Assyrians, thrived reasonably well throughout the reign of Nebuchadrezzar. By the time of his death, a constellation of factors existed which heralded the deep troubles about to beset the kingdom. These included excessive economic inflation in Babylon precipitated in part by extravagant royal building projects, Median, Lydian, and Egyptian pressures on trade routes leading into Mesopotamia, and a lack of effective leadership among the royal family.

A quick succession of rulers followed Nebuchadrezzar. His son Amel-marduk (561–560 B.C.E.), the Evil-merodach of II Kings 25:27 and Jer. 52:31 who released Jehoiachin from prison, reigned for only two years before being killed in a revolution. A son-in-law of Nebuchadrezzar, Neriglissar (the Nergal-sharezer of Jer. 39:3), succeeded to the throne. His reign (559–556 B.C.E.) witnessed a Babylonian campaign into southeastern Asia Minor against King Appuashu of Pirindu, who had invaded Syria (*ABC* 103–4). Following his mysterious death upon returning to Babylon, the young son of Neriglissar, Labashi-marduk, "a minor who had not yet learned how to behave" (*ANET* 309), assumed the throne but ruled only for a short time before being replaced in a rebellion led by officers of the kingdom.

The new ruler, Nabonidus (555–539 B.C.E.), a Babylonian military commander from Haran in northern Syria, was the son of a nobleman and the high priestess of the moon-god Sin in his native city. Although Nabonidus' reign would mark the end of the Babylonian kingdom and he himself would be remembered in popular tradition as the mad monarch par excellence, he seems to have made some gallant efforts to stabilize the tottering kingdom.

First of all, Nabonidus sought to reform Babylonian religion and to use the worship of the moon-god Sin as a unifying force in the empire. His emphasis on the worship of Sin was, of course, not to the exclusion of the other religious cults. The moon-god, unlike Marduk, a Babylonian sun deity, was worshiped by many peoples in the empire, including the Arabs and the Arameans. The king took as his pious duty the restoration of the Sin sanctuary (Ehulhul) in Haran where his high priestess mother survived to the age of 104 years (see *ANET* 560–62). The sanctuary had been destroyed in 610 B.C.E. and subsequently held by the Medes until military pressure from Cyrus forced their withdrawal from the area. In addition, Nabonidus constructed a special Sin sanctuary at Ur and installed his daughter as high priestess. His support and encouragement of the worship of Sin alienated elements of the religious establishment in Babylon headed by the Marduk priesthood.

Most of Nabonidus' military activity and economic interests were centered in the west. In his early years as king, he was active in eastern Asia Minor and Syria, in Hume in Cilicia and Hamath in Syria. After a short stay and period of sickness in the Anti-Lebanon, Nabonidus turned his attention to the Arabian Desert (*ANET* 305). He stayed there for over a decade without returning to the capital city, where his son Bel-shar-usur (the Belshazzar of Dan. 5:22; 7:1; 8:1) served as regent. Nabonidus notes the following reasons for leaving the capital city and for his stay in Arabia:

> But the citizens of Babylon, Borsippa, Nippur, Ur, Uruk and Larsa, the administrators and the inhabitants of the urban centers of Babylonia acted evil, careless and even sinned against his (Sin's) great divine power, having not yet experienced the awfulness of the wrath of the Divine Crescent, the king of all gods; they disregarded his rites and there was much irreligious and disloyal talk. They devoured one another like dogs, caused disease and hunger to appear among them. He (Sin) decimated the inhabitants of the country, but he made me leave my city Babylon on the road to Tema, Dadanu, Padakku, Hibra, Jadihu even as far as Jatribu [later Muslim Medina]. For ten years I was moving around among these cities and did not enter my own city Babylon. (*ANET* 562)

The activity and stay of Nabonidus in the Eastern Mediterranean Seaboard and in Arabia were probably necessitated by economic and trade considerations. He must have been attempting to establish and exercise control over the overland trade routes in the region. There is a strong possibility that Jewish soldiers and families accompanied him to Arabia, because practically all the oases he claims to have visited were later strong centers of Jewish settlement. As we shall see in the next chapter, by the time Nabonidus returned to Babylon his former ally King Cyrus II of Anshan had risen to a position of dominance throughout Mesopotomia and was merely waiting for the proper occasion to seize the Babylonian capital.

The Diaspora

Nebuchadrezzar's deportations of Judeans to Babylonia and the flight of many others to Egypt greatly increased the number of Judeans and Israelites living outside the Palestinian area. The fate of most of these deportees is unknown, although later Jewish communities in many areas throughout the

Middle East may have originated from these exiled groups. The families of some of these exiles eventually returned to Palestine and were a strong influence on Jewish life in the area during the Persian period. Although we shall consider the return of these exiles in the next chapter, a discussion of the exiled groups is appropriate at this point, since the dispersion of groups from Palestine reached a climax in the Babylonian period.

The diaspora did not have its beginnings in the days following the destruction of Jerusalem. The Assyrians had exiled peoples from Galilee and Transjordan in 733–732 B.C.E. (II Kings 15:29; *ANET* 283). After Samaria fell in 722 B.C.E., according to his inscriptions Sargon II deported 27,290 persons from the land of Samaria (*ANET* 284–85) and resettled them in Assyrian provinces in Upper Mesopotamia and Media (II Kings 17:6, 18; 18:11; I Chron. 5:26). After Sennacherib's successful campaign in Judah in 701 B.C.E., he claimed to have counted 200,150 persons driven from Hezekiah's towns as booty (*ANET* 288). Certainly some of these must have been exiled and settled elsewhere (see Isa. 5:13; 11:12–16; 27:8; Micah 1:16; and above, Text X). One of Sennacherib's palace reliefs in Nineveh depicts the deportation of Judeans from Lachish. Nebuchadrezzar's deportations of 597, 586, and 582 B.C.E. (Jer. 52:29) only increased the number of Israelites and Judeans living in the east; it did not inaugurate the diaspora.

The Judeans who fled to Egypt after the assassination of Gedaliah increased the population from Palestine already in Egypt. Several texts make references to these earlier Jewish communities there. Isaiah 11:11 mentions Judeans dwelling in various regions along the Nile. Jeremiah 44:1 introduces the words of Jeremiah addressed to his countrymen living in Egypt at Migdol, Tahpanhes (Daphnae), and Memphis and in the land of Pathros (Upper Egypt; see Jer. 46:14). This presupposes widespread Jewish settlements in Egypt. The Elephantine archives, which we will describe below, note that this community was founded before Cambyses' capture of Egypt in 525 B.C.E. (*ANET* 492; see below, Text XVIII). As we have noted, the *Letter of Aristeas* (paragraph 13) states that Jews were sent to Egypt as mercenary soldiers during the reign of Pharaoh Psammetichus (probably Psammetichus I rather than II). Similarly, Judean troops had been taken to Egypt during the reign of Manasseh (*ANET* 294). (Note the reference to being taken to Egypt in ships in Deut. 28:68.) In both of these cases, Jewish troops may have subsequently been stationed in Egypt as military garrisons. In addition to Mesopotamia and Egypt, Judean refugees and emigrants were found also in those small nations surrounding Judah (see Jer. 40:11–12; 41:15).

What can be known about Jewish life in the diaspora? Of the two main centers of the dispersed—Mesopotamia and Egypt—the former was by far the most significant in terms both of its contribution to the later development of Jewish faith and its role in Jewish life in the Persian period. Before we discuss what can be known about diaspora life, a word about the extent and nature of the available primary source material on the issue is in order.

The Biblical Source Material

Very little biblical material is directly descriptive of life in the diaspora. Neither of the two main historical sources—Genesis-II Kings and I-II Chronicles—covers the period following the fall of Jerusalem or overtly concerns itself with life and culture outside Palestine. Our primary biblical sources are the books of the prophets Jeremiah and Ezekiel and chs. 40–55 of Isaiah.

Jeremiah was a witness to both captures of the city of Jerusalem (in 597 and 586 B.C.E.) and he participated in the life of the Judean community during the rule of Gedaliah. After the latter's assassination, Jeremiah was carried to Egypt and some of his book relates to this period (Jer. 43–44). The prophet had earlier carried on correspondence with the exiles deported to Babylonia in 597 B.C.E. and he appears to have been informed about conditions there (see Jer. 28–29; 50–51). Thus the Book of Jeremiah supplies some valuable but very limited information about both the Babylonian and the Egyptian diasporas.

The ministry of the prophet Ezekiel seems to have been carried out completely in the Babylonian exile. His career spanned the period from 593 (Ezek. 1:2) to at least 571 B.C.E. (Ezek. 29:17). The sermons and narratives in the Book of Ezekiel thus provide many insights into the life of the exiles in Babylonia.

Much of Isaiah 40–55 is now dated by many scholars to the closing years of the Babylonian exile. The anonymous prophet, frequently referred to as Deutero-Isaiah, who produced this material saw in the rise of the Persians under Cyrus grounds for renewal and hope for the exiles. The historical conditions reflected in the book shed light on the circumstances of the Babylonian Jewish exilic communities at the transition point between the Babylonian and Persian periods.

Nonbiblical Sources

Nonbiblical texts from both Babylonia and Egypt cast some, although not extensive, light on the life and status of Jews living in the diaspora. Among the Babylonian materials are royal cuneiform tablets that refer to Jehoiachin in exile (see *ANET* 308). In addition, Jewish names appear in tablets discovered at the site of Nippur in 1893 which reveal the commercial and land-leasing activity of the Marashu firm. These tablets, although dating from the second half of the fifth century (455 to 403 B.C.E.) and thus from the Persian period, provide evidence of the involvement of Jews in the economic life of the communities where they were settled.

Numerous documents in Aramaic from Egypt provide information related to the Egyptian diaspora. The most significant of these are the so-called Elephantine papyri. Discovered in Egypt at Elephantine Island opposite Aswan, these legal and epistolary documents were found in three major caches near the turn of the last century. The papyri came from a Jewish military settlement and present us with many facets of the legal and religious conditions existing in the colony. Although again dating from the Persian period (495 to 399 B.C.E.), they can be used to reconstruct the life of Jews in Egypt during the Babylonian period, since it is probable that this community was already in existence during the preceding Assyrian period and probably changed little over the years.

The Exiles in Babylonia

The Babylonian treatment of exiled Judeans was probably varied. Many captives who had leadership roles in the revolt were sent into exile in chains and were presumably imprisoned or confined. This was the case with both Judean kings—Jehoiachin (II Kings 25:27) and Zedekiah (II Kings 25:7)—and other members of the royal family. Those, however, who were deported in order to weaken the rebellious nation, or to siphon off the superpatriots, or to provide service for the conquerors were treated differently.

Elephantine Papyrus. This and other documents from the Jewish colony at Elephantine in Egypt were published in three groups, one in 1906, another in 1911, and a third in 1953. Consisting mostly of letters and legal documents, these Persian period writings shed light on religious and legal conditions in a Jewish colony in the diaspora (see Text XVIII, p. 466). *(Brooklyn Museum)*

The Babylonian texts which refer to Jehoiachin as king of Judah mention foodstuffs provided him and his five sons as pensionary payments (*ANET* 308). Such payments were made to numerous persons, of diverse national backgrounds (even Greeks!), status, and professions. They do not in themselves reflect any preferential position but do suggest the humane treatment given Jehoiachin and Judean nobles. Seal impressions discovered at several Judean sites inscribed "Belonging to Eliakim steward of Yaukin (Jehoiachin)" could suggest that even after being exiled Jehoiachin was allowed to retain possession of some Judean crown property which was administered by Eliakim. Jehoiachin, in the thirty-seventh year of his exile (561/60 B.C.E.), was released from prison by the Babylonian king Evil-merodach (Amel-marduk) and given, in the terms of the text, "a seat above the seats of the kings who were with him in Babylon" (II Kings 25:27–30), although what this status involved is unexplained. The royal family seems to have remained intact; the cuneiform texts that mention Jehoiachin also refer to his sons.

The exiles were not forced to live in inhuman conditions. There seems to have been no opposition to them or limitation of their privileges because of their origin or religion. They were treated like the exiles from any other nation. Something of the nature of exilic conditions can be seen in Jeremiah's recommendations to the Judeans carried away in 597 B.C.E.: "Build houses and live in them; plant gardens and eat their produce. Take wives and have sons and daughters; take wives for your sons, and give your daughters in marriage, that they may bear sons and daughters; multiply there, and do not decrease. But seek the welfare of the city where I have sent you into exile, and pray to Yahweh on its behalf, for in its welfare you will find your welfare" (Jer. 29:5–7; see also II Kings 18:31–32, where the Assyrian Rabshakeh describes the conditions of exilic life).

Exiles were settled by both Assyrians and Babylonians not only in ruined cities that needed rebuilding and in areas that needed agricultural development but also in administrative centers. The appearance of the term "tel" in various place-names where Judean exiles lived (Tel-Melah, Tel-Harsha, Tel-Abib) could suggest that Judeans were sometimes settled on abandoned sites, since "tel" may mean "mound" (often a city ruin). The prophet Ezekiel lived in Tel-Abib on the River Chebar (Ezek. 1:3; 3:15). Thus the Jews received land to till and sites to rebuild and settle and as tenants to the king would have provided labor, paid taxes, and served in the military. The appearance of Jewish names in about 8 percent of the prosaic business texts of the Marashu firm illustrate that Judean exiles became involved in various commercial activities. Biblical texts indicate that they could own property (Jer. 29:5), even slaves (Ezra 2:65), and many became quite wealthy (Ezra 1:6; 2:68–69). Administrative positions were open to them as to the exiles of other nations.

The exiles remained relatively free and certainly should not be understood as slaves. They would have been under no overt pressure to assimilate and lose their identities. Like many other exiled groups, the Jews preserved some communal cohesion and national identity and may have formed their own ethnic corporations in various towns. References to "the elders of Judah/Israel" (Ezek. 8:1; 14:1; 20:1, 3) and "the elders of the exile" (Jer. 29:1) indicate a state of limited internal autonomy in which they were able to live and govern themselves according to traditional customs and to preserve their family structures. The presence of Davidic family members probably contributed to the sense of identity and to some optimism about the future. Years were reckoned by reference to Jehoiachin's reign (Ezek. 1:2; 33:21; 40:1). While the practices of ritual purity, Sabbath observance, and circumcision tended to isolate Jews from the local culture, they also contributed to the people's sense of distinctiveness and communal cohesion.

Transferred peoples could continue to practice their national religion in the land of their exile, although there was also the tendency to combine this with some form of worship of the gods of the lands in which they dwelt (see Ezek. 14:3; 20:29). The foreigners who were settled in Samaria, for example, continued the worship of their gods while also serving the god of Israel (see II

Kings 17:24–33). Many Judeans taken to Babylonia probably continued their ancestral religion and traditional worship. For some this meant the continuation of syncretistic worship and the service of many gods (see Ezek. 14; 20:31; Deut. 4:27–28; 28:36, 64). Many of the exiles, strongly Yahwistic, continued to advocate the worship of only one god.

Little is known about the practice of Yahwism in exile. The Jews at Elephantine in Egypt possessed their own temple where sacrifice was offered, but whether similar conditions prevailed in Babylonia is uncertain. Ezekiel 11:16 is sometimes taken to refer to a "temporary sanctuary." According to Ezra 8:15–20, Temple personnel were congregated at the "place" Casiphia. Since *maqom* (= place) can denote a temple precinct, this text has been understood as specifying a temple. Such argumentation, however, is founded as much on conjecture as on evidence. Jews in Mesopotamia probably worshiped in a nonsacrificial cult in which prayer, praise, and the reading and exposition of the law were characteristic. Sermons, such as those found in Ezekiel and the prose passages of Jeremiah, were perhaps also commonplace. This type of worship could function anywhere, requiring only a meeting place ("synagogue" in Greek). Exilic worship no doubt possessed many of the characteristics of the later synagogue services.

Jewish life in an alien culture naturally led to some cultural assimilation even among the most conservative. The use of the Aramaic language and the square Aramaic script became widespread, although they did not totally replace Hebrew and the older script. The presence of Babylonian names among the exiles illustrates some accommodation to the host culture, although many Jews continued to give their children Hebrew names, and the fact that a Jewish person bore a theophoric name referring to a god other than Yahweh does not in itself denote conversion. Babylonian names for the months replaced the old Canaanite-Hebrew names used in Palestine. Political and economic pressures no doubt were influential in the level of assimilation among persons of prominence. Undoubtedly many Judeans, like most of the Israelites exiled by the Assyrians, assimilated the culture so thoroughly as to lose their Jewish identity.

Prophets as radically different as Ezekiel and Second Isaiah (the author of Isa. 40–55) wrote and preached during the exile. Ezekiel, with his priestly orientation, especially condemned his contemporaries for their abominations and impurities, their adherence to idolatry, and their syncretistic worship of other gods in addition to Yahweh. Ezekiel held out hope to the exiles that they would return to the land and purge it of its detestable things and abominations (see Ezek. 11:14–25). Like Jeremiah, in his earlier preaching, Ezekiel saw the exiles as the hope for the people—they were the "very good figs, like first-ripe figs" and those left in Judah were the "very bad figs, so bad that they could not be eaten" (Jer. 24:2; but compare Jer. 42:7–22). Like Ezekiel, Jeremiah or his followers and editors spoke of the transformed persons that would live in the renewed land (see Ezek. 11:19–20; Jer. 31:31–34; 32:36–41) when Israel and Judah would exist together again as one. Ezekiel or his circle of associates proceeded to draw up a blueprint for the idyllic life in a transformed Palestine

(Ezek. 40–48). Second Isaiah, about whom more will be said in the next chapter, gave expression to an elevated monotheism which declared all gods besides Yahweh to be merely impotent idols and other religions to be mere delusions: "Thus says Yahweh, the King of Israel and his Redeemer, Yahweh of hosts: 'I am the first and I am the last; besides me there is no god' " (Isa. 44:6).

The Egyptian Diaspora

The Egyptian diaspora was less significant for the immediate future of Judaism, and the status and life of the Judeans there are even less known than the Mesopotamian diaspora. The only direct, firsthand information, except for the material in the Book of Jeremiah (Jer. 43–44; 46), comes from the legal documents and letters of the Elephantine archives (see *ANET* 491–92, 548–49, and *AP*). These texts, even though from the later Persian period, reveal a number of interesting features about life in the Egyptian diaspora. (1) The Elephantine community was a small military colony which included women and children. Since it was a military outpost protecting the southern border and Nile commerce, the soldiers received payments as well as land grants from their overlords. Jewish settlements at Migdol, Tahpanhes, and Memphis were probably military garrisons similar to Elephantine (see Jer. 46:14). (2) There was intermarriage with Egyptians and assimilation in both directions. There is evidence of Egyptians becoming members of the Jewish community, and no doubt the reverse conditions also obtained. (3) Some Jewish persons rose to high position in local administrative matters and some accumulated significant wealth. (4) The community retained contact with the religious authorities in both Jerusalem and Samaria. (5) The colony possessed limited internal autonomy and governed itself according to the customs of their ancestors. Contracts and legal documents suggest that there was a great similarity between the practices of the Jewish community and Egyptian culture. At Elephantine, for example, a woman apparently possessed the right to divorce her husband. This may, however, reflect an ancient Israelite practice rather than a modification of Jewish legal procedures in an alien culture. (6) The community was at least aware of many traditional Jewish practices, including observance of the Sabbath and such festivals as Passover and Unleavened Bread. (7) They possessed a temple that bore structural similarity to the one in Jerusalem, and in which the ancestral god Yahweh (Yahu) was worshiped and sacrifices were offered. The existence of such a temple in Egypt would not necessarily have been understood as an infringement of the provision in the Deuteronomic law specifying only one place of sacrifice to Yahweh, since the biblical law speaks of conditions pertaining "in the land," that is, within Canaan (see Deut. 12:1, 10). Isaiah 19:19 speaks in a positive tone of the day when "there will be an altar to Yahweh in the midst of the land of Egypt, and a pillar to Yahweh at its border" and thus seems to endorse a sacrificial cult outside Palestine. (8) Indications suggest that the Jews at Elephantine were syncretistic in their worship. Oaths and blessings and other evidence refer to a variety of Syro-Palestinian deities venerated in the Elephantine and

surrounding Aramaic community: Anat, Sati, Bethel, Harambethel, Asham-
bethel, and so on. (For reference to some of these deities in Palestine in the
Assyrian period, see *ANET* 534.)

Biblical texts in general take a decidedly negative attitude toward the members of the Egyptian diaspora. This is especially the case with the prophet
Jeremiah: "Behold, I have sworn by my great name, says Yahweh, that my name
shall no more be invoked by the mouth of any man of Judah in all the land of
Egypt, saying, 'As Yahweh GOD lives.' Behold, I am watching over them for
evil and not for good; all the men of Judah who are in the land of Egypt shall
be consumed by the sword and by famine, until there is an end of them. And
those who escape the sword shall return from the land of Egypt to the land of
Judah, few in number" (Jer. 44:26–28).

CHAPTER 14

The Era
of the Persian Empire

The middle decades of the sixth century (559–539 B.C.E.) witnessed the rise of a new ruling power in the Near East. The Persians, an Indo-European people whose origins and center of power lay in the territory north and east of the Fertile Crescent, quickly established the most comprehensive Near Eastern empire that had existed until that time.

The architect for the new empire was Cyrus II. His meteoric career and far-flung conquests took advantage of the weaknesses of the Babylonian, Lydian, Median, and Egyptian kingdoms and appealed to those who favored internationalism over the more limited ethnic kingdoms that had temporarily replaced the Assyrian empire. Cyrus' son Cambyses added Egypt to the Persian holdings. Darius I, the third of the Persian rulers, further expanded the imperial holdings and gave organizational structure to the huge Persian empire.

For over two centuries, from the Persian capture of Babylon in 539 B.C.E. until the fall of Tyre to Alexander the Great in 332 B.C.E., Palestine and the Jewish community in Judah were under Persian hegemony. The most significant events in Jewish history during this period, at least from the perspective of the final editors of the Hebrew Bible, were the return of exiles from Babylonia, the reconstruction of the Jerusalem Temple, the refortification of the city of Jerusalem, and the attempts to reform Judean life by two returning Jewish leaders from the diaspora—Ezra and Nehemiah. Unfortunately, as we shall see, the biblical materials, our primary explicit sources for Jewish history in the land of Palestine during this period, by focusing on the restoration efforts of exilic returnees, practically ignore the ongoing life and history of the Judean community that remained in the land and never experienced the exile. Thus any reconstruction of the history of Palestinian Judaism for this period is at the mercy of the narrow documentation that has survived.

The basic Jewish sources for the period are the historical books of Ezra and Nehemiah, the prophetical books of Haggai and Zechariah (Zech. 1–8), the apocryphal book of 1 Esdras, and Josephus' *Antiquities* (Book XI). (Although given a Persian setting, the Book of Esther is a romantic novel and supplies no precise historical information on the period.) Ezra 1 reports that Cyrus granted permission for exiled Judeans to return and rebuild the Temple (Ezra 1:1–4; compare 6:1–5) and that he restored the Temple vessels taken into exile by Nebuchadrezzar sending these home under the care of Shesh-bazzar "the prince of Judah" (1:5–11). After supplying a list of the returnees (Ezra 2; see Neh. 7:6–73), the story of the returning exiles focuses on the work of reconstructing the Temple led by Jeshua and Zerubbabel (Ezra 3:1–4:5; see 5:13–16), on opposition to the work of the returnees (4:6–24), and on the eventual rededication of the sanctuary (6:1–22). The remainder of Ezra-Nehemiah is taken up with the stories about Ezra (Ezra 7–10; Neh. 7:73b–10:39) and Nehemiah (Neh. 1:1–7:73a; 11–13). I Esdras offers a summary in Greek of the Book of Ezra and Neh. 7:38–8:12 along with II Chron. 35–36. Josephus offers little not paralleled in the biblical sources. Since the biblical sources supply only a few vignettes of Jewish life for this period, the story is best carried by the narrative of the larger Persian history.

The Rise of Cyrus and the Persians

The ancient world was familiar with several legends about the origins and early career of Cyrus (Herodotus I. 95). The account based on the motif of the threatened child who grows up to be a great leader (see *ANET* 119; Ex. 2; Matt. 2) fascinated Herodotus (I.107–30) but probably provides little of historical value. Cyrus, apparently the son of King Cambyses I, of the minor kingdom of Anshan, and Mandane, the daughter of the Median king Astyages (about 585–550 B.C.E.), began his career as ruler in his father's rather insignificant province in southwestern Persia. Cyrus was able to expand his power at the expense of his Median overlord and grandfather Astyages and probably with the blessings of the Babylonian king Nabonidus, who was suspicious of Median power. A fragmentary portion of the Nabonidus Chronicle reports that Cyrus acquired Astyages' kingdom in 550 B.C.E. as a consequence of the desertion of the Median forces:

> King Ishtumegu (Astyages) called up his troops and marched against Cyrus, king of Anshan, in order to meet him in battle. The army of Ishtumegu revolted against him and in fetters they delivered him to Cyrus. Cyrus marched against the country Agamtanu (Ecbatana); the royal residence he seized; silver, gold, other valuables . . . of the country Agamtanu he took as booty and brought them to Anshan. (*ANET* 305)

Thus Cyrus took control over the Median empire. Instead of moving against Babylonia, as might have been expected, Cyrus turned his attention westward. According to Herodotus (I. 73–90), he carried on negotiations with the Greek city-states in Ionia and attacked Croesus, the legendary king of Lydia who had initially attacked Cyrus to get revenge for the latter's actions against Astyages, a brother-in-law of Croesus (so Herodotus I.73). Following up an inconclusive victory, Cyrus unconventionally attacked Croesus, after the latter had dismissed his provincial levies, prior to the onset of winter. After fourteen days, Cyrus had taken Sardis the capital city (see *ANET* 306). In addition to Lydia and Lycia, the Greek states in Asia Minor were subdued and added to Cyrus' holdings in Armenia, Cappadocia, and Cilicia which he had taken on his march to fight Croesus. It was probably during Cyrus' campaign into western Asia Minor that Cyprus voluntarily submitted to Persian control (Herodotus III.19). Thus two of the major powers of the time—Media and Lydia—fell to the Persians.

Before moving against the third major power, Babylonia, Cyrus extended his control to the east, securing the entire Iranian plateau and the territory extending to northwest India. In Babylonia itself, discontent with Nabonidus and pro-Cyrus support accelerated. Probably three classes especially hoped for a Persian triumph. (1) The Marduk priesthood was strongly opposed to Naboni dus' predilection for the god Sin, even through he had continued to worship and support the other Babylonian deities. The absence of the king from Babylon during his stay in Tema had curbed religious celebrations. In strongly anti-Nabonidus tones, the Nabonidus Chronicle monotonously demurs: "The king stayed in Tema; the crown prince, the officials and his army were in Akkad (Babylonia). The king did not come to Babylon for the ceremonies of the month Nisan, . . . Nebo did not come to Babylon, . . . Bel did not go out of Esagila in procession, the festival of the New Year was omitted" (*ANET* 306). (2) Babylonian merchants who had seen their markets disrupted and trade routes disappear probably yearned for the renewal of an empire where far-flung trade routes and ever-increasing markets created demands and stimulated supplies. (3) Thousands of foreigners now living in Babylon must have felt that chances for return to their homelands were better under anyone other than the ruling establishment.

Nabonidus was an old man, perhaps past seventy, when he returned from Arabia, probably in 540 B.C.E., to prepare the capital city for the inevitable invasion of the Persians. He hastily sought to fortify the city of Babylon and the outlying regions for the onslaught of Cyrus and participated in the spring new year festival which his absence had suspended for a decade. But the city and the region—torn by internal dissensions, cut off from external trade and military aid, defended primarily by mercenary seminomads, and plagued by famine and inflation—were no match for Persian forces now joined by defectors from the Babylonian military hierarchy. In September 539 B.C.E., the Babylonian army was defeated at Opis, and the ancient city of Akkad was destroyed and its population slaughtered by Cyrus. The pro-Persian chronicles report the capture of Babylon itself in the following terms:

> On the sixteenth day [of the month Tishri = 16 October 639] Gobryas (Ugbaru), governor of the Guti, and the army of Cyrus entered Babylon without a battle. Afterwards, after Nabonidus, retreated, he was captured in Babylon. Until the end of the month, the shield-bearing troops of the Guti surrounded the gates of Esagila. But there was no interruption of rites in Esagila or the other temples and no date for a performance was missed. On the third day of the month Marchesvan [= 29 October 639] Cyrus entered Babylon. . . . There was peace in the city while Cyrus spoke his greeting to all of Babylon. (*ABC* 109–10)

With the fall of the capital city, Babylonia—the third major Near Eastern power of the sixth century—fell to Persian control. The territory ruled by Nabonidus —Babylonia proper, Arabia and the Transjordan, and the Eastern Mediterranean Seaboard—was all added, theoretically at least, to the Persian empire.

Cyrus as Liberator and Propagandist

It is not accidental that history has remembered Cyrus as a great liberator of captured peoples. (See Text XVII.) It is an image which he and his officials sought to foster and which the historical conditions of the time facilitated. Here he was building upon and exploiting an age-old royal tradition. The portrait of the good ruler as "the gatherer of the dispersed" and "the restorer of the gods and their sanctuaries" was a common feature of Near Eastern royal ideology. Already in the eighteenth century B.C.E., Hammurabi could boast that he was the one "who collected the scattered people" (*ANET* 164). Such motifs were especially stressed by the Assyrian rulers Esarhaddon and Ashurbanipal. For example, after Sennacherib had destroyed Babylon and its Esagila temple in 689 B.C.E., Esarhaddon depicted himself as the great restorer of people and temple. The following quotes from texts concerning Esarhaddon's rebuilding of Babylon illustrate the point:

> Seventy years as the period of its (Esagila's) desolation he (Marduk) wrote down in the Book of Fate. But the merciful Marduk—his anger lasted but a moment— turned the book upside down and ordered its restoration in the eleventh [a reversed 70 in cuneiform script] year. (*ARAB* II, §650)

> As for the enslaved Babylonians, who had been the feudatories, the clients, of the gods Anu and Enlil, their freedom I established anew. The "capitalists," who had been brought into slavery, who had been apportioned to the yoke and fetter, I gathered together and accounted them for Babylonians.
>   Their plundered possessions I restored. The naked I clothed and turned their feet into the road to Babylon. To resettle the city, to rebuild the temple, to set out plantations, to dig irrigation-ditches I encouraged them. Their clientship which had lapsed, which had slipped out of their hands, I restored. The tablet (charter) of their freedom I wrote anew. Toward the four winds of heaven I opened up their ways so that, establishing their tongue (language) in every land, they might carry out their plans. (*ARAB* II, §659E)

The building inscriptions of Ashurbanipal abound with similar claims about how he "renewed the sanctuaries of all the metropolises and revived in them the ancient cults and restored their regular offerings which had ceased" (*ARAB*, §956). Similarly, Nabonidus repaid the god Sin for raising him to the throne by restoring his city and cult:

> I carefully executed the command of his (Sin's) great godhead, I was not careless nor negligent but set in motion people from Babylon and Upper Syria, from the border of Egypt on the Upper Sea to the Lower Sea, all those whom Sin, the king of the gods, had entrusted to me, thus I build anew the Ehulhul, the temple of Sin,

and completed this work. I then led in procession Sin, Ningal, Nusku and Sadar-nunna, from Shuanna in Babylon, my royal city, and brought them in joy and happiness into the temple, installing them on a permanent dais. I made abundant offerings before them and lavished gifts on them. (*ANET* 563)

With a grand flair for propagandistic impact, Cyrus too played the role of liberator, accepting and acknowledging the patronage of the gods worshiped by those capitulating to and supporting him. The so-called Cyrus Cylinder, reflective of and modeled on earlier inscriptions of Esarhaddon and Ashurbanipal, for example, ascribed his success in Babylon to Marduk, who "scanned and looked through all the countries, searching for a righteous ruler willing to lead him in the annual procession. Then he pronounced the name of Cyrus, king of Anshan, declared him to be the ruler of all the world" (*ANET* 315; see Text XVII).

Against this background, the hope of the Judean exiles to return home and Second Isaiah's preaching and expectations become more understandable. This prophet sought, in poetry of great lyrical expression and in an enormously persuasive rhetoric, to convince his fellow exiles that the activity of Cyrus and the international developments of the time were under the control of Yahweh and that all of this forebode a good future for the exiles. The prophet hailed Cyrus as savior and redeemer, as the chosen of Yahweh: "I [Yahweh] stirred up one from the north, and he has come, from the rising of the sun, and he shall call on my name; he shall trample on rulers as on mortar, as the potter treads clay" (Isa. 41:25). In order to emphasize Cyrus as Yahweh's "chosen," he even bestowed upon Cyrus the title borne by Davidic kings: "Thus says Yahweh to his messiah, to Cyrus, whose right hand I have grasped, to subdue nations before him and ungird the loins of kings, to open doors before him that gates may not be closed" (Isa. 45:1). The prophet has Yahweh address Cyrus personally (see Isa. 45:1–7) and proclaim the fall of Babylon (Isa. 46–47). The hope for the future is already placed in the mouth of Yahweh and the hands of Cyrus: " 'He is my shepherd, and he shall fulfil all my purpose'; saying of Jerusalem, 'She shall be built,' and of the temple, 'Your foundation shall be laid' " (Isa. 44:28). The words of the prophet must be seen therefore as not only intended for his exilic audience but also for the Persians to demonstrate that it was also Yahweh who had chosen Cyrus and that his people expected reciprocation (Isa. 45:13). Josephus reports that Cyrus took his lenient attitude toward the Judean exiles after reading Isaiah's prophecy about Cyrus, written 210 years before the Persian took Babylon (*Ant.* XI. 1–9). This, of course, assumes too much; Josephus did not know about a Second Isaiah. However, it is not beyond the range of possibility to assume that Cyrus and the Persians knew the Jewish sentiments reflected in Isaiah 40–48, if not the material itself.

Cyrus' treatment of groups that had been deported and settled throughout the Assyrian and Babylonian empires probably varied from case to case. The Cyrus Cylinder, obviously seeking to gain as much propagandistic mileage as possible, probably presents an accurate picture of Cyrus' policy toward people and cults in the Babylonian area. (See Text XVII.)

TEXT XVII. An Inscription of Cyrus

Upon their complaints the lord of the gods (Marduk) became terribly angry and [he departed from] their region, (also) the (other) gods living among them left their mansions, wroth that he (Nabonidus) had brought (them) into Babylon. (But) Marduk [who does care for] . . . on account of (the fact that) the sanctuaries of all their settlements were in ruins and the inhabitants of Sumer and Akkad had become like (living) dead, turned back (his countenance) his an[ger] [abated] and he had mercy (upon them). He scanned and looked (through) all the countries, searching for a righteous ruler willing to lead him (i.e. Marduk) (in the annual procession). (Then) he pronounced the name of Cyrus, king of Anshan, declared him (lit.: pronounced [his] name) to be (come) the ruler of all the world. He made the Guti country and all the Manda-hordes bow in submission to his (i.e. Cyrus') feet. And he (Cyrus) did always endeavour to treat according to justice the black-headed whom he (Marduk) has made him conquer. Marduk, the great lord, a protector of his people/worshipers, beheld with pleasure his (i.e. Cyrus') good deeds and his upright mind (lit.: heart) (and therefore) ordered him to march against his city Babylon. He made him set out on the road to Babylon going at his side like a real friend. His widespread troops—their number, like that of the water of a river, could not be established—strolled along, their weapons packed away. Without any battle, he made him enter his town Babylon, sparing Babylon any calamity. He delivered into his (i.e. Cyrus') hands Nabonidus, the king who did not worship him (i.e. Marduk). All the inhabitants of Babylon as well as of the entire country of Sumer and Akkad, princes and governors (included), bowed to him (Cyrus) and kissed his feet, jubilant that he (had received) the kingship, and with shining faces. Happily they greeted him as a master through whose help they had come (again) to life from death (and) had all been spared damage and disaster, and they worshiped his (very) name. . . . .

When I entered Babylon as a friend and (when) I established the seat of the government in the palace of the ruler under jubilation and rejoicing, Marduk, the great lord, [induced] the magnanimous inhabitants of Babylon [to love me], and I was daily endeavouring to worship him. My numerous troops walked around in Babylon in peace, I did not allow anybody to terrorize (any place) of the [country of Sumer] and Akkad. I strove for peace in Babylon and in all his (other) sacred cities. As to the inhabitants of Babylon, [who] against the will of the gods [had/were . . . , I abolished] the corvée (lit.: yoke) which was against their (social) standing. I brought relief to their dilapidated housing, putting (thus) an end to their (main) complaints. Marduk, the great lord, was well pleased with my deeds and sent friendly blessings to myself, Cyrus, the king who worships him, to Cambyses, my son, the offspring of [my] loins, as well as to all my troops, and we all [praised] his great [godhead] joyously, standing before him in peace.

> All the kings of the entire world from the Upper to the Lower Sea, those who are seated in throne rooms, (those who) live in other [types of buildings as well as] all the kings of the West land living in tents, brought their heavy tributes and kissed my feet in Babylon. (As to the region) from . . . as far as Ashur and Susa, Agade, Eshnunna, the towns Zamban, Me-Turnu, Der as well as the region of the Gutians, I returned to (these) sacred cities on the other side of the Tigris, the sanctuaries of which have been ruins for a long time, the images which (used) to live therein and established for them permanent sanctuaries. I (also) gathered all their (former) inhabitants and returned (to them) their habitations. Furthermore, I resettled upon the command of Marduk, the great lord, all the gods of Sumer and Akkad whom Nabonidus has brought into Babylon to the anger of the lord of the gods, unharmed, in their (former) chapels, the places which make them happy. (*ANET* 315–16) (See photograph on p. 444.)

It can be safely assumed that a similar attitude prevailed toward other regions and cults, especially in those sensitive areas where it would have been especially advantageous to have centers sympathetic to Persian authority. Judah would surely have been such a region, since it lay on the road to Egypt, the fourth major Near Eastern power of the time and the one kingdom still unconquered by Cyrus.

Although Cyrus and his successors earned a reputation for tolerance and benevolence, it should be noted that Persian kings could be as harsh in their treatment of subject peoples as others, depending upon the needs of the situation. For example, later kings often took harsh actions against their subjects, even against cultic centers: Darius I had the temple at Didyma in Asia Minor destroyed (Herodotus VI. 20), Xerxes destroyed Babylon in reprisal for a revolt (Herodotus I.183), the residents of Barca in Lydia were resettled in Bactria by Darius I (Herodotus IV.204), the Paeonians were moved from Thrace to Phrygia (Herodotus V.13–16), citizens of Miletus were resettled on the Persian Gulf (Herodotus VI.20), and late in Persian history, Sidonians were exiled to Babylon and Susa (*ABC* 114).

Persian Policy Toward the Judean Exiles

The Book of Ezra contains two ordinances dated to the "first year" of Cyrus, presumably the year following his capture of Babylon (539 B.C.E.), which speak of a return of the Jews from exile and of the restoration of the Temple. One is written in Aramaic and is described as the official record of Cyrus' edict preserved in the official archives at Ecbatana in Persia (Ezra 6:1–5). This document has Cyrus stipulate that the Temple should be rebuilt according to certain dimensions and specifications, that royal funds should be used for the project, and that the vessels taken from the old Temple to Babylon should be restored (compare Ezra 5:13–15). The other ordinance, written in Hebrew, is described

Cyrus Cylinder. This inscription details Persian attitudes of tolerance and sympathy toward local religions of conquered peoples (see Text XVII, p. 442); it thereby displays some consistency with the tradition of the Edict of Cyrus (Ezra 6:2–5). *(The British Museum)*

as a proclamation distributed in writing throughout the kingdom (Ezra 1:2–4). This latter text notes that Cyrus was charged by Yahweh the God of heaven to reconstruct the Temple in Jerusalem. Further, it notes that permission was granted to any Yahweh worshipers wishing to return to work on the rebuilding to do so; Jews not returning might contribute toward the expense of those who did return as well as to the cost of Temple restoration.

The differences in these ordinances are significant. Ezra 6:3–5 concentrates on the rebuilding of the Temple at royal expense but makes no reference to returning exiles. Ezra 1:2–4, on the other hand, focuses on the issue of returning exiles and contains no particulars about Temple reconstruction. If both texts are authentic and from the first year of Cyrus' reign, as they purport, then these could be seen as two types of Persian administrative documents with different functions. The Hebrew text in Ezra 1 would be a form of the message that was proclaimed by official heralds in various Jewish communities and subsequently posted in written form. The second, the Aramaic text in Ezra 6, would represent the form of an official memorandum stored in the royal archives. Such memoranda presumably were based on royal decrees and were written down on clay tablets for filing or on papyrus sheets which were glued together to form archival scrolls.

If these texts refer to two different decrees but have in common their interest in the restoration of the Temple, then the text in Ezra 6:3–5 may be seen as Cyrus' decree ordering Temple reconstruction and the return of the sacred vessels. (Note that in this text, the reference to "the first year of Cyrus" appears to be part of the document.) The decree in Ezra 1:2–4 would then be a subsequent decree granting the right of Jews to return and aid in restoration but making no reference to the vessels or Temple specifications, since these were covered in the earlier decree. (Note that in Ezra 1:1–5, the dating of the decree is part of the editorial frame rather than a part of the document.) Even if these decrees came from two different occasions in the reign of Cyrus or served two different functions, there is no real reason to doubt their historical value, although their wording may have been shaped by the biblical editors.

Such a decree or decrees concerning the reconstruction of the Temple and the return of the exiles should not be taken as an expression of Persian favoritism toward the Jews. In the first place, such action as we have seen was typical of Cyrus when such a policy was judged in the best interests of the Persian cause. Second, his affirmation that it was Yahweh who had given him all the kingdoms of the earth was comparable to similar affirmations made about Marduk. Third, such actions could be viewed as reciprocation for the pro-Persian sentiments held by many Judean exiles, such as Second Isaiah. Fourth, by providing support for the Jerusalem Temple, Cyrus was assuming the role of successor to Jerusalemite royalty, since the Temple had been a "royal shrine" under the special care of the king. Fifth, the political realities on the southwestern borders of his empire could have made expedient such a friendly and supportive gesture. Although "all the kings of the West land living in tents" had submitted to Cyrus shortly after his capture of Babylon, bringing tribute and kissing his feet (*ANET* 316), others may not have submitted so readily, if at all. Egypt was still ruled by the aged Pharaoh Amasis (570–526 B.C.E.), a former ally of Croesus. The inevitable attack against Egypt could only be aided, not hindered, by a Judean community favorably disposed to the Persians.

Two final matters should be noted about these decrees. (1) They did not require or allow for the gathering of the dispersed Jews throughout the Persian empire. Thus no return en masse was envisioned. (2) The decrees are primarily concerned with the reconstruction of the Temple, not the return of exiles per se.

The Political Situation in Judah

Unfortunately all the Jewish historical sources for the Persian period focus almost exclusively on the exilic returnees and their efforts to affect life in the province of Judah. One might say that practically all of these sources assume that Judah existed during the Babylonian period as an occupational vacuum awaiting repopulation from those taken into exile and that all the major impulses of the time came from the returnees. As we noted in the last chapter, however, one should assume that a vigorous life continued in the area, although with a reduced population.

If our conclusions are correct, headed by political life Judeans continued to function in the area. As we noted, the important aristocratic family of Shaphan had moved into leadership following the destruction of Jerusalem. Gedaliah was appointed as king. After Gedaliah's assassination, we should assume that Nebuchadrezzar appointed a successor, although the ruler may not have held monarchical office. Presumably Mizpah continued as the capital for the region.

In the early chapters of Ezra, there appears the figure of Shesh-bazzar described as "the prince of Judah" (Ezra 1:8) and said to have been appointed as governor by Cyrus (Ezra 5:14). Although it must remain in the arena of speculation, it could be surmised that Shesh-bazzar, who bore a Babylonian name, was the incumbent ruler of the Judean province at the time of Cyrus' triumph. As such, the title "prince of Judah" either would be equivalent to the term king, as perhaps in the Book of Ezekiel (Ezek. 45:7–8), or would be the Hebrew equivalent of a Babylonian title. After assuming authority in the area, Cyrus continued Shesh-bazzar in office but with the title "governor" (Ezra 5:14).

The province or district of Judah, if we may judge from the evidence of the books of Ezra and Nehemiah, was composed of the territory extending from just north of Bethel to south of Beth-zur and from the Jordan River to just west of Emmaus and Azekah. This would give an area of about twenty-five miles north to south and thirty or so miles east to west, or an area of about eight hundred square miles. This would probably have corresponded to the boundaries established by Nebuchadrezzar following the fall of Jerusalem.

The Extent of the Return

Surprisingly, the biblical materials contain practically no information on the return of exiles from Babylon during the early years of Persian rule. (This contrasts noticeably with the accounts of returns at the time of Ezra [Ezra 7–8] and Nehemiah [Neh. 2:1–10].) Mention is made of the fact that Temple vessels were turned over to Shesh-bazzar to be returned (Ezra 1:7–11; 5:14–15). The transport of these cultic artifacts is noted also in Second Isaiah:

> Depart, depart, go out thence,
>   touch no unclean thing;
> go out from the midst of her [Babylon], purify yourselves,
>   you who bear the vessels of Yahweh.
> For you shall not go out in haste,
>   and you shall not go in flight,
> for Yahweh will go before you,
>   and the God of Israel will be your rear guard.
>   (Isa. 52:11–12)

Otherwise, we are only told that "then rose up the heads of the fathers' houses of Judah and Benjamin, and the priests and the Levites, every one whose spirit God had stirred to go up to rebuild the house of Yahweh which is in Jerusalem" (Ezra 1:5).

Two lists of returnees, almost identical, appear in Ezra 2 and Nehemiah 7. The appearance of the list in Ezra 2 immediately following the comments about Shesh-bazzar would imply that the list should be associated with the return, of about fifty thousand persons (see Ezra 2:64–67), under Shesh-bazzar. The officials associated with the list, however, are not Shesh-bazzar but Zerubbabel, Jeshua, Nehemiah, and others who belong to later periods (Ezra 2:2; Neh. 7:7). Thus, if the document is a genuine list of returnees, it probably comes from a time later than Shesh-bazzar. Doubts can be raised, however, about whether it is even an authentic tabulation of returnees at all. The list contains no indication of date or any references to Cyrus. It may be some census count, a tax document, or a population count (see Ezra 5:4–10) from a later period which has been incorporated into the text and treated as a list of returnees.

In all probability, the initial return from Babylon was a rather limited matter. Several factors indicate this. (1) The permission to return was related to reconstruction work on the Temple and not a full-fledged grant of exilic repatriation. Thus only those "whose spirit God had stirred to go up to rebuild the temple of Yahweh" (Ezra 1:5) would have left Babylon. (2) The Persians apparently did not move into southern Syria-Palestine in force until the time of Cambyses' invasion of Egypt in 526/5 B.C.E. Thus conditions prior to this time were not conducive to mass movement of exiled Judeans to the area. (3) The books of Haggai and Zechariah, concerned with the period around 520 B.C.E., do not indicate any large conglomerate of returnees anxious to complete Temple construction. (4) The rather favorable status of the exiles in Babylonia vis-à-vis conditions in Palestine may have made it more desirable for Jews to remain in Babylon, "being unwilling to leave their possessions" (*Ant.* XI.8).

Perhaps we should think of only an initial return of small numbers which may, however, have swelled with the movement of Persian forces into Palestine during the reign of Cambyses (530–522 B.C.E.). The outbreak of troubles which especially plagued the city of Babylon at the time of Cambyses' death and the subsequent turmoil in the early years of Darius I (522–486 B.C.E.) may have encouraged migration back to Canaan.

The Reconstruction of the Jerusalem Temple

A temple to Yahweh in Jerusalem built with Cyrus' patronage never became a reality during his reign. The rebuilt Temple was not dedicated until the reign of Darius I (Ezra 6:15). This, of course, does not call into question either the authenticity of Cyrus' decrees concerning the Temple or his utilization of the orders for propaganda purposes. The issuing of the decree and the assumption of the role of "restorer of the old order" were apparently as consequential as the execution of the role itself. Esarhaddon's inscriptions, for example, speak of him as the one who rebuilt Esagila and Babylon, protected their arrangements, and returned the deported gods taken to Ashur. Yet it was twelve years later and long after his death, during the reign of his successor Ashurbanipal, when his decree was brought to fruition.

Various interpretations and differing accounts of the "restoration" of authentic Jewish existence after the calamitous judgment of Yahweh in the fall of Jerusalem are found in Jewish tradition. Underlying these are the assumptions that the exile marked a radical break in authentic existence, that proper restoration was the work of those who had actually experienced being in exile, and that the renewed community must in some sense be new and uncontaminated and yet stand in continuity with conditions that had existed prior to the exile.

Diverse narratives and traditions thus exist about when, under whom, and how this restoration was effected. This can be seen in the various ways in which Temple restoration and renewal of worship in Jerusalem are described. In one form, it was Ezra who was the real restorer. This can be seen in the biblical traditions about Ezra as well as in the apocryphal book of II Esdras. Another form is found in II Macc. 1:18–2:15, where it is Nehemiah who is the restorer of Temple and altar. I Esdras, Josephus who follows I Esdras, and some of the biblical texts in Ezra, Haggai, and Zechariah assign Zerubbabel a unique role as restorer. (One can say that for the author of the Book of Daniel [see Dan. 9], true restoration of people and Temple was to be realized finally in the second century B.C.E.)

In Ezra 1–6 there appear to be three different presentations of the Temple restoration. One line of tradition, in Ezra 1 + 5:6–17, sees Shesh-bazzar as the initiator of work on Temple rebuilding at the time of Cyrus which continues uninterrupted into the time of Darius I. A second line of tradition, in Ezra 3 + 6:19–22, sees Zerubbabel and Jeshua as the restorers. A final form, in Ezra 5:1–5 + 6:1–18 and in Haggai and Zechariah, assigns the restoration work to Zerubbabel and Joshua, but they carry out the work in conjunction with the prophetical activity of Haggai and Zechariah.

One plausible interpretation of the restoration of the Jerusalem Temple, which we follow here, sees reconstruction as having been begun under Shesh-bazzar and then reaching a new phase under the leadership of Zerubbabel and Joshua at the time of Darius' accession to the throne. Our approach to the matter, however, assumes that Shesh-bazzar was not necessarily an exile, or if so, he had already been appointed as head of the Judean community prior to the rise of Cyrus and the Persians. Shesh-bazzar would have been given custody of the Temple vessels to return them to Jerusalem where a continuing cult existed. (The figures for the Temple vessels in Ezra 1:9–11, however, appear to be greatly exaggerated.) He also began, in his position as Persian-appointed governor of the province, to carry out the decree of Cyrus. Thus work was begun on reconstructing the Temple (Ezra 5:16), but Shesh-bazzar did not bring the task to completion. We are not told what happened to him. Perhaps he functioned as governor until his death and was succeeded in his post by Zerubbabel.

Under Zerubbabel, reconstruction entered a new phase but a phase reflective of and with a new impetus given by conditions under the successors of Cyrus, to which we shall now turn.

Cambyses

Cyrus died fighting in the east in 530 B.C.E. Before his final battle he had designated his son Cambyses as heir apparent and had had Cambyses accompany him on much of the march eastward, probably to familiarize the subjects with the king's successor (Herodotus I.208). After his father's death, Cambyses, who was remembered in tradition as a harsh ruler, "being naturally bad" (so Josephus, *Ant.* XI.26), subdued the eastern region of the empire and then invaded Egypt in 526/5 B.C.E. He assembled his invasion force at the Palestinian coastal town of Acco (Strabo XVI.2.25). Arabic tribes aided the Persian forces in their march through the Sinai desert, supplying them with water (Herodotus II.7–9) as they had the Assyrians in an earlier era. Speaking of these Arabs, Herodotus claims they "never submitted to the Persian yoke, but were on friendly terms, and gave Cambyses a free passage into Egypt; for, without the consent of the Arabians, the Persians could not have penetrated into Egypt" (Herodotus III.88). Cyprus, along with the Phoenicians, supplied ships for the Persian expedition.

The aged and resourceful Egyptian pharaoh Amasis died, after a reign of forty-four years, while the Persian force was moving toward Egypt. The new pharaoh, Psammetichus III, was defeated after a hard-fought battle in the Delta and withdrew to Memphis, where he was quickly overcome. Persian conquest was apparently aided by the defection of Udjahorresne the commander of the Egyptian fleet.

Cambyses remained in Egypt for three years. Udjahorresne, who was also a leading priest, prepared a royal titulature for the Persian monarch, who was duly crowned as the legitimate pharaoh of Upper and Lower Egypt. Cambyses apparently wanted to be seen as the legitimate successor of the old Saitic dynasty whose last king Apries had been replaced by Amasis. The latter's name was removed from many Egyptian monuments. A legend that Cambyses was the son of a daughter of Apries circulated in various forms (see Herodotus I.1–3) and may have been part of Persian propaganda. During his stay in Egypt, where he was later remembered, perhaps somewhat falsely, as an intolerant madman, Cambyses carried out several expeditions, with only limited success: a campaign against Ethiopia apparently achieved some objectives, a force sent into the desert to the oasis of Amun disappeared in a sandstorm, and an expedition to Carthage failed when the Phoenicians refused to fight against their kinsmen. (Much of the material provided by Herodotus [III.1–38] on Cambyses' invasion and stay in Egypt is colored by the Egyptian disdain for the monarch.)

Something of Cambyses' interest in local life and religion in Egypt and probably a more realistic and unbiased view of the king can be seen in the autobiographical inscription of the much rewarded Udjahorresne (see *AEL* III.36–41). According to this text, Cambyses, "the Great Ruler of Egypt and Great Chief of all foreign lands," not only visited the temple of the goddess Neith (mother of the sun-god Re) in Sais and provided offerings but also ordered that the temple be purged of all foreigners and purified for its proper ritual, and that all the priestly personnel be returned to the sanctuary. The reconsecration of the temple, which had been the cult sanctuary and dynastic center for the Saite Dynasty, and the restoration of normalcy after the turmoil of invasion were supervised by Udjahorresne, who requested in his inscription that his pious deeds be remembered by the gods:

I am a man who is good in his town. I rescued its inhabitants from the very great turmoil when it happened in the whole land, the like of which had not happened in this land. I defended the weak against the strong. I rescued the timid man when misfortune came to him. I did for them every beneficence when it was time to act for them. . . .

One honored by Neith is he who shall say: "O great gods who are in Sais! Remember all the benefactions done by the chief physician, Udjahorresne. And may you do to him all benefactions! May you make his good name endure in this land forever!" (*AEL* III.39–40)

(Later, Udjahorresne was with Darius in Elam and was sent back to Egypt by the Persian king to restore the establishment called the House of Life where medicine, theology, temple administration, and ritual were studied and practiced.)

Cambyses was far less tolerant and benevolent with regard to other temples in Egypt. Surprised at the extent of temple and priestly revenues, he curtailed the income and powers of many sanctuaries.

When Cambyses was in Syria (at Ecbatana according to Herodotus; in Damascus according to Josephus in *Ant.* XI.30) on his return home, he learned that his brother, Bardiya (or Smerdis), had usurped the throne (Herodotus III.62). Cambyses, however, never made it home to suppress the revolt. He died in Syria of uncertain causes: Herodotus speaks of an accidental stabbing while mounting his steed (III.64); in the Behistun Inscription, Darius I reports that Cambyses died by his own hand (*OP* 120, §11).

Although Cambyses passed through Palestine on his journeys to and from Egypt and his forces congregated at Acco for the invasion, no reference in contemporary documents refers to any contacts between him and the Jewish community. (I Esdras 2:16–25 and Josephus in *Ant.* XI.20–30 do, however, associate the content of Ezra 4:7–24 with Cambyses rather than Darius.) One thing is clear: by the time of Cambyses, Palestine and the Eastern Mediterranean Seaboard were securely in Persian hands.

Darius I

The rebellion in Persia was probably led by Cambyses' true brother and thus the son of Cyrus rather than by a pretender as later claimed by Darius. Even among the Persians, Cambyses was considered a tyrant, "severe and arrogant" (Herodotus III.89), and the widespread extent of the support for Bardiya prior to the death of Cambyses suggests that he had a large following. Darius admitted that "all the people became rebellious from Cambyses, and went over to him (Bardiya), both Persia and Media and the other provinces" (*OP* 120, §11). In the Behistun Inscription, Darius gives the following account of how matters occurred:

A son of Cyrus, Cambyses by name, of our family—he was king here. Of that Cambyses there was a brother, Smerdis (Bardiya) by name, having the same mother and the same father as Cambyses. Afterwards, Cambyses slew that Smerdis. When Cambyses slew Smerdis, it did not become known to the people that Smerdis had been slain. Afterwards, Cambyses went to Egypt. When Cambyses had gone off to Egypt, after that the people became evil. After that the Lie waxed great in the country, both in Persia and in Media and in other provinces. . . . Afterwards, there was one man, a Magian, Gaumata by name; he rose up. . . . He lied to the people thus: "I am Smerdis, the son of Cyrus, brother of Cambyses." After that, all the people became rebellious. (*OP* 119–20, §§10–11)

This version of events, reported in the massive Behistun Inscription recorded in three languages—Elamite, Akkadian, and Old Persian—was widely circulated and apparently believed in the ancient world (see Herodotus' version in III.61–69). A version of the Behistun Inscription in Aramaic was found at Elephantine (*AP* 251–59). In all probability, Darius, supported by an inner circle of seven prominent leaders, took over the throne from the usurper Bardiya, who had sought to take advantage of the absence and dislike for his brother Cambyses to seize power. Darius, although from the same ancestral line as Cyrus, was not from the immediate ruling branch.

Three factors about the early years of Darius (522–486 B.C.E.) are significant for the subsequent course of events in Judah.

Widespread Revolts at the Beginning of His Reign. At the beginning of his reign, Darius was confronted with numerous political and military obstacles. These involved suppressing the popular support given Bardiya and the subsequent major revolts that followed Darius' assumption of power. Although Bardiya reigned for only a short time—Herodotus says seven months (III.67); the Behistun Inscription gives three months (*OP* 120, §§11–13)—his support was widespread. Darius assumed power without popular support, and opposition to his rule broke out in various regions. He notes that rebellions occurred in the provinces of Persia, Elam, Media, Assyria, Egypt, Parthia, Margiana, Sattagydia, and Scythia (*OP* 123, §22). Some of the strongest opposition was in Babylon, which had quickly recognized Bardiya as king. After his death, Nebuchadrezzar III, the son of Nabonidus, whom Darius called Nidintu-Bel, was acclaimed king in Babylon and other cities. After defeating the Babylonian army, Darius entered Babylon and executed Nidintu-Bel and the city's leading citizens. A second revolt in Babylon broke out in August 521 B.C.E., led by Nebuchadrezzar IV, and was finally suppressed in November. Herodotus reports that this second capture involved harsh treatment of the population:

> When Darius had made himself master of the Babylonians, first of all he demolished the walls and bore away all the gates; for when Cyrus had taken Babylon before, he did neither of these things; and, secondly, Darius impaled about three thousand of the principal citizens, and allowed the rest of the Babylonians to inhabit the city. (Herodotus III.159)

The extent of troubles throughout the empire can be seen in Darius' claim that he fought nineteen battles and took nine kings captive in a single year (*OP* 131,

CHART XVI. The Persian Empire

Persian Rulers	*Events in Palestine*
Cyrus II (559–530) Became king of Anshan (559) Conquered Astyages of Media (550) Defeated Croesus of Lydia (546) Captured Babylon (539) Edict allowing Jews to return and rebuild the Temple (538)	Judah as a Babylonian province or subject kingdom Shesh-bazzar as head of Judean province First return of Jews from Babylonia (538?) Work begun on Jerusalem Temple restoration(?)
Cambyses (530–522)	Zerubbabel as governor Palestine fully under Persian control Work begun on Jerusalem Temple restoration(?)
Conquest of Egypt (525) Political turmoil after the death of Cambyses (522–520)	
Darius I (522–486) Codification of Egyptian laws under Persian supervision Ionian cities, aided by Athens, revolt against Persians (499) Persian expedition against Athens defeated at the Battle of Marathon (490) Egypt rebelled against Persia just before Darius' death (486)	Prophets Haggai and Zechariah active in Jerusalem (520) Jerusalem Temple rebuilt (520–515)
Xerxes I (486–465) Egyptian revolt suppressed (483) Persians invaded Greece; Persian fleet defeated at Battle of Salamis (480) Persian army defeated by Greeks at the Battle of Plataea; Persian fleet destroyed at the Battle of Mount Mykale; Persia lost control of Macedon, Thrace, and Cyrenaica (479) Delian League formed by Athens to liberate Greek cities from Persians (478)	

Artaxerxes I Longimanus (465–424)
  Egyptians, under Inaros and aided by
    Athens, again rebel against Persians
    (465–455)

Ezra's mission to Jerusalem (458?)

Rebellion of satrap Megabyzus (449/8)
Peace of Callias between Persia and
  Athens (449)

Nehemiah sent to Jerusalem to
  refortify the city (445)

Peloponnesian War in Greece
  (431–404)

Darius II Nothus (424/3–405/4)
  Greek cities in Asia Minor reclaimed
    by Persia (404)

Elephantine Jews appealed to
  Jerusalem and Samaria for help
  in rebuilding their temple (407)

Artaxerxes II Memnon (405/4–359/8)
  Egypt regained its freedom from Persia
    (after 401)

Egyptians moved into southern
  Palestine for a time (about 399)
Ezra's mission (398?)
Egyptians moved back into
  southern Palestine for a short
  time (360)

Revolt of several satraps (366–360)

Philip II came to power in Macedon
  (359)

Artaxerxes III Ochus (359/8–338/7)

Revolt of Phoenicians led by
  Tennes (about 350)

Persians regain control of Egypt (342)

Arses (338/7–336)

Darius III Comodamus (336–330)
  Philip assassinated (336)
  Alexander the Great invaded the
    Persian empire (334)
  Darius defeated at Issus (333)
  Capture of Tyre (332)
  Death of Darius (330)

---

§52). That Babylon was ravaged by turmoil for months may have been an
encouragement to Jewish exiles to leave the region and return to Palestine.

Administrative Reforms. The struggles of Darius to secure his throne in 522–
519 B.C.E. were followed by his efforts to provide the empire with an effective
administrative system. According to Herodotus, Darius was remembered above

all for his organizational skills: "The Persians say Darius was a trader, Cambyses a master, and Cyrus a father. The first, because he made profit of everything; the second, because he was severe and arrogant; the latter, because he was mild, and always aimed at the good of his people" (Herodotus III. 89). This assessment is given in the context of a discussion of Darius' organization of the empire into provinces, or satrapies, each with its assigned tribute. Darius reorganized his empire, but the exact details and geography are somewhat uncertain. The Behistun Inscription claims twenty-two regions plus Persia as Darius' domain (*OP* 119, §6). Herodotus claims that twenty satrapies existed (Herodotus III. 89–97) which may reflect the condition of his own time, that is, the middle of the fifth century. Later texts suggest a different number. (See Map 27.)

When Darius began the reorganization into provinces, or satrapies, cannot be determined, but indications point to a period early in his reign immediately following the turmoil that accompanied his rise to power. Each satrapy was subdivided into smaller provinces. Palestine fell, according to Herodotus (III.91), into the fifth satrapy, called Abar Nahara ("Beyond the River," or "Trans-Euphrates" as viewed from Mesopotamia), an administrative division already known in Assyrian times. This satrapy was composed of "Phoenicia, Syria called Palestine, and Cyprus" and extended "from the city of Posidium . . . down to Egypt, except a district belonging to the Arabians, which was exempt from taxation." The fifth satrapy thus included the Eastern Mediterranean Seaboard and Cyprus, with which the seaboard was closely associated. The territory comprising the fifth satrapy plus Babylonia had been part of the territory Cyrus inherited from Nabonidus, and the two areas formed one administrative unit for a time. When Babylonia and Abar Nahara were separated still remains a disputed point. Gobryas, father-in-law of Darius, for example, served as satrap over Babylon and Abar Nahara under Cambyses, yet such a text as Ezra 5:3 suggests that the two were separate early in the reign of Darius, although there is some evidence to suggest that a certain Ushtani was satrap over Babylonia and Abar Nahara under Darius. If Darius created the separate satrap of Abar Nahara, then the rebellions of Nebuchadrezzar III (522 B.C.E.) and Nebuchadrezzar IV (521 B.C.E.) may have led to this separation which was intended to facilitate better control over the Babylonian area. It may, however, have been later, at the time of troubles under Xerxes, that the two satrapies were created.

Darius seems to have taken a personal interest in specific matters of rather limited administrative concern throughout the empire, a factor reflected in his concern with the Jerusalem cult. We have already noted his interest in local Egyptian matters in his commission of Udjahorresne's revival of the House of Life at Sais. Additional actions are also indicative. Darius ordered his satrap Ariandes to collect wise men from the military, scribes, and priests of Egypt to collect and write down the laws of Egypt in effect at the death of Amasis. The commission worked for sixteen years, and the results were made available in both the Egyptian (demotic) and Aramaic languages. Such codification of earlier laws prior to Cambyses' restriction of Temple privileges endeared Darius to the Egyptian priesthood. The later Demotic Chronicle preserves the fact that Darius

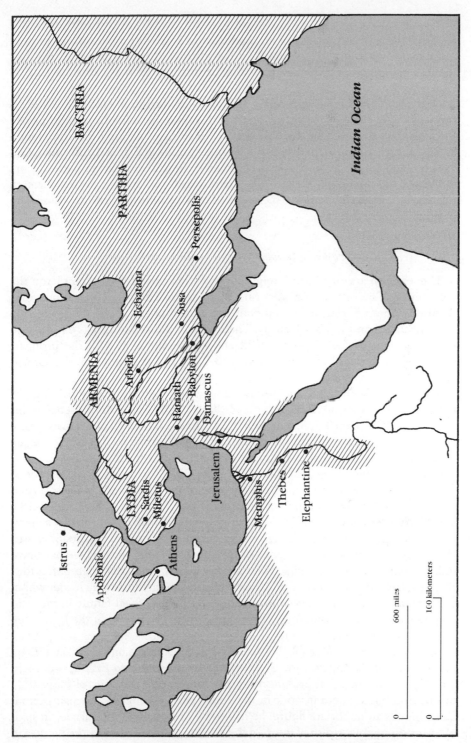

MAP 27. The Persian Empire at Its Greatest Extent

reversed some of the policies of his predecessor. Various temples were restored and a major sanctuary to Ammon-Re was constructed at El-Kharga. As we shall see in the next section, Darius took similar interests in the Jerusalem cult.

Darius in Egypt. Darius apparently visited Egypt during the fourth year of his reign (518–517 B.C.E.). It was probably at this time that a flotilla of ships passed through the canal joining the Nile and the Red Sea, marking the completion of a project partially realized by Neco II. Inscriptions in Elamite, Akkadian, Old Persian, and Egyptian hieroglyphs commemorating the occasion were set up.

On his trip to Egypt, Darius, like Cambyses, would have passed through Palestine and the conditions there could have come under his immediate perusal.

The Completion of Temple Reconstruction

The early years of Darius' reign form the historical background for the completion of reconstruction work on the Jerusalem Temple. Restoration work, begun by Shesh-bazzar, apparently entered a new phase under the leadership of Zerubbabel and Jeshua (Joshua). Their role in the rebuilding is emphasized in the account of Ezra 3 + 6:19–22 and, in conjunction with the prophets Haggai and Zechariah, in Ezra 5:1–5 + 6:1–18 and the books of Haggai and Zechariah (Zech. 1–8).

Who were Zerubbabel and Jeshua? In Ezra-Nehemiah, Zerubbabel is referred to only by name (Ezra 2:2; 4:2–3; Neh. 12:47) or with reference to his father, Shealtiel (Ezra 3:2, 8; 5:2; Neh. 12:1). Ezra-Nehemiah never assigns him a title, unless he is the person called ruler or governor in Ezra 2:63; 6:7. Haggai clearly refers to Zerubbabel as governor (Hag. 1:1, 14; 2:2, 21) and presents him as a "messianic" figure (Hag. 2:2–9, 20–23). Zechariah likewise stresses Zerubbabel's important role, calling him one of the "anointeds" (Zech. 4) and seems to apply to him the political-messianic title "Branch" (Zech. 6:12–13). The Chronicler (in I Chron. 3:17–24) unequivocally makes Zerubbabel a member of the Davidic family, although listing him as a son of Pedaiah, not Shealtiel. If Zerubbabel had been a member of the Davidic family line, it seems almost unbelievable that neither Ezra, Nehemiah, Haggai, nor Zechariah noted this. In all probability, therefore, Zerubbabel was a non-Davidic Jewish leader whom the Chronicler has made into a member of the Judean royal family in order to emphasize what he considered to be essential—the continuity of the leadership in preexilic and postexilic times.

Whether and when Zerubbabel returned from exile are unknown data. Ezra-Nehemiah clearly depicts him as a returnee from exile (see Ezra 2:1–2; Neh. 7:6–7), but this material presents only the returnees, "the sons of the exile," as carrying out significant work in the community during the Persian period. Since he was an important figure, he had to be presented as a returnee. In spite of the questionable nature of much of the traditions, there seems to be no reason to doubt that Zerubbabel served for a time as governor of Judah, perhaps having succeeded Shesh-bazzar already in the days before Darius (see Ezra 3:7; 4:3–5). It is far more uncertain that he was a returnee from exile.

Associated with Zerubbabel in work on the Temple was the priest Joshua (Jeshua), son of Jozadak. As with Zerubbabel, Ezra-Nehemiah does not assign Joshua any title but refers to him either by name alone (Ezra 2:2, 36; 4:3, Neh. 12:1, 7, 10) or with reference to his father (Ezra 3:2, 8; 5:2; 10:18; Neh. 12:26). He is called "the high priest" in both Haggai (Hag. 1:1, 12, 14; 2:2, 4) and Zechariah (Zech. 3:1, 8; 6:11). In I Chron. 6:1–15, the Chronicler provides a "genealogy" of the high priests from Aaron to Jozadak (Jehozadak). This list notes twelve high priests from Aaron to the building of the Temple and then seems to have supplied eleven high priests from the building of the Temple until Jehozadak (Jozadak), who "went into exile." Joshua would thus be the twelfth high priest following the construction of the first Temple. Such a listing is schematic in the extreme, being calculated on two successions of twelve high priests, one before and one after the building of the Temple, with forty-year reigns each. Jehozadak (Jozadak) appears nowhere in the biblical traditions except in the texts we have noted and is associated with the "official" line of Jerusalem priests only by the Chronicler. II Kings 25:18–21 reports that Seraiah the chief priest at the time of the Babylonian capture of Jerusalem, and father of Jehozadak according to I Chron. 6:14, was put to death by Nebuchadrezzar, but no reference is made to Jehozadak or the family of Seraiah as having been carried into captivity.

Two possibilities exist for understanding Joshua's predecessor and origins. (1) Joshua's father could have been a son of Seraiah, have been carried into captivity, have died there, and have been "succeeded" by Joshua. Thus Joshua would have been a priest descended from the family of Zadok, the ruling priestly family in Jerusalem. This, of course, is the assumption behind I Chron. 6:14–15 and fits the view of those biblical compilers who claimed or believed that all the significant persons involved in the restoration returned from exile. At the same time, this would satisfy the Chronicler's desire to have continuity between the preexilic and postexilic priesthood. (2) It could be assumed that Joshua's ancestor had functioned as the chief priest in the cult that continued in Judah after the destruction of the Temple, either at the site of the old Temple in Jerusalem or, more likely, at the provincial capital at Mizpah. If one assumes this view, then Jehozadak (Jozadak) may not have been a son of the high priest ruling at the time of Jerusalem's destruction. He would have risen to prominence as chief priest in the province after the city's destruction. His son Joshua then would simply have been his successor in the land of Judah.

A major problem that has baffled biblical interpreters for years has been the issue of when the Aaronite priestly line came to dominance. There is no evidence, other than genealogical references in the Chronicler, that Zadok and his successors in the Jerusalem Temple were Aaronite, yet the final editing of the biblical materials gives the Aaronites dominance and subsumes other groups under them. Jehozadak and Joshua may have been representatives of the Aaronite priestly line which, we suggested earlier (see above, p. 113), had connections with Bethel, Mizpah, and other northern sanctuary centers. The period following the fall of Jerusalem may have been the time when the Aaronites, represented by Jehozadak and Joshua, came to prominence. Of course, one must realize that it is finally impossible to have any real certainty about the origins of the priestly line represented by Joshua.

The concerted Jewish effort that finally rebuilt the Temple cannot be understood apart from developments on the international scene from the time of Cambyses' death until the early years of Darius and the expectations these stirred in the Judean community. The widespread turmoil, dissension, and revolts in the Persian empire, which we noted in the preceding section, ignited prophetic fervor among the Jewish community and incited renewed efforts on Temple reconstruction. The prophets Haggai and Zechariah, active during the early years of Darius' reign, proclaimed a radical, impending action of God that would transform the status of the community and the world (see Hag. 2:6–7; 21:22). Zerubbabel was cast by these prophets in the role of the new ruler-to-be of the Jewish community (see Hag. 2:23; Zech. 4:6–10; 6:9–14). How personally involved Zerubbabel became in this zealous enthusiasm cannot be determined.

Within the biblical traditions, especially in the books of Ezra and Zechariah, there is evidence that suggests conflicts and tensions between groups in Judah during the time of Zerubbabel and the Temple reconstruction. The nature of these tensions is more hinted at than discussed. In addition, the material in Ezra related to this period (Ezra. 1–6) reached its final form after the other traditions in Ezra-Nehemiah; and further, its presentation has been colored by the descriptions of the Judean opponents of this later period. The editor of the material in Ezra 1–6 has attempted to reinterpret all opposition as being from outside the local community (see Ezra 4:1), even reading back material descriptive of a later period into this era (Ezra 4:7–23). The hostility between the community in Jerusalem and the surrounding peoples dates primarily from the time of Ezra and Nehemiah and nearer to the editor's time than to the period of Temple reconstruction.

There were some apparently who opposed any reconstruction of the Jerusalem Temple. This is hinted at in Isa. 66:1–3, which may come from this period. Neither the rationale for this position nor any indication of the extent of this opposition is noted. A primary tension of the time seems to have centered around conflicts between "the people of the land" (those who had not gone into exile) and "the sons of the exile" (those returning from exile). Nonreturning Yahweh worshipers, who no doubt included some persons from the province of Samaria, sought to participate in the rebuilding of the Temple but were rebuffed by the returnees: "You have nothing to do with us in building a house to our God; but we alone will build to Yahweh, the God of Israel, as King Cyrus the king of Persia has commanded us" (Ezra 4:3). This exclusivism of the returnees and rejection of the offer of help were probably partially based on economic conflict over the rights to property that had been taken over by those not exiled (see Jer. 39:10; II Kings 25:12; Ezek. 11:15). The people of the land opposed the returnees (see already Ezra 3:3) and "hired counselors against them to frustrate their purpose, all the days of Cyrus king of Persia, even until the reign of Darius king of Persia" (Ezra 4:4–5). Legal measures to defend the land rights and privileges they held under the Babylonians may not have been the only means used to frustrate the dominance of the returnees, since Zech. 8:10 reports that there was no safety in the city since the laying of the Temple's foundation.

Most of the returnees were strongly Yahwistic and seem to have operated on the basis of the nationalistic and exclusivistic theology of Deuteronomy, thus advocating a strict adherence to Deuteronomic law on behalf of the worshipers. This meant that one considered impure by the strict Yahwists would have been admissible to the Jerusalem cult only after he had "separated himself from the pollutions of the peoples of the land to worship Yahweh, the God of Israel" (Ezra 6:21). The visions of the prophet Zechariah show even the high priest Joshua as originally falling short of this strict Yahwism: "The angel said to those who were standing before him [Joshua], 'Remove the filthy garments from him.' And to him he said, 'Behold, I have taken your iniquity away from you, and I will clothe you with rich apparel' " (Zech. 3:4). This opposition could have been based on the fact that Joshua was not a "son of the exile" and a returnee. On the other hand, priestly theology with its radical but universalizing monotheism was less concerned with election and nationalism than was the Deuteronomic theology. The high priest Joshua, like many of his later successors, seems to have been less exclusive and ritually demanding than stricter Yahwists wished. Before he was acceptable to function as high priest, to have legal charge of the Temple and its courts, and to be a mediator of revelation, Joshua was required to agree to walk in Yahweh's ways, that is, agree to follow the law as interpreted by the strict Yahwists (Zech. 3:6–10). For the strict Yahwists, he was at best only "a brand plucked from the fire" (Zech. 3:2). The work on the Temple could not proceed harmoniously until a compromise between the strict Yahwists, led by Zerubbabel, and the less strict Yahwists, represented by Joshua, had produced a "peaceful understanding" and cooperation (Zech. 6:13).

Whether these tensions within the Judean community, the messianic fervor associated with Temple restoration, or some other reason explains Zerubbabel's removal from office remains uncertain. He simply disappears from history. The references to him in Zechariah 4 are dated to February 519 B.C.E., probably just prior to the time when Darius marched through Palestine on his way to Egypt. According to Ezra 5:3–6:15, however, when the authority to rebuild the Temple was questioned by Tattenai, the governor of the province "Beyond the River" to which Judah belonged, search was made for a copy of Cyrus' permission and a memorandum was found. Darius gave his approval and order for work to continue. This cooperative spirit of the Persians does not suggest that the Jewish messianic enthusiasm of the time was interpreted as rebellion. However, no reference is made in the correspondence with the Persian court to Zerubbabel's presence, nor is mention made of his later work on the Temple, or of his presence at the Temple dedication (in 515 B.C.E.; Ezra 6:15). Was Zerubbabel exterminated by the Persians? Removed from office and exiled? Or did he simply die? An enigmatic passage in Zechariah, sometimes related to Zerubbabel, could suggest that he may have been killed, perhaps by a pro-Davidic faction as a result of an internal dispute: "I will pour out on the house of David and the inhabitants of Jerusalem a spirit of compassion and supplication, so that, when they look on him whom they have pierced, they shall mourn for him, as one mourns for an only child, and weep bitterly over him, as one weeps over a first-born" (Zech. 12:10). Any theory about what happened to Zerubbabel is, of course, purely speculative. At any rate, it was Joshua, the high priest, who ended up wearing a crown as the only "anointed" (= messiah) in the community (Zech. 6:9–14).

Judah as a Persian Province After Darius I

Under the organizational scheme of Darius I, the tiny province of Judah took its place in the massive Persian empire and for decades practically disappeared from view (see Map 28). Darius not only secured the territory held by Cyrus and Cambyses but also extended the Persian frontier, so that he ruled over the largest empire the world had seen. It stretched from the Indus Valley in southeast Asia to the Danube River in the Balkans, from the steppes of southern Russia to Libya in North Africa. As the "King" in the kingdom, the Persian monarch claimed absolute control and ruled under the "shadow" of the god Ahura-Mazda. It was the king, not the Persians, whom Ahura-Mazda had made to rule (see *ANET* 316–17).

Under Darius the families of his original supporters filled most major posts, both at the court and in the military, as well as governorships of the satrapies. "The King's ears," special intelligence inspectors, and cooperative local officials served to keep the monarch informed on matters throughout the kingdom. Although Indo-Europeans—as Xerxes I says, "Aryan of Aryan descent" (*ANET* 316)—the Persians utilized Aramaic as the official language, thus providing some linguistic unity for the empire. An international bureaucracy and army, capable courier service, royal coinage, extensive trade, and limited local freedom created a generally widespread sense of security and cooperation among the various national groups but as in the case of most alien overlordships did not totally win over the hearts and loyalty of the king's subjects or extinguish the embers of a dormant hostility. The satraps posed, especially later when their positions tended to become hereditary and private armies developed, more of a threat to the peace of the empire than national uprisings. The size of the empire, however, meant that Persia's external enemies were too widely separated to cooperate effectively.

As a small subprovince, Judah was a part of the administrative satrapy Abar Nahara ("Beyond the River") which lay west and south of the Euphrates River and was made up of Syria, Phoenicia, Palestine, and Cyprus. Judah occupied the plateau lying between the Dead Sea and the coastal piedmont (the Judean

**MAP 28. The Persian Province of Judah Among the Other Provinces
"Beyond the River"**

Shephelah). As a distinct political unit, Judah probably continued to be ruled by an appointed governor. The biblical text provides no names of the holders of this office between Zerubbabel and Nehemiah. From archaeological remains such as seals, bullae, and stamped jar handles, the names of other governors are known. It is uncertain, however, whether some of these governors preceded or followed Nehemiah. The recently recovered names of the governors Elnathan, Yehoezer, and Ahzai are Jewish—which suggests that the Persians appointed rulers from among the local populace. Except when Persian affairs were directly involved, self-government was apparently enjoyed by the province. The collection of taxes for the royal coffers was a primary responsibility of the governor (Neh. 5:15). The evidence from the time of Nehemiah (Neh. 3) suggests that the province of Judah was divided into five subunits or districts each with its ruler or rulers: Jerusalem (Neh. 3:9–12), Beth-haccherem (Neh. 3:14), Mizpah (Neh. 3:15), Beth-zur (Neh. 3:16), and Keilah (Neh. 3:17–18). (See Map 29.)

Persia and the West from Darius I to Artaxerxes III

After highlighting the return from exile and the reconstruction of the Jerusalem Temple, the biblical traditions move to focus on the activity of Ezra and Nehemiah. Unfortunately, numerous problems plague any reconstruction of their work. It is impossible to know with any certainty, for example, to what particular historical period or periods the careers of the men belong. Josephus assigns them consecutive careers during the reign of Xerxes I (486–465 B.C.E.). I Esdras describes the work of Ezra without mention of Nehemiah. The present books of Ezra-Nehemiah present them as having overlapping careers and assign both to the reign of an Artaxerxes but do not specify which Artaxerxes of the three Persian kings who bore this name.

Both Ezra and Nehemiah, like the Egyptian official Udjahorresne, whom we mentioned earlier, conducted their reforming and restoration work with the permission and under a commission from the Persian authorities (see Ezra 7:11–26; Neh. 2:1–8). Their activity, therefore, was not only condoned but also encouraged by the ruling government and thus must have been viewed as in the best interests of the Persians. This means that their activities must be understood not just in terms of the religious conditions and needs of the Jewish community in Palestine but in terms of the political interests of the Persians in Syria-Palestine. In this section we shall outline the main events in Persian history during the fifth and fourth centuries, especially noting those periods of tension in the western part of the empire, tension which may have made special intervention into Judean life by the Persians both timely and opportune.

Of prime significance during the later reign of Darius I (522–486 B.C.E.) was the beginning of Greco-Persian hostilities. In 512 B.C.E., Darius extended his empire westward into Europe, crossing the Bosphorus, conquering Thrace, and pursuing the Scythians to the mouth of the Danube (Herodotus IV. 83–144). East and west, Asia and Europe now became embroiled in a struggle that would

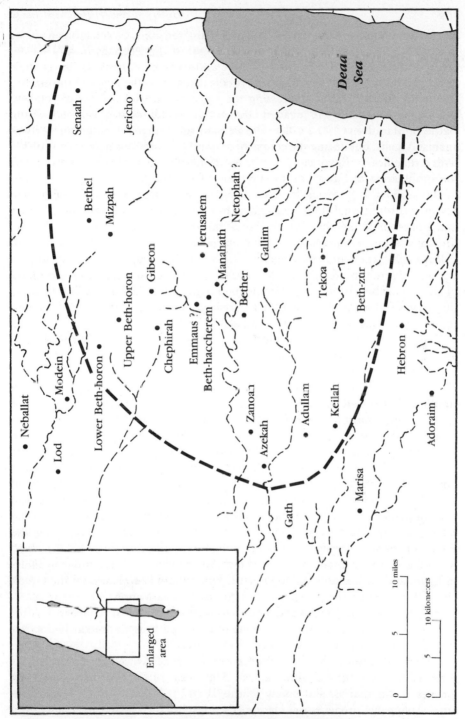

MAP 29. The Persian Province of Judah
(See also Map 28)

last for generations. After a period of increasing tensions, Greek (Ionian) cities in Asia Minor as well as Cyprus rebelled against the Persians in 499 B.C.E., being encouraged and supported in their endeavor by Athens. Utilizing their naval strength to good advantage, the rebels threatened the peace of the empire for half a decade. After suppressing the uprising, Darius set out to retaliate against the Athenians. He invaded Greece but was humiliated especially at the Battle of Marathon (490 B.C.E.). The Persian ruler hoped to wage further war against Athens, but during the course of making preparations he was confronted with a rebellion in Egypt early in 486 B.C.E. Darius' death later in the year left the subjugation of Egypt and the invasion of Greece to his successor, Xerxes I (486–465 B.C.E.), Darius' son by Atossa, the daughter of Cyrus. The Egyptian revolt was suppressed three years later, but only after heavy fighting. The fact that Xerxes appointed his own brother as satrap in Egypt might suggest that the previous satrap was implicated in the uprising.

Before Xerxes could move against Greece, revolt erupted again in Babylon but was severely repressed. By 481 B.C.E., Xerxes ceased calling himself king of Babylon, which suggests governmental restructuring in the area. It is possible that it was following this revolt that Babylonia was made into an independent satrapy and separated from Abar Nahara.

Xerxes' great expedition against Greece, begun in 481 B.C.E., proved to be a Persian fiasco. In battles at Artemisium, Thermopylae, and Salamis, the Greeks routed the Persians from most of Europe. The Greek allies took the fight into Asia Minor and Cyprus. At Plataea, Mykale, and Eurymedon, the Greeks won significant victories. Xerxes gave up the struggle with the Greeks and was subsequently murdered by his vizier Artabanus. Xerxes' youngest son, Artaxerxes I (465–424 B.C.E.), fought his way to dominance at the Persian court. The Egyptian Inaros, a son of Psammetichus III, took the occasion of the struggle over the throne to organize a revolt. Athens not only encouraged the uprising but also dispatched naval forces to aid the effort. The main Egyptian rebels and an Athenian fleet were defeated and Egypt was brought back under Persian control in 455 B.C.E. after a lengthy war led on the Persian side by Arsames the satrap of Egypt and Megabyzus the satrap of Abar Nahara. Following the Egyptian uprising, Persia and Athens, in the Peace of Callias (449 B.C.E.) which was adhered to for some time, agreed that Athens would not intervene in affairs in Egypt and Cyprus and that the Persian king would keep hands off the Greek cities along the southern and western coasts of Asia Minor.

In 448 B.C.E., Megabyzus and his two sons rebelled against Artaxerxes. After two victories over forces sent to subdue him, Megabyzus was reconciled to the Persian king and peace was restored to the area.

Additional fraternal strife erupted at the death of Artaxerxes. Three of his sons assumed the throne within a year. The "year of the four emperors" saw Xerxes II, Sogdianos, and finally Darius II (424/3–405/4 B.C.E.) each rule after slaying his predecessor. Darius II's reign also witnessed troubles in the west. Revolts broke out in Anatolia and Syria. Arsames was recalled from Egypt to assist in suppressing the opposition. In his absence, widespread discontent occurred in Egypt and the Yahwistic temple in the Jewish military colony at Elephantine was destroyed (see Text XVIII).

Under Artaxerxes II (405/4–359/8 B.C.E.), Persian control in the west collapsed further. The Egyptians, led by Pharaoh Amyrteus (404–399 B.C.E.), gained their independence when Artaxerxes was forced to fight his brother Cyrus to retain the throne. For sixty years (404–343 B.C.E.) and during the rule of three dynasties (Twenty-eighth to Thirtieth), Egypt retained its independence and in fact launched a counteroffensive against Persia that involved the invasion of Syria-Palestine. Persia considered Egypt to be nothing more than a rebellious province and expended enormous effort in an attempt to return the renegade to the fold.

In alliances, first with Sparta, then with King Evagoras ruler of the Cypriot kingdom of Salamis, and then with Athens, Egyptian rulers sought friends wherever they could find a Mediterranean opponent of the Persians. Archaeological and inscriptional evidence indicates that pharaohs Nepherites I (399–393 B.C.E.) and Achoris (393–380 B.C.E.) extended their influence along the coastal plain of Palestine and into Phoenician territory. For a time, the Egyptians, with the aid of Evagoras, held Tyre and Sidon. Two major efforts by the Persians, including the amassing of a fleet and thousands of Greek mercenaries at Acco, pushed the Egyptians out of Palestine-Phoenicia temporarily but failed to resubjugate Egypt proper. The "revolt of the satraps" in the 360s B.C.E. raised havoc in many parts of the empire. In 360 B.C.E., Pharaoh Tachos pushed north toward Syria, but dissension in Egypt led to the abortion of his campaign and Tachos' surrender to the Persians.

When the aged monarch Artaxerxes II, an octogenarian, died, he was succeeded by his ambitious and ruthless son Ochos (Artaxerxes III—359/8–338/7 B.C.E.). Under his administration, some of the old glory of the empire was restored. After subduing the revolting satraps, he set out to reconquer Egypt (Diodorus XVI. 40–52.8). The initial effort, after a year's fighting (351–350 B.C.E.), was abandoned. Ochos' failure triggered widespread revolt along the Eastern Mediterranean Seaboard. Phoenicia and Cyprus, encouraged and aided by Pharaoh Nectanebo II (359–341 B.C.E.), were the prime movers in the area. Sidon, under King Tennes, took an important role but was eventually subdued by the Persians when its leaders betrayed the city. The city was destroyed and its surviving inhabitants deported (see *ABC* 114). Another assault was made on Egypt, led by the Persian king's associate Bagoas and Mentor of Rhodes, the latter having been earlier in the employ of the Egyptian pharaoh. In 342 B.C.E., Egypt was reconquered and in spite of occasional disturbances remained under Persian control until it was "liberated" by Alexander the Great in 332 B.C.E.

The Activity of Ezra and Nehemiah

This larger world of the Persian empire receives little consideration in the biblical traditions and we are left to wonder about the course of life in the Palestinian Jewish community during the time. Only two snippets of biblical

TEXT XVIII. Correspondence on Rebuilding the Elephantine Temple

To our lord Bagoas, governor of Judah, your servants Yedoniah and his colleagues, the priests who are in the fortress of Elephantine. May the God of Heaven seek after the welfare of our lord exceedingly at all times and give you favor before King Darius and the nobles a thousand times more than now. May you be happy and healthy at all times. Now, your servant Yedoniah and his colleagues depose as follows: In the month of Tammuz in the 14th year of King Darius [410 B.C.E.], when Arsames departed and went to the king, the priests of the god Khnub, who is in the fortress of Elephantine, conspired with Vidaranag, who was commander-in-chief here, to wipe out the temple of the god Yaho from the fortress of Elephantine. So that wretch Vidaranag sent to his son Nefayan, who was in command of the garrison of the fortress of Syene, this order, "The temple of the god Yaho in the fortress of Yeb is to be destroyed." Nefayan thereupon led the Egyptians with the other troops. Coming with their weapons to the fortress of Elephantine, they entered that temple and razed it to the ground. The stone pillars that were there they smashed. Five "great" gateways built with hewn blocks of stone which were in that temple they demolished, but their doors *are standing,* and the hinges of those doors are of bronze; and *their* roof of cedarwood, all of it, with the . . . and whatever else was there, everything they burnt with fire. As for the basins of gold and silver and other articles that were in that temple, they carried all of them off and made them their own.—Now, our forefathers built this temple in the fortress of Elephantine back in the days of the kingdom of Egypt, and when Cambyses came to Egypt he found it built. They knocked down all the temples of the gods of Egypt, but no one did any damage to this temple. But when this happened, we and our wives and our children wore sackcloth, and fasted, and prayed to Yaho the Lord of Heaven, who has let us see our desire upon that Vidaranag. The dogs took the fetter out of his feet, and any property he had gained was lost; and any men who have sought to do evil to this temple have all been killed and we have seen our desire upon them.—We have also sent a letter before now, when this evil was done to us, (to) our lord and to the high priest Johanan and his colleagues the priests in Jerusalem and to Ostanes the brother of Anani and the nobles of the Jews. Never a letter have they sent to us. Also, from the month of Tammuz, year 14 of King Darius, to this day, we have been wearing sackcloth and fasting, making our wives as widows, not anointing ourselves with oil or drinking wine. Also, from then to now, in the year 17 of King Darius, no meal-offering, in[cen]se, nor burnt offering have been offered in this temple. Now your servants Yedoniah, and his colleagues, and the Jews, the citizens of Elephantine, all say thus: If it please our lord, take thought of this temple to rebuild it, since they do not let us rebuild it. Look to your well-wishers and friends here in Egypt. Let a letter be sent from you to them concerning the temple of the god Yaho to build it in the fortress of Elephantine as it was built before; and the meal-offering, incense, and burnt offering will be offered in your name, and we shall pray for you at all times, we, and our wives, and our children, and the Jews who are here, all of them, if you do thus, so that that temple is rebuilt. And you shall have a merit before Yaho the God of Heaven more than a man who offers to him burnt offering and sacrifices worth a thousand talents of silver and gold. Because of this we have written to inform you. We have also set the whole matter forth in a letter in our name to Delaiah and Shelemiah, the sons of Sanballat the governor of Samaria. Also, Arsames knew nothing of all that was done to us. On the 20th of Marheshwan, year 17 of King Darius [407 B.C.E.].

Memorandum of what Bagoas and Delaiah said to me: Let this be an instruction to you in Egypt to say before Arsames about the house of offering of the God of Heaven which had been in existence in the fortress of Elephantine since ancient times, before Cambyses, and was destroyed by that wretch Vidaranag in the year 14 of King Darius: to rebuild it on its site as it was before, and the meal-offering and incense to be made on that altar as it used to be.

Your servants Yedoniah the son of Ge[mariah] by name 1, Ma'uzi the son of Nathan by name [1], Shemaiah the son of Haggai by name 1, Hosea the son of Yatom by name 1, Hosea the son of Nathun by name 1, 5 men in all, Syenians who [ho]ld proper[ty] in the fortress of Elephantine, say as follows: If your lordship is [favo]rable, and the temple of ou[r] God Yaho [is rebuilt] in the fortress of Elephantine as it was for[merly buil]t, and n[o] *sheep*, ox, or goat are offered there as burnt offering, but (only) incense, meal-offering, [and drink-offering], and (if) your lordship giv[es] orders [to that effect, then] we shall pay into your lordship's house the s[um of . . . and] a thous-[and] *ardabs* of barley. (*ANET* 492) (See photograph on p. 432.)

tradition, except for the materials about Ezra and Nehemiah, have been preserved relating to this period. These, in Ezra 4:6–23, have been preserved out of chronological order, as if they belonged to the period between Cyrus and Darius I. They have been employed to illustrate the theme of "opposition to restoration," the topic of Ezra 4. The first, in Ezra 4:6, merely notes that an accusatory letter was written against the inhabitants of Judah and Jerusalem. If the Ahasuerus of the biblical text was King Xerxes I, then this letter written in the beginning of his reign (his accession year, 486/5 B.C.E.) would date to the time of the Egyptian revolt (486–483 B.C.E.) suppressed by Xerxes. The sending of such a letter of accusation might indicate that Judah was suspected or implicated in the anti-Persian activity in the region, but this is only speculation, since nothing is given of the letter's content. The second tradition, in Ezra 4:7–23, reports that officials of the province Abar Nahara wrote to Artaxerxes warning against the rebuilding of the city of Jerusalem undertaken by Jewish returnees. The king ordered that work on the reconstruction cease. Again it is impossible to determine the actual historical context of this interchange. If the monarch was Artaxerxes I, then the attempted rebuilding of the city could have been related in some fashion to the Egyptian revolt led by Inaros (465–455 B.C.E.).

Unlike the fragmentary items in Ezra 4:6–23, the biblical traditions about Ezra and Nehemiah are rather extensive. The present form of these traditions, in Ezra 7–10 and the Book of Nehemiah, apparently is based on originally independent collections. The Ezra traditions are found in Ezra 7–10 and Neh. 7:73b–10:39. Some of these are composed in a first person account, the so-called "memoirs of Ezra" (Ezra 7:12–9:15). The first person "memoirs of Nehemiah" are found in Neh. 1:1–7:73a; 11–13. (Serious questions, however, can be raised about whether all the material in Neh. 7:5b–73a and 9:1–13:3 belonged to the Nehemiah source used by the editor.) These memoirs, especially those of Nehemiah, are similar in form to the autobiographical inscription of the Egyptian official Udjahorresne, whom we noted earlier and who, like Nehemiah, operated as a Persian appointee. The Ezra and Nehemiah traditions have been edited to make their activity contemporaneous, and, in describing the work of one, the editor makes occasional reference to the other (see Neh. 8:9; 12:26, 36). The lack of any real interaction between the two and the indication of the traditions' original independence, however, suggest that their careers were unrelated.

The Chronological Problem

As we noted earlier, the historical contexts within which Ezra and Nehemiah worked remain uncertain. Ezra 7:7–8 and Neh. 2:1 associate both with an Artaxerxes; Ezra with the seventh year of the king's reign and Nehemiah with the twentieth. If both worked under Artaxerxes I, then Ezra would have returned to Jerusalem in 458 B.C.E. and Nehemiah in 445 B.C.E.; if under Artaxerxes II, then the years would have been 398 B.C.E. and 384 B.C.E. Artaxerxes III (359/8–338/7 B.C.E.) might be a candidate for Ezra's mission, but Neh. 5:14, which refers to the thirty-second year of Artaxerxes, rules out this latter Persian as the monarch under whom Nehemiah functioned.

Any conclusions about the relationship of the work of the two men and the historical contexts to which they belonged must remain highly uncertain and rely on intuitive speculation. We assume that Nehemiah preceded Ezra and that the former worked under Artaxerxes I and the latter under Artaxerxes II. Placing Nehemiah before Ezra, and thus discounting the present biblical order, is based on several considerations. (1) Chronological precision, as we noted in discussing Ezra 4:6–23, is not characteristic of the editing of the material in Ezra-Nehemiah where thematic interests are more evident. (2) Ezra is considered by the final biblical editor to be the real restorer of Jewish life after the exile and this could have led to giving him priority over Nehemiah. In the traditions about Ezra, he is presented as the true successor to the preexilic high priests (Ezra 7:1–5), his activity is seen as the true continuation of activity following Temple restoration (the subject of Ezra 1–6), and the return under Ezra is depicted as a second exodus under this postexilic "Moses" (Ezra 7). (3) Ezra's work in Jerusalem seems to presuppose a reconstructed and repopulated city; conditions not restored until the work of Nehemiah. (4) The high priest at the time of Nehemiah was Eliashib (Neh. 3:1, 20; 13:4), whereas at the time of Ezra the high priest was Jehohanan the son of Eliashib (Ezra 10:6). One of the Elephantine letters, written to Bagoas the governor of Judah in 407 B.C.E. requesting permission to rebuild the temple of Yahweh previously burned at the direction of Egyptian priests, makes reference to a recently written letter addressed "to the high priest Johanan and his colleagues the priests in Jerusalem" (*ANET* 492). If this Johanan can be identified with the Jehohanan of Ezra's day, then this would place Ezra near the end of the fifth or the beginning of the fourth century.

The names and order of the high priests in the Persian period are, however, a complex issue. Nehemiah 12:10–11 supplies the following order: Jeshua, Joiakim, Eliashib, Joiada, Jonathan, and Jaddua, while Neh. 12:22 supplies an alternative list of the same group or else a list extending the line to the time of "Darius the Persian" (Darius III?): Eliashib, Joiada, Johanan, and Jaddua. From Josephus, it is possible to reconstruct the following order: Jeshua, Joiakim, Eliashib, Johanan, Joiakim, Eliashib, Joiada, Johanan, and Jaddua (*Ant.* XI.121, 147, 158, 297, 302). The association of Eliashib-Nehemiah and Jehohanan (= Johanan) —Ezra would, at any rate, suggest the priority of Nehemiah.

The correlation of Nehemiah with the twentieth year of Artaxerxes I and Ezra with the seventh year of Artaxerxes II makes it possible to relate their activity in Palestine with times when having Jewish support in the area would have been especially advantageous to the Persians. The year of Nehemiah's return, 445 B.C.E., was a time just following a long Egyptian revolt as well as the revolt of the satrap over the province Beyond the River. It was thus a time for reestablishing firm Persian support in the region. The year of Ezra's return, 398 B.C.E., was at a time when Egypt not only had asserted its independence from Persia but also had begun to move into the coastal region of Syria-Palestine.

The Work of Nehemiah

Thus Nehemiah, if we are correct in our dating, rose to the office of cupbearer to King Artaxerxes I (Neh. 2:1), a position that gave him opportunity for personal contact with the king. The occasion of Nehemiah's interest in returning to Jerusalem is said to have been the arrival at Susa of persons coming from Judah (Neh. 1:1–2). Perhaps this group consisted of an embassy hoping to make an appeal directly to the royal court regarding the rebuilding of Jerusalem, thereby bypassing the uncooperative administrators of the satrapy Beyond the River (see Ezra 4:7–23). Nehemiah was informed that "the wall of Jerusalem is broken down, and its gates are destroyed by fire" (Neh. 1:3). Nehemiah requested and was granted permission by Artaxerxes to return to Jerusalem and rebuild the city (Neh. 2:1–8). He left for Jerusalem, probably in 445 B.C.E., in the company of "Persian troops and cavalry" and with the authority of letters that vouchsafed passage to Judah and, once there, use of timber from the royal estates (Neh. 2:7–9). Although no mention is made of it in connection with the initial arrangements of Artaxerxes, apparently he had been appointed governor of the district (Neh. 5:14). He may also have returned to Judah not just to refortify Jerusalem but also to establish the restored city as the capital of the province.

After a nocturnal, secret survey of the conditions of the city's fortifications, Nehemiah rallied support for reconstruction (Neh. 2:11–20). Various segments in the society including the priesthood, landed gentry, and district rulers worked on different sections of the wall (Neh. 3). Opposition to the refortification came from the leaders of neighboring provinces—Sanballat the Horonite in Samaria, Tobiah the Ammonite, Geshem the Arabian, and the citizens of Ashdod (Neh. 2: 10, 19; 4:7). Since these groups were on generally good terms with the local Judeans (Neh. 6:17–19; 13:4–5, 23, 28), these opponents must have seen correctly that the refortification and Nehemiah's leadership were a threat to their authority and influence in the area. Work was carried out with special military precautions, utilization of the Persian forces, speed, and long hours of work (Neh. 4), although the biblical text says nothing about any actual enemy force being employed to frustrate reconstruction. Nehemiah's opponents sought to entice him away from Jerusalem to do him harm and threatened to file an accusation charging him with fomenting a rebellion and pretensions to kingship (Neh. 6:1–9). In addition, local prophecies were circulated seeking to discourage him. Apparently some of the prophets opposed to his work were Judeans (see Neh. 6:10–14, especially 6:14). Other occasional hints of the unwillingness of some Judeans to aid the restoration are noted (Neh. 3:5; 4:10). Nonetheless, the city wall was restored in fifty-two days, according to Neh. 6:15 (Josephus in *Ant.* XI.179 says the work required two years and four months). Such work, which necessarily would have involved arousing support, organizing labor, and securing necessary stone and timber, certainly could not have been carried out immediately after Nehemiah's arrival in Jerusalem but must have required some period for planning and preparation.

Two economic moves were made by Nehemiah to alleviate the exploitation of the poorer classes by the landed gentry and provincial officers. Some of the poorer Judean classes complained of poverty, others protested that conditions demanded the mortgaging of their property, while some argued that they were forced to sell members of their families into slavery. Such complaints were made against the exploitation by their Judean brothers (Neh. 5:1–5). Plotting his moves to secure the greatest public support for himself and his cause and to produce the greatest pressure on the oppressors, Nehemiah confronted the nobles and officials in a public assembly (Neh. 5:6–13). Noting that he and his party had redeemed Judeans sold into foreign slavery, he pointed out that the local men of wealth, on the other hand, had engaged in the slave traffic by selling Judeans. Admitting that he, his family, and his servants had lent Judeans money at interest contrary to the law (see Deut. 23:19–20), Nehemiah swore that this interest would not be collected and challenged his countrymen to return property taken at interest and to cease the practice. The leaders submitted and agreed to the abolition of interest and the return of property seized for nonpayment of debts.

A second economic measure was Nehemiah's remission of taxes that previous governors had imposed for the support of themselves and their staff; the taxes consisted of food, wine, and forty shekels of silver (Neh. 5:14–15). He was apparently able to do so since he was a man of means. There was evidently no subsequent reduction of the standard of living at the governor's palace, since Nehemiah brags that "there were at my table a hundred and fifty men, Jews and officials, besides those who came to us from the nations which were about us [foreign visitors]. Now that which was prepared for one day was one ox and six choice sheep; fowls likewise were prepared for me, and every ten days skins of wine in abundance" (Neh. 5:17–18).

Nehemiah 11:1–2 reports that Jerusalem was repopulated by moving one tenth of the people into the city. Nehemiah is not explicitly referred to in the description of this action (but see Neh. 7:4–5), and much of the material in Nehemiah 11–12 does not appear to have been part of his memoirs. Thus it is impossible to say anything certain about Nehemiah's role in the resettlement. The period just following the restoration of the city's fortification, however, would seem to have been a natural time for such a repopulation of the city which may have coincided with making the city the province's capital.

After twelve years (but compare Neh. 13:6 with 5:14), Nehemiah returned to the Persian court for a time. No reason is given for this trip, but he may have had to defend himself against charges brought by his opponents in the neighboring provinces (see Neh. 2:19; 6:5–9). After his return to Jerusalem, Nehemiah initiated action geared to produce several religious reforms. The first move was the expulsion of Tobiah the Ammonite (see Deut. 23:3–6) from a special chamber in the Temple where he had been installed by the high priest Eliashib (Neh. 13:4–9). Apparently Tobiah was a Yahwist. His reason for having a special chamber in the Temple is uncertain, although he was an influential person in Judean circles especially among the Judean nobles or landed gentry. The role of Eliashib in granting Tobiah such a prerogative demonstrates that the high priest and the priesthood were far more open to religious relationships with foreigners and their participation in the cult than such strong Yahwists as Nehemiah and his followers. Thus Nehemiah must be viewed as a strong lay representative of a strict Yahwism which sought to bring the priesthood and religious establishment into conformity with a conservative position, a position based primarily on the laws of the book of Deuteronomy. His further actions confirm this.

The Levites had been deprived of their income and status in the Temple and thus forced to make their livelihoods completely from agricultural pursuits. Nehemiah gathered and reinstated these strong Yahwists in the Temple, outlined their duties vis-à-vis the priests, put some in places of leadership, and ensured that the tithe of grain, wine, and oil, or a portion thereof, went for their upkeep (Neh. 13:10–13, 30). Probably to placate the priests for this dimunition of their power, he made arrangements for "the wood offering, at appointed times, and for the first fruits" (Neh. 13:31). He found that there was also great laxity in Sabbath observance. Rural Judeans were working and, along with Tyrians, were running markets in Jerusalem on the Sabbath. Nehemiah remonstrated with the nobles, ordered the city gates closed and guarded during the Sabbath, and gave the Levites power to supervise and enforce observance of the day as a holy occasion (Neh. 13:15–22).

The move to prevent mixed marriages, oriented toward producing a purified Judean community, was probably the most controversial of Nehemiah's actions (Neh. 13:23–28). Judean men had married women from Ashdod, Ammon, and Moab, and children of such marriages were giving up speaking the language of Judah. Nehemiah sought to force the Judean community to desist from such practice by taking an oath in the name of God not to give their daughters or marry their sons or themselves to aliens. One of the high priest's grandsons was apparently banished for having married the daughter of Sanballat the Horonite. The tyrannical nature of Nehemiah's rule can be seen in his confession that in order to secure agreement to such an oath he had to resort to drastic measures: "I contended with them and cursed them and beat some of them and pulled out their hair" (Neh. 13:25).

Ezra's Attempted Reform

Ezra returned to Jerusalem with a special commission from the Persian king, probably Artaxerxes II, in 398/7 B.C.E. (Ezra 7:7). He is described as "the priest, the scribe of the law of the God of heaven" (Ezra 7:12). His genealogy in Ezra 7:1, which makes him a descendant of the preexilic high-priestly family, appears very suspicious, since he is listed as the son of Seraiah, who was executed in 586 B.C.E.

The royal decree designating Ezra as a special commissioner and outlining his work (Ezra 7:11–26) contained a number of stipulations. (1) Permission was granted for any of the people of Israel, their priests, or Levites to return with Ezra. (According to the list in Ezra 8:1–14, about five thousand returned with him.) (2) Ezra was commissioned to investigate conditions in Judah and Jerusalem in the light of the law of God in his hand. (3) Silver and gold contributed by the king and his counselors were to be carried to Jerusalem, along with the gifts and freewill offerings made by the members of the diaspora as well as special vessels prepared for the Temple. (4) Treasurers in the satrapy Beyond the River were ordered to cooperate with Ezra and provide, within limits, all necessary assistance and funds, as well as exemption from taxation for all religious personnel associated with the Temple. (5) Ezra was granted authority to appoint magistrates and judges to administer and teach the law of God and to execute punishments for failure to obey the law of God (and the law of the

Persian monarch!). This last stipulation may be a later addition to the original mandate, since the present form of the king's decree first speaks about Ezra (Ezra 7:12–20), then the treasurers of the provinces (Ezra 7:21–24), and then, once again, of Ezra (Ezra 7:25–26). This hardly seems original.

The concern of the Persian monarchs with the law of subject peoples has already been noted in the case of Darius I and Egypt. Often they were concerned with various elements in the local cults: one of the Elephantine letters, dated to 419 B.C.E., refers to the fact that Darius II had written to Arsames the satrap in Egypt about the regulation of the observance of the Jewish feast of Unleavened Bread in the Elephantine community (*ANET* 491).

Ezra and his followers are reported to have returned to Jerusalem in festive procession without military escort as a mighty pilgrimage to the holy land. In his hand was the law of God. The identity of Ezra's book of law has been a much-debated issue. Attempts to define its contents have ranged from the suggestion that it was a special, but no longer extant, code developed under Persian supervision to the hypothesis that it was the Pentateuch in basically its present form. About this law, we are told (1) that it was in Ezra's hand (although nothing is said about the law being already known in Jerusalem), (2) that the people requested Ezra to read as if they were unfamiliar with the law (Neh. 8:1), (3) that the people reacted unexpectedly or perhaps ceremoniously and wept after hearing the law (Neh. 8:9–10), (4) that the Levites had to aid the people in understanding the law (Neh. 8:7–8), and (5) that the Feast of Tabernacles which was celebrated on the basis of Ezra's law was so innovative that "from the days of Jeshua the son of Nun to that day the people of Israel had not done so" (Neh. 8:17). The stress on the innovative aspect of the law, however may be partly a literary device used by the editor to heighten the significance of the law's promulgation (see II Kings 23:21–23). The contents of Ezra's law, perhaps recently codified, can no longer be determined with any exactitude. Some of its content may have been subsequently incorporated into the Pentateuch.

Ezra presented the law code to the people in a public reading (Neh. 8:1–12), led them to observe the Festival of Tabernacles according to the code's stipulations (Neh. 8:13–18), and secured a covenant of the people to obey the law (Neh. 9:38).

Ezra learned that intermarriage with foreign women was widespread, "so that the holy race has mixed itself with the peoples of the lands. And in this faithlessness the hand of the officials and chief men has been foremost" (Ezra 9:2). He led the people to take an oath that they would make "a covenant with our God to put away all these wives and their children" (Ezra 10:3). Here Ezra moved beyond the intention of Nehemiah, who sought only to stop intermarriage with foreigners but did not seek to force the dissolution of such existing marriages. An assembly was called to deal with the matter and to implement the policy of divorcing foreign women, but it was shortened by a heavy rain or winter cold (Ezra 10:9–15). A commission was appointed to examine the matter and investi-

gate the extent of the intermarriage. After three months the committee produced a list of offenders which included some priests and Levites (Ezra 10:
16–43).

Unfortunately nothing is known about the final outcome of Ezra's work and
his effort to force the divorce of foreign women and thus purify the "holy race."
After providing a list of offenders, the final chapter of Ezra concludes abruptly
and enigmatically: "All of these took foreign wives and there are still wives of
theirs and they have had (or put) sons" (Ezra 10:44; so the Hebrew text). All
appearances suggest that Ezra's work was aborted and never carried to completion. Had he been successful, this would surely have been reported. One can
speculate that his policy aroused such opposition from the officials in neighboring provinces and from the local constituency that he was either forced to retire
or was removed from the scene.

Later Developments in the Period

We know practically nothing about the history of the Jewish community
between Ezra-Nehemiah and the conquest of Alexander the Great. What effect
the Persian-Egyptian wars, the revolt of the satraps, the Phoenician rebellion
initiated by Tennes, and the Persian reconquest of Egypt may have had on the
Jerusalem community remains unknown. Josephus, in *Ant.* XI.297–301, reports
one incident which, in spite of problems of interpretation, probably relates to
the reign of Artaxerxes III. According to this account, the Jewish high priest
Johanan slew his brother Jeshua in the Temple. Jeshua had sought to acquire
the high priesthood with the help of his friend, the Persian general Bagoas. As
a consequence of the murder and the Jewish protest against his entry of the
Temple, according to Josephus, Bagoas "made the Jews suffer seven years" by
imposing a special tribute tax on every sacrifice made in the Temple (*Ant.*
XI.297, 301). This general Bagoas appears to be the same Bagoas, who, according to Diodorus Siculus, was Artaxerxes III's closest associate (Diodorus XVI.
47.2). He was a major leader in the Persian conquest of Egypt and a king maker
at the royal court. Diodorus describes him as "master of the kingdom, and
Artaxerxes did nothing without his advice. And after Artaxerxes' death he
designated in every case the successor to the throne and enjoyed all the functions of kingship save the title" (Diodorus XVI.50.8). Diodorus also reports
that, after the Persian troops plundered the Egyptian shrines in 342 B.C.E.,
carrying off the inscribed records from the ancient temples, Bagoas returned
these to the Egyptian priests "on the payment of huge sums by way of ransom"
(Diodorus XVI.51.2). Eventually he murdered Artaxerxes and then, disappointed with his own selection as successor, Arses (338/7–336 B.C.E.), Bagoas
had him and most of the royal line put to death as well (Diodorus XVII.5.3–6),
before he himself was poisoned.

Unfortunately this little vignette provided by Josephus casts no major light
on the course and shape of Jewish history. Attempts to relate this event to the
larger Persian history, such as the fourth-century Egyptian invasion of Syria-

Palestine or the rebellion of Tennes, have failed. Nonetheless, three factors are noteworthy. (1) The friendship of Jeshua of the Jerusalem high-priestly family with a member of the upper echelon of Persian administration suggests that the Jewish community was not without standing in the Persian empire and that Jewish affairs were not isolated for the larger world. (2) Bagoas' intervention in the life of the Jerusalem Temple illustrates the exercise of tight Persian control and supervision over many facets of life throughout the empire. (3) The struggle between Johanan and Jeshua illustrates the internal conflicts that could tear at Jerusalem life especially over such an important post as high priest and particularly when exacerbated by the intervention of outside powers.

Bibliography

Recent Histories of Israel and Judah

Albright, W. F. *The Biblical Period from Abraham to Ezra.* New York: Harper Torchbooks, 1963.

Ben-Sasson, H. H. (ed.). *History of the Jewish People.* London/Cambridge: Weidenfeld & Nicolson/Harvard University Press, 1976.

Bright, J. *A History of Israel.* 3d ed. Philadelphia/London: Westminster Press/SCM Press, 1981.

Castel, F. *The History of Israel and Judah in Old Testament Times.* Mahwah, N.J.: Paulist Press, 1985.

Cazelles, H. *Histoire politique d'Israël des origins à Alexandre le Grand.* Paris: Desclée, 1982.

Donner, H. *Geschichte des Volkes Israel und seiner Nachbarn in Grundzugen.* 2 vols. Göttingen: Vandenhoeck & Ruprecht, 1984–85.

Ehrlich, E. *A Concise History of Israel from the Earliest Times to the Destruction of the Temple in AD 70.* London/New York: Darton, Longman & Todd/Harper Torchbooks, 1962/1965.

Fohrer, G. *Geschichte Israels: Von den Anfängen bis zur Gegenwart.* 3d ed. Heidelberg: Quelle & Meyer, 1982.

Grant, M. *The History of Ancient Israel.* London/New York: Weidenfeld & Nicolson/Charles Scribner's Sons, 1984.

Gunneweg, A. H. J. *Geschichte Israels bis Bar Kochba.* Stuttgart: W. Kohlhammer, 1972.

Hayes, J. H., and J. M. Miller (eds.). *Israelite and Judaean History.* Old Testament Library. Philadelphia/London: Westminster Press/SCM Press, 1977.

Herrmann, S. *A History of Israel in Old Testament Times.* Rev. ed. London/Philadelphia: SCM Press/Fortress Press, 1981.

Jagersma, H. *A History of Israel in the Old Testament Period.* London/Philadelphia: SCM Press/Fortress Press, 1983.

Lemaire, A. *Histoire du peuple Hébreu.* Paris: Presses Universitaires de France, 1981.

Mazar, B. (ed.). *The World History of the Jewish People.* Jerusalem: Massada Publishing, 1961–.

Metzger, M. *Grundriss der Geschichte Israels.* Neukirchen-Vluyn: Neukirchener Verlag, 1963.

Noth, M. *The History of Israel.* 2d ed. London/New York: A. & C. Black/Harper & Row, 1960.

Oesterley, W. O. E., and T. H. Robinson. *A History of Israel.* 2 vols. London: Oxford University Press, 1932.

Orlinsky, H. M. *Ancient Israel.* 2d ed. Ithaca, N.Y.: Cornell University Press, 1960.

Soggin, J. A. *A History of Israel: From the Beginnings to the Bar Kochba Revolt, A.D. 135.* London/Philadelphia: SCM Press/Westminster Press, 1984/1985.

de Vaux, R. *The Early History of Israel.* London/Philadelphia: Darton, Longman & Todd/Westminster Press, 1978.

Chapter 1: The Setting

Abel, F.-M. *Géographie de la Palestine.* 2 vols. Paris: J. Gabalda, 1933, 1938.

Aharoni, Y. *The Land of the Bible: A Historical Geography.* Rev. ed. by A. F. Rainey. Philadelphia/London: Westminster Press/Burns & Oates, 1980.

———. *The Archaeology of the Land of Israel.* Philadelphia/London: Westminster Press/SCM Press, 1982.

Aharoni, Y., and M. Avi-Yonah. *The Macmillan Bible Atlas.* New York/London: Macmillan/Collier Macmillan, 1977.

Albright, W. F. *The Archaeology of Palestine.* New ed.; revised by W. G. Dever. Gloucester, Mass.: Peter Smith, 1976.

Avi-Yonah, M. *The Holy Land from the Persian to the Arab Conquest (536 BC to AD 640): A Historical Geography.* Rev. ed. Grand Rapids, Mich.: Baker Book House, 1977.

——— (ed.). *Encyclopedia of Archaeological Excavations in the Holy Land.* 4 vols. London/Englewood Cliffs, N.J.: Oxford University Press/Prentice-Hall, 1976–1979.

Baly, D. *Geographical Companion to the Bible.* New York/London: McGraw-Hill/Lutterworth Press, 1963.

———. *The Geography of the Bible.* 2d ed. New York/London: Harper & Row/Lutterworth Press, 1979.

Beyerlin, W. (ed.). *Near Eastern Religious Texts Relating to the Old Testament.* Old Testament Library. London/Philadelphia: SCM Press/Westminster Press, 1978.

Bickerman, E., and M. Smith. *The Ancient History of Western Civilization.* New York/London: Harper & Row, 1976.

Finegan, J. *Handbook of Biblical Chronology: Principles of Reckoning in the Ancient World and Problems of Chronology in the Bible.* Princeton: Princeton University Press, 1964.

———. *The Archaeology of the New Testament: The Life of Jesus and the Beginning of the Early Church.* Princeton: Princeton University Press, 1969.

———. *Archaeological History of the Ancient Middle East.* Boulder, Colo./Folkestone, England: Westview Press/Dawson & Sons, 1979.

Gardiner, A. *Egypt of the Pharaohs: An Introduction.* London/New York: Oxford University Press, 1961.

Grollenberg, L. H. *Atlas of the Bible.* London/New York: Thomas Nelson & Sons, 1956.

Hallo, W. W., and W. K. Simpson. *The Ancient Near East: A History.* New York: Harcourt Brace Jovanovich, 1971.

Harrison, R. K. *Old Testament Times.* Grand Rapids, Mich./Leicester, England: Wm. B. Eerdmans Publishing Co./Inter-Varsity Press, 1970/1972.

Heaton, E. W. *Everyday Life in Old Testament Times.* London/New York: B. T. Batsford/Charles Scribner's Sons, 1956.

Keel, O., M. Küchler et al. *Orte und Landschaften der Bibel. Ein Handbuch und Studienreiseführer zum Heiligen Land.* 4 vols. Zurich/Göttingen: Benzinger/Vandenhoeck & Ruprecht, 1982–1986.

Kenyon, K. M. *The Bible and Recent Archaeology.* London/Atlanta: British Museum/John Knox Press, 1978.

———. *Archaeology in the Holy Land.* 4th ed. London/New York: Ernest Benn/W. W. Norton & Co., 1979.

May, H. G. *Oxford Bible Atlas.* 3d ed. London/New York: Oxford University Press, 1984.

Noth, M. *The Old Testament World.* London/Philadelphia: A. & C. Black/Fortress Press, 1966.

Oppenheim, A. L. *Ancient Mesopotamia: Portrait of a Dead Civilization.* Chicago/London: University of Chicago Press, 1964.

Saggs, H. W. F. *The Greatness That Was Babylon: A Sketch of the Ancient Civilization of the Tigris-Euphrates Valley.* London/New York: Sidgwick & Jackson/Hawthorn Books, 1962.

Simon, J. *The Geographical and Topographical Texts of the Old Testament.* Leiden: E. J. Brill, 1959.

Smith, G. A. *Historical Geography of the Holy Land.* 4th ed. London: Hodder & Stoughton, 1896; reprinted by various publishers.

Thomas, D. W. (ed.). *Documents from Old Testament Times.* London: Oxford University Press, 1958.

———. *Archaeology and Old Testament Study.* London: Oxford University Press, 1967.

de Vaux, R. *Ancient Israel: Its Life and Institutions.* London/New York: Darton, Longman & Todd/McGraw-Hill, 1961.

Vogel, E. "Bibliography of Holy Land Sites," *HUCA* 42 (1971): 1–96.

Vogel, E., and B. Holtzclaw. "Bibliography of Holy Land Sites: Part II," *HUCA* 52 (1981): 1–92.

Wiseman, D. J. (ed.). *Peoples from Old Testament Times.* London: Oxford University Press, 1973.

Wright, G. E. *Biblical Archaeology.* Rev. ed. Philadelphia/London: Westminster Press/Gerald Duckworth & Co., 1962.

Chapter 2: The Question of Origins

Albright, W. F. "The Israelite Conquest of Canaan in the Light of Archaeology," *BASOR* 74 (1939): 11–23.

Bimson, J. *Redating the Exodus and Conquest.* Sheffield, England: JSOT Press, 1978.

Bright, J. *Early Israel in Recent History Writing.* London: SCM Press, 1956.

Dever, W. G. *Archaeology and Biblical Studies: Retrospects and Prospects.* Evanston, Ill.: Seabury-Western Theological Seminary, 1974.

Glueck, N. *The Other Side of the Jordan.* New Haven: American Schools of Oriental Research, 1940.

Greenberg, M. *The Hab/piru.* New Haven: American Oriental Society, 1955.

Hallo, W. W. "Biblical History in Its Near Eastern Setting." In *Scripture in Context: Essays on the Comparative Method,* edited by C. D. Evans et al., 1–26. Pittsburgh: Pickwick Press, 1980.

Ibrahim, M. "The Collared-Rim Jar of the Early Iron Age." In *Archaeology in the Levant,* edited by R. Moorey and P. Parr, 116–26. Warminster, England: Aris & Phillips, 1978.

Kallai, Z. "Judah and Israel: A Study in Israelite Historiography," *IEJ* 28 (1978): 251–61.

Mendenhall, G. E. *The Tenth Generation: The Origins of the Biblical Tradition.* Baltimore:
Johns Hopkins University Press, 1973.

Millard, A. R., and D. J. Wiseman (eds.). *Essays on the Patriarchal Narratives.* Leicester/
Winona Lake, Ind.: Inter-Varsity Press/Eisenbrauns, 1980/1983.

Ramsey, G. W. *The Quest for the Historical Israel: Reconstructing Israel's Early History.*
Atlanta/London: John Knox Press/SCM Press, 1981/1982.

Rowley, H. H. *From Joseph to Joshua.* London: Oxford University Press, 1950.

Sasson, J. M. "On Choosing Models for Recreating Pre-Monarchical Israel," *JSOT* 21
(1981): 3–24.

Soggin, J. A. "The History of Israel: A Study in Some Questions of Method," *EI* 14
(1978): 44–51.

Thompson, T. L. *The Historicity of the Patriarchal Narratives: The Quest for the Historical
Abraham.* Berlin/New York: Walter de Gruyter, 1974.

Van Seters, J. *Abraham in History and Tradition.* New Haven/London: Yale University
Press, 1975.

————. *In Search of History: Historiography in the Ancient World and the Origins of Biblical
History.* New Haven/London: Yale University Press, 1983.

Chapter 3: Before Any King Ruled in Israel

Alt, A. "The Settlement of the Israelites in Palestine." In his *Essays on Old Testament
History and Religion,* 135–169. Oxford/Garden City, N.Y.: B. H. Blackwell/Double-
day & Co., 1966/1967.

Coote, R. B., and K. W. Whitelam, *The Emergence of Israel in Historical Perspective.* Sheffield, England: Almond, 1986.

Cross, F. M. *Canaanite Myth and Hebrew Epic: Essays in the History of the Religion of Israel.*
Cambridge: Harvard University Press, 1973.

Dothan, T. *The Philistines and Their Material Culture.* New Haven/London: Yale University Press, 1982.

Emerton, J. A. "New Light on Israelite Religion: The Implications of the Inscriptions
from Kuntillet 'Ajrud," *ZAW* 94 (1982): 2–20.

Freedman, D. N., and D. F. Graf (eds.). *Palestine in Transition: The Emergence of Ancient
Israel.* Sheffield, England: Almond Press, 1983.

de Geus, C. H. J. "The Importance of Archaeological Research Into the Palestinian
Agricultural Terraces," *PEQ* 107 (1975): 65–74.

————. *The Tribes of Israel: An Investigation Into Some of the Presuppositions of Martin Noth's
Amphictyony Hypothesis.* Assen: Van Gorcum, 1976.

Gottwald, N. K. *The Tribes of Yahweh: A Sociology of the Religion of Liberated Israel, 1250–
1000 B.C.* Maryknoll, N.Y./London: Orbis Books/SCM Press, 1979/1980.

Halpern, B. *The Emergence of Israel in Canaan.* Chico, Calif.: Scholars Press, 1983.

Hopkins, D. C. *The Highlands of Canaan: Agricultural Life in the Early Iron Age.* Decatur,
Ga.: Almond Press, 1985.

Lapp, P. "The Conquest of Palestine in the Light of Archaeology," *CTM* 38 (1967):
283–300.

Lindars, B. "The Israelite Tribes in Judges," *SVT* 30 (1979): 95–112.

Mayes, A. D. H. *Israel in the Period of the Judges.* London: SCM Press, 1974.

McKenzie, J. L. *The World of the Judges.* Englewood Cliffs, N.J./London: Prentice-
Hall/Geoffrey Chapman, 1966.

Mendenhall, G. E. "The Hebrew Conquest of Palestine," *BA* 25 (1962): 66–87 = *BAR* 3 (1970): 100–120.

Niemann, H. M. *Die Daniten. Studien zur Geschichte eines altisraelitischen Stammes.* Göttingen: Vandenhoeck & Ruprecht, 1985.

Schunck, K.-D. *Benjamin. Untersuchungen zur Entstehung und Geschichte eines israelitischen Stammes.* Berlin/New York: Walter de Gruyter, 1963.

Strobel, A. *Der spätbronzezeitliche Seevölkersturm.* Berlin/New York: Walter de Gruyter, 1976.

Tadmor, H. "The Decline of Empires in Western Asia ca. 1200 BCE." In *Symposia: Celebrating the Seventy-fifth Anniversary of the Founding of the American Schools of Oriental Research (1900–1975),* edited by F. M. Cross, 1–14. Cambridge: American Schools of Oriental Research, 1979.

Weippert, M. *The Settlement of the Israelite Tribes in Palestine.* London: SCM Press, 1971.

Chapter 4: The Early Israelite Monarchy

Ahlström, G. W. *Royal Administration and National Religion in Ancient Palestine.* Leiden: E. J. Brill, 1982.

Alt, A. "The Formation of the Israelite State in Palestine." In his *Essays on Old Testament History and Religion,* 171–237.

Birch, B. C. "The Development of the Tradition on the Anointing of Saul in I Samuel 9:1–10:16," *JBL* 90 (1971): 55–68.

———. *The Rise of the Israelite Monarchy: The Growth and Development of I Samuel 7–15.* Missoula, Mont.: Scholars Press, 1976.

Blenkinsopp, J. *Gibeon and Israel: The Role of Gibeon and the Gibeonites in the Political and Religious History of Early Israel.* Cambridge: Cambridge University Press, 1972.

———. "Did Saul Make Gibeon His Capital?" *VT* 24 (1974): 1–7.

———. "The Quest of the Historical Saul." In *No Famine in the Land,* edited by J. W. Flanagan and A. W. Robinson, 75–99. Missoula, Mont.: Scholars Press, 1975.

Bucellati, G. *Cities and Nations of Ancient Syria: An Essay on Political Institutions with Special Reference to the Israelite Kingdoms.* Rome: Istitutio di Studi del Vicino Oriente, 1967.

Campbell, A. F. *The Ark Narrative (I Sam. 4–6, II Sam. 6): A Form-Critical and Traditio-Historical Study.* Missoula, Mont.: Scholars Press, 1975.

Clements, R. E. "The Deuteronomistic Interpretation of the Founding of the Monarchy in I Sam. VIII," *VT* 24 (1974): 398–410.

Cohen, M. A. "The Role of the Shilonite Priesthood in the United Monarchy of Ancient Israel," *HUCA* 36 (1965): 59–98.

Donner, H. *Die Verwerfung des Königs Saul.* Wiesbaden: Otto Harrassowitz, 1983.

Evans, W. E. "An Historical Reconstruction of the Emergence of Israelite Kingship and the Reign of Saul." In *Scripture in Context II: More Essays on the Comparative Method,* edited by W. W. Hallo et al., 61–77. Winona Lake, Ind.: Eisenbrauns, 1983.

Frick, F. S. *The Formation of the State in Ancient Israel: A Survey of Models and Theories.* Decatur, Ga.: Almond Press, 1985.

Gunn, D. M. *The Fate of King Saul.* Sheffield, England: JSOT Press, 1980.

Halpern, B. *The Constitution of the Monarchy in Israel.* Chico, Calif.: Scholars Press, 1981.

Humphreys, W. L. "From Tragic Hero to Villain: A Study of the Figure of Saul and the Development of I Samuel," *JSOT* 22 (1982): 95–117.

Langlamet, F. "David et la maison de Saul," *RB* 86 (1979): 194–213; 87 (1980): 161–210; 88 (1981): 321–32.

Mayes, A. D. H. "The Rise of the Israelite Monarchy," *ZAW* 90 (1978): 1–19.

McKenzie, J. L. "The Four Samuels," *BR* 7 (1962): 1–16.

Miller, J. M. "Saul's Rise to Power: Some Observations Concerning I Samuel 9:1–10:16, 10:26–11:15, and 13:2–14:46," *CBQ* 36 (1974): 157–74.

———. "Geba/Gibeath of Benjamin," *VT* 25 (1975): 145–66.

Miller, P. D., and J. J. M. Roberts. *The Hand of the Lord: A Reassessment of the "Ark Narrative" of I Samuel.* Baltimore: Johns Hopkins University Press, 1977.

North, R. "Social Dynamics from Saul to Jehu," *BTB* 12 (1982): 109–19.

Schmidt, L. *Menschlicher Erfolg und Jahwes Initiative. Studien zu Tradition, Interpretation, und Historie in den Überlieferungen von Gideon, Saul, und David.* Neukirchen-Vluyn: Neukirchener Verlag, 1970.

Whitelam, K. W. *The Just King: Monarchial Judicial Authority in Ancient Israel.* Sheffield, England: JOST Press, 1979.

Chapter 5: David, King of Jerusalem

Ackroyd, P. R. "The Succession Narrative (so-called)," *Int* 35 (1981): 383–96.

Auld, A. G. "The 'Levitical Cities': Texts and History," *ZAW* 91 (1979): 194–206.

Ben-Barak, Z. "The Legal Background to the Restoration of Michal to David," *SVT* 30 (1979): 15–29.

———. "Meribaal and the System of Land Grants in Ancient Israel," *Bib* 62 (1981): 73–91.

Cohen, M. A. "The Rebellions During the Reign of David: An Inquiry Into Social Dynamics in Ancient Israel." In *Studies in Jewish Bibliography, History and Literature,* edited by C. Berlin, 91–112. New York: KTAV, 1971.

Conrad, J. "Der Gegenstand und die Intention der Geschichte von der Thronfolge Davids," *ThLZ* 108 (1983): 161–76.

Crüsemann, F. *Der Widerstand gegen das Königtum. Die antiköniglichen Texte des Alten Testaments und der Kampf um den frühen israelitischen Staat.* 2d ed. Neukirchen-Vluyn: Neukirchener Verlag, 1985.

Flanagan, J. W. "Court History or Succession Document? A Study of 2 Samuel 9–20 and I Kings 1–2," *JBL* 91 (1972): 172–81.

———. "The Relocation of the Davidic Capital," *JAAR* 47 (1979): 233–44.

Fokkelman, J. *King David: Narrative Art and Poetry in the Books of Samuel.* Assen: Van Gorcum, 1981–.

Ishida, T. *The Royal Dynasties in Ancient Israel: A Study on the Formation and Development of Royal-Dynastic Ideology.* Berlin/New York: Walter de Gruyter, 1977.

——— (ed.). *Studies in the Period of David and Solomon and Other Essays.* Winona Lake, Ind.: Eisenbrauns, 1982.

Katzenstein, H. J. *The History of Tyre.* Jerusalem: Schocken Institute for Jewish Research of the Jewish Theological Seminary of America, 1973.

Kenyon, K. M. *Royal Cities of the Old Testament.* London/New York: Barrie & Jenkins/Schocken Books, 1971.

Lemche, N. P. "David's Rise," *JSOT* 10 (1978): 2–25.

Levenson, J. D., and B. Halpern. "The Political Import of David's Marriages," *JBL* 99 (1980): 507–18.

Malamat, A. "Aspects of the Foreign Politics of David and Solomon," *JNES* 22 (1963): 1–17.

──────. *Das davidische und salomonische Königreich und seine Beziehungen zu Ägypten und Syrien.* Vienna: Österreichischen Akademie der Wissenschaften, 1983.

McCarter, P. K. "The Apology of David," *JBL* 99 (1980): 489–504.

Mettinger, T. N. D. *King and Messiah: The Civil and Sacral Legitimation of the Israelite Kings.* Lund: CWK Gleerup, 1976.

Miller, J. M. "Jebus and Jerusalem: A Case of Mistaken Identity," *ZDPV* 90 (1974): 115–27.

Olyan, S. "Zadok's Origins and the Tribal Politics of David," *JBL* 101 (1982): 177–93.

VanderKam, J. C. "Davidic Complicity in the Deaths of Abner and Eshbaal: A Historical and Redactional Study," *JBL* 99 (1980): 521–39.

Veijola, T. *Die ewige Dynastie. David und die Entstehung seiner Dynastie nach der deuteronomistischen Darstellung.* Helsinki: Annales Academiae Scientiarum Fennicae, 1975.

Weingreen, J. "The Rebellion of Absalom," *VT* 19 (1969): 263–66.

Whitelam, K. W. "The Defence of David," *JSOT* 29 (1984): 61–87.

Würthwein, E. *Die Erzählung von der Thronfolge Davids. Theologische oder politische Geschichtsschreibung?* Zurich: Theologische Verlag, 1974.

Chapter 6: The Reign of Solomon

Bin-Nun, S. R. "Formulas from the Royal Records of Israel and of Judah," *VT* 18 (1968): 414–32.

Busink, T. A. *Der Tempel von Jerusalem. Von Salomo bis Herodes.* 2 vols. Leiden: E. J. Brill, 1970, 1980.

Cody, A. *A History of the Old Testament Priesthood.* Rome: Pontifical Biblical Institute, 1969.

Delekat, L. "Tendez und Theologie der David-Salomo-Erzählung." In *Das Ferne und Nahe Wort: Festschrift für L. Rost,* edited by F. Maass, 26–36. Berlin: Alfred Töpelmann, 1967.

Donner, H. "Israel und Tyrus in Zeitalter Davids und Salomos. Zur gegenseitigen Abhängigkeit von Innen- und Aussenpolitik," *JNSL* 10 (1982): 43–52.

Hauer, C. "The Economics of National Security in Solomonic Israel," *JSOT* 18 (1980): 63–73.

Heaton, E. W. *Solomon's New Men: The Emergence of Ancient Israel as a National State.* London: Thames & Hudson, 1974.

Johnson, A. R. *Sacral Kingship in Ancient Israel.* 2d ed. Cardiff: University of Wales Press, 1967.

Kitchen, K. A. *The Third Intermediate Period in Egypt 1100–650 BC.* Warminster, England: Aris & Phillips, 1973.

Liver, J. "The Book of the Acts of Solomon," *Bib* 48 (1967): 75–101.

Maly, E. *The World of David and Solomon.* Englewood Cliffs, N.J./London: Prentice-Hall/Geoffrey Chapman, 1966.

Mettinger, T. N. D. *Solomonic State Officials: A Study of the Civil Government Officials of the Israelite Monarchy.* Lund: CWK Gleerup, 1971.

Pritchard, J. B. (ed.). *Solomon and Sheba.* London/New York: Phaidon/Praeger, 1974.

Redford, D. B. "Studies in Relations Between Palestine and Egypt During the First Millennium B.C.:I—The Taxation System of Solomon." In *Studies in the Ancient Palestinian World,* edited by J. W. Wevers and D. B. Redford, 141–56. Toronto: University of Toronto, 1972.

Roberts, J. J. M. "The Davidic Origin of the Zion Tradition," *JBL* 92 (1973): 329–44.
Wright, G. E. "The Provinces of Solomon," *EI* 8 (1967): 58–68.
Yadin, Y. *Hazor: The Head of All Those Kingdoms.* London: British Academy, 1972.
———. *Hazor: The Rediscovery of a Great Citadel of the Bible.* London/New York: Weidenfeld & Nicolson/Random House, 1975.

Chapter 7: Separate Kingdoms

Albright, W. F. "The Chronology of the Divided Monarchy of Israel," *BASOR* 100 (1945): 16–22.
Alt, A. "The Monarchy in Israel and Judah." In his *Essays on Old Testament History and Religion,* 239–59.
Auerbach, M., and L. Smolar. "Aaron, Jeroboam and the Golden Calves," *JBL* 86 (1967): 129–40.
Begrich, J. *Die Chronologie der Könige von Israel und Judah.* Tübingen: J. C. B. Mohr [Paul Siebeck], 1929.
Debus, J. *Die Sünde Jerobeams. Studien zur Darstellung Jerobeams und der Geschichte des Nordreichs in der deuteronomistischen Geschichtsschreibung.* Göttingen: Vandenhoeck & Ruprecht, 1967.
Fritz, V. "The 'List of Rehoboam's Fortresses' in 2 Chr. 11:5–12—A Document from the Time of Josiah," *EI* 15 (1981): 46–53.
Herrmann, S. "Operationen Pharao Schoschenks I. im östlichen Ephraim," *ZDPV* 80 (1964): 55–79.
Mayes, A. D. H. *The Story of Israel Between Settlement and Exile: A Redactional Study of the Deuteronomic History.* London: SCM Press, 1983.
Mazar, B. "The Campaign of Pharaoh Shishak to Palestine," *SVT* 4 (1957): 57–66.
———. "The Cities of the Priests and the Levites," *SVT* 7 (1959): 193–205.
Miller, J. M. "Another Look at the Chronology of the Early Divided Monarchy," *JBL* 86 (1967): 276–88.
Redford, D. B. "Studies in the Relationship Between Palestine and Egypt During the First Millennium BC: II—The Twenty-second Dynasty," *JAOS* 93 (1973): 3–17.
Schenkel, J. D. *Chronology and Recensional Development in the Greek Text of Kings.* Cambridge: Harvard University Press, 1968.
Thiele, E. *A Chronology of the Hebrew Kings.* Grand Rapids, Mich.: Zondervan, 1977.
———. *The Mysterious Numbers of the Hebrew Kings: A Reconstruction of the Chronology of the Kingdoms of Israel and Judah.* Rev. ed. Grand Rapids, Mich.: Zondervan, 1984.
Wifall, W. R. "The Chronology of the Divided Monarchy of Israel," *ZAW* 80 (1968): 319–37.

Chapter 8: The Omride Era

Elat, M. "The Campaign of Shalmaneser III Against Aram and Israel," *IEJ* 25 (1975): 25–35.
Lipinski, E. "Le Ben-hadad II de la Bible et l'histoire." In *Fifth World Congress of Jewish Studies I,* 157–73. Jerusalem: World Union of Jewish Studies, 1969.
Miller, J. M. "The Elisha Cycle and the Accounts of the Omride Wars," *JBL* 85 (1966): 441–55.
———. "The Rest of the Acts of Jehoahaz (I Kings 20; 22: 1–38)," *ZAW* 80 (1968): 337–42.

————. "So Tibni Died (I Kings 16:22)," *VT* 18 (1968): 392–94.

Parrot, A. *Samaria: The Capital of the Kingdom of Israel.* London: SCM Press, 1958.

Pienaar, D. N. "The Role of the Fortified Cities in the Northern Kingdom During the Reign of the Omride Dynasty," *JNSL* 9 (1981): 151–57.

Schmitt, H. C. *Elisa. Traditionsgeschichtliche Untersuchungen zur vorklassischen nordisraelitischen Prophetie.* Gütersloh: Gerd Mohn, 1972.

Steck, O. D. *Überlieferung und Zeitgeschichte in den Elia-Erzählungen.* Neukirchen-Vluyn: Neukirchener Verlag, 1968.

Strange, J. "Joram, King of Israel and Judah," *VT* 25 (1975): 191–201.

Timm, S. "Die territoriale Ausdehnung des Staates Israel zur Zeit der Omriden," *ZDPV* 96 (1980): 20–40.

————. *Die Dynastie Omri. Quellen und Untersuchungen zur Geschichte Israels im 9. Jahrhundert vor Christus.* Göttingen: Vandenhoeck & Ruprecht, 1982.

Whitley, C. F. "The Deuteronomic Presentation of the House of Omri," *VT* 2 (1952): 137–52.

Chapter 9: The Century of the Jehu Dynasty

Andersen, F. I. "The Socio-Juridical Background of the Naboth Incident," *JBL* 85 (1966): 46–57.

Astour, C. "841 B.C.: The First Assyrian Invasion of Israel," *JAOS* 91 (1971): 383–89.

Dearman, J. A. *Property Rights in the Eighth-Century Prophets: The Conflict and Its Background.* Ph.D. dissertation, Emory University, 1981.

Dearman, J. A., and J. M. Miller. "The Melqart Stele and the Ben Hadads of Damascus: Two Studies," *PEQ* 115 (1983): 95–101.

Eph'al, I. *The Ancient Arabs: Nomads on the Borders of the Fertile Crescent 9th–5th Centuries B.C.* Jerusalem/Leiden: Magnes Press/E. J. Brill, 1982.

Gottwald, N. K. *All the Kingdoms of the Earth: Israelite Prophecy and International Relations in the Ancient Near East.* New York/London: Harper & Row, 1964.

Haran, M. "The Rise and Decline of the Empire of Jeroboam ben Joash," *VT* 17 (1967): 266–97.

Jepsen, A. "Israel und Damaskus," *AfO* 14 (1941–1944): 153–72.

Millard, A. R., and H. Tadmor. "Adad-nirari III in Syria: Another Stela Fragment and the Dates of His Campaigns," *Iraq* 35 (1973): 57–64.

Miller, J. M. "The Fall of the House of Ahab," *VT* 17 (1967): 307–24.

————. "The Moabite Stone as a Memorial Stela," *PEQ* 106 (1974): 9–18.

Page, S. "A Stela of Adad-nirari III and Nergal-ereš from Tell al Rimah," *Iraq* 30 (1968): 139–53.

Pitard, W. T. *Ancient Damascus: A Historical Study of the Syrian City-State from Earliest Times Until Its Fall to the Assyrians in 732 B.C.E.* Winona Lake, Ind.: Eisenbrauns, 1986.

Tadmor, H. "The Historical Inscriptions of Adad-nirari III," *Iraq* 35 (1973): 141–50.

Yeivin, S. "Did the Kingdoms of Israel Have a Maritime Policy?" *JQR* 50 (1960): 193–228.

Chapter 10: The Era of Assyrian Domination: The End of the Kingdom of Israel

Alt, A. "Das System der assyrischen Provinzen auf dem Boden des Reiches Israel," *ZDPV* 52 (1929): 220–42 = his *KS* II, 188–205.

Asurmendi, J. M. *La Guerra Siro-Efraimita: Historia y Profetas.* Valencia/Jerusalem: Institución San Jerónimo, 1982.

Begrich, J. "Der syrisch-ephraimitische Krieg und seine weltpolitischen Zusammenhänge," *ZDMG* 83 (1929): 213–37 = his *GS,* 99–120.

Borger, R. "Das Ende des ägyptischen Feldherrn Sib'e = Sô,' " *JNES* 19 (1960): 49–53.

Borger, R., and H. Tadmor. "Zwei Beiträge zur alttestamentlichen Wissenschaft aufgrund der Inschriften Tiglatpilesers III," *ZAW* 94 (1982): 244–51.

Cazelles, H. "Problèmes de la guerre Syro-Ephraimite," *EI* 14 (1978): 70–78.

Cook, H. J. "Pekah," *VT* 14 (1964): 121–35.

Donner, H. *Israel unter den Völkern. Die Stellung der klassichen Propheten des 8. Jahrhunderts v. Chr. zur Aussenpolitik der Könige von Israel und Juda.* Leiden: E. J. Brill, 1964.

Forrer, E. *Die Provinzeinteilung des assyrischen Reiches.* Leipzig: J. C. Hinrichs, 1920.

Frankenstein, S. "The Phoenicians in the Far West: A Function of Neo-Assyrian Imperialism." In *Power and Propaganda: A Symposium on Ancient Empires,* edited by M. T. Larsen, 263–94. Copenhagen: Akademisk Forlag, 1979.

Goedicke, H. "The End of 'So, King of Egypt,' " *BASOR* 171 (1963): 64–66.

Hallo, W. W. "From Qarqar to Carchemish: Assyria and Israel in the Light of New Discoveries," *BA* 23 (1960): 34–61 = *BAR* II, 152–88.

Levine, L. D. "Menahem and Tiglath-Pileser: A New Synchronism," *BASOR* 206 (1972): 40–42.

———. *Two Neo-Assyrian Stelae from Iran.* Toronto: Royal Ontario Museum, 1972.

Na'aman, N. "The Brook of Egypt and Assyrian Policy on the Border of Egypt," *TA* 6 (1979): 68–90.

Oded, B. "The Historical Background of the Syro-Ephraimite War Reconsidered," *CBQ* 34 (1972): 153–65.

———. "The Phoenician Cities and the Assyrian Empire in the Time of Tiglath-pileser III," *ZDPV* 90 (1974): 38–49.

———. *Mass Deportations and Deportees in the Neo-Assyrian Empire.* Wiesbaden: Dr. Ludwig Reichert Verlag, 1979.

Otzen, B. "Israel Under the Assyrians: Reflections on the Imperial Policy in Palestine," *ASTI* 11 (1977): 96–110 = "Israel Under the Assyrians," in *Power and Propaganda: A Symposium on Ancient Empires,* edited by M. T. Larsen, 251–61. Copenhagen: Akademisk Forlag, 1979.

Saggs, H. W. F. "Assyrian Warfare in the Sargonid Period," *Iraq* 25 (1963): 145–55.

———. *The Might That Was Assyria.* London: Sidgwick & Jackson, 1984.

Tadmor, H. "The Southern Border of Aram," *IEJ* 12 (1962): 114–22.

———. "Philistia Under Assyrian Rule," *BA* 29 (1966): 86–102.

———. "Introductory Remarks to a New Edition of the Annals of Tiglath-Pileser III," *Proceedings of the Israel Academy of Sciences and Humanities,* II/9 (1967): 168–87.

———. "Assyria and the West: The Ninth Century and Its Aftermath." In *Unity and Diversity: Essays in the History, Literature and Religion of the Ancient Near East,* edited by H. Goedicke and J. J. M. Roberts, 36–48. Baltimore: Johns Hopkins University Press, 1975.

Talmon, S. "Polemics and Apology in Biblical Historiography—2 Kings 17:24–41." In *The Creation of Sacred Literature: Composition and Redaction of the Biblical Text,* edited by R. E. Friedman, 57–68. Berkeley/London: University of California Press, 1981.

Vogt, E. "Die Texte Tiglat-Pilesers III. über die Eroberung Palästinas," *Bib* 45 (1964): 348–54.

Weippert, M. "Menahem von Israel und seine Zeitgenossen in einer Steleninschrift des assyrischen Königs Tiglath-pileser III aus dem Iran," *ZDPV* 89 (1973): 26–53.

Wiseman, D. J. "Two Historical Inscriptions from Nimrud," *Iraq* 13 (1951): 21–26.

———. "A Fragmentary Inscription of Tiglath-pileser III from Nimrud," *Iraq* 18 (1956): 117–29.

Chapter 11: The Era of Assyrian Domination: Judean History from Ahaz to Amon

Ackroyd, P. R. "The Biblical Interpretation of the Reigns of Ahaz and Hezekiah." In *In the Shelter of Elyon*, edited by W. B. Barrick and J. R. Spencer, 247–59. Sheffield, England: JSOT Press, 1984.

Alt, A. "Neue assyrische Nachrichten über Palästina," *ZDPV* 67 (1945): 128–46 = his *KS* II, 226–41.

———. "Tiglathpilesers III. erster Feldzug nach Palästina," *KS* II, 150–62.

Brinkman, J. A. "Merodach-Baladan II." In *Studies Presented to A. Leo Oppenheim*, edited by R. D. Biggs and J. A. Brinkman, 6–53. Chicago: Oriental Institute, 1964.

Broski, M. "The Expansion of Jerusalem in the Reigns of Hezekiah and Manasseh," *IEJ* 24 (1974): 21–26.

Bulbach, S. W. *Judah in the Reign of Manasseh as Evidenced in Texts During the Neo-Assyrian Period and in the Archaeology of the Iron Age*. Ph.D. dissertation, New York University, 1981.

Childs, B. S. *Isaiah and the Assyrian Crisis*. London: SCM Press, 1967.

Clements, R. E. *Isaiah and the Deliverance of Jerusalem: A Study of the Interpretation of Prophecy in the Old Testament*. Sheffield, England: JSOT Press, 1980.

Cogan, M. *Imperialism and Religion: Assyria, Judah and Israel in the Eighth and Seventh Centuries B.C.E.* Missoula, Mont.: Scholars Press, 1974.

Elat, E. "The Economic Relations of the Neo-Assyrian Empire with Egypt," *JAOS* 98 (1978): 20–34.

Evans, C. D. "Judah's Foreign Policy from Hezekiah to Josiah," *Scripture in Context: Essays on the Comparative Method*, edited by C. D. Evans et al., 157–78. Pittsburgh: Pickwick Press, 1980.

Gadd, C. J. "Inscribed Prisms of Sargon II from Nimrud," *Iraq* 16 (1954): 173–201.

Malamat, A. "The Historical Background of the Assassination of Amon King of Judah," *IEJ* 3 (1953): 26–29.

McKay, J. *Religion in Judah Under the Assyrians*. London: SCM Press, 1973.

Mommsen, H., et al. "The Provenience of the *lmlk* Jars," *IEJ* 34 (1984): 89–113.

Moriarty, F. L. "The Chronicler's Account of Hezekiah's Reform," *CBQ* 27 (1965): 399–406.

Na'aman, N. "Sennacherib's 'Letter to God' on His Campaign to Judah," *BASOR* 214 (1974): 25–39.

———. "Sennacherib's Campaign to Judah and the Date of the Stamps," *VT* 29 (1979): 61–86.

Reade, J. E. "Sargon's Campaigns of 720, 716, and 715 B.C.: Evidence from the Sculptures," *JNES* 35 (1976): 95–104.

Reich, R. "The Identification of the 'Sealed *kāru* of Egypt,' " *IEJ* 34 (1984): 132–38.

Rowley, H. H. "Hezekiah's Reform and Rebellion," *BJRL* 44 (1961–1962): 395–461 = his *Men of God: Studies in Old Testament History and Prophecy*, 98–132. London/New York: Thomas Nelson & Sons, 1963.

Shea, W. H. "Sennacherib's Second Campaign," *JBL* 104 (1985): 401–18.

Spieckermann, H. *Juda unter Assur in der Sargonidenzeit.* Göttingen: Vandenhoeck & Ruprecht, 1982.

Stohlmann, S. "The Judaean Exile After 701 B.C.E." In *Scripture in Context II: More Essays on the Comparative Method,* edited by W. W. Hallo et al., 147–75. Winona Lake, Ind.: Eisenbrauns, 1983.

Tadmor, H. "The Campaigns of Sargon II of Assur: A Chronological Historical Study," *JCS* 12 (1958): 22–40, 77–100.

Tadmor, H., and M. Cogan. "Ahaz and Tiglath-pileser in the Book of Kings: Historiographic Considerations," *Bib* 60 (1979): 491–508.

Thompson, M. E. W. *Situation and Theology: Old Testament Interpretation of the Syro-Ephraimitic War.* Sheffield, England: Almond Press, 1982.

Ussishkin, D. "The Destruction of Lachish by Sennacherib and the Dating of the Royal Judean Storage Jars," *TA* 4 (1977): 28–60.

Vanel, A. "Ṭâbe'él en Is. VII 6 et le roi Tubail de Tyr," *SVT* 26 (1974): 17–24.

Welten, P. *Die Königs-Stempel. Ein Beitrag zur Militärpolitik Judas unter Hiskia und Josia.* Wiesbaden: Deutscher Palästina-Verein, 1969.

Chapter 12: The Last Years of the Davidic Kingdom

Aharoni, Y. *The Arad Inscriptions.* Jerusalem: Israel Exploration Society, 1981.

Albright, W. F. "The Seal of Eliakim and the Latest Preexilic History of Judah," *JBL* 51 (1932): 77–106.

Avigad, N. "The Chief of the Corvée," *IEJ* 30 (1980): 170–73.

Cazelles, H. "La vie de Jérémie dans son contexte national et international," *BETL* 54 (1981): 21–39.

Claburn, W. E. "The Fiscal Basis of Josiah's Reforms," *JBL* 92 (1973): 11–22.

Cogan, M., and H. Tadmor. "Gyges and Ashurbanipal: A Study in Literary Transmission," *Or* 46 (1977): 66–85.

Elat, M. "The Political Status of the Kingdom of Judah Within the Assyrian Empire in the 7th Century B.C.E." In *Investigations at Lachish: The Sanctuary and the Residency (Lachish V),* edited by Y. Aharoni, 61–70. Tel Aviv: Gateway Publishers, 1975.

Frankena, R. "The Vassal Treaties of Esarhaddon and the Dating of Deuteronomy," *OTS* 14 (1965): 122–54.

Freedy, K. S., and D. B. Redford. "The Dates in Ezekiel in Relation to Biblical, Babylonian, and Egyptian Sources," *JAOS* 90 (1970): 462–85.

Frost, S. B. "The Death of Josiah: A Conspiracy of Silence," *JBL* 87 (1968): 369–82.

Greenberg, M. "Ezekiel 17 and the Policy of Psammetichus II," *JBL* 76 (1967): 304–9.

Gyles, M. F. *Pharaonic Policies and Administration, 663 to 323 B.C.* Chapel Hill: University of North Carolina Press, 1959.

Kienitz, F. *Die politische Geschichte Ägyptens vom 7. bis zum 4. Jahrhundert vor der Zeitwende.* Berlin: Akademie-Verlag, 1953.

Kutsch, E. "Das Jahr der Katastrophe: 587 v. Chr.," *Bib* 55 (1974): 520–45.

Malamat, A. "The Twilight of Judah: In the Egyptian-Babylonian Maelstrom," *SVT* 28 (1955): 123–45.

———. "The Last Kings of Judah and the Fall of Jerusalem," *IEJ* 18 (1968): 137–56.

———. "Josiah's Bid for Armageddon," *JANES* 5 (1973): 267–78.

Milgrom, J. "The Date of Jeremiah, Chapter 2," *JNES* 14 (1955): 65–69.

Millard, A. R. "The Scythian Problem." In *Orbis Aegyptiorum Speculum—Glimpses of Ancient Egypt,* edited by John Ruffle et al., 119–22. Warminster, England: Aris & Phillips, 1979.

Nelson, R. "*Realpolitik* in Judah (687–609 B.C.E.)." In *Scripture in Context II,* 177–89.

Nicholson, E. W. "The Centralization of the Cult in Deuteronomy," *VT* 13 (1963): 380–89.

———. *Deuteronomy and Tradition: Literary and Historical Problems in the Book of Deuteronomy.* Oxford/Philadelphia: Basil Blackwell/Fortress Press, 1967.

Ogden, G. S. "The Northern Extent of Josiah's Reform," *ABR* 26 (1978): 26–34.

Perlitt, L. *Bundestheologie im Alten Testament.* Neukirchen-Vluyn: Neukirchener Verlag, 1969.

Porten, B. "The Identity of King Adon," *BA* 44 (1981): 36–52.

Reade, J. "The Accession of Sinsharishkun," *JCS* 23 (1970): 1–9.

Sarna, N. M. "Zedekiah's Emancipation of Slaves and the Sabbatical Year," *AOAT* 22 (1973): 143–49.

———. "The Abortive Insurrection in Zedekiah's Day (Jer. 27–29)," *EI* 14 (1978): 89–96.

Spalinger, A. J. "Assurbanipal and Egypt: A Source Study," *JAOS* 94 (1974): 316–28.

———. "Esarhaddon and Egypt: An Analysis of the First Invasion of Egypt," *Or* 43 (1974): 295–326.

———. "Psammetichus, King of Egypt: I," *JARCE* 13 (1976): 133–47.

———. "Egypt and Babylonia: A Survey (c. 620 B.C.–550 B.C.)," *SAK* 5 (1977): 228–44.

———. "Psammetichus, King of Egypt: II," *JARCE* 15 (1978): 49–57.

———. "The Concept of the Monarchy During the Saite Epoch—An Essay of Synthesis," *Or* 47 (1978): 12–36.

———. "The Date of the Death of Gyges and Its Historical Implications," *JAOS* 98 (1978): 400–409.

Stern, E. "Israel at the Close of the Monarchy," *BA* 38 (1975): 26–54.

Thomas, D. W. "The Sixth Century B.C.: A Creative Epoch in the History of Israel," *JSS* 6 (1961): 33–46.

Tsevat, M. "The Neo-Assyrian and Neo-Babylonian Vassal Oaths and the Prophet Ezekiel," *JBL* 78 (1959): 199–204.

Vaggione, R. P. "Over All Asia? The Extent of the Scythian Domination in Herodotus," *JBL* 92 (1973): 523–30.

Weinfeld, M. "Cult Centralization in Israel in the Light of a Neo-Babylonian Analogy," *JNES* 23 (1964): 202–12.

———. *Deuteronomy and the Deuteronomic School.* Oxford: Clarendon Press, 1972.

Williamson, H. G. M. "The Death of Josiah and the Continuing Development of the Deuteronomic History," *VT* 32 (1982): 242–48.

Chapter 13: The Period of Babylonian Domination

Ackroyd, P. R. *Exile and Restoration: A Study of Hebrew Thought of the Sixth Century B.C.* Old Testament Library. London/Philadelphia: SCM Press/Westminster Press, 1968.

Coogan, M. D. "Life in the Diaspora: Jews at Nippur in the Fifth Century B.C.," *BA* 37 (1974): 6–12.

———. *West Semitic Personal Names in the Marušû Documents.* Missoula, Mont.: Scholars Press, 1976.

Friedman, R. E. *The Exile and Biblical Narrative: The Formation of the Deuteronomistic and Priestly Works.* Chico, Calif.: Scholars Press, 1981.

Gadd, C. J. "The Haran Inscriptions of Nabonidus," *AnSt* 8 (1958): 35–92.

Janssen, E. *Juda in der Exilszeit. Ein Beitrag zur Frage der Entstehung des Judentums.* Göttingen: Vandenhoeck & Ruprecht, 1956.

Lindsay, J. "The Babylonian Kings and Edom, 605–550 B.C.," *PEQ* 108 (1976): 23–39.

Porten, B. *Archives from Elephantine: The Life of an Ancient Jewish Military Colony.* Los Angeles/London: University of California Press/Cambridge University Press, 1968.

Weidner, E. F. "Jojachin, König von Juda, in babylonischen Keilschrifttexten." In *Mélanges syriens offerts à M. René Dussaud,* II, 923–35. Paris: Paul Guethner, 1939.

Weinberg, S. S. "Post-Exilic Palestine: An Archaeological Report," *IASHP* 4 (1971): 78–97.

Whitley, C. F. *The Exilic Age.* London/Philadelphia: Longmans, Green & Co./Westminster Press, 1957.

Zadok, R. "Notes on the Early History of the Israelites and Judeans in Mesopotamia," *Or* 51 (1982): 391–93.

Chapter 14: The Era of the Persian Empire

Ackroyd, P. R. *Israel Under Babylonia and Persia.* London: Oxford University Press, 1970.

———. "Archaeology, Politics, and Religion: The Persian Period," *Iliff Review* 39 (1982): 5–23.

Andersen, F. I. "Who Built the Second Temple?" *ABR* 6 (1958): 1–35.

Avigad, N. *Bullae and Seals from a Post-Exilic Judean Archive.* Jerusalem: Institute of Archaeology/Hebrew University of Jerusalem, 1976.

Barag, D. "The Effects of the Tennes Rebellion on Palestine," *BASOR* 183 (1966): 6–12.

Bickerman, E. J. "The Edict of Cyrus in Ezra 1," *JBL* 65 (1946): 249–75.

Coggins, R. J. *Samaritans and Jews: The Origins of Samaritanism Reconsidered.* Oxford/Atlanta: Basil Blackwell/John Knox Press, 1975.

Cook, J. M. *The Persian Empire.* London/New York: J. M. Dent & Sons/Schocken Books, 1983.

Cross, F. M. "A Reconstruction of the Judean Restoration," *JBL* 94 (1975): 4–18.

Davies, W. D., and L. Finkelstein (eds.). *The Cambridge History of Judaism. I: Introduction; The Persian Period.* Cambridge/New York: Cambridge University Press, 1984.

Driver, G. R. *Aramaic Documents of the Fifth Century BC.* London: Oxford University Press, 1954; abridged and revised edition, 1957.

Emerton, J. A. "Did Ezra Go to Jerusalem in 428 BC?" *JTS* XVII (1966): 1–19.

Galling, K. *Studien zur Geschichte Israels im persischen Zeitalter.* Tübingen: J. C. B. Mohr [Paul Siebeck], 1964.

Gelston, A. "The Foundations of the Second Temple," *VT* 16 (1966): 232–35.

Houtman, C. "Ezra and the Law," *OTS* 21 (1981): 91–115.

In der Smitten, W. T. *Esra. Quellen, Überlieferung, und Geschichte.* Assen: Van Gorcum, 1973.

Japhet, S. "Sheshbazzar and Zerubbabel: Against the Background of the Historical and Religious Tendencies of Ezra-Nehemiah," *ZAW* 94 (1982): 66–98; 95 (1983): 218–29.

Kellermann, U., *Nehemia. Quellen, Überlieferung, und Geschichte.* Berlin: Alfred Töpelmann, 1967.

―――. "Erwägungen zum Problem der Esradatierung," *ZAW* 80 (1968): 55–87.

Koch, K. "Ezra and the Origins of Judaism," *JSS* 19 (1974): 173–97.

Kraeling, E. G. *The Brooklyn Museum Aramaic Papyri: New Documents of the Fifth Century B.C. from the Jewish Colony at Elephantine.* New Haven/London: Yale University Press/ Oxford University Press, 1953.

Kuhrt, A. K. "The Cyrus Cylinder and Achaemenid Imperial Politics," *JSOT* 25 (1983): 83–97.

McEvenue, S. E. "The Political Structure in Judah from Cyrus to Nehemiah," *CBQ* 44 (1981): 353–64.

Meyer, E. *Der Papyrusfund von Elephantine.* 2d ed. Leipzig: J. C. Hinrichs, 1912.

Myers, J. M. *The World of the Restoration.* Englewood Cliffs, N.J./London: Prentice-Hall/Geoffrey Chapman, 1968.

Olmstead, A. T. *History of the Persian Empire.* Chicago/London: University of Chicago Press/Cambridge University Press, 1948.

von Rad, G. "Die Nehemia-Denkschrift," *ZAW* 76 (1964): 176–87.

Rainey, A. F. "The Satrapy 'Beyond the River,'" *AJBA* 1 (1969): 51–78.

Rowley, H. H. "The Chronological Order of Ezra and Nehemiah." In *Ignace Goldhizer Memorial Volume,* I, edited by S. Lowinger and J. Somogyi, 117–49. Budapest: Globus, 1948. Also in his *The Servant of the Lord,* 135–68. Oxford: Basil Blackwell, 1965.

―――. "Nehemiah's Mission and Its Background," *BJRL* 37 (1954–1955): 528–61 = his *Men of God,* 211–45.

Saley, R. J. "The Date of Nehemiah Reconsidered." In *Biblical and Near Eastern Studies: Essays in Honor of William Sanford LaSor,* edited by G. A. Tuttle, 151–65. Grand Rapids, Mich.: Wm. B. Eerdmans, 1978.

Smith, M. "II Isaiah and the Persians," *JAOS* 83 (1963): 415–21.

―――. *Palestinian Parties and Politics That Shaped the Old Testament.* New York: Columbia University Press, 1971.

Stern, E. *The Material Culture of the Land of the Bible in the Persian Period 538–332 B.C.* Warminster, England/Jerusalem: Aris & Phillips/Israel Exploration Society, 1982.

Tuland, C. G. "Josephus, *Antiquities.* Book XI. Correction or Confirmation of Biblical Post-Exilic Records," *AUSS* IV (1966): 176–92.

de Vaux, R. "The Decrees of Cyrus and Darius on the Rebuilding of the Temple." In his *The Bible and the Ancient Near East,* 63–96. London/Garden City, N.Y.: Darton, Longman, & Todd/Doubleday & Co., 1971.

Widengren, G. "Yahweh's Gathering of the Dispersed." In *In the Shelter of Elyon: Essays on Ancient Palestinian Life and Literature,* edited by W. B. Barrick and J. R. Spencer, 227–45. Sheffield, England: JSOT Press, 1984.

Williamson, H. G. M. "The Historical Value of Josephus' *Jewish Antiquities* XI. 297–301," *JTS* 38 (1977): 49–66.

Name Index

Scripture Index